From Master Student to
MASTER EMPLOYEE

Third Edition

Based on Dave Ellis' Becoming a Master Student

Doug Toft
Contributing Editor

WADSWORTH
CENGAGE Learning™

AUSTRALIA • BRAZIL • JAPAN • KOREA • MEXICO • SPAIN • UNITED KINGDOM • UNITED STATES

WADSWORTH
CENGAGE Learning™

From Master Student to Master Employee, Third Edition
Ellis

Senior Publisher: Lyn Uhl

Senior Sponsoring Editor: Shani Fisher

Development Editor: Daisuke Yasutake

Editorial Assistant: Cat Salerno

Senior Marketing Manager: Kirsten Stoller

Marketing Coordinator: Ryan Ahern

Marketing Communications Manager: Martha Pfeiffer

Content Project Manager: Jessica Rasile

Senior Art Director: Pam Galbreath

Text Designer: Susan Gilday

Print Buyer: Julio Esperas

Senior Rights Specialist: Katie Huha

Photo Manager: Jennifer Meyer Dare

Photo Researcher: Walter Kopec

Cover Designer: Yvo Riezebos

Cover Image: Ted Humble-Smith/RF/Getty

Production Service/Compositor: S4Carlisle Publishing Services

For product information and technology assistance, contact us at
Cengage Learning Customer & Sales Support, 1-800-354-9706
For permission to use material from this text or product,
submit all requests online at **cengage.com/permissions**
Further permissions questions can be emailed to
permissionrequest@cengage.com

Library of Congress Control Number: 2010923020

Student Edition:

ISBN-13: 978-0-495-91304-7

ISBN-10: 0-495-91304-9

Annotated Instructor's Edition:

ISBN-13: 978-0-495-91314-6

ISBN-10: 0-495-91314-6

Wadsworth
20 Channel Center Street
Boston, MA 02210
USA

Cengage Learning is a leading provider of customized learning solutions with office locations around the globe, including Singapore, the United Kingdom, Australia, Mexico, Brazil and Japan. Locate your local office at **international.cengage.com/region**

Cengage Learning products are represented in Canada by Nelson Education, Ltd.

For your course and learning solutions, visit **www.cengage.com**.

Purchase any of our products at your local college store or at our preferred online store **www.CengageBrain.com**.

Printed in the United States of America
2 3 4 5 6 7 14 13 12 11 10

Advisory Board

Kinaya J. Ade'
Medix College, GA

Mike Bohn
Westwood College, TX

Justina Boyd
Colorado University

Judy Brandon
Clovis Community College, NM

Carl Bridges
Career Education Corporation, IL

Julie Brown
Corinthian Colleges, Inc., CA

Jodi Caldwell
Georgia Southern University

Marla Cartwright
Kaplan University

Jennifer Combs
Fullerton College, CA

Audra Cooke
Rock Valley College, IL

David Cooper
Northwest Business College, IL

Katharine Davis
Mississippi Delta Community College

Sylvia Edwards-Borens
Texas State Technical College, Waco, TX

Steven Epstein
SUNY—Suffolk Community College, NY

Mary Etter
Davenport University, MI

Marie Feuer
Mt. Sierra College, CA

Mominka Fileva
Davenport University, MI

Carol Forrey
Kaplan University

Richard Gargan
Florida Metropolitan University, Orlando, FL

James George
Westwood College, Chicago Loop, IL

Vicki Gidney
International Business College, TX

Dr. Andrea Goldstein
South University, GA

Paul Gore
University of Utah

Anne Gupton
Mott Community College, MI

Dorothy Herndon
National College of Business and Technology, VA

Pat Hunnicutt
ITT-Technical Institutes, Little Rock, AR

Evelyn Hyde
Brown Mackie College-Salina, KS

Jane Jepson
Cypress College, CA

Martha Johnson
Texas A&M University

James Jones
Southwest Florida College, FL

Jill Jurgens
Old Dominion University, VA

Linda Kester
Erie Institute of Technology, PA

Pamela King
Southwest Florida College, FL

Patsy Krech
University of Memphis, TN

Stephen Lewis
Westwood College, O'Hare Campus, IL

Susan Loffredo
Northeastern University, MA

Blake Mackesy
Wilkes University, PA

Carole Mackewich
Clark College, WA

Dean Mancina
Golden West College, CA

Forrest Marston
Sanford Brown Institute, FL

Eldon L. McMurray
Utah Valley State College

Amanda Millard
Westwood College, Chicago Loop, IL

Katrina Neckuty-Fodness
Globe University/Minnesota School of Business, MN

Linda Nelson
Davenport University, IN

Diane Noraas
Baker College, MI

Sharon Occipinti
Florida Metropolitan University, Tampa, FL

Keri O'Malley
ECPI Technical College at Greensboro, NC

Rebecca Owens
Colorado Technical University, CO

Nancy Porretto
Katherine Gibbs Schools, Melville, NY

Margaret Puckett
North Central State College, OH

Tracey Robinson
DeVry University–South FL

Tara Ross
Virginia College Online, AL

Advisory Board

Diane Savoca
St. Louis Community College, MO

Kathlene Scholljegeredes
Bethel College, MN

Deidre Sepp
Marist College, NY

Valerie Smolek
Westwood College, Torrance, IL

Jake Sneva
University at Buffalo, NY

David Southwell
*Westwood College,
O'Hare Campus, IL*

Jeffrey Swanberg
Rockford Business College, IL

Pat Twaddle
*Moberly Area Community College,
MO*

Dr. Pamela D. Walker
Northwestern College, IL

Debra Watson
*Mississippi Gulf Coast
Community College*

Diane Williams
PIMA Medical Institute, AZ

Jean Wisuri
American Education Centers, KY

Eric S. Wormsley
PIMA Community College

Student Advisory Board

Wylonda Bernstein
East-West University

Valerie Cordes
Alpena Community College

William Couch
University of Maryland College Park

Jesse Decker
Ocean County College

Theresa Francis
Southwestern Illinois College

Alecia Jackson
*Phillips Community College of the
University of Arizona*

Kanisha Jackson
Ohio University

Bradford Johnson
Tallahassee Community College

Steven Kelley
Drexel University

Joyce King
Broward College

Kevin Kunz, Jr.
Mesa Community College

Sally LaFleure
Alpena Community College

Jose Ledesma II
San Diego Mesa College

Jess Maggi
Le Moyne College

Ashley Molton
Central Texas College

Lindsay M. Ordone
Delgado Community College

Christian Penaherrera
University at Buffalo

Melody Reese
Kent State University

Christopher Sampson
University of Houston-Downtown

Jason Shah
University of New Orleans

Lisa Shelley
University of Texas at Arlington

Vanessa Silva
Pace University

Ivory D. Wiggins
Mesa College

Jamila Williams
SUNY— University at Buffalo

Katherine Wood
Washington and Lee University

Brief Table of Contents

Image Source/Alamy

© Tom Grill/Corbis

© Masterfile Royalty Free

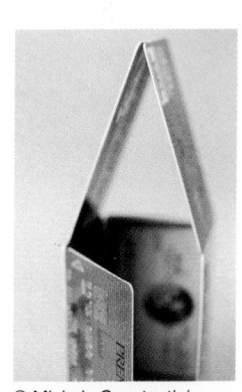
© Michele Constantini, PhotoAlto/Getty

Table of Contents

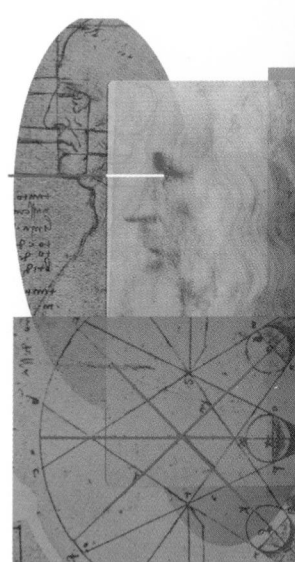

Table of Contents

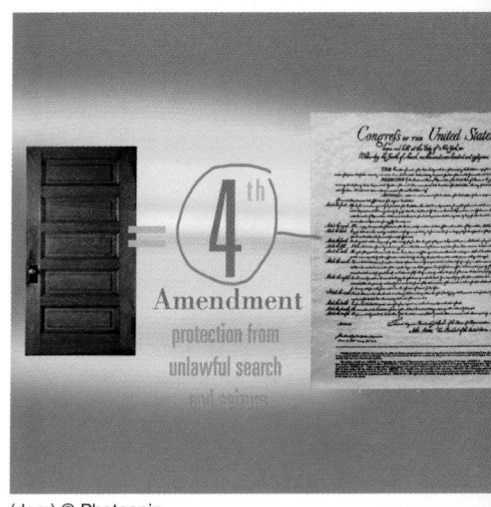

(door) © Photospin

© Graham Bell/Corbis

Table of Contents

Thinkstock/Getty

© image100/Corbis

Table of Contents

Stockbyte/Getty

ZenShui/Alix Minde/Getty

Mastering Transitions

Master Student Map

as you read, ask yourself

what if . . .

I could use the strategies that help me succeed in school to also succeed in the workplace?

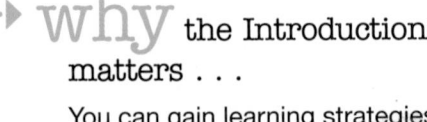

why the Introduction matters . . .

You can gain learning strategies that will help you make a successful transition to higher education.

what is included . . .

how you can use this Introduction . . .

- Keep a journal that translates insights into new behaviors.
- Learn to make transitions in ways that will assist you for the rest of your life.

MASTER EMPLOYEE in *action*

I had a lot of difficulties in interviews, especially when an interviewer would ask me to describe myself. Looking back now, I realize that I was lucky I wasn't hired for any of those positions. It forced me to stop and be more critical about the type of person I was, and the type of job that would truly suit me. When I finally found a job opening that interested me, I discovered that I didn't have any problem in the interview.

—MATT CARLE, GRAPHIC DESIGNER

Photo courtesy of Matt Carle

From master student to master employee

ONCE UPON A TIME, people thought of education as an enterprise set apart from the business of daily life. The halls of colleges, universities, and other schools were described as ivory towers—places where scholars retreated from the world of work to pursue knowledge.

Today, a different point of view prevails. The boundaries between classroom, office, and factory floor are fluid and flexible. Learning includes practicum experience, internships, work-study assignments, and other career-related experiences. Many students work full-time while attending classes.

Instead of competing, workplaces and classrooms can now complement each other. This development mirrors some key discoveries in the psychology of learning: that we learn by immersing ourselves in concrete experiences, reflecting on them, constructing theories, and then testing those theories in action.

Pioneers of both liberal education and modern work methods would agree. In his classic book *The Idea of a University,* John Henry Newman wrote that "all Knowledge is a whole and the separate Sciences parts of one"—leaving no room to divorce theory from practice or knowledge from application.[1] And Henry Ford said, "The only real security that a person can have in this world is a reserve of knowledge, experience, and ability. Without these qualities, money is practically useless."[2]

The purpose of this book is to build two kinds of bridges between your classroom experiences and your career. One is the bridge of skills—your ability to perform tasks that are valued by employers. The other is the bridge of learning—the ability to update your skills and acquire new ones any time you choose.

As a student, you are now involved in a multibillion-dollar enterprise called higher education. By focusing on the skills you acquire and the results you create, you can move between the role of student and the role of employee as easily as you change clothes. As a student, you are also at work, performing in ways that produce measurable results. This is natural because both roles draw on a common set of skills. The phrases *master student* and *master employee* are terms for qualities that live inside you, waiting only to be discovered. ✳

critical thinking exercise

1 Textbook reconnaissance

Start becoming a master student this moment by doing a 15-minute "textbook reconnaissance." Here's how.

First, read this book's Table of Contents. Do it in three minutes or less. Next, look at every page in the book. Move quickly. Scan headlines. Look at pictures. Notice forms, charts, and diagrams. Don't forget the last few pages in back, which include extra copies of planning forms that you might find useful.

A textbook reconnaissance shows you where a course is going. It gives you the big picture. That's useful because brains work best when going from the general to the specific. Getting the big picture before you start makes it easier to recall and understand details later on.

Your textbook reconnaissance will work even better if, as you scan, you look for ideas you can use. When you find one, write the page number and a short description of the idea. If you run out of room, just continue your list on a separate sheet of paper. You also can use Post-It Notes to flag the pages that look useful. You could even use notes of different colors to signal priority, such as green for ideas to use right away and yellow for suggestions to apply later. The idea behind this technique is simple: It's easier to learn when you're excited, and it's easier to get excited about a course if you know it's going to be useful, interesting, or fun.

Remember, look at every page, and do it quickly. Another useful tip for the master student is this: Do it now.

Page Number   **Description**

_____

_____

_____

_____

_____

(www) Complete this exercise online.

This book is worthless— if you just read it

FROM MASTER STUDENT TO MASTER EMPLOYEE is worthless, *if* reading it is all you do. Until you take action and use the ideas to change your behavior, this book will make little difference in your life.

The purpose of this book is to help you make successful transitions to higher education and the workplace, and to set up a pattern of success that will last the rest of your life. You probably won't take action and use the ideas in this book until you are convinced that you have something to gain. That's one reason for providing this Introduction—to persuade you to use this book actively.

Before you stiffen up and resist this sales pitch, remember that you have already bought the book. Now you can get something for your money by committing yourself to take action—in other words, by committing yourself to becoming a master student. Here's what's in it for you.

Andersen Ross/Getty

Pitch #1: You can save money now and make more money later. Start with money. Your college education is one of the most expensive things you will ever buy. You might find yourself paying $30 to $100 an hour to sit in class. (See Critical Thinking Exercise 37: "Education by the Hour" on page 291 to come up with a specific figure that applies to your own education.)

As a master student, you control the value you get out of your education, and that value can be considerable. The joy of learning aside, college graduates make more money during their lifetimes than do their non-degreed peers.[3] The income advantage you might gain through higher education could total hundreds of thousands of dollars. It pays to be a master student.

Pitch #2: You can rediscover the natural learner in you. Joy is important, too. As you become a master student, you will learn to gain knowledge in the most effective way possible—by discovering the joyful, natural learner within you.

Children are great natural students. They quickly master complex skills, such as language, and they have fun doing it. For young children, learning is a high-energy process involving experimentation, discovery, and sometimes broken dishes. Then comes school. For some students, drill and drudgery replace discovery and dish breaking. Learning can become a drag. You can use this book to reverse that process and rediscover what you knew as a child—that laughter and learning go hand in hand.

Sometimes—and especially in college—learning does take effort. As you become a master student, you will learn many ways to work hard and have fun.

Pitch #3: You can choose from hundreds of techniques.

From Master Student to Master Employee is packed with hundreds of practical, nuts-and-bolts techniques. The best part is, you can begin using them immediately. For example, during Critical Thinking Exercise 1: "Textbook Reconnaissance" on page 1, you might find three powerful learning techniques in one 15-minute exercise. Even if you doze in lectures, drift off during tests, or dawdle on term papers, you'll find ideas in this book that you can use to become a more effective student.

Not all of these ideas will work for you. That's why there are so many of them in this book. You can experiment with the techniques. As you discover what works, you will develop a unique style of learning that you can use for the rest of your life.

Pitch #4: You get the best suggestions from thousands of students.

The concepts and techniques in this book are here not just because learning theorists, educators, and psychologists say they work. They are here because tens of thousands of students from all kinds of backgrounds have tried them and agree that they work. These people are students who dreaded giving speeches, couldn't read their own notes, and fell behind in their course work. Then they figured out how to solve those problems. Now you can use their ideas.

Pitch #5: You can learn about yourself.

The process of self-discovery is an important theme in *From Master Student to Master Employee*. Throughout the book, you can use Discovery Statements and Intention Statements for everything from organizing your desk to choosing long-term goals. Studying for an organic chemistry quiz is a lot easier with a clean desk and a clear idea of the course's importance to you.

Pitch #6: You can use a proven product.

The previous editions of this book have proved successful for thousands of students. Student feedback has been positive. In particular, students with successful histories have praised the techniques in this book.

Pitch #7: You can learn the secret of student success.

If this sales pitch still hasn't persuaded you to use this book actively, maybe it's time to reveal the secret of student success. (Provide your own drum roll here.) The secret is . . . there are no secrets. Perhaps the ultimate formula is to give up formulas, keep experimenting, and find strategies that actually help you meet your goals.

The strategies that successful students use are well known. You have hundreds of them at your fingertips right now, in this book. Use them. Modify them. Invent new ones. You're the authority on what works for you.

However, what makes any technique work is commitment—and action. Without them, the pages of *From Master Student to Master Employee* are just two pounds of expensive mulch. Add your participation to the mulch, and these pages become priceless. ✳

This book is worth $1,000

Cengage Learning is proud to present three students each year with a $1,000 scholarship for tuition reimbursement. Any post-secondary school in the United States and Canada can nominate one student for the scholarship. To be considered, the student must write an essay that answers the question, "How do you define success?"

 For more details, visit the *From Master Student to Master Employee* Web site.

Get the most out of this book

1. Get used to a new look and tone. This book looks different from traditional textbooks. *From Master Student to Master Employee* presents major ideas in magazine-style articles. You will discover lots of lists, blurbs, one-liners, pictures, charts, graphs, illustrations, and even a joke or two.

Note: As a strategy for avoiding sexist language, this book alternates the use of feminine and masculine pronouns.

2. Rip 'em out. The pages of *From Master Student to Master Employee* are perforated because some of the information here is too important to leave in the book, and there are some pages your instructor might want to see. For example, Journal Entry 2 asks you to list some important things you want to get out of your education. To keep yourself focused on these goals, you could rip that page out and post it on your bathroom mirror or some other place where you'll see it several times a day.

You can reinsert the pages later by sticking them into the spine of the book. A piece of tape will hold them in place.

3. Skip around. You can use this book in several different ways. Read it straight through. Or pick it up, turn to any page, and find an idea you can use. Look for ideas you can use right now. For example, if you are about to choose a major or want to learn how to set goals, skip directly to the articles on these topics on pages 78 and 94, respectively.

You might find that this book presents similar ideas in several places. This repetition is intentional. Repetition reinforces key points. Also, a technique that works in one area of your life might work in others as well. Look especially to the Power Processes in this text for ideas that you can apply in many ways.

4. If it works, use it. If it doesn't, lose it. If there are sections of this book that don't apply to you at all, skip them—unless, of course, they are assigned. In that case, see if you can gain value from those sections anyway. When you are committed to getting value from this book, even an idea that seems irrelevant or ineffective at first can turn out to be a powerful tool.

5. Put yourself into the book. As you read about techniques in this book, create your own scenarios and cast yourself in the title role. For example, when reading through Critical Thinking Exercise 1: "Textbook Reconnaissance," picture yourself using this technique on your math textbook.

6. Listen to your peers. At the beginning of each chapter you will find a feature titled "Master Employee in Action." These include quotations from people who demonstrate the attitudes and strategies presented in this text. As you dig into each chapter, think about what you would say if you could add your voice to theirs.

7. Own this book. Right now, put your name, address, and related information on the inside cover of this book. Don't stop there, though. Determine what you want to get out of school, and create a record of how you intend to get it by reading the Power Processes and completing the Journal Entries in this Introduction. Every time your pen touches a page, you move closer to mastery.

8. Do the Critical Thinking Exercises. Critical Thinking Exercises appear throughout this book. Their purpose is to help you stretch your mind and get some practice in solving problems. Use these exercises to explore new ways of thinking about chapter topics. Note that other elements of this text, including Chapter 8: "Thinking" and Journal Entries, also promote critical thinking.

The Critical Thinking Exercises are based on a single idea: Ideas are meant to be *used*. Exercises invite you to write, touch, feel, move, see, search, ponder, speak, listen, recall, choose, commit, and create. You might even sing and dance. Learning often works best when it involves action.

To get the most out of this book, do most of the exercises. Also remember that it's never too late to go back and do the ones you skipped.

9. Learn about learning styles. Check out the Learning Styles Inventory and related articles in Chapter 1: "First Steps." This material can help you discover your preferred learning styles and allow you to explore new styles. Then, throughout the rest of this book, you'll find suggestions for applying your knowledge of learning styles. The modes of learning can be accessed by asking four basic questions: *Why? What? How?* and *What if?*

10. Navigate through learning experiences with the Master Student Map. You can orient yourself for maximum learning every time you open this book by asking those same four questions: *Why? What? How?* and *What if?* That's the idea behind the Master Student Map included on the first page of each chapter, which includes sample answers to those questions. Remember that you can use the four-part structure of this map to cycle through several learning styles and effectively learn anything.

11. Link to the Web. Throughout this book, you'll notice reminders to visit the Web site for *From Master Student to Master Employee.* When you see these notices, go to the Web site for articles, online exercises, and links to other useful Web sites.

12. Read the sidebars. Look for sidebars—short bursts of words and pictures placed between longer articles—throughout this book. These short pieces might offer insights that transform your experience of higher education. ✳

(2) critical thinking exercise
Commitment

This book is worthless unless you actively participate in its activities and exercises. One powerful way to begin taking action is to make a commitment. Conversely, if you don't make a commitment, then sustained action is unlikely. The result is a worthless book. Therefore, in the interest of saving your valuable time and energy, this exercise gives you a chance to declare your level of involvement upfront. From the following options, choose the sentence that best reflects your commitment to using this book. Write the number in the space provided at the end of the list.

1. "Well, I'm reading this book right now, aren't I?"

2. "I will skim the book and read the interesting parts."

3. "I will read the book, think about it, and do the exercises that look interesting."

4. "I will read the book, do some exercises, and complete some of the Journal Entries."

5. "I will read the book, do some exercises and Journal Entries, and use some of the techniques."

6. "I will read the book, do most of the exercises and Journal Entries, and use some of the techniques."

7. "I will study this book, do most of the exercises and Journal Entries, and use some of the techniques."

8. "I will study this book, do most of the exercises and Journal Entries, and experiment with many of the techniques in order to discover what works best for me."

9. "I promise myself that I will create value from this course by studying this book, doing all the exercises and Journal Entries, and experimenting with most of the techniques."

10. "I will use this book as if the quality of my education depends on it—doing all the exercises and Journal Entries, experimenting with most of the techniques, inventing techniques of my own, and planning to reread this book in the future."

Enter your commitment level and today's date here:

Commitment level _____ Date _____

If you selected commitment level 1 or 2, you might consider passing this book on to a friend. If your commitment level is 9 or 10, you are on your way to terrific success in school. If your level is somewhere in between, experiment with the techniques and learning strategies you will find in this book. If you find that they work, consider returning to this exercise and raising your level of commitment.

 Complete this exercise online.

Link to the work world

ONE THEORY of education separates life into two distinct domains: work and school. One is the "real" world. The other is the place where you attend classes to prepare for the real world.

Consider another point of view: Success in higher education promotes success on the job. You can link school experiences to the work world, starting today.

When you graduate from school, you don't leave your capacity for mastery locked inside a classroom. Excellence in one setting paves the way for excellence in other settings. A student who knows how to show up for class on time is ready to show up for work on time. And a student who's worked cooperatively in a study group brings people skills to the table when joining a project team at work.

To stimulate your thinking, experiment with this strategy: Whenever you go to class, imagine that you're actually at work. Then act accordingly. When you read, think like an employee who is gathering information to include in a bid for a multimillion-dollar project. When you take notes, imagine that you're documenting the results of a corporate board meeting. Whenever you complete a class assignment, imagine that you're about to be paid for the quality of your work.

This is not a far-fetched idea. In some career and technical schools, students are required to dress as they would in the workplace. They know that *dressing* the part of an employee makes it easier for them to *act* the part.

Psychologist William James promoted this strategy nearly a century ago. He wrote that when you act repeatedly in a new and constructive way, you're likely to stimulate new feelings and gain new habits in the process.[4] Another name for this is the "act as if" technique. In other words, act as if you are a master employee right now.

Starting with this page, read this book with a mental filter in place. Ask yourself:

- How can I use these ideas to meet my career goals?
- How can I use these techniques at my current job?
- How can these strategies help me to get a better job—one with more pay, more recognition, and more opportunities to do what I love to do?

For example, suggestions from "*Making the Transition to Higher Education*" (page 13) can also help you make the transition to a new career.

The techniques presented in "*Setting and Achieving Goals*" (page 94) can help you plan and complete work-related projects on time.

The article "*20 Memory Techniques*" (page 122) will come in handy as you learn the policies and procedures for a new job.

Use the techniques presented in Chapter 5: "Reading," starting with "*How Muscle Reading Works*" (page 140), to keep up with journals and books in your career field. This set of techniques can also help you extract valuable information from Web sites, keep up with ever-increasing volumes of e-mail, and reduce mountains of interoffice memos to manageable proportions.

Adapt the ideas mentioned in "*Cooperative Learning: Working in Teams*" (page 193) in order to collaborate more effectively with coworkers.

The suggestions in "*Thriving with Diversity*" (page 252) can assist you in adapting to the culture of a new company.

Ideas from "*Managing Conflict*" (page 255) can help you defuse tensions among coworkers.

These are just a few examples. Take any idea that you gain from this book and put it to the test. Use it, modify it, expand it, or replace it with one of your own. When you start looking for ways to break down the barriers between higher education and higher achievement on the job, there's no limit to the possibilities. ✴

The Discovery and Intention Journal Entry system

One way to become a better student is to grit your teeth and try harder. There is a better way: The Discovery and Intention Journal Entry system. This system can increase your effectiveness by showing you how to focus your energy.

USING THE DISCOVERY and Intention Journal Entry system is a little like flying an airplane. Airplanes are seldom exactly on course. Human and automatic pilots are always checking an airplane's positions and making corrections. The resulting flight path looks like a zigzag. The plane is almost always flying in the wrong direction, but because of constant observation and course correction, it arrives at the right destination.

As a student, you can use a similar approach. Journal Entries throughout this book are labeled as Discovery Statements, Intention Statements, or Discovery/Intention Statements. Each Journal Entry will contain a short set of instructions to direct your writing.

Through Discovery Statements, you gain awareness of "where you are." These statements are a record of what you are learning about yourself as a student—both your strengths and your weaknesses. Discovery Statements can also be declarations of your goals, descriptions of your attitudes, statements of your feelings, transcripts of your thoughts, and chronicles of your behavior.

Sometimes Discovery Statements chronicle an "aha!" moment—a flash of insight that results when you connect a new idea with your prior experiences, preferred styles of learning, or both. Perhaps a solution to a long-standing problem suddenly occurs to you, or a life-changing insight wells up from the deepest recesses of your mind. Don't let such moments disappear. Capture them in Discovery Statements.

Intention Statements can be used to alter your course. These statements are about your commitment to take action based on increased awareness. An intention arises out of your choice to direct your energy toward a specific task and to aim at a particular goal. The processes of discovery and intention reinforce each other.

Even simple changes in behavior can produce results. If you feel like procrastinating, then tackle just one small, specific task related to your intention. Find something you can complete in five minutes or less, and do it *now*. For example, access just one Web site related to the topic of your next assigned paper. Spend just three minutes previewing a reading assignment. Taking "baby steps" like these can move you into action with grace and ease.

That's the system in a nutshell. Discovery leads to awareness. Intention leads to commitment. And *intention leads naturally to focused action.*

The process of discovery, intention, and action creates a dynamic and efficient cycle. The purpose of this system is not to get you pumped up and excited

to go out there and try harder. In fact, Discovery and Intention Statements are intended to help you work smarter rather than harder.

First, you write Discovery Statements about where you are now. Next, you write Intention Statements about where you want to be, and the specific steps you will take to get there. Finally, you follow up with action—the sooner, the better.

Then you start the cycle again. Write Discovery Statements about whether or how you act on your Intention Statements—and what you learn in the process. Follow up with more Intention Statements about what you will do differently in the future. Then move into action and describe what happens next.

This process never ends. Each time you repeat the cycle, you get new results. It's all about getting what you want and becoming more effective in everything you do. This is the path of mastery—a path that you can travel for the rest of your life.

Sometimes a Discovery or Intention Statement will be long and detailed. Usually, it will be short—maybe just a line or two. With practice, the cycle will become automatic.

Don't panic when you fail to complete an intended task. Straying off course is normal. Simply make the necessary corrections. Mastery is not an end state or final goal. Rather, mastery is a process that never ends.

Miraculous progress might not come immediately. Do not be concerned. Stay with the cycle. Give it time. Use Discovery Statements to get a clear view of your world. Then use Intention Statements to direct your actions. Whenever you notice progress, record it.

Even if the following statement strikes you as improbable, just consider the possibilities: It can take the same amount of energy to get what you *don't* want in school as it takes to get what you *do* want. Sometimes getting what you don't want takes even more effort. An airplane burns the same amount of fuel flying away from its destination as it does flying toward it. It pays to stay on course.

You can use the Discovery and Intention Journal Entry system to stay on your own course and get what you want out of school. Start with the Journal Entries included in the text. Then go beyond them. Write Discovery and Intention Statements of your own at any time, for any purpose. Create new strategies whenever you need them, based on your current situation.

Once you get the hang of it, you might discover you can fly. ✳

Hello Author I Agree ☺

Rewrite this book

Some books should be preserved in pristine condition. This book isn't one of them.

Something happens when you interact with your book by writing in it. *From Master Student to Master Employee* is about learning, and learning results when you are active. When you make notes in the margin, you can hear yourself talking with the author. When you doodle and underline, you see the author's ideas taking shape. You can even argue with the author and come up with your own theories and explanations. In all of these ways, you can become a coauthor of this book. Rewrite it to make it yours.

While you're at it, you can create symbols or codes that will help you when reviewing the text later on. You might insert a "Q" where you have questions or put exclamation points next to important ideas. You could also circle words to look up in a dictionary.

Remember, if any idea in this book doesn't work for you, you can rewrite it. Change the exercises to fit your needs. Create a new technique by combining several others. Create a technique out of thin air!

Find something you agree or disagree with on this page, and write a short note in the margin about it. Or draw a diagram. Better yet, do both. Let creativity be your guide. Have fun.

Begin rewriting now.

Discovery and Intention Statement guidelines

Discovery Statements

1 Record the specifics about your thoughts, feelings, and behavior. Thoughts include inner voices. We talk to ourselves constantly in our heads. When internal chatter gets in your way, write down what you are telling yourself. If this seems difficult at first, just start writing. The act of writing can trigger a flood of thoughts.

Thoughts also include mental pictures. These images are especially powerful. Picturing yourself flunking a test is like a rehearsal to do just that. One way to take away the power of negative images in your mind is to describe them in detail.

Also notice how you feel when you function well. Use Discovery Statements to pinpoint exactly where and when you learn most effectively.

In addition, observe your actions and record them accurately. Use facts. If you spent 90 minutes chatting online with a favorite cousin instead of reading your anatomy text, write about it and include the details, such as when you did it, where you did it, and how it felt. Record your observations quickly, as soon as you make them.

2 Use discomfort as a signal. When you approach a daunting task, such as a difficult math problem, notice your physical sensations—a churning stomach, perhaps, or shallow breathing or yawning. Feeling uncomfortable, bored, or tired might be a signal that you're about to do valuable work. Stick with it. Tell yourself you can handle the discomfort just a little bit longer. You will be rewarded.

You can experience those rewards at any time. Just think of the problem that poses the biggest potential barrier to your success in school. Choose a problem that you face right now, today. (Hint: It might be the thing that's distracting you from reading this article.) If you have a lot of emotion tied up in this problem, that's even better. Write a Discovery Statement about it.

3 Suspend judgment. When you are discovering yourself, be gentle. Suspend self-judgment. If you continually judge your behaviors as "bad" or "stupid" or "galactically imbecilic," sooner or later your mind will revolt. Rather than put up with the abuse, it will quit making discoveries. For your own benefit, be kind to yourself.

4 Tell the truth. Suspending judgment helps you tell the truth about yourself. The saying "The truth will set you free" endures for a reason. The closer you get to the truth, the more powerful your Discovery Statements will be. And if you notice that you are avoiding the truth, don't blame yourself. Just tell the truth about it.

Intention Statements

1 Make intentions positive. The purpose of writing Intention Statements is to focus on what you want rather than what you don't want. Instead of writing "I will not fall asleep while studying chemistry," write, "I intend to stay awake when studying chemistry." Also avoid the word *try*. Trying is not doing. When we hedge our bets with *try*, we can always tell ourselves, "Well, I *tried* to stay awake." We end up fooling ourselves into thinking we succeeded.

2 Make intentions observable. Experiment with an idea from educational trainer Robert Mager, who suggests that goals be defined through behaviors that can be observed and measured.[5] Rather than writing "I intend to work harder on my history assignments," write, "I intend to review my class notes, and I intend to make summary sheets of my reading." Then, when you review your progress, you can determine more precisely whether you have accomplished what you intended.

3 Make intentions small and achievable. Give yourself opportunities to succeed by setting goals you can meet. Break large goals into small, specific tasks that can be accomplished quickly. Small and simple changes in behavior—when practiced consistently over time—can have large and lasting effects. If you want to get an A in biology, ask yourself, "What can I do today?" You might choose to study biology for an extra hour. Make that your intention.

When setting your goals, anticipate self-sabotage. Be aware of what you might do, consciously or unconsciously, to undermine your best intentions. If you intend to study differential equations at 9 p.m., notice what you're doing when you sit down to watch a two-hour movie that starts at 8 p.m.

Also, be careful with intentions that depend on other people. If you write that you intend for your study group to complete an assignment by Monday, then your success depends on the other students in the group.

4 Set timelines that include rewards. Timelines can focus your attention. For example, if you are assigned to write a paper, break the assignment into small tasks and set a precise due date for each one. You might write, "I intend to select a topic for my paper by 9 a.m. Wednesday."

Timelines are especially useful when your intention is to experiment with a technique suggested in this book. The sooner you act on a new idea, the better. Consider practicing a new behavior within four hours after you first learn about it.

Remember that you create timelines to help yourself, not to feel guilty. In addition, you can always change a timeline.

When you meet your goal on time, reward yourself. Rewards that are an integral part of a goal are powerful. For example, your reward for earning a degree might be the career you've always dreamed of. External rewards, such as a movie or an afternoon in the park, are also valuable. These rewards work best when you're willing to withhold them. If you plan to take a nap on Sunday afternoon whether or not you've finished your English chemistry assignment, the nap is not an effective reward.

Another way to reward yourself is to sit quietly after you have finished your task and savor the feeling. One reason why success breeds success is that it feels good. ✳

journal entry ①

Discovery Statement

Recalling excellence

Welcome to the first Journal Entry in this book. You'll find Journal Entries in every chapter, all with a similar design that allows space for you to write.

Reflect on your personal experience of mastery. In the following space, write a description of a time in your life when you did something well. This experience does not need to be related to school. Describe the details of the situation, including the place, time, and people involved. Also describe the physical sensations and emotions you associate with the event.

I discovered that . . .

_____

_____

_____

_____

_____

_____

_____

_____

_____

_____

_____

_____

_____

_____

_____

_____

_____

_____

The value of higher education

THE POTENTIAL BENEFITS of higher education are enormous. To begin with, there are economic benefits. Over their lifetimes, college graduates on average earn much more than high school graduates. That's just one potential payoff. Consider the others explained in the following text.

Gain a broad vision

It's been said that a large corporation is a collection of departments connected only by a plumbing system. As workers in different fields become more specialized, they run the risk of forgetting how to talk to one another.

Higher education can change that. One benefit of studying the liberal arts is the chance to gain a broad vision. People with a liberal arts background are aware of the various kinds of problems tackled in psychology and theology, philosophy and physics, literature and mathematics. They understand how people in all of these fields arrive at conclusions and how these fields relate.

(money) © Don Farrall/Getty, (statue) © Ron Dahlquist/Getty, (nurse, woman in pink) © Masterfile Royalty Free, (nest) © Judith Collins/Alamy

Master the liberal arts

According to one traditional model, education means mastering two essential tasks: the use of language and the use of numbers. To acquire these skills, students once immersed themselves in seven subjects: grammar, rhetoric, logic, arithmetic, geometry, music, and astronomy. These subjects, called the liberal arts, complemented the fine arts (such as poetry) and the practical arts (such as farming).

This model of liberal arts education still has something to offer. Today we master the use of language through the basic processes of communication: reading, writing, speaking, and listening. In addition, courses in mathematics and science help us understand the world in quantitative terms. The abilities to communicate and calculate are essential to almost every profession.

The word *liberal* comes from the Latin verb *libero*, which means "to free." Liberal arts are those that

promote critical thinking. Studying them can free us from irrational ideas, half-truths, racism, and prejudice. The liberal arts grant us freedom to explore alternatives and create a system of personal values. These benefits are the very basis of personal fulfillment and political freedom.

Discover your values

Our values define how we spend our time and money. Higher education offers the opportunity to question and refine our values.

In addition, we do not spend all of our waking hours at our jobs. That fact leaves us with a decision that affects the quality of our lives: how to spend leisure time. By cultivating our interest in the arts and community affairs, the liberal arts provide us with many options for activities outside work. Our studies add a dimension to life that goes beyond having a job and paying the bills.

Discover new interests

Taking a broad range of courses has the potential to change your direction in life. A student previously committed to a career in science might try out a drawing class and eventually switch to a degree in studio arts. Or a person who swears that she has no aptitude for technical subjects might change her major to computer science after taking an introductory computer course.

To make effective choices about your long-term goals, base those choices on a variety of academic and personal experiences. Even if you don't change majors or switch career directions, you might discover an important avocation or gain a complementary skill. For example, science majors who will eventually write for professional journals can benefit from taking English courses.

Hang out with the greats

The poet Ezra Pound defined literature as "news that stays news."[6] Most of the writing in newspapers and magazines becomes dated quickly. In contrast, many of the books you read in higher education have passed the hardest test of all—time. Such works have created value for people for decades, sometimes for centuries. These creations are inexhaustible. We can return to them time after time and gain new insights. These are the works we can justifiably deem great. Hanging out with them transforms us. Getting to know them exercises our minds, just as running exercises our bodies.

Learn skills that apply across careers

Jobs that involve responsibility, prestige, and higher incomes depend on self-management skills. These skills include knowing ways to manage time, resolve conflicts, set goals, learn new skills, and relate to people of diverse cultures. Higher education is a place to learn and practice such skills.

Join the conversation

Long ago, before the advent of printing presses, televisions, and computers, people educated themselves by conversing with each other. Students in ancient Athens were often called *peripatetic* (a word that means "walking around") because they were frequently seen strolling around the city, engaged in heated philosophical debate.

Since then, the debate has deepened and broadened. The world's finest scientists and artists have joined voices in a conversation that spans centuries and crosses cultures. This conversation is about the nature of truth and beauty, knowledge and compassion, good and evil—ideas that form the very basis of human society.

Robert Hutchins, former president of the University of Chicago, called this exchange the "great conversation."[7] By studying this conversation, we take on the most basic human challenges: coping with death and suffering, helping create a just global society, living with meaning and purpose.

Our greatest thinkers have left behind tangible records. You'll find them in libraries, concert halls, museums, and scientific laboratories across the world. Through higher education, you gain a front-row seat for the great conversation—and an opportunity to add your own voice. ✳

You don't *need* this course— but you might *want* it

Some students don't believe they need a student success course. They might be right. These students may tell you that many schools don't even offer such a class. That's true.

Consider the benefits of taking this course anyway.

Start with a single question: What's one new thing that you could do on a regular basis to make a significant, positive difference in your life? This question might be the most important thing you ask yourself this term. The answer does not have to involve a huge behavior change. Over weeks and months, even a small shift in the way you take notes, read a textbook, or interact with instructors can make a major difference in how well you do in school.

Students who open up to this idea experience benefits. These comments from a recent student success course evaluation are typical:

> *I didn't expect to get anything out of this course except an easy 'A.' Boy, was I ever wrong. This course has changed my life.*

> *I entered college with no confidence. Now that I have taken this class, I feel like I can succeed in any class.*

> *This course has truly showed that I have the power to change any situation for the better.*

> *I am now ready for the rest of my college years.*

A student success course gives you dozens of strategies for creating the life of your dreams. It's possible that you might arrive at these strategies on your own, given enough time. Why wait, however? Approach this book and your course as if the quality of your education depends on them. Then watch the benefits start to unfold.

You share one thing in common with other students at your career school, college, or university: Entering higher education represents a major change in your life. You've joined a new culture with its own set of rules, both spoken and unspoken.

© Andresr/Shutterstock

Making the transition to higher education

WHETHER YOU'VE JUST GRADUATED from high school or have been out of the classroom for decades, you'll discover many differences between secondary and post-secondary education. The sooner you understand such differences, the sooner you can deal with them. Some examples of what you might face include the following:

- *New academic standards.* Once you enter higher education, you'll probably find yourself working harder in school than ever before. Instructors will often present more material at a faster pace. There probably will be fewer tests in higher education than in high school, and the grading might be tougher. Compared to high school, you'll have more to read, more to write, more problems to solve, and more to remember.

- *A new level of independence.* College instructors typically give less guidance about how or when to study. You may not get reminders about when assignments are due or when quizzes and tests will take place. You probably won't get study sheets the night before a test. And anything that's said in class or included in assigned readings might appear on an exam. Overall, you might receive less consistent feedback about how well you are doing in each of

your courses. Don't let this tempt you into putting off work until the last minute. You will still be held accountable for all course work.

- *Differences in teaching styles.* Instructors at colleges, universities, and vocational schools are often steeped in their subject matter. Many did not take courses on how to teach and might not be as interesting as some of your high school teachers. In addition, some professors might seem more focused on research than on teaching.

- *A larger playing field.* The institution you've just joined might seem immense, impersonal, and even frightening. The sheer size of the campus, the variety of courses offered, the large number of departments—all of these opportunities can add up to a confusing array of options.

- *More students and more diversity.* The school you're attending right now might enroll hundreds or thousands more students than your high school. And the range of diversity among these students might surprise you.

In summary, you are now responsible for structuring your time and creating new relationships. Perhaps more than ever before, you'll find that your life is your own creation. You are free to set different goals, explore alternative ways of thinking, change habits, and expand your circle of friends. All this can add up to a new identity—a new way of being in the world.

At first, this world of choices might seem overwhelming or even frightening. You might feel that you're just going through the motions of being a student or playing a role that you've never rehearsed.

That feeling is understandable. Use it to your advantage. Consider that you *are* assuming a new role in life—that of being a student in higher education. And just as actors enter the minds of the characters that they portray, you can take on the character of a master student.

When you're willing to take responsibility for the quality of your education, you can create the future of your dreams. Keep the following strategies in mind.

Decrease the unknowns. Before classes begin, get a map of the school property and walk through your first day's schedule, perhaps with a classmate or friend. Visit your instructors in their offices and introduce yourself. Anything you can do to get familiar with the new routine will help.

Admit your feelings—whatever they are. School can be an intimidating experience for new students. Anyone can feel anxious, isolated, homesick, or worried. People of diverse cultures, adult learners, commuters, and people with disabilities may feel excluded.

Those emotions are common among new students, and there's nothing wrong with them. Simply admitting the truth about how you feel—to yourself and to someone else—can help you cope. And you can almost always do something constructive in the present moment, no matter how you feel.

If your feelings about this transition make it hard for you to carry out the activities of daily life—going to class, working, studying, and relating to people—then get professional help. Start with a counselor at the student health service on your campus. The mere act of seeking help can make a difference.

Allow time for transition. You don't have to master the transition to higher education right away. Give it some time. Also, plan your academic schedule with your needs in mind. Balance time-intensive courses with others that don't make as many demands.

Find resources. A supercharger increases the air supply to an internal combustion engine. The resulting difference in power can be dramatic. You can make just as powerful a difference in your education if you supercharge it by using all of the resources available to students. In this case, your "air supply" includes people, campus clubs and organizations, and school and community services.

Of all resources, people are the most important. You can isolate yourself, study hard, and get a good education. However, doing this is not the most powerful use of your tuition money. When you establish relationships with teachers, staff members, fellow students, and employers, you can get a *great* education. Build a network of people who will personally support your success in school.

Accessing resources is especially important if you are the first person in your family to enter higher education. As a first-generation student, you are having experiences that people in your family may not understand. Talk to your relatives about your activities at school. If they ask how they can help you, give specific answers. Also, ask your instructors about programs for first-generation students on your campus.

Meet with your academic advisor. One person in particular—your academic advisor—can help you access resources and make the transition to higher education. Meet with this person regularly. Advisors generally know about course requirements, options for declaring majors, and the resources available at your school. Peer advisors might also be available.

When you work with an advisor, remember that you're a paying customer and have a right to be satisfied with the service you get. Don't be afraid to change advisors when that seems appropriate.

Learn the language of higher education. Terms such as *grade point average (GPA), prerequisite, accreditation, matriculation, tenure,* and *syllabus* might be new to you. Ease your transition to higher education by checking your school catalog or school Web site for definitions of these words and others that you don't understand. Also ask your academic advisor for clarification.

Show up for class. In higher education, teachers generally don't take attendance. Yet you'll find that attending class is essential to your success. The amount that you pay in tuition and fees makes a powerful argument for going to classes regularly and getting your money's worth. In large part, the material that you're tested on comes from events that take place in class.

Showing up for class occurs on two levels. The most visible level is being physically present in the classroom. Even more important, though, is showing up mentally. This kind of attendance includes taking detailed notes, asking questions, and contributing to class discussions.

Research on college freshmen indicates a link between regular class attendance and academic success.[8] Succeeding in school can help you get almost anything you want, including the career, income, and relationships you desire. Attending class is an investment in yourself.

Manage out-of-class time. For students in higher education, time management takes on a new meaning. What you do *outside* class matters as much as—or even more than—what you do in class. Instructors give you the raw materials for understanding a subject while a class meets. You then take those materials, combine them, and *teach yourself* outside of class.

To allow for this process, schedule two hours of study time for each hour that you spend in class. Also, get a calendar that covers the entire academic year. With the syllabus for each of your courses in hand, note key events for the entire term—dates for tests, papers, and other projects. Getting a big picture of your course load makes it easier to get assignments done on time and avoid all-night study sessions.

Experiment with new ways to study. You can cope with increased workloads and higher academic expectations by putting all of your study habits on the table and evaluating them. Don't assume that the learning strategies you used in the past—in high school or the workplace—will automatically transfer to your new role in higher education. Keep the habits that serve you, drop those that hold you back, and adopt new ones to promote your success. On every page of this book, you'll find helpful suggestions.

Classroom civility—what's in it for you

A student arrives 15 minutes late to a lecture and lets the door slam behind her. She pulls a fast-food burger out of a paper bag (hear the sound of that crackling paper). Then her cell phone rings at full volume—and she answers it. Behaviors like these send a message to everyone in the room: "I'm ignoring you."

Civility means treating people with politeness and respect. Even a small problem with classroom civility can create a barrier for everyone. Learning gets interrupted. Trust breaks down. Your tuition dollars go down the drain.

When you treat instructors with respect, you're more likely to be treated that way in return. A respectful relationship with an instructor could turn into a favorable reference letter, a mentorship, a job referral, or a friendship that lasts for years after you graduate from school. Politeness pays.

Classroom civility does not mean that you have to be passive or insincere. You can present your opinions with passion and even disagree with an instructor. And you can do so in a way that leaves everyone enriched rather than threatened.

Many schools have formal policies about classroom civility. Find out what policies apply to you.

The basics of classroom civility are summarized in the following suggestions. They reflect common sense, and they make an uncommon difference.

Attend classes regularly. Show up for classes on time. If you know that you're going to miss a class or be late, then let your instructor know. Take the initiative to ask your instructor or another student about what you missed.

If you arrive late, do not disrupt class. Close the door quietly and take a seat. When you know that you will have to leave class early, tell your instructor before class begins, and sit near an exit. If you leave class to use the restroom or handle an emergency, do so quietly.

During class, participate fully. Take notes and join in discussions. Turn off your cell phone or any other electronic device that you don't need for class. Remember that sleeping, texting, or doing work for another class is a waste of your time and money.

Instructors often give assignments or make a key point at the end of a class period. Be there when it happens. Wait until class has been dismissed before you pack up your notebook and other materials.

Communicate respect. When you speak in class, begin by addressing your instructor as *Ms., Mrs., Mr., Professor,* or whatever the teacher prefers.

Discussions gain value when everyone gets a chance to speak. Show respect for others by not monopolizing class discussions. Refrain from side conversations and profanity. When presenting viewpoints that conflict with those of classmates or your instructor, combine passion for your opinion with respect for the opinions of others.

Respect gets communicated in the smallest details. Maintain good hygiene. Avoid making distracting noises, and cover your mouth if you yawn or cough. Also avoid wearing inappropriate revealing clothing. Even if you meet your future spouse in class, refrain from public displays of affection.

If you disagree with a class requirement or grade you received, then talk to your instructor about it after class. Your ideas will get more attention if they are expressed in a private setting and in a respectful manner.

See civility as a contribution. Every class you enter has the potential to become a community of people who talk openly, listen fully, share laughter, and arrive at life-changing insights. Anything you do to make that vision a reality is a contribution to your community.

Take the initiative in meeting new people.
Take time before or after class to introduce yourself to classmates and instructors. Most of the people in this new world of higher education are waiting to be welcomed. Plugging into the social networks at any school takes time, but it's worth the effort. Connecting to school socially as well as academically promotes your success and your enjoyment.

Become a self-regulated learner. Reflect on your transition to higher education. Think about what's working well, what you'd like to change, and ways to make those changes. Psychologists use the term *self-regulation* to describe this kind of thinking.[9] Self-regulated learners set goals, monitor their progress toward those goals, and change their behavior based on the results they get.

From Master Student to Master Employee promotes self-regulation through the ongoing cycle of discovery, intention, and action. Write Discovery Statements to monitor your behavior and evaluate the results you're currently creating in any area of your life. Write about your level of commitment to school, your satisfaction with your classes and grades, your social life, and your family's support for your education.

Based on your discoveries, write Intention Statements about your goals for this term, this year, next year, and the rest of your college career. Describe exactly what you will do to create new results in each of these time frames. Then follow through with action. In this way, you take charge of your transition to higher education, starting now. ✳

 Find more strategies for mastering the art of transition online.

Extracurricular activities: Reap the benefits

As you enter higher education, you may find that you are busier than you've ever been before. Often that's due to the variety of extracurricular activities available to you: athletics, fraternities, sororities, student newspapers, debate teams, study groups, service learning projects, internships, student government, and political action groups, to name just a few. Your school might also offer conferences, films, concerts, museums, art galleries, and speakers—all for free or reduced prices. Student organizations help to make these activities possible, and you can join any of them.

Extracurricular involvement comes with potential benefits. People who participate in extracurricular activities are often excellent students. Such activities help them bridge the worlds inside and outside the classroom. They develop new skills, explore possible careers, build contacts for jobs, and build a lifelong habit of giving back to their communities. They make new friends among both students and faculty, work with people from other cultures, and sharpen their conflict resolution skills.

Getting involved in these organizations also comes with some risks. When students don't balance extracurricular activities with class work, their success in school can suffer. They can also compromise their health by losing sleep, neglecting exercise, skipping meals, or relying on fast food. These costs are easier to avoid if you keep a few suggestions in mind:

- *Make conscious choices* about how to divide your time between schoolwork and extracurricular activities. Decide up-front how many hours each week or month you can devote to a student organization. Leave room in your schedule for relaxing and for unplanned events. For more ideas, see Chapter 3: "Time."

- *Look to the future* when making commitments. Write down three or four of the most important goals you'd like to achieve in your lifetime. Then choose extracurricular activities that directly support those goals.

- *Create a career plan* that includes a list of skills needed for your next job. Then choose extracurricular activities to develop those skills. If you're unsure of your career choice, then get involved in campus organizations to explore your options.

- *Whenever possible, develop leadership experience* by holding an office in an organization. If that's too much of a commitment, then volunteer to lead a committee or plan a special event.

- *Get involved in a variety of extracurricular activities.* Varying your activities demonstrates to future employers that you can work with a variety of people in a range of settings.

- *Recognize reluctance* to follow through on a commitment. You might agree to attend meetings and find yourself forgetting them or consistently showing up late. If that happens, write a Discovery Statement about the way you're using time. Follow that with an Intention Statement about ways to keep your agreements—or consider renegotiating those agreements.

- *Check out the rules* before joining any student organization. Ask about dues and attendance requirements.

Connect to resources

AS A STUDENT IN higher education, you can access a world of student services and community resources. Any of them can help you succeed in school. Many of them are free.

Name a problem that you're facing right now or that you anticipate facing in the future: finding money to pay for classes, resolving conflicts with a teacher, lining up a job after graduation. Chances are that a school or community resource can help you. The ability to access resources is a skill that will serve you long after you've graduated.

Resources often go unused. Following are some examples of resources that might be available to you. Check your school and city Web sites for more options.

Academic advisors can help you select courses, choose a major, plan your career, and adjust in general to the culture of higher education.

Arts organizations connect you to local museums, concert venues, clubs, and stadiums.

Athletic centers often open weight rooms, swimming pools, indoor tracks, basketball courts, and racquetball and tennis courts to all students.

Child care is sometimes made available to students at a reasonable cost through the early childhood education department on campus or community agencies.

Churches, synagogues, mosques, and temples have members who are happy to welcome fellow worshippers who are away from home.

Computer labs on campus are places where students can go to work on projects and access the Internet. Computer access is often available off-campus as well. Check public libraries for this service. Some students get permission to use computers at their workplace after hours.

Consumer credit counseling can help even if you've really blown your budget. Best of all, it's usually free. Do your research, and choose a reputable and not-for-profit consumer credit counselor.

Counseling centers in the community can assist you with a problem when you can't get help at school. Look for career-planning services, rehabilitation offices, outreach programs for veterans, and mental health clinics.

The *financial aid office* assists students with loans, scholarships, work-study, and grants.

Governments (city, county, state, and federal) often have programs for students. Check the government listings in your local telephone directory.

Hotlines offer a way to get emergency care, personal counseling, and other kinds of help via a phone call. Do an Internet search on *phone hotlines* in your area that assist with the specific kind of help you're looking for, and check your school catalog for more resources.

Job placement offices can help you find part-time employment while you are in school and a full-time job after you graduate.

Legal aid services provide free or inexpensive assistance to low-income people.

Libraries are a treasure on campus and in any community. They employ people who are happy to help you locate information.

Newspapers published on campus and in the local community list events and services that are free or inexpensive.

The *school catalog* lists course descriptions and tuition fees, requirements for graduation, and information on everything from the school's history to its grading practices.

School security agencies can tell you what's safe and what's not. They can also provide information about parking, bicycle regulations, and traffic rules.

Special needs and disability services assist college students who have learning disabilities or other disabilities.

Student health clinics often provide free or inexpensive counseling and other medical treatment.

Student organizations present opportunities for extracurricular activities. Explore student government, fraternities, sororities, service clubs, religious groups, sports clubs, and political groups. Find women's centers; multicultural student centers; and organizations for international students, students with disabilities, and gay and lesbian students.

Support groups exist for people with almost any problem, from drug addiction to cancer. You can find people with problems who meet every week to share suggestions, information, and concerns about problems they share.

Tutoring is usually free and is available through academic departments or counseling centers. ✳

Leading the way—succeeding as a first-generation student

AMERICAN HISTORY CONFIRMS that people who are the first in their family to enter higher education can succeed. Examples range from the former slaves who enrolled in the country's first African-American colleges to the ex-soldiers who used the GI Bill to win advanced degrees. From their collective experience, you can take some life-changing lessons.

Remember your strengths

The fact that you're reading this book right now is a sign of your accomplishments. You applied to school. You got admitted. You've already taken a huge step to success: You showed up.

Celebrate every one of your successes in higher education, no matter how small they seem. Every assignment you complete, every paper you turn in, and every quiz question you answer is a measurable and meaningful step to getting a degree.

Discover more of your strengths by taking any fact that others might see as a barrier and looking for the hidden advantage. Did you grow up in a family that struggled to make ends meet financially? Then you know about living on a limited budget. Did you work to help support your family while you were in high school? Then you know about managing your time to balance major commitments. Did you grow up in a neighborhood with people of many races, religions, and levels of income? Then you already have an advantage when it comes to thriving with diversity.

Put your strengths in writing. Write Discovery Statements about specific personal, academic, and financial challenges you faced in the past. Describe how you coped with them. Then follow up with Intention Statements about ways to meet the challenges of higher education.

Also keep showing up. Going to every class, lab session, and study group meeting is a way to squeeze the most value from your tuition bills.

Expect change—and discomfort

Entering higher education means walking into a new culture. At times you might feel that all the ground rules have changed, and you have no idea how to fit in. This is normal.

When you walked into your first class this semester, you carried your personal hopes for the future along with the expectations of your parents, siblings, and other relatives. Those people might assume that you'll return home and be the same person you were last year.

The reality is that you will change while you're in school. Your beliefs, your friends, and your career goals may all shift. You might feel critical of people back home and think that some of their ideas are limited. And in turn, they might criticize you.

First-generation students sometimes talk about standing between two worlds. They know that they're changing. At the same time, they are uncertain about what the future holds.

This, too, is normal. Education is all about change. It can be exciting, frustrating, and frightening—all at once. Making mistakes and moving through disappointments is part of the process.

Ask for support

You don't have to go it alone. Your tuition buys access to many services. These are sources of academic and personal support. You'll find examples listed in "Connect to Resources" on page 17. Ask your school about any programs geared specifically to first-generation students.

The key point is to *ask for help right away*. Do this as soon as you feel stuck in class or experience conflict in a relationship.

Also keep a list of every person who stands behind you—relatives, friends, instructors, advisors, mentors, tutors, and counselors. Remind yourself that you are surrounded by people who want you to succeed. Furthermore, thank each of them for their help.

Pay it forward

You are an inspiration to your family, friends, and fellow students. Several people you know might apply to school on the strength of your example. Talk to these people about what you've learned. Your presence in their lives is a contribution. ✳

Succeeding in higher education— at any age

David Buffington/BlendImages/Getty

BEING AN ADULT LEARNER puts you on strong footing. With a rich store of life experiences, you can ask meaningful questions and make connections between course work and daily life.

Following are some suggestions for adult learners who want to ease their transition to higher education. If you're a younger student, commuting student, or community college student, look for useful ideas here as well.

Be clear about why you're back in school. Deborah Davis, author of *The Adult Learner's Companion*, suggests that you state your reason for entering higher education in a single sentence or phrase.[10] For example:

- To be a role model for my family.
- To finish a degree that I started work on years ago.
- To advance in my current job.
- To increase my income and career prospects over the long term.

Make your statement brief, memorable, and personally inspiring. Recall it whenever you're buried in the details of writing papers, reading textbooks, and studying for tests.

Ease into it. If you're new to higher education, consider easing into it. You can choose to attend school part-time before making a full-time commitment. If you've taken college-level classes in the past, find out if any of those credits will transfer into your current program.

Plan your week. Many adult learners report that their number one problem is time. One solution is to plan your week. By planning ahead a week at a time, you get a bigger picture of your multiple roles as a student, an employee, and a family member. With that awareness, you can make conscious adjustments in the number of hours you devote to each domain of activity. For many more suggestions on this topic, see Chapter 3: "Time."

Delegate tasks. Consider hiring others to do some of your household work or errands. Yes, this costs money. It's also an investment in your education and future earning power.

If you have children, delegate some of the chores to them. Or start a meal co-op in your neighborhood. Cook dinner for yourself and someone else one night each week. In return, ask that person to furnish you with a meal on another night. A similar strategy can apply to child care and other household tasks.

Get to know other returning students. Introduce yourself to other adult learners. Being in the same classroom gives you an immediate bond. You can exchange work, home, or cell phone numbers and build a network of mutual support. Some students adopt a buddy system, pairing up with another student in each class to complete assignments and prepare for tests.

Find common ground with traditional students. You share a central goal with younger students: to succeed in school. It's easier to get past the generation gap when you keep this in mind. Traditional and nontraditional students have many things in common. They seek to gain knowledge and skills for their chosen careers. They desire financial stability and personal fulfillment. And, like their older peers, many younger students are concerned about whether they have the skills to succeed in higher education.

Consider pooling resources with younger students. Share notes, edit papers, and form study groups. Look for ways to build on each other's strengths. If you want help with using a computer for assignments, you might find a younger student to help. In group projects and case studies, expand the discussion by sharing insights from your experiences.

David Buffington/BlendImages/Getty

Enlist your employer's support. Employers often promote continuing education. Further education can increase your skills in a specific field while enhancing your ability to work with people. That makes you a more valuable employee or consultant.

Let your employer in on your educational plans. Point out how the skills you gain in class will help you meet work objectives. Offer informal seminars at work to share what you're learning in school.

Get extra mileage out of your current tasks. You can look for specific ways to merge your work and school lives. Some schools offer academic credit for work and life experience. Your company might reimburse its employees for some tuition costs or even grant time off to attend classes.

Experiment with combining tasks. For example, when you're assigned a research paper, choose a topic that relates to your current job tasks.

Look for child care. For some students, returning to class means looking for child care outside the home. Many schools offer childcare facilities at reduced rates for students.

Review your subjects before you start classes. Say that you're registered for trigonometry and you haven't taken a math class since high school. Consider brushing up on the subject before classes begin. Also talk with future instructors about ways to prepare for their classes.

Be willing to adopt new study habits. Rather than returning to study habits from previous school experiences, many adult learners find it more effective to treat their school assignments exactly as they would treat a project at work. They use the same tactics in the library as they do on the job, which often helps them learn more actively.

Integrate class work with daily experiences. You can start by remembering two words: *why* and *how*.

Why prompts you to look for a purpose and benefit in what you're learning. Say that your psychology teacher lectures about Abraham Maslow's ideas on the hierarchy of human needs. Maslow stated that the need for self-actualization is just as important as the need for safety, security, or love.[11]

As you learn what Maslow meant by *self-actualization,* ask yourself why this concept would make a difference in your life. Perhaps your reason for entering higher education is connected to your own quest for self-actualization, that is, for maximizing your fulfillment in life and living up to your highest potential. The theory of self-actualization could clarify your goals and help you get the most out of school.

How means looking for immediate application. Invent ways to use and test concepts in your daily life—the sooner, the better. For example, how could you restructure your life for greater self-actualization? What would you do differently on a daily basis? What things would you acquire that you don't have now? And how would you be different in your moment-to-moment relationships with people?

"Publish" your schedule. After you plan your study and class sessions for the week, hang your schedule in a place where others who live with you will see it.

Enroll family and friends in your success. The fact that you're in school will affect the key relationships in your life. Attending classes and doing homework could mean less time to spend with others. You can prepare family members by discussing these issues ahead of time. For ways to prevent and resolve conflict, see Chapter 9: "Communicating."

You can also involve your spouse, partner, children, or close friends in your schooling. Offer to give them a tour of the campus and encourage them to attend social events at school with you.

Take this process a step further and ask the key people in your life for help. Share your reason for getting a degree, and talk about what your whole family has to gain from this change in your life. Ask them to think of ways that they can support your success in school. Make your own education a joint mission that benefits everyone. ✶

Discovery Statement

Choosing your purpose

Success is a choice—your choice. To *get* what you want, it helps to *know* what you want. That is the purpose of this two-part Journal Entry.

You can begin choosing success by completing this Journal Entry right now. If you choose to do it later, plan a date, time, and place and then block out the time on your calendar.

Date: _____

Time: _____

Place: _____

Part 1

Select a time and place when you know you will not be disturbed for at least 20 minutes. (The library is a good place to do this exercise.) Relax for two or three minutes, clearing your mind. Next, complete the following sentences—and then keep writing.

When you run out of things to write, stick with it just a bit longer. Be willing to experience a little discomfort. Keep writing. What you discover might be well worth the extra effort.

What I want from my education is . . .

_____

_____

_____

_____

When I complete my education, I want to be able to . . .

_____

_____

_____

_____

I also want . . .

_____

_____

_____

_____

_____

Part 2

After completing Part 1, take a short break. Reward yourself by doing something that you enjoy. Then come back to this Journal Entry.

Now, review the list you just created of things that you want from your education. See if you can summarize them in one sentence. Start this sentence with; "My purpose for being in school is. . . ."

Allow yourself to write many drafts of this mission statement, and review it periodically as you continue your education. With each draft, see if you can capture the essence of what you want from higher education and from your life. State it in a vivid way—in a short sentence that you can easily memorize, one that sparks your enthusiasm and makes you want to get up in the morning.

You might find it difficult to express your purpose statement in one sentence. If so, write a paragraph or more. Then look for the sentence that seems most charged with energy for you.

Following are some sample purpose statements:

- My purpose for being in school is to gain skills that I can use to contribute to others.
- My purpose for being in school is to live an abundant life that is filled with happiness, health, love, and wealth.
- My purpose for being in school is to enjoy myself by making lasting friendships and following the lead of my interests.

Write at least one draft of your purpose statement in the following space:

_____

_____

_____

_____

_____

_____

_____

_____

_____

THE Power Processes

A User's Guide

A *Power Process* is a suggestion to shift your perspective and try on a new habit or way of seeing the world. This book includes a baker's dozen of them. Reviewers of *From Master Student to Master Employee* consistently refer to the power of the Power Processes. Many students point to these short, offbeat, and occasionally outrageous articles as their favorite part of the book.

Why use the Power Processes?

People operate like holograms. Holograms are three-dimensional pictures made by using lasers and a special kind of film. You can cut holographic film into tiny pieces and reproduce the entire image from any piece. Each piece contains the whole.

Scientists have observed the same principle at work in biology, physics, sociology, politics, and management. Biologists know that the chromosomes in each cell are the blueprints for that whole organism. Careful study of any one cell can show a plan for the entire body.

The hologram-like nature of human behavior can be summed up in the word *process*. We have a natural tendency to live in patterns—to act out of habit. You can harness this idea for practical benefit. Altering a single attitude or basic behavior is like changing the blueprint for your life. One small change can open the door to many other changes, with a cascading series of positive effects. That's the reason why the word *power* goes with the term *process*.

Becoming a master student means setting up patterns of success that will last the rest of your life. The Power Processes in this book offer many more examples of this approach.

How do I use the Power Processes?

Approach each Power Process with an open mind. Then experiment with it right away. See if it works for you.

Psychologists have written thousands of pages on the subject of personal change. You can find countless personality theories, techniques for reinforcing behaviors, and other complex schemes.

As an alternative, consider that personal change is simple. Just do something differently. Do it now. Then see what happens.

People often make personal change more complicated. They spend years trying to enhance their self-discipline, unearth their childhood memories, search for their hidden sources of motivation, discover their higher self, and on and on.

Another option is to just change, starting today. That's the idea behind the Power Processes. You'll find 13 of them in this book:

- Discover what you want, page 23
- Ideas are tools, page 49
- Risk being a fool, page 81
- Be here now, page 113
- Love your problems (and experience your barriers), page 133
- Notice your pictures and let them go, page 159
- I create it all, page 183
- Detach, page 211
- Find a bigger problem, page 239
- Employ your word, page 271
- Choose your conversations (and your community), page 293
- Surrender, page 313
- Be it, page 353

To start unleashing the power, turn the page now. ✳

Discover What You Want

Excerpts from Creating Your Future.
Copyright © 1998 by David B. Ellis.
Reprinted with permission of the author.

Imagine a person who walks up to a counter at the airport to buy a plane ticket for his next vacation. "Just give me a ticket," he says to the reservation agent. "Anywhere will do."

The agent stares back at him in disbelief. "I'm sorry, sir," she replies. "I'll need some more details. Just minor things—such as the name of your destination city and your arrival and departure dates."

"Oh, I'm not fussy," says the would-be vacationer. "I just want to get away. You choose for me."

Compare this scene with that of another traveler who walks up to the counter and says, "I'd like a ticket to Ixtapa, Mexico, departing on Saturday, March 23, and returning Sunday, April 7. Please give me a window seat, first class, with vegetarian meals."

Now, ask yourself which traveler is more likely to end up with an enjoyable vacation. The same principle applies in any area of life. Knowing where we want to go increases the probability that we will arrive at our destination. Discovering what we want makes it more likely that we'll attain it. Once our goals are defined precisely, our brains reorient our thinking and behavior to align with those goals—and we're well on the way there.

The example about the traveler with no destination seems far-fetched. Before you dismiss it, though, do an informal experiment: Ask three other students what they want to get out of their education. Be prepared for hemming and hawing, vague generalities, and maybe even a helping of pie-in-the-sky à la mode.

These responses are amazing, considering the stakes involved. Our hypothetical vacationer is about to invest a couple weeks of his time and hundreds of dollars, all with no destination in mind. Students routinely invest years of their lives and thousands of dollars with an equally hazy idea of their destination in life.

Now suppose that you ask someone what she wants from her education and you get this answer: "I plan to get a degree in journalism with double minors in earth science and Portuguese so that I can work as a reporter covering the environment in Brazil." Chances are you've found a master student. The details of a person's vision offer a clue to mastery.

Discovering what you want greatly enhances your odds of succeeding in higher education. Many students quit school simply because they are unsure about what they want from it. With well-defined goals in mind, you can look for connections between what you want and what you study. The more connections you discover, the more likely you'll stay in school—and the more likely you'll get what you want in every area of life.[12]

Learn more about using this Power Process online.

1 First Steps

Master Student Map

as you read, ask yourself

what if . . .

I could discover my interests, skills, and passions—and build a successful education and career with them?

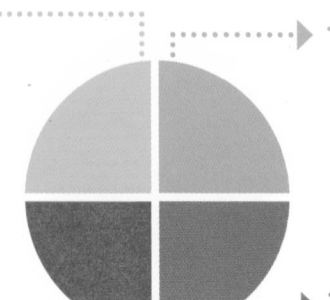

why this chapter matters . . .

Visible measures of success—such as top grades and a career that you love—start with the willingness to discover who you are and what you want.

what is included . . .

how you can use this chapter . . .

- Experience the power of telling the truth about your current skills.
- Discover your preferred learning styles and develop new ones.
- Define what you want from your education and your career.

MASTER EMPLOYEE in *action*

> The skills I learned in college are initiative and being pro-active. Similar to making the effort to attend office hours to speak with a professor about a project, I have been pro-active in reaching out to people within my division to learn more about their job responsibilities. Through doing so, I have been able to gain insights as to areas I may want to learn more about as well as further my knowledge about how our jobs are connected.

—KRISTEN OATS, FINANCIAL ANALYST

Photo courtesy of Kristen Oats

First Step:
Truth is a key to mastery

THE FIRST STEP technique is simple: Tell the truth about who you are and what you want. End of discussion. Now proceed to Chapter 2: "Careers."

Well, it's not *quite* that simple.

The First Step is one of the most valuable tools in this book. It magnifies the power of all the other techniques. It is a key to becoming a master student.

Urging you to tell the truth sounds like moralizing, but there is nothing moralizing about a First Step. It is a practical, down-to-earth way to change behavior. No technique in this book has been field-tested more often or more successfully—or under tougher circumstances.

The principle of telling the truth is applied universally by people who want to turn their lives around. For members of Alcoholics Anonymous, the First Step is acknowledging that they are powerless over alcohol. For people who join Weight Watchers, the First Step is admitting how much they weigh.

It's not easy to tell the truth about our weaknesses. For some of us, it's even harder to recognize our strengths. Maybe we don't want to brag. Maybe we're attached to a poor self-image. Yet using the First Step technique in *From Master Student to Master Employee* means we must tell the truth about our positive qualities, too.

It might help to remember that weaknesses are often strengths taken to an extreme. The student who carefully revises her writing can make significant improvements in a term paper. If she revises too much and hands in the paper late, though, her grade might suffer. Any success strategy carried too far can backfire.

Whether written or verbal, the ways that we express our First Steps are more powerful when they are specific rather than judgmental. For example, if you want to improve your note-taking skills, you might write, "I am an awful note taker." It would be more effective to write, "I can't read 80 percent of the notes I took in Introduction to Psychology last week, and I have no idea what was important in that class." Be just as specific about what you plan to achieve. You might declare, "I want to take legible notes that help me predict what questions will be on the final exam."

Completing the exercises in this chapter can help you tap resources you never knew you had. They're all First Steps. It's just that simple. The truth has power. ✳

journal entry 3

Discovery/Intention Statement

Create value from this chapter

Take five minutes to skim the Discovery Wheel exercise starting on page 27. Find one statement that describes a skill you already possess—a personal strength that will promote your success in school. Write that statement here:

_____

_____

_____

_____

The Discovery Wheel might also prompt some thoughts about skills you want to acquire. Describe one of those skills by completing the following sentence.

I discovered that . . .

_____

_____

_____

_____

Now, skim the appropriate chapter in this book for at least three articles that could help you develop this skill. For example, if you want to take more effective notes, turn to Chapter 6: "Notes." List the names of your chosen articles here.

I intend to read . . .

_____

_____

_____

_____

_____

critical thinking exercise
③ Taking the First Step

The purpose of this exercise is to give you a chance to discover and acknowledge your own strengths, as well as areas for improvement. For many students, this exercise is the most difficult one in the book. To make the exercise worthwhile, do it with courage.

Some people suggest that looking at areas for improvement means focusing on personal weaknesses. They view it as a negative approach that runs counter to positive thinking. Well, perhaps. Positive thinking is a great technique. So is telling the truth, especially when we see the whole picture—the negative aspects as well as the positive ones.

If you admit that you can't add or subtract and that's the truth, then you have taken a strong, positive First Step toward learning basic math. On the other hand, if you say that you are a terrible math student and that's not the truth, then you are programming yourself to accept unnecessary failure.

The point is to tell the truth. This exercise is similar to the Discovery Statements that appear in every chapter. The difference is that, in this case, for reasons of confidentiality, you won't write down your discoveries in the book.

Be brave. If you approach this exercise with courage, you are likely to disclose some things about yourself that you wouldn't want others to read. You might even write down some truths that could get you into trouble. Do this exercise on separate sheets of paper; then hide or destroy them. Protect your privacy.

To make this exercise work, follow these suggestions.

Be specific. It is not effective to write, "I can improve my communication skills." Of course you can. Instead, write down precisely what you can *do* to improve your communication skills—for example, "I can spend more time really listening while the other person is talking, instead of thinking about what I'm going to say next."

Look beyond the classroom. What goes on outside school often has the greatest impact on your ability to be an effective student. Consider your strengths and weaknesses that you may think have nothing to do with school.

Be courageous. This exercise is a waste of time if it is done half-heartedly. Be willing to take risks. You might open a door that reveals a part of yourself that you didn't want to admit was there. The power of this technique is that once you know what is there, you can do something about it.

Part 1

Time yourself, and for 10 minutes write as fast as you can, completing each of the following sentences at least 10 times with anything that comes to mind. If you get stuck, don't stop. Just write something—even if it seems crazy.

- I never succeed when I . . .
- I'm not very good at . . .
- Something I'd like to change about myself is . . .

Part 2

When you have completed the first part of the exercise, review what you have written, crossing off things that don't make any sense. The sentences that remain suggest possible goals for becoming a master student.

Part 3

Here's the tough part. Time yourself, and for 10 minutes write as fast as you can, completing the following sentences with anything that comes to mind. As in Part 1, complete each sentence at least 10 times. Just keep writing, even if it sounds silly.

- I always succeed when I . . .
- I am very good at . . .
- Something I like about myself is . . .

Part 4

Review what you have written, and circle the things that you can fully celebrate. This list is a good thing to keep for those times when you question your own value and worth.

 Complete this exercise online.

critical thinking exercise
4 The Discovery Wheel

The Discovery Wheel is another opportunity to tell the truth about the kind of student you are and the kind of student you want to become.

This is not a test. There are no trick questions, and the answers will have meaning only for yourself.

Here are two suggestions to make this exercise more effective. First, think of it as the beginning of an opportunity to change. There is another Discovery Wheel at the end of this book. You will have a chance to measure your progress there, so be honest about where you are now. Second, lighten up. A little laughter can make self-evaluations a lot more effective.

Here's how the Discovery Wheel works. By the end of this exercise, you will have filled in a circle similar to the one on this page. The Discovery Wheel circle is a picture of how you see yourself as a student. The closer the shading comes to the outer edge of the circle, the higher the evaluation of a specific skill. In the example to the right, the student has rated her reading skills low and her note-taking skills high.

The terms *high* and *low* are not meant to reflect judgment. The Discovery Wheel is not a permanent picture of who you are. It is a picture of how you view your strengths and weaknesses as a student today. To begin this exercise, read the following statements and award yourself points for each one, using the point system described below. Then add up your point total for each section, and shade the Discovery Wheel on page 30 to the appropriate level.

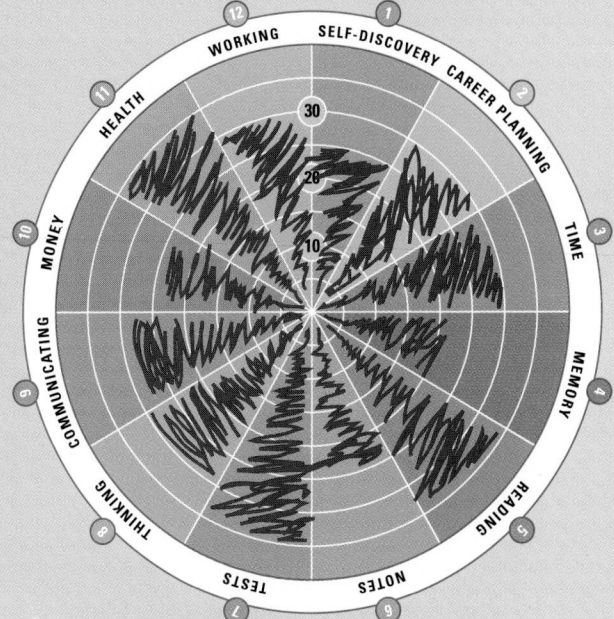

5 points: This statement is always or almost always true of me.

4 points: This statement is often true of me.

3 points: This statement is true of me about half the time.

2 points: This statement is seldom true of me.

1 point: This statement is never or almost never true of me.

 Complete this exercise online.

1. _____ I enjoy learning.

2. _____ I understand and apply the concept of multiple intelligences.

3. _____ I connect my courses to my purpose for being in school.

4. _____ I make a habit of assessing my personal strengths and areas for improvement.

5. _____ I am satisfied with how I am progressing toward achieving my goals.

6. _____ I use my knowledge of learning styles to support my success in school.

7. _____ I am willing to consider any idea that can help me succeed in school—even if I initially disagree with that idea.

8. _____ I regularly remind myself of the benefits I intend to get from my education.

_____ **Total score (1) Self-discovery**

1. _____ I relate school to what I plan to do for the rest of my life.

2. _____ I plan my career with a detailed knowledge of my skills.

3. _____ I relate my career plan to my interests, attitudes, and core values.

FIRST STEPS

4. _____ I can effectively use a variety of resources to research possible careers.

5. _____ I use the career planning services offered by my school.

6. _____ I am planning a career that contributes something worthwhile to the world.

7. _____ I have a written career plan and I update it regularly.

8. _____ I use internships, extracurricular activities, information interviews, and on-the-job experiences to test and refine my career plan.

_____ Total score (2) Career Planning

1. _____ I set long-term goals and periodically review them.

2. _____ I set short-term goals to support my long-term goals.

3. _____ I write a plan for each day and each week.

4. _____ I assign priorities to what I choose to do each day.

5. _____ I plan review time so I don't have to cram before tests.

6. _____ I plan regular recreation time.

7. _____ I adjust my study time to meet the demands of individual courses.

8. _____ I have adequate time each day to accomplish what I plan.

_____ Total score (3) Time

1. _____ I am confident of my ability to remember.

2. _____ I can remember people's names.

3. _____ At the end of a lecture, I can summarize what was presented.

4. _____ I apply techniques that enhance my memory skills.

5. _____ I can recall information when I'm under pressure.

6. _____ I remember important information clearly and easily.

7. _____ I can jog my memory when I have difficulty recalling.

8. _____ I can relate new information to what I've already learned.

_____ Total score (4) Memory

1. _____ I preview and review reading assignments.

2. _____ When reading, I ask myself questions about the material.

3. _____ I underline or highlight important passages when reading.

4. _____ When I read textbooks, I am alert and awake.

5. _____ I relate what I read to my life.

6. _____ I select a reading strategy to fit the type of material I'm reading.

7. _____ I take effective notes when I read.

8. _____ When I don't understand what I'm reading, I note my questions and find answers.

_____ Total score (5) Reading

1. _____ When I am in class, I focus my attention.

2. _____ I take notes in class.

3. _____ I am aware of various methods for taking notes and choose those that work best for me.

4. _____ I distinguish important material and note key phrases in a lecture.

5. _____ I copy down material that the instructor writes out and displays to the class.

6. _____ I can put important concepts into my own words.

7. _____ My notes are valuable for review.

8. _____ I review class notes within 24 hours.

_____ Total score (6) Notes

1. _____ I use techniques to manage stress related to exams.

2. _____ I manage my time during exams and am able to complete them.

3. _____ I am able to predict test questions.

4. _____ I adapt my test-taking strategy to the kind of test I'm taking.

5. _____ I understand what essay questions ask and can answer them completely and accurately.

6. _____ I start reviewing for tests at the beginning of the term.

7. _____ I continue reviewing for tests throughout the term.

8. _____ My sense of personal worth is independent of my test scores.

_____ **Total score (7) Tests**

1. _____ I have flashes of insight and think of solutions to problems at unusual times.

2. _____ I use brainstorming to generate solutions to a variety of problems.

3. _____ When I get stuck on a creative project, I use specific methods to get unstuck.

4. _____ I see problems and tough choices as opportunities for learning and personal growth.

5. _____ I am willing to consider different points of view and alternative solutions.

6. _____ I can detect common errors in logic.

7. _____ I construct viewpoints by drawing on information and ideas from many sources.

8. _____ As I share my viewpoints with others, I am open to their feedback.

_____ **Total score (8) Thinking**

1. _____ I am candid with others about who I am, what I feel, and what I want.

2. _____ Other people tell me that I am a good listener.

3. _____ I can communicate my upset and anger without blaming others.

4. _____ I can make friends and create valuable relationships in a new setting.

5. _____ I am open to being with people I don't especially like in order to learn from them.

6. _____ I can effectively plan and research a large writing assignment.

7. _____ I create first drafts without criticizing my writing, then edit later for clarity, accuracy, and coherence.

8. _____ I know ways to prepare and deliver effective speeches.

_____ **Total score (9) Communicating**

1. _____ I am in control of my personal finances.

2. _____ I can access a variety of resources to finance my education.

3. _____ I am confident that I will have enough money to complete my education.

4. _____ I take on debts carefully and repay them on time.

5. _____ I have long-range financial goals and a plan to meet them.

6. _____ I make regular deposits to a savings account.

7. _____ I pay off the balance on credit card accounts each month.

8. _____ I can have fun without spending money.

_____ **Total score (10) Money**

1. _____ I have enough energy to study and work—and still enjoy other areas of my life.

2. _____ If the situation calls for it, I have enough reserve energy to put in a long day.

3. _____ The way I eat supports my long-term health.

4. _____ The way I eat is independent of my feelings of self-worth.

5. _____ I exercise regularly to maintain a healthy weight.

6. _____ My emotional health supports my ability to learn.

7. _____ I notice changes in my physical condition and respond effectively.

8. _____ I am in control of any alcohol or other drugs I put into my body.

_____ **Total score (11) Health**

1. _____ In work settings, I look for models of success and cultivate mentors.

2. _____ My work creates value for my employer.

3. _____ I see working as a way to pursue my interests, expand my skills, and develop mastery.

4. _____ I support other people in their career planning and job hunting—and am willing to accept their support.

5. _____ I can function effectively in corporate cultures and cope positively with office politics.

6. _____ I am skilled at discovering job openings and moving through the hiring process.

7. _____ I regularly update and take action on my career plan.

8. _____ I see learning as a lifelong process that includes experiences inside and outside the classroom.

_____ **Total score (12) Working**

Filling in your Discovery Wheel

Using the total score from each category, shade in each section of the Discovery Wheel. Use different colors, if you want. For example, you could use green to denote areas you want to work on. When you have finished, complete Journal Entry 4.

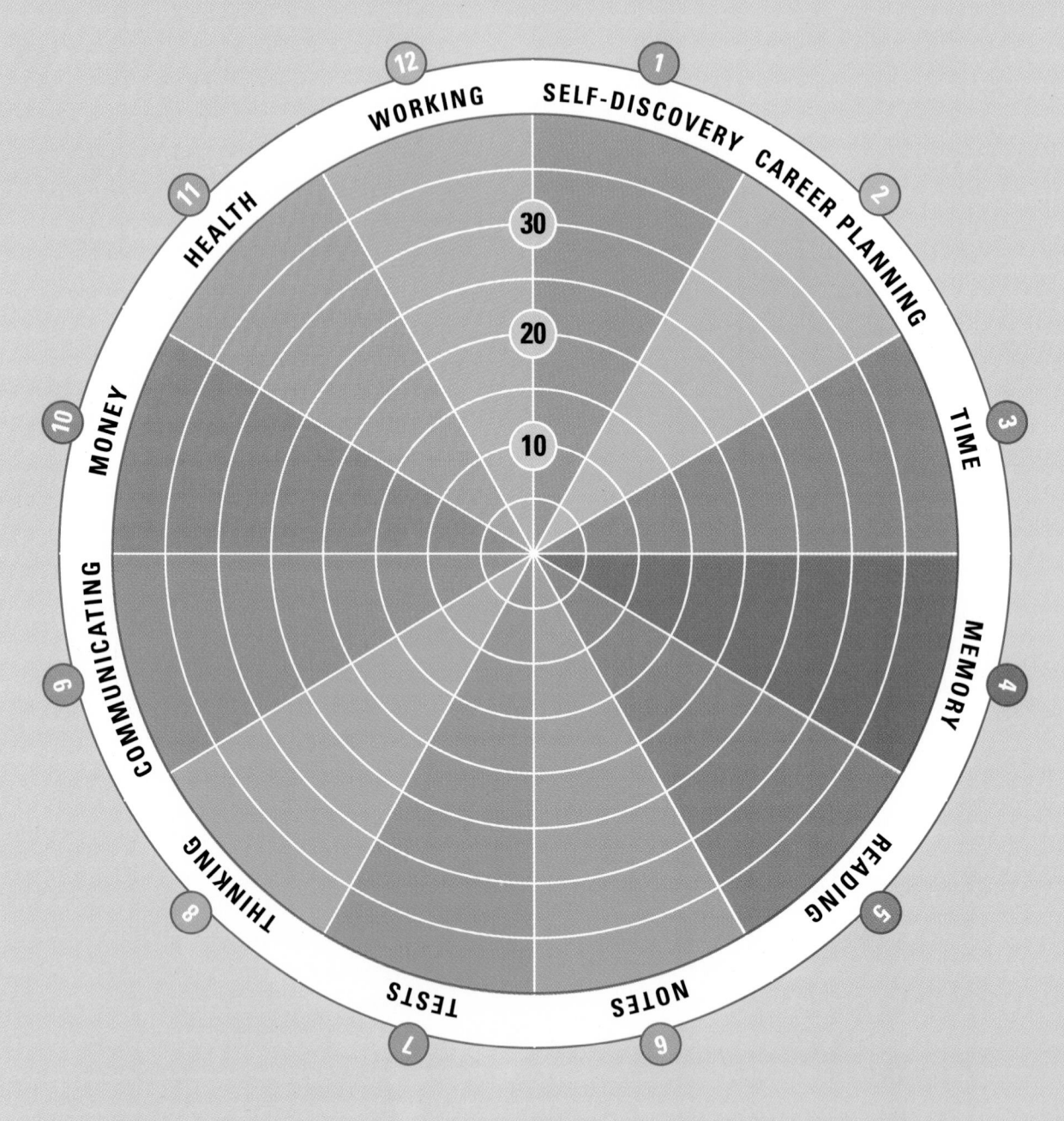

Discovery/Intention Statement

Roll your Discovery Wheel

Now that you have completed your Discovery Wheel, it's time to get a sense of its weight, shape, and balance. Can you imagine running your hands around it? If you could lift it, would it feel light or heavy? How would it sound if it rolled down a hill? Would it roll very far? Would it wobble? Make your observations without judging the wheel as good or bad. Simply be with the picture you have created.

After you have spent a few minutes studying your Discovery Wheel, complete the following sentences in the spaces below them. Don't worry about what to write. Just put down whatever comes to mind. Remember, this is not a test.

This wheel is an accurate picture of my ability as a student because . . .

_____

_____

_____

_____

_____

My self-evaluation surprises me because . . .

_____

_____

_____

_____

The two areas in which I am strongest are . . .

_____

_____

_____

_____

_____

The areas in which I want to improve are . . .

_____

_____

_____

_____

_____

_____

_____

I want to concentrate on improving these areas because . . .

_____

_____

_____

_____

_____

_____

_____

Now, select one of your discoveries, and describe how you intend to benefit from it. Complete the statement below. To gain some practical value from this discovery, I will . . .

_____

_____

_____

_____

_____

_____

Learning styles: Discovering how you learn

what if ◄ ⋯⋯⋯► why

how ◄ ⋯⋯⋯ ►what

RIGHT NOW, you are investing substantial amounts of time, money, and energy in your education. What you get in return for this investment depends on how well you understand the process of learning and use it to your advantage.

If you don't understand learning, you might feel bored or confused in class. After getting a low grade, you might have no idea how to respond. Over time, frustration can mount to the point where you question the value of being in school.

Some students answer that question by dropping out of school. These students lose a chance to create the life they want, and society loses the contributions of educated workers.

You can prevent that outcome. Gain strategies for going beyond boredom and confusion. Discover new options for achieving goals, solving problems, listening more fully, speaking more persuasively, and resolving conflicts between people. Start by understanding the different ways that people create meaning from their experience and change their behavior. In other words, learn about *how* we learn.

We learn by perceiving and processing

When we learn well, says psychologist David Kolb, two things happen.[1] First, we *perceive*—that is, we notice events and "take in" new experiences. Second, we *process,* or "deal with," experiences in a way that helps us make sense of them.

Some people especially enjoy perceiving through *concrete experience.* They like to absorb information through their five senses. They learn by getting directly involved in new experiences. When solving problems, they rely on intuition as much as intellect. These people typically function well in unstructured classes that allow them to take initiative.

Other people favor perceiving by *abstract conceptualization.* They take in information best when they can think about it as a subject separate from themselves. They analyze, intellectualize, and create

theories. Often these people take a scientific approach to problem solving and excel in traditional classrooms.

People also process experiences differently. Some people favor processing information by *reflective observation.* They prefer to stand back, watch what is going on, and think about it. They consider several points of view as they attempt to make sense of things and generate many ideas about how something happens. They value patience, good judgment, and a thorough approach to learning.

Other people like to process experience by *active experimentation.* They prefer to jump in and start doing things immediately. These people do not mind taking risks as they attempt to make sense of things; this helps them learn. They are results-oriented and look for practical ways to apply what they have learned.

Perceiving and processing—an example

Suppose that you get a new cell phone. It has more features than any phone you've used before. You have many options for learning how to use it. For example, you could do any of the following:

- Just get your hands on the phone right away, press some buttons, and see if you can dial a number or send a text message.

- Read the instruction manual and view help screens on the phone before you try to make a call.

- Recall experiences you've had with phones in the past and what you've learned by watching other people use their cell phones.

- Ask a friend who owns the same type of phone to coach you as you experiment with making calls and sending messages.

These actions illustrate the different ways of perceiving and processing:

- Getting your hands on the phone right away and seeing if you can make it work is an example of learning through concrete experience.

- Reading the manual and help screens before you use the phone is an example of learning through abstract conceptualization.
- Recalling what you've experienced in the past is an example of learning through reflective observation.
- Asking a friend to coach you through a "hands-on" activity with the phone is an example of learning through active experimentation.

Four modes of learning and four questions

Your learning style is the unique way in which you blend the possible ways of perceiving and processing experience. Learning styles can be described in many ways. To keep things simple, just think in terms of four *modes* of learning.

Mode 1 learners are concrete and reflective. They seek a purpose for new information and a personal connection with the content. They want to know that a course matters, and how it challenges or fits in with what they already know. These learners embrace new ideas that relate directly to their current interests and career plans. In summary, Mode 1 learners ask, *Why* learn this?

Mode 2 learners are abstract and reflective. They crave information. When learning something, they want to know the main facts, ideas, and procedures. They seek a theory to explain events and are interested in what experts have to say. Often these learners like ideas that are presented in a logical, organized way. They break a subject down into its key elements or steps and master each one in a systematic way. Mode 2 learners ask, *What* is the content?

Mode 3 learners are abstract and active. They hunger for an opportunity to try out what they're studying. They want to take theories and test them by putting them into practice. These learners thrive when they have well-defined tasks, guided practice, and frequent feedback. Mode 3 learners ask, *How* does this work?

Mode 4 learners are concrete and active. They get excited about going beyond classroom assignments. They apply what they're learning in various situations and use theories to solve real problems. Mode 4 learners ask, *What if* I tried this in a different setting?

The four modes—an example

From Master Student to Master Employee is specifically designed to move you through all four modes of learning.

At the beginning of each chapter, you complete a Journal Entry designed to connect the chapter content to your current life experience. The aim is to help you see the chapter's possible benefits and discover a purpose for reading further. You answer the Mode 1 question—*Why* learn this?

Next, you read articles that are filled with ideas and suggestions for succeeding in school and the workplace. All these readings are answers to the Mode 2 question—*What* is the content?

You also use exercises to practice new skills with and get feedback from your instructor and other students. These exercises are answers to the Mode 3 question—*How* does this work?

Finally, at the end of each chapter, a "Career Application" article and "Focus on Transferable Skills" exercise helps you apply the chapter content to different situations and choose your next step toward mastery. You discover answers to the Mode 4 question—*What if* I tried this in a different setting?

Also notice the Master Student Map at the beginning of each chapter. It presents the chapter content as answers to these four questions. For example, the Master Student Map for this chapter (page 24) suggests *why* this chapter matters: "Success starts with telling the truth about what *is* working—and what *isn't*—in our lives right now." There's a list of *what* topics are included and suggestions for *how* you can use this chapter. Finally, you're encouraged to ask, "*What if* I could create new outcomes in my life by accepting the way I am right now?"

Becoming a flexible learner

Kolb believes that effective learners are flexible. They can learn using all four modes. They consistently ask *Why? What? How?* and *What if?*—and use a full range of activities to find the answers.

Becoming a flexible learner promotes your success in school and in the workplace. By developing all four modes of learning, you can excel in many types of courses. You can learn from instructors with many different styles of teaching. You can expand your options for declaring a major and choosing a career. You can experiment with a variety of strategies and create new options for learning *anything*.

Above all, you can recover your natural gift for learning. Rediscover a world where the boundaries between learning and fun, between work and play, all disappear. While immersing yourself in new experiences, blend the sophistication of an adult with the wonder of a child. This path is one that you can travel for the rest of your life.

The following elements of this chapter are designed to help you take the next steps toward becoming a flexible learner:

- To discover how you currently prefer to learn, take the Learning Style Inventory on this page.

- Read the article "Using Your Learning Style Profile to Succeed" to learn ways to expand on your preferences.

- For additional perspectives on learning styles, see the articles "Claim Your Multiple Intelligences" and "Learning by Seeing, Hearing, and Moving—The VAK System."

Directions for completing the Learning Style Inventory

To help you become more aware of learning styles, Kolb developed the Learning Style Inventory (LSI). This inventory is included on the next several pages. Responding to the items in the LSI can help you discover a lot about ways you learn.

The LSI is not a test. There are no right or wrong answers. Your goal is simply to develop a profile of your current learning style. So, take the LSI quickly. You might find it useful to recall a recent time when you learned something new at school, at home, or at work. However, do not agonize over your responses.

Note that the LSI consists of twelve sentences, each with four different endings. You will read each sentence, and then write a "4" next to the ending that best describes the way you currently learn. Then you will continue ranking the other endings with a "3," "2," or "1," representing the ending that least describes you. You must rank each ending. *Do not leave any endings blank.* Use each number only once for each question.

Following are more specific directions:

1. Read the instructions at the top of page LSI-1. When you understand example A, you are ready to begin.

2. Before you write on page LSI-1, remove the sheet of paper following page LSI-2.

3. While writing on page LSI-1, *press firmly* so that your answers will show up on page LSI-3.

4. After you complete the twelve items on page LSI-1, go to page LSI-3. ✻

 Find more information and examples related to learning styles online.

 journal entry

Discovery Statement

Prepare for the Learning Style Inventory

As a "warm-up" for the LSI and articles that follow, spend a minute or two thinking about times in the past when you felt successful at learning. Underline or highlight any of the following statements that describe those situations:

I was in a highly structured setting, with a lot of directions about what to do and feedback on how well I did at each step. I was free to learn at my own pace and in my own way.

I learned as part of a small group.

I learned mainly by working alone in a quiet place.

I learned in a place where there was a lot of activity going on.

I learned by forming pictures in my mind.

I learned by *doing* something—moving around, touching something, or trying out a process for myself.

I learned by talking to myself or explaining ideas to other people.

I got the "big picture" before I tried to understand the details.

I listened to a lecture and then thought about it after class.

I read a book or article and then thought about it afterward.

I used a variety of media—such as videos, films, audio recordings, or computers—to assist my learning.

I went beyond taking notes and wrote in a personal journal.

I was considering where to attend school and knew I had to actually set foot on each campus before choosing.

I was shopping for a car and paid more attention to how I felt about test driving each one than to the sticker prices or mileage estimates.

I was thinking about going to a movie and carefully read the reviews before choosing one.

Reviewing this list, do you see any patterns in the way you prefer to learn? If you do see any patterns, briefly describe them here.

_____

_____

_____

_____

Learning Style Inventory

Before completing the items, remove the sheet of paper following this page. While writing, press firmly.

1. When I learn: _____ I like to deal with my feelings. _____ I like to think about ideas. _____ I like to be doing things. _____ I like to watch and listen.

2. I learn best when: _____ I listen and watch carefully. _____ I rely on logical thinking. _____ I trust my hunches and feelings. _____ I work hard to get things done.

3. When I am learning: _____ I tend to reason things out. _____ I am responsible about things. _____ I am quiet and reserved. _____ I have strong feelings and reactions.

4. I learn by: _____ feeling. _____ doing. _____ watching. _____ thinking.

5. When I learn: _____ I am open to new experiences. _____ I look at all sides of issues. _____ I like to analyze things, breaking them down into their parts. _____ I like to try things out.

6. When I am learning: _____ I am an observing person. _____ I am an active person. _____ I am an intuitive person _____ I am a logical person.

7. I learn best from: _____ observation. _____ personal relationships. _____ rational theories. _____ a chance to try out and practice.

8. When I learn: _____ I like to see results from my work. _____ I like ideas and theories. _____ I take my time before acting. _____ I feel personally involved in things.

9. I learn best when: _____ I rely on my observations. _____ I rely on my feelings. _____ I can try things out for myself. _____ I rely on my ideas.

10. When I am learning: _____ I am a reserved person. _____ I am an accepting person. _____ I am a responsible person. _____ I am a rational person.

11. When I learn: _____ I get involved. _____ I like to observe. _____ I evaluate things. _____ I like to be active.

12. I learn best when: _____ I analyze ideas. _____ I am receptive and open-minded. _____ I am careful. _____ I am practical.

Take a snapshot of your learning styles

This page is intended to be completed as a culminating exercise. Before you work on this exercise, complete the Learning Styles Inventory and read the following articles:

Learning styles: Discovering how you learn, page 32

Using your learning style profile to succeed, page 35

Claim your multiple intelligences, page 37

Learning by seeing, hearing, and moving—the VAK system, page 39

An inventory of your learning styles is just a snapshot that gives a picture of who you are today. Your answers are not right or wrong. Your score does not dictate who you can become in the future. The key questions are simply "How do I currently learn?" and "How can I become a more successful learner?"

Take a few minutes right now to complete the following sentences describing your latest insights into the way you learn. When you finish, plan to follow up on those insights.

If someone asked me, "What do you mean by learning styles, and can you give me an example?" I'd say . . .

I would describe my current learning style(s) as . . .

If someone asked me to define intelligence, I'd say . . .

When learning well, I tend to use the following senses . . .

I apply my knowledge of learning styles and multiple intelligences by using certain strategies, such as . . .

When I study or work with people whose learning styles differ from mine, I will respond by . . .

To explore new learning styles, I will . . .

Remove this sheet before completing the Learning Style Inventory.

This page is inserted to ensure that the other writing you do in this book doesn't show through on page LSI-3.

Remove this sheet before completing the Learning Style Inventory.

This page is inserted to ensure that the other writing you do in this book doesn't show through on page LSI-3.

Scoring your Inventory

Now that you have taken the Learning Style Inventory, it's time to fill out the Learning Style Graph (page LSI-5) and interpret your results. To do this, please follow the next five steps.

1 First, add up all of the numbers you gave to the items marked with brown **F** letters. Then write down that total to the right in the blank next to "**Brown** F." Next, add up all of the numbers for "**Teal** W,"

"**Purple** T," and "**Orange** D," and also write down those totals in the blanks to the right.

2 Add the four totals to arrive at a GRAND TOTAL and write down that figure in the blank to the right. (Note: The grand total should equal 120. If you have a different amount, go back and re-add the colored letters; it was probably just an addition error.) Now remove this page and continue with Step 3 on page LSI-5.

F	T	D	W
W	T	F	D
T	D	W	F
F	D	W	T
F	W	T	D
W	D	F	T
W	F	T	D
D	T	W	F
W	F	D	T
W	F	D	T
F	W	T	D
T	F	W	D

Remove this page after you have
completed Steps 1 and 2 on page LSI-3.
Then continue with Step 3 on page LSI-5.

Learning Style Graph

3 Remove the sheet of paper that follows this page. Then transfer your totals from Step 1 on page LSI-3 to the lines on the Learning Style Graph below. On the brown (F) line, find the number that corresponds to your "**Brown F**" total from page LSI-3. Then write an X on this number. Do the same for your "**Teal W**," "**Purple T**," and "**Orange D**" totals. The graph on this page is yours to keep and to refer to and the graph on page LSI-7 is for you to turn into your professor if he or she requires it.

4 Now, pressing firmly, draw four straight lines to connect the four X's and shade in the area to form a kite. (For an example, see the illustration to the right.) This is your learning style profile. Each X that you placed on these lines indicates your preference for a different aspect of learning:

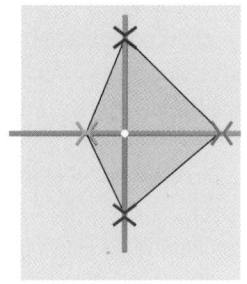

Concrete experience ("feeling"). The number where you put your X on this line indicates your preference for learning things that have personal meaning and have connections to experiences in your life. The higher your score on this line, the more you like to learn things that you feel are important and relevant to yourself.

Reflective observation ("watching"). Your number on this line indicates how important it is for you to reflect on the things you are learning. If your score is high on this line, you probably find it important to watch others as they learn about an assignment and then report on it to the class. You probably like to plan things out and take the time to make sure that you fully understand a topic.

Abstract conceptualization ("thinking"). Your number on this line indicates your preference for learning ideas, facts, and figures. If your score is high on this line, you probably like to absorb many concepts and gather lots of information on a new topic.

Active experimentation ("doing"). Your number on this line indicates your preference for applying ideas, using trial and error, and practicing what you learn. If your score is high on this line, you probably enjoy hands-on activities that allow you to test out ideas to see what works.

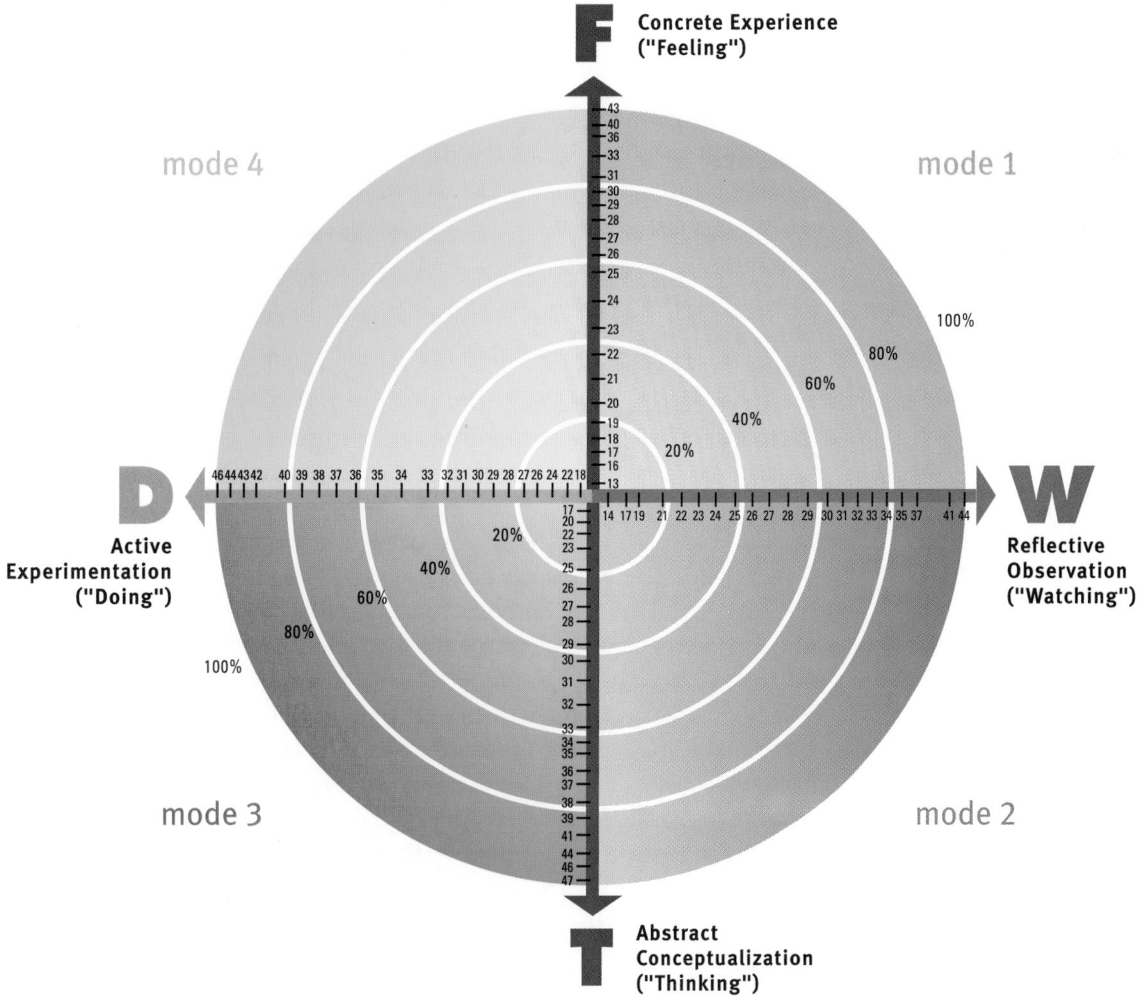

Learning styles across the curriculum

You can get another perspective on learning styles by thinking about ways to succeed in the various subjects that you study. For example, a math course will draw on different ways of perceiving and processing information than a course in African-American literature or modern dance. When you feel stuck in a particular subject, see if you can get unstuck by applying a strategy based on your knowledge of learning styles. The following chart offers some examples. Start with them, and create more on your own.

Subject Area	Possible Strategies for Mastery
Humanities: English, literature, public speaking, history, religion, philosophy, fine arts	• Deepen your reading skills by previewing and reviewing each assignment (see Chapter 5: "Reading"). • Keep a dictionary handy and create an updated list of new words and their definitions. • Experiment with several different formats for taking notes (see Chapter 6: "Notes"). • Keep a personal journal to practice writing and make connections between the authors and ideas that you're studying. • Take part in class discussions and welcome chances to speak in front of groups.
Math and natural sciences: algebra, geometry, calculus, chemistry, biology, physics	• Before registering for a course, make sure that you are adequately prepared through prior course work. • In your notes, highlight basic principles—definitions, assumptions, axioms. • Learn concepts in the sequence presented by your instructor. • If you feel confused, ask a question immediately. • Attend all classes, practice solving problems every day, and check your work carefully. • Translate word problems into images or symbols; translate images and symbols into words. • Balance abstract ideas with concrete experiences, including laboratory sessions and study groups. • Take math courses back to back so you can apply what you learn in one level of a math course immediately to the next level.
Social sciences: sociology, psychology, economics, political science, anthropology, geography	• Pay special attention to theories—key terms and statements that are used to explain relationships between observations and predict events. • Expect complex and contradictory theories, and ask your instructor about ways to resolve disagreements among experts in the field. • Ask your instructor to explain the scientific method and how it is used to arrive at theories in each social science. • Ask about the current state of evidence for each theory. • Ask for examples of a theory and look for them in your daily life.
Foreign languages: learning to speak, read, and write any language that is new to you	• Pay special attention to the "rules"—principles of grammar, noun forms, and verb tense. For each principle, list correct and incorrect examples. • Spend some time reading, writing, or speaking the language every day. • Welcome the opportunity to practice speaking in class, where you can get immediate feedback. • Start or join a study group in each of your language classes. • Spend time with people who are already skilled in speaking the language. • Travel to a country where the language is widely spoken. • Similar to math courses, take your language courses back to back to ensure fluency.

Remove this sheet before completing the Learning Style Graph

This page is inserted to ensure that the other writing you do in this book doesn't show through on page LSI-7.

Remove this sheet before completing the Learning Style Graph

This page is inserted to ensure that the other writing you do in this book doesn't show through on page LSI-7.

Returning to the big picture about learning styles

This chapter introduces many ideas about how people learn—four modes, multiple intelligences, and the VAK system. That's a lot of information! And these are just a few of the available theories. You may have heard about inventories other than the Learning Style Inventory, such as the Myers-Briggs Type Indicator® (MBTI®) Instrument.* Do an Internet search on *learning styles,* and you'll find many more.

To prevent confusion, remember that there is one big idea behind these theories about learning styles. They all promote *metacognition* (pronounced "metta-cog-NI-shun"). *Meta* means "beyond" or "above." *Cognition* refers to everything that goes on inside your brain—perceiving, thinking, and feeling. So, metacognition refers to your ability to view your attitudes and behaviors from beyond—that is, understand more fully the way you learn. From that perspective, you can choose to think and act in new ways. *Metacognition is one of the main benefits of higher education.*

In addition, theories about learning styles share the following insights:

- People differ in important ways.
- We can see differences as strengths—not deficits.
- Relationships improve when we take differences into account.
- Learning is continuous—it is a *process,* as well as a series of outcomes.
- We *create* knowledge rather than simply absorbing it.
- We have our own preferences for learning.
- We can often succeed by matching our activities with our preferences.
- Our preferences can expand as we experiment with new learning strategies.
- The deepest learning takes place when we embrace a variety of styles and strategies.

Remember that teachers in your life will come and go. Some will be more skilled than others. None of them will be perfect. With a working knowledge of learning styles, you can view any course as one step along a path to learning what you want, using the ways that *you* choose to learn. Along this path toward mastery, you become your own best teacher.

*MBTI and Myer-Briggs Type Indicator are registered trademarks of Consulting Psychologists Press, Inc.

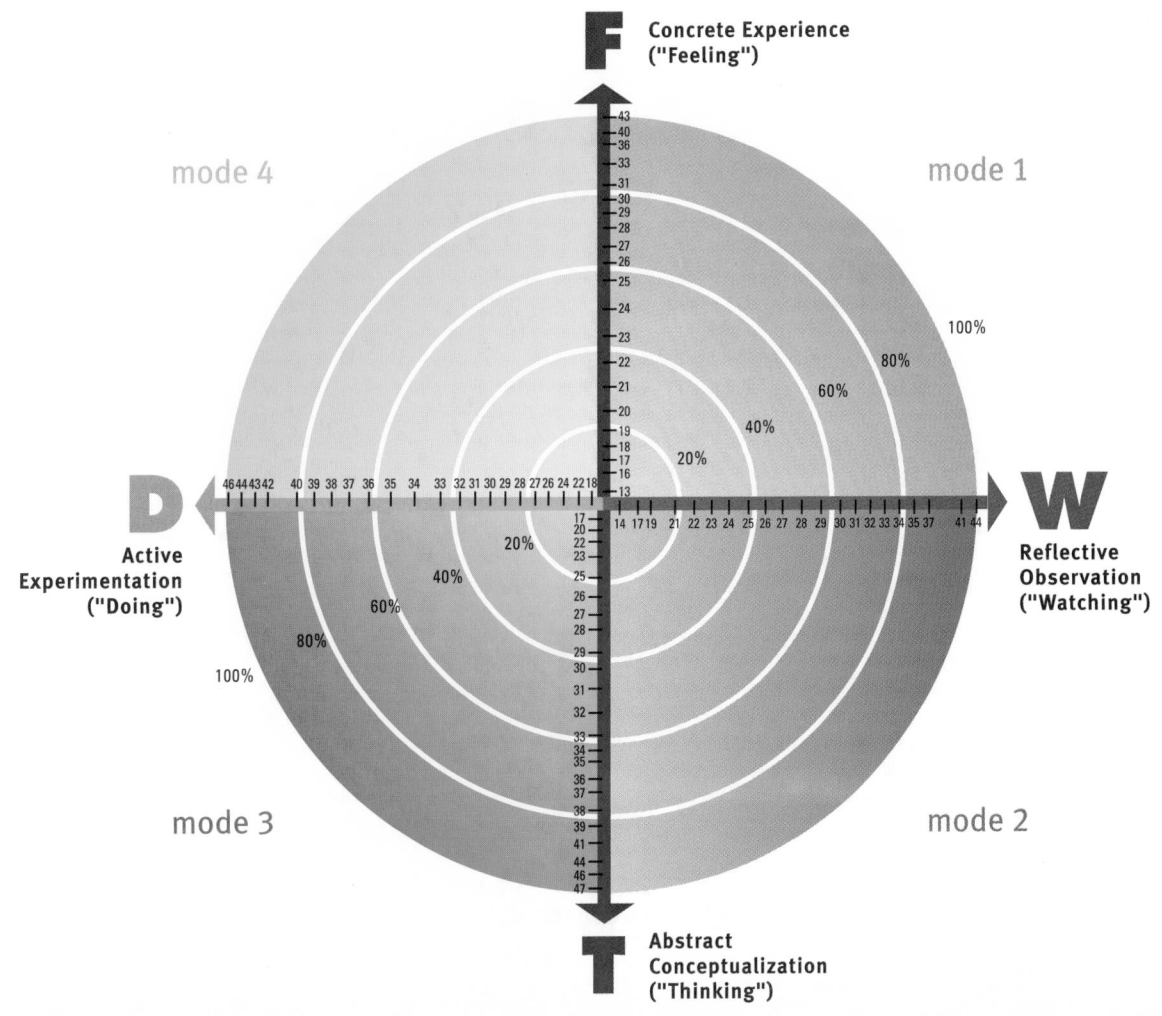

Balancing your preferences

The chart below identifies some of the natural talents as well as challenges for people who have a strong preference for any one mode of learning. For example, if most of your kite is in Mode 2 of the Learning Style Graph, then look at the lower right-hand corner of the following chart to see if this is an accurate description of yourself.

After reviewing the description of your preferred learning mode, read all of the sections for the other modes that start with the words "People with other preferred modes." These sections explain what actions you can take to become a more balanced learner.

Concrete Experience

mode 4

Strengths:
- Getting things done
- Leadership
- Risk taking

Too much of this mode can lead to:
- Trivial improvements
- Meaningless activity

Too little of this mode can lead to:
- Work not completed on time
- Impractical plans
- Lack of motivation to achieve goals

People with other preferred modes can develop Mode 4 by:
- Making a commitment to objectives
- Seeking new opportunities
- Influencing and leading others
- Being personally involved
- Dealing with people

mode 1

Strengths:
- Imaginative ability
- Understanding people
- Recognizing problems
- Brainstorming

Too much of this mode can lead to:
- Feeling paralyzed by alternatives
- Inability to make decisions

Too little of this mode can lead to:
- Lack of ideas
- Not recognizing problems and opportunities

People with other preferred modes can develop Mode 1 by:
- Being aware of other people's feelings
- Being sensitive to values
- Listening with an open mind
- Gathering information
- Imagining the implications of ambiguous situations

Active Experimentation ← → **Reflective Observation**

Strengths:
- Problem solving
- Decision making
- Deductive reasoning
- Defining problems

Too much of this mode can lead to:
- Solving the wrong problem
- Hasty decision making

Too little of this mode can lead to:
- Lack of focus
- Reluctance to consider alternatives
- Scattered thoughts

People with other preferred modes can develop Mode 3 by:
- Creating new ways of thinking and doing
- Experimenting with fresh ideas
- Choosing the best solution
- Setting goals
- Making decisions

mode 3

Strengths:
- Planning
- Creating models
- Defining problems
- Developing theories

Too much of this mode can lead to:
- Vague ideals ("castles in the air")
- Lack of practical application

Too little of this mode can lead to:
- Inability to learn from mistakes
- No sound basis for work
- No systematic approach

People with other preferred modes can develop Mode 2 by:
- Organizing information
- Building conceptual models
- Testing theories and ideas
- Designing experiments
- Analyzing quantitative data

mode 2

Abstract Conceptualization

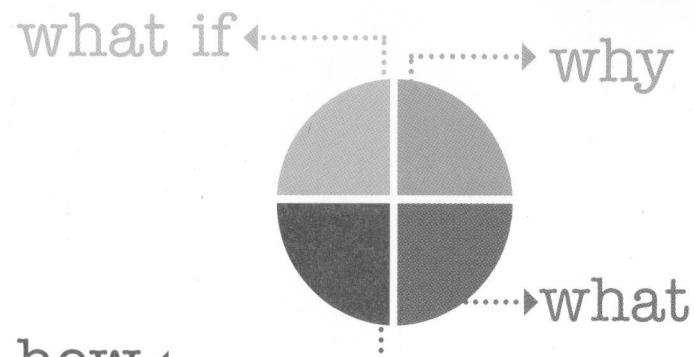

Using your learning style profile to succeed

Develop all four modes of learning

Each mode of learning highlighted in the Learning Style Inventory represents a unique blend of concrete experience, reflective observation, abstract conceptualization, and active experimentation. You can explore new learning styles simply by adopting new habits related to each of these activities. Consider the following suggestions as places to start. Also remember that any insight derived from exploring learning styles will make a difference in your life only when it leads to changes in your behavior.

To gain concrete experiences:

■ Attend a live demonstration or performance related to your course content.

■ Engage your emotions by reading a novel or seeing a video related to your course.

■ Interview an expert in the subject you're learning or a master practitioner of a skill you want to gain.

■ Conduct role-plays, exercises, or games based on your courses.

■ Conduct an informational interview with someone in your chosen career or "shadow" that person for a day on the job.

■ Look for a part-time job, internship, or volunteer experience that complements what you do in class.

■ Deepen your understanding of another culture and extend your foreign language skills by studying abroad.

To become more reflective:

■ Keep a personal journal, and write about connections among your courses.

■ Form a study group to discuss and debate topics related to your courses.

■ Set up a Web site, computer bulletin board, e-mail listserv, or online chat room related to your major.

■ Create analogies to make sense of concepts; for instance, see if you can find similarities between career planning and putting together a puzzle.

■ Visit your course instructor during office hours to ask questions.

■ Take time during social events with friends and relatives to briefly explain what your courses are about.

To develop abstract thinking:

■ Take notes on your reading in outline form; consider using word-processing software with an outlining feature.

■ Supplement assigned texts with other books, magazine and newspaper articles, and related Web sites.

■ Attend lectures given by your current instructors and others who teach the same subjects.

■ Take ideas presented in text or lectures and translate them into visual form—tables, charts, diagrams, and maps (see Chapter 6: "Notes").

■ Create visuals and use computer software to recreate them with more complex graphics and animation.

To become more active:

■ Conduct laboratory experiments or field observations.

■ Go to settings where theories are being applied or tested; for example, volunteer at a local business or observe a lab school classroom.

■ Make predictions based on theories you learn, and then see if events in your daily life confirm your predictions.

■ Try out a new behavior described in a lecture or reading, and observe its consequences in your life.

Use the modes to explore your major

If you enjoy learning in Mode 1, you probably value creativity and human relationships. When choosing a major, consider the arts, English, psychology, or political science.

If Mode 2 is your preference, then you enjoy gathering information and building theories. A major related to math or science might be ideal for you.

If Mode 3 is your favorite, then you like to diagnose problems, arrive at solutions, and use technology. Again, a major related to health care, engineering, or economics is a logical choice for you.

And if your preference is Mode 4, you probably enjoy taking the initiative, implementing decisions, teaching, managing projects, and moving quickly from planning into action. Consider a major in business or education.

As you prepare to declare a major, remain flexible. Use your knowledge of learning styles to open up possibilities rather than restrict them.

Use the modes of learning to explore your career

People who excel at Mode 1 are often skilled at "tuning in" to the feelings of clients and coworkers. These people can listen with an open mind, tolerate confusion, be sensitive to people's feelings, open up to problems that are difficult to define, and brainstorm a variety of solutions. If you like Mode 1, you may be drawn to a career in counseling, social services, the ministry, or another field that centers on human relationships. You might also enjoy a career in the performing arts.

People who prefer Mode 2 like to do research and work with ideas. They are skilled at gathering data, interpreting information, and summarizing—activities that help them arrive at the "big picture." They may excel at careers that center on science, math, technical communications, or planning. Mode 2 learners may also work as college teachers, lawyers, technical writers, or journalists.

People who like Mode 3 are drawn to solving problems, making decisions, and checking on progress toward goals. Careers in medicine, engineering, information technology, or another applied science are often ideal for them.

People who enjoy Mode 4 like to influence and lead others. These people are often described as "doers" and "risk takers." They like to take action and complete projects. Mode 4 learners often excel at managing, negotiating, selling, training, and teaching. They might also work for a government agency.

Keep in mind that there is no strict match between certain learning styles and certain careers. Learning is essential to success in all careers. Also, any career can attract people with a variety of learning styles.

Accommodate differing styles

Once you've discovered differences in styles, look for ways to accommodate them in your dealings with other people.

Remember that some people want to reflect on the "big picture" first. When introducing a project plan, you might say, "This process has four major steps." Before explaining the plan in detail, talk about the purpose of the project and the benefits of completing each step.

Allow time for active experimentation and concrete experience. Offer people a chance to try out a new product or process for themselves—to literally "get the feel of it."

Allow for abstract conceptualization. When leading a study group or conducting a training session, provide handouts that include plenty of visuals and step-by-step instructions. Visual learners and people who like to think abstractly will appreciate these materials. Also schedule periods for questions and answers.

When working on teams, look for ways that members can complement one another's strengths. If you're skilled at planning, find someone who excels at doing. Also seek people who can reflect on and interpret the team's experience. Pooling different styles allows you to draw on everyone's strengths. ✳

Use the modes to learn from *any* instructor

Students who experience difficulty in school might say, "The tests are too hard for me." Or "In class, we never have time for questions." Or "The instructor doesn't teach to my learning style."

Such statements prevent you from taking responsibility for your education. To stay in charge of your learning, consider adopting attitudes such as the following:

I will look for the value in this information.

I can learn something useful in any situation.

I will experiment with this suggestion to see if it works.

No matter who's teaching this course, I am responsible for what I learn.

I will master this subject by using several modes of learning.

You can take action on such statements even if you don't fully agree with them. One way to change your attitudes is to adopt new behaviors, see how they work, and watch for new results.

Claim your multiple intelligences

(man) © Tanya Constantine/Getty, (fern) © Tim Laman/Getty, (ballet shoes) © Scott T. Baxter/Getty, (protractor) © Vladimir Godnik/Getty, (meditating woman) © Meg Takamura, (easel) © Stockbyte/Getty, (microphone) © George Doyle/Getty, (holding hands) © DougMenuez/Getty, (music) © Gregor Schuster/Getty

PEOPLE OFTEN THINK that being smart means the same thing as having a high IQ, and that having a high IQ automatically leads to success. However, psychologists are finding that IQ scores do not always foretell which students will do well in academic settings—or after they graduate.[2]

Howard Gardner of Harvard University believes that no single measure of intelligence can tell us how smart we are. Instead, Gardner defines intelligence in a flexible way as "the ability to solve problems, or to create products, that are valued within one or more cultural settings." He also identifies several types of intelligence:[3]

People using **verbal/linguistic intelligence** are adept at language skills and learn best by speaking, writing, reading, and listening.

People who use **mathematical/logical intelligence** are good with numbers, logic, problem solving, patterns, relationships, and categories.

When people learn visually and by organizing things spatially, they display **visual/spatial intelligence.**

People using **bodily/kinesthetic intelligence** prefer physical activity, and they would rather participate in games than just watch.

Individuals using **musical/rhythmic intelligence** enjoy musical expression through songs, rhythms, and musical instruments.

People using **intrapersonal intelligence** are generally reserved, self-motivated, and intuitive.

Outgoing people show evidence of **interpersonal intelligence** and do well with cooperative learning, often making good leaders.

People using **naturalist intelligence** love the outdoors and recognize details in plants, animals, rocks, clouds, and other natural formations.

Experiment with learning in ways that draw on a variety of intelligences. When we acknowledge all of our intelligences, we can constantly explore new ways of being smart. ✳

5 critical thinking exercise
Develop your multiple intelligences

In the following chart, place a check mark next to any of the "Possible Characteristics" that describe you. Also check off the "Possible Learning Strategies" that you intend to use. Finally, underline or highlight any of the "Possible Careers" that spark your interest.

Remember that the chart is *not* an exhaustive list or a formal inventory. Take what you find merely as points of departure. You can identify other characteristics and invent strategies of your own to cultivate different intelligences.

Type of intelligence	Possible characteristics	Possible learning strategies	Possible careers
Verbal/linguistic	❏ You enjoy writing letters, stories, and papers. ❏ You take excellent notes from textbooks and lectures.	❏ Highlight, underline, and write notes in your textbooks. ❏ Rewrite and edit your class notes.	English teacher, editor, journalist, lawyer, librarian, radio or television announcer
Mathematical/logical	❏ You prefer math or science class over English class. ❏ You want to know how and why things work.	❏ Group concepts into categories, and look for underlying patterns. ❏ Convert text into tables, charts, and graphs.	Accountant, actuary, auditor, computer programmer, economist, mathematician, math or science teacher, tax preparer
Visual/spatial	❏ You draw pictures to give an example or clarify an explanation. ❏ You assemble things from illustrated instructions.	❏ When taking notes, create concept maps, mind maps, and other visuals (see Chapter 6). ❏ When your attention wanders, focus it by sketching or drawing.	Architect, cartographer, commercial artist, engineer, fine artist, graphic designer, interior decorator, photographer
Bodily/kinesthetic	❏ You tend not to sit still for long periods of time. ❏ You enjoy working with your hands.	❏ Carry materials with you and practice studying in several different locations. ❏ Create hands-on activities related to key concepts.	Actor, athlete, athletic coach, chiropractor, dancer, physical education teacher, physical therapist
Musical/rhythmic	❏ You often sing in the car or shower. ❏ You play a musical instrument.	❏ During a study break, play music or dance to restore energy. ❏ Relate key concepts to songs you know.	Musician, music teacher, music therapist
Intrapersonal	❏ You enjoy writing in a journal and being alone with your thoughts. ❏ You prefer to work on individual projects over group projects.	❏ Connect course content to your personal values and goals. ❏ Connect readings and lectures to a strong feeling or significant past experience.	Freelance writer, owner of a home-based business
Interpersonal	❏ You have plenty of friends and regularly spend time with them. ❏ You prefer talking and listening over reading or writing.	❏ Create flash cards and use them to quiz study partners. ❏ Volunteer to give a speech or lead group presentations.	Counselor, manager, nurse, school administrator, teacher
Naturalist	❏ You enjoy being outdoors. ❏ You find that important insights occur during times you spend in nature.	❏ Post pictures of outdoor scenes where you study and play recordings of outdoor sounds while you read. ❏ Invite classmates to discuss course work while taking a hike.	Biologist, construction worker, environmental activist, park ranger, recreation supervisor, woodworker

Learning by seeing, hearing, and moving: The VAK system

YOU CAN APPROACH the topic of learning styles with a simple and powerful system—one that focuses on just three ways of perceiving through your senses:

- Seeing, or *visual learning*.
- Hearing, or *auditory learning*.
- Movement, or *kinesthetic learning*.

To recall this system, remember the letters *VAK*, which stand for visual, auditory, and kinesthetic. The theory is that each of us prefers to learn through one of these sense channels. In addition, we can enrich our learning with activities that draw on the other channels.

To reflect on your VAK preferences, answer the following questions. Each question has three possible answers. Circle the answer that best describes how you would respond in the stated situation. This is not a formal inventory—just a way to prompt some self-discovery.

When you have problems spelling a word, you prefer to:

1. Look it up in the dictionary.
2. Say the word out loud several times before you write it down.
3. Write out the word with several different spellings and then choose one.

You enjoy courses the most when you get to:

1. View slides, overhead displays, videos, and readings with plenty of charts, tables, and illustrations.
2. Ask questions, engage in small-group discussions, and listen to guest speakers.
3. Take field trips, participate in lab sessions, or apply the course content while working as a volunteer or intern.

When giving someone directions on how to drive to a destination, you prefer to:

1. Pull out a piece of paper and sketch a map.
2. Give verbal instructions.
3. Say, "I'm driving to a place near there, so just follow me."

When planning an extended vacation to a new destination, you prefer to:

1. Read colorful, illustrated brochures or articles about that place.
2. Talk directly to someone who's been there.
3. Spend a day or two at that destination on a work-related trip before taking a vacation there.

You've made a commitment to learn to play the guitar. The first thing you do is:

1. Go to a library or music store and find an instruction book with plenty of diagrams and chord charts.
2. Pull out your favorite CDs, listen closely to the guitar solos, and see if you can sing along with them.
3. Buy or borrow a guitar, pluck the strings, and ask someone to show you how to play a few chords.

You've saved up enough money to lease a car. When choosing from among several new models, the most important factor in your decision is:

1. The car's appearance.
2. The information you get by talking to people who own the cars you're considering.
3. The overall impression you get by taking each car on a test drive.

You've just bought a new computer system. When setting up the system, the first thing you do is:

1. Skim through the printed instructions that come with the equipment.

2. Call up someone with a similar system and ask her for directions.

3. Assemble the components as best as you can, see if everything works, and consult the instructions only as a last resort.

You get a scholarship to study abroad next semester, which starts in just three months. You will travel to a country where French is the most widely spoken language. To learn as much French as you can before you depart, you:

1. Buy a video-based language course that's recorded on a DVD.

2. Set up tutoring sessions with a friend who's fluent in French.

3. Sign up for a short immersion course in an environment in which you speak only French, starting with the first class.

Now take a few minutes to reflect on the meaning of your responses. All of the answers numbered "1" are examples of visual learning. The "2" refer to auditory learning, and the "3" illustrate kinesthetic learning. Finding a consistent pattern in your answers indicates that you prefer learning through one sense channel more than the others. Or you might find that your preferences are fairly balanced.

The following list includes suggestions for learning through each sense channel. Experiment with these examples, and create more techniques of your own. Use the suggestions to build on your current preferences and develop new options for learning.

To enhance visual learning:

■ Preview reading assignments by looking for elements that are highlighted visually—bold headlines, charts, graphs, illustrations, and photographs.

■ When taking notes in class, leave plenty of room to add your own charts, diagrams, tables, and other visuals later.

■ Whenever an instructor writes information on a blackboard or other display, copy it exactly in your notes.

■ Transfer your handwritten notes to your computer. Use word-processing software that allows you to format your notes in lists, add headings in different fonts, and create visuals in color.

■ Before you begin an exam, quickly sketch a diagram on scratch paper. Use this diagram to summarize the key formulas or facts you want to remember.

■ During tests, see if you can visualize pages from your handwritten notes or images from your computer-based notes.

To enhance auditory learning:

■ Reinforce memory of your notes and readings by talking about them. When studying, stop often to recite key points and examples in your own words.

■ After reciting several summaries of key points and examples, record your favorite version or write it out.

■ Read difficult passages in your textbooks slowly and out loud.

■ Join study groups, and create short presentations about course topics.

■ Visit your instructors during office hours to ask questions.

To enhance kinesthetic learning:

■ Look for ways to translate course content into three-dimensional models that you can build. While studying biology, for example, create a model of a human cell using different colors of clay.

■ Supplement lectures with trips to museums, field observations, lab sessions, tutorials, and other hands-on activities.

■ Recite key concepts from your courses while you walk or exercise.

■ Intentionally set up situations in which you can learn by trial and error.

■ Create a practice test, and write out the answers in the room where you will actually take the exam.

One variation of the VAK system has been called VARK.[4] The *R* describes a preference for learning by reading and writing. People with this preference might benefit from translating charts and diagrams into statements, taking notes in lists, and converting those lists into possible items on a multiple-choice test. ✳

> *Reminder: Go back to page LSI-2 to complete the "Take a Snapshot of Your Learning Styles" exercise.*

In 1482, Leonardo da Vinci wrote a letter to a wealthy baron, applying for work. Here is an excerpt from the letter: "I can contrive various and endless means of offense and defense. . . . I have all sorts of extremely light and strong bridges adapted to be most easily carried . . . I have methods for destroying every turret or fortress. . . . I will make covered chariots, safe and unassailable. . . . In case of need I will make big guns, mortars, and light ordnance of fine and useful forms out of the common type." And then he added, almost as an afterthought, "In times of peace I believe I can give perfect satisfaction and to the equal of any other in architecture . . . can carry out sculpture . . . and also I can do in painting whatever may be done."
The *Mona Lisa*, for example.

The Master Student

THIS BOOK IS about something that cannot be taught. It's about becoming a master student.

Mastery means attaining a level of skill that goes beyond technique. For a master, methods and procedures are automatic responses to the needs of the task. Work is effortless; struggle evaporates. The master carpenter is so familiar with her tools that they are part of her. To a master chef, utensils are old friends. Because these masters don't have to think about the details of the process, they bring more of themselves to their work.

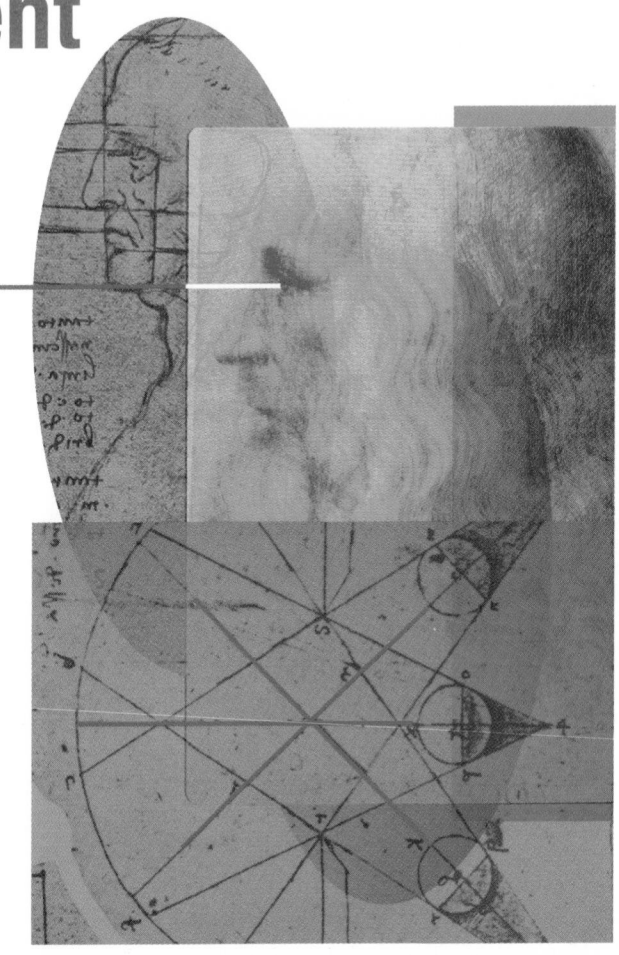

Mastery can lead to flashy results—an incredible painting, for example, or a gem of a short story. In basketball, mastery might result in an unbelievable shot at the buzzer. For a musician, it might be the performance of a lifetime—the moment when everything comes together.

Psychologist Mihaly Csikszentmihalyi describes mastery as the experience of *flow*. During this experience, our attention is completely focused: "Self-consciousness disappears, yet one feels stronger than usual. The sense of time is distorted: hours seem to pass by in minutes . . . whatever one does becomes worth doing for its own sake; living becomes its own justification."[5]

When the master student is in such a state, she makes learning look easy. She works hard without seeming to make any effort. She's relaxed *and* alert, disciplined *and* spontaneous, focused *and* fun-loving.

You might say that those statements don't make sense. Mastery, in fact, doesn't make sense. It cannot be captured with words. It defies analysis. Mastery cannot be taught. It can only be learned and experienced.

Examine the following list of characteristics of master students in light of your own experience. The list is not complete. It merely points in a direction. Look in that direction and you'll begin to see the endless diversity of master students. These people are old and young, male and female. They exist in every period of history. And they come from every culture, race, and ethnic group.

Also remember to look to yourself. No one can teach us to be master students; we already are master students. We are natural learners by design. As students, we can discover that every day.

Following are some traits shared by master students.

Inquisitive. The master student is curious about everything. By posing questions, she can generate interest in the most mundane, humdrum situations. When she is bored during a biology lecture, she thinks to herself, "I always get bored when I listen to this instructor. Why is that? Maybe it's because he reminds me of my boring Uncle Ralph, who always tells those endless fishing stories. He even looks like Uncle Ralph. Amazing! Boredom is certainly interesting." Then she asks herself, "What can I do to get value out of this lecture, even though it seems boring?" And she finds an answer.

Able to focus attention. Watch a 2-year-old at play. Pay attention to his eyes. The wide-eyed look reveals an energy and a capacity for amazement that keep his attention absolutely focused in the here and now. The master student's focused attention has a childlike quality. The world, to a child, is always new. Because the master student can focus attention, to him the world is always new, too.

Willing to change. The unknown does not frighten the master student. In fact, she welcomes it—even the unknown in herself. We all have pictures of who we think we are, and these pictures can be useful. However, they also can prevent learning and growth. The master student is open to changes in her environment and in herself.

Able to organize and sort. The master student can take a large body of information and sift through it to discover relationships. He can play with information, organizing data by size, color, function, timeliness, and hundreds of other categories.

Competent. Mastery of skills is important to the master student. When she learns mathematical formulas, she studies them until they become second nature. She practices until she knows them cold, then puts in a few extra minutes. She also is able to apply what she learns to new and different situations.

Positive. The master student doesn't give in to negative thoughts or feelings. He is able to cope and deal with problems of daily life.

Able to suspend judgment. The master student has opinions and positions, and she is able to let go of them when appropriate. She realizes she is more than her thoughts. She can quiet her internal dialogue and listen to an opposing viewpoint. She doesn't let judgment get in the way of learning. Rather than approaching discussions with a "Prove it to me and then I'll believe it" attitude, she asks herself, "What if this is true?" and explores possibilities.

Energetic. Notice the student with a spring in his step—the one who is enthusiastic and involved in class. When he reads, he often sits on the very edge of his chair, and he plays with the same intensity. He is a master student.

Well. Health is important to the master student, though not necessarily in the sense of being free of illness. Rather, she values her body and treats it with respect. She tends to her emotional and spiritual health, as well as her physical health.

Self-aware. The master student is willing to evaluate himself and his behavior. He regularly tells the truth about his strengths and those aspects that could be improved.

Responsible. There is a difference between responsibility and blame, and the master student knows it well. She is willing to take responsibility for everything in her life—even for events that most people would blame on others.

For example, if a master student takes a required class that most students consider boring, she chooses to take responsibility for her interest level. She looks for ways to link the class to one of her goals. She sees the class as an opportunity to experiment with new study techniques that will enhance her performance in any course. She remembers that by choosing her thoughts and behaviors, she can create interesting classes, enjoyable relationships, fulfilling work experiences, or just about anything else she wants.

Willing to take risks. The master student often takes on projects with no guarantee of success. He participates in class dialogues at the risk of looking foolish. He tackles difficult subjects in term papers. He welcomes the risk of a challenging course.

Willing to participate. Don't look for the master student on the sidelines. She's in the game. She is a player who can be counted on. She is willing to make a commitment and to follow through on it.

A generalist. The master student is interested in everything around him. He has a broad base of knowledge in many fields and can apply it to his specialties.

Willing to accept paradox. The word *paradox* comes from two Greek words, *para* ("beyond") and *doxen* ("opinion"). A paradox is something that is beyond opinion or, more accurately, something that might seem contradictory or absurd yet might actually have meaning.

For example, the master student can be committed to managing money and reaching her financial goals. At the same time, she can be totally detached from money, knowing that her real worth is independent of how much money she has. The master student recognizes the limitations of the mind and is at home with paradox. She can accept that ambiguity.

Courageous. The master student admits his fear and fully experiences it. For example, he will approach a tough exam as an opportunity to explore feelings of anxiety and tension related to the pressure to perform. He does not deny fear; he embraces it.

Self-directed. Rewards or punishments provided by others do not motivate the master student. Her motivation to learn comes from within.

Spontaneous. The master student is truly in the here and now. He is able to respond to the moment in fresh, surprising, and unplanned ways.

Relaxed about grades. Grades make the master student neither depressed nor euphoric. She recognizes that sometimes grades are important. At the same time, grades are not the only reason she studies. She does not measure her worth as a human being by the grades she receives.

Intuitive. The master student has an inner sense that cannot be explained by logic. He has learned to trust his feelings, and he works to develop this intuitive sense.

Creative. Where others see dull details and trivia, the master student sees opportunities to create. She can gather pieces of knowledge from a wide range of subjects and put them together in new ways. The master student is creative in every aspect of her life.

Willing to be uncomfortable. The master student does not place comfort first. When discomfort is necessary to reach a goal, he is willing to experience it. He can endure personal hardships and can look at unpleasant things with detachment.

Optimistic. The master student sees setbacks as temporary and isolated, knowing that she can choose her response to any circumstance.

Willing to laugh. The master student might laugh at any moment, and his sense of humor includes the ability to laugh at himself.

Going to school is a big investment. The stakes are high. It's OK to be serious about that, but the master student knows he doesn't have to go to school on the deferred-fun program. He celebrates learning, and understands one of the best ways to do that is to have a laugh now and then.

Hungry. Human beings begin life with a natural appetite for knowledge. In some people it soon gets dulled. The master student has tapped that hunger, and it gives her a desire to learn for the sake of learning.

Willing to work. Once inspired, the master student is willing to follow through with sweat. He knows that genius and creativity are the results of persistence and work. When in high gear, the master student works with the intensity of a child at play.

Caring. A master student cares about knowledge and has a passion for ideas. She also cares about people and appreciates learning from others. She flourishes in a community that values win/win outcomes, cooperation, and love.

The master student in you. The master student is in all of us. By design, human beings are learning machines. We have an innate ability to learn, and all of us have room to grow and improve.

It is important to understand the difference between learning and being taught. Human beings can resist being taught anything. Psychologist Carl Rogers goes so far as to say that anything that can be taught to a human being is either inconsequential or just plain harmful.[6] What is important in education, Rogers asserts, is learning. And everyone has the ability to learn.

Unfortunately, people also learn to hide that ability. As they experience the pain that sometimes accompanies learning, they shut down. If a child experiences embarrassment in front of a group of people, he may learn to avoid similar situations. In doing so, he restricts his possibilities.

Some children "learn" that they are slow learners. If they learn it well enough, their behavior starts to match that label.

As people grow older, they sometimes accumulate a growing list of ideas to defend—a catalog of familiar experiences that discourages them from learning anything new.

Still, the master student within survives. To tap that resource, you don't need to acquire anything. You already have everything you need. Every day you can rediscover the natural learner within you. ✳

olly/Shutterstock

Motivation—getting beyond "I'm just not in the mood"

THERE ARE at least two ways to think about motivation. One way is to use the terms *self-discipline,* *willpower,* and *motivation* to describe something missing in ourselves. We use these words to explain another person's success—or our own shortcomings: "If I were more motivated, I'd get more involved in school." "Of course she got an A. She has self-discipline." "If I had more willpower, I'd lose weight." It seems that certain people are born with lots of motivation, while others miss out on it.

A second approach to thinking about motivation is to stop assuming that motivation is mysterious, determined at birth, or hard to come by. Perhaps there's nothing in you that's missing. What we call motivation could be something that you already possess—the ability to do a task even when you don't feel like it. This is a habit that you can develop with practice. The following suggestions offer ways to do that.

Promise it. Motivation can come simply from being clear about your goals and acting on them. Say that you want to start a study group. You can commit yourself to inviting people and setting a time and place to meet. Promise your classmates that you'll do this, and ask them to hold you accountable. Self-discipline, willpower, motivation—none of these mysterious characteristics needs to get in your way. Just make a promise and keep your word.

Befriend your discomfort. Begin by investigating the discomfort. Notice the thoughts running through your head, and speak them out loud: "I'd rather walk on a bed of coals than do this." "This is the last thing I want to do right now."

Also observe what's happening with your body. For example, are you breathing faster or slower than usual?

Is your breathing shallow or deep? Are your shoulders tight? Do you feel any tension in your stomach?

Once you're in contact with your mind and body, stay with the discomfort a few minutes longer. Don't judge it as good or bad. Accepting the thoughts and body sensations robs them of power. They might still be there, but in time they can stop being a barrier for you.

Discomfort can be a gift—an opportunity to do valuable work on yourself. On the other side of discomfort lies mastery.

Change your mind—and your body. You can also get past discomfort by planting new thoughts in your mind or changing your physical stance. For example, instead of slumping in a chair, sit up straight or stand up. You can also get physically active by taking a short walk. Notice what happens to your discomfort.

Work with your thoughts, also. Replace "I can't stand this" with "I'll feel great when this is done" or "Doing this will help me get something I want."

Sweeten the task. Sometimes it's just one aspect of a task that holds you back. You can stop procrastinating merely by changing that aspect. If distaste for your physical environment keeps you from studying, you can change that environment. Reading about social psychology might seem like a yawner when you're alone in a dark corner of the house. Moving to a cheery, well-lit library can sweeten the task.

Talk about how bad it is. One way to get past negative attitudes is to take them to an extreme. When faced with an unpleasant task, launch into a no-holds-barred gripe session. Pull out all the stops: "There's no way I can start my income taxes now. This is terrible beyond words—an absolute disaster. This is a

Galina Barskaya/Shutterstock

catastrophe of global proportions!" Griping taken this far can restore perspective. It shows how self-talk can turn inconveniences into crises.

Turn up the pressure. Sometimes motivation is a luxury. Pretend that the due date for your project has been moved up one day, one week, or one month. Raising the stress level slightly can spur you into action. Then the issue of motivation seems beside the point, and meeting the due date moves to the forefront.

Turn down the pressure. The mere thought of starting a huge task can induce anxiety. To get past this feeling, turn down the pressure by taking "baby steps." Divide a large project into small tasks. In 30 minutes or less, you could preview a book, create a rough outline for a paper, or solve two or three math problems. Careful planning can help you discover many such steps to make a big job doable.

Ask for support. Other people can become your allies in overcoming procrastination. For example, form a support group and declare what you intend to accomplish before each meeting. Then ask members to hold you accountable. If you want to begin exercising regularly, ask another person to walk with you three times weekly. People in support groups ranging from Alcoholics Anonymous to Weight Watchers know the power of this strategy.

Adopt a model. One strategy for succeeding at any task is to hang around the masters. Find someone you consider successful, and spend time with her. Observe this person and use her as a model for your own behavior. You can "try on" this person's actions and attitudes. Look for tools that feel right for you. This person can become a mentor to you.

Compare the payoffs to the costs. All behaviors have payoffs and costs. Even unwanted behaviors such as cramming for exams or neglecting exercise have payoffs. Cramming might give you more time that's free of commitments. Neglecting exercise can give you more time to sleep.

We can openly acknowledge the payoffs and then follow up with the next step—determining the costs. For example, skipping a reading assignment can give you time to go to the movies. However, you might be unprepared for class and have twice as much to read the following week.

Maybe there is another way to get the payoff (going to the movies) without paying the cost (skipping the reading assignment). With some thoughtful weekly planning, you might choose to give up a few hours of television and end up with enough time to read the assignment *and* go to the movies.

Comparing the costs and benefits of any behavior can fuel our motivation. We can choose new behaviors because they align with what we want most.

Do it later. At times, it's effective to save a task for later. For example, writing a résumé can wait until you've taken the time to analyze your job skills and map out your career goals. Putting it off does not show a lack of motivation—it shows planning.

Heed the message. Sometimes lack of motivation carries a message that's worth heeding. For example, consider the student who majors in accounting but seizes every chance to be with children. His chronic reluctance to read accounting textbooks might not be a problem. Instead, it might reveal his desire to major in elementary education. His original career choice might have come from the belief that "real men don't teach kindergarten." In such cases, an apparent lack of motivation signals a deeper wisdom trying to get through. ✳

Ways to change a habit

CONSIDER A NEW WAY to think about the word *habit*. Imagine for a moment that many of our most troublesome problems and even our most basic traits are just habits.

The expanding waistline that your friend is blaming on her spouse's cooking—maybe that's just a habit called overeating.

The fit of rage that a student blames on a teacher—maybe that's just the student's habit of closing the door to new ideas.

Procrastination, stress, and money shortages might just be names that we give to collections of habits—scores of simple, small, repeated behaviors that combine to create a huge result. The same goes for health, wealth, love, and many of the other things that we want from life.

One way to change your thinking about success and failure is to focus on habits. Behaviors such as failing to complete reading assignments or skipping class might be habits leading to outcomes that "could not" be avoided, including dropping out of school. In the same way, behaviors such as completing assignments and attending class might lead to the outcome of getting an "A."

When you confront a behavior that undermines your goals or creates a circumstance that you don't want, consider a new attitude: That behavior is just a habit. And it can be changed.

Thinking about ourselves as creatures of habit actually gives us power. Then we are not faced with the monumental task of changing our very nature. Rather, we can take on the doable job of changing our habits. One change in behavior that seems insignificant at first can have effects that ripple throughout your life.

Tell the truth. Telling the truth about any habit—from chewing our fingernails to cheating on tests—frees us. Without taking this step, our efforts to change might be as ineffective as rearranging the deck chairs on the *Titanic.* Telling the truth allows us to see what's actually sinking the ship.

When we admit what's really going on in our lives, our defenses come down. We become open to accepting help from others. The support we need to change a habit has an opportunity to make an impact.

© EyeWire Collection/Getty

© Ryan McVay/Getty

© Daniel Allan/Getty

Choose and commit to a new behavior. It often helps to choose a new habit to replace an old one. First, make a commitment to practice the new habit. Tell key people in your life about your decision to change. Set up a plan for when and how. Answer questions such as these: When will I apply the new habit? Where will I be? Who will be with me? What will I be seeing, hearing, touching, saying, or doing? Exactly how will I think, speak, or act differently?

For example, consider the student who always snacks when he studies. Each time he sits down to read, he positions a bag of potato chips within easy reach. For him, opening a book is a cue to start chewing. Snacking is especially easy, given the place he chooses to study: the kitchen. He decides to change this habit by studying at a desk in his bedroom instead of at the kitchen table. And every time he feels the urge to bite into a potato chip, he drinks from a glass of water instead.

Richard Malott, a psychologist who specializes in helping people overcome procrastination, lists three key steps in committing to a new behavior.[7] First, *specify* your goal in numerical terms whenever possible. For example, commit to reading 30 pages per day, Monday through Friday. Second, *observe* your behavior and record the results—in this case, the number of pages that you actually read every day. Finally, set up a small *consequence* for failing to keep your commitment. For instance, pay a friend one quarter for each day that you read less than 30 pages.

Affirm your intention. You can pave the way for a new behavior by clearing a mental path for it. Before you apply the new behavior, rehearse it in your mind. Mentally picture what actions you will take and in what order.

Say that you plan to improve your handwriting when taking notes. Imagine yourself in class with a blank notebook poised before you. See yourself taking up a finely crafted pen. Notice how comfortable it feels in your hand. See yourself writing clearly and legibly. You can even picture how you will make individual letters: the *e*'s, *i*'s, and *r*'s. Then, when class is over, see yourself reviewing your notes and taking pleasure in how easy they are to read.

Start with a small change. You can sometimes rearrange a whole pattern of behaviors by changing one small habit. If you have a habit of always being late for classes, then be on time for one class. As soon as you change the old pattern by getting ready and going on time to one class, you might find yourself arriving at all of your classes on time. You might even start arriving everywhere else on time, too. The joy of this process is watching one small change of habit ripple through your whole life.

Get feedback and support. Getting feedback and support is a crucial step in adopting a new behavior. It is also a point at which many plans for change break down. It's easy to practice your new behavior with great enthusiasm for a few days. After the initial rush of excitement, though, things can get a little tougher. You begin to find excuses for slipping back into old habits: "One more cigarette won't hurt." "I can get back to my diet tomorrow." "It's been a tough day. I deserve this beer."

One way to get feedback is to bring other people into the picture. Ask others to remind you that you are changing your habit if they see you backsliding. If you want to stop an old behavior, such as cramming for tests, then tell everyone about your goal. When you want to start a new behavior, though, consider telling only a few people—those who truly support your efforts.

Starting new habits might call for the more focused, long-lasting support that close friends or family members can give. Support from others can be as simple as a quick phone call: "Hi. Have you started that outline for your research paper yet?" Or it can be as formal as a support group that meets once a week to review everyone's goals and action plans.

You can also be an effective source of feedback. You know yourself better than anyone else does and can design a system to monitor your behavior. Create your own charts to track your behavior, or write about your progress in your journal. Figure out a way to monitor your progress.

Practice, practice, practice—without self-judgment. Psychologist B. F. Skinner defines learning as a stable change in behavior that comes as a result of practice.[8] This widely accepted idea is key to changing habits. Act on your intention over and over again. If you fail or forget, let go of any self-judgment. Just keep practicing the new habit. Allow whatever time it takes to make a change.

Accept the feelings of discomfort that might come with a new habit. Keep practicing the new behavior, even if it feels unnatural. Trust the process. Grow into the new behavior. However, if this new habit doesn't work, simply note what happened (without guilt or blame), select a new behavior, and begin this cycle of steps over again.

Making mistakes as you practice doesn't mean that you've failed. Even when you don't get the results you want from a new behavior, you learn something valuable in the process. Once you understand ways to change one habit, you will be able to change almost any habit. ✳

© EyeWire Collection/Getty

© Stockbyte   © Jules Frazier/Getty

Master Student Profiles

Each chapter of this text includes a Master Student Profile of a person who embodies one or more qualities of a master student. As you read about these people and others like them, ask yourself: "How can I apply this?" Look for the timeless qualities in the people you read about. Many of the master students used tools that you can use today.

The people profiled in this book were chosen because they demonstrate unusual and effective ways to learn. Remember that these are just 12 examples of master students (one for each chapter). You can read more about these master students and others in the Master Student Hall of Fame on the Web site.

As you read the Master Student Profiles, ask yourself questions based on each mode of learning: Why is this person considered a master student? What attitudes or behaviors helped to create her mastery? How can I develop those qualities? What if I could use his example to create positive new results in my own life?

Also reflect on other master students you've read about or know personally. Focus on people who excel at learning. The master student is not a vague or remote ideal. Rather, master students move freely among us.

In fact, there's one living inside your skin.

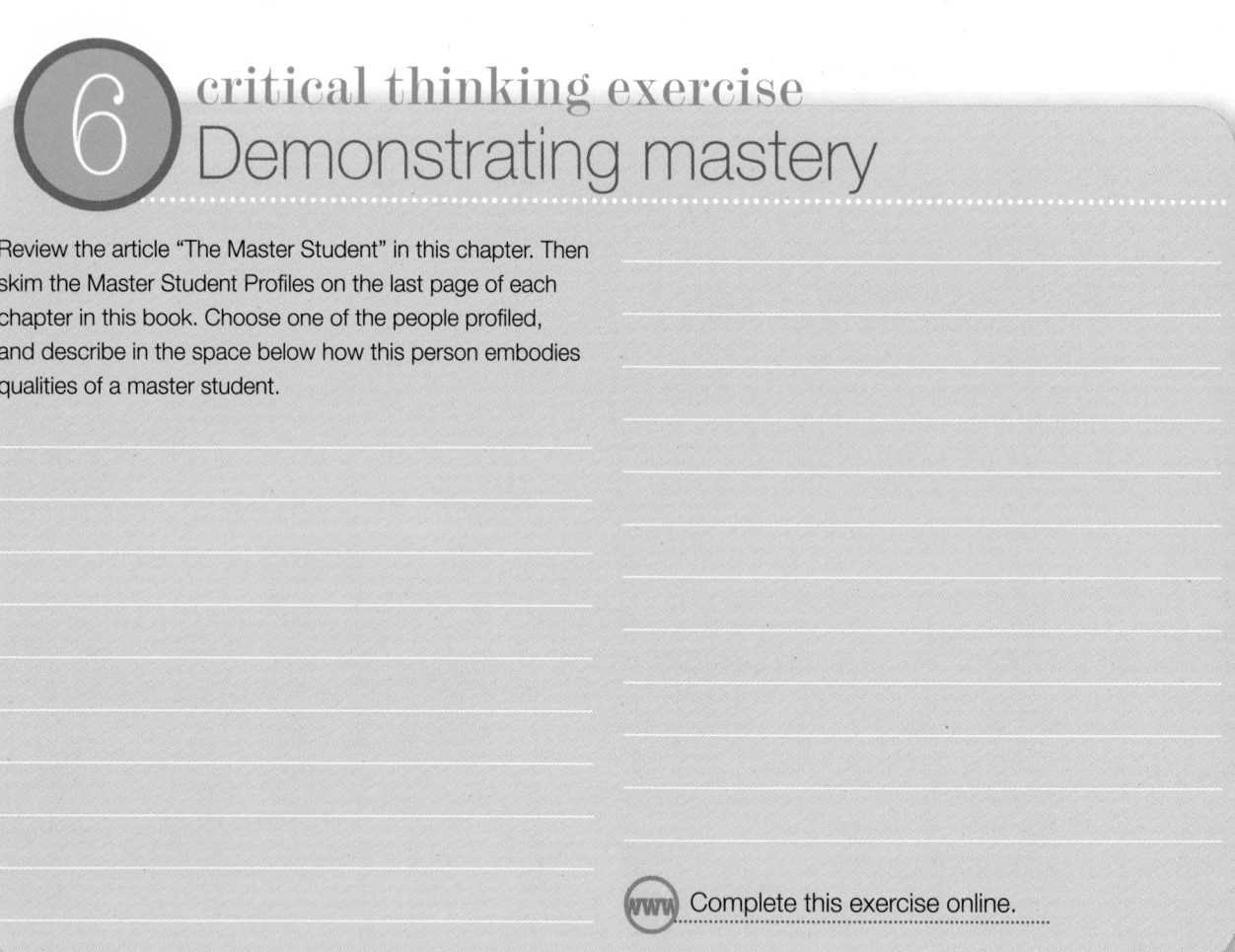

6 critical thinking exercise
Demonstrating mastery

Review the article "The Master Student" in this chapter. Then skim the Master Student Profiles on the last page of each chapter in this book. Choose one of the people profiled, and describe in the space below how this person embodies qualities of a master student.

(www) Complete this exercise online.

Ideas Are Tools

There are many ideas in this book. When you first encounter them, don't believe any of them. Instead, think of the ideas as tools.

For example, you use a hammer for a purpose—to drive a nail. You don't try to figure out whether the hammer is "right." You just use it. If it works, you use it again. If it doesn't work, you get a different hammer.

People have plenty of room in their lives for different kinds of hammers, but they tend to limit their openness for different kinds of ideas. A new idea, at some level, is a threat to their very being—unlike a new hammer, which is simply a new hammer.

Most of us have a built-in desire to be right. Our ideas, we often think, represent ourselves.

Some ideas are worth believing. But please note: This book does not contain any of those ideas. The ideas on these pages are strictly "hammers."

Imagine someone defending a hammer. Picture this person holding up a hammer and declaring, "I hold this hammer to be self-evident. Give me this hammer or give me death. Those other hammers are flawed. There are only two kinds of people in this world: people who believe in this hammer and people who don't."

That ridiculous picture makes a point. This book is not a manifesto or set of beliefs. It's a toolbox, and tools are meant to be used.

If you read about a tool in this book that doesn't sound "right" or one that sounds a little goofy, remember that the ideas here are for using, not necessarily for believing. Suspend your judgment. Test the idea for yourself. If it works, use it. If it doesn't, don't use it.

Any tool—whether it's a hammer, a computer program, or a study technique—is designed to do a specific job. A master mechanic carries a variety of tools, because no single tool works for all jobs. If you throw a tool away because it doesn't work in one situation, you won't be able to pull it out later when it's just what you need. So if an idea doesn't work for you and you are satisfied that you gave it a fair chance, don't throw it away. File it away instead. The idea might come in handy soon.

And remember, this book is not about figuring out the "right" way. Even the "ideas-are-tools" approach is not "right."

It's a hammer . . . (or maybe a saw).

Complete this exercise online.

Edmond Van Hoorick/Digital Vision/Getty Images

Career Application

Shortly after graduating with an A.A. degree in Business Administration, Sylvia Lopez was thrilled to land a job as a staff accountant at a market research firm. After one week, she wanted to quit. She didn't think she would ever learn to deal with her coworkers. Their personalities just seemed too different.

For example, there was the account coordinator, Ed Washington. He spent hours a day on the phone calling prospective customers who responded to the corporate Web site. Since Ed's office door was always open and he had a loud voice, people inevitably overheard his calls. It seemed to Sylvia that he spent a lot of time socializing with clients— asking about their hobbies and family lives. Even though Ed was regarded as a skilled salesperson, Sylvia wondered when he actually got any work done.

Sylvia also felt uncomfortable with Linda Martinez, the firm's accounting analyst and her direct supervisor. Linda kept her office door closed most of the time. In contrast to Ed, Linda hardly ever stopped to chat informally. Instead of taking lunch breaks, she typically packed a bag lunch and ate it while checking e-mail or updating the company databases. Linda had a reputation as a top-notch employee. Yet the only time people saw her was at scheduled staff meetings. Linda led those meetings and distributed a detailed agenda in advance. Although Ed was on a first-name basis with everyone in the office, Linda made it clear that she wished to be addressed as "Ms. Martinez."

After worrying for several days about how to deal with the differences among her coworkers, Sylvia scheduled times to meet with Ed and Linda individually about her concerns. Before each meeting, she carefully prepared her opening remarks, writing them out. For Ed, her notes included this comment: "Since I'm new on the job and feel pressed for time, I'd like to get your help in making the most efficient use of our meeting time." And for Linda she wrote: "I'd like to make sure my performance is up to par. Is there any way I can get regular feedback from you about how I'm doing?"

Andrew Taylor/Shutterstock

Reflecting on this scenario

List at least two strategies from this chapter that would be useful to Sylvia in this situation. Briefly describe how she could apply each one.

_____

_____

_____

_____

_____

_____

_____

_____

_____

Quiz

chapter 1

- Career Application
◄ ◄ ◄ ◄ ◄
- Transferable Skills
- Master Student Profile

Name_____   Date____/____/____

1. Take the following statement and rewrite it as a more effective First Step: "I am terrible at managing money."

2. Define the term *mastery* as it is used in this chapter.

3. The First Step technique refers only to telling the truth about your areas for improvement. True or false? Explain your answer.

4. The four modes of learning are associated with certain questions. Give the appropriate question for each mode.

5. Give two examples of ways that you can accommodate people with different learning styles.

6. According to the text, thinking of ourselves as creatures of habit can actually empower us. True or false? Explain your answer.

7. List three types of intelligence defined by Howard Gardner. Then describe one learning strategy related to each type of intelligence that you listed.

8. According to the Power Process: "Ideas Are Tools." If you want the ideas in this book to work, you must believe in them. True or false? Explain your answer.

9. Define the word *metacognition*.

10. This chapter presents two views of the nature of motivation. Briefly explain the difference between them.

Focus on Transferable Skills

The Discovery Wheel in this chapter includes a section labeled *Self-discovery*. For the next 10 to 15 minutes, go beyond your initial responses to that exercise by completing the following statements. Take a snapshot of your current transferable skills related to self-discovery. Then focus on a new skill that you'd like to develop, or an existing skill that you can take to a deeper level.

Before completing the following items, you might find it useful to jump ahead to Chapter 2 to review the articles "Jumpstart Your Education with Transferable Skills" on page 58 and "101 Transferable Skills" on page 60.

SELF-AWARENESS

Three things I do well as a student are . . .

Three ways that I excel as an employee are . . .

STYLES

If asked to describe my learning style in one sentence, I would say that I am . . .

To become a more flexible learner, I could . . .

FLEXIBILITY

When I disagree with what someone else says about me, my first response is usually to . . .

In these situations, I could be more effective by . . .

NEXT ACTION

The transferable skill related to self-awareness, styles, or flexibility that I'd most like to develop is . . .

To develop that skill, the most important thing I can do next is to . . .

Master Student PROFILE

Jerry Yang

. . . is inquisitive

© TAO CHUAN YEH/Getty Images

(1968–) Founder and CEO of Yahoo!

In 1994, David Filo and Jerry Yang were in typical start-up mode—working 20 hours a day, sleeping in the office, juiced on the idea that people were discovering their concept and plugging in. There was only one difference between them and most new entrepreneurs: They weren't making any money. We're not talking about an absence of profitability. We're talking about an absence of revenue. There were no sales. None. And, the fact is, the Yahoo! founders didn't care. Filo and Yang were working like maniacs for the sheer joy of it.

Their mission? Bringing order to the terrible, tangled World Wide Web. Back then—in the pre-history of the Internet—plenty of interesting Websites existed. But the forum wasn't organized; there was no system that enabled people to find the sites they wanted in an easy, orderly way . . .

. . . By 1995, the service had become so popular, the partners were able to raise $1 million in venture capital to expand the business. There was no trail to follow, however; back then, Internet commerce was still in its infancy. But the partners knew they had a tiger by the tail. "What we did took 20 hours a day," says Yang, 29. "But we were one of the first to [try to organize the Web], and we did it better than anyone."

Yang, born in Taiwan and raised in San Jose, California, was named Chief Executive Officer of Yahoo! on June 18, 2007. Yang reflected on his vision and the future of the company on Yahoo's! blog, Yodel Anecdotal™:

The title of Chief Yahoo takes on new meaning today. I have the great honor of stepping into the role of Yahoo!'s Chief Executive Officer. Yahoo! has an incredibly bright future and I make this move with deep conviction and enthusiasm. I've partnered closely with our executive teams for 12 years to steer our strategy and direction and today I'm ready for this challenge.

What is [my] vision? A Yahoo! that executes with speed, clarity and discipline. A Yahoo! that increases its focus on differentiating its products and investing in creativity and innovation. A Yahoo! that better monetizes its audience. A Yahoo! whose great talent is galvanized to address its challenges. And a Yahoo! that is better focused on what's important to its users, customers, and employees.

. . . We have incredible assets. This company has massive potential, drive, determination and skills, and we won't be satisfied until the external perception of Yahoo! accurately reflects that reality.

I have absolute conviction about Yahoo!'s potential for long-term success as an Internet leader. Yahoo! is a company that started with a vision and a dream and, make no mistake, that dream is very much alive. I'm committed to doing whatever it takes to transform Yahoo! into an even greater success in the future.

The time for me is right. The time is now. The Internet is still young, the opportunities ahead are tremendous, and I'm ready to rally our nearly 12,000 Yahoos around the world to help seize them.

Adapted from "Unconventional Thinking," *Entrepreneur Magazine*, September, 1997; and Jerry Yang, "Yodel Anectotal™", June 18th, 2007, yodel.yahoo.com/2007/06/18/my-new-job. Reproduced with permission of Yahoo! Inc.® 2007 by Yahoo! Inc. Yahoo! and the Yahoo! logo are trademarks of Yahoo! Inc.

Learn more about Jerry Yang and other master students at the Master Student Hall of Fame.

2 Careers

Master Student Map

as you read, ask yourself

what if . . .

I could create the career of my dreams—starting today?

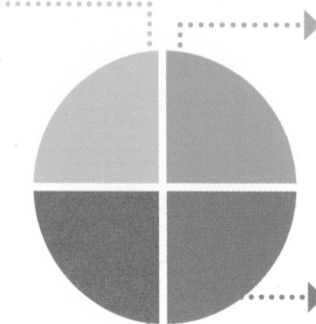

why this chapter matters . . .

By learning about the job market and discovering your skills, you can plan to channel your passions into a successful career.

how

you can use this chapter . . .

- Expand your career options.
- Find your place in the world of work through concrete experiences—informational interviews, internships, and more.
- Choose a career that aligns with your interests, skills, and values.
- Create a career plan.

what is included . . .

MASTER EMPLOYEE in *action*

While the courses were important, the personal/social aspects of my college career were perhaps more important. Through those aspects I learned about time management, project management, and people management skills.

—ANDY FISHER, EXECUTIVE MARKETING MANAGER

Photo courtesy of Andy Fisher

Choosing who you want to be

WHEN PEOPLE ASK about your choice of career, they often pose this question: "What do you want to be?"

One response is to name a job. "I want to be a computer technician." "I want to be a recording engineer." "I want to be a chef." These answers really suggest what we want to *do*.

Another response is to describe a certain income level or lifestyle. "I want to be rich, with all the free time in the world." "I want to sell all my belongings, move to Hawaii, and live on the beach." These statements are actually about what we'd like to *have*.

Yet another option is to describe what you want your life to stand for—the kind of person you want to become. You could talk about being trustworthy, fun-loving, compassionate, creative, honest, productive, and accountable. These are just a few examples of the core values you can bring to any job or lifestyle that you choose.

Career planning does not begin with grinding out résumés, churning out cover letters, poring over want ads, saving for an MBA, or completing a 100-question career assessment. Those steps might be important or even essential—later. But they could be useless unless you take time to exercise your imagination and consider what you want most of all. Career planning starts with dreaming about who you want to *be*.

Dreaming makes sense in a hard-nosed, practical way. Consider people who change careers in midlife. Many of these people have been in the work force for several decades. They've raised families, received promotions, and acquired possessions. They've spent a lifetime being "practical." These people are looking for more than just another job. They want a career that pays the bills *and* excites their passions.

Bring up the subject of career planning and someone might say, "Well, just remember that even if you hate your job, you can always do what you want in your free time." Consider that *all* your time is free time. You give your time freely to your employers or clients, and you do this for your own purposes. All of us are "self-employed," even if we work full-time for someone else.

There's no need to wait 10, 20, or 30 years to discover your passions. You can start now by reading and completing the exercises in this chapter.[1] ✳

journal entry 6

Discovery/Intention Statement

Create value from this chapter

Recall a time when you felt powerful, competent, and fulfilled. Examples might include writing a paper when the words flowed effortlessly, skillfully leading a bar mitzvah service, or working in a restaurant and creating a new dish that won rave reviews. Mentally re-create this experience and the feelings that came with it.

Now, reflect on this experience. Briefly describe the skills that you were using at that moment, the values you were demonstrating, or both.

I discovered that I . . .

_____

_____

Next, review what you just wrote. Convert one of the skills or values that you listed into an intention that could guide your overall career plan. For example, you might write, "I intend, no matter what job I have, to be an effective leader." Or "I intend to create a career that gives free expression to my creativity."

I intend to . . .

_____

_____

Now scan this chapter for ideas that can help you act on your intention. List at least four ideas, along with the page numbers where you can read more about them.

Strategy	Page number

Digital Vision/Photodisc/Getty

You've got a world of choices

Our society offers a limitless array of careers. You no longer have to confine yourself to a handful of traditional categories, such as business, education, government, or manufacturing.

PEOPLE ARE CONSTANTLY creating new products and services to meet emerging demands. The number of job titles is expanding so rapidly that we can barely track them. Many of these jobs fall outside the 9-to-5 office setting. Here are some examples.

There are people who work as *ritual consultants*, helping people to plan weddings, anniversaries, graduations, and other ceremonies.

Space planners help individuals and organizations to efficiently arrange furniture and equipment.

Auto brokers visit dealers, shop around, and buy a car for you.

Professional organizers walk into your home or office and coach you on managing time and paperwork.

Pet psychologists help you raise a happy and healthy animal.

Life coaches assist you in setting and achieving goals related to your career or anything else. Some coaches specialize in working with executives, a form of self-employment that can lead to a six-figure annual income.

Court reporters produce court transcripts, but they can also use their skills for lucrative gigs outside the courtroom, including real-time captioning for television shows and Webcasts.

Photographers and advertising agencies hire *food stylists* to make meals look mouth-watering and awe-inspiring at the same time.

Sommeliers match foods with fine wines to enhance the flavors of both.

Videographers work for agencies as well as video production firms and large corporations.

Pilots can transform a love of flying into a lucrative career. *Yacht captains* do the same with their passions for sailing and fresh air.

If you're a self-employed graphic designer, an *artists' representative* can help you find well-paying work. And if you're in the mood for climbing a mountain or two, an *adventure tour guide* will lead the way.

The global marketplace creates even more options for you. Through Internet connections and communication satellites that bounce phone calls around the planet, you can exchange messages with almost anyone, anywhere. Your customers or clients could be located in Colorado or China, Pennsylvania or Panama. You can track packages worldwide in real time and stay on top of investment opportunities as they emerge. Your skills in thinking globally could help you create a new product or service for a new market—and perhaps a career that does not even exist today.

In addition to choosing the *content* of your career, you have many options for integrating work into the context of your life. You can work full-time. You can work part-time. You can commute to a cubicle in a major corporation. Or you can work at home and take the one-minute commute from your bedroom to your desk. You can join a thriving business—or create one of your own.

If the idea of self-employment seems far-fetched, consider that as a student you already *are* self-employed. You are setting your own goals, structuring your time, making your own financial decisions, and monitoring your performance. These are all transferable skills that you can use to become your own boss.

Reading this chapter and completing its exercises and Journal Entries will help you start gathering information on possible careers. Just remember that there is no reason to limit your choices. You've got the world to choose from.[2] ✳

The world of work—an overview

PERHAPS THE MOST comprehensive guide to the work world is the O*NET OnLine system (the Occupational Information Network). O*NET classifies American workers into 16 career clusters outside the military. Those clusters are listed below, along with a few examples of the many careers included in each cluster. Go online to **http://online.onetcenter.org/find/** for more information. Also check out O*NET's companion Web sites for career planning at **http://online.onetcenter.org/**

Agriculture, Food, and Natural Resources
Gas plant operators
Geological and petroleum technicians
Veterinarians and veterinary assistants

Architecture and Construction
Architects
Construction and building inspectors
Interior designers
Solar thermal installers and technicians

Arts, Audio/Video Technology, and Communications
Audio and video equipment technicians
Choreographers
Film and video editors
Writers and authors

Business, Management, and Administration
Administrative assistants
Legal and medical secretaries
Management analysts
Operations research analysts

Education and Training
Education administrators
Librarians and library technicians
Instructional designers and technologists
Teachers

Finance
Bill and account collectors
Credit analysts
Financial analysts
Risk management specialists

Government and Public Administration
Climate change analysts
Government property inspectors and investigators
Transportation inspectors
Urban and regional planners

Health Science
Cardiovascular technologists and technicians
Health educators
Medical and clinical laboratory technicians
Medical records and health information technicians

Hospitality and Tourism
Chefs and head cooks
Food service managers and lodging managers
Recreation workers

Human Services
Child, family, and school social workers
Fitness trainers and aerobics instructors
Marriage and family therapists
Medical and public health social workers

Information Technology
Computer security specialists
Computer software engineers
Computer support specialists
Network and computer systems administrators

Law, Public Safety, Corrections, and Security
Arbitrators, mediators, and conciliators
Criminal investigators and special agents
Emergency medical technicians and paramedics
Firefighters and police detectives

Manufacturing
Chemical plant and system operators
Electrical and electronics repairers
Industrial engineering technicians
Industrial machinery mechanics

Marketing, Sales, and Service
Green marketers
Market research analysts
Real estate appraisers
Sales engineers

Science, Technology, Engineering, and Mathematics
Automotive engineers
Biochemical engineers
Energy engineers

Transportation, Distribution, and Logistics
Automotive master mechanics
Commercial pilots
Industrial safety and health engineers ✳

Jumpstart your education with transferable skills

When meeting with an academic advisor, you may be tempted to say, "I've just been taking general education and liberal arts courses. I don't have any marketable skills." Think again.

(pool player) Glow Images/Getty, (surveryor) Monty Rakusen/Getty

FEW WORDS ARE as widely misunderstood as *skill*. Defining it carefully can have an immediate and positive impact on your career planning.

Identify two kinds of skills

One dictionary defines *skill* as "the ability to do something well, usually gained by training or experience." Some skills—such as the ability to repair fiber-optic cables or do brain surgery—are acquired through formal schooling, on-the-job training, or both. These abilities are called *technical skills*. People with such skills have mastered a specialized body of knowledge needed to do a specific kind of work.

However, there is another category of skills that we develop through experiences both inside and outside the classroom. We may never receive formal training to develop these abilities, yet they are key to success in the workplace. These are *transferable skills*. Transferable skills indicate the kind of abilities that help people thrive in any job—no matter what technical skills they have. These are all transferable skills.

Perhaps you've heard someone described this way: "She's really smart and knows what she's doing, but she's got lousy people skills." People skills—such as *listening* and *negotiating*—are prime examples of transferable skills.

Succeed in many situations

Transferable skills are often invisible to us. The problem begins when we assume that a given skill can be used in only one context, such as being in school or working at a particular job. Thinking in this way places an artificial limit on our possibilities.

As an alternative, think about the things you routinely do to succeed in school. Analyze your activities to isolate specific skills. Then brainstorm a list of jobs where you could use the same skills.

Consider the task of writing a research paper. This calls for the following skills:

- *Planning*, including setting goals for completing your outline, first draft, second draft, and final draft.
- *Managing time* to meet your writing goals.
- *Interviewing* people who know a lot about the topic of your paper.
- *Researching* using the Internet and campus library to discover key facts and ideas to include in your paper.
- *Writing* to present those facts and ideas in an original way.
- *Editing* your drafts for clarity and correctness.

Now consider the kinds of jobs that draw on these skills.

For example, you could transfer your skill at writing papers to a possible career in journalism, technical writing, or advertising copywriting.

You could use your editing skills to work in the field of publishing as a magazine or book editor.

Interviewing and research skills could help you enter the field of market research. And the abilities to plan, manage time, and meet deadlines will help you succeed in all the jobs mentioned so far.

Use the same kind of analysis to think about transferring skills from one job to another. Say that you work part-time as an administrative assistant at a computer dealer that sells a variety of hardware and software. You take phone calls from potential customers, help current customers solve problems using their computers, and attend meetings where your coworkers plan ways to market new products. You are developing skills at *selling, serving customers,* and *working on teams.* These skills could help you land a job as a sales representative for a computer manufacturer or software developer.

The basic idea is to take a cue from the word *transferable.* Almost any skill you use to succeed in one situation can *transfer* to success in another situation.

The concept of transferable skills creates a powerful link between higher education and the work world. Skills are the core elements of any job. While taking any course, list the specific skills you are developing and how you can transfer them to the work world. Almost everything you do in school can be applied to your career—if you consistently pursue this line of thought.

Ask four questions

To experiment further with this concept of transferable skills, ask and answer four questions derived from the Master Student Map.

Why identify my transferable skills? Getting past the "I-don't-have-any-skills" syndrome means that you can approach job hunting with more confidence. As you uncover these hidden assets, your list of qualifications will grow as if by magic. You won't be padding your résumé. You'll simply be using action words to tell the full truth about what you can do.

Identifying your transferable skills takes a little time. However, the payoffs are numerous. A complete and accurate list of transferable skills can help you land jobs that involve more responsibility, more variety, more freedom to structure your time, and more money. Careers can be made—or broken—by the skills that allow you to define your job, manage your workload, and get along with people.

Transferable skills help you thrive in the midst of constant change. Technology will continue to develop. Ongoing discoveries in many fields could render current knowledge obsolete. Jobs that exist today may disappear in a few years, only to be replaced by entirely new ones.

In the economy of the twenty-first century, you might not be able to count on job security. What you *can* count on is "skills security"—abilities that you can carry from one career to another or acquire as needed.

What are my transferable skills? Discover your transferable skills by reflecting on key experiences. Recall a time when you performed at the peak of your ability, overcame obstacles, won an award, gained a high grade, or met a significant goal. List the skills you used to create those successes. List those skills as "-ing" words derived from action verbs. Examples are *acting, auditing, building, coaching, collecting, inspecting, managing, teaching,* and *training.* You'll find a longer list of transferable skills in the next article.

For a more complete picture of your transferable skills, describe the object of your action. Say that one of the skills on your list is *organizing.* This could refer to organizing ideas, organizing people, or organizing objects in a room. Specify the kind of organizing that you like to do.

How do I perform these skills? You can bring your transferable skills into even sharper focus by adding adverbs—words that describe *how* you take action. You might say that you edit *accurately* or learn *quickly.*

In summary, you can use a three-column chart to list your transferable skills. For example:

Verb	Object	Adverb
Organizing	Records	Effectively
Serving	Customers	Courteously
Coordinating	Special events	Efficiently

Add a specific example of each transferable skill to your skills list, and you're well on your way to an engaging résumé and a winning job interview.

What if I could expand my transferable skills? In addition to thinking about the skills you already have, consider the skills you'd like to acquire. Describe them in detail. List experiences that can help you develop them. Let your list of transferable skills grow and develop as you do. ✳

 Learn more about transferable skills online.

101 transferable skills

THERE ARE LITERALLY hundreds of transferable skills. The following list offers 101 examples. Use this list as a tool to jog your thinking when you take an inventory of *your* transferable skills.

To learn more about transferable skills, check out O*NET OnLine, a Web site from the federal government at **http://online.onetcenter.org**. There you'll find tools for discovering your skills and matching them to specific occupations. Additional information on careers and job hunting is available through CareerOneStop at **http://www.careeronestop.org**.

Self-discovery skills

Assessing your current knowledge and skills

Choosing and applying learning strategies

Selecting strategies to acquire new knowledge and skills

Showing flexibility by adopting new attitudes and behaviors

For more information on self-discovery skills, see Chapter 1.

Career planning skills

Discovering career-related values and interests

Discovering content and transferable skills

Discovering options for possible careers

Setting career goals

Updating career goals to reflect new insights and work experience

For more information about career planning skills, keep reading this chapter.

Time-management skills

Choosing materials and facilities needed to meet goals

Choosing technology and applying it to goal-related tasks

Delivering projects and outcomes on schedule

Designing other processes, procedures, or systems to meet goals

Managing multiple projects at the same time

Monitoring progress toward goals

Persisting in order to meet goals

Planning projects for teams

Planning special events

Scheduling due dates for project outcomes

Scheduling time for goal-related tasks

Working independently to meet goals

For more information about time-management skills, see Chapter 3.

Memory skills

Focusing attention to learn new information and ideas

Selecting key information and ideas to remember

Associating new information and ideas with prior knowledge

Discovering meaningful ways to organize new information and ideas

Encoding new information and ideas in ways that appeal to the senses

For more information about memory skills, see Chapter 4.

Reading skills

Reading for detail

Reading for key ideas and major themes

Reading to discover strategies for solving problems or meeting goals

Reading to follow instructions

Reading to synthesize ideas and information from several sources

For more information about reading skills, see Chapter 5.

Note-taking skills

Creating pictures, graphs, and other visuals to summarize and clarify information

Gathering information online or in the library

Gathering information through field research, interviews, and primary sources

Organizing information and ideas in digital and paper-based forms

Taking legible, meaningful, and accurate notes

For more information about note-taking skills, see Chapter 6.

Test-taking and related skills

Applying scientific findings and methods to solve problems

Assessing personal performance at school or at work

Managing stress

Using mathematics to do basic computations and solve problems

Using test results and other assessments to improve performance

Working cooperatively in study groups and project teams

For more information about skills related to test taking, see Chapter 7.

Thinking skills

Choosing and implementing solutions

Choosing appropriate strategies for making decisions

Choosing ethical behaviors

Diagnosing the sources of problems

Evaluating material presented verbally, in print, or online

Evaluating products, services, or programs

Generating possible solutions to problems

Interpreting information needed for problem solving or decision making

Stating problems accurately

Thinking to create new ideas, products, or services

Thinking to evaluate ideas, products, or services

Summarizing information in numerical form in graphs or tables

For more information about thinking skills, see Chapter 8.

Communication skills

Assigning and delegating tasks

Coaching

Consulting

Counseling

Conversing informally on a one-to-one basis

Giving people feedback about the quality of their performance

Interpreting and responding to nonverbal messages

Interviewing people for assessment purposes (such as performance reviews)

Interviewing people for hiring purposes

Leading meetings

Leading project teams

Listening fully (without judgment or distraction)

Managing relationships with vendors or suppliers

Meeting the public

Persuading people to buy a product or service or adopt an idea

Researching by conducting focus groups

Maintaining accurate records and accessing them when needed

Resolving conflicts

Responding to complaints

Responding to requests

Selling products, programs, or services

Serving clients and customers

Speaking to explain ideas, information, or procedures

Speaking to diverse audiences

Speaking to persuade people to adopt policies or take action

Supervising people while they perform assigned tasks

Teaching

Training

Tutoring

Writing and editing

For more information about communication skills, see Chapter 9.

Money skills

Decreasing expenses

Increasing income

Monitoring income and expenses

Preparing budgets

Using credit responsibly

For more information about money skills, see Chapter 10.

Health skills

Changing habits that affect health

Making health-related decisions based on sound information

Maintaining reserves of energy and alertness for the tasks of daily life

Managing stress and negative emotions in constructive ways

Monitoring habits that affect health

For more information about health skills, see Chapter 11.

Skills for adapting to work environments

Finding employment based on self-knowledge and accurate information about the work world

Finding and learning from a mentor

Taking the initiative with tasks and going beyond the minimum requirements of a job

Updating skills continuously

Adapting to the culture of an organization while maintaining personal values

Practicing integrity and honesty

Working well with people from a variety of backgrounds

For more information about workplace adaptation skills, see Chapter 12. ✳

This exercise is about discovering the full range of your skills. Before you begin, gather at least 100 index cards (3 × 5) and a pen or pencil. Allow about one hour for this exploration. Warning: The results may be personally empowering!

Step 1

Think back over your activities during the past month. See if you can remember every activity during which you demonstrated *any* skill. The idea behind this exercise is to list as many such activities as possible.

Write down each of these many activities, listing each one on a *separate* 3 × 5 card. Some of your cards might read "cooked meals," "tuned up my car," or "weeded a garden." Spend 10 minutes on this step.

Step 2

Now spend another 10 minutes reflecting on your school activities. Focus especially on those that involved some extra effort on your part. Examples might include:

- Class presentations or speeches
- Independent study, theses, or capstone projects
- Teaching or research assistantships
- Tutoring or mentoring assignments
- Work on a student newspaper, radio station, or Web site
- Student government activities

Again, describe any such activities in a word or short phrase. List each one on a 3 × 5 card.

Step 3

Your next step is to spend another 10 minutes reviewing work experiences, both paid and unpaid. Start by listing as many major job activities as you can recall. Remember to include internships and volunteer work.

Step 4

This step is for any skill-developing activities that haven't occurred to you so far. Keep brainstorming and filling up cards!

Have you planned special trips or vacations? Write those down.

Have you published anything—a recipe, letter to the editor, newsletter article, family history, blog, or Web site? List those also.

Also create cards for:

- Hobbies
- Special licenses or credentials
- Continuing education credits
- Workshops, conferences, seminars, and training experiences
- Membership in Girl Scouts, Boy Scouts, or related groups
- Activities for your church, synagogue, mosque, meditation community, or other spiritual group

Step 5

For the next few minutes, take a well-deserved break. Then quickly scan all the cards you just created. After you finish your scan, take another 10 minutes to list any specialized knowledge or procedures needed to complete those activities.

For example, tutoring a French class requires a working knowledge of that language. Tuning up a car requires knowing how to adjust a car's timing and replace spark plugs. You could list several such skills for any one activity.

These are your *technical skills*. Write each one on a separate card and label it "Content."

Step 6

Go over your activity cards one more time. Look for examples of *transferable skills*. For instance, giving a speech or working as a salesperson in a computer store requires the ability to persuade people. That's a transferable skill. Tuning up a car means that you can attend to details and troubleshoot. Tutoring in French requires teaching, listening, and speaking skills.

Write each of your transferable skills on a separate card and label each card "Transferable."

Step 7

Congratulations—you now have a detailed picture of your technical and transferable skills. The work you've just done will pay off every time that you revise your résumé, prepare for job interviews, and complete other career-planning and job-hunting tasks.

CAREERS

2

8 critical thinking exercise
Use informal ways to discover yourself

During career planning, take time to explore your interests in an informal and playful way. The results can be revealing and useful.

Answer the following questions by writing the first ideas that come to mind. Use additional paper as needed or create a computer file for your writing. Have fun and stay open to new insights.

Imagine that you're at a party and you're having a fascinating conversation with someone you just met. What does this person do for a living? What is your conversation about?

_____

_____

_____

_____

_____

_____

What do you enjoy doing most with your unscheduled time? List any hobby or other activity that you do not currently define as "work."

_____

_____

_____

_____

Think about the kinds of books, newspaper and magazine articles, and television shows that are most likely to capture your attention. What subjects or situations do they involve?

_____

_____

_____

_____

_____

If you bookmark Web sites in your Internet browser, review that list. What interests do these sites reveal?

_____

_____

_____

_____

_____

_____

_____

What kinds of problems do you most enjoy solving—those that involve ideas, people, or products? Give an example.

_____

_____

_____

_____

_____

Finally, reread your answers to the previous questions. List three to five interests that are critical to your choice of career.

_____

_____

_____

_____

_____

_____

_____

Ways to learn about careers

TO DISCOVER THE full range of jobs that exist, you can turn to friends, family members, teachers, classmates, coworkers. Also check out the following sources of career information.

Publications

Visit the career planning and job-hunting sections in bookstores and libraries. Look for books, magazines, videos, and other nonprint materials related to career planning. Libraries may subscribe to trade journals and industry newsletters.

Career counseling

Your school may offer career counseling as well as links to similar services in the off-campus community. Private consultants and companies offer career counseling for a fee. Ask around to find someone who's seen a career counselor and get some recommendations.

The Internet

Through your own searching and suggestions from others, you can find useful Web sites devoted to job hunting and career planning. One place to start is **JobHuntersBible.com**, which includes links to sites screened by Richard Bolles, author of *What Color Is Your Parachute?*

Also visit the Occupational Information Network (O*NET) site posted by the U.S. Department of Labor at **http://online.onetcenter.org**. Here you'll find information on hundreds of jobs that you can search by using keywords or browsing a complete list. You'll also find Skills Search, an online tool that helps you list your skills and then matches the list with potential jobs.

At CareerOneStop, **http://www.careeronestop.org**, you can view over 1 million job postings, get labor market trends and tips, and post your résumé for thousands of employers.

Use America's Career InfoNet at **http://www .careerinfonet.org** to identify your skills, match them to specific occupations, use a résumé tutorial, and learn about effective strategies for job hunting.

Also check out America's Job Bank at **http://www .jobbankinfo.org**. Here you can post your résumé, create a cover letter, and research employers in your area.

The Riley Guide at **http://www.rileyguide.com/** is one of the most comprehensive guides to careers and job hunting on the Internet. Besides career information, you'll find suggestions for using the Internet while career planning and job hunting.

Job-Hunt at **http://www.job-hunt.com** includes over 6,000 links to career-planning and job-hunting resources in all 50 states.

Organizations

Professional associations exist for people in almost any career. One function of these associations is to publicize career options and job openings of interest to their members. Search the Internet with the keywords *professional associations* and follow the links that interest you. Many organizations offer student membership rates.

Working people

One powerful way to sort through all this information is to seek out people working in the careers that interest you. Working people can update you on the latest terminology and trends in their field.[3] *

There's an old saying: "If you enjoy what you do, you'll never work another day in your life." If you clearly define your career goals and your strategy for reaching them, you can plan your education effectively and create a seamless transition from school to the workplace.

Stockbyte

Create your career

You already know a lot about your career plan

When people learn study skills and life skills, they usually start with finding out things they don't know. That means discovering new strategies for taking notes, reading, writing, managing time, and the other subjects covered in this book.

Career planning is different. You can begin your career planning education by realizing how much you know right now. You've already made many decisions about your career. This is true for young people who say, "I don't have any idea what I want to be when I grow up." It's also true for midlife career changers.

Consider the student who can't decide if she wants to be a cost accountant or a tax accountant and then jumps to the conclusion that she is totally lost when it comes to career planning. It's the same with the student who doesn't know if he wants to be a veterinary assistant or a nurse.

These people forget that they already know a lot about their career choices. The person who couldn't decide between veterinary assistance and nursing had already ruled out becoming a lawyer, computer programmer, or teacher. He just didn't know yet whether he had the right bedside manner for horses or for people. The person who was debating tax accounting versus cost accounting already knew she didn't want to be a doctor, playwright, or taxicab driver. She did know she liked working with numbers and balancing books.

In each case, these people have already narrowed their list of career choices to a number of jobs in the same field—jobs that draw on the same core skills. In general, they already know what they want to be when they grow up.

Demonstrate this for yourself. Find a long list of occupations. Talk to a librarian, or go online to **http://online.onetcenter.org/find/**. Using a stack of 3×5 cards, write down about a hundred randomly selected job titles, one title per card. Sort through the cards, and divide them into two piles. Label one pile "Careers I've Definitely Ruled Out for Now." Label the other pile "Possibilities I'm Willing to Consider."

You might go through a stack of 100 such cards and end up with 95 in the "definitely ruled out" pile and 5 in the "possibilities" pile. This demonstrates that you already have a career in mind.

Your career is a choice, not a discovery

Many people approach career planning as if they were panning for gold. They keep sifting through the dirt, clearing the dust, and throwing out the rocks. They are hoping to strike it rich and discover the perfect career.

Other people believe that they'll wake up one morning, see the heavens part, and suddenly know what they're supposed to do. Many of them are still waiting for that magical day to dawn.

You can approach career planning in a different way. Instead of seeing a career as something you discover, you can see it as something you choose. You don't find the right career. You create it.

There's a big difference between these two approaches. Thinking that there's only one "correct" choice for your career can lead to a lot of anxiety: "Did I choose the right one?" "What if I made a mistake?"

Viewing your career as your creation helps you relax. Instead of anguishing over finding the right career, you can stay open to possibilities. You can choose one career today, knowing that you can choose again later.

Suppose that you've narrowed your list of possible careers to five, and you still can't decide. Then just choose one. Any one. Many people will have five careers in a lifetime anyway. You might be able to pursue all five of your careers, and you can do any one of them first. The important thing is to choose.

One caution is in order. Choosing your career is not something to do in an information vacuum. Rather, choose after you've done a lot of research. That includes research into yourself—your skills and interests—and a thorough knowledge of what careers are available.

After you've gathered all of the data, there's only one person who can choose your career: you. This choice does not have to be a weighty one. In fact, it can be like going into your favorite restaurant and choosing from a menu that includes only your favorite dishes. At that point, it's difficult to make a mistake. Whatever your choice, you know you'll enjoy it.

Plan by naming names

One key to making your career plan real and to ensuring that you can act on it is naming. Go back over your plan to see if you can include specific names whenever they're called for:

- *Name your job.* List the skills you enjoy using, and find out which jobs use them (the *Occupational Outlook Handbook* is a good resource for this activity). What are those jobs called? List them. Note that the same job might have different names.

- *Name your company—the agency or organization you want to work for.* If you want to be self-employed or start your own business, name the product or service you'd sell. Also list some possible names for your business. If you plan to work for others, name the organizations or agencies that are high on your list.

- *Name your location.* Ask if your career choices are consistent with your preferences about where to live and work. For example, someone who wants to make a living as a studio musician might consider living in a large city such as New York or Toronto. This contrasts with the freelance graphic artist who conducts his business mainly by phone, fax, and e-mail. He might be able to live anywhere and still pursue his career.

- *Name your contacts.* Take the list of organizations you just compiled. Find out which people in these organizations are responsible for hiring. List those

people, and contact them directly. If you choose self-employment, list the names of possible customers or clients. All of these people are job contacts.

Now expand your list of contacts by brainstorming with your family and friends. Come up with a list of names—anyone who can help you with career planning and job hunting. Write each of these names on a 3 × 5 card or Rolodex card. You can also use a spiral-bound notebook, computer, or personal digital assistant.

Next, call the key people on your list. Ask them about their career experiences, tell them about the career path you're considering, and probe their knowledge of the industry you're interested in. After you speak with them, make brief notes about what you discussed. Also jot down any actions you agreed to take, such as a follow-up call.

Consider everyone you meet as a potential member of your job network. Be prepared to talk about what you do. Develop a "pitch"—a short statement of your career goal that you can easily share with your contacts. For example: "After I graduate, I plan to work in the travel business. I'm looking for an internship in a travel agency for next summer. Do you know of any agencies that take interns?"

Describe your ideal lifestyle

In addition to choosing the content of your career, you have many options for integrating work into the context of your life. You can work full-time. You can work part-time. You can commute to a cubicle in a major corporation. Or you can work at home and take the 30-second commute from your bedroom to your desk.

Close your eyes. Visualize an ideal day in your life after graduation. Vividly imagine the following:

- Your work setting
- Your coworkers
- Your calendar and to-do list for that day
- Other sights and sounds in your work environment

This visualization emphasizes the importance of finding a match between your career and your lifestyle preferences—the amount of flexibility in your schedule, the number of people you see each day, the variety in your tasks, and the ways that you balance work with other activities.

Consider self-employment

Instead of joining a thriving business, you could create one of your own. As a student, you are already practicing many of the skills needed for self-employment, including goal setting, structuring your time, making your own financial decisions, and monitoring your performance. Remember that many successful businesses—including Facebook and Yahoo!—were started by college students.

Test your choice—and be willing to change

Career-planning materials and counselors can help you test your choice and change it if you decide to do so. Read books about careers. Search for career-planning Web sites. Ask career counselors about skills assessments that can help you discover more about your skills and identify jobs that call for those skills. Take career-planning courses and workshops sponsored by your school. Visit the career-planning and job placement offices on campus.

Once you have a career choice, translate it into workplace experience. For example:

- Contact people who are actually doing the job you're researching, and ask them a lot of questions about what it's like (an *information interview*).

- Choose an internship or volunteer position in a field that interests you.

- Get a part-time or summer job in your career field.

If you find that you enjoy your experiences, you've probably made a wise career choice. And the people you meet are possible sources of recommendations, referrals, and employment in the future. If you did *not* enjoy your experiences, celebrate what you learned about yourself. Now you're free to refine your initial career choice or go in a new direction.

Career planning is not a once-and-for-all proposition. Rather, career plans are made to be changed and refined as you gain new information about yourself and the world. You might get a useful new idea by striking up a conversation with a stranger with a fascinating career. Or you might bump into a friend you haven't seen for years—someone who offers you a job you've never considered. Such events cannot be planned. Nonetheless, they can change your life.

Career planning never ends. If your present career no longer feels right, you can choose again—no matter what stage of life you're in. The process is the same, whether you're choosing your first career or your fifth.[5] ✳

 Find more strategies online for career planning.

9 critical thinking exercise
Dig out the "life story" of a product

All the goods and services in our society result from work done by people. Pondering this fact may give you new possibilities for career planning.

For example, pick up any object near the place where you are sitting or standing right now—perhaps a computer, notebook, pen, pencil, CD, DVD, or piece of clothing. If possible, choose something that holds a special interest for you.

Next, reflect for a moment on the path that this product took from its creator into your hands. On a separate sheet of paper, list the job title of every person who helped to plan, produce, distribute, and sell this item. If you're not sure, just brainstorm answers. After doing this exercise, you can do some research to confirm your answers.

Finally, scan this list for any jobs that interest you. To find out more about them, use the resources listed in the article "Ways to Learn about Careers."

As you do this exercise, think creatively and keep your options open. You might think of titles for jobs that don't exist yet. Instead of tossing out these ideas, consider them as starting points in creating an entirely new career for yourself.[4]

10 critical thinking exercise
Create a support team

To fuel your energy for career planning, create your own support team. Begin by listing the names of at least five people with whom you can share your frustrations and successes in career planning and job hunting. These can be friends, family members, coworkers, or classmates. Include each person's name, telephone number, and e-mail address. Begin your list in the following space.

From this list, recruit people to be on your support team. Tell each team member your goals and intended actions. Ask them to help in holding you accountable to your plan. Keep touching base with each member of your team and support them in return.[6]

11 critical thinking exercise
Brainstorm career options

It's time to take another step toward your career plan. Nothing too heavy or serious is required. Just be willing to dream and dwell in possibilities for a few minutes. In fact, be prepared to create some exciting and even outrageous ideas.

Remember that you can eventually refine these ideas and turn them into a practical plan for action. That step is important, and it will come later in this chapter.

Schedule an hour to do this exercise. If you can set aside even more time, you may get more interesting results. Feel free to take a break between steps or spread the exercise over several sessions. Use additional paper as needed to write your responses to each step.

Step 1: Imagine a wonderful life.

In the space provided, write a paragraph that describes an ideal day for you. Mentally remove your current limitations and let your imagination run free. What would you be doing right now if you had enough money to live on for the rest of your life and nothing scheduled on your calendar?

Describe one day from this perspective. Write in the present tense. Include some details about where you live, what you own, what you're doing, and the important people in your life. Above all, give yourself permission to create a compelling vision, and don't worry for now about how "practical" it is.

Step 2: Create a personal definition of success.

Now reflect for a moment on how you define success. Many of the advertisements you see every day offer visions of what success means—fat bank accounts, big homes, luxury cars, great clothes, good looks, and friends who look like fashion models. However, these visions may have nothing to do with *your* definition of success. Complete the following sentence:

To me, success means . . .

Step 3: Look "back" on a successful career.

Next, take a mental trip at least 10 years into the future. (If you can, extend that timeline even more, to 20 or 30 years from today.) After completing this amount of time in the work world, you are talking to a newspaper reporter who is writing a feature story about people who have successful careers.

Write a paragraph describing what you will tell this reporter about the highlights of your career. Include any awards, recognitions, major accomplishments, or special events that marked this period of your life.

Step 4: Describe your career in more detail.

Fill in some more details about the career you just described. More specifically, describe two or three of your primary job activities, and write in the present tense.

Do you interact primarily with ideas and information, people, or pieces of technology? And what are the main results or outcomes of your work? Explain.

Also describe the conditions in which you work. Do you work primarily alone or with other people? Do you work at home or away from home? What does your office look like?

What do you value most about your work? Salary and benefits? Leadership roles? Opportunities for advancement? Tangible results? Working on teams? Working independently? Social contribution? These are just a few examples. List your core career values in the following space.

Step 5: List the careers that interest you most.

Congratulations for completing all the creative thinking you've been asked to do. There's just one more step to this exercise.

Find a long list of possible jobs or careers. (One source is the Occupational Information Network, published by the U.S. Department of Labor and available online at **http://online .onetcenter.org/find/**. A reference librarian can help you find other sources.

Spend five minutes scanning the list. Keeping in mind all the values and preferences you described in steps 1 to 4 of this exercise, list the five jobs or careers from the list that interest you most right now.[7]

Sample formats for career plans

FOLLOWING ARE EXCERPTS from career plans in several different formats. You can review these samples for useful ideas. Your career plan can combine several of these formats—and others that you create.[8]

Sample #1: Timeline. One simple format for a career plan is the humble timeline. Simply draw a line and plot dates for major events that you'd like to see take place. Your timeline could also include dates for events related to family life, recreation, and other areas of life. Notice that the sample timeline includes a date years into the future. This person's plan is to take part in projects that will go well beyond his death.

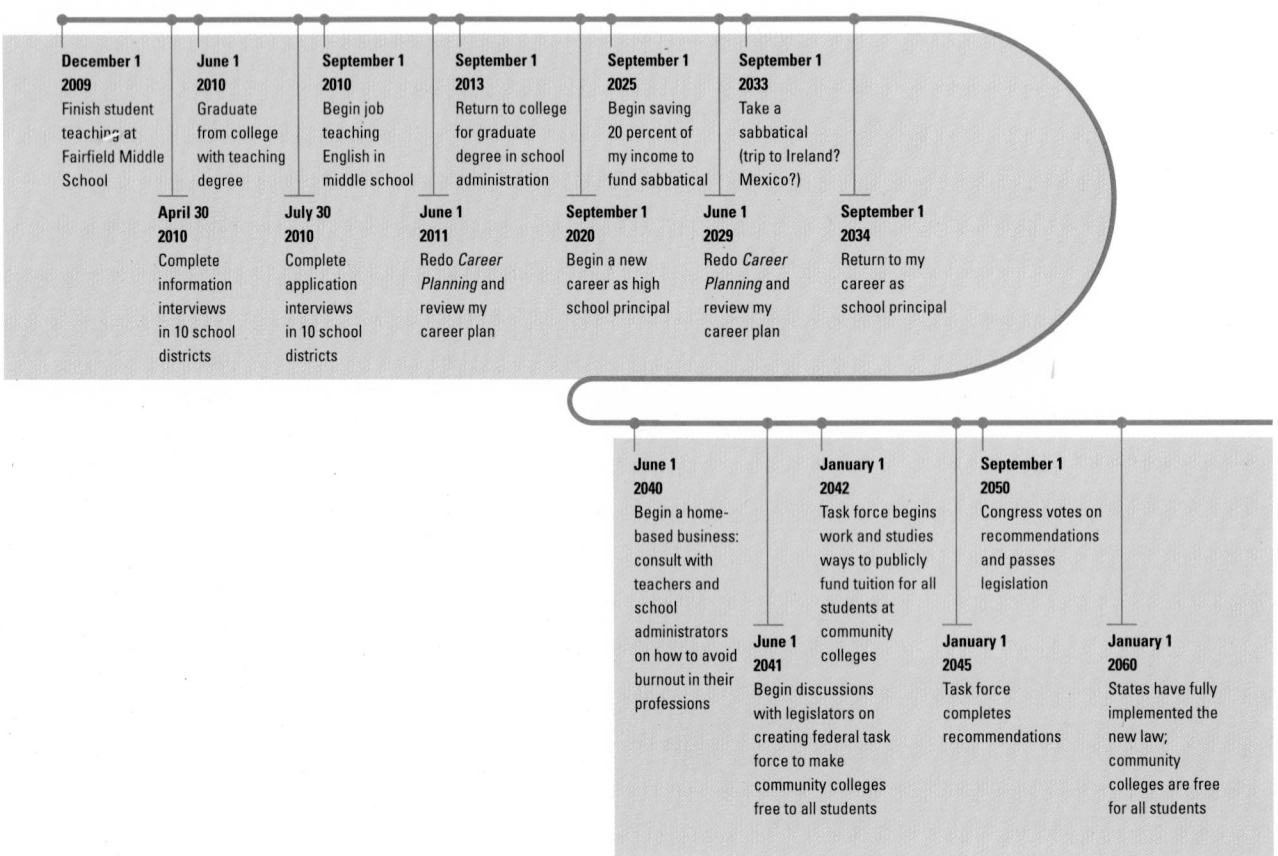

December 1 2009
Finish student teaching at Fairfield Middle School

June 1 2010
Graduate from college with teaching degree

September 1 2010
Begin job teaching English in middle school

September 1 2013
Return to college for graduate degree in school administration

September 1 2025
Begin saving 20 percent of my income to fund sabbatical

September 1 2033
Take a sabbatical (trip to Ireland? Mexico?)

April 30 2010
Complete information interviews in 10 school districts

July 30 2010
Complete application interviews in 10 school districts

June 1 2011
Redo *Career Planning* and review my career plan

September 1 2020
Begin a new career as high school principal

June 1 2029
Redo *Career Planning* and review my career plan

September 1 2034
Return to my career as school principal

June 1 2040
Begin a home-based business: consult with teachers and school administrators on how to avoid burnout in their professions

January 1 2042
Task force begins work and studies ways to publicly fund tuition for all students at community colleges

September 1 2050
Congress votes on recommendations and passes legislation

June 1 2041
Begin discussions with legislators on creating federal task force to make community colleges free to all students

January 1 2045
Task force completes recommendations

January 1 2060
States have fully implemented the new law; community colleges are free for all students

Sample #2: Mind map. You can create a mind map that links personal values to the skills that you want to develop and use. You might find that these skills can be used in several careers.

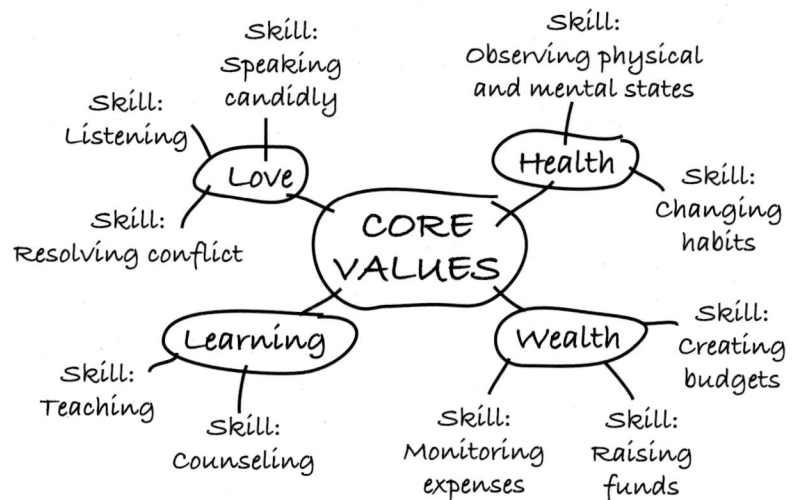

Sample #3: Pie chart. With a pie chart, you visualize the amounts of time that you want to devote to career-related activities.

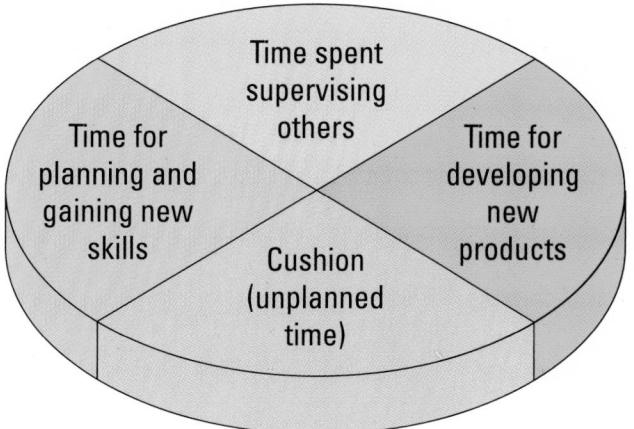

Sample #4: Prioritize. Another option is to list your career goals and sort them by priority. Assign each goal a number from 1 to 100. Higher numbers denote higher priority.

- Consult college career services department on law school options (100)
- Prepare rigorously for LSAT and do well (100)
- Get into top-10 law school (95)
- Get position as editor on *Law Review* (90)
- Graduate in top of class at law school (85)
- Work for state district attorney's office (80)
- Use my position and influence to gain political and judicial contacts (75)

- Found private law firm focused on protection of workers' rights (70)
- Win major lawsuits in defense of individual liberties in the workplace (60)
- Leave law practice to travel to developing countries in aid of poor for two years (60)
- Found international agency in protection of human rights (50)
- Win Nobel Prize (30)

Find more sample career plans online.

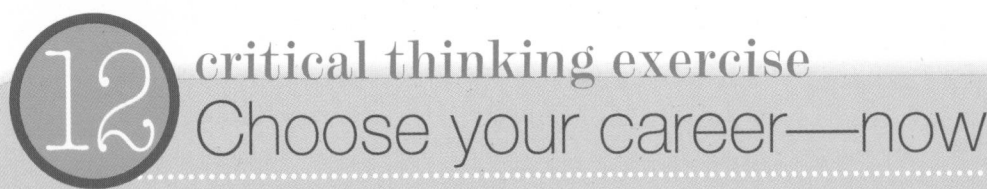

12 critical thinking exercise
Choose your career—now

This exercise offers you the opportunity to make a trial career choice. Now.

Remember that this is a *trial choice.* You can choose again later based on new insights into yourself and the job market. You may change your mind several times during your stay in higher education based on what you learn from courses, internships, work-study assignments, information interviews, part-time jobs, and other work experiences. These experiences are ways to test your career choices. With each choice, you'll come closer to a career that provides you with rewarding work on a daily basis.

In addition to choosing a career, make your choice come alive. Determine the very next actions that you will take to make your choice a reality. This can be just a rough draft of your career plan, which you can revise many times. The point is to start getting your ideas in visible form, and to do it now.

The format of your career plan is up to you. You could include many details, such as the next job title you'd like to have, the courses required for your major, and other training that you want to complete. You could list companies to research and people that could hire you. You could also include target dates to complete each of these tasks. Another option is to represent your plan visually through flow charts, timelines, mind maps, drawings, paintings, sculpture, computer animation, songs, or any other medium that inspires you. No matter what format you choose, get started now and do what works.

Come back to this exercise once each semester and do it again. Include your latest discoveries and intentions. Make your career plan a living document that grows and changes as you do.

To get started, just complete the following sentences. Use the space here and continue on additional paper or other materials.

The career I choose for now is . . .

The next steps that will lead me to this career are . . .

1.

2.

3.

4.

5.

Gearing up for a global economy

ONE GENERATION AGO, only low-skilled factory workers worried about automation—being laid off and replaced by machines. Today, even skilled employees fear losing their jobs to computer-driven robots, or to workers across the globe who will do the same job for a fraction of the wages.

You are entering a global economy. Your toughest competitors for a new job might be people from India or China with technical skills and a blazing fast Internet connection.

One big reason for this change is technology. Much of what workers produce now ends up in digital form. Books, music, movies, television shows, radio programs, technical publications, drawings and designs, slide presentations, X-rays—all can be created on a computer, saved to a CD or DVD, and sent instantly across the world.

This means that employers can hire from a global work force. Project teams in the future might include people from several nations who connect via e-mail, cell phones, teleconferencing, and digital devices that have yet to be invented.

You can thrive in this global economy with the following strategies.

Complete your education. According to *Tough Choices or Tough Times: The Report of the New Commission on the Skills of the American Workforce*, the United States will remain an economic powerhouse only if its citizens are educated to do creative work—research, development, design, marketing, sales, and management. Careers in these areas are the least likely to be outsourced.[9]

The authors of *Tough Choices* note that people with computer skills and strong backgrounds in mathematics and science will have key tools to succeed in the new global economy. Yet they will also need to work with abstract ideas, think creatively, learn quickly, write well, develop new products, and work on culturally diverse project teams. The development of skills is a potential benefit of higher education.

Create a long-term career plan. When planning your career, look beyond your next job. Think in terms of a career *path*. Discover opportunities for advancement and innovation over the long term.

If you're a computer programmer, think about what you could do beyond writing code—perhaps by becoming a systems analyst or software engineer. If you're a musician, find out how you can use the Internet to promote your band, book gigs, and distribute recordings. And if you're a stockbroker, plan to offer more than advice about buying and selling. Help your clients plan their retirement and fund their children's college education as well.

No matter what your plan, consider cultivating sales and marketing skills. Every organization depends on people who can bring in new customers and clients. If you can attract new sources of revenue, you'll be harder to replace.

Develop two key sets of skills. In *The New Division of Labor: How Computers Are Creating the Next Job Market*, Frank Levy and Richard J. Murnane describe two sets of skills that will not be taken over by robots or computers.[10]

First is *expert thinking*. This is the ability to handle problems that cannot be solved simply by applying rules. The doctor who successfully treats a person with a rare set of symptoms offers an example of expert thinking. So does the mechanic who repairs a car engine defect that the computer diagnostics missed.

Second is *complex communication*—the ability to find information, explain it to other people, and persuade them how to use it. An example is the engineer who convinces his colleagues that his design for a DVD player will outstrip the competition and reduce production costs. Complex communication is essential to education, sales, marketing, and management.

Even in a high-tech world, there will always be a need for the human touch. Learn to lead meetings, guide project teams, mentor people, nurture new talent, and create long-term business relationships. Use creative thinking to develop new products and services, reduce expenses, save energy, and attract new customers and clients. Then use critical thinking skills to refine your ideas and turn them into reality. You'll offer employers something that they cannot get from a software package, robot, or any other source. ✳

Explore career assessments

Career assessments, also called vocational aptitude tests, skill inventories, or interest assessments, can be a helpful resource for self-discovery and career planning. They can provide useful information about your personality and work preferences.

YOUR SCHOOL'S CAREER planning or counseling center may offer one or more career assessments. To get the most out of them, keep the following ideas in mind.

Add the human touch. Meet with an experienced career counselor at your school. A counselor can help you select appropriate assessments and understand the results. (This is true even when an assessment is listed as "self-directed.") A counselor can also suggest next steps for creating your career plan and connect you with other services.

Bear in mind that assessments are not tests. Even though some assessments include the word *test* in their title, there are no right or wrong answers to the questions they include.

Ask about cost. Many assessments are available online for free. Others require payment. Check with the career center at your school as well to find out which free assessments they offer. Pay for an assessment only when you're convinced that the benefits will justify the cost.

Remember that assessments differ in quality. Some assessments are backed by decades of research. Others were created last week. Do not expect *any* single assessment—free or fee-based—to give a comprehensive picture of your personality and career interests.

Take several assessments and compare the results. Some assessments will help you identify major aspects of your personality and give only general guidelines for choosing a career. Other assessments will crank out a list of specific job titles for you to consider. Take both kinds of assessments and see what they have to offer.

Keep the results on file. If you take an assessment online, print out the results. Keep them in a folder along with other career planning documents.

Consider taking an assessment more than once—for example, once during this semester and again next year. Doing so will allow you to compare the new results with the earlier results and see if they differ. This can lead to useful insights about your changing career interests.

Combine assessments with other forms of self-discovery. Assessments are just one way to gather ideas for your career plan. Use activities such as the Journal Entries and Critical Thinking Exercises in this book to round out any assessment results.

Remember that what you do with the results is always a personal choice. No assessment can dictate your career direction or substitute for your gut instincts. If the result of an assessment seems wildly off base to you, then it probably is. Take what seems most valuable from each assessment and leave the rest.

Have fun. Approach assessments with a spirit of adventure and play. You're just gathering data—not putting yourself on trial. The purpose of taking any assessment and planning your career is to discover new paths to fulfillment—and create the life of your dreams.

With these guidelines in mind, look for useful assessments. You can start by doing an Internet search with the keywords *career assessment* or *self-assessment*. Inspect the results of your search carefully. Some of the most reputable assessments you might find are the:

- *Campbell Interest and Skill Survey*, a well-known assessment that includes several hundred multiple-choice items. This assessment links to specific information about 60 possible careers.

- *Keirsey Temperament Sorter*, based on the Myers-Briggs Type Indicator®, a prominent personality assessment. Use the Keirsey results as a basis for taking more career-focused assessments.

- *Career Liftoff Interest Inventory (CLII)*, a 240-item assessment linked to a set of codes for classifying job interests.

- *Career Maze*, an online assessment that aims to provide an 82-item list of your personal characteristics and ways to connect them with specific jobs.[11] ✳

Testing your career plan— jump into the job market

Do information interviews. Talk to people who actually do the kind of work that you'd like to do. Schedule an informational interview to ask them about their work. With their permission, go to their job sites. Spend time with them during a workday. Hang around. Ask questions.

To find people you can interview, ask friends and family members for ideas. Perhaps they know someone who works in your chosen field. Also check with a career counselor and alumni office at your school.

When scheduling an informational interview, make it clear that your purpose is to gain information—not get a job. If you set up an informational interview and then use the occasion to ask for a job, you send mixed messages and risk making a negative impression.

Prepare for the interview by researching the particular business or organization you're going to visit. Also list questions to ask the person that you will interview, such as:

- How did you prepare for your career?
- How did you find this job?
- What skills does this job require?
- What other jobs call for a similar set of skills?
- What are your major tasks and responsibilities?
- What kinds of decisions do you regularly make at work?
- Does this job require travel or hours outside a typical work day?
- What do you like most—and least—about your job?
- What changes are occurring in this field?
- What are the salary ranges and opportunities for employment and promotion?
- How can I effectively prepare to work in this career?
- Can you recommend someone else for me to interview?

While informational interviews are often one-time events, they can also involve multiple visits to several people at the same work site. You might even spend several days or weeks following people on the job. Such extended experience is sometimes referred to as job-shadowing.

Volunteer. Volunteering offers another path to work experience that you can list on your résumé. To gain the most from this experience, research and choose volunteer positions as carefully as you would a full-time, salaried job. Identify organizations that are doing the kind of work that excites you. Contact them and ask for the person who supervises volunteers. Then schedule a face-to-face meeting to find out more.

Work. To find out more about working, go to work. Beyond gaining experience, you'll get insights that can change your life. A short-term job assignment can help you define your current skills, develop new ones, refine your career plan, develop contacts, and even lead to doing work that you love.

Cooperative (co-op) education programs offer one option. These programs combine specific classroom assignments with carefully supervised work experience. In addition to getting academic credit, most co-op students get paid and function as productive employees.

Other options include freelancing and temporary work. Rather than becoming an employee, a freelancer works for organizations on specific projects. Rates of payment, due dates, and other details are specified by contract. Freelancers typically work off-site at their own office. A temporary worker (temp) also works on contract but reports to an organization's work site.

Share the process with others. Consider forming a career-planning group. Working in groups allows you to give and receive career coaching. Group members can brainstorm options for each other's careers, research the work world, share information of mutual interest, trade contacts, and pair up for informational interviews. This is one way to raise your energy level for career planning.

Taking part in a group can open you up to your dream career. Others can point out ideas and information you've overlooked. They may alert you to opportunities you never considered or skills you were not aware you had. Working with such a group gives you a firm foundation for networking and relationships that can lead directly to a job offer. For more ideas on networking, see Chapter 12: "Working."[12] ✳

Gaining experience as an intern

Wonderfile

ONE WAY TO launch into your career is an internship. As an intern, you work in a job that relates directly to your career interests. Internships blend classroom learning with on-the-job experience. You get to put your technical and transferable skills into action.

Internships often offer academic credit. Some involve paid positions, while other internships are volunteer opportunities. Interns usually prepare for their assignments by completing courses in a specific field.

Note that internships may be called by other names, such as *co-op experience, practicum, externship,* and *field experience.*

Find internships. To find an internship, make an appointment with someone at the career planning or counseling office on your campus. There you can connect with employers in your area who are looking for interns. You will likely submit a résumé and cover letter explaining your career interests. This is valuable in itself as experience in applying for jobs.

You can also locate organizations that interest you and contact them directly about internships. Even companies that do not have formal internship programs may accept applications.

Other suggestions to keep in mind:

- *Start early.* During a fall semester, for example, start searching for internships for the spring or summer.

- *Network.* Talk to friends, parents, family, neighbors, and instructors to discover if they know about internships for you.

- *Surf the Internet.* Use Internet search engines to find employment or internship listings. Research organizations that interest you and contact them directly.

- *Use the library.* Ask a reference librarian to help you find internship guides. Some look like college catalogs, listing popular positions with key contacts and due dates for applications.

Succeed at your internship. To get the most from your internships, act professionally every moment that you're on the job. In addition:

- *Get direction.* Find an internship supervisor and meet with that person regularly. Ask this person to explain your tasks and offer feedback on how you're doing.

- *Set a goal.* Think about what you'd most like to gain from your internship. For example, your main goal might be to gain information about a career that you can't get from any other source, clarify your choice of a major, or meet people who can recommend you for a job in the future.

- *Ask questions.* You are not expected to be an expert. If you are in doubt about how to complete any task, ask for help.

- *Meet people.* Some internships allow you to work in several areas of a company. If yours does not, then attend company events where you can meet a variety of people.

- *Take the initiative.* If you see a way to save time or money for the organization, then suggest it to your supervisor. If your idea works, be sure to share the credit with her.

- *Look for value in any experience.* Interns are sometimes asked to make photocopies, run errands, and do other "grunt" work. Complete these tasks with a constructive attitude. Use them to demonstrate that you have integrity and a strong work ethic. These are key transferable skills.

Remember that any internship might lead you to a full-time, professional job following graduation. Keep in touch with the people you meet. Even if they are working at another company when you graduate, they can help you find job openings.

Reflect on your internship. Internships offer a great way to test a career choice, even if you find out that you don't like a particular job. You can benefit from ruling out a career choice early on—especially if it involves a major with a lot of required courses.

Write Discovery Statements about what you learn from your internships. List details about what you accomplished. Also write Intention Statements about what you want from your next work experience. You'll find these journal entries useful when you write your résumé—no matter what career you eventually choose. ✳

Service-learning:
Career planning as contribution

AS PART OF a service-learning project for a sociology course, students volunteer at a community center for older adults. For another service-learning project, history students interview people in veterans' hospitals about their war experiences. These students plan to share their interview results with a psychiatrist on the hospital staff.

These examples of actual projects from the National Service-Learning Clearinghouse demonstrate the working premise of service-learning: Volunteer work and other forms of contributing can become a vehicle for higher education.

Service-learning generally includes three elements: meaningful community service, a formal academic curriculum, and time for students to reflect on what they learn from service. That reflection can include speaking, journal writing, and paper writing.

Service-learning creates a win/win scenario. For one thing, students gain the satisfaction of contributing. They also gain experiences that can guide their career choices and help them develop job skills.

When you design or participate in a service-learning project, consider these suggestions:

■ *Choose partners carefully.* Work with a community agency that has experience with students. Make sure that the agency has liability insurance to cover volunteers.

■ *Handle logistics.* Integrating service-learning into your schedule can call for detailed planning. If your volunteer work takes place off campus, arrange for transportation, and allow for travel time.

■ *Reflect on your service-learning project.* Write Discovery Statements about what you want to gain from service-learning and how you feel about what you're doing. Follow up with Intention Statements about what you'll do differently for your next volunteer experience.

■ *Explore the cycle of learning.* You can learn from your service-learning in ways that blend abstract thinking, concrete experience, reflection, and action. For example, write a case study based on your experience or conduct a panel discussion. Create a documentary film, play, photographic exhibit, or song cycle. You can also publish a Web site with audio and video elements that you update on a regular basis.

■ *Include ways to evaluate your project.* From your Intention Statements, create action goals and outcome goals. *Action goals* state what you plan to do and how many people you intend to serve; for instance, "We plan to provide 100 hours of literacy tutoring to 10 people in the community." *Outcome goals* describe the actual impact that your project will have: "At the end of our project, 60 percent of the people we tutor will be able to write a résumé and fill out a job application." Build numbers into your goals whenever possible. That makes it easier to evaluate the success of your project.

■ *Build long-term impact into your project.* One potential drawback of service-learning is that the programs are often short-lived. After students pack up and return to campus, programs can die. Make sure that other students or community members are willing to step in and take over for you when the semester ends.

■ *Build transferable skills.* Review the list of 101 transferable skills on page 60 to stimulate your thinking. List the specific skills that you're developing through service-learning. Keep this list. It will come in handy when you write a résumé and fill out job applications. Before you plan to do another service-learning project, think about the skills you'd like to develop from that experience.

■ *Celebrate mistakes.* If your project fails to meet its goals, have a party. State—in writing—the obstacles you encountered and ways to overcome them. The solutions you offer will be worth gold to the people who follow in your footsteps. ✳

Choosing your major

ONE DECISION THAT troubles many students in higher education is the choice of an academic major. The following four suggestions can guide you through the process of choosing an academic major.

1. Discover options

Follow the fun. See if you can find lasting patterns in the subjects and extracurricular activities that you've enjoyed over the years. Look for a major that allows you to continue and expand on these experiences.

Also, sit down with a stack of 3 × 5 cards and brainstorm answers to the following questions, many of which are similar to the career plan questions you answered in Critical Thinking Exercise 8: "Use Informal Ways to Discover Yourself" on page 63.

- What do you enjoy doing most with your unscheduled time?

- Imagine that you're at a party and having a fascinating conversation. What is this conversation about?

- What Web sites do you frequently visit or have bookmarked in a Web browser?

- What kinds of problems do you enjoy solving—those that involve people? products? ideas?

- What interests are revealed by your choices of reading material, television shows, and other entertainment?

- What would an ideal day look like for you? Describe where you'd live, who would be with you, and what you'd do throughout the day.

Consider your abilities. In addition to considering what you enjoy, think about times and places when you excelled. List the courses that you aced, the work assignments that you mastered, and the hobbies that led to rewards or recognition. Let your choice of a major reflect a discovery of your passions *and* potentials.

Use formal techniques for self-discovery. Writing is a path to the kind of self-knowledge involved in choosing your major. Start with the Critical Thinking Exercises and Journal Entries in this book. Review what you've written, looking for statements about your interests and abilities.

Also consider questionnaires and inventories that are designed to correlate your interests with specific majors. Examples include the Strong Interest Inventory and the Self-Directed Search. Your academic advisor or someone in your school's job placement office can give you more details about these and related inventories.

For a fun and helpful exercise, take several of them and meet with an advisor to interpret the results.

Remember that there is no questionnaire, inventory, test, or formula for choosing a major or career. Likewise, there is no expert who can make these choices for you. Inventories can help you gain self-knowledge, and other people can offer valuable perspectives. However, what you *do* with all this input is entirely up to you.

Link to long-term goals. Your choice of a major can fall into place once you determine what you want in life. Before you choose a major, you should back up to view a bigger picture. List your core values, such as contributing to society, achieving financial security and professional recognition, enjoying good health, or making time for fun. Also write down specific goals that you want to accomplish 5 years, 10 years, or even 50 years from today.

Many students find that the prospect of getting what they want in life justifies all of the time, money, and effort invested in going to school. Having a major gives you a powerful incentive for attending classes, taking part in discussions, reading textbooks, writing papers, and completing other assignments. When you see a clear connection between finishing school and creating the life of your dreams, the daily tasks of higher education become charged with meaning.

Studies indicate that a major factor associated with completing a degree is commitment to personal goals.[13] A choice of major reflects those goals.

Ask other people. Ask key people in your life for their ideas, and listen with an open mind. At the same time, distance yourself from any pressure to choose a major or career that fails to interest you. If you make a choice based solely on the expectations of other people, you could end up with a major—or even a career—you don't enjoy.

Gather information. Check your school's catalog or Web site for a list of available majors. Take a quick glance, and highlight all the majors that interest you. Then talk to students who have declared them. Also read descriptions of courses required for these majors. Chat with instructors who teach courses in these areas, and ask for copies of their class syllabi. Go to the bookstore and browse required texts.

Based on this information, write a list of prospective majors. Discuss them with an academic advisor and someone at your school's career-planning center.

Invent a major. When choosing a major, you might not need to limit yourself to those listed in your school catalog. Many schools now have flexible programs that allow for independent study. Through such programs, you might be able to combine two existing majors or invent an entirely new one of your own.

Consider a complementary minor. You can add flexibility to your academic program by choosing a minor to complement or contrast with your major. The student with a major in psychology might choose a minor in business administration, with the idea of managing a counseling service some day. An effective choice of a minor can expand your skills and career options.

Think critically about the link between your major and your career. Your career goals might have a significant impact on your choice of major. You might be able to pursue a rewarding career by choosing among *several* different majors. Even students planning to apply for law school or medical school have flexibility in their choice of majors. In addition, after graduation, many people are employed in jobs with little relationship to their major. Likewise, you might choose a career in the future that is unrelated to any currently available major.

Remember that many students who choose an "impractical" major go on to prosper in their careers. According to the National Committee for Latin and Greek, people who majored in classical civilizations and literature range from Ted Turner (founder of CNN) to J. K. Rowling (author of the Harry Potter novels).[14]

Also remember that your required courses can benefit you no matter what major or career you choose. For instance, English composition can help chemistry majors who will publish technical articles.

2. Make a trial choice

At many schools, declaring a major offers some benefits. For example, you might get priority when registering for certain classes and qualify for scholarships or grants.

Don't delay such benefits. Even if you feel undecided, you probably have a good idea about what major you will choose. One way to verify this is to conduct a simple experiment. Pretend that you have to choose a major today. Based on the options for a major that you've already discovered, write down the first three ideas that come to mind. Review the list for a few minutes, and then just choose one. This is one way to choose a trial major. Critical Thinking Exercise 13, "Make a Trial Choice of Major," suggests another way to narrow down your choices.

Hold on to your list, however. It reflects your current intuition, or "gut feelings," and it may come in handy during the next step. Step 3 might confirm your trial choice of major—or return you to one of the other prospective majors in your original list.

3. Evaluate your trial choice

When you've made a trial choice of major, take on the role of a scientist. Treat your choice as a hypothesis, and then design a series of experiments to evaluate and test it. For example:

- Schedule office meetings with instructors who teach courses in the major. Ask about required course work and career options in the field.

- Discuss your trial choice with an academic advisor or career counselor.

- Enroll in a course related to your possible major. Remember that introductory courses might not give you a realistic picture of the workloads involved in advanced courses.

- Find a volunteer experience, internship, part-time job, or service learning experience related to the major.

- Interview students who have declared the same major. Ask them in detail about their experiences and suggestions for success.

- Interview someone who works in a field related to the major.

- Think about whether you can complete your major given the amount of time and money that you plan to invest in higher education.

- Consider whether declaring this major would require a transfer to another program.

If your "experiments" confirm your choice of major, celebrate that fact. If they result in choosing a new major, celebrate that outcome as well.

Also remember that higher education represents a safe place to test your choice of major—and to change your mind. As you sort through your options, help is always available from administrators, instructors, advisors, and peers.

4. Choose again

Keep your choice of a major in perspective. There is probably no single "correct" choice. Your unique collection of skills is likely to provide the basis for majoring in several fields.

Odds are that you'll change your major at least once—and that you'll change careers several times during your life. One benefit of higher education is mobility. You gain the general skills and knowledge that can help you move into a new major or career field at any time.

Viewing a major as a one-time choice that determines your entire future can raise your stress levels. Instead, look at choosing a major as the start of a continuing path of discovery and action. ✳

 Find more strategies for choosing a major.

13 critical thinking exercise
Make a trial choice of major

This exercise presents another method for choosing a major. Look at your school's catalog for a list of majors, and cross out all of the majors that you already know are not right for you. You will probably eliminate well over half the list.

Now scan the remaining majors. Next to the ones that definitely interest you, write "yes." Next to majors that you're willing to consider and are still unsure about, write "maybe."

Focus on your "yes" choices. See if you can narrow them down to three majors. List those here.

_____

_____

_____

Finally, put an asterisk next to the major that interests you most right now. This is your trial choice of major.

journal entry 7

Discovery/Intention Statement

Reflect on choosing a major

Reflect for a moment on your experience with Critical Thinking Exercise 13: "Make a Trial Choice of Major." If you had already chosen a major, did it confirm that choice? Did you uncover any new or surprising possibilities for declaring a major?

I discovered that I . . .

_____

_____

_____

_____

Now, list the major that is your top choice for right now.

_____

_____

_____

_____

Next list publications you will find and people you intend to consult to gather more information about this major.

I intend to . . .

_____

_____

_____

_____

_____

_____

_____

Plan to repeat this Journal Entry and the preceding Critical Thinking Exercise several times. You may find yourself researching several majors and changing your mind. That's fine. The aim is to start thinking about your major now.

Risk Being a Fool

A master student has the courage to take risks. Part of taking risks is being willing to fail sometimes—even being willing to be a fool. This idea can work for you because you already are a fool.

Don't be upset. All of us are fools at one time or another. There are no exceptions. If you doubt it, think back to that stupid thing you did just a few days ago. You know the one. Yes . . . *that* one. It was embarrassing, and you tried to hide it. You pretended you weren't a fool. This happens to everyone.

We are all fallible human beings. Most of us, however, spend too much time and energy trying to hide our foolhood. No one is really tricked by this—not even ourselves. It's OK to look ridiculous while dancing. It's all

right to sound silly when singing to your kids. Sometimes it's OK to be absurd. It comes with taking risks.

This Power Process comes with a warning label: Taking risks does *not* mean escaping responsibility for our actions. "Risk being a fool" is not a suggestion to get drunk at a party and make a fool of yourself. It is not a suggestion to fool around or do things badly. Mediocrity is not the goal.

The point is that mastery in most activities calls for the willingness to do something new, to fail, to make corrections, to fail again, and so on.

"Risk being a fool" means that foolishness—along with courage, cowardice, grace, and clumsiness—is a human characteristic. We all share it. You might as well risk being a fool

because you already are one, and nothing in the world can change that. Why not enjoy it once in a while?

There's one sure-fire way to avoid any risk of being a fool, and that's to avoid life. The writer who never finishes a book will never have to worry about getting negative reviews. The center fielder who sits out every game is safe from making any errors. And the comedian who never performs in front of an audience is certain to avoid telling jokes that fall flat. The possibility of succeeding at any venture increases when we're comfortable with making mistakes—that is, with the risk of being a fool.

 Learn more about taking risks online.

Ted Humble-Smith/Getty

Career Application

Tiana Kabiri earned her B.A. in computer science and found a job in her field within a month after she graduated.

© Tom Grill/Corbis

She now works as a systems programmer for a large bank with seven local branches. Tiana was the first person in her family to gain a college degree. Her friends and relatives are thrilled with her accomplishments.

While in school, Tiana took part in several workshops on career planning. However, she never did many of the suggested exercises and largely downplayed the concept of career planning. Defining her interests, thinking about the skills she most wanted to develop, and researching employment trends just seemed like too much work.

Besides, according to the National Association of Colleges and Employers, starting salary offers for graduates with a bachelor's degree in computer programming averaged $45,558 a year in 2003. When Tiana heard this, she figured that was all the information she needed to choose her career.

One day at work, Tiana received an e-mail from a friend who was still in school—a student majoring in computer science and actively engaged in career planning. The message included these quotations from the Web site published by the U.S. Department of Labor:

Employment of computer programmers is expected to decline slowly, decreasing by 4 percent from 2006 to 2016. The consolidation and centralization of systems and applications, developments in packaged software, advances in programming languages and tools, and the growing ability of users to design, write, and implement more of their own programs mean that more programming functions can be performed by other types of information workers, such as computer software engineers.[15]

Tiana read this and felt a wave of panic. As an entry-level programmer, she was now worried about her long-term job security. She was happy with her salary, and her job seemed secure for the near future. But she worried that her skills would eventually become obsolete or that her job would be outsourced and eliminated.

Reflecting on this scenario.

Looking beyond Tiana's skills in programming, list five transferable skills that you would recommend Tiana to develop that will help her in the future.

_____

_____

_____

_____

_____

_____

_____

_____

_____

_____

_____

_____

Quiz

Name_____   Date____/____/____

1. List five ways to test your choice of a major.

2. The text suggests that you add specifics to your career plan by "naming names." List three examples of these specifics.

3. The Power Process "Risk Being a Fool" calls for taking risks without considering the consequences. True or false? Explain your answer.

4. Explain how service-learning can contribute to your career plan.

5. The best way to get useful information from a career assessment is to take one and make it a blueprint for choosing your career. True or false? Explain your answer.

6. List three questions that you could ask during an information interview.

7. Briefly describe a strategy that you can use to prosper in a global economy.

8. Briefly explain the difference between career planning as a process of *discovery* and career planning as a process of *choice*.

9. Explain the difference between technical skills and transferable skills.

10. List three examples of technical skills and three examples of transferable skills.

Focus on Transferable Skills

The Discovery Wheel in Chapter 1: "First Steps" includes a section labeled *Career planning*. For the next 10 to 15 minutes, go beyond your initial responses to that exercise. Take a snapshot of those skills that help you link your passions with the world of work. Also choose a related skill to develop in the near future.

You might want to prepare for this exercise by reviewing the articles "Jumpstart Your Education with Transferable Skills" on page 58 and "101 Transferable Skills" on page 60.

DISCOVERING SKILLS

When asked to list my transferable skills, the most common examples I include are . . .

When asked to list my technical skills, the most common examples I include are . . .

DISCOVERING POSSIBLE CAREERS

The careers that most interest me right now are . . .

To expand my list of career possibilities, I would turn to the following sources of information:

CREATING AND TESTING A CAREER PLAN

The format that I find most useful in creating a career plan is . . .

To test my career plan, I am planning to . . .

NEXT ACTION

The transferable skill related to career planning that I would most like to develop is . . .

To develop that skill, the most important thing I can do next is to . . .

Master Student PROFILE

Lisa Price
. . . is willing to take risks

© Bennett Raglin/WireImage/Getty Images

Today I am a successful businesswoman. But when I was twenty-eight years old, I filed for personal bankruptcy. I had spent a number of years chasing dreams, living over my head and hoping that I would be able to pay for it later. Well . . . I did pay—just not the way I had hoped. I reached a point where my credit-card balances were sky high. And I would later learn that with penalties and interest, I was also about $33,000 in debt to the Internal Revenue Service. I wasn't even thirty and I had already screwed up my life. . . .

. . . Over the next ten years, I focused on turning my life around—and did. . . . In my early thirties, I had taken one hundred dollars and created a business out of my love of good scents and lifelong hobby of creating fragrances. I started selling perfumes at flea markets as a way of supplementing my income, always reinvesting the profit back into my business. As it turns out, people liked my products and my venture began to blossom. My hobby-turned-business grew slowly, without bank loans or credit cards—my finances were too bad to qualify for either. . . . In time, my company, Carol's Daughter: Beauty by Nature, transformed itself into a successful boutique in the Fort Greene neighborhood of Brooklyn and online business. . . .

. . . How did I get myself into such a tough situation—and, more importantly, how did I dig myself out? Like many people I overextended myself by trying to keep up with others. . . . But when we're open to it, life's difficulties can teach us lessons . . . . I stopped trying to keep up with the Joneses and began to pay attention to myself—my inner Self. I learned to listen to the internal voice that spoke to me without fail, each and every day, whether or not I paid attention.

. . . As this was happening I learned to trust my gifts and talents. In my case I literally followed my nose out of my difficulties and into a life I could never have imagined.

. . . As I run my company, teach classes, and speak to people, many tell me they long to do work that they love. Most tell me that financial fear keeps them stuck where they are. Not too long ago I felt trapped in a dead-end job like the seekers I describe. I want more women and men to experience the feeling of exhilaration and sense of satisfaction that living your passion brings.

From *Success Never Smelled So Sweet* by Lisa Price and Hillary Beard. Copyright © 2004 by Lisa Price and Hillary Beard. Used by permission of Ballantine Books, a division of Random House, Inc. and the William Morris Agency.

(1962–) Author of *Success Never Smelled So Sweet: How I Followed My Nose and Found My Passion*

Learn more about Lisa Price and other master students at the Master Student Hall of Fame.

3 Time

Master Student Map

as you read, ask yourself

what if . . .

I could meet my goals with time to spare?

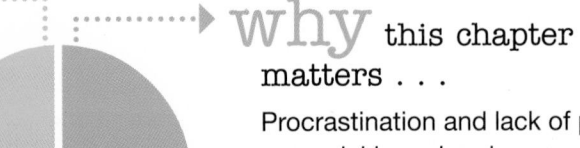

why this chapter matters . . .

Procrastination and lack of planning can quickly undermine your success in school and at work.

what is included . . .

how you can use this chapter . . .

- Discover the details about how you currently use time.
- Set goals that make a difference in the quality of your life.
- Know exactly what to do today, this week, and this month to achieve your goals.
- Eliminate procrastination.

MASTER EMPLOYEE in *action*

In my college classes I would get syllabi from professors that laid out the whole year. Assignments were never mentioned again and it was up to me to do them on time. At work, I have a whole series of tasks to complete on my own from week to week. And I now know how/when to do those things without being asked.

—KARLIS BRYAN, ASSISTANT MEDIA BUYER

Photo courtesy of Karlis Bryan

You've got the time

THE WORDS *time management* may call forth images of restriction and control. You might visualize a prune-faced Scrooge hunched over your shoulder, stopwatch in hand, telling you what to do every minute. The whole situation is bad news.

Here's the good news: You do have enough time for the things you want to do. All it takes is thinking about the possibilities and making conscious choices.

Time is an equal opportunity resource. All of us, regardless of gender, race, creed, or national origin, have exactly the same number of hours in a week. No matter how famous we are, no matter how rich or poor, we get 168 hours to spend each week—no more, no less.

Time is also an unusual commodity. It cannot be saved. You can't stockpile time like wood for the stove or food for the winter. It can't be seen, heard, touched, tasted, or smelled. You can't sense time directly. Even scientists and philosophers find it hard to describe. Because time is so elusive, it is easy to ignore. That doesn't bother time at all. Time is perfectly content to remain hidden until you are nearly out of it. And when you are out of it, you are completely out of it.

Time is a nonrenewable resource. If you're out of wood, you can chop some more. If you're out of money, you can earn a little extra. If you're out of love, there is still hope. If you're out of health, it can often be restored. But when you're out of time, that's it. When this minute is gone, it's gone.

Time seems to pass at varying speeds. Sometimes it crawls. On Friday afternoons, classroom clocks can creep. After you've worked a 10-hour day, reading the last few pages of an economics assignment can turn minutes into hours. A year in school can stretch out to an eternity.

At the other end of the spectrum, time flies. There are moments when you are so absorbed in what you're doing that hours disappear like magic.

Approach time as if you are in control. Sometimes it seems that your friends control your time, that your boss controls your time, that your teachers or your parents or your kids or somebody else controls your time. Maybe that is not true, though. When you say you don't have enough time, you might really be saying that you are not spending the time you *do* have in the way that you want.

Everything written about time management boils down to two topics. One involves knowing exactly

what you want. The other involves knowing *how* to get what you want. State your wants as written goals. Then choose activities that will help you meet those goals.

You should spend your most valuable resource in the way you choose. Start by observing how you use time. Critical Thinking Exercise 14: "The Time Monitor/Time Plan Process" gives you this opportunity. ✳

journal entry 8

Discovery/Intention Statement

Create value from this chapter

Think back to a time during the past year when you rushed to finish a project or when you did not find time for an activity that was important to you. List one thing you might have done that created this outcome.

I discovered that I . . .

_____

_____

_____

_____

_____

Now take a few minutes to skim this chapter. Find five techniques that you intend to use. List them below, along with their associated page numbers.

Strategy	Page Number

critical thinking exercise

14 The Time Monitor/ Time Plan process

The purpose of this exercise is to transform time into a knowable and predictable resource. Complete this exercise over a two-week period:

- During the first week, you *monitor* your activities to get detailed information about how you actually spend your time.

- After you analyze your first week in Journal Entry 9, you *plan* the second week.

- During the second week, you *monitor* your activity again and compare it with your plan.

- Based on everything you've learned, you *plan* again.

For this exercise, monitor your time in 15-minute intervals, 24 hours a day, for seven days. Record how much time you spend sleeping, eating, studying, attending lectures, traveling to and from class, working, watching television, listening to music, taking care of the kids, running errands—everything.

If this sounds crazy, hang on for a minute. This exercise is not about keeping track of the rest of your life in 15-minute intervals. It is an opportunity to become conscious of how you spend your time—your life. Use the Time Monitor/Time Plan process only for as long as it helps you do that.

When you know exactly how you spend your time, you can make choices with open eyes. You can spend more time on the things that are most important to you and less time on the unimportant. Monitoring your time puts you in control of your life.

Here's an eye opener for many students. If you think you already have a good idea of how you manage time, predict how many hours you will spend in a week on each category of activity listed in the form on page 90 (Four categories are already provided; you can add more at any time.) Make your predictions before your first week of monitoring. Write them in the margin to the left of each category. After monitoring your time for one week, see how accurate your predictions were.

The following charts are used for monitoring and planning, and include instructions for using them. Some students choose other materials, such as 3 x 5 cards, calendars, campus planners, or time management software. You might even develop your own way to monitor your time.

www Do this exercise online.

1. **Get to know the Time Monitor/Time Plan.** Look at the sample Time Monitor/Time Plan on page 89. Note that each day has two columns—one labeled "Monitor" and the other labeled "Plan." During the first week, you will use only the "Monitor" column, just like this student did.

   On Monday, the student in this example got up at 6:45 a.m., showered, and got dressed. He finished this activity and began breakfast at 7:15. He put this new activity in at the time he began and drew a line just above it. He ate from 7:15 to 7:45. It took him 15 minutes to walk to class (7:45 to 8:00), and he attended classes from 8:00 to 11:00.

   When you begin an activity, write it down next to the time you begin. Round off to the nearest 15 minutes. If, for example, you begin eating at 8:06, enter your starting time as 8:00. Over time, it will probably even out. In any case, you will be close enough to realize the benefits of this exercise.

   Keep your Time Monitor/Time Plan with you every minute you are awake for one week. Take a few moments every two or three hours to record what you've done. Or enter a note each time you change activities.

2. **Remember to use your Time Monitor/Time Plan.** It might be easy to forget to fill out your Time Monitor/Time Plan. One way to remember is to create a visual reminder for yourself. You can use this technique for any activity you want to remember.

   Relax for a moment, close your eyes, and imagine that you see your Time Monitor/Time Plan. Imagine that it has arms and legs and is as big as a person. Picture the form sitting at your desk at home, in your car, in one of your classrooms, or in your favorite chair. Visualize it sitting wherever you're likely to sit. When you sit down, the Time Monitor/Time Plan will get squashed unless you pick it up and use it.

   You can make this image more effective by adding sound effects. The Time Monitor/Time Plan might scream, "Get off me!" Or since time can be related to money, you might associate the Time Monitor/Time Plan with the sound of an old-fashioned cash register. Imagine that every time you sit down, a cash register rings to remind you it's there.

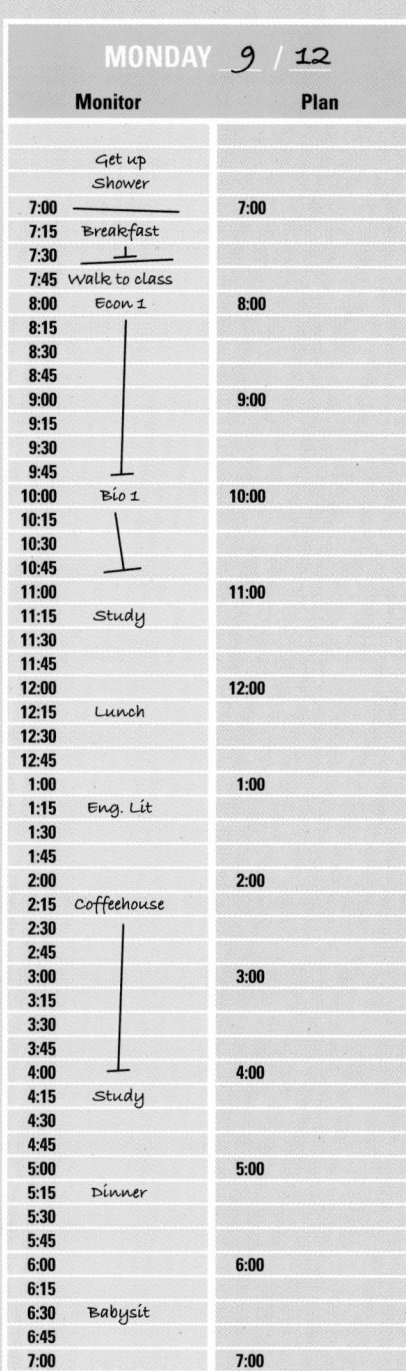

MONDAY _9_ / _12_	
Monitor	**Plan**
Get up	
Shower	
7:00 ———	7:00
7:15 Breakfast	
7:30	
7:45 Walk to class	
8:00 Econ 1	8:00
8:15	
8:30	
8:45	
9:00	9:00
9:15	
9:30	
9:45	
10:00 Bio 1	10:00
10:15	
10:30	
10:45	
11:00	11:00
11:15 Study	
11:30	
11:45	
12:00	12:00
12:15 Lunch	
12:30	
12:45	
1:00	1:00
1:15 Eng. Lit	
1:30	
1:45	
2:00	2:00
2:15 Coffeehouse	
2:30	
2:45	
3:00	3:00
3:15	
3:30	
3:45	
4:00	4:00
4:15 Study	
4:30	
4:45	
5:00	5:00
5:15 Dinner	
5:30	
5:45	
6:00	6:00
6:15	
6:30 Babysit	
6:45	
7:00	7:00

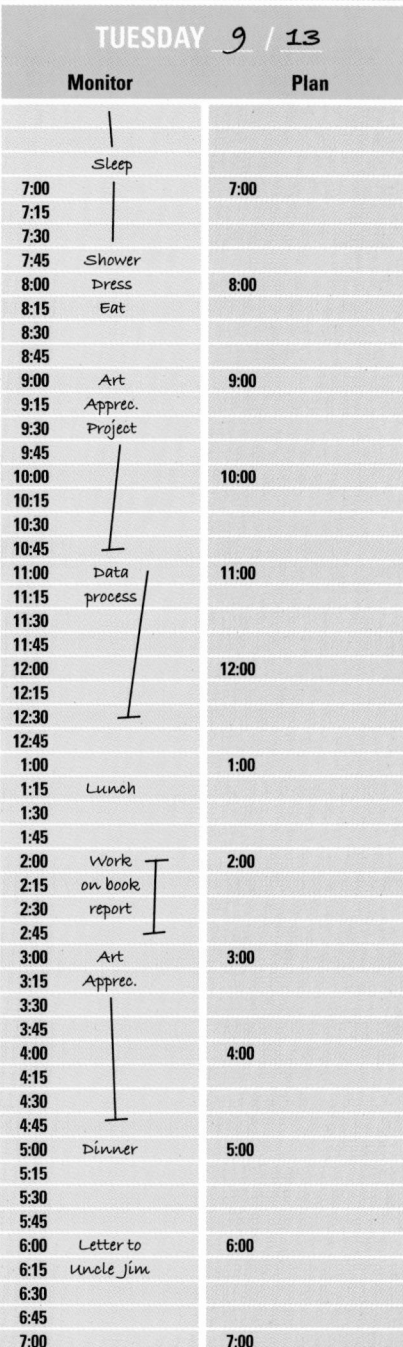

TUESDAY _9_ / _13_	
Monitor	**Plan**
Sleep	
7:00	7:00
7:15	
7:30	
7:45 Shower	
8:00 Dress	8:00
8:15 Eat	
8:30	
8:45	
9:00 Art	9:00
9:15 Apprec.	
9:30 Project	
9:45	
10:00	10:00
10:15	
10:30	
10:45	
11:00 Data	11:00
11:15 process	
11:30	
11:45	
12:00	12:00
12:15	
12:30	
12:45	
1:00	1:00
1:15 Lunch	
1:30	
1:45	
2:00 Work	2:00
2:15 on book	
2:30 report	
2:45	
3:00 Art	3:00
3:15 Apprec.	
3:30	
3:45	
4:00	4:00
4:15	
4:30	
4:45	
5:00 Dinner	5:00
5:15	
5:30	
5:45	
6:00 Letter to	6:00
6:15 Uncle Jim	
6:30	
6:45	
7:00	7:00

3. **Evaluate the Time Monitor/Time Plan.** After you've monitored your time for one week, group your activities together by categories. The form on page 90 lists the categories "Sleep," "Class," "Study," and "Meals." Think of other categories you could add. "Grooming" might include showering, putting on makeup, brushing teeth, and getting dressed. "Travel" could include walking, driving, taking the bus, and riding your bike. Other categories might be "Exercise," "Entertainment," "Work," "Television," "Domestic," and "Children."

Write in the categories that work for you, and then do the following:

• Guess how many hours you *think* you spent on each category of activity. List these hours in the "Estimated" column.

- List the *actual* number of hours you spent on each activity, adding up the figures from your daily time monitoring. List these hours in the "Monitored" column. Make sure that the grand total of all categories is 168 hours.

- Now take a minute and let these numbers sink in. Compare the totals in the "Estimated" and "Monitored" columns.

Notice your reactions. You might be surprised. You might feel disappointed or even angry about where your time goes.

Use those feelings as motivation to plan your time differently. Go to the "Planned" column and choose how much time you *want* to spend on various categories during the coming week. As you do this, allow yourself to have fun. Approach planning in the spirit of adventure. Think of yourself as an artist who's creating a new life.

In several months you might want to take another detailed look at how you spend your life. Fill in the "Monitor" and "Plan" columns on pages 91–92 simultaneously. Use a continuous cycle of monitoring and planning to get the full benefits of this exercise for the rest of your life. Let time management become more than a technique. Transform it into a habit—a constant awareness of how you spend your lifetime.

WEEK OF ___ / ___ / ___ /			
Category	Estimated	Monitored	Planned
Sleep			
Class			
Study			
Meals			

MONDAY __ / __ / __ /		TUESDAY __ / __ / __ /		WEDNESDAY __ / __ / __ /	
Monitor	Plan	Monitor	Plan	Monitor	Plan
7:00	7:00	7:00	7:00	7:00	7:00
7:15		7:15		7:15	
7:30		7:30		7:30	
7:45		7:45		7:45	
8:00	8:00	8:00	8:00	8:00	8:00
8:15		8:15		8:15	
8:30		8:30		8:30	
8:45		8:45		8:45	
9:00	9:00	9:00	9:00	9:00	9:00
9:15		9:15		9:15	
9:30		9:30		9:30	
9:45		9:45		9:45	
10:00	10:00	10:00	10:00	10:00	10:00
10:15		10:15		10:15	
10:30		10:30		10:30	
10:45		10:45		10:45	
11:00	11:00	11:00	11:00	11:00	11:00
11:15		11:15		11:15	
11:30		11:30		11:30	
11:45		11:45		11:45	
12:00	12:00	12:00	12:00	12:00	12:00
12:15		12:15		12:15	
12:30		12:30		12:30	
12:45		12:45		12:45	
1:00	1:00	1:00	1:00	1:00	1:00
1:15		1:15		1:15	
1:30		1:30		1:30	
1:45		1:45		1:45	
2:00	2:00	2:00	2:00	2:00	2:00
2:15		2:15		2:15	
2:30		2:30		2:30	
2:45		2:45		2:45	
3:00	3:00	3:00	3:00	3:00	3:00
3:15		3:15		3:15	
3:30		3:30		3:30	
3:45		3:45		3:45	
4:00	4:00	4:00	4:00	4:00	4:00
4:15		4:15		4:15	
4:30		4:30		4:30	
4:45		4:45		4:45	
5:00	5:00	5:00	5:00	5:00	5:00
5:15		5:15		5:15	
5:30		5:30		5:30	
5:45		5:45		5:45	
6:00	6:00	6:00	6:00	6:00	6:00
6:15		6:15		6:15	
6:30		6:30		6:30	
6:45		6:45		6:45	
7:00	7:00	7:00	7:00	7:00	7:00
7:15		7:15		7:15	
7:30		7:30		7:30	
7:45		7:45		7:45	
8:00	8:00	8:00	8:00	8:00	8:00
8:15		8:15		8:15	
8:30		8:30		8:30	
8:45		8:45		8:45	
9:00	9:00	9:00	9:00	9:00	9:00
9:15		9:15		9:15	
9:30		9:30		9:30	
9:45		9:45		9:45	
10:00	10:00	10:00	10:00	10:00	10:00
10:15		10:15		10:15	
10:30		10:30		10:30	
10:45		10:45		10:45	
11:00	11:00	11:00	11:00	11:00	11:00
11:15		11:15		11:15	
11:30		11:30		11:30	
11:45		11:45		11:45	
12:00	12:00	12:00	12:00	12:00	12:00

THURSDAY ___ / ___ / ___ /		FRIDAY ___ / ___ / ___ /		SATURDAY ___ / ___ / ___ /	
Monitor	Plan	Monitor	Plan	Monitor	Plan
7:00	7:00	7:00	7:00		
7:15		7:15			
7:30		7:30			
7:45		7:45			
8:00	8:00	8:00	8:00		
8:15		8:15			
8:30		8:30			
8:45		8:45			
9:00	9:00	9:00	9:00		
9:15		9:15			
9:30		9:30			
9:45		9:45			
10:00	10:00	10:00	10:00		
10:15		10:15			
10:30		10:30			
10:45		10:45			
11:00	11:00	11:00	11:00		
11:15		11:15			
11:30		11:30			
11:45		11:45			
12:00	12:00	12:00	12:00		
12:15		12:15			
12:30		12:30			
12:45		12:45			
1:00	1:00	1:00	1:00		
1:15		1:15			
1:30		1:30			
1:45		1:45			
2:00	2:00	2:00	2:00		
2:15		2:15			
2:30		2:30			
2:45		2:45			
3:00	3:00	3:00	3:00		
3:15		3:15			
3:30		3:30			
3:45		3:45			
4:00	4:00	4:00	4:00		
4:15		4:15			
4:30		4:30			
4:45		4:45			
5:00	5:00	5:00	5:00		
5:15		5:15			
5:30		5:30			
5:45		5:45			
6:00	6:00	6:00	6:00		

SUNDAY ___ / ___ / ___ /	
Monitor	Plan

THURSDAY (cont.)		FRIDAY (cont.)		SUNDAY	
6:15		6:15			
6:30		6:30			
6:45		6:45			
7:00	7:00	7:00	7:00		
7:15		7:15			
7:30		7:30			
7:45		7:45			
8:00	8:00	8:00	8:00		
8:15		8:15			
8:30		8:30			
8:45		8:45			
9:00	9:00	9:00	9:00		
9:15		9:15			
9:30		9:30			
9:45		9:45			
10:00	10:00	10:00	10:00		
10:15		10:15			
10:30		10:30			
10:45		10:45			
11:00	11:00	11:00	11:00		
11:15		11:15			
11:30		11:30			
11:45		11:45			
12:00	12:00	12:00	12:00		

Discovery Statement

Reflecting on how you spend the time of your life

Now that you have monitored one week, reflect on how you spend the time of your life:

    After one week of monitoring my time, I discovered that . . .

_____

_____

_____

_____

_____

_____

_____

I want to spend more time on . . .

_____

_____

_____

_____

_____

_____

I want to spend less time on . . .

_____

_____

_____

_____

_____

_____

_____

_____

I was surprised that I spent so much time on . . .

_____

_____

_____

_____

_____

_____

_____

_____

_____

_____

I was surprised that I spent so little time on . . .

_____

_____

_____

_____

_____

_____

_____

_____

TIME

3

Setting and achieving goals

Many of us have vague, idealized notions of what we want out of life. These notions float among the clouds in our heads. They are wonderful, fuzzy, safe thoughts such as "I want to be a good person," "I want to be financially secure," or "I want to be happy."

Jon Feingersh/Blend Images/Getty

SUCH OUTCOMES ARE great possible goals. When we keep these goals in a generalized form, however, we may become confused about ways to actually achieve them. If you really want to meet a goal, translate it into specific, concrete behaviors. Find out what that goal looks like. Listen to what it sounds like. Pick it up and feel how heavy that goal is. Inspect the switches, valves, joints, cogs, and fastenings of the goal. Make your goal as real as a chain saw. There is nothing vague or fuzzy about chain saws. You can see them, feel them, and hear them. They have a clear function. Goals can be every bit as real and useful.

Writing down your goals exponentially increases your chances of meeting them. Writing exposes undefined terms, unrealistic time frames, and other symptoms of fuzzy thinking. If you've been completing Intention Statements as explained in the Introduction to this book, then you've already had experience writing goals. Both goals and Intention Statements address changes you want to make in your behavior, your values, or your circumstances—or in all of these areas. To keep track of your goals, write each one on a separate 3 x 5 card, or key them all into a word-processing file on your computer.

There are many useful methods for setting goals. You're about to learn one of them. This method is based on writing specific goals that relate to several time frames and areas of your life. Experiment with this method and modify it as you see fit. Also, reflect regularly on your goals. The keywords to remember are *specific, time, areas,* and *reflect.* Combine the first letter of each word and you get *STAR.* Use this acronym to remember the suggestions that follow.

Write specific goals. In writing, state your goals as observable actions or measurable results. Think in detail about how things will be different once your goals are attained. List the changes in what you'd see, feel, touch, taste, hear, be, do, or have.

Suppose that one of your goals is to become a better student by studying harder. You're headed in a powerful direction; now translate that goal into a concrete action, such as "I will study two hours for every hour I'm in class." Specific goals make clear what actions are needed or what results are expected. Consider these examples:

Vague goal	Specific goal
Get a good education.	Graduate with B.S. degree in engineering, with honors, by 2014.
Enhance my spiritual life.	Meditate for 15 minutes daily.
Improve my appearance.	Lose 6 pounds during the next 6 months.
Get a good job.	Work as a computer security specialist at a mid-sized company where I can continue to learn and advance to higher positions.
Get more friends.	Introduce myself to at least one new person each week.
Be debt-free.	Pay off at least 50 percent of the total balance on my credit card each month.
Be happy.	Learn simple and effective ways to release negative emotions in the moment that they occur.

When stated specifically, a goal might look different to you. If you examine it closely, a goal you once thought you wanted might not be something you want after all. Or you might discover that you want to choose a new path to achieve a goal that you are sure you want.

Write goals in several time frames. To get a comprehensive vision of your future, write down the following:

- *Long-term goals.* Long-term goals represent major targets in your life. These goals can take 5 to 20 years to achieve. In some cases, they will take a lifetime. They can include goals in education, careers, personal relationships, travel, financial security—whatever is important to you. Consider the answers to the following questions as you create your long-term goals: What do you want to accomplish in your life? Do you want your life to make a statement? If so, what is that statement?

- *Mid-term goals.* Mid-term goals are objectives you can accomplish in one to five years. They include goals such as completing a course of education, paying off a car loan, or achieving a specific career level. These goals usually support your long-term goals.

- *Short-term goals.* Short-term goals are the ones you can accomplish in a year or less. These goals are specific achievements, such as completing a particular course or group of courses, hiking down the Appalachian Trail, or organizing a family reunion. A short-term financial goal would probably include an exact dollar amount. Whatever your short-term goals are, they will require action now or in the near future.

Write goals in several areas of life. People who set goals in only one area of life—such as their career—may find that their personal growth becomes one-sided.

They might experience success at work while neglecting their health or relationships with family members and friends.

To avoid this outcome, set goals in a variety of categories. Consider what you want to experience in your:

- Education
- Career
- Financial life
- Family life
- Social life
- Spiritual life
- Level of health

Add goals in other areas as they occur to you.

Reflect on your goals. Each week, take a few minutes to think about your goals. You can perform the following spot checks:

- *Check in with your feelings.* Think about how the process of setting your goals felt. Consider the satisfaction you'll gain in attaining your objectives. If you don't feel a significant emotional connection with a written goal, consider letting it go or filing it away to review later.

- *Check for alignment.* Look for connections among your goals. Do your short-term goals align with your mid-term goals? Will your mid-term goals help you achieve your long-term goals? Look for a fit between all of your goals and your purpose for taking part in higher education, as well as your overall purpose in life.

- *Check for obstacles.* All kinds of things can come between you and your goals, such as constraints on time and money. Anticipate obstacles, and start looking now for workable solutions.

- *Check for immediate steps.* Here's a way to link goal setting to time management. Create a list of small, achievable steps you can take right away to accomplish each of your short-term goals. Ask yourself: What is the physical action that I could take to achieve my goal? Add these actions to your to-do list on an appropriate day. If you want to take one of these actions on a certain date, then enter it into a calendar that you consult daily. Over the coming weeks, review your to-do list and calendar. Take note of your progress, and celebrate your successes. ✳

Huntstock/Getty

Get real with your goals

One way to make goals effective is to examine them up close. That's what this exercise is about. Using a process of brainstorming and evaluation, you can break a long-term goal into smaller segments until you have taken it completely apart. When you analyze a goal to this level of detail, you're well on the way to meeting it. For this exercise, you will use a pen, extra paper, and a watch with a second hand. (A digital watch with a built-in stopwatch feature is even better.) Timing is an important part of the brainstorming process, so follow the stated time limits. This entire exercise takes about an hour.

Part 1: Long-term goals

Brainstorm.   Begin with an eight-minute brainstorm. Use a separate sheet of paper for this part of the exercise. For eight minutes, write down everything you think you want in your life. Write as fast as you can, and write whatever comes into your head. Leave no thought out. Don't worry about accuracy. The object of a brainstorm is to generate as many ideas as possible.

Evaluate.   After you have finished brainstorming, spend the next six minutes looking over your list. Analyze what you wrote. Read the list out loud. If something is missing, add it. Look for common themes or relationships among your goals. Then select three long-term goals that are important to you—goals that will take many years to achieve. Write these goals in the following space provided.

_____

_____

_____

Before you continue, take a minute to reflect on the process you've used so far. What criteria did you use to select your top three goals?

Part 2: Mid-term goals

Brainstorm.   Read out loud the three long-term goals you selected in Part 1. Choose one of them. Then brainstorm a list of goals you might achieve in the next one to five years that would lead to the accomplishment of that one long-term goal. These are mid-term goals. Spend eight minutes on this brainstorm. Go for quantity.

Evaluate.   Analyze your brainstorm of mid-term goals. Then select three that you determine to be important in meeting the long-term goal you picked. Allow yourself six minutes for this part of the exercise. Write your selections in the following space provided.

_____

_____

_____

Again, pause for reflection before going on to the next part of this exercise. Why do you see these three goals as more important than the other mid-term goals you generated? On a separate sheet of paper, write about your reasons for selecting these three goals.

Part 3: Short-term goals

Brainstorm.   Review your list of mid-term goals, and select one. In another eight-minute brainstorm, generate a list of short-term goals—those you can accomplish in a year or less that will lead to the attainment of that mid-term goal. Write down everything that comes to mind. Do not evaluate or judge these ideas yet. For now, the more ideas you write down, the better.

Evaluate.   Analyze your list of short-term goals. The most effective brainstorms are conducted by suspending judgment, so you might find some bizarre ideas on your list. That's fine. Now is the time to cross them out. Next, evaluate your remaining short-term goals, and select three that you are willing and able to accomplish. Allow yourself six minutes for this part of the exercise. Then write your selections in the following space provided.

_____

_____

_____

The more you practice, the more effective you can be at choosing goals that have meaning for you. You can repeat this exercise, employing the other long-term goals you generated or creating new ones.

 Complete this exercise online.

One of the most effective ways to stay on track and actually get things done is to use a daily to-do list. While the Time Monitor/Time Plan gives you a general picture of the week, your daily to-do list shows specific tasks you want to complete within the next 24 hours.

The ABC daily to-do list

© Deborah Jaffe/Getty

ONE ADVANTAGE OF keeping a daily to-do list is that you don't have to remember what to do next. It's on the list. A typical day in the life of a student is full of separate, often unrelated tasks—reading, attending lectures, reviewing notes, working at a job, writing papers, researching special projects, running errands. It's easy to forget an important task on a busy day. When that task is written down, you don't have to rely on your memory.

The following steps present one method for creating and using to-do lists. This method involves ranking each item on your list according to three levels of importance—A, B, and C. Experiment with these steps, modify them as you see fit, and invent new techniques that work for you.

Step 1. Brainstorm tasks

To get started, list all of the tasks you want to get done tomorrow. Each task will become an item on a to-do list. Don't worry about putting the entries in order or scheduling them yet. Just list everything you want to accomplish on a sheet of paper or planning calendar, or in a special notebook. You can also use 3 x 5 cards, writing one task on each card. Cards work well because you can slip them into your pocket or rearrange them, and you never have to copy to-do items from one list to another.

Step 2. Estimate time

For each task you wrote down in Step 1, estimate how long it will take you to complete it. This can be tricky. If you allow too little time, you end up feeling rushed. If you allow too much time, you become less productive. For now, give it your best guess. If you are unsure, overestimate rather than underestimate how long it will take for each task. Overestimating has two benefits: (1) it avoids a schedule that is too tight, missed deadlines, and the resulting feelings of frustration and failure; and (2) it allows time for the unexpected things that come up every day—the spontaneous to-dos. Now pull out your calendar or Time Monitor/Time Plan. You've probably scheduled some hours for activities such as classes or work. This leaves the unscheduled hours for tackling your to-do lists.

Add up the time needed to complete all your to-do items. Also add up the number of unscheduled hours in your day. Then compare the two totals. The power of this step is that you can spot overload in advance. If you have eight hours' worth of to-do items but only four unscheduled hours, that's a potential problem. To solve it, proceed to Step 3.

Step 3. Rate each task by priority

To prevent overscheduling, decide which to-do items are the most important, given the time you have available. One suggestion for making this decision comes from the book *How to Get Control of Your Time and Your Life* by Alan Lakein: Simply label each task A, B, or C.[1]

The A's on your list are those things that are the most critical. They include assignments that are coming due or jobs that need to be done immediately. Also included are activities that lead directly to your short-term goals.

The B's on your list are important, but less so than the A's. Although B's might someday become A's, for the present these tasks are not as urgent as A's. They can be postponed, if necessary, for another day.

The C's do not require immediate attention. C priorities include activities such as "shop for a new blender" and "research genealogy on the Internet." C's are often small, easy jobs with no set timeline. They, too, can be postponed.

Once you've labeled the items on your to-do list, schedule time for all of the A's. The B's and C's can be done randomly during the day when you are in-between tasks and are not yet ready to start the next A.

Step 4. Cross off tasks

Keep your to-do list with you at all times. Cross off activities when you finish them, and add new ones when you think of them. If you're using 3 x 5 cards, you can toss away or recycle the cards with completed items. Crossing off tasks and releasing cards can be fun—a visible reward for your diligence. This step fosters a sense of accomplishment.

When using the ABC priority method, you might experience an ailment common to students: C fever. Symptoms include the uncontrollable urge to drop that A task and begin crossing C's off your to-do list. If your history paper is due tomorrow, you might feel compelled to vacuum the rug, call your third cousin in Tulsa, and make a trip to the store for shoelaces. The

reason C fever is so common is that A tasks are usually more difficult or time-consuming to achieve, with a higher risk of failure.

If you notice symptoms of C fever, ask yourself, "Does this job really need to be done now? Do I really need to alphabetize my DVD collection, or might I better use this time to study for tomorrow's data-processing exam?" Use your to-do list to keep yourself on task, working on your A's. But don't panic or berate yourself when you realize that in the last six hours, you have completed 11 C's and not a single A. Just calmly return to the A's.

Step 5. Evaluate

At the end of the day, evaluate your performance. Look for A priorities you didn't complete. Look for items that repeatedly turn up as B's or C's on your list and never seem to get done. Consider changing them to A's or dropping them altogether. Similarly, you might consider changing an A that didn't get done to a B or C priority. When you're done evaluating, start on tomorrow's to-do list. Be willing to admit mistakes. You might at first rank some items as A's only to realize later that they are actually C's. And some of the C's that lurk at the bottom of your list day after day might really be A's. When you keep a daily to-do list, you can adjust these priorities *before* they become problems.

In any case, make starting your own to-do list an A priority. ✳

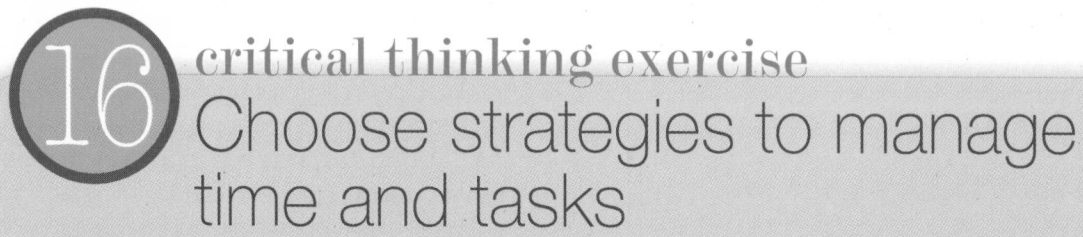

16 critical thinking exercise
Choose strategies to manage time and tasks

After reading the article "The ABC Daily To-Do List," choose one technique to apply—preferably within the next 24 hours. In the following space, summarize that technique in one sentence:

After using the technique for at least one week and observing the results, use the following space to describe how well it worked for you. If the technique worked well, consider making it a habit. If it did *not* work well, list a way to modify the strategy so that it becomes a better fit for you:

Stop procrastination NOW

CONSIDER A BOLD idea: To stop procrastinating, just stop procrastinating. Now. Giving up procrastination is actually a simple choice. People just *tell* themselves that it takes months or even years to give up this habit.

Test this idea for yourself. Think of something that you've been putting off. Choose a small, specific task—one that you can complete in five minutes or less. Then do that task today.

Tomorrow, choose another task and do it. Repeat this strategy each day for one week. Notice what happens to your habit of procrastination. In addition, experiment with the following ideas.

Discover the costs. Find out if procrastination keeps you from getting what you want. Clearly seeing the side effects of procrastination can help you kick the habit.

Discover your procrastination style. Psychologist Linda Sapadin identifies different styles of procrastination.[2] For example, *dreamers* have big goals that they seldom translate into specific plans. *Worriers* focus on the worst-case scenario and are likely to talk more about problems than about solutions. *Defiers* resist new tasks or promise to do them and then don't follow through. *Overdoers* create extra work for themselves by refusing to delegate tasks and neglecting to set priorities. And *perfectionists* put off tasks for fear of making a mistake.

Awareness of your procrastination style is a key to changing your behavior. If you exhibit the characteristics of an overdoer, for example, then say no to new projects. Also ask for help in completing your current projects.

To discover your procrastination style, observe your behavior. Avoid judgments. Just be a scientist: Record the facts. Write Discovery Statements about specific ways you procrastinate. Follow up with Intention Statements about what to do differently.

Trick yourself into getting started. If you have a 50-page chapter to read, then grab the book and say to yourself, "I'm not really going to read this chapter right now. I'm just going to flip through the pages and scan the headings for 10 minutes." Tricks like these can get you started on a task you've been dreading.

Let feelings follow action. If you put off exercising until you feel energetic, you might wait for months. Instead, get moving now. Then watch your feelings change. After five minutes of brisk walking, you might be in the mood for a 20-minute run. This principle—action generates motivation—can apply to any task that you've put on the back burner.

Choose to work under pressure. Sometimes people thrive under pressure. As one writer puts it, "I don't do my *best* work under deadline. I do my *only* work under deadline." Used selectively, this strategy might also work for you. Put yourself in control. If you choose to work with a due date staring you right in the face, then schedule a big block of time during the preceding week. Until then, enjoy!

Think ahead. Use the monthly calendar on page 109 or the long-term planner on pages 111–112 to list due dates for assignments in all your courses. Using these tools, you can anticipate heavy demands on your time and take action to prevent last-minute crunches. Make *From Master Student to Master Employee* your home base—the first place to turn in taking control of your schedule.

Give up "someday." Procrastination rests on this vague notion: *I'll do it someday.* Other people reinforce this notion by telling you that your life will *really* start when you. . . . (Fill in the blank with phrases like *graduate from college, get married, have kids, get promoted,* or *retire.*) Using this logic, you could wait your whole life to start living. Avoid this fate. Take action today.

Create goals that draw you forward. A goal that grabs you by the heartstrings is an inspiration to act now. If you're procrastinating, then set some goals that excite you. Then you might wake up one day and discover that procrastination is part of your past. ✳

 Find more strategies for ending procrastination.

TIME

25 ways to get the most out of now

The following techniques are about getting the most from study time. They're listed in four categories:

■ When to study.
■ Where to study.
■ Ways to handle the rest of the world.
■ Things to ask yourself if you get stuck.

Don't feel pressured to use all of the techniques or to tackle them in order. As you read, note the suggestions you think will be helpful. Pick one technique to use now. When it becomes a habit, come back to this article and select another one. Repeat this cycle, and enjoy the results as they unfold in your life.

Ferenc Szelepcsenyi/Shutterstock

When to study

Study difficult (or boring) subjects first. If your chemistry problems put you to sleep, get to them first, while you are fresh. We tend to give top priority to what we enjoy studying, yet the courses that we find most difficult often require the most creative energy. Save your favorite subjects for later. If you find yourself avoiding a particular subject, get up an hour earlier to study it before breakfast. With that chore out of the way, the rest of the day can be a breeze.

Be aware of your best time of day. Many people learn best in daylight hours. If this is true for you, schedule study time for your most difficult subjects before nightfall.

Unless you grew up on a farm, the idea of being conscious at 5 a.m. might seem ridiculous. Yet many successful businesspeople begin the day at 5 a.m. or earlier. Athletes and yoga practitioners use the early morning, too. Some writers complete their best work before 9 a.m.

Others experience the same benefits by staying up late. They flourish after midnight. If you aren't convinced, then experiment. When you're in a time crunch, get up early or stay up late. You might even see a sunrise.

Use waiting time. Five minutes waiting for a subway, 20 minutes waiting for the dentist, 10 minutes in-between classes—waiting time adds up fast. Have short study tasks ready to do during these periods. For example, you can carry 3 x 5 cards with facts, formulas, or definitions and pull them out anywhere.

A CD or mp3 player can help you use commuting time to your advantage. Use your computer to make a recording of yourself reading your notes. Then transfer that recording onto a CD or mp3 player. Play it as you drive, or listen through headphones as you ride on the bus or subway.

Study two hours for every hour you're in class. Students in higher education are regularly advised to allow two hours of study time for every hour spent in class. If you are taking 15 credit hours, then plan to spend 30 hours a week studying. The benefits of following this advice will be apparent at exam time.

Keep in mind that the "two hours for one" rule doesn't distinguish between focused time and unfocused time. In one four-hour block of study time, it's possible to use up two of those hours with phone calls, breaks, daydreaming, and doodling. With study time, quality counts as much as quantity.

Avoid marathon study sessions. When possible, study in shorter sessions. Three 3-hour sessions are usually more productive than one 9-hour session. If you must study in a large block of time, work on several subjects, and avoid studying similar topics one after the other.

Where to study

Use a regular study area. Your body and your mind know where you are. Using the same place to study, day after day, helps train your responses. When you arrive at that particular place, you can focus your attention more quickly.

Study where you'll be alert. In bed, your body gets a signal. For most students, that signal is more likely to be "Time to sleep!" than "Time to study!" Just as you train your body to be alert at your desk, you also train it to slow down near your bed. For that reason, don't study where you sleep.

Easy chairs and sofas are also dangerous places to study. Learning requires energy. Give your body a message that energy is needed. Put yourself in a situation that supports this message. For example, some schools offer empty classrooms as places to study. Many students report that they find themselves studying effectively in a classroom setting.

Use a library. Libraries are designed for learning. The lighting is perfect. The noise level is low. A wealth of material is available. Entering a library is a signal to focus the mind and get to work. Many students can get

more done in a shorter time frame at the library than anywhere else. Experiment for yourself.

Ways to handle the rest of the world

Pay attention to your attention. Breaks in concentration are often caused by internal interruptions. Your own thoughts jump in to divert you from your studies. When this happens, notice these thoughts and then let them go. Perhaps the thought of getting something else done is distracting you. One option is to handle that other task now and study later. You can also write yourself a note about it, or schedule a specific time to do it.

Agree with living mates about study time. This agreement includes roommates, spouses, and children. Make the rules about study time clear, and be sure to follow them yourself. Explicit agreements—even written contracts—work well. One student always wears a colorful hat when he wants to study. When his wife and children see the hat, they respect his wish to be left alone.

Get off the phone. The phone is the ultimate interrupter. People who wouldn't think of distracting you in person might call or text you at the worst times because they can't see that you are studying. You don't have to be a victim of your cell phone. If a simple "I can't talk; I'm studying" doesn't work, use dead silence.

Keep on going?

Some people keep on going, even when they get stuck or fail again and again. To such people belongs the world. Consider the hapless politician who compiled this record:

- Failed in business, 1831.
- Defeated for legislature, 1832.
- Failed in business a second time, 1833.
- Suffered a nervous breakdown, 1836.
- Defeated for speaker of the house, 1838.
- Defeated for elector, 1840.
- Defeated for Congress, 1843.
- Defeated for Senate, 1855.
- Defeated for vice president, 1856.
- Defeated for Senate, 1858.
- Elected president, 1860.

Who was the fool who kept on going in spite of so many failures?

Answer: The fool was Abraham Lincoln.

It's a conversation killer. Another idea is to short-circuit the whole problem: Turn off your phone or silence it.

Learn to say no. Saying no is a time-saver and a valuable life skill for everyone. Some people feel it is rude to refuse a request. However, you can say no effectively and courteously. Others want you to succeed as a student. When you tell them that you can't do what they ask because you are busy educating yourself, most people will understand.

Hang a "do not disturb" sign on your door. Many hotels will give you a free "do not disturb" sign for the advertising. You can also create a sign yourself. They work. Using signs can relieve you of making a decision about cutting off each interruption—a time-saver in itself.

Get ready the night before. Completing a few simple tasks just before you go to bed can help you get in gear the next day. If you need to make some phone calls first thing in the morning, look up those numbers, write them on 3 x 5 cards, and set them near the phone. If you need to drive to a new location, make a note of the address and check the directions online, then put them next to your car keys. If you plan to spend the next afternoon writing a paper, get your materials together: dictionary, notes, outline, paper, pencil, flash drive, laptop—whatever you need. Pack your lunch or put gas in the car. Organize the baby's diaper bag and your briefcase or backpack.

Remember cultural differences

There are as many different styles for managing time as there are people. These styles vary across cultures.

In the United States and England, for example, business meetings typically start on time. That's also true in Scandinavian countries such as Norway and Sweden. However, travelers to Panama might find that meetings start about a half-hour late. Furthermore, people who complain about late meetings while doing business in Mexico might be considered rude.

When you study or work with people of different races and ethnic backgrounds, look for differences in their approach to time. A behavior that you might view as rude or careless—such as showing up late for appointments—could simply result from seeing the world in a different way.

Call ahead. We often think of talking on the telephone as a prime time-waster. Used wisely, though, the telephone can actually help manage time. Before you go shopping, call the store to see if it carries the items you're looking for. If you're driving, call for directions to your destination (or look them up online). A few seconds on the phone or computer can save hours in wasted trips and wrong turns.

Avoid noise distractions. To promote concentration, avoid studying in front of the television, and turn off the radio. Many students insist that they study better with background noise, and it might be true. Some students report good results with carefully selected and controlled music. For many others, silence is the best form of music to study by.

At times noise levels might be out of your control. A neighbor or roommate might decide to find out how far she can turn up her music before the walls crumble. Meanwhile, your ability to concentrate on the principles of sociology goes down the drain. To avoid this scenario, schedule study sessions during periods when your living environment is usually quiet. If you live in a residence hall, ask if study rooms are available. Otherwise, go somewhere else where it's quiet, such as the library. Some students have even found refuge in quiet coffee shops, self-service laundries, and places of worship.

Manage interruptions. Notice how others misuse your time. Be aware of repeat offenders. Ask yourself if there are certain friends or relatives who consistently interrupt your study time.

If avoiding the interrupter is impractical, send a clear message. Sometimes others don't realize that they are breaking your concentration. You can give them a gentle, yet firm, reminder: "What you're saying is important. Can we schedule a time to talk about it when I can give you my full attention?" If this strategy doesn't work, there are other ways to make your message more effective. For more ideas, see Chapter 9: "Communicating."

See if you can "firewall" yourself for selected study periods each week. Find a place where you can count on being alone and working without interruption.

However, sometimes interruptions still happen. Therefore, create a system for dealing with them. One option is to take an index card and write a quick note about what you're doing the moment an interruption occurs. As soon as possible, return to the card and pick up the task where you left off.

Things to ask yourself if you get stuck

Ask: "What is one task I can accomplish toward achieving my goal?" This technique is helpful when you face a big, imposing job. Pick out one small accomplishment, preferably one you can complete in about five minutes; then do it. The satisfaction of getting one thing done can spur you on to get one more thing done. Meanwhile, the job gets smaller.

Ask: "Am I being too hard on myself?" If you are feeling frustrated with a reading assignment, if your attention wanders repeatedly, or if you've fallen behind on math problems that are due tomorrow, take a minute to listen to the messages you are giving yourself. Are you scolding yourself too harshly? Lighten up. Allow yourself to feel a little foolish, and then get on with the task at hand. Don't add to the problem by berating yourself.

Worrying about the future is another way people beat themselves up: "How will I ever get all this done?" "What if every paper I'm assigned turns out to be this hard?" "If I can't do the simple calculations now, how will I ever pass the final?" Instead of promoting learning, such questions fuel anxiety.

Labeling and generalizing weaknesses are other ways people are hard on themselves. Being objective and specific in the messages you send yourself will help eliminate this form of self-punishment and will likely generate new possibilities. An alternative to saying "I'm terrible in algebra" is to say "I don't understand factoring equations." This rewording suggests a plan to improve.

You might be able to lighten the load by discovering how your learning styles affect your behavior. For example, you may have a bias toward concrete experience rather than abstract thinking. If so, after setting a goal, you might want to move directly into action.

In large part, the ability to learn through concrete experience is a valuable trait. After all, action is necessary to achieve goals. At the same time, you might find it helpful to allow extra time to plan. Careful planning can help you avoid unnecessary activity. Instead of using a planner that shows a day at a time, experiment with a calendar that displays a week or month at a glance. The expanded format can help you look farther into the future and stay on track as you set out to meet long-term goals.

Ask: "Is this a piano?" Carpenters who construct rough frames for buildings have a saying they use when they bend a nail or accidentally hack a chunk out of a two-by-four: "Well, this ain't no piano." It means that perfection is not necessary. Ask yourself if what you are doing needs to be perfect. Perhaps you don't have to apply the same standards of grammar to lecture notes that you would apply to a term paper. If you can complete a job 95 percent perfectly in two hours and 100 percent perfectly in four hours, ask yourself whether the additional 5 percent improvement is worth doubling the amount of time you spend.

Sometimes, though, it *is* a piano. A tiny miscalculation can ruin an entire lab experiment. A misstep in solving a complex math problem can negate hours of work. Computers are notorious for turning little errors into nightmares. Accept lower standards only when appropriate.

A related suggestion is to weed out low-priority tasks. The to-do list for a large project can include dozens of items, not all of which are equally important. Some can be done later, while others can be skipped altogether, if time is short.

Apply this idea when you study. In a long reading assignment, look for pages you can skim or skip. When it's appropriate, read chapter summaries or article abstracts. As you review your notes, look for material that might not be covered on a test, and decide whether you want to study it.

Ask: "Would I pay myself for what I'm doing right now?" If you were employed as a student, would you be earning your wages? Ask yourself this question when you notice that you've taken your third snack break in 30 minutes. Then remember that you are, in fact, employed as a student. You are investing in your own productivity and are paying a big price for the privilege of being a student. Doing a mediocre job now might result in fewer opportunities in the future.

Ask: "Can I do just one more thing?" Ask yourself this question at the end of a long day. Almost always you will have enough energy to do just one more short task. The overall increase in your productivity might surprise you.

Ask: "Am I making time for things that are important but not urgent?" If we spend most of our time putting out fires, we can feel drained and frustrated. According to Stephen R. Covey, this chain of events occurs when we forget to take time for things that are not urgent but are truly important.[3] Examples of truly important activities include exercising regularly, reading, praying or meditating, spending quality time alone or with family members and friends, traveling, and cooking nutritious meals. Each of these activities can contribute directly to a long-term goal or life mission. Yet when schedules get tight, we often forgo these things, waiting for that elusive day when we'll "finally have more time."

That day won't come until we choose to make time for what's truly important. Knowing this, we can use some of the suggestions in this chapter to free up more time.

Ask: "Can I delegate this?" Instead of slogging through complicated tasks alone, you can draw on the talents and energy of other people. Busy executives know the value of delegating tasks to coworkers. Without delegation, many projects would flounder or die.

You can apply the same principle in your life. Instead of doing all the housework or cooking by yourself, for example, you can assign some of the tasks to family members or roommates. Rather than making a trip to the library to look up a simple fact, you can call and ask a library assistant to research it for you. Instead of driving across town to deliver a package, you can hire a delivery service to do so. All of these tactics can free up extra hours for studying.

It's not practical to delegate certain study tasks, such as writing term papers or completing reading assignments. However, you can still draw on the ideas of others in completing such tasks. For instance, form a writing group to edit and critique papers, brainstorm topics or titles, and develop lists of sources.

If you're absent from a class, find a classmate to summarize the lecture, discussion, and any upcoming assignments. Presidents depend on briefings. You can use the same technique.

Ask: "How did I just waste time?" Notice when time passes and you haven't accomplished what you had planned to do. Take a minute to review your actions, and note the specific ways you wasted time. We tend to operate by habit, wasting time in the same ways over and over again. When you are aware of things you do that drain your time, you are more likely to catch yourself in the act next time. Observing one small quirk might save you hours. But keep this in mind: Asking you to notice how you waste time is not intended to make you feel guilty. The point is to increase your skill by getting specific information about how you use time.

Ask: "Could I find the time if I really wanted to?" The next time you're tempted to say, "I just don't have time," pause for a minute. Question the truth of this statement. Could you find four more hours this week for studying? Suppose that someone offered to pay you $10,000 to find those four hours. Suppose, too, that

Commuter students: Manage the demands on your time

Some commuter students talk about the "3 C" problem—going from the *car* to *class* and straight back to the *car*. These students feel isolated from campus life. You can avoid that fate and still honor your current commitments:

Focus on a few high-priority activities. Reflect on the main commitments in your life. See if you can reduce them to three or four major activities, such as work, family, and school. Tackle other major projects, such as finding a new job, after you get your degree.

Join a study group. In addition to boosting your test scores, study groups can help you meet people and feel more connected to school.

Meet with your instructors. Once each week or two, set aside an extra 15 minutes to chat with one of your instructors before or after class. Also schedule regular times to meet with instructors during their office hours.

Attend a weekend event on campus. Invite your family and friends to attend concerts, plays, speakers, and other school-related events.

Ask about programs for commuter students. Your school might have a lounge with lockers, desks, and computers that commuter students can use. Search out these spaces and look for notices of special events and services for commuter students.

TIME

3

you will get paid only if you don't lose sleep, call in sick for work, or sacrifice anything important to you. Could you find the time if vast sums of money were involved?

Remember that when it comes to school, vast sums of money *are* involved.

Ask: "Am I willing to promise it?" This time-management idea might be the most powerful of all: If you want to find time for a task, promise yourself—and others—that you'll get it done.

One way to accomplish big things in life is to make big promises. There's little reward in promising what's safe or predictable. No athlete promises to place seventh at the Olympics. Chances are that if you're not making big promises, you're not stretching yourself.

The point of making a promise is not to chain yourself to a rigid schedule or impossible expectations.

You can promise to reach goals without unbearable stress. You can keep schedules flexible and carry out your plans with ease, joy, and satisfaction.

At times, though, you might go too far. Some promises may be truly beyond you, and you might break them. However, failing to keep a promise is just that—failing to keep a promise. A broken promise is not the end of the world.

Promises can work magic. When your word is on the line, it's possible to discover reserves of time and energy you didn't know existed. Promises can push you to exceed your expectations. ✳

 Discover even more ways to get the most out of now.

The 7-day antiprocrastination plan

Listed here are seven strategies you can use to reduce or eliminate many sources of procrastination. The suggestions are tied to the days of the week to help you remember them. Use this list to remind yourself that each day of your life presents an opportunity to stop the cycle of procrastination.

MONDAY Make it Meaningful What is important about the task you've been putting off? List all the benefits of completing that task. Look at it in relation to your short-, mid-, or long-term goals. Be specific about the rewards for getting it done, including how you will feel when the task is completed. To remember this strategy, keep in mind that it starts with the letter *M,* as in the word *Monday.*

TUESDAY Take it Apart Break big jobs into a series of small ones you can do in 15 minutes or less. If a long reading assignment intimidates you, divide it into two- or three-page sections. Make a list of the sections, and cross them off as you complete them so you can see your progress. Even the biggest projects can be broken down into a series of small tasks. This strategy starts with the letter *T,* so mentally tie it to *Tuesday.*

WEDNESDAY Write an Intention Statement If you can't get started on a term paper, you might write, "I intend to write a list of at least ten possible topics by 9 p.m. I will reward myself with an hour of guilt-free recreational reading." Write your intention on a 3x5 card. Carry it with you or post it in your study area, where you can see it often. In your memory, file the first word in this strategy—*write*—with *Wednesday.*

THURSDAY Tell Everyone Publicly announce your intention to get a task done. Tell a friend that you intend to learn ten irregular French verbs by Saturday. Tell your spouse, roommate, parents, and children. Include anyone who will ask whether you've completed the assignment or who will suggest ways to get it done. Make the world your support group. Associate *tell* with *Thursday.*

FRIDAY Find a Reward Construct rewards to yourself carefully. Be willing to withhold them if you do not complete the task. Don't pick a movie as a reward for studying biology if you plan to go to the movie anyway. And when you legitimately reap your reward, notice how it feels. Remember that *Friday* is a fine day to *find* a reward. (Of course, you can find a reward on any day of the week. Rhyming *Friday* with *fine* day is just a memory trick.)

SATURDAY Settle it Now Do it now. The minute you notice yourself procrastinating, plunge into the task. Imagine yourself at a cold mountain lake, poised to dive. Gradual immersion would be slow torture. It's often less painful to leap. Then be sure to savor the feeling of having the task behind you. Link *settle* with *Saturday.*

SUNDAY Say No When you keep pushing a task into a low-priority category, reexamine your purpose for doing that task at all. If you realize that you really don't intend to do something, quit telling yourself that you will. That's procrastinating. Just say no. Then you're not procrastinating. You don't have to carry around the baggage of an undone task. *Sunday*—the last day of this 7-day plan—is a great day to finally let go and just *say* no.

Image Source/Alamy

Organizing time and tasks at work

TO SUCCEED AT getting organized, think in terms of two broad strategies. First, get the big picture—what you intend to accomplish this month, this quarter, this year, and beyond. Second, set priorities for your day-to-day, hour-to-hour tasks.

Get real with project due dates. The more complicated the project, the more you can benefit from getting organized. This is especially true with projects that extend well into the future. Start by scheduling a long-term goal—for example, the due date for the final product. Next, set interim due dates for the work you'll produce at key points leading up to that final date. These interim dates function as mid-term goals. In turn, each mid-term goal can lead you to more immediate, short-term goals.

For example, say that you're a computer technician and your team plans to complete a major hardware and software upgrade for your company in one year (long-term goal). As a team, set goals for finishing major parts of this project, such as due dates for installing new computers in individual departments (mid-term goals). You could also set up meetings with each department head over the next month to update them on your plans (short-term goals).

You may end up juggling several major projects at once. To plan effectively, enter all the relevant due dates in a monthly calendar so that you can see several of them at a glance.

Monitor work time and tasks. Another way to get a big picture of your work life is to look for broad patterns in how you currently spend your work time. Use the Time Monitor/Time Plan explained earlier in this chapter to do this analysis. Find out which tasks burn up most of your hours on the job.

With this data in hand, you can make immediate choices to minimize downtime and boost your productivity. Start by looking for low-value activities to eliminate. Also note your peak periods of energy during the workday. Schedule your most challenging tasks for these times.

Schedule fixed blocks of time first. Start with recurring meetings, for instance. These time periods are usually determined in advance and occur at regular times each week or month. Be realistic about how much time you need for such events. Then schedule other tasks around them.

Set clear starting and stopping times. Tasks often expand to fill the time we allot for them. "It always takes me two hours just to deal with my e-mails each day" might become a self-fulfilling prophecy. As an alternative, schedule a certain amount of time for reading and responding to e-mail. Set a timer and stick to it. People often find that they can gradually decrease such time by forcing themselves to work a little more efficiently. This can usually be done without sacrificing the quality of your work.

Clean your desk. For starters, purge your cubicle and files of everything you don't need. Start tossing junk mail the moment that it arrives. Next, start a "to read" file for documents that you can review at any time. Pack this folder for your next plane trip or bus ride. Finally, avoid the habit of writing reminder notes on random scraps of paper. Store all your to-do items in a unified system, such as a stack of 3 x 5 cards or a single file on your computer. Having an uncluttered desk makes it easier for you to find things. And that saves time. ✳

BananaStock/Alamy

Beyond time management:
Staying focused on what matters

Ask some people about managing time, and a dreaded image appears in their minds.

THEY SEE A person with a 100-item to-do list clutching a calendar chock full of appointments. They imagine a robot who values cold efficiency, compulsively accounts for every minute, and has no time for people.

It might help you to think beyond time management to the larger concept of *planning*. The point of planning is not to load your schedule with obligations. Instead, planning is about getting the important things done and still having time to be human. An effective planner is productive and relaxed at the same time.

Discover your style. If you find it hard to work from a conventional to-do list, you can try plotting your day on a mind map. (Mind maps are explained in Chapter 6: "Notes.") Doing so might feel especially comfortable if you're blessed with a natural visual intelligence, as explained in the discussion of Howard Gardner's theory of multiple intelligences in Chapter 1: "First Steps."

Another approach might be to write to-do items, one per 3 x 5 card, in any order in which tasks occur to you. Later you can edit, sort, and rank the cards, choosing which items to do. This method will probably appeal to you if you learn best through active experimentation and using your kinesthetic intelligence, which involves movement and the sense of touch.

Do less. Planning is as much about dropping worthless activities as about adding new ones. See if you can reduce or eliminate activities that contribute little to your values. When you add a new item to your calendar or to-do list, consider dropping a current one.

Buy less. Before you purchase an item, estimate how much time it will take to locate, assemble, use, repair, and maintain it. You might be able to free up hours by doing without.

Slow down. Sometimes it's useful to hurry, such as when you're late for a meeting or about to miss a plane. At other times, haste is a choice that serves no real purpose. If you're speeding through the day like a launched missile, consider what would happen if you got to your next destination a few minutes later than planned. Rushing might not be worth the added strain.

Handle it now. A long to-do list can result from postponing decisions and procrastinating. An alternative is to handle a task or decision immediately. Answer that letter now. Make that phone call as soon as it occurs to you. Then you don't have to add the task to your calendar or to-do list.

Remember people. Few people on their deathbeds ever say, "I wish I'd spent more time at the office." They're more likely to say, "I wish I'd spent more time with my family and friends." The pace of daily life can lead us to neglect the people we cherish.

Efficiency is a concept that applies to things—not people. When it comes to maintaining and nurturing relationships, we can often benefit from loosening up our schedules. We can allow extra time for spontaneous visits and free-ranging conversations.

Forget about time. Take time away from time. Schedule downtime—a space in your day when you ignore to-do lists, appointments, and accomplishments. This period is when you're accountable to no one else and have nothing to accomplish. Even a few minutes spent in this way can yield a sense of renewal. One way to manage time is periodically to forget about it.

Strictly speaking, time cannot be managed. The minutes, hours, days, and years simply march ahead. What we can do is manage *ourselves* with respect to time. A few basic principles can help us do that just as effectively as a truckload of cold-blooded techniques. ✳

17 critical thinking exercise
Master monthly calendar

This exercise will give you an opportunity to step back from the details of your daily schedule and get a bigger picture of your life. The more difficult it is for you to plan beyond the current day or week, the greater the benefit of this exercise.

Your basic tool is a one-month calendar. Use it to block out specific times for upcoming events such as study group meetings, due dates for assignments, review periods before tests, and other time-sensitive tasks.

To get started, you might want to copy the blank monthly calendar on page 109 onto both sides of a sheet of paper. You can also make several copies of these pages and tape them together so that you can see several months at a glance.

Be creative. Experiment with a variety of uses for your monthly calendar. For instance, you can note day-to-day changes in your health or moods, list the places you visit while you are on vacation, or circle each day that you practice a new habit. For examples of filled-in monthly calendars, see the following example.

Find printable copies of this monthly calendar online.

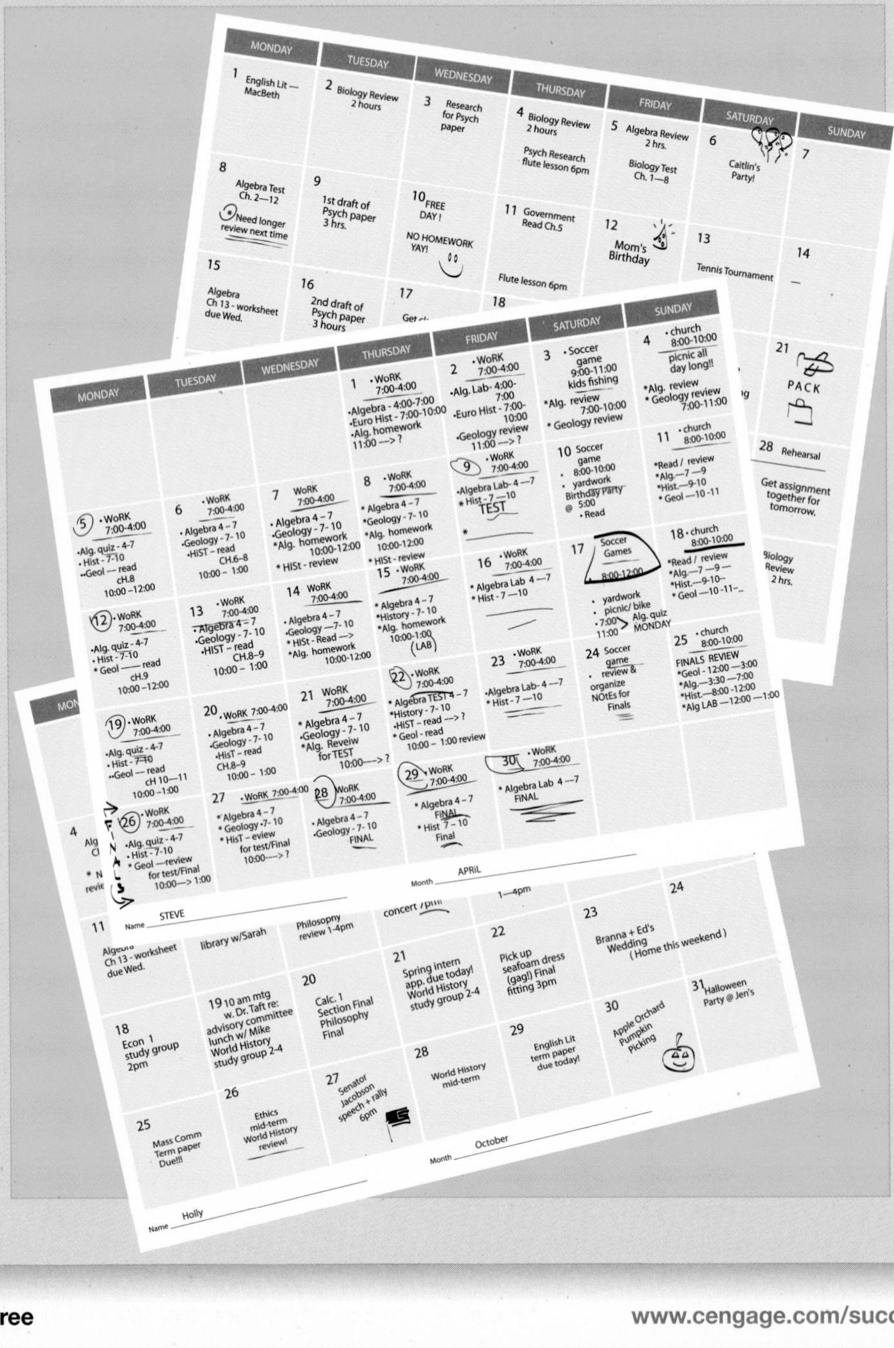

MONDAY	TUESDAY	WEDNESDAY	THURSDAY	FRIDAY	SATURDAY	SUNDAY

Name

Month

TIME

3

Gearing up:
Using a long-term planner

Planning a day, a week, or a month ahead is a powerful practice. Using a long-term planner—one that displays an entire quarter, semester, or year at a glance—can yield even more benefits.

WITH A LONG-TERM planner, you can eliminate a lot of unpleasant surprises. Long-term planning allows you to avoid scheduling conflicts—the kind that obligate you to be in two places at the same time three weeks from now. You can also anticipate busy periods, and start preparing for them now. Say good-bye to all-night cram sessions; say hello to serenity.

Find a long-term planner, or make your own. Many office supply stores carry academic planners in paper form that cover an entire school year. Computer software for time management offers the same features. You can also be creative and make your own long-term planner. A big roll of newsprint pinned to a bulletin board or taped to a wall will do nicely.

Enter scheduled dates that extend into the future. Use your long-term planner to list commitments that extend beyond the current month. Enter test dates, lab sessions, days that classes will be canceled, and other events that will take place over this term and next term.

Create a master assignment list. Find the syllabus for each course you're currently taking. Then, in your long-term planner, enter the due dates for all of the assignments in all of your courses.

The purpose of this technique is not to make you feel overwhelmed. Rather, its aim is to help you take a First Step toward recognizing the demands on your time. Armed with the truth about how you use your time, you can make more accurate plans.

Include nonacademic events. In addition to tracking academic commitments, you can use your long-term planner to mark significant events in your life outside school. Include birthdays, doctors' appointments, concert dates, credit card payment due dates, and car maintenance schedules.

Use your long-term planner to divide and conquer. Big assignments such as term papers or major presentations pose a special risk. When you have three months to do a project, you might say to yourself, "That looks like a lot of work, but I've got plenty of time. No problem." But two months, three weeks, and six days from now, it could suddenly be a huge problem.

For some people, academic life is a series of last-minute crises punctuated by periods of exhaustion. You can avoid that fate. The trick is to set due dates *before* the final due date.

When planning to write a term paper, for instance, enter the final due date in your long-term planner. Then set individual due dates for each milestone in the writing process—creating an outline, completing your research, finishing a first draft, editing the draft, and preparing the final copy. By meeting these interim due dates, you make steady progress on the assignment throughout the term. ✳

 Find printable copies of this long-term planner online.

Week of	Monday	Tuesday	Wednesday	Thursday	Friday	Saturday	Sunday
9 / 5							
9 / 12		English quiz					
9 / 19			English paper due		Speech #1		
9 / 26	Chemistry test					Skiing at the lake	
10 / 3		English quiz			Speech #2		
10 / 10				Geography project due			
10 / 17				--- No classes ---			

TIME

3

LONG-TERM PLANNER ___ / ___ / ___ to ___ / ___ / ___

Week of	Monday	Tuesday	Wednesday	Thursday	Friday	Saturday	Sunday
___ / ___							
___ / ___							
___ / ___							
___ / ___							
___ / ___							
___ / ___							
___ / ___							
___ / ___							
___ / ___							
___ / ___							
___ / ___							
___ / ___							
___ / ___							
___ / ___							
___ / ___							
___ / ___							
___ / ___							
___ / ___							
___ / ___							
___ / ___							
___ / ___							
___ / ___							
___ / ___							
___ / ___							
___ / ___							
___ / ___							
___ / ___							
___ / ___							
___ / ___							

3

TIME

LONG-TERM PLANNER ___ / ___ / ___ to ___ / ___ / ___

Week of	Monday	Tuesday	Wednesday	Thursday	Friday	Saturday	Sunday
__ / __							
__ / __							
__ / __							
__ / __							
__ / __							
__ / __							
__ / __							
__ / __							
__ / __							
__ / __							
__ / __							
__ / __							
__ / __							
__ / __							
__ / __							
__ / __							
__ / __							
__ / __							
__ / __							
__ / __							
__ / __							
__ / __							
__ / __							
__ / __							
__ / __							
__ / __							
__ / __							
__ / __							
__ / __							
__ / __							
__ / __							
__ / __							

TIME

3

Be Here Now

Being right here, right now is such a simple idea. It seems obvious. Where else can you be but where you are? When else can you be there but when you are there?

The answer is that you can be somewhere else at any time—in your head. It's common for our thoughts to distract us from where we've chosen to be. When we let this happen, we lose the benefits of focusing our attention on what's important to us in the present moment.

To "be here now" means to do what you're doing when you're doing it. It means to be where you are when you're there. Students consistently report that focusing attention on the here and now is one of the most powerful tools in this book.

We all have a voice in our head that hardly ever shuts up. If you don't believe it, conduct this experiment: Close your eyes for 10 seconds, and pay attention to what is going on in your head. Please do this right now.

Notice something? Perhaps a voice in your head was saying, "Forget it. I'm in a hurry." Another might have said, "I wonder when 10 seconds is up." Another could have been saying, "What little voice? I don't hear any little voice."

That's the voice.

This voice can take you anywhere at any time—especially when you are studying. When the voice takes you away, you might appear to be studying, but your brain is at the beach.

All of us have experienced this voice, as well as the absence of it.

When our inner voices are silent, time no longer seems to exist. We forget worries, aches, pains, reasons, excuses, and justifications. We fully experience the here and now. Life is magic.

Do not expect to be rid of daydreams entirely. That is neither possible nor desirable. Inner voices serve a purpose. They enable us to analyze, predict, classify, and understand events out there in the "real" world. The trick is to consciously choose when to be with your inner voice and when to let it go.

Instead of trying to force a stray thought out of your head—a futile enterprise—simply notice it. Accept it. Tell yourself, "There's that thought again." Then gently return your attention to the task at hand. That thought, or another, will come back. Your mind will drift. Simply notice again where your thoughts take you, and gently bring yourself back to the here and now.

The idea behind this Power Process is simple. When you plan for the future, plan for the future. When you listen to a lecture, listen to a lecture. When you read this book, read this book. And when you choose to daydream, daydream. Do what you're doing when you're doing it.

Be where you are when you're there. Be here now . . . and now . . . and now.

 Learn more about this Power Process online.

© Luca Tettoni/Corbis

Career Application

Steve Carlson is a technical writer for DCS, a company that makes products for multimedia teleconferencing: digital video cameras, large-screen televisions, and software. He joined DCS two years ago, after graduating with a B.A. in Technical Communications. This is his first full-time, professional job.

Steve works in a five-person documentation department. The department creates sales brochures, user manuals, and other documents about DCS products. Working with his manager, Louise Chao, Steve helps decide which documents are needed for each DCS product. He then writes documents, edits documents written by others, and works closely with a graphic designer who oversees document production.

On a Friday afternoon, Louise knocks on the door of Steve's office. She wants Steve to handle a rush project—a new product brochure to be researched, written, designed, and printed in two weeks. Louise is on the way to another meeting and only has five minutes to talk.

Steve's schedule is already full of projects. For the last month, he has been working Saturdays to stay on top of his workload. As Louise describes the project, Steve listens without comment. When Louise is finished, Steve points to a large wallboard in his office.

This wallboard is a chart that shows all of Steve's active projects. This chart includes a visual time line for each project that shows due dates for researching, outlining, drafting, and revising each document. Steve has negotiated these dates with the product development teams. Each time line is color-coded—red for urgent projects, green for other active projects, and yellow for planned projects that are not yet active. Steve uses the wallboard to plan his day-to-day tasks and visually represent his workload.

"I estimate that it would take me at least three full days to research and write the document you're talking about," Steve says. "In addition, meetings with my designer would take up another two days. So doing the brochure means that I'd need to free up at least one week of my time."

Steve then points to the projects shown in red on his wallboard. "Louise, I know this new product brochure is important to you," he says. "Can we schedule a time to choose which of these urgent projects I could delay for a week to meet your request?"

Asia Images Group/Getty

Reflecting on this scenario

List at least two strategies from this chapter that would be useful to Steve in this situation. Briefly describe how he could apply each one.

_____

_____

_____

_____

_____

_____

_____

_____

_____

Quiz

Name _____   Date ____/____/____

1. Briefly explain how making promises can help you manage time.

2. Rewrite the statement "study harder" so that it becomes a specific goal.

3. The text suggests that you set long-term goals. Write one example of a long-term goal.

4. Write a mid-term and short-term goal that can help you achieve the long-term goal that you listed for Question 3.

5. Describe three strategies for managing time and tasks at work.

6. In time management terms, what is meant by "This ain't no piano"?

7. Define *C fever* as it applies to the ABC priority method.

8. Describe three strategies for overcoming procrastination.

9. According to the text, overcoming procrastination is a complex process that can take months or even years. True or false? Explain your answer.

10. Describe three ways to get the most value from using a long-term planner.

Focus on Transferable Skills

The Discovery Wheel in Chapter 1: "First Steps" includes a section labeled "Time." For the next 10 to 15 minutes, go beyond your initial responses to that exercise. Take a snapshot of your current transferable skills related to time management and goal setting. Then focus on a skill that you'd like to develop next.

You might want to prepare for this exercise by reviewing the articles "Jumpstart Your Education with Transferable Skills" on page 58 and "101 Transferable Skills" on page 60.

GOALS

I would describe my ability to set specific goals as . . .

The most important goal for me to achieve during this school year is . . .

DAILY PLANNING

When setting priorities for what to do each day, the first thing I consider is . . .

I keep track of my daily to-do items by . . .

PROCRASTINATION

The kinds of tasks on which I tend to procrastinate include . . .

My strategies for overcoming procrastination currently include . . .

BALANCE

My ability to balance recreation with working and studying can be described as . . .

If I sense that I'm not making enough time for family and friends, I respond by . . .

NEXT ACTION

The transferable skill related to time that I would most like to develop is . . .

To develop that skill, the most important thing I can do next is to . . .

Master Student PROFILE

Richard Anderson

. . . is responsible

Mark Wilson/RM/
Getty Images News

**(1955–) CEO of
Delta Airlines**

Q. What was the most important leadership lesson you learned?

A. I've learned to be patient and not lose my temper. And the reason that's important is everything you do is an example, and people look at everything you do and take a signal from everything you do. And when you lose your temper, it really squelches debate and sends the wrong signal about how you want your organization to run. . . .

Q. Are there other things that you've learned to do more of, or less?

A. You've got to be thankful to the people who get the work done, and you've got to be thankful to your customers. So, I find myself, more and more, writing hand-written notes to people. I must write a half a dozen a day.

Q. Looking back over your career, even to the early years, do you recall an insight that set you on a different trajectory?

A. Yes, and it was actually at my first job while I went to night law school at South Texas College of Law. And I had a good full-time job as the administrative assistant to the D.A. And what you understood was you really needed to be a problem-solver, not a problem-creator. You know, don't bring a Rubik's cube to the table, unless you have an idea on how you're going to try to get an answer. And always try to be a leader that comes up with the creative answers to the hard problems.

Q. And what about advice on your career?

A. If you just focus on getting your job done and being a good colleague and a team player in an organization, and not focused about being overly ambitious and wanting pay raises and promotions and the like, and just doing your job and being a part of a team, the rest of it all takes care of itself.

Q. Did somebody give you that advice, or was that something that you came to understand yourself?

A. My mother and father died from cancer when I was 20, and so I was working full time, and I was pretty fortunate to be around a lot of good people that had that kind of culture and approach to things. It was just by osmosis that I came to those kinds of conclusions. . . .

Q. And is there any change in the kind of qualities you're looking for [in job candidates] compared with 5, 10 years ago?

A. I think this communication point is getting more and more important. People really have to be able to handle the written and spoken word. And when I say written word, I don't mean PowerPoints. I don't think PowerPoints help people think as clearly as they should because you don't have to put a complete thought in place. You can just put a phrase with a bullet in front of it. And it doesn't have a subject, a verb and an object, so you aren't expressing complete thoughts. . . .

Q. What about time management?

A. Only touch paper once. No. 2, always have your homework done. No. 3, return your calls very promptly. No. 4, stick to your schedule. I keep my watch about 10 minutes ahead. It's important to run on time, particularly at an airline. And use your time wisely. And then, once a month, take the rest of the calendar year, or the next six months and re-review how you are using your time and reprioritize what you're doing.

Learn more about Richard Anderson and other master students at the Master Student Hall of Fame.

4 Memory

Master Student Map

as you read, ask yourself

what if . . .

I could use my memory to its full potential?

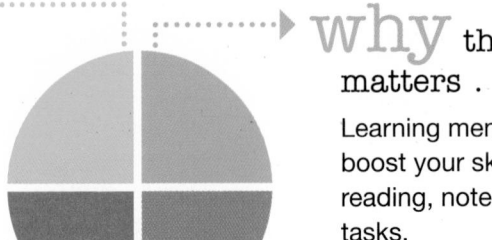

why this chapter matters . . .

Learning memory techniques can boost your skills at test taking, reading, note taking, and many other tasks.

what is included . . .

how you can use this chapter . . .

- Focus your attention.
- Make conscious choices about what to remember.
- Recall facts and ideas with more ease.

MASTER EMPLOYEE in *action*

My field is contantly developing, and I have to memorize new code, programs, and even programming languages on a monthly basis. Whenever a new program is introduced into our office, I find that it's easiest if I take it home and play with it. By interacting with it creatively, I can transform it from something I need to memorize into a tool I can use.

—RAUL OLIVO, SOFTWARE ENGINEER

Photo courtesy of Raul Olivo

Take your memory out of the closet

ONCE UPON A TIME, people talked about human memory as if it were a closet. You stored individual memories there as you would old shirts and stray socks. Remembering something was a matter of rummaging through all that stuff. If you were lucky, you found what you wanted.

This view of memory creates some problems. For one thing, closets can get crowded. Things too easily disappear. Even with the biggest closet, you eventually run out of space. If you want to pack some new memories in there—well, too bad. There's no room.

Brain researchers shattered this image to bits. Memory is not a closet. It's not a place or a thing. Instead, memory is a *process.*

On a conscious level, memories appear as distinct and unconnected mental events: words, sensations, and images. They can include details from the distant past— the smell of cookies baking in your grandmother's kitchen or the feel of sunlight warming your face through the window of your first-grade classroom.

On a biological level, each of those memories involves millions of nerve cells, or neurons, firing chemical messages to one another. If you could observe these exchanges in real time, you'd see regions of cells all over the brain glowing with electrical charges at speeds that would put a computer to shame.

When a series of cells connects several times in a similar pattern, the result is a memory. Psychologist Donald Hebb uses this aphorism to describe this principle: "Neurons which fire together, wire together."[1] It means that memories are not really stored. Instead, remembering is a process in which you *encode* information as links between active neurons that fire together. You also *decode,* or reactivate, neurons that wired together in the past.

Memory is the probability that certain patterns of brain activity will occur again in the future. In effect, you recreate a memory each time you recall it.

Whenever you learn something new, your brain changes physically by growing more connections between neurons. The more you learn, the greater the number of connections. For all practical purposes, there's no limit to how many memories your brain can encode.

There's a lot you can do to wire those neural networks into place. That's where the memory techniques described in this chapter come into play. Step out of your crowded mental closet into a world of infinite possibilities. ✻

journal entry 10

Discovery/Intention Statement

Create value from this chapter

Write a sentence or two describing the way you feel when you want to remember something but have trouble doing so. Think of a specific incident in which you experienced this problem, such as a time when you tried to remember someone's name or a fact you needed during a test.

I discovered that I . . .

_____

_____

_____

_____

_____

Now spend five minutes skimming this chapter, and find three to five memory strategies you intend to use. List the strategies in the following space, and note the page numbers where they are explained.

Strategy	Page Number

The memory jungle

© Photodisc

Think of your memory as a vast, overgrown jungle. This memory jungle is thick with wild plants, exotic shrubs, twisted trees, and creeping vines. It spreads over thousands of square miles—dense, tangled, forbidding.

4

MEMORY

IMAGINE THAT THE jungle is encompassed on all sides by towering mountains. There is only one entrance to the jungle, a small meadow that is reached by a narrow pass through the mountains.

In the jungle there are animals, millions of them. The animals represent all of the information in your memory. Imagine that every thought, mental picture, or perception you ever had is represented by an animal in this jungle. Every single event ever perceived by any of your five senses—sight, touch, hearing, smell, or taste—is a thought animal that has also passed through the meadow and entered the jungle. Some of the thought animals, such as the color of your seventh-grade teacher's favorite sweater, are well hidden. Other thoughts, such as your cell phone number or the position of the reverse gear in your car, are easier to find.

The memory jungle has two rules: Each thought animal must pass through the meadow at the entrance to the jungle. And once an animal enters the jungle, it never leaves.

The meadow represents short-term memory. You use this kind of memory when you look up a telephone number and hold it in your memory long enough to make a call. Short-term memory appears to have a limited capacity (the meadow is small) and disappears fast (animals pass through the meadow quickly).

The jungle itself represents long-term memory. This kind of memory allows you to recall information from day to day, week to week, and year to year. Remember that thought animals never leave the long-term memory jungle. The following visualizations can help you recall useful concepts about memory.

Visualization 1: A well-worn path

© Photodisc

Imagine what happens as a thought—in this case, we'll call it an elephant—charges across short-term memory and into the jungle. The elephant leaves a trail of broken twigs and hoof prints that you can follow. Brain research suggests that thoughts can wear paths in the brain.[2] These paths are called *neural traces*. The more well-worn a neural trace, the easier it is to retrieve (find) the thought. In other words, the more often the elephant retraces the path, the clearer the path becomes. The more often you recall information, and the more often you put the same information into your memory, the easier it is to find. When you buy a new car, for example, the first few times you try to find reverse, you have to think for a moment. After you have found reverse gear every day for a week, the path is worn into your memory. After a year, the path is so well-worn that when you dream about driving your car backward, you even dream the correct motion for putting the gear in reverse.

Visualization 2: A herd of thoughts

© Photodisc

The second picture you can use to your advantage in recalling concepts about memory is the picture of many animals gathering at a clearing—like thoughts gathering at a central location in memory. It is easier to retrieve thoughts that are grouped together, just as it is easier to find a herd of animals than it is to find a single elephant.

Pieces of information are easier to recall if you can associate them with similar information. For example, you can more readily remember a particular player's batting average if you can associate it with other baseball statistics.

Visualization 3: Turning your back

© Photodisc

Imagine releasing the elephant into the jungle, turning your back, and counting to 10. When you turn around, the elephant is gone. This is exactly what happens to most of the information you receive.

Generally, we can recall only 50 percent of the material we have just read. Within 24 hours, most of us can recall only about 20 percent. This means that 80 percent of the material has not been encoded and is wandering around, lost in the memory jungle.[3]

The remedy is simple: Review quickly. Do not take your eyes off the thought animal as it crosses the short-term memory meadow. Look at it again (review it) soon after it enters the long-term memory jungle. Wear a path in your memory immediately.

Visualization 4: Directing the animal traffic

© Photodisc

The fourth picture is one you are in. You are standing at the entrance to the short-term memory meadow, directing herds of thought animals as they file through the pass, across the meadow, and into your long-term memory. You are taking an active role in the learning process. You are paying attention. You are doing more than sitting on a rock and watching the animals file past into your brain. You have become part of the process; in doing so, you have taken control of your memory. ✳

(WWW) Find guided visualizations based on the memory jungle online.

20 memory techniques

Experiment with these techniques to develop a flexible, custom-made memory system that fits your style of learning.

THE 20 TECHNIQUES that follow are divided into four categories, each of which represents a general principle for improving memory:

Organize it. Organized information is easier to find.

Use your body. Learning is an active process; get all of your senses involved.

Use your brain. Work *with* your memory, not *against* it.

Recall it. Regularly retrieve and apply key information.

Read this article while thinking about ways to use the techniques. Mark the technique you like best, and apply it right away. Then come back to this article for more. Also look for ways to combine techniques.

Organize it

1 Be selective. During your stay in higher education, you will be exposed to thousands of facts and ideas. No one expects you to memorize all of them. To a large degree, the art of memory is the art of selecting what to remember in the first place.

As you dig into your textbooks and notes, make choices about what is most important to learn. Imagine that you are going to create a test on the material, and consider the questions you would ask.

When reading, look for chapter previews, summaries, and review questions. Pay attention to anything printed in bold type. Also notice visual elements—tables, charts, graphs, and illustrations. They are all clues pointing to what's important. During lectures, notice what the instructor emphasizes. Anything that's presented visually—on the board, in overheads, or with slides—is probably key.

2 Make it meaningful. You remember things better if they have meaning for you. For this reason, avoid memorizing things that you don't truly understand. First see if you can express a concept in your words and give some examples of it.

One way to create meaning is to learn from the general to the specific. Before you begin your next reading assignment, skim the passage to locate the main idea. You can use the same techniques you learned in Critical Thinking Exercise 1: "Textbook Reconnaissance" on page 1. If you're ever lost, step back and look at the big picture. The details then might make more sense.

You can organize any list of items—even random items—in a meaningful way to make them easier to remember. One simple and useful technique is to simply "chunk" long items into smaller units. Say that you want to remember a social security number: 681711945. Divide it into smaller chunks: 681-71-1945. Also make the last four digits meaningful by associating them with the year that World War II ended (1945).

In his book *Information Anxiety*, Richard Saul Wurman proposes five principles for organizing any body of ideas, facts, or objects:[4]

Principle	Example
Organize by **time**	Events in history or in a novel flow in chronological order.
Organize by **location**	Addresses for a large company's regional offices are grouped by state and city.
Organize by **category**	Nonfiction library materials are organized by subject categories.
Organize by **continuum**	Products rated in most consumer guides or online stores are grouped from highest in price to lowest in price, or highest in quality to lowest in quality.
Organize by **alphabet**	Entries in a book index are listed in ABC order.

From INFORMATION ANXIETY by Richard Saul Wurman, copyright © 1989 by Richard Saul Wurman. Used by permission of Doubleday, a division of Bantam Doubleday Dell Publishing Group, Inc.

3 Create associations. The data already encoded in your neural networks are arranged according to a scheme that makes sense to you. When you introduce new data, you can remember them more effectively if you associate them with similar or related data.

Your favorite courses probably relate to subjects that you already know something about. If you have been interested in politics over the last few years, you'll find it easier to remember the facts in a modern history course. Even when you're tackling a new subject, you can build a mental store of basic background information—the raw material for creating associations. Preview reading assignments, and complete those readings before you attend lectures. Before taking upper-level courses, master the prerequisites.

Use your body

4 Learn actively. Action is a great memory enhancer. You can use simple, direct methods to infuse your learning with action. When you sit at your desk, sit up straight. Sit on the edge of your chair, as if you were about to spring out of it and sprint across the room.

Also experiment with standing up when you study. It's harder to fall asleep in this position. Some people insist that their brains work better when they stand. Pace back and forth and gesture as you recite material out loud. Use your hands. Get your body moving.

Don't forget to move your mouth. During a lecture, ask questions. With your textbooks, read key passages out loud. Use a louder voice for the main points.

Active learning also involves a variety of learning styles. In Chapter 1: "First Steps," the article "Learning Styles: Discovering How You Learn" explains four methods of learning: concrete experience, abstract conceptualization, active experimentation, and reflective observation. Many courses in higher education lean heavily toward abstract conceptualization—lectures, papers, and reading. These courses might not offer chances to actively experiment with ideas or test them in concrete experience.

Create those opportunities yourself. For example, your introductory psychology textbook probably offers some theories about how people remember information. Choose one of those theories and test it on yourself. See if you can discover a new memory technique. Your sociology class might include a discussion about how groups of people resolve conflict. See if you can apply any of those ideas to resolving conflict in your own family.

The point behind each of these examples is the same: To remember an idea, go beyond thinking about it. *Do* something with it. Instead of reviewing material in a passive way (such as scanning paragraphs in a textbook), get active: Create flash cards, write out the main points, recite those points while taking a brisk walk, or do anything else that moves information down into your muscles.

5 Relax. When you're relaxed, you absorb new information quickly and recall it with greater ease and accuracy. Students who can't recall information under the stress of a final exam can often recite the same facts later when they are relaxed.

Relaxing might seem to contradict the idea of active learning as explained in technique 4, but it doesn't. Being relaxed is not the same as being drowsy, zoned out, or asleep. Relaxation is a state of alertness, free of tension, during which your mind can play with new information, roll it around, create associations with it, and apply many of the other memory techniques. You can be active *and* relaxed. See Critical Thinking Exercise 21: "Relax" on page 147 in Chapter 5: "Reading" for some tips on how to relax.

6 Create pictures. Draw diagrams. Make cartoons. Use these images to connect facts and illustrate relationships. You can "see" and recall associations within and among abstract concepts more easily when you visualize both the concepts and the associations. The key is to use your imagination. Creating pictures reinforces visual and kinesthetic learning styles.

For example, Boyle's law states that at a constant temperature, the volume of a confined ideal gas varies inversely with its pressure. Simply put, cutting the volume in half doubles the pressure. To remember this concept, you might picture someone "doubled over" using a bicycle pump. As she increases the pressure in the pump by decreasing the volume in the pump cylinder, she seems to be getting angrier. By the time she has doubled the pressure (and halved the volume), she is boiling ("Boyle-ing") mad.

Another reason to create pictures is that visual information is associated with a part of the brain that is different from the part that processes verbal information. When you create a picture of a concept, you are anchoring the information in a second part of your brain. Doing so increases your chances of recalling that information.

To visualize abstract relationships effectively, create an action-oriented image, such as the person using the pump. Make the picture vivid, too. The person's face could be bright red. Be sure to involve all of your senses. Imagine how the cold metal of the pump would feel, and how the person would grunt as she struggled with it.

You can also create pictures as you study by using *graphic organizers*. The purpose of these preformatted charts is to help you visualize relationships among facts and ideas.

One example is a *topic-point-details* chart. At the top of this chart, write the main topic of a lecture or reading assignment. In the left column, list the main points you want to remember. In the right column, list key details related to each point. Following is the beginning of a chart based on this article:

Example 1

20 MEMORY TECHNIQUES

Point	Details
1. Be selective	Choose what not to remember. Look for clues to important material.
2. Make it meaningful	Organize by time, location, category, continuum, or alphabet.
3. Create associations	Link new facts with facts you already know.
4. Learn actively	Sit straight. Stand while studying. Recite while walking.
5. Relax	Release tension. Remain alert.

Example 2

STIMULATE THE ECONOMY WITH TAX CUTS?

Opinion	Support
Yes	Savings from tax cuts allow businesses to invest money in new equipment. Tax cuts encourage businesses to expand and hire new employees.
No	Years of tax cuts under the Bush administration failed to prevent the mortgage credit crisis. Tax cuts create budget deficits.
Maybe	Tax cuts might work in some economic conditions. Budget deficits might be only temporary.

You could use a similar chart to prompt critical thinking about an issue. Express that issue as a question, and write it at the top. In the left column, note your opinion about the issue. In the right column, list notable facts, expert opinions, reasons, and examples that support each opinion. Example 2 in the right column is about tax cuts as a strategy for stimulating the economy.

Sometimes you'll want to remember the main actions in a story or historical event. Create a time line by drawing a straight line. Place points in order on that line to represent key events. Place earlier events toward the left end of the line and later events toward the right. Example 3 to the right shows the start of a time line of events relating to the U.S. war with Iraq.

When you want to compare or contrast two things, play with a Venn diagram. Represent each thing as a circle. Draw the circles so that they overlap. In the overlapping area, list characteristics that the two things share. In the outer parts of each circle, list the unique characteristics of each thing. Example 4 on page 125 compares the two types of journal entries included in this book—Discovery Statements and Intention Statements.

The graphic organizers described here are just a few of the many kinds available. Search online for more examples. Have fun, and invent graphic organizers of your own.

7 Recite and repeat. When you repeat something out loud, you anchor the information in two different senses. First, you get the physical sensation in your throat, tongue, and lips when voicing the concept. Second, you hear it. The combined result is synergistic, just as it is when you create pictures. That is, the effect of using two different senses is greater than the sum of their individual effects.

The "out loud" part is important. Reciting silently in your head can be useful—in the library, for example— but it is not as effective as making noise. Your mind can

Example 3

3/19/03	3/30/03	4/9/03	5/1/03	5/29/03
U.S. invades Iraq	Rumsfeld announces location of WMD	Soldiers topple statue of Saddam	Bush declares mission accomplished	Bush: We found WMD

MEMORY

4

Example 4

Discovery Statements   Intention Statements

Discovery Statements
- Describe specific thoughts
- Describe specific feelings
- Describe current and past behaviors

(overlap)
- Are a type of journal entry
- Are based on telling the truth
- Can be written at any time on any topic
- Can lead to action

Intention Statements
- Describe future behaviors
- Can include time lines
- Can include rewards

trick itself into thinking it knows something when it doesn't. Your ears are harder to fool.

The repetition part is important, too. Repetition is a common memory device because it works. Repetition blazes a trail through the pathways of your brain, making the information easier to find. Repeat a concept out loud until you know it; then say it five more times.

Recitation works best when you recite concepts in your own words. For example, if you want to remember that the acceleration of a falling body due to gravity at sea level equals 32 feet per second per second, you might say, "Gravity makes an object accelerate 32 feet per second faster for each second that it's in the air at sea level." Putting a concept into your own words forces you to think about it.

Have some fun with this technique. Recite by writing a song about what you're learning. Sing it in the shower. Use any style you want.

Or imitate someone. Imagine your textbook being read by Will Ferrell, Madonna, or Clint Eastwood.

8 Write it down. The technique of writing things down is obvious, yet easy to forget. Writing a note to yourself helps you remember an idea, even if you never look at the note again.

You can extend this technique by writing down an idea not just once, but many times. When you choose to remember something, repetitive writing is a powerful tool.

Writing engages a different kind of memory than speaking. Writing prompts us to be more logical, coherent, and complete. Written reviews reveal gaps in knowledge that oral reviews miss, just as oral reviews reveal gaps that written reviews miss.

Another advantage of written reviews is that they more closely match the way you're asked to remember materials in school. During your academic career, you'll probably take far more written exams than oral exams. Writing can be an effective way to prepare for such tests.

Finally, writing is physical. Your arm, your hand, and your fingers join in. Remember, learning is an active process—you remember what you *do*.

Use your brain

9 Engage your emotions. The human brain is designed for finding protection in dangerous physical environments. Brains thrive on challenges: moving muscles, solving problems, and remembering information that ensures survival and success.

One powerful way to enhance your memory is to befriend your amygdala. This area of your brain lights up with extra neural activity each time you feel a strong emotion. When a topic excites love, laughter, or fear, the amygdala sends a flurry of chemical messages that say, in effect: *This information is important. Don't forget it.*

You're more likely to remember course material when you relate it to a goal—whether academic, personal, or career. This is one reason why it pays to be specific about what you want. The more goals you have and the more clearly they are defined, the more channels you create for incoming information.

You can use this strategy even when a subject seems boring at first. If you're not naturally interested in a topic, then create interest. Find a study partner in the class or form a study group. Also consider getting to know the instructor personally. When a course creates a bridge to human relationships, you engage the content in a more emotional way.

10 Overlearn. One way to fight mental fuzziness is to learn more than you need to know about a subject simply to pass a test. You can pick a subject apart, examine it, add to it, and go over it until it becomes second nature.

This technique is especially effective for problem solving. Do the assigned problems, and then do more problems. Find another textbook, and work similar problems. Then make up your own problems and solve them. When you pretest yourself in this way, the potential rewards are speed, accuracy, and greater confidence at exam time.

11 Escape the short-term memory trap. Short-term memory is different from the kind of memory you'll need during exam week. For example, most of us can look at an unfamiliar seven-digit phone number once and remember it long enough to dial it. See if you can recall that number the next day. Short-term memory can fade after a few minutes, and it rarely lasts more than several hours.

To escape this trap, do a short review within minutes or hours of a study session. This can move material from short-term memory into long-term memory—and perhaps save hours of study time when exams roll around.

12 Use your times of peak energy. Study your most difficult subjects during the times when your energy peaks. Some people can concentrate more effectively during daylight hours. The early morning hours can be especially productive, even for those who hate to get up with the sun. Observe the peaks and valleys in your energy flow during the day, and adjust study times accordingly. Perhaps you experience surges in memory power during the late afternoon or evening.

13 Distribute learning. As an alternative to marathon study sessions, experiment with several shorter sessions spaced out over time. You might find that you can get far more done in three 2-hour sessions than in one 6-hour session.

For example, when you are preparing for your American history exam, study for an hour or two and then wash the dishes. While you are washing the dishes, part of your mind will be reviewing what you studied. Return to American history for a while, then call a friend. Even when you are deep in conversation, part of your mind will be reviewing history.

You can get more done if you take regular breaks. You can even use the breaks as mini-rewards. After a productive study session, give yourself permission to log on and check your e-mail, listen to a song, or play 10 minutes of hide-and-seek with your kids.

Distributing your learning is a brain-friendly activity. You cannot absorb new information and ideas during all of your waking hours. If you overload your brain, it will find a way to shut down for a rest—whether you plan for it or not. By taking periodic breaks while studying, you allow information to sink in. During these breaks, your brain is taking the time to rewire itself by growing new connections between cells. Psychologists call this process *consolidation*.[5]

The idea of allowing time for consolidation does have an exception. When you are so engrossed in a textbook that you cannot put it down, when you are consumed by an idea for a term paper and cannot think of anything else—keep going. The master student within you has taken over. Enjoy the ride.

14 Be aware of attitudes. People who think history is boring tend to have trouble remembering dates and historical events. People who believe math is difficult often have a hard time recalling mathematical equations and formulas. All of us can forget information that contradicts our opinions.

If you think a subject is boring, remind yourself that everything is related to everything else. Look for connections that relate to your own interests.

For example, consider a person who is fanatical about cars. He can rebuild a motor in a weekend and has a good time doing so. From this apparently specialized interest, he can explore a wide realm of knowledge. He can relate the workings of an engine to principles of physics, math, and chemistry. Computerized parts in newer cars can lead him to the study of data processing. He can research how the automobile industry has changed our cities and helped create suburbs, a topic that relates to urban planning, sociology, business, economics, psychology, and history.

Being aware of your attitudes is not the same as fighting them or struggling to give them up. Just notice your attitudes and be willing to put them on hold.

15 Elaborate. According to Harvard psychologist Daniel Schacter, all courses in memory improvement are based on a single technique—elaboration. *Elaboration* means consciously encoding new information. Repetition is one basic way to elaborate. However, current brain research indicates that other types of elaboration are more effective for long-term memory.[6]

One way to elaborate is to ask yourself questions about incoming information: *Does this remind me of something or someone I already know? Can I find an example of this in my own life? How would I say this in my own words? How can I use this information?*

When you first learned to recognize Italy on a world map, your teacher probably pointed out that the country is shaped like a boot. This is a simple form of elaboration.

The same idea applies to more complex material. When you meet someone new, for example, ask yourself, "Does she remind me of someone else?" When reading this book, preview the material using the Master Student Map that opens each chapter to explore how it applies to you.

16 Intend to remember. To instantly enhance your memory, form the simple intention to *learn it now* rather than later. The intention to remember can be more powerful than any single memory technique.

You can build on your intention with simple tricks. During a lecture, for example, pretend that you'll be quizzed on the key points at the end of the period. Imagine that you'll get a $5 reward for every correct answer.

Also pay attention to your attention. Each time your mind wanders during class, make a tick mark in the margins of your notes. The act of writing reengages your attention.

If your mind keeps returning to an urgent or incomplete task, then write an Intention Statement about how you will handle it. With your intention safely recorded, return to what's important in the present moment.

Recall it

17 Remember something else. When you are stuck and can't remember something that you're sure you know, remember something else that is related to it.

If you can't remember your great-aunt's name, remember your great-uncle's name. During an economics exam, if you can't remember anything about the aggregate demand curve, recall what you do know about the aggregate supply curve. If you cannot recall specific facts, remember the example that the instructor used during her lecture. Any piece of information is encoded in the same area of the brain as a similar piece of information. You can unblock your recall by stimulating that area of your memory.

A brainstorm is a good memory jog. If you are stumped when taking a test, start writing down lots of answers to related questions, and—pop!—the answer you need is likely to appear.

A variation on this technique is something that psychologists call *context-dependent memory*: You're more likely to recall something if you're in the same physical environment where you learned it. Taken literally, this would mean studying for a test in the same room where you will *take* the test. That's not always practical. Yet you can still use the context effect by attending every class, taking careful notes, and sitting in the same approximate spot in the room. If that doesn't work, then experiment with *reducing* the context effect: Study in several different locations while reviewing the same key ideas and information.

18 Notice when you do remember. Everyone has a different memory style. Some people are best at recalling information they've read. Others have an easier time remembering what they've heard, seen, or done.

To develop your memory, notice when you recall information easily, and ask yourself what memory techniques you're using naturally. Also notice when you find it difficult to recall information. Be a reporter. Get the facts, and then adjust your learning techniques. In addition, remember to congratulate yourself when you remember.

19 Use it before you lose it. Even information encoded in long-term memory becomes difficult to recall when we don't use it regularly. The pathways to the information become faint from disuse. For example, you can probably remember your current phone number. However, what was your phone number 10 years ago?

This example points to a powerful memory technique. To remember something, access it a lot. Read it, write it, speak it, listen to it, apply it—find some way to make contact with the material regularly. Each time you do so, you widen the neural pathway to the material and make it easier to recall the next time.

Another way to make contact with the material is to teach it. Teaching demands mastery. When you explain the function of the pancreas to a fellow student, you discover quickly whether you really understand it yourself.

Study groups are especially effective because they put you on stage. The friendly pressure of knowing that you'll teach the group helps focus your attention.

20 Adopt the attitude that you never forget. You might not believe that an idea or a thought never leaves your memory. That's OK. In fact, it doesn't matter whether you agree with the idea or not. It can work for you anyway.

Test the concept. Instead of saying, "I don't remember," you can say, "It will come to me." The latter statement implies that the information you want is encoded in your brain and that you can retrieve it—just not right now. You'll probably be surprised to find that the information was in there all along.

People who use the flip side of this technique often get the opposite results. "I never remember anything," they say over and over again. "I've always had a poor memory. I'm such a scatterbrain." That kind of negative talk is self-fulfilling.

Instead, use positive affirmations that support you in developing your memory: "I recall information easily and accurately." "At any time I choose, I will be able to recall key facts and ideas." "My memory serves me well." ✳

 Find more memory strategies online.

18 critical thinking exercise
Remembering your car keys— or anything else

Pick something you frequently forget or misplace. Some people chronically lose their car keys or forget to write down checks in their check register. Others let anniversaries and birthdays slip by.

Pick an item or a task you're prone to forget. Then design a strategy for remembering it. Use any of the techniques from this chapter, research others, or make up your own from scratch. Describe your technique and the results in the following space.

_____

_____

_____

_____

_____

_____

_____

_____

In this exercise, as in most of the exercises in this book, a failure is also a success. Don't be concerned with whether your technique will work. Design it, and then find out if it works. If it doesn't work for you this time, use another method.

Keep your brain fit for life

Memories are encoded as physical changes in the brain. Your brain is an organ that needs regular care and exercise. Higher education gives you plenty of chances to exercise that organ. Don't let those benefits fade after you leave school. Starting now, adopt habits to keep your brain lean and fit for life. Consider these research-based suggestions from the Alzheimer's Association.[7]

Stay mentally active   If you sit at a desk most of the workday, take a class. If you seldom travel, start reading maps of new locations and plan a cross-country trip. Seek out museums, theaters, concerts, and other cultural events. Even after you graduate, consider learning another language or taking up a musical instrument. Learning gives your brain a workout, much like sit-ups condition your abs.

Stay socially active   Having a network of supportive friends can reduce stress levels. In turn, stress management helps to maintain connections between brain cells. Stay socially active by working, volunteering, and joining clubs.

Stay physically active   Physical activity promotes blood flow to the brain. It also reduces the risk of diabetes, cardiovascular disease, and other diseases that can impair brain function.

Adopt a brain-healthy diet   A diet rich in dark-skinned fruits and vegetables boosts your supply of antioxidants—natural chemicals that nourish your brain. Examples of these foods are raisins, blueberries, blackberries, strawberries, raspberries, kale, spinach, brussels sprouts, alfalfa sprouts, and broccoli. Avoid foods that are high in saturated fat and cholesterol, which may increase the risk of Alzheimer's disease.

Drink alcohol moderately, if at all   A common definition of moderate consumption for people of legal drinking age is a limit of one drink per day for women and two drinks per day for men. Heavier drinking can affect memory.

Protect your heart   In general, what's good for your heart is good for your brain. Protect both organs by eating well, exercising regularly, managing your weight, staying tobacco-free, and getting plenty of sleep. These habits reduce your risk of heart attack, stroke, and other cardiovascular conditions that interfere with blood flow to the brain.

4

MEMORY

(door) © Photospin, (iilustration) Walter Kopec

Mnemonic devices

It's pronounced ne-MON-ik. The word refers to tricks that can increase your ability to recall everything from grocery lists to speeches.

SOME ENTERTAINERS USE mnemonic devices to perform "impossible" feats of memory, such as recalling the names of everyone in a large audience after hearing them just once. Using mnemonic devices, speakers can go for hours without looking at their notes. The possibilities for students are endless.

There is a catch, though. Mnemonic devices have three serious limitations:

- They don't always help you understand or digest material. Mnemonics rely only on rote memorization.
- The mnemonic device itself is sometimes complicated to learn and time-consuming to develop.
- Mnemonic devices can be forgotten.

In spite of their limitations, mnemonic devices can be powerful. These devices fall into five general categories: new words, creative sentences, rhymes and songs, the loci system, and the peg system.

Make up new words. Acronyms are words created from the initial letters of a series of words. Examples include NASA (National Aeronautics and Space Administration) and laser (light amplification by stimulated emission of radiation).

You can make up your own acronyms to recall a series of facts. A common mnemonic acronym is Roy G. Biv, which has helped millions of students remember the colors of the visible spectrum (red, orange, yellow, green, blue, indigo, and violet). IPMAT helps biology students remember the stages of cell division (interphase, prophase, metaphase, anaphase, and telophase).

If you take an introductory psychology course, you might find the acronym OCEAN to be useful. It stands for the five major personality traits: open-mindedness, conscientiousness, extraversion, agreeableness, and neuroticism. In addition, your knowledge of United States geography might be enhanced by HOMES, an acronym for the names of the Great Lakes: Huron, Ontario, Michigan, Erie, and Superior.

Use creative sentences. Acrostics are sentences that help you remember a series of letters that stand for something. For example, the first letters of the words in the sentence *Every good boy does fine* (E, G, B, D, and F) are the music notes associated with the lines of the treble clef staff.

Create rhymes and songs. Madison Avenue advertising executives spend billions of dollars a year on advertisements designed to burn their messages into your memory. The song "It's the Real Thing" was used to market Coca-Cola, despite the soda's artificial ingredients.

Rhymes have been used for centuries to teach basic facts. "*I before e, except after c*" has helped many a student on spelling tests.

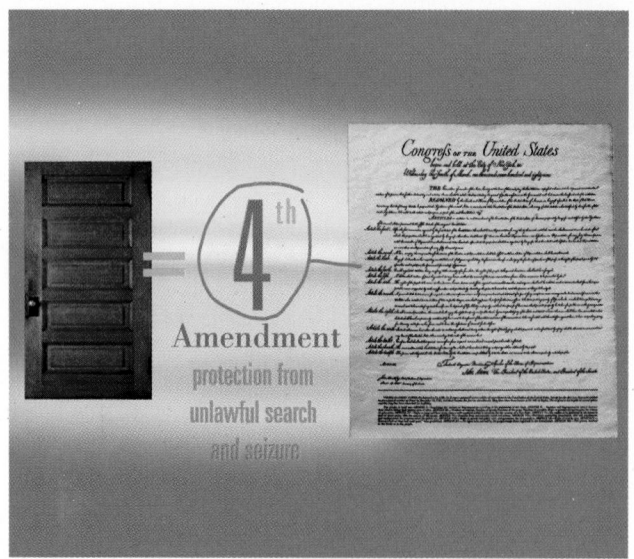

(door) © Photospin

Use the loci system. The word *loci* is the plural of *locus,* a synonym for *place* or *location.* Use the loci system to create visual associations with familiar locations. Unusual associations are the easiest to remember.

The loci system is an old one. Ancient Greek orators used it to remember long speeches, and politicians use it today. For example, if a politician's position was that road taxes must be raised to pay for school equipment, his loci visualizations before a speech might have looked like the following.

First, as he walks in the door of his house, he imagines a large *porpoise* jumping through a hoop. This reminds him to begin by telling the audience the *purpose* of his speech.

Next, he visualizes his living room floor covered with paving stones, forming a road leading into the kitchen. In the kitchen, he pictures dozens of schoolchildren sitting on the floor because they have no desks.

Now it's the day of the big speech. The politician is nervous. He's perspiring so much that his clothes stick to his body. He stands up to give his speech, and his mind goes blank. Then he starts thinking to himself:

I can remember the rooms in my house. Let's see, I'm walking in the front door and—wow!—I see a porpoise. That reminds me to talk about the purpose of my speech. And then there's that road leading to the kitchen. Say, what are all those kids doing there on the floor? Oh, yeah, now I remember—they have no desks! We need to raise taxes on roads to pay for their desks and the other stuff they need in classrooms.

Use the peg system. The peg system is a technique that employs keywords that are paired with numbers. Each word forms a "peg" on which you can "hang" mental associations. To use this system effectively, learn the following peg words and their associated numbers well:

bun goes with 1

shoe goes with 2

tree goes with 3

door goes with 4

hive goes with 5

sticks goes with 6

heaven goes with 7

gate goes with 8

wine goes with 9

hen goes with 10

You can use the peg system to remember the Bill of Rights (the first 10 amendments to the U.S. Constitution). For example, amendment number *four* is about protection from unlawful search and seizure. Imagine people knocking at your *door* who are demanding to search your home. This amendment means that you do not have to open your door unless those people have a proper search warrant. ✳

19 critical thinking exercise
Get creative

Construct your own mnemonic device for remembering some of the memory techniques in this chapter. Make up a poem, jingle, acronym, or acrostic. Or use another mnemonic system. Describe your mnemonic device in the following space.

Remembering names

New friendships, job contacts, and business relationships all start with remembering names. Here are some suggestions for remembering them.

Recite and repeat in conversation   When you hear a person's name, repeat it. Immediately say it to yourself several times without moving your lips. You can also repeat the name out loud in a way that does not sound forced or artificial: "I'm pleased to meet you, Maria."

Ask the other person to recite and repeat
After you've been introduced to someone, ask that person to spell his name and pronounce it correctly for you. Most people will be flattered by the effort you're making to learn their names.

Visualize   After the conversation, construct a brief visual image of the person. For a memorable image, make it unusual. Imagine the name painted in hot pink fluorescent letters on the person's forehead.

Admit you don't know   Admitting that you can't remember someone's name can actually put people at ease. Most of them will sympathize if you say, "I'm working to remember names better. Yours is right on the tip of my tongue. What is it again?"

Introduce yourself again   If you miss a name the first time around, reintroduce yourself: "We met earlier. I'm Jesse. Please tell me your name again."

Use associations   Link each person you meet with one characteristic that you find interesting or unusual. For example, you could make a mental note: "Vicki Cheng—long, black hair" or "James Washington—horn-rimmed glasses."

Limit the number of new names you learn at one time   When meeting a large group of people, concentrate on remembering just two or three names. Few of the people in mass introductions expect you to remember their names, anyway.

Ask for photos   For example, a small business where you work might have a brochure with pictures of all the employees.

Intend to remember   The next time you're introduced to someone, direct 100 percent of your attention to hearing that person's name. Do this consistently, and see what happens to your ability to remember names.

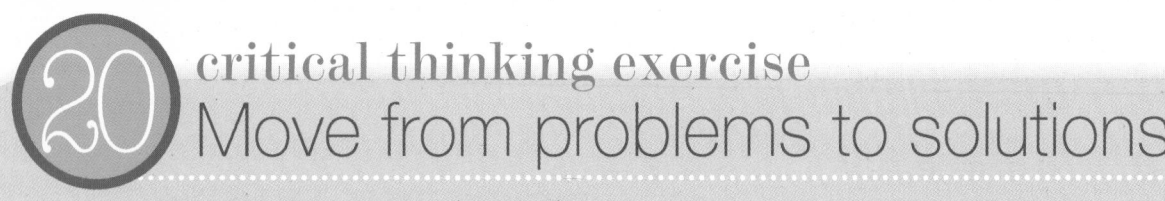

Many students find it easy to complain about school and to dwell on problems. This exercise gives you an opportunity to change that habit and respond creatively to any problem you're currently experiencing—whether it be with memorizing or some other aspect of school or life.

The key is to dwell more on solutions than on problems. Do that by inventing as many solutions as possible for any given problem. See if you can turn a problem into a *project* (a plan of action) or a *promise* to change some aspect of your life. Shifting the emphasis of your conversation from problems to solutions can raise your sense of possibility and unleash the master learner within you.

In the following space, describe three problems that could interfere with your success as a student. The problems can be related to courses, teachers, personal relationships, finances, or anything else that might get in the way of your success.

My problem is that . . .

My problem is that . . .

My problem is that . . .

Next, brainstorm at least five possible solutions to each of those problems. Ten solutions would be even better. (You can continue brainstorming on a separate piece of paper or on a computer.) You might find it hard to come up with that many ideas. That's OK. Stick with it. Stay in the inquiry, give yourself time, and ask other people for ideas.

I can solve my problem by . . .

I can solve my problem by . . .

I can solve my problem by . . .

Love Your Problems
(and Experience Your Barriers)

We all have problems and barriers that block our progress or prevent us from moving into new areas. Often, the way we respond to our problems places limitations on what we can be, do, and have.

Problems often work like barriers. When we bump up against one of our problems, we usually turn away and start walking along a different path. All of a sudden—bump!—we've struck another barrier. And we turn away again.

As we continue to bump into problems and turn away from them, our lives stay inside the same old boundaries. Inside these boundaries, we are unlikely to have new adventures. We are unlikely to keep learning.

If we respond to problems by loving them instead of resisting them, we can expand the boundaries in which we live our lives.

The word *love* might sound like an overstatement. In this Power Process, the word means to unconditionally accept the fact that your problems exist. The more we deny or resist a problem, the stronger it seems to become. When we accept the fact that we have a problem, we can find effective ways to deal with it.

Suppose one of your barriers is being afraid of speaking in front of a group. You could get up in front of the group and pretend that you're not afraid. Or you could tell yourself, "I'm not going to be scared," and then try to keep your knees from knocking. Generally, these strategies don't work.

A more effective approach is to love your fear. Go to the front of the room, look out into the audience, and say to yourself, "I am scared. I notice that my knees are shaking and my mouth feels dry, and I'm having a rush of thoughts about what might happen if I say the

wrong thing. Yup, I'm scared, and I'm not going to fight it. I'm going to give this speech anyway."

The beauty of this Power Process is that you continue to take action— giving your speech, for example—no matter what you feel. You walk right up to the barrier and then *through* it. You might even find that if you totally accept and experience a barrier, such as fear, it shrinks or disappears. Even if that does not happen right away, you still open up to new experiences and gain new chances to learn.

Loving a problem does not need to stop us from solving it. In fact, fully accepting and admitting a problem usually helps us take effective action— which can free us of the problem once and for all.

 Discover more ways to love your problems online.

Career Application

After declaring a major in hospitality and tourism management, Anne Nelson was lucky enough to get an internship in a large theme park just a few miles down the road from her career school. Her first assignment was to "shadow" a concierge named Juan at a five-star hotel near the park's main entrance.

Juan greeted Anne with a firm handshake and wide smile. "Welcome to my world," he said. "I've been in this business for 30 years, and every day on the job is different than the one before. As a concierge, you are expected to do the impossible—everything from hailing a cab to finding an aromatherapist. My goal is to honor the wishes of every hotel guest, even the people with really strange requests."

Anne was stunned by Juan's range of knowledge. He effortlessly recalled the names of restaurants, spas, nightclubs, and limousine services within a 25-mile range of the hotel. In addition, he could refer guests to a particular massage therapist, server, chef, bartender, or driver at those places.

"When you get there," he often told guests with a wink, "tell them that Juan sent you."

"You must have a long list of local businesses and contact people stashed away somewhere," Anne said to Juan. "Do you keep that on paper, or do you use an iPhone or Blackberry or something like that?"

"None of the above," Juan replied. "When I first started, I wrote notes on hotel stationery, napkins, or whatever else I could find. But before long I chose to just keep a lot of information on the tip of my tongue. And, anyway, my thumbs are too big for those tiny phones! Most of what I know is stored up here," Juan said, pointing to his forehead.

Andersen Ross/Getty

"Say," Juan added, "there's a big staff at this hotel. Since it's your first day, I'd like you to meet everybody. Let's start with the 10 people at the front desk."

Anne smiled but felt a wave of panic. *How am I ever going to remember everyone's name,* she said to herself, *let alone recall even 1 percent of everything else that Juan knows?*

Reflecting on this scenario

List two or three strategies from this chapter that would be useful to Anne in this situation. In a sentence or two, describe specifically how she could use each strategy.

_____

_____

_____

_____

_____

_____

_____

_____

_____

_____

_____

_____

_____

_____

_____

_____

_____

_____

_____

_____

_____

_____

_____

Name _____   Date ____/____/____

1. In the article about the memory jungle, the meadow:
   (a) Is a place that every animal (thought or perception) must pass through.
   (b) Represents short-term memory.
   (c) Represents the idea that short-term memory has a limited capacity.
   (d) All of the above.

2. Explain the purpose of graphic organizers and give two examples of them.

3. Give two examples of ways in which you can organize a long list of items.

4. Define *acronym,* and give an example of one.

5. Memorization on a deep level can take place if you:
   (a) Repeat the idea.
   (b) Repeat the idea.
   (c) Repeat the idea.
   (d) All of the above.

6. Mnemonic devices are the most efficient ways to memorize facts and ideas. True or false? Explain your answer.

7. Briefly describe at least three memory techniques other than mnemonics.

8. List two techniques that can be used to remember the names of three specific people you've recently met.

9. Briefly define the word *love* as it is used in the Power Process: "Love Your Problems (and Experience Your Barriers)."

10. According to the text, "One powerful way to enhance your memory is to make friends with your amygdala." Briefly explain the meaning of this sentence.

Focus on Transferable Skills

The Discovery Wheel in Chapter 1: "First Steps" includes a section labeled "Memory." For the next 10 to 15 minutes, go beyond your initial responses to that exercise. Take a detailed snapshot of your transferable skills related to memory. Then focus on a skill that you'd like to develop next.

You might want to prepare for this exercise by reviewing the articles "Jumpstart Your Education with Transferable Skills" on page 58 and "101 Transferable Skills" on page 60.

GENERAL MEMORY SKILLS

Memory techniques that I already use include . . .

If someone asked me to rate the effectiveness of these techniques, I would say that . . .

A new memory technique that I would like to experiment with is . . .

REMEMBERING NAMES

The last time that I was introduced to someone, I discovered that my skill in remembering that person's name was . . .

A high level of skill in remembering names could help me to . . .

NEXT ACTION

I'll know that I've reached a new level of mastery in remembering ideas and information when . . .

To reach that level of mastery, the most important thing I can do next is to . . .

Master Student PROFILE

Scott Heiferman
. . . is willing to change

I grew up with four siblings who were 12 to 17 years older, so I was exposed early to the fields they were interested in and the diversity influenced me. When I was a preteen, I programmed an Apple II computer to manage the inventory for my parents' paint store.

I was 16 when my mother died, and I realized that life is short. It motivated me to take risks and have fun.

I studied engineering at the University of Iowa, but I wasn't good enough in math to focus solely on engineering, so I got a business degree. I wasn't much interested in the business classes, but I saw business as a means to bring innovation to a large number of people. . . .

During senior year, I had two job offers, one in Silicon Valley and one at Sony in Montvale, N.J. When I looked at a map, Montvale seemed as if it was practically New York City, so I chose the job there. But Montvale isn't New York City and I lasted less than a year there.

I moved to Queens and in 1995 started an online ad agency called i-traffic, which was bought by Agency.com in 1999.

I was 27, with a staff of more than 100, when Agency.com bought the company, and I was totally over my head managing a large operation. I left the company in 2000. I was so sick of working with lawyers and accountants and investment bankers that I worked the counter at a McDonald's in Manhattan for a couple of weeks.

The attacks on Sept. 11 got me thinking and I came up with 30 ideas for my next project. I narrowed them to two.

One, which I developed with a co-founder, was a company called Fotolog, now a social network that is big in South America. The other was Meetup, a way for people to self-organize locally. I pulled a team together and we started Meetup.com in 2002.

A Meetup is about the simple idea of using the Internet to get people off the Internet. People feel a need to commiserate or get together and talk about what's important to them.

When we were designing the site, we were wrong about almost everything we thought people would want to use it for. I thought it would be a niche lifestyle venture, perhaps for fan clubs. I had no idea that people would form new types of P.T.A.'s, chambers of commerce or health support groups. And we weren't thinking that anyone would want to meet about politics, but there are thousands of these Meetups.

People have organized more than 200,000 monthly Meetups in more than 100 countries. There's nothing more powerful than a community coming together around a purpose. We spend increasingly more time in front of screens. We're more connected technologically, but we're less connected physically.

Meetup earns most of its revenue from the small monthly fee charged to organizers, 1 percent of our users. There are 60 of us in our Manhattan office, and we had our first profitable month in July.

Critics have predicted our death three times. If no one is predicting your company's death, then you're not taking enough risks in what you're doing.

In 2008, I married Emily Krasnor, a human-rights professional. In a few years, we hope to move to a developing country, perhaps in Africa. She'll continue her human-rights work while I will help expand Meetup's operations around the world.

As told to Patricia R. Olsen.

Scott Heiferman, "The Pursuit of Community," *New York Times,* September 5, 2009, http://www.nytimes.com/2009/09/06/jobs/06boss.html?emc=eta1.

Scott J. Ferrell/Congressional Quarterly/Getty Images

Founder and CEO of Meetup, a Web site for organizing local groups

Learn more about Scott Heiferman and other master students at the Master Student Hall of Fame.

5 Reading

Master Student Map

as you read, ask yourself

what if . . .

I could finish my reading with time to spare, easily recall the key points, and put the ideas I read about into action?

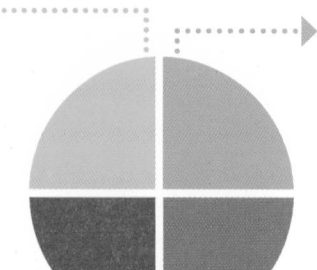

why this chapter matters . . .

Success in the workplace and in higher education requires extensive reading.

what is included . . .

how you can use this chapter . . .

- Analyze what effective readers do and experiment with new techniques.
- Increase your vocabulary and adjust your reading speed for different types of material.
- Comprehend difficult content with more ease.

MASTER EMPLOYEE in *action*

College gave me the tools to understand the technical data involved in maps and scientific reports, but in my job, it isn't enough to simply understand the technical aspects. I also have to be able to translate this data into a format that a layperson can understand. This means that I have to be able to read my own writing from the perspective of someone who doesn't necessarily have my technical background. —**MONICA EDMONDS, HYDROLOGIST**

Photo courtesy of Monica Edmonds

Muscle Reading

PICTURE YOURSELF SITTING at a desk with a book in your hands. Your eyes are open, and it looks as if you're reading. Suddenly your head jerks up. You blink. You realize your eyes have been scanning the page for 10 minutes, and you can't remember a single thing you have read.

Or picture this: You've had a hard day. You were up at 6 a.m. to get the kids ready for school. A coworker called in sick, and you missed your lunch trying to do his job as well as your own. You picked up the kids, then had to shop for dinner. Dinner was late, of course, and the kids were grumpy.

Finally, you get to your books at 8 p.m. You begin a reading assignment on something called "the equity method of accounting for common stock investments."

"I am preparing for the future," you tell yourself, as you plod through two paragraphs and begin the third.

Suddenly, everything in the room looks different. Your head is resting on your elbow, which is resting on the equity method of accounting. The clock reads 11:00 p.m. Say good-bye to three hours.

Sometimes the only difference between a sleeping pill and a textbook is that the textbook doesn't have a warning on the label about operating heavy machinery.

Muscle Reading—the subject of this chapter—is a way to avoid mental mini-vacations and reduce the number of unscheduled naps during study time, even after a hard day.

The abilities to focus attention on reading, locate main ideas, and find relevant details are transferable skills that you can develop through Muscle Reading. And they apply to all kinds of reading beyond textbooks. Use Muscle Reading to get what you want from work-related reading materials as well.

Muscle Reading is a way to decrease your difficulties and struggles by increasing your energy and skills. Once you learn this system, you can actually spend less time on your reading and get more out of it.

This is not to say that Muscle Reading will make your education a breeze. Learning to use Muscle Reading can take some effort. In fact, skilled readers enter into a dialogue with an author. They ask questions of a text,

and they demand answers. They reflect on what they read and look for applications. Effective reading is an active, energy-consuming, sit-on-the-edge-of-your-seat business. That's why this strategy is called Muscle Reading. ✴

journal entry 11

Discovery/Intention Statement

Discover what you want from this chapter

Recall a time when you encountered problems with reading, such as words you didn't understand or paragraphs you paused to reread more than once. Sum up the experience and how you felt about it by completing the following statement.

I discovered that I . . .

_____

_____

_____

_____

Now list three to five specific reading skills you want to gain from this chapter.

I intend to . . .

_____

_____

_____

_____

_____

How Muscle Reading works

© Masterfile Royalty Free

MUSCLE READING IS a three-phase technique you can use to extract the ideas and information you want.

Phase 1 includes steps to take *before* you read.

Phase 2 includes steps to take *while* you read.

Phase 3 includes steps to take *after* you read.

Each phase has three steps.

> **PHASE ONE:**
> **Before you read**
> Step 1: **Preview**
> Step 2: **Outline**
> Step 3: **Question**
>
> **PHASE TWO:**
> **While you read**
> Step 4: **Read**
> Step 5: **Underline**
> Step 6: **Answer**
>
> **PHASE THREE:**
> **After you read**
> Step 7: **Recite**
> Step 8: **Review**
> Step 9: **Review again**

To assist your recall of Muscle Reading strategies, memorize three short sentences:

$P_{ry} O_{ut} Q_{uestions.}$

$R_{oot} U_p A_{nswers.}$

$R_{ecite,} R_{eview, and} R_{eview again.}$

These three sentences correspond to the three phases of the Muscle Reading technique. Each sentence is an acrostic: The first letter of each word stands for one of the nine steps previously listed.

Take a moment to invent images for each of those sentences.

For *Phase 1,* visualize or feel yourself prying out questions from a text. These questions are ones you want answered based on a brief survey of the assignment. Make a mental picture of yourself scanning the material, spotting a question, and reaching into the text to pry it out. Hear yourself saying, "I've got it. Here's my question."

Then for *Phase 2,* get your muscles involved. Feel the tips of your fingers digging into the text as you root up the answers to your questions.

Finally, you enter *Phase 3.* Hear your voice reciting what you have learned. Listen to yourself making a speech or singing a song about the material as you review it.

To jog your memory, write the first letters of the Muscle Reading acrostic in a margin or at the top of your notes. Then check off the steps you intend to follow. Alternatively, you can write the Muscle Reading steps on 3 x 5 cards and then use them for bookmarks.

Muscle Reading might take a little time to learn. At first you might feel it's slowing you down. That's natural when you're gaining a new skill. Mastery comes with time and practice.

PHASE 1

Before *you* read.

Preview

Outline

Question

© Masterfile Royalty Free

Step 1: Preview

Before you start reading, preview the entire assignment. You don't have to memorize what you preview to get value from this step. Previewing sets the stage for incoming information by warming up a space in your mental storage area.

If you are starting a new book, look over the table of contents and flip through the text page by page. If you're going to read one chapter, flip through the pages of that chapter. Even if your assignment is merely a few pages in a book, you can benefit from a brief preview of the table of contents.

Keep the preview short. If the entire reading assignment will take less than an hour, your preview might take five minutes. Previewing is also a way to get yourself started when an assignment looks too big to handle. It is an easy way to step into the material.

Keep an eye out for summary statements. Many textbooks have summaries in the introduction or at the end of each chapter. If the assignment is long or complex, read the summary first.

Read all chapter headings and subheadings. Like the headlines in a newspaper, these headings are usually printed in large, bold type. Often headings are brief summaries in themselves.

When previewing, seek out familiar concepts, facts, or ideas. These items can help increase comprehension by linking new information to previously learned material. Also look for ideas that spark your imagination or curiosity. Inspect drawings, diagrams, charts, tables, graphs, and photographs. Imagine what kinds of questions will show up on a test.

Previewing helps to clarify your purpose for reading. Ask yourself what you will do with this material and how it can relate to your long-term goals. Will you be reading just to get the main points? Key supporting details? Additional details? All of the above? Your answers will guide what you do with each step that follows.

Step 2: Outline

With complex material, take time to understand the structure of what you are about to read. Outlining actively organizes your thoughts about the assignment and can help make complex information easier to understand.

If your textbook provides chapter outlines, spend some time studying them. When an outline is not provided, sketch a brief one in the margin of your book or at the beginning of your notes on a separate sheet of paper. Later, as you read and take notes, you can add to your outline.

Headings in the text can serve as major and minor entries in your outline. For example, the heading for this article is "Phase 1: Before You Read," and the subheadings list the three steps in this phase. When you outline, feel free to rewrite headings so that they are more meaningful to you.

The amount of time you spend on this outlining step will vary. For some assignments, a 10-second mental outline is all you might need. For other assignments (fiction and poetry, for example), you can skip this step altogether.

Step 3: Question

Before you begin a careful reading, determine what you want from the assignment. Then write down a list of questions, including any questions that resulted from your preview of the materials.

Another useful technique is to turn chapter headings and subheadings into questions. For example, if a heading is "Transference and Suggestion," you can ask yourself, "What are *transference* and *suggestion*? How does *transference* relate to *suggestion*?" Make up a quiz as if you were teaching this subject to your classmates.

If there are no headings, look for key sentences and turn them into questions. These sentences usually show up at the beginnings or ends of paragraphs and sections.

Have fun with this technique. Make the questions playful or creative. You don't need to answer every question that you ask. The purpose of making up questions is to get your brain involved in the assignment. Take your unanswered questions to class, where they can be springboards for class discussion.

Demand your money's worth from your textbook. If you do not understand a concept, write specific questions about it. The more detailed your questions, the more powerful this technique becomes.

 Find examples of Phase 1 strategies online.

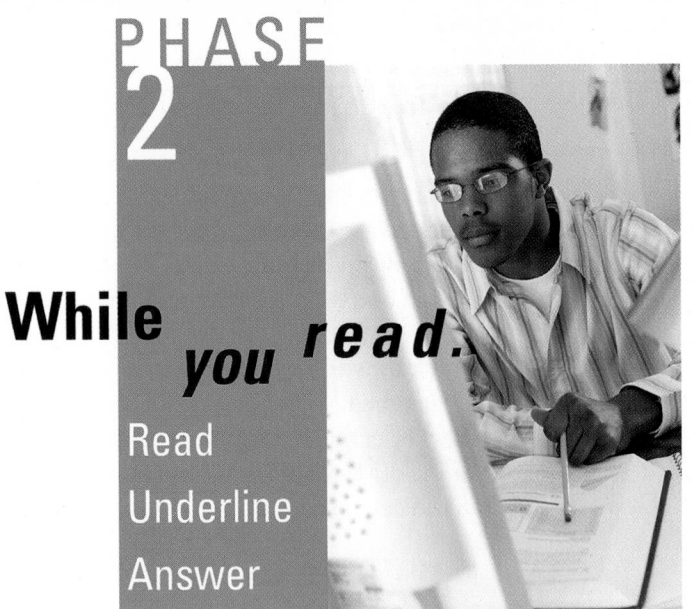

While you read.

Read
Underline
Answer

© Masterfile Royalty Free

Step 4: Read

Before you dive into the first paragraph, take a few moments to reflect on what you already know about this subject. Do so even if you think you know nothing. This technique prepares your brain to accept the information that follows.

As you read, be conscious of where you are and what you are doing. Use the Power Process: "Be Here Now" in Chapter 3: "Time." When you notice your attention wandering, gently bring it back to the present moment.

One way to stay focused is to avoid marathon reading sessions. Schedule breaks, and set a reasonable goal for the entire session. Then reward yourself with an enjoyable activity for 5 or 10 minutes every hour or two.

For difficult reading, set more limited goals. Read for a half-hour and then take a break. Most students find that shorter periods of reading distributed throughout the day and week can be more effective than long sessions.

You can also use the following four techniques to stay focused as you read.

First, visualize the material. Form mental pictures of the concepts as they are presented. If you read that a voucher system can help control cash disbursements, picture a voucher handing out dollar bills. Using visual imagery in this way can help deepen your understanding of the text while allowing information to be transferred into your long-term memory.

Second, read the material out loud, especially if it is complicated. Some of us remember better and understand more quickly when we hear an idea.

Third, get a "feel" for the subject. For example, let's say you are reading about a microorganism—a

paramecium—in your biology text. Imagine what it would feel like to run your finger around the long, cigar-shaped body of the organism. Imagine feeling the large fold of its gullet on one side and the tickle of the hairy little cilia as they wiggle in your hand.

Fourth, remember that a goal of your reading is to answer the questions you listed during Phase 1. After you've identified the key questions, predict how the author will answer them. Then read to find out if your predictions were accurate.

A final note: It's easy to fool yourself about reading. Just having an open book in your hand and moving your eyes across a page doesn't mean you are reading effectively. Reading textbooks takes energy, even if you do it while sitting down.

If you do an informal study of chief executive officers, you'll find some who wear out the front of their chairs first. Approach your reading assignment as a company president would. Sit up. Keep your spine straight. Use the edge of your chair. And avoid reading in bed—except for fun.

Step 5: Underline

Deface your books. Have fun writing in them. Indulge yourself as you never could with your grade school books.

The purpose of making marks in a text is to call out important concepts or information that you will need to review later. Be aware, though, that underlining a text with a pen can make underlined sections—the important parts—harder to read. As an alternative, many students underline in pencil or use colored highlighters to flag keywords and sentences. Using a highlighter to mark key information can save lots of time when you are studying for tests.

Underlining offers a secondary benefit. When you read with a highlighter, pen, or pencil in your hand, you involve your kinesthetic senses of touch and motion. Being physical with your books can help build strong neural pathways in your memory.

Avoid underlining too soon. Sometimes, underlining after you read each paragraph works best. At other times, you may want to wait until you complete a chapter or section to make sure you know the key points. Then mark up the text.

Underline sparingly—usually less than 10 percent of the text. If you mark up too much on a page, you defeat the purpose—to flag the most important material for review.

In addition to underlining, you can mark up a text in the following ways:

- Place an asterisk (*) or an exclamation point (!) in the margin next to an especially important sentence or term.

- Circle key terms and words to look up later in a dictionary.

- Write short definitions of key terms in the margin.

- Write a *Q* in the margin to highlight possible test questions, passages you don't understand, and questions to ask in class.

- Write personal comments in the margin—points of agreement or disagreement with the author.

- Write mini-indexes in the margin—that is, the numbers of other pages in the book where the same topic is discussed.

- Write summaries by listing the main points or key events covered in a chapter.

- Rewrite chapter titles, headings, and subheadings so that they're more meaningful to you.

- Draw diagrams, pictures, tables, or maps that translate text into visual terms.

- Number each step in a list or series of related points.

Step 6: Answer

As you read, seek out the answers to your questions and write them down. Fill in your outline. Jot down new questions, and note when you don't find the answers you are looking for. Use these notes to ask questions in class, or see your instructor personally.

When you read, create an image of yourself as a person in search of the answers. You are a detective, watching for every clue, sitting erect in your straight-back chair, demanding that your textbook give you what you want—the answers.

 Find examples of Phase 2 strategies online.

Five smart ways to highlight a text

Excessive highlighting leads to wasted time during reviews and can also spoil the appearance of your books. Get the most out of all that money you pay for books. Highlight in an efficient way that leaves texts readable for years to come.

Read carefully first Read an entire paragraph, section, or chapter at least once before you begin highlighting. Don't be in a hurry to mark up your book.

Make choices up front about what to highlight Perhaps you can accomplish your purposes by highlighting only certain chapters or sections of a text. Look for passages that directly answer the questions you posed during Step 3 of Muscle Reading. Within these passages, highlight individual words, phrases, or sentences rather than whole paragraphs.

Recite first You might want to apply Step 7 of Muscle Reading before you highlight. Recite first; then go back and highlight. You'll probably highlight more selectively.

Underline, then highlight Underline key passages lightly in pencil. Then close your text and come back to it later. Perhaps you can highlight less than you underlined and still capture the key points.

Use highlighting to monitor your comprehension Stop reading periodically, and look back over the sentences you've highlighted. See if you are making accurate distinctions between main points and supporting material. Highlighting too much—more than 10 percent of the text—can be a sign that you're not making this distinction and that you don't fully understand what you're reading. See the article "When reading is tough" later in this chapter for suggestions that can help.

 Find an example of smart highlighting online.

PHASE 3

After *you read.*

Recite

Review

Review again

© Masterfile Royalty Free

Step 7: Recite

Talk to yourself about what you've read. Or talk to someone else. When you finish a reading assignment, make a speech about it.

One way to get yourself to recite is to look at each underlined point. Note what you marked; then put the book down and start talking out loud. Explain as much as you can about that particular point.

To make this technique more effective, do it in front of a mirror. It might seem silly, but the benefits can be enormous. Reap them at exam time.

Classmates are even better than mirrors. Form a group, and practice teaching one another what you have read. One of the best ways to learn anything is to teach it to someone else.

In addition, talk about your reading whenever you can. Tell friends and family members what you're learning from your textbooks.

Step 8: Review

Plan to do your first complete review within 24 hours of reading the material. Sound the trumpets! This point is critical: A review within 24 hours moves information from your short-term memory to your long-term memory.

Review within one day. If you read it on Wednesday, review it on Thursday. During this review, look over your notes and clear up anything you don't understand. Recite some of the main points again.

This review can be short. You might spend as little as 15 minutes reviewing a difficult two-hour reading assignment. Investing that time now can save you hours later when studying for exams.

Step 9: Review again

The final step in Muscle Reading is the weekly or monthly review. This step can be very short—perhaps only four or five minutes per assignment. Simply go over your notes. Read the highlighted parts of your text. Recite one or two of the more complicated points.

The purpose of these reviews is to keep the neural pathways to the information open and to make them more distinct. That way, the information can be easier to recall. You can accomplish these short reviews anytime, anywhere, if you are prepared.

Conduct a five-minute review while you are waiting for a bus to arrive, your socks to dry, or the water to boil. You can use 3 x 5 cards as a handy review tool. Write ideas, formulas, concepts, and facts on cards, and carry them with you. These short review periods can be effortless and fun.

Sometimes longer review periods are appropriate. For example, if you found an assignment difficult, consider rereading it. Start over, as if you had never seen the material before. Sometimes a second reading will provide you with surprising insights.

 Find examples of Phase 3 strategies online.

Muscle Reading—a leaner approach

Keep in mind that Muscle Reading is an overall approach, not a rigid, step-by-step procedure. Here's a shorter variation that students have found helpful. Practice it with any chapter in this book:

• ***Preview and question.*** Flip through the pages, looking at anything that catches your eye—headings, subheadings, illustrations, photographs. Turn the title of each article into a question. For example, "How Muscle Reading Works" can become "How Does Muscle Reading Work?" List your questions on a separate sheet of paper, or write each question on a 3 x 5 card.

• ***Read to answer your questions.*** Read each article. Then go back over the text and underline or highlight answers to the appropriate questions on your list.

• ***Recite and review.*** When you're done with the chapter, close the book. Recite by reading each question—and answering it—out loud. Review the chapter by looking up the answers to your questions. (It's easy—they're already highlighted.) Review again by quizzing yourself one more time with your list of questions.

READING

5

When reading is tough

© Graham Bell/Corbis

Read it again. Make several passes through any reading material. During a preview, just scan the text to look for keywords and highlighted material. Next, skim the entire chapter or article again, spending a little more time and taking in more than you did during your preview. Finally, read in more depth, proceeding word by word through some or all of the text.

Difficult material—such as the technical writing in science texts—is often easier the second or third time around. Isolate difficult passages and read them again, slowly.

If you read an assignment and are completely lost, do not despair. Sleep on it. When you return to the assignment the next day, you'll see it with fresh eyes.[1]

Look for essential words. If you are stuck on a paragraph, mentally cross out all of the adjectives and adverbs, and then read the sentences without them. Find the important words—usually verbs and nouns.

Hold a mini-review. Pause briefly to summarize—either verbally or in writing—what you've read so far. Stop at the end of a paragraph and recite, in your own words, what you have just read. Jot down some notes, or create a short outline or summary.

Read it out loud. Make noise. Read a passage out loud several times, each time using a different inflection and emphasizing a different part of the sentence. Be creative. Imagine that you are the author talking.

Talk to your instructor. Admit when you are stuck, and make an appointment with your instructor. Most teachers welcome the opportunity to work individually with students. Be specific about your confusion. Specify the passage that you had the most trouble with.

Stand up. Changing positions periodically can combat fatigue. Experiment with standing as you read, especially if you get stuck on a tough passage and decide to read it out loud.

Skip around. Jump to the next section or to the end of a tough article or chapter. You might have lost the big picture. Simply seeing the next step, the next main point, or a summary might be all you need to put the details in context. Retrace the steps in a chain of ideas, and look for examples. Absorb facts and ideas in whatever order works for you.

Find a tutor. Many schools provide free tutoring services. If your school does not, other students who have completed the course can assist you.

Use another text. Find a similar text in the library. Sometimes a concept is easier to understand if it is expressed another way. Children's encyclopedias, for example, can provide useful overviews of baffling subjects.

Pretend you understand, and then explain it. We often understand more than we think we do. Pretend that the material is clear as a bell and explain it to another person, or even to yourself. Write down your explanation. You might be amazed by what you know.

Stop reading. When none of these suggestions work, do not despair. Admit your confusion and then take a break. Catch a movie, go for a walk, study another subject, or sleep on it. The concepts you've already absorbed might come together at a subconscious level as you move on to other activities. When you return to the reading material, see it with fresh eyes. ✳

5

READING

Building your vocabulary

HAVING A LARGE vocabulary makes reading more enjoyable and increases the range of materials you can explore. In addition, building your vocabulary gives you more options for self-expression when speaking or writing.

Strengthen your vocabulary by taking delight in words. Look up unfamiliar terms. Pay special attention to words that arouse your curiosity.

Students regularly use two kinds of paper dictionaries: the desk dictionary and the unabridged dictionary. A desk dictionary is an easy-to-handle abridged dictionary that you can use many times in the course of a day. Keep this book within easy reach (maybe in your lap) so you can look up unfamiliar words while reading. You can find a large, unabridged dictionary in a library or bookstore. It provides more complete information about words and definitions not included in your desk dictionary. Unabridged dictionaries also include synonyms, usage notes, and word histories.

Alternatively, you may prefer using one of several online dictionaries. To discover some options, search the Internet with the keywords *online dictionary*.

Construct a word stack. When you come across an unfamiliar word, write it down on a 3 x 5 card. Below the word, copy the sentence in which it was used, along with the page number. You can look up each word immediately, or you can accumulate a stack of these cards and look up the words later. Write the definition of each word on the back of the 3 x 5 card, adding diacritics—the marks that tell you how to pronounce it. A related option is to store your list of words and definitions in a computer file.

To expand your vocabulary and learn the history behind the words, take your stack of cards or list to an unabridged dictionary. As you find related words in the dictionary, add them to your stack. These cards become a portable study aid that you can review in your spare moments.

Learn—even when your dictionary is across town. When you are listening to a lecture and hear an unusual word, or when you are reading on the bus and encounter a word you don't know, you can still build your word stack. Pull out a 3 x 5 card and write down the word and its sentence. Later, you can look up the definition and write it on the back of the card.

Divide words into parts. Another suggestion for building your vocabulary is to divide an unfamiliar word into syllables and look for familiar parts. This strategy works well if you make it a point to learn common prefixes (beginning syllables) and suffixes (ending syllables). For example, the suffix *-tude* usually refers to a condition or state of being. Knowing this makes it easier to conclude that *habitude* refers to a usual way of doing something and that *similitude* means being similar or having a quality of resemblance.

Infer the meaning of words from their context. You can often deduce the meaning of an unfamiliar word simply by paying attention to its context—the surrounding words, phrases, sentences, paragraphs, or images. Later, you can confirm your deduction by consulting a dictionary.

Practice looking for context clues such as these:

- *Definitions.* A keyword might be defined right in the text. Look for phrases such as *defined as* or *in other words.*

- *Examples.* Authors often provide examples to clarify a word meaning. If the word is not explicitly defined, then study the examples. They're often preceded by the phrases *for example, for instance,* or *such as.*

- *Lists.* When a word is listed in a series, pay attention to the other items in the series. They might define the unfamiliar word through association.

- *Comparisons.* You might find a new word surrounded by synonyms—words with a similar meaning. Look for synonyms after words such as *like* and *as.*

- *Contrasts.* A writer might juxtapose a word with its antonym. Look for phrases such as *on the contrary* and *on the other hand.* ✳

Reading *fast*

One way to read faster is to read faster. This idea might sound like double-talk, but it is a serious suggestion. The fact is, you can probably read faster simply by making a conscious effort to do so.

EXPERIMENT WITH THE "just do it" method right now. Read the rest of this article as fast as you can. After you finish, come back and reread the same paragraphs at your usual rate. Note how much you remember from your first sprint through the text. Build on that success by experimenting with the following guidelines.

Set a time limit. When you read, use a clock or a digital watch with a built-in stopwatch feature to time yourself. You are not aiming to set speed records, so be realistic. For example, set a goal to read two or three sections of a chapter in an hour, using all of the Muscle Reading steps. If that works, set a goal of 50 minutes for reading the same number of sections. Test your limits. The idea is to give yourself a gentle push, increasing your reading speed without sacrificing comprehension.

Move your eyes faster. When we read, our eyes leap across the page in short bursts called *saccades* (pronounced *să-käds*). A saccade is also a sharp jerk on the reins of a horse—a violent pull to stop the animal quickly. Our eyes stop like that, too, in pauses called *fixations*.

Although we experience the illusion of continuously scanning each line, our eyes actually take in groups of words, usually about three at a time. For more than 90 percent of reading time, our eyes are at a dead stop in those fixations.

One way to decrease saccades is to follow your finger as you read. The faster your finger moves, the faster your eyes move. You can also use a pen, pencil, or 3 x 5 card as a guide.

Your eyes can move faster if they take in more words with each burst—for example, six instead of three. To practice taking in more words between fixations, find a newspaper with narrow columns. Then read down one column at a time, and fixate only once per line.

In addition to using these techniques, simply make a conscious effort to fixate less. You might feel a little uncomfortable at first. That's normal. Just practice often, for short periods of time.

Notice and release ineffective habits. Our eyes make regressions; that is, they back up and reread words. You can reduce regressions by paying attention to them. Awareness helps you regress less frequently.

You can also increase your speed if you don't subvocalize—that is, if you don't mentally "hear" the words as you read them. To stop doing it, just be aware of it.

Stay flexible. When you're in a hurry, experiment by skimming the assignment instead of reading the whole thing. Also remember that speed isn't everything. Skillful readers vary their reading rate according to their purpose and the nature of the material. An advanced text in analytic geometry usually calls for a different reading rate than a comic book.

You also can use different reading rates on the same material. For example, you might first sprint through an assignment for the keywords and ideas, and then return to the difficult parts for a slower and more thorough reading. ✳

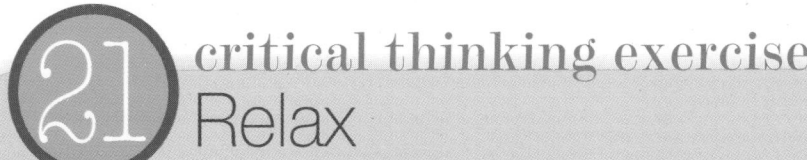

㉑ critical thinking exercise
Relax

Eyestrain can be the result of continuous stress. Take a break from your reading and use this exercise to release tension.

1. Sit on a chair or lie down, and take a few moments to breathe deeply.

2. Close your eyes, place your palms over them, and visualize a perfect field of black.

3. Continue to be aware of the blackness for two or three minutes while you breathe deeply.

4. Now remove your hands from your eyes, and open your eyes slowly.

5. Relax for a minute more; then continue reading.

Becoming an online learner

© Brand X Pictures/Alamy

IF YOU'RE RETURNING to school after a long break from the classroom, you might be surprised at all the online reading you're asked to do. You might go online to read textbooks and articles, do exercises, complete assignments, download ebooks, view PowerPoint presentations, use e-mail, join chat room sessions, and more. Use these online learning experiences to develop technology skills that you can apply to any job. Also remember that online learning gives you ways to continually update your skills and renew your career.

Of course, it's fine to print out online reading material. You can treat these printouts like conventional textbooks and apply the strategies for Muscle Reading. In addition, consider the following ways to succeed with online learning.

Set up your workspace

If possible, choose a single computer to use for your online learning. This allows you to access the same hardware, software, and set of files every time you study. If you will be using several locations for your online learning, then choose computers with similar configurations. Also plan to carry the files that you'll need on a USB drive or another portable storage device.

Next, consider the fact that you'll spend many hours at a screen and keyboard. To preserve your energy and alertness, set up a comfortable workspace:

- Use a keyboard that you can tilt to a comfortable angle for typing.
- Position the keyboard so that it allows your forearms to be in a straight line and parallel with the floor.
- Find a chair with an adjustable seat that supports your lower back.
- Get a lamp that illuminates your entire desk without glaring in the computer screen.
- Set up your desk so that you're not facing a window or looking directly into another light source.

Also develop some useful habits. Rest your eyes periodically by closing them for a minute or shifting your gaze away from the computer screen. Check your posture to make sure that your spine is erect and yet relaxed. In addition, get up once an hour to stretch or take a short walk.

Check out hardware and software requirements

If you're new to online learning and register for a course that depends on technology, contact the instructor before the first class. Ask about the kind of computer and software you'll be expected to use.

Install the software and learn it as soon as possible. This gives you time to troubleshoot your system and ask for help. If you do need help, get it well before the first assignment is due.

Your school might offer discounts on word processing, spreadsheet, presentation, and other common applications. Check at the bookstore. Also search your school's Web site for free workshops available about how to use those applications.

Ask about antivirus software. Your school might have a site license that makes this software free to students.

When an instructor hands out the course syllabus, read it carefully for information related to online learning, including:

- The instructor's e-mail address, phone number, and other contact information.
- The instructor's office hours, including times that she is available online.
- Policies for class attendance, including chat sessions and other online sessions.

- Requirements for submitting assignments online.
- Ways to check grades and get other feedback online.

Set up folders and files for easy reference

Before classes meet, create a separate folder for each class on your computer's hard drive. Give each folder a meaningful name, such as *biology-spring-2012*. Place all files related to a course in the appropriate folder. Doing this can save you from one of the main technology-related time-wasters—searching for lost files.

Also name individual files with care. Check with your instructor for guidelines. If you will submit several drafts of an assignment, ask how to name those files so that you can separate the current draft from earlier ones. For example, you might be asked to use a consistent file name along with a date, such as *assignment2-10/15/12*.

Avoid changing extensions that identify different types of files, such as .ppt for PowerPoint presentations or .pdf for files in the Adobe Reader portable document format. If you change extensions, you could have problems finding files later or sharing them with other users.

You'll probably send and receive e-mail as part of your online course work. Set up a separate folder in your e-mail software for each course. Also give each e-mail a brief and clear subject line. Again, check with your instructor about how to do this. You might be required to include the course title or another specific piece of information in each subject line.

If your course includes online chats or discussion boards, consider saving them. You can print them and review them like a textbook.

Get technical support

If you feel intimidated by technology, remember that there are living, breathing human beings who can help. These include instructors, librarians, and people who staff computer labs and help desks. Find the contact information for those services on your school's Web site. Computer dealers and manufacturers might offer similar resources, such as online help and toll-free numbers for customer service.

Murphy's Law of Computer Crashes states that technology tends to break down at the moment of greatest inconvenience. Prepare for it in advance:

- Identify several on-campus computer labs with the technology you need.
- Find a technology buddy in each of your classes—someone who can update you on assignments and contact the instructor if you lose Internet access.
- Set up a backup e-mail account in case your primary one goes offline.

- Get complete contact information—address and phone numbers—for your instructors in case you lose Internet access.
- Keep extra printer supplies—paper and toner or ink cartridges—always on hand.

Back up your files

Anyone with computer experience knows the sickening feeling that arises when a crucial file is accidentally deleted. A paper or another assignment that took hours to finish can simply disappear into the digital void.

To avoid this fate, use the save command often when working with files, or set up your software to save files every few minutes. Then make backup copies of your files every day. Copy those files onto a USB drive, external hard drive, or shared server space.

Get online early—and often

Verify your access to course-related Web sites. Ask your instructors for any usernames and passwords that you'll need. Then make sure that you can get online to each site and follow all the links.

Some students act as if they have all the time in the world to complete their online assignments. The temptation to procrastinate can be strongest with courses that take place mostly or totally online.

The reality is that completing online course work can take far more time that you expect. To prevent last-minute crunches, front-load your efforts. Log on to your online courses at a consistent time each day. Look for announcements relating to assignments, tests, chat sessions, and other online course events. Check discussion boards to read the latest postings.

Also download or print out online course materials as soon as they're posted on the class Web site. These materials might not be available later in the term.

Schedule yourself for success. Set aside regular blocks of time each week to complete online assignments. Give those scheduled sessions the same priority as regular classroom meetings. Let your roommates or family members know that you plan to be online during those times and "offline" for other activities.

In addition:

- Early in the term, create a detailed timeline with a due date for each assignment.
- Break big assignments into smaller steps and list a due date for each step.
- Check off those steps as you complete them.
- If you have any questions about an online assignment, e-mail questions immediately.
- If you want to meet with an instructor in person, request an appointment several days in advance.

Ask for feedback

To get the most from online learning, ask for regular feedback on papers, quizzes, tests, and other assignments. If your questions are too complex for an e-mail message, then schedule time for a phone call with your instructor. Otherwise, make a visit during office hours. Ask for help as soon as you have a question or need to solve a problem.

Connect with other students

Online learning can be isolating. It also can be a way to connect with other students and even find new friends. The difference lies in your approach.

Though online learning often includes audio and video files, much of your course-related communication will take place through good old-fashioned text. Classmates and instructors will get to know you largely through the content and tone of your writing.

- *Be conversational.* Writing teachers often ask you to express ideas in the fewest possible words. That is a sound guideline that you can temper occasionally during online communication. Stick to the point, but avoid being so brief that your message sounds clipped or blunt. Adding an occasional joke and emoticon such as :) is another way to lighten up.

- *Keep the tone positive.* When you enjoy a class activity or read a comment that you especially like, mention it and express your appreciation. If you're confused by or disagree with someone's comment, use "I"

Muscle Reading for ebooks

Today you can read ebooks on many platforms—computers, mobile phones, and dedicated devices such as the Amazon Kindle and Sony Reader. Muscle your way into this new medium by using features that are not available with printed books. Though ebook features vary, try the following with whatever device you use.

Check compatibility   Some ebooks can be viewed only with a certain type of ebook reader. Check with your instructor about which device to use.

Find navigation tools   To flip electronic pages, look for *previous* and *next* buttons or arrows on the right and left borders of each page. Many ebooks also offer a "go to page" feature that allows you to key in a specific page number.

For a bigger picture of the text, look for a table of contents that lists chapter headings and subheadings. Click on any of these headings to expand the text for that part of the book. Note that charts, illustrations, photos, tables, diagrams, and other visuals might be listed separately in the table of contents.

Search   Look for a search box that allows you to enter keywords. Then you can find all the places in the text where those words appear.

Customize page appearance   For a more readable text, adjust the font size or zoom in on a page.

Look for links to related information   Many ebook readers will supply a definition of any word in the text. All you need to do is highlight a word and click on it. Also find out if your ebook reader will connect you to Web sites related to the topic of your ebook.

Mark it up   Look for ways to electronically underline or highlight text. In addition, see if you can annotate the book by keying in your own notes tied to specific pages.

You might be able to tag each note with a keyword and then sort your notes into categories based on these words.

Print   See if you can connect your ebook device to a printer. You might find it easier to study difficult passages on paper. Note that some ebook publishers impose a limit on how much text you can print.

Sit back and listen   Some ebook readers will convert highlighted text into speech. Let your book read itself out loud.

Monitor battery life   Recharge the battery for your ebook device or laptop computer so that it has enough power to last throughout your work or school day. Seeing your screen go dark when you're in the middle of a paragraph could be a one-way ticket to frustration.

Generate notes automatically   Some ebooks will summarize any text that you highlight. Though these summaries are no substitute for your own written summaries, they can be useful starting points.

Consult the print version   Sometimes it's hard to beat a good old-fashioned book—especially when they include dense tables, complex illustrations, and large, color-coded charts. These features might not translate well to a small screen. Go to the library or bookstore to see if you can find those pages in a printed copy of your ebook.

Copy and paste   See if you can copy and paste highlighted text to a word processing file. This is a fast way to create summaries of a reading assignment and take notes while writing papers or creating presentations. To avoid plagiarism, put quotation marks around the text that you copy and paste. Also record the source for each copied passage.

messages to overcome confusion and resolve conflict; for example: "I'm confused by your response to my previous post. Could you please explain what you mean by. . .?" For more suggestions, see Chapter 9: "Communicating."

- *Review before sending or posting.* Remember that participants in online courses often lack the cues that come from hearing the tone of your voice or seeing your facial expressions. Before hitting the "send" button, consider how your instructor or virtual classmates might react to your message. Reword to avoid confusion.

- *Establish an online presence.* Contribute regularly to chat rooms and discussion threads. This keeps you engaged in the course. It also helps other people to get to know you.

When possible, make personal contact with at least one other student in each of your classes—especially those that involve lots of online course work. Meet with this person to share notes, quiz each other, edit papers, and do other cooperative learning tasks. This source of support can help you keep current with online work and promote your success. In addition, explore the option of creating a face-to-face study group for each online course.

Build online learning into any course

You can integrate information technology into daily study tasks, even for courses that do not meet online.

For example, you can turn any study group into an active online community. Experiment with e-mail, bulletin boards, chat rooms, and instant messaging software. Online applications such as Google Docs, Zoho Writer, and PBwiki allow any group member to create and edit documents. You could even create a Web site or Facebook page for your study group. Add a group calendar for scheduling meetings and links for uploading and downloading files. These tools can be lifesavers when your group finds it too difficult to meet in person.

Pull the plug on distractions

Some students are used to being online while watching television, listening to music, or sending text messages. When applied to online reading, these habits can reduce your learning and imperil your grades. To succeed with technology, turn off the television, quit online chat sessions, and turn down the music. Use the Power Process: "Be Here Now" on page 113 to stay in charge of your attention and the results you get from online learning. ✳

 Find out if you're prepared for online learning with the E-Learning Readiness Self-Assessment.

READING

5

Gaining information literacy

INFORMATION LITERACY allows you to research, write, create presentations, gain new knowledge, update your skills, and succeed as a "knowledge worker" in the twenty-first century. This is the intellectual equivalent of mountain climbing. You'll make observations, gather facts, trek into new intellectual territory, and ascend from one plateau of insight to another.

Information literacy means asking questions, finding sources of answers, determining the quality of those sources, collecting information, and reflecting on what you find to arrive at your own ideas. These are transferable skills that promote your success in any career.

List questions you want to answer. Information literacy starts with asking questions. The questions that you ask will guide your research—and greatly influence the quality of the answers that you get.

Begin with your main question. This is the one that gets to the heart of your paper, presentation, or personal interest.

To discover your main question, define your topic carefully. Say that you are interested in why many Internet-based businesses started up during the 1990s and eventually failed. This was a decade in which some "dot-com" companies got financial backing even though they had no clear products, services, or business plans.

So, your topic is *the failure of "dot-com" companies during the 1990s.* Now take this topic and turn it into a question: *What led to the failure of dot-com companies during the 1990s?* This is your main question.

Chances are that you can think of questions that relate to your main question. These are your *supporting questions.* Examples could include:

- What were some of the major dot-com companies during the 1990s?
- What products or services did these companies offer?
- What problems existed in the business plans for these companies?
- Did anyone see these problems?
- How did successful dot-com companies differ from those that failed?

Translate your questions into keywords. Print materials, Internet sources, and other online sources are catalogued in searchable databases. The art of searching them lies in choosing keywords to describe what you want to find.

You can take keywords directly from your main and supporting questions. For example, keywords from the previous list include *dot-com companies, 1990s,* and *failures.*

Search for sources of information. Next, enter combinations of your keywords into an online search engine such as Google.com, Yahoo.com, or Ask.com. Experiment with different combinations of keywords.

There's a simple way to determine the quality of your keywords: the number of relevant "hits" (search results) that you get. If you get many hits that seem unrelated to your topic, then use more specific keywords. If you get only a few hits, use more general keywords or a different search engine.

In addition, make a visit to a library. There are three benefits to doing this. First, much published material is still available only in printed form, and much of that printed material is stored in libraries.

Second, many libraries have access to special databases that are not available on the Internet.

Third, libraries give you access to a resource that goes beyond the pages of a book or a Web site—a librarian. Librarians are trained explorers who can guide your expedition into the information jungle. Asking a librarian for help can save you hours.

Librarians have different specialties. Start with a reference librarian. If the library has the material that you want, this person will find it. If not, he will direct you to another source.

Libraries—from the smallest one in your hometown to the Smithsonian in Washington, D.C.—consist of just three basic elements:

- *Catalogs*—online databases that list all of the library's accessible sources.
- *Collections*—materials, such as periodicals (magazines and newspapers), books, pamphlets, audio and video materials, and materials available from other collections via interlibrary loan.
- *Computer resources*—Internet access and specialized databases.

Before you start your next research project, take some time to investigate all three elements of your campus and community library. Sign up for a library orientation session or tour. Step into each room and ask what's available there.

Also find out whether the library houses any special collections. You might find one related to your major or another special interest.

Distinguish between types of sources. *Primary sources* are often the researcher's dream. These sources offer firsthand access to original work. Examples include personal journals, letters, e-mails, speeches, works of art, field observations, archeological digs, and other collections of data. You can also go directly to subject matter experts—another primary source—and ask them your questions directly.

Secondary sources explain, report about, and comment on primary sources. Examples are newspapers, trade magazines, scholarly journals, Web sites, and popular magazines such as *Newsweek* and *Rolling Stone*. Secondary sources are useful places to start your research by getting an overview of your topic. They might even give you all you need for informal research.

Tertiary sources include dictionaries, encyclopedias, handbooks, almanacs, atlases, and other reference works. (*Tertiary* means "third level.") These sources list, summarize, and index the other two kinds of sources.

Spotting the differences between the three types of sources can be tricky. Ask a librarian for help.

Evaluate your sources. Once you find materials with answers to your questions, inspect them with a critical eye. Allow sufficient time for this step. Scan all the sources to find the most useful ones, and read those several times. Do this in a place where you can write notes—not while you're riding a stationary bike or watching TV.

With print sources, give special attention to the preface, publication data, table of contents, bibliography, glossary, endnotes, and index. (Nonprint materials, including online documents, often include similar types of information.) Also scan any headings, subheadings, and summaries. If you have time, read a chapter or section. Then evaluate sources according to the following criteria:

Relevance. Find sources that directly answer your research questions. If you're in doubt about the relevance of a particular source, then ask yourself: Will this material help me achieve the purpose of my research and support my thesis?

Find what you want on the Internet

At one level, searching the Internet is simple. Just go online to a site such as Ask, Google, or Yahoo! Look for the search box, and enter a keyword or two to describe what you want to find. Then hit the enter key.

You might find exactly what you're looking for in this way. If you don't, then take your Internet searches to the next level:

Use specific keywords Entering *firefox* or *safari* will give you more focused results than entering *web browser*. *Reading strategies* or *note-taking strategies* will get more specific results than *study strategies*.

Use unique keywords Whenever possible, use proper names. Enter *Beatles* or *Radiohead* rather than *British rock bands*. If you're looking for nearby restaurants, enter *restaurant* and your zip code rather than the name of your city.

Start with fewer keywords rather than more Instead of *ways to develop your career plan,* just enter *career plan*. The extra words might lead to irrelevant results or narrow your search too much.

If you're looking for certain words in a certain order, use quotation marks *"Audacity of hope"* will return a list of pages with that exact phrase.

Search within a site If you're looking only for articles about college tuition from the *New York Times,* then add *new york times* or *nytimes.com* to the search box.

When you're not sure of a keyword, add a wild card character In most search engines, that character is the asterisk (*). If you're looking for the title of a film directed by Clint Eastwood and just can't remember the name, enter *clint eastwood directed* *.

Look for more search options The previous suggestions will keep you from drowning in a sea of useless search results. Many search engines also offer advanced search features and explain how to use them. Look for the word *advanced* or *more* on the site's home page, and click on the link.

Experiment with meta-search engines Meta-search engines combine results from several search engines. Examples include Dogpile and Clusty.

Create your own search engine Google allows you to customize your search engine. Go online to **www.google.com/coop/cse**.

Currentness. Notice the publication date of your source material. If your topic is time sensitive, set some guidelines about how current you want your sources to be.

Credibility. Scan the source for biographical information about the author. Look for education, training, and work experience that qualifies this person to publish on the topic. Also notice any possible sources of bias, such as political affiliations or funding sources that might color the author's point of view.

For ways to evaluate online sources, see "Think Critically about Information on the Internet" on page 231.

Reflect on your sources. Take notes on your sources using the suggestions in Chapter 6: "Notes." Allow time to digest your first impressions of the facts and ideas that you've gathered. Take a walk—outdoors, if possible—and ask yourself the following questions:

- What are the main points that the authors of these sources made?

- What are the authors' main areas of agreement and disagreement?

- If I could meet with these authors in person, what would I ask them?

- What personal experiences do I have with the topic of my research?

- If I were limited to only one 3 x 5 card to express my main thoughts on this topic, what would I write?

- If I could interview someone about this topic on a talk show, what would I say?

Asking these questions uses the work of others to get to the heart of an issue and stimulate your *own* thinking. It's amazing how many students go through higher education without doing this. Some even get an advanced degree even though they fail to get deeply acquainted with their own mind.

Discover the pleasures of solitary reflection, emerging insights, and sudden inspiration. A library furnished with plush chairs and wooden bookcases is a traditional setting for these experiences. Add computer technology and library skills to the mix, and you get an ideal environment for gaining information literacy.[2] ✳

English as a Second Language

If you grew up reading and speaking a language other than English and are new to the English language, you might fall under the category of an English as a Second Language (ESL) student or an English Language Learner (ELL). Experiment with the following suggestions to learn English with more success.

Build confidence by seeing mistakes as teachers. Many ESL/ELL students feel insecure about using English in social settings, including the classroom. Choosing not to speak, however, can delay your mastery of English and isolate you from other students.

As an alternative, make it your intention to speak up in class. List several questions beforehand, and plan to ask them. Also schedule a time to meet with your instructors during office hours to discuss any material that you find confusing. These strategies can help you build relationships while developing English skills.

In addition, start a conversation with at least one native speaker of English in each of your classes. For openers, ask about their favorite instructors or ideas for future courses to take.

Remember that the terms *English as a Second Language* and *English Language Learner* describe a difference—not a deficiency. The fact that you've entered a new culture and are mastering another language gives you a broader perspective than people who speak only one language. If you currently speak two or more languages, you've already demonstrated your ability to learn.

Analyze errors in using English. To learn from your errors, make a list of those that are most common for you. Next to the error, write a corrected version. Remember that native speakers of English also use this technique—for instance, by making lists of words they frequently misspell.

Learn by speaking and listening. You probably started your English studies by using textbooks. Writing and reading in English are important. Both can help you add to your English vocabulary and master grammar. To gain greater fluency and improve your pronunciation, also make it your goal to *hear* and *speak* English.

For example, listen to radio talk shows. Imitate the speaker's pronunciation by repeating phrases and sentences that you hear. During conversations, notice the facial expressions and gestures that accompany certain English words and phrases.

If you speak English with an accent, do not be concerned. Many people speak clear, accented English. Work on your accent only if you can't be easily understood.

Take advantage of opportunities to read and hear English at the same time. For instance, turn on English subtitles when watching a film on DVD. Also, check your library for books on tape or CD. Check out the printed book, and follow along as you listen.

Use computer resources. Some online dictionaries allow you to hear words pronounced. They include Answers.com (**www.answers.com**) and Merriam-Webster Online (**www.m-w.com**). Other resources include online book sites with a read-aloud feature. An example is Project Gutenberg (**www.gutenberg .org**; search on "Audio Books"). Speaks for Itself (**www.speaksforitself.com**) is a free download that allows you to hear text from Web sites read aloud.

Also, check general Web sites for ESL students. A popular one is Dave's ESL Café (**www.eslcafe.com**), which will lead you to others.

Celebrate your gains. Every time you analyze and correct an error in English, you make a small gain. Celebrate those gains. Taken together over time, they add up to major progress in mastering English as a Second Language. ✳

Reading with children underfoot

© Digital Vision/Picture Quest

IT IS POSSIBLE to have effective study time as well as quality time to spend with your children. The following suggestions come mostly from students who are also parents. The specific strategies you use will depend on your schedule and the ages of your children.

Attend to your children first. When you first come home from school, keep your books out of sight. Spend at least 10 minutes with your children before you settle in to study. Give them hugs, and ask about their day. Then explain that you have some work to do. Your children might reward you with 30 minutes of quiet time. A short time of full, focused attention from a parent can be more satisfying than longer periods of partial attention.

Of course, this suggestion won't work with the youngest children. If your children are infants or toddlers, schedule sessions of concentrated study for when they are asleep.

Use "pockets" of time. See if you can arrange study time at school before you come home. If you arrive at school 15 minutes earlier and stay 15 minutes later, you can squeeze in an extra half-hour of study time that day. Also look for opportunities to study between classes.

Before you shuttle children to soccer games or dance classes, throw a book in the car. While your children are warming up for the game or changing clothes, steal another 15 minutes to read.

Plan special activities for your child. Find a regular playmate for your child. Some children can pair off with close friends and safely retreat to their rooms for hours of private play. You can check on them occasionally and still get lots of reading done.

Another option is to take your children to a public playground. While they swing, slide, and dig in the sand, you can dig into your textbooks. Lots of physical activity will tire out your children in constructive ways. If they go to bed a little early, that's extra time for you to read.

After you set up appropriate activities for your children, don't attend to them every second, even if you're nearby as they play. Obviously, you want to break up fights, stop unsafe activity, and handle emergencies. Short of such incidents, though, you're free to read.

Create a special space for your child. Set aside one room or area of your home as a play space. Child-proof this space. The goal is to create a place where children can roam freely and play with minimal supervision. Consider allowing your child in this area *only* when you study. Your homework time then becomes your child's reward.

If you're cramped for space, just set aside some special toys for your child to play with during your study time. When you're sitting at your desk, your child might enjoy sitting at a small table and doing an "assignment." While she plays with stickers or flips through some children's books, you can review your notes.

Use television responsibly. Another option is to use television as a babysitter—when you can control the programming. Rent a videotape or DVD for your child to watch as you study. If you're concerned about your child becoming a couch potato, select educational programs that keep his mind active and engaged.

See if your child can use headphones while watching television. That way, the house stays quiet while you study.

Allow for interruptions. It's possible that you'll be interrupted even if you set up special activities for your child in advance. If so, schedule the kind of studying that can be interrupted. For instance, you could write out or review flash cards with key terms and definitions.

Save the tasks that require sustained attention for other times.

Plan study breaks with children. Another option is to spend 10 minutes with your children for every 50 minutes that you study. View this time not as an interruption but as a study break.

Alternatively, you can schedule time to be with your children when you've finished studying. Let your children in on the plan: "I'll be done reading at 7:30. That gives us a whole hour to play before you go to bed."

Many children love visible reminders that "their time" is approaching. An oven timer works well for this purpose. Set it for 15 minutes of quiet time. Follow that with five minutes of show-and-tell, storybooks, or another activity with your child. Then set the timer for another 15 minutes of studying, another break, and so on.

Develop a routine. Many young children love routines. They often feel more comfortable and secure when they know what to expect. You can use this characteristic to your benefit. One option is to develop a regular time for studying and let your child know this schedule: "I have to do my homework between 4 p.m. and 5 p.m. every day." Then enforce it.

Bargain with children. Reward them for respecting your schedule. In return for quiet time, give your child an extra allowance or a special treat. Children might enjoy gaining "credits" for this purpose. Each time they give you an hour of quiet time for studying, make an entry on a chart, put a star on their bulletin board, or give them a coupon. After they've accumulated a certain number of entries, stars, or coupons, they can cash them in for a big reward—a movie or a trip to the zoo.

Ask other adults for help. This suggestion for studying with children relates to a message repeated throughout the book: Enlist other people to help support your success. Getting help can be as simple as asking your spouse, partner, neighbor, or fellow student to take care of the children while you study. Offer to trade child care with a neighbor: You will take his kids and yours for two hours on Thursday night if he'll take them for two hours on Saturday morning. Some parents start block-wide babysitting co-ops based on the same idea.

Find community activities and services. Ask if your school provides a day care service. In some cases, these services are available to students at a reduced cost. Community agencies such as the YMCA might offer similar programs.

You can also find special events that appeal to children. Storytelling hour at the library is one example. While your child is being entertained and supervised, you can stay close by. Use the time in this quiet setting to read a chapter or review class notes.

Make it a game. Reading a chemistry textbook with a 3-year-old in the same room is not as preposterous as it sounds. The secret is to involve your child. For instance, use this time to recite. Make funny faces as you say the properties of the transition elements in the periodic table. Talk in a weird voice as you repeat Faraday's laws. Draw pictures and make up an exciting story about the process of titration.

Read out loud to your children, or use them as an audience for a speech. If you invent rhymes, poems, or songs to help you remember formulas or dates, teach them to your children. Be playful. Kids are attracted to energy and enthusiasm.

Whenever possible, involve family members in tasks related to reading. Older children can help you with research tasks—finding books at the library, looking up news articles, or even helping with typing.

When you can't read everything, just read something. Your objection to reading with children nearby may sound like this: "I just can't concentrate. There's no way I can get it all done while children are around."

That's OK. Even if you can't absorb an entire chapter while the kids are running past your desk, you can skim the chapter. Or you might only read the introduction and summary. When you can't get it *all* done, just get *something* done.

Caution: If you always read this way, your education might be compromised. Supplement this strategy with others so that you can get all of your reading done. ✳

 Discover more ways to study with children underfoot.

critical thinking exercise
22 Revisit your goals

One powerful way to achieve any goal is to periodically assess your progress in meeting it. This step is especially important with long-term goals—those that can take years to achieve.

When you did Critical Thinking Exercise 15: "Get Real with Your Goals" on page 96, you focused on one long-term goal and planned a detailed way to achieve it. This process involved setting mid-term and short-term goals that will lead to achieving your long-term goal. Take a minute to review that exercise and revisit the goals you set. Then complete the following steps.

1. Take your long-term goal from Critical Thinking Exercise 15 and rewrite it in the following space. If you can think of a more precise way to state it, feel free to change the wording.

_____

_____

_____

2. Next, check in with yourself. How do you feel about this goal? Does it still excite your interest and enthusiasm? On a scale of 1 to 10, how committed are you to achieving this goal? Write down your level of commitment in the following space.

_____

3. If your level of commitment is 5 or less, you might want to drop the goal and replace it with a new one. To set a new goal, just turn back to Critical Thinking Exercise 15 and do it again. Be sure to release any self-judgment about dropping your original long-term goal. Letting go of one goal creates space in your life to set and achieve a new one.

4. If you're committed to the goal you listed in Step 1 of this exercise, consider whether you're still on track to achieve it. Have you met any of the short-term goals related to this long-term goal? If so, list your completed goals here.

_____

_____

Before going on to the next step, take a minute to congratulate yourself and celebrate your success.

5. Finally, consider any adjustments you'd like to make to your plan. For example, write additional short-term or mid-term goals that will take you closer to your long-term goal. You can also cross out any goals that you no longer deem necessary. Make a copy of your current plan in the following space.
Long-term goal (to achieve within your lifetime):

_____

_____

Supporting mid-term goals (to achieve in one to five years):

_____

_____

_____

Supporting short-term goals (to achieve within the coming year):

_____

_____

_____

Notice Your Pictures and Let Them Go

One of the brain's primary jobs is to manufacture images. We use mental pictures to make predictions about the world, and we base much of our behavior on those predictions.

Pictures can sometimes get in our way. Take the student who plans to attend a school he hasn't visited. He chose this school for its strong curriculum and good academic standing, but his brain didn't stop there. In his mind, the campus has historic buildings with ivy-covered walls and tree-lined avenues. The professors, he imagines, will be as articulate as Barack Obama and as entertaining as Conan O'Brien. The cafeteria will be a cozy nook serving everything from delicate quiche to strong coffee. He will gather there with fellow students for hours of stimulating, intellectual conversation. The library will have every book, while the computer lab will boast the newest technology.

The school turns out to be four gray buildings situated downtown next to the bus station. The first class he attends is taught by an overweight, balding professor wearing a purple and orange bird-of-paradise tie. The cafeteria is a nondescript hall with machine-dispensed food, and the student's apartment is barely large enough to accommodate his roommate's tuba. This hypothetical student gets depressed. He begins to think about dropping out of school.

The problem with pictures is that they can prevent us from seeing what is really there. That is what happened to the student in this story. His pictures prevented him from noticing that his school is in the heart of a culturally vital city—close to theaters, museums, government offices, clubs, and all kinds of stores. The professor with the weird tie is not only an expert in his field but also a superior teacher. The school cafeteria is skimpy because it can't compete with the variety of inexpensive restaurants in the area.

Our pictures often lead to our being angry or disappointed. We set up expectations of events before they occur. Sometimes we don't even realize that we have these expectations. The next time you discover you are angry, disappointed, or frustrated, look to see which of your pictures aren't being fulfilled.

When you notice that pictures are getting in your way, in the most gentle manner possible, let your pictures go. Let them drift away like wisps of smoke picked up by a gentle wind.

Sometimes when we let go of old pictures, it's helpful to replace them with new, positive pictures. These new images can help you take a fresh perspective. The new pictures might not feel as comfortable and genuine as your old ones, but it's important to let those pictures go. No matter what picture is in your head, you can still be yourself.

 Learn more about this Power Process online.

Career Application

Sachin Aggarwal worked as a bank teller during the summers while he was in school. After earning an Associate in Science degree in Marketing, he was promoted and gained a new job title: personal banker. When bank customers want to open a new account or take out a car loan, Sachin is the first person they see.

PhotosIndia.com/Getty

His career plan is to stay at this job for two years and then transfer his credits to a college where he can earn a four-year degree. While working as a teller, Sachin gained a reputation as a quick study. When the bank installed a new computer system, he completed the online tutorials and stayed on top of the software updates. Within a few weeks, Sachin was training new tellers to use the system.

In addition, he often fielded questions from some of the bank's older employees who described themselves as "computer challenged." Sachin's most recent performance review acknowledged his patience and ability to adapt his explanations to people with various levels of computer experience.

Right now, Sachin's biggest challenge is job-related reading. He never anticipated the number of documents—both printed and online—that would cross his desk after he got promoted. His supervisor has asked him to read technical manuals for each of the bank's services and account plans. He's also taking a customer service course with a 400-page textbook. In addition, he gets about 10 e-mail messages each day, some of them several screens long.

Within the first week after his promotion, Sachin often asked himself, "Why am I being bombarded with all this material? Most of it doesn't seem relevant to my job." Even so, he decided to put these reactions on hold and just dig into his reading stack. He figures the best way to proceed is to start with any document at random and read it straight through before starting another one. Eventually, he hopes, he'll see a use for it all.

Reflecting on this scenario

List two or three strategies from this chapter that would be useful to Sachin in this situation. In a sentence or two, describe specifically how he could use each strategy.

_____

_____

_____

_____

_____

_____

_____

_____

_____

_____

_____

_____

_____

_____

Quiz

Name _____   Date ____/____/____

1. Name the acrostic that can help you remember the steps of Muscle Reading.

2. Define the term *information literacy*.

3. Give three examples of what to look for when previewing a reading assignment.

4. List three ways to evaluate sources of information.

5. In addition to underlining and highlighting, there are other ways to mark up a text. List three other techniques.

6. To remember what you read, wait at least 24 hours before doing a review. True or false? Explain your answer.

7. Explain at least three techniques you can use when reading is tough.

8. The Power Process in this chapter includes this sentence: "Our pictures often lead to our being angry or disappointed." Give an example from your own experience.

9. Ways to infer the meaning of a word from context include:
   a) Looking for definitions included in the text.
   b) Looking for examples of the word's meaning.
   c) Looking for synonyms of the word.
   d) Looking for antonyms of the word.
   e) All of the above.

10. List at least three techniques for increasing your reading speed.

Focus on Transferable Skills

The Discovery Wheel in Chapter 1: "First Steps" includes a section labeled "Reading." For the next 10 to 15 minutes, go beyond your initial responses to that exercise. Take a detailed snapshot of your transferable skills related to reading. Then focus on a skill that you'd like to develop next.

You might want to prepare for this exercise by reviewing the articles "Jumpstart Your Education with Transferable Skills" on page 58 and "101 Transferable Skills" on page 60.

BEFORE YOU READ

If someone asked me how well I keep up with my assigned reading, I would say that...

To get the most out of a long reading assignment, I start by...

WHILE YOU READ

To focus my attention while I read, I...

When I take notes on my reading, my usual method is to...

AFTER YOU READ

When it's important for me to remember what I read, I...

When I don't understand something that I've read, I overcome confusion by...

NEXT ACTION

To become a more effective reader, the most important skill I could develop next is...

To develop that skill, I intend to...

Master Student PROFILE

Bert and John Jacobs

. . . are positive

© John Rich Photography

Bert Jacobs (1965–) and John Jacobs (1968–), whose job titles are "chief executive optimist" and "chief creative optimist," started their business by selling T-shirts out of the back of a van. "Life is good" says the T-shirt, the hoodie, the baseball cap, and the onesie, to which one might reasonably respond in these days of doom and gloom: Really?

When Bert and John Jacobs launched their self-described optimistic apparel company out of a Boston apartment 15 years ago, we were smack in the middle of the go-go '90s and those three little words—part lifestyle, part mantra, part last ditch effort by a pair of struggling T-shirt entrepreneurs to make rent money—seemed to mirror the national mood.

Today, not so much. Which oddly enough might make this something of a golden moment for the Life is good company.

"It is generally people who face the greatest adversity who embrace this message the most," says Bert Jacobs, whose company website features a section of "inspiring letters that fuel us all to keep spreading good vibes." The letters include testimonials from survivors of a grizzly bear attack, a young amputee, and a soldier stationed in Iraq. "People have a higher sense and appreciation of the simple things when they've been through something difficult. It's our job to see the glass half full."

Life is good doesn't have a demographic, the brothers like to say, but rather a psychographic: the optimists. And while one might imagine that their numbers are dwindling at roughly the same rate as their retirement accounts, some observers suggest otherwise. . . .

That's not to say Life is good is immune to the downturn, but in this company's case it's all relative. . . .

Until last year the company, whose annual sales top $100 million, had never had a year with less than 30 percent growth. In 2008 it grew only 10 percent, a slowdown that Jacobs notes (in apropos parlance) is "not exactly something you bum out about." Especially since the company hasn't spent a dime on advertising. . . .

Life is good was tested once before, not by the company's customers but its employees. In the days following 9/11 a number of managers approached Bert Jacobs and said that they weren't feeling right about spreading the company's signature tidings. Some had lost friends in the attacks. The news was all about anthrax and terrorism and tips on turning your basement into a bunker. Maybe life wasn't so good, and maybe this was not the message the American people wanted to hear.

But the company forged ahead, launching its first (wildly successful) nationwide fundraiser. Jacobs calls it the pivotal moment in his business life. "Our company has this fantastic positive energy and our brand is capable of bringing people together," he says. "We know there's trauma and violence and hardship. Life is good isn't the land of Willy Wonka. We're not throwing Frisbees all day. We live in the real world. But you can look around you and find good things any time."

Learn more about Bert and John Jacobs and other master students at the Master Student Hall of Fame.

6 Notes

Master Student Map

as you read, ask yourself

what if . . .

I could take notes that remain useful for weeks, months, or even years to come?

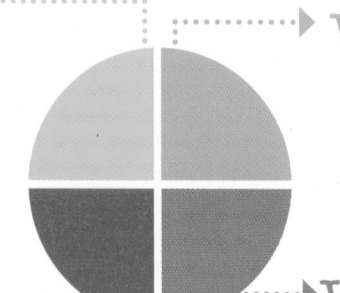

why this chapter matters . . .

Note taking makes you an active learner, enhances memory, and influences how well you do on tests and other evaluations.

what is included . . .

how you can use this chapter . . .

- Experiment with several formats for note taking.
- Create a note-taking format that works especially well for you.
- Take effective notes in special situations—while reading, when speakers talk fast, and during meetings.

MASTER EMPLOYEE in *action*

It is essential that I am meticulous about the information I record on the various documents that pass through my hand each day. Thankfully in college I was introduced to various note taking strategies. After trying out several, I was able to come up with a system that is now second nature to me.

—JOANN ADAMS, COURT CLERK

Photo courtesy of Joann Adams

The note-taking process flows

ONE WAY TO understand note taking is to realize that taking notes is just one part of the process. Effective note taking consists of three parts: observing, recording, and reviewing. First, you observe an "event"—a statement by an instructor, a lab experiment, a slide show of an artist's works, or a chapter of required reading. Then you record your observations of that event; that is, you "take notes." Finally, you review what you have recorded.

Each part of the note-taking process is essential, and each depends on the others. Your observations determine what you record. What you record determines what you review. And the quality of your review can determine how effective your next observations will be. For example, if you review your notes on the Sino-Japanese War of 1894, the next day's lecture on the Boxer Rebellion of 1900 will make more sense.

Legible and speedy handwriting is also useful in taking notes. Knowledge about outlining is handy, too. A nifty pen, a new notebook, and a laptop computer are all great note-taking devices. However, they're all worthless—unless you participate as an energetic observer *in* class and regularly review your notes *after* class. If you take those two steps, you can turn even the most disorganized chicken scratches into a powerful tool.

Sometimes note taking looks like a passive affair, especially in large lecture classes. One person at the front of the room does most of the talking. Everyone else is seated and silent, taking notes. The lecturer seems to be doing all of the work.

Don't be deceived. Observe more closely, and you'll see some students taking notes in a way that radiates energy. They're awake and alert, poised on the edge of their seats. They're writing—a physical activity that expresses mental engagement. These students listen for levels of ideas and information, make choices about what to record, and compile materials to review.

In higher education, you might spend hundreds of hours taking notes. Making them more effective is a direct investment in your success. Think of your notes as a textbook that *you* create—one that's more current and more in tune with your learning preferences than any textbook you could buy. ✳

6

NOTES

journal entry

Discovery/Intention Statement

Get what you want from this chapter

Think about the possible benefits of improving your skills at note taking. Recall a recent incident in which you had difficulty taking notes. Perhaps you were listening to an instructor who talked fast, or you got confused and stopped taking notes altogether. Describe the incident in the following space.

_____

_____

_____

Now preview this chapter to find at least five strategies that you can use right away to help you take better notes. Sum up each of those strategies in a few words, and then note page numbers where you can find out more about each suggestion.

Strategy   **Page number**

_____

_____

_____

Reflect on your intention to experiment actively with this chapter. Describe a specific situation in which you promise to apply the strategies you previously listed. If possible, choose a situation that will occur within the next 24 hours.

I intend to . . .

_____

_____

_____

OBSERVE
The note-taking process flows

SHERLOCK HOLMES, a fictional master detective and student of the obvious, could track down a villain by observing the fold of his scarf and the mud on his shoes. In real life, a doctor can save a life by observing a mole—one a patient has always had—that undergoes a rapid change.

An accountant can save a client thousands of dollars by observing the details of a spreadsheet. A student can save hours of study time by observing that she gets twice as much done at a particular time of day.

Keen observers see facts and relationships. They know ways to focus their attention on the details and then tap their creative energy to discover patterns. To sharpen your classroom observation skills, experiment with the following techniques, and continue to use those that you find most valuable. Many of these strategies can be adapted to the notes you take while reading.

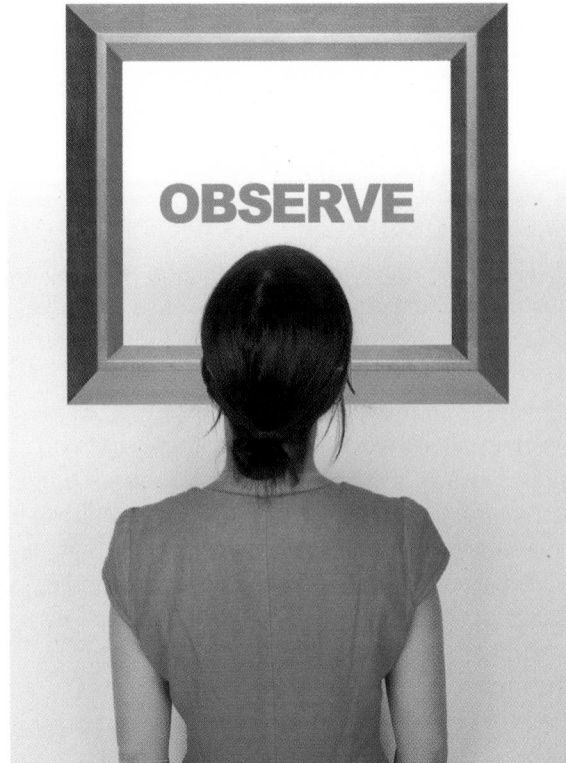

(woman) ballyscanlon/Getty, (frame) mike.irwin/Shutterstock

Set the stage

Complete outside assignments. Nothing is more discouraging (or boring) than sitting through a lecture about the relationship of Le Chatelier's principle to the study of kinetics if you've never heard of Henri Louis Le Chatelier or kinetics. The more familiar you are with a subject, the more easily you can absorb important information during class lectures. Instructors usually assume that students will complete assignments, and they construct their lectures accordingly.

Bring materials. A good pen does not make you a good observer, but the lack of a pen or notebook can be distracting enough to take the fine edge off your concentration. Make sure you have a pen, pencil, notebook, or any other materials you need. Bring your textbook to class, especially if the lectures relate closely to the text.

If you are consistently unprepared for a class, that might suggest something about your intentions concerning the course. Find out if it does. The next time you're in a frantic scramble to borrow pen and paper 37 seconds before the class begins, notice the cost. Use the borrowed pen and paper to write a Discovery Statement about your lack of preparation. Consider whether you intend to be successful in the course.

Sit front and center. Students who get as close as possible to the front and center of the classroom often

do better on tests for several reasons. The closer you sit to the lecturer, the harder it is to fall asleep. The closer you sit to the front, the fewer interesting or distracting classmates are situated between you and the instructor. Material on the board is easier to read from up front. Also, the instructor can see you more easily when you have a question.

Instructors are usually not trained to perform. Some can project their energy to a large audience, but some cannot. A professor who sounds boring from the back of the room might sound more interesting up close.

Sitting up front enables you to become a constructive force in the classroom. By returning the positive energy that an engaged teacher gives out, you can reinforce the teacher's enthusiasm and enhance your experience of the class.

In addition, sound waves from the human voice begin to degrade at a distance of 8 to 12 feet. If you sit more than 15 feet from the speaker, your ability to hear and take effective notes might be compromised. Get close to the source of the sound. Get close to the energy.

Sitting close to the front is a way to commit yourself to getting what you want out of school. One reason students gravitate to the back of the classroom is that they think the instructor is less likely to call on them. Sitting in back can signal a lack of commitment. When you sit up front, you are declaring your willingness to take a risk and participate.

Conduct a short preclass review. Arrive early, and then put your brain in gear by reviewing your notes

NOTES

6

What to do when you miss a class

For most courses, you'll benefit by attending every class session. If you miss a class, catch up as quickly as possible. Following are some way to do that:

Clarify policies on missed classes On the first day of classes, find out about your instructors' policies on absences. See if you will be allowed to make up assignments, quizzes, and tests. You should also inquire about doing extra-credit assignments.

Contact a classmate Early in the semester, identify a student in each class who seems responsible and dependable. Exchange e-mail addresses and phone numbers. If you know you won't be in class, contact this student ahead of time. When you notice that your classmate is absent, pick up extra copies of handouts, make assignment lists, and offer copies of your notes.

Contact your instructor If you miss a class, e-mail, phone, or fax your instructor, or put a note in his mailbox. Ask if he has another section of the same course that you can attend so you won't miss the lecture information. Also ask about getting handouts you might need before the next class meeting.

Consider technology If there is a Web site for your class, check it for assignments and the availability of handouts you missed. Free online services such as NoteMesh allow students to share notes with one another. These services use wiki software, which allows you to create and edit Web pages using any browser. Before using such tools, however, check with your instructors for their policies on note sharing.

from the previous class. Scan your reading assignment. Look at the sections you have underlined or highlighted. Review assigned problems and exercises. Note questions you intend to ask.

Clarify your intentions. Take a 3×5 card to class with you. On that card, write a short Intention Statement about what you plan to get from the class. Describe your intended level of participation or the quality of attention you will bring to the subject. Be specific. If you found your previous class notes to be inadequate, write down what you intend to do to make your notes from this class session more useful.

"Be here now" in class

Accept your wandering mind. The techniques in Chapter 3's Power Process: "Be Here Now" can be especially useful when your head soars into the clouds. Don't fight daydreaming. When you notice your mind wandering during class, look at it as an opportunity to refocus your attention. Accept the fact that you are in class listening to a lecture and not somewhere else. If thermodynamics is losing out to beach parties, let go of the beach.

Notice your writing. When you discover yourself slipping into a fantasyland, feel the weight of your pen in your hand. Notice how your notes look. Paying attention to the act of writing can bring you back to the here and now.

You also can use writing in a more direct way to clear your mind of distracting thoughts. Pause for a few seconds, and write those thoughts down. If you're distracted by thoughts of errands you need to run after class, list them on a 3×5 card that you will stick in your pocket. You can also simply put a symbol, such as an arrow or asterisk, in your notes to mark the

places where your mind started to wander. Once your distractions are out of your mind and safely stored on paper, you can gently return your attention to taking notes.

Be with the instructor. In your mind, put yourself right up front with the instructor. Imagine that you and the instructor are the only ones in the room and that the lecture is a personal conversation between the two of you. Pay attention to the instructor's body language and facial expressions. Look the instructor in the eye.

Remember that the power of this suggestion is immediately reduced by digital distractions—Web surfing, e-mail checking, or text messaging. Taking notes is a way to stay focused. The physical act of taking notes signals your mind to stay in the same room as the instructor.

Notice your environment. When you become aware of yourself daydreaming, bring yourself back to class by paying attention to the temperature in the room, the feel of your chair, or the quality of light coming through the window. Run your hand along the surface of your desk. Listen to the chalk on the blackboard or the sound of the teacher's voice. Be in that environment. Once your attention is back in the room, you can focus on what's happening in class.

Postpone debate. When you hear something you disagree with, note your disagreement and let it go. Don't allow your internal dialogue to drown out subsequent material. If your disagreement is persistent and strong, make note of it and then move on. Internal debate can prevent you from absorbing new information. It is OK to absorb information you don't agree with. Just absorb it with the mental tag "My instructor says . . . , and I don't agree with it."

Let go of judgments about lecture styles.
Human beings are judgment machines. We evaluate everything, especially other people. If another person's eyebrows are too close together (or too far apart), if she walks a certain way, or if she speaks with an unusual accent, we instantly make up a story about her. We do this so quickly that the process is usually not a conscious one.

Don't let your attitude about an instructor's lecture style, habits, or appearance get in the way of your education. You can decrease the power of your judgments if you pay attention to them and let them go.

You can even let go of judgments about rambling, unorganized lectures. Turn them to your advantage. Take the initiative, and organize the material yourself. While taking notes, separate the key points from the examples and supporting evidence. Note the places where you got confused, and make a list of questions to ask.

Participate in class activities. Ask questions. Volunteer for demonstrations. Join in class discussions. Be willing to take a risk or look foolish, if that's what it takes for you to learn. Chances are, the question you think is dumb is also on the minds of several of your classmates.

Relate the class to your goals. If you have trouble staying awake in a particular class, write at the top of your notes how that class relates to a specific goal. Identify the reward or payoff for reaching that goal.

Think critically about what you hear. This suggestion might seem contrary to the previously mentioned technique "postpone debate." It's not. You might choose not to think critically about the instructor's ideas during the lecture. That's fine. Do it later, as you review and edit your notes. This is the time to list questions or write down your agreements and disagreements.

Watch for clues

Be alert to repetition. When an instructor repeats a phrase or an idea, make a note of it. Repetition is a signal that the instructor thinks the information is important.

Listen for introductory, concluding, and transition words and phrases. Introductory, concluding, and transition words and phrases include phrases such as *the following three factors, in conclusion, the most important consideration, in addition to,* and *on the other hand.* These phrases and others signal relationships, definitions, new subjects, conclusions, cause and effect, and examples. They reveal the structure of the lecture. You can use these phrases to organize your notes.

Watch the board or PowerPoint presentation. If an instructor takes the time to write something down on the board or show it in a PowerPoint presentation, consider the material to be important. Copy all diagrams and drawings, equations, names, places, dates, statistics, and definitions.

Watch the instructor's eyes. If an instructor glances at his notes and then makes a point, it is probably a signal that the information is especially important. Anything he reads from his notes is a potential test question.

Highlight the obvious clues. Instructors often hint strongly or tell students point-blank that certain information is likely to appear on an exam. Make stars or other special marks in your notes next to this information. Instructors are not trying to hide what's important.

Notice the instructor's interest level. If the instructor is excited about a topic, it is more likely to appear on an exam. Pay attention when she seems more animated than usual.

www Find more strategies for observing online.

journal entry 13

Discovery/Intention Statement

Create more value from lectures

Think back on the last few lectures you have attended. How do you currently observe (listen to) lectures? What specific behaviors do you have as you sit and listen? Briefly describe your responses in the following space.

I discovered that I . . .

_____

_____

_____

Now write an Intention Statement about any changes you want to make in the way you respond to lectures.

I intend to . . .

_____

_____

_____

RECORD
The note-taking process flows

THE FORMAT AND STRUCTURE of your notes are more important than how fast you write or the elegance of your handwriting. The following techniques can improve the effectiveness of your notes.

General techniques for note taking

Use keywords. An easy way to sort the extraneous material from the important points is to take notes using keywords. Keywords contain the essence of communication. The two main kinds of keywords are:

- Concepts, technical terms, names, and numbers.
- Linking words, including those that describe action, relationship, and degree (for example, *most*, *least*, and *faster*).

Keywords evoke images and associations with other words and ideas. They trigger your memory. That characteristic makes them powerful review tools. One keyword can initiate the recall of a whole cluster of ideas. A few keywords can form a chain from which you can reconstruct an entire lecture.

To see how keywords work, take yourself to an imaginary classroom. You are now in the middle of an anatomy lecture. Picture what the room looks like, what it feels like, how it smells. You hear the instructor say:

OK, what happens when we look directly over our heads and see a piano falling out of the sky? How do we take that signal and translate it into the action of getting out of the way? The first thing that happens is that a stimulus is generated in the neurons—receptor neurons—of the eye. Light reflected from the piano reaches our eyes. In other words, we see the piano.

The receptor neurons in the eye transmit that sensory signal—the sight of the piano—to the body's nervous system. That's all they can do—pass on information. So we've got a sensory signal coming into the nervous system. But the neurons that initiate movement in our legs are effector neurons. The information from the sensory neurons must be transmitted to effector neurons or we will get squashed by the piano. There must be some kind of interconnection between receptor and effector neurons. What happens between the two? What is the connection?

Keywords you might note in this example include *stimulus, generated, receptor neurons, transmit, sensory*

signals, nervous system, effector neurons, and *connection.* You can reduce the instructor's 163 words to these 12 keywords. With a few transitional words, your notes might look like this:

> Stimulus (piano) generated in receptor neurons (eye)
>
> Sensory signals transmitted by nervous system to effector neurons (legs)
>
> What connects receptor to effector?

Note the last keyword of the previous lecture: *connection.* This word is part of the instructor's question and leads to the next point in the lecture. Be on the lookout for questions like this. They can help you organize your notes and are often clues for test questions.

Use pictures and diagrams. Make relationships visual. Copy all diagrams from the board, and invent your own.

A drawing of a piano falling on someone who is looking up, for example, might be used to demonstrate the relationship of receptor neurons to effector neurons. Label the eyes "receptor" and the feet "effector." This picture implies that the sight of the piano must be translated into a motor response. By connecting the explanation of the process with the unusual picture of the piano falling, you can link the elements of the process together.

Write notes in paragraphs. When it is difficult to follow the organization of a lecture or put information into outline form, create a series of informal paragraphs. These paragraphs should contain few complete sentences. Reserve complete sentences for precise definitions, direct quotations, and important points that the instructor emphasizes by repetition or other signals—such as the phrase "This is an important point."

RECORD

(woman) ballyscanlon/Getty, (hands/camera) tezzstock/Shutterstock,
(frame) Jenson/Shutterstock

Copy material from the board and a PowerPoint presentation. Record all formulas, diagrams, and problems that the teacher presents on the board or in a PowerPoint presentation. Copy dates, numbers, names, places, and other facts. If it's presented visually in class, put it in your notes. You can even use your own signals or codes to flag that material.

Use a three-ring binder. Three-ring binders have several advantages over other kinds of notebooks. First, pages can be removed and spread out when you review. This way, you can get a complete picture of a lecture. Second, the three-ring-binder format allows you to insert handouts right into your notes. Third, you can insert your own out-of-class notes in the correct order.

Use only one side of a piece of paper. When you use one side of a page, you can review and organize all your notes by spreading them out side by side. Most students find the benefit well worth the cost of the paper. Perhaps you're concerned about the environmental impact of consuming more paper. If so, you can use the blank side of old notes and use recycled paper.

Use 3×5 cards. As an alternative to using notebook paper, use 3×5 cards to take lecture notes. Copy each new concept onto a separate 3×5 card.

Keep your own thoughts separate. For the most part, avoid making editorial comments in your lecture notes. The danger is that when you return to your notes, you might mistake your own ideas for those of the instructor. If you want to make a comment, clearly label it as your own.

Use an "I'm lost" signal. No matter how attentive and alert you are during a lecture, you might get lost or confused at some point. If it is inappropriate to interrupt the instructor to ask a question, record in your notes that you were lost. Invent your own signal—for example, a circled question mark. When you write down your code for "I'm lost," leave space for the explanation or clarification that you will get it later. The space will also be a signal that you missed something. Later, you can speak to your instructor or ask to see a fellow student's notes.

Label, number, and date all notes. Develop the habit of labeling and dating your notes at the beginning of each class. Number the page, too. Sometimes the sequence of material in a lecture is important. Write your name and phone number in each notebook in case you lose it.

Use standard abbreviations. Be consistent with your abbreviations. If you make up your own abbreviations or symbols, write a key explaining them in your notes. Avoid vague abbreviations. When you use an abbreviation such as *comm.* for *committee,* you run the risk of not being able to remember whether you meant *committee, commission, common,* or *commit.* One way to abbreviate is to leave out vowels. For example, *talk* becomes *tlk, said* becomes *sd, American* becomes *Amrcn.*

Leave blank space. Notes tightly crammed into every corner of the page are hard to read and difficult to use for review. Give your eyes a break by leaving plenty of space.

Later, when you review, you can use the blank spaces in your notes to clarify points, write questions, and add other material.

Take notes in different colors. You can use colors as highly visible organizers. For example, you can signal important points with red or use one color of ink for notes about the text and another color for lecture notes.

Use graphic signals. The following ideas can be used with any note-taking format:

- Use brackets, parentheses, circles, and squares to group information that belongs together.
- Use stars, arrows, and underlining to indicate important points. Flag the most important points with double stars, double arrows, or double underlines.
- Use arrows and connecting lines to link related groups.
- Use equal signs, greater-than signs, and less-than signs to indicate compared quantities.

To avoid creating confusion with graphic symbols, use them carefully and consistently. Write a "dictionary" of your symbols in the front of your notebooks; an example is on the next page.

[I, ( ), ◯, ▭ = info
   that belongs together

∗, ↘, — = important

∗∗, ↘↘, ≡, !!! = extra important

> = greater than   < = less than
= = equal to

⟶ = leads to, becomes
   Ex: school ⟶ job ⟶ money

? = huh?, lost

?? = big trouble, clear up
   immediately

Use recorders effectively. Some students record lectures with audio recorders, but there are persuasive arguments against doing so. When you record a lecture, there is a strong temptation to daydream. After all, you can always listen to the lecture again later on. Unfortunately, if you let the recorder do all of the work, you are skipping a valuable part of the learning process.

There are other potential problems as well. Listening to recorded lectures can take a lot of time—more time than reviewing written notes. Recorders can't answer the questions you didn't ask in class. Also, recording devices malfunction. In fact, the unscientific Hypothesis of Recording Glitches states that the tendency of recorders to malfunction is directly proportional to the importance of the material.

With those warnings in mind, you can use a recorder effectively if you choose. For example, you can use recordings as backups to written notes. (Check with your instructor first. Some prefer not to be recorded.) Turn the recorder on; then take notes as if it weren't there. Recordings can be especially useful if an instructor speaks fast.

The Cornell method

A note-taking system that has worked for students around the world is the *Cornell method*.[1] Originally developed by Walter Pauk at Cornell University during the 1950s, this approach continues to be taught across the United States and in other countries as well.

The cornerstone of this method is what Pauk calls the *cue column*—a wide margin on the left-hand side of the paper. The cue column is the key to the Cornell method's many benefits. Here's how to use it.

Format your paper. On each sheet of your notepaper, draw a vertical line, top to bottom, about two inches from the left edge of the paper. This line

creates the cue column—the space to the left of the line. You can also find Web sites that allow you to print out pages in this format. Just do an Internet search using the keywords *cornell method pdf*.

Take notes, leaving the cue column blank. As you read an assignment or listen to a lecture, take notes on the right-hand side of the paper. Fill up this column with sentences, paragraphs, outlines, charts, or drawings. Do not write in the cue column. You'll use this space later, as you do the next steps.

Condense your notes in the cue column. Think of the notes you took on the right-hand side of the paper as a set of answers. In the cue column, list potential test questions that correspond to your notes. Write one question for each major term or point.

As an alternative to questions, you can list keywords from your notes. Yet another option is to pretend that your notes are a series of articles on different topics. In the cue column, write a newspaper-style headline for each "article." In any case, be brief. If you cram the cue column full of words, you defeat its purpose of reducing the number of words and length of your notes.

Write a summary. Pauk recommends that you reduce your notes even more by writing a brief summary at the bottom of each page. This step offers you another way to engage actively with the material.

Cue column	Notes
What are the 3 phases of Muscle Reading?	Phase 1: Before you read Phase 2: While you read Phase 3: After you read
What are the steps in phase 1?	1. Preview 2. Outline 3. Question
What are the steps in phase 2?	4. Read 5. Underline 6. Answer
What are the steps in phase 3?	7. Recite 8. Review 9. Review again
What is an acronym for Muscle Reading?	Pry = preview Out = outline Questions = question Root = read Up = underline Answers = answer Recite Review Review again

Summary
Muscle Reading includes 3 phases: before, during, and after reading. Each phase includes 3 steps. Use the acronym to recall all the steps.

Use the cue column to recite. Cover the right-hand side of your notes with a blank sheet of paper. Leave only the cue column showing. Then look at each item you wrote in the cue column and talk about it. If you wrote questions, answer each question. If you wrote keywords, define each word and talk about why it's important. If you wrote headlines in the cue column, explain what each one means and offer supporting details. After reciting, uncover your notes and look for any important points you missed.

Mind mapping

Mind mapping, a system developed by Tony Buzan,[2] can be used in conjunction with the Cornell method to take notes. In some circumstances, you might want to use mind maps exclusively.

To understand mind maps, first review the features of traditional note taking. Outlines (explained in the next section) divide major topics into minor topics, which, in turn, are subdivided further. They organize information in a sequential, linear way.

The traditional outline reflects only a limited range of brain function—a point that is often made in discussions about "left-brain" and "right-brain" activities. People often use the term *right brain* when referring to creative, pattern-making, visual, intuitive brain activity. They use the term *left brain* when talking about orderly, logical, step-by-step characteristics of thought. Writing teacher Gabrielle Rico uses another metaphor. She refers to the left-brain mode as our "sign mind" (concerned with words) and the right-brain mode as our "design mind" (concerned with visuals).[3] A mind map uses both kinds of brain functions. Mind maps can contain lists and sequences and show relationships. They can also provide a picture of a subject. They work on both verbal and nonverbal levels.

One benefit of mind maps is that they quickly, vividly, and accurately show the relationships between ideas. Also, mind mapping helps you think from general to specific. By choosing a main topic, you focus first on the big picture, then zero in on subordinate details. By using only keywords, you can condense a large subject into a small area on a mind map. You can review more quickly by looking at the keywords on a mind map than by reading notes word for word.

Give yourself plenty of room. To create a mind map, use blank paper that measures at least 11 by 17 inches. If that's not available, turn regular notebook paper on its side so that you can take notes in a horizontal (instead of vertical) format. If you use a computer to take notes in class, consider investing in software that allows you to create digital mind maps that can include graphics, photos, and URL links.

Determine the main concept of the lecture, article, or chapter. As you listen to a lecture or read from your text, figure out the main concept. Write it in the center of the paper and circle it, underline it, or highlight it with color. You can also write the concept in large letters. Record concepts related to the main concept on lines that radiate outward from the center. An alternative is to circle or box in these concepts.

Use keywords only. Whenever possible, reduce each concept to a single word per line, circle, or box in your mind map. Although this reduction might seem awkward at first, it prompts you to summarize and condense ideas to their essence. That results in fewer words for you to write now and fewer to review when it's time to prepare for tests. (Using shorthand symbols and abbreviations can help.) Keywords are usually nouns and verbs that communicate the bulk of the speaker's ideas. Choose words that are rich in associations and that can help you recreate the lecture.

Create links. A single mind map doesn't have to include all of the ideas contained in a lecture, book, or article. Instead, you can link mind maps. For example, draw a mind map that sums up the five key points in a chapter, and then make a separate, more detailed mind map for each of those key points. Within each mind map, include references to the other mind maps. This technique helps explain and reinforce the relationships among many ideas. Some students pin several mind maps next to one another on a bulletin board or tape them to a wall. This allows for a dramatic—and effective—look at the big picture.

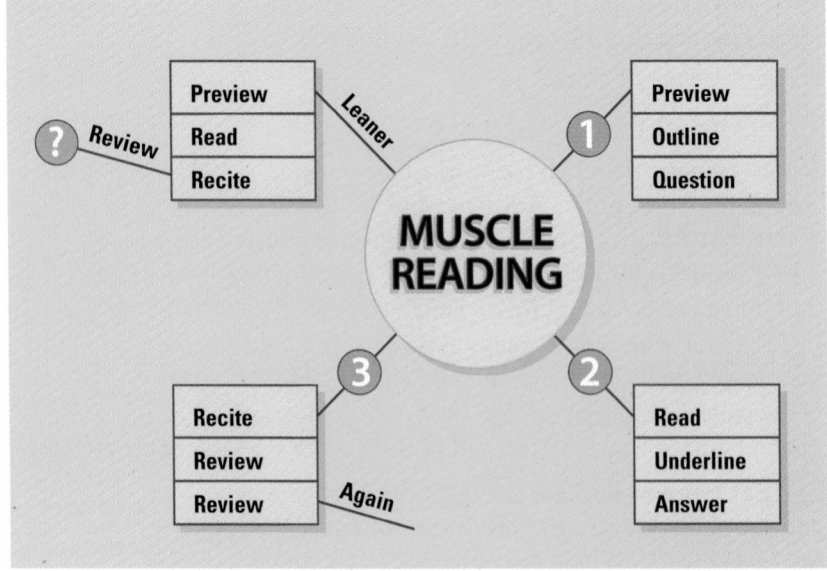

Outlining

A traditional outline shows the relationships among major points and supporting ideas. One benefit of taking notes in the outline format is that doing so can totally occupy your attention. You are recording ideas and also organizing them. This process can be an advantage if the material has been presented in a disorganized way. By playing with variations, you can discover the power of outlining to reveal relationships among ideas. Technically, each word, phrase, or sentence that appears in an outline is called a *heading*. Headings are arranged in different levels:

- In the first, or top, level of headings, note the major topics presented in a lecture or reading assignment.

- In the second level of headings, record the key points that relate to each topic in the first-level headings.

- In the third level of headings, record specific facts and details that support or explain each of your second-level headings. Each additional level of subordinate heading supports the ideas in the previous level of heading.

Roman numerals offer one way to illustrate the difference between levels of headings. See the following examples below and to the right.

First-level heading

Second-level heading

Third-level heading

I. Muscle Reading includes 3 phases.
 A. Phase 1: Before you read
  1. Preview
  2. Outline
  3. Question
 B. Phase 2: While you read
  4. Read
  5. Underline
  6. Answer
 C. Phase 3: After you read
  7. Recite
  8. Review
  9. Review again

Combining formats

Feel free to use different note-taking systems for different subjects and to combine formats. Do what works for you.

For example, combine mind maps with the Cornell method. You can modify the Cornell format by dividing your notepaper in half. Reserve one half for mind maps and the other for linear information such as lists, graphs, and outlines, as well as equations, long

Distinguish levels with indentations only:

Muscle Reading includes 3 phases
 Phase 1: Before you read
  Preview

Distinguish levels with bullets and dashes:

MUSCLE READING INCLUDES 3 PHASES
 • Phase 1: Before you read
  – Preview

Distinguish headings by size:

MUSCLE READING INCLUDES 3 PHASES
Phase 1: Before you read
Preview

explanations, and word-for-word definitions. You can incorporate a mind map into your paragraph-style notes whenever you feel one is appropriate. Mind maps are also useful for summarizing notes taken in the Cornell format.

John Sperry, a teacher at Utah Valley State College, developed a note-taking system that can include all of the formats discussed in this article:

- Fill up a three-ring binder with fresh paper. Open your notebook so that you see two blank pages—one on the left and one on the right. Plan to take notes across this entire two-page spread.

- During class or while reading, write your notes only on the left-hand page. Place a large dash next to each main topic or point. If your instructor skips a step or switches topics unexpectedly, just keep writing.

- Later, use the right-hand page to review and elaborate on the notes that you took earlier. Use this page for anything you want. For example, add visuals such as mind maps. Write review questions, headlines, possible test questions, summaries, outlines, mnemonics, or analogies that link new concepts to your current knowledge.

- To keep ideas in sequence, place appropriate numbers on top of the dashes in your notes on the left-hand page. Even if concepts are presented out of order during class, they'll still be numbered correctly in your notes. ✳

 See more examples of notes in various formats online.

REVIEW
The note-taking process flows

THINK OF REVIEWING as an integral part of note taking rather than an added task. To make new information useful, encode it in a way that connects that information to your long-term memory. The key is reviewing.

Review within 24 hours. In Chapter 5: "Reading," when you read the suggestion to review what you've read within 24 hours, you were asked to sound the trumpet. If you have one, get it out and sound it again. This note-taking technique might be the most powerful one you can use. In fact, it might save you hours of review time later in the term.

Many students are surprised that they can remember the content of a lecture in the minutes and hours after class. They are even more surprised by how well they can read the sloppiest of notes at that time. Unfortunately, short-term memory deteriorates quickly. The good news is that if you review your notes soon enough, you can move that information from short-term to long-term memory. Best of all, you can do it in just a few minutes—often 10 minutes or less.

The sooner you review your notes, the better, especially if the content is difficult. In fact, you can start reviewing during class. When your instructor pauses to set up the overhead display or erase the board, scan your notes. Dot the *i*'s, cross the *t*'s, and write out unclear abbreviations. Another way to use this technique is to get to your next class as quickly as you can. Then use the four or five minutes before the lecture begins to review the notes you just took in the previous class. If you do not get to your notes immediately after class, you can still benefit by reviewing them later in the day. A review right before you go to sleep can also be valuable.

Think of the day's unreviewed notes as leaky faucets, constantly dripping and losing precious information until you shut them off with a quick review. Remember, it's possible to forget most of the material within 24 hours—unless you review.

Edit your notes. During your first review, fix words that are illegible. Write out abbreviated words that might be unclear to you later. Make sure you can read everything. If you can't read something or don't understand something you *can* read, mark it and make a note to ask your instructor or another student about it. Check to see that your notes are labeled with the date and class and that the pages are numbered.

(woman) ballyscanlon/Getty, (frames) Vladimir Wrangel/Shutterstock

Fill in keywords in the left-hand column. This task is important if you are to get the full benefit of using the Cornell method. Using the keyword principles described earlier in this chapter, go through your notes and write keywords or phrases in the left-hand column.

These keywords will speed up the review process later.

Use your keywords as cues to recite. Cover your notes with a blank sheet of paper so that you can see only the keywords in the left-hand margin. Take each keyword in order, and recite as much as you can about the point. Then uncover your notes and look for any important points you missed.

Conduct short weekly review periods. Once a week, review all of your notes again. These review sessions don't need to take a lot of time. Even a 20-minute weekly review period is valuable. Some students find that a weekend review—say, on Sunday afternoon—helps them stay in continuous touch with the material. Scheduling regular review sessions on your calendar helps develop the habit.

As you review, step back to see the larger picture. In addition to reciting or repeating the material to yourself, ask questions about it: Does this relate to my goals? How does this compare to information I already know, in this field or another? Will I be tested on this material? What will I do with this material? How can I associate it with something that deeply interests me?

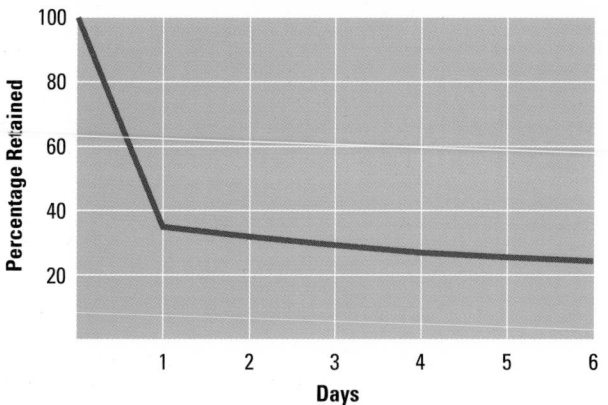

To study the process of memory and forgetting, Hermann Ebbinghaus devised a method for testing memory. The results, shown here in what has come to be known as the Ebbinghaus forgetting curve, demonstrate that forgetting occurs most rapidly shortly after learning and then gradually declines over time.

Consider typing your notes. Some students type up their handwritten notes on the computer. The argument for doing so is threefold. First, typed notes are easier to read. Second, they take up less space. Third, the process of typing them forces you to review the material.

Another alternative is to bypass handwriting altogether and take notes in class on a laptop. This solution has a potential drawback, though: Computer errors can wipe out your notes files. If you like using this method of taking notes, save your files frequently, and back up your work onto a jump drive or other portable drive.

Create summaries. Mind mapping is an excellent way to summarize large sections of your course notes or reading assignments. Create one map that shows all the main topics you want to remember. Then create another map about each main topic. After drawing your maps, look at your original notes and fill in anything you missed. This system is fun and quick.

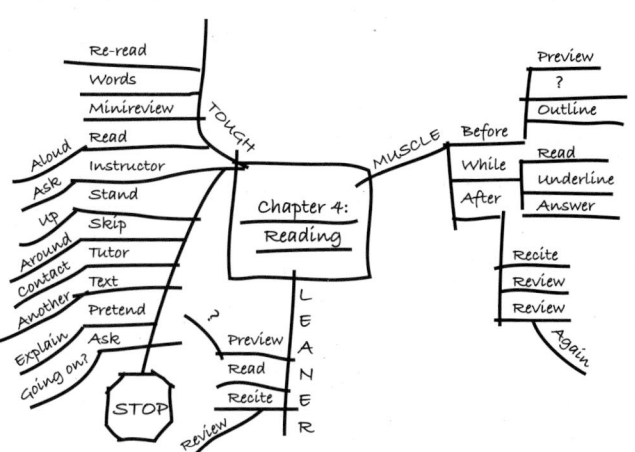

Another option is to create a "cheat sheet." There's only one guideline: Fit all your review notes on a single sheet of paper. Use any note-taking format that you want—mind map, outline, Cornell method, or a combination of all of them. The beauty of this technique is that it forces you to pick out main ideas and key details. There's not enough room for anything else!

If you're feeling adventurous, create your cheat sheet on a single index card. Start with the larger sizes (5×7 or 4×6) and then work down to a 3×5 card.

Some instructors might let you use a summary sheet during an exam. But even if you can't use it, you'll benefit from creating one while you study for the test. Summarizing is a powerful way to review. ✳

journal entry 14

Discovery Statement

Reflect on your review habits

Think about the way you have conducted reviews of your notes in the past. Respond to the following statements by checking "Always," "Often," "Sometimes," "Seldom," or "Never" after each.

1. I review my notes immediately after class.

_____ Always _____ Often _____ Sometimes

_____ Seldom _____ Never

2. I conduct weekly reviews of my notes.

_____ Always _____ Often _____ Sometimes

_____ Seldom _____ Never

3. I make summary sheets of my notes.

_____ Always _____ Often _____ Sometimes

_____ Seldom _____ Never

4. I edit my notes within 24 hours.

_____ Always _____ Often _____ Sometimes

_____ Seldom _____ Never

5. Before class, I conduct a brief review of the notes I took in the previous class.

_____ Always _____ Often _____ Sometimes

_____ Seldom _____ Never

Observe, record, and review at work

TAKING NOTES AT WORK allows you to apply many of the transferable skills covered in this book—listening, remembering, writing, and critical thinking. Remember that the ability to take clear and concise notes is one way to make yourself valuable to an employer. It might even help you get promoted.

Be prepared

Before meetings, complete background reading on the topics to be discussed, including minutes from relevant meetings in the past. Doing this sets the stage for taking better notes in upcoming meetings. It's easier to make sense of what people say when you already know something about the meeting topics.

Experiment with formats

During meetings, experiment with Cornell format notes, mind mapping, outlining, concept mapping, or some combination of these. Feel free to add boldface headings, charts, tables, graphs, and other visuals that make the main ideas stand out. If you're taking notes to distribute to coworkers, they will appreciate it if you get to the point and keep paragraphs short.

Your employer may have specific guidelines for taking meeting notes. Ask your supervisor about this. Note that in some cases—such as minutes taken during a board of directors meeting—notes may function as legal documents reviewed by the IRS or another independent auditor.

Keep up with speakers

When taking notes during fast-paced meetings and conference calls, use suggestions from the article "When a Speaker Talks *Fast*" in this chapter. Immediately after the call or meeting, review and edit your notes.

Notice your handwriting

Colleagues may read your handwriting often. If your penmanship creates communication problems or does not convey a positive image, simply notice this fact. Then

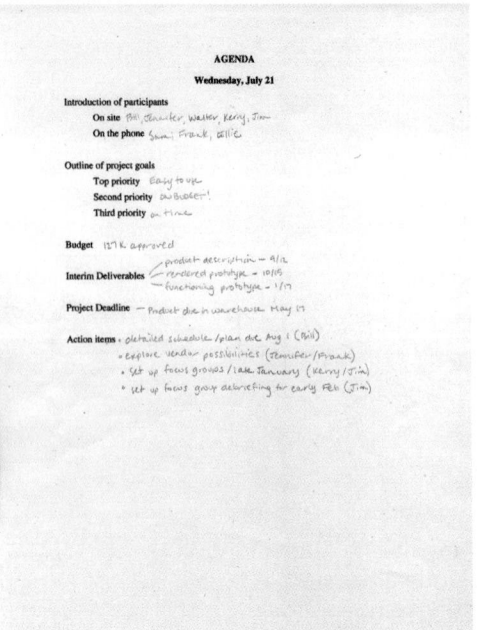

pay conscious attention to your handwriting as you take notes.

Remember the "four A's"

Consider adding the following topics to your notes:

- *Attendance.* In many organizations, people expect meeting notes to include a list of attendees. For large meetings, see if you can get an advance list of the people who are expected to attend. Bring this to the meeting and check off peoples' names as they enter the room. Along with your list of attendees, include the name of your department, the date, the time, and the name of the person who led the meeting.

- *Agenda.* Think of the agenda as a road map—a way to keep the discussion on track. Skilled planners often put an agenda in writing and distribute it in advance of a meeting. Use this agenda while you take notes.

- *Agreements.* The purpose of most meetings is to reach an agreement about something—a policy, project, or plan. Focus on capturing the details about each agreement.

- *Actions.* During meetings, people often commit to take some type of action in the future. Record each follow-up action and who agreed to do it.

Follow-up action is often a make-or-break point for project teams. One mark of exceptional teams is that people make agreements about what they will do—and then keep those agreements.

You can set a powerful example. Ask whether any of the points you included in your notes call for follow-up action on your part. Highlight such items in your notes. Then add them to your calendar or to-do list and follow through.

Review

After meetings, review the notes you took. Edit or rewrite your notes for clarity and accuracy. If you took handwritten notes, consider entering the important points into a computer file. ✻

Get to the bones of your book with concept maps

CONCEPT MAPPING, pioneered by Joseph Novak and D. Bob Gowin, is a tool to make major ideas in a book leap off the page.[4] In creating a concept map, you reduce an author's message to its essence—its bare bones. Concept maps can also be used to display the organization of lectures and discussions.

Concepts and links are the building blocks of knowledge. A *concept* is a name for a group of related things or ideas. *Links* are words or phrases that describe the relationship between concepts. Consider the following paragraph:

> Muscle Reading consists of three phases. Phase 1 includes tasks to complete before reading. Phase 2 tasks take place during reading. Finally, Phase 3 includes tasks to complete after reading.

In this paragraph, examples of concepts are *Muscle Reading, reading, phases, tasks, Phase 1, Phase 2,* and *Phase 3.* Links include *consists of, includes, before, during,* and *after.*

To create a concept map, list concepts and then arrange them in a meaningful order from general to specific. Then fill in the links between concepts, forming meaningful statements.

Concept mapping promotes critical thinking. It alerts you to missing concepts or faulty links between concepts. In addition, concept mapping mirrors the way that your brain learns—that is, by linking new concepts to concepts that you already know.

To create a concept map, use the following steps:

1. **List the key concepts in the text.** Aim to express each concept in three words or less. Most concept words are nouns, including terms and proper names. At this point, you can list the concepts in any order.

2. **Rank the concepts so that they flow from general to specific.** On a large sheet of paper, write the main concept at the top of the page. Place the most specific concepts near the bottom. Arrange the rest of the concepts in appropriate positions throughout the middle of the page. Circle each concept.

3. **Draw lines that connect the concepts.** On these connecting lines, add words that describe the relationship between the concepts. Again, limit yourself to the fewest words needed to make an accurate link—three words or less. Linking words are often verbs, verb phrases, or prepositions.

4. **Finally, review your map.** Look for any concepts that are repeated in several places on the map. You can avoid these repetitions by adding more links between concepts. ✳

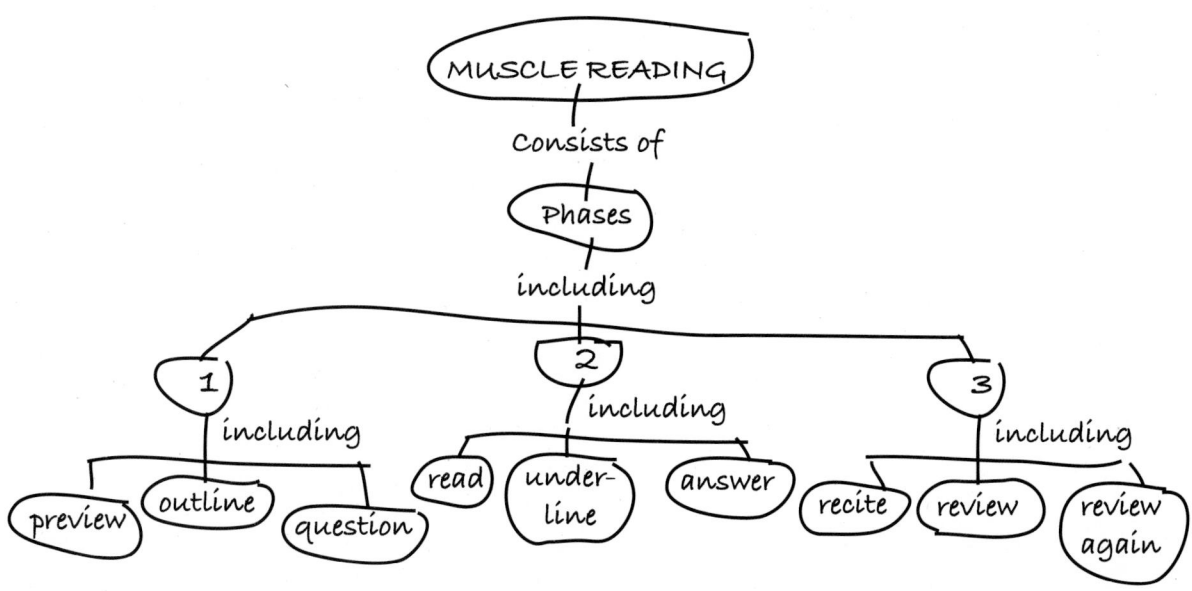

Taking notes while reading

TAKING NOTES WHILE READING requires the same skills that apply to taking class notes: observing, recording, and reviewing. Use these skills to take notes for review and for research.

Review notes

Take review notes when you want more detailed notes than writing in the margin of your text allows. You might want to single out a particularly difficult section of a text and make separate notes. You can also make summaries of overlapping lecture and text material. Since you can't underline or make notes in library books, these sources will require separate notes, too.

To take more effective review notes, follow these suggestions:

- ■ *Use a variety of formats.* Translate text into Cornell notes, mind maps, or outlines. Combine these formats to create your own. Translate diagrams, charts, and other visual elements into words. Then reverse the process by translating straight text into visual elements.

- ■ *However, don't let the creation of formats get in your way.* Even a simple list of key points and examples can become a powerful review tool.

- ■ *Condense a passage to key quotes.* Authors embed their essential ideas in key sentences. As you read, continually ask yourself, "What's the point?" Then see if you can point to a specific sentence on the page to answer your question. Look especially at headings, subheadings, and topic sentences of paragraphs. Write these key sentences word for word in your notes, and put them within quotation marks. Copy as few sentences as you can and still retain the core meaning of the passage.

- ■ *Condense by paraphrasing.* Pretend that you have to summarize a chapter, article, or book on a postcard. Limit yourself to a single paragraph—or a single sentence—and use your own words. This is a great way to test your understanding of the material.

- ■ *Take a cue from the table of contents.* Look at the table of contents in your book. Write each major heading on a piece of paper, or key those headings into a word-processing file on your computer. Include page numbers. Next, see if you can improve on the table of contents. Substitute your own headings for those that appear in the book. Turn single words or phrases into complete sentences, and use words that are meaningful to you.

- ■ *Note special concepts in math and science.* When you read mathematical, scientific, or other technical materials, copy important formulas or equations. Recreate important diagrams, and draw your own visual representations of concepts. Also write down data that might appear on an exam.

Research notes

Take research notes when preparing to write a paper or deliver a speech. One traditional method of research is to take notes on index cards. You write one idea, fact, or quotation per card. The advantage of limiting each card to one item of information is that you can easily arrange cards according to the sequence of your outline—and ongoing changes in your outline.

Taking notes on a computer offers the same flexibility as index cards. In addition, you can take advantage of software features that help you create tables of contents, indexes, graphics, and other elements you might want to use in your project later on.

No matter which method you use, your research notes will fall into two main categories.

The first category includes information about your sources. For example, a source card for a book will show the author, title, date and place of publication, and publisher. You'll need such information later in the writing process as you create a formal list of your sources—especially sources of quotes or paraphrased material that is included in the body of your paper or presentation. By keeping track of your sources as you conduct research, you create a working bibliography. Ask your instructor about what source information to record (and also see the sidebar to this article). When recording your own ideas, simply note the source as "me."

The second category of research notes includes the actual ideas and facts that you will use to create the content of your paper or presentation. Again, if you're using index cards, write only *one* piece of information on each information card—a single quotation, fact, or concept. Doing so makes it easier for you to sort cards later.

Be sure to avoid plagiarism. When people take words or images from a source and present them as their own, they are committing plagiarism. Even when plagiarism is accidental, the consequences can be harsh. For essential information on this topic, see the "Avoiding Plagiarism" sidebar in Chapter 8 on page 238.

If you're taking notes on a computer and using Internet sources, be especially careful to avoid plagiarism. When you copy text or images from a Web site, separate those notes from your own ideas. Use a different font for copied material, or enclose it in quotation marks.

Schedule time to review all the information and ideas that your research has produced. By allowing time for rereading and reflecting on all the notes you've taken, you create the conditions for genuine understanding.

Start by summarizing major points of view on your topic. Note points of agreement and disagreement among your sources.

Also see if you can find direct answers to the questions that you had when you started researching. These answers could become headings in your paper.

Look for connections between the ideas, facts, and examples that appear in your resource materials. Also look for connections between your research and your life—ideas that you can verify based on personal experience.

Adapt to special cases. The style of your notes can vary according to the nature of the reading material. For example, if you are assigned a short story or poem, read the entire work once without taking any notes. On your first reading, simply enjoy the piece. When you finish, write down your immediate impressions. Then go over the piece and make brief notes on characters, images, symbols, settings, plot, point of view, or other aspects of the work. ✳

 Find examples of effective research and review notes online.

Note this information about your sources

The following text features checklists of the information to record about various types of sources. Whenever possible, print out or make photocopies of each source. For books, include a copy of the title page and copyright page, both of which are found in the front matter. For magazines and scholarly journals, copy the table of contents.

For each book you consult, record the following:

☐ Author

☐ Editor (if listed)

☐ Translator (if listed)

☐ Edition number (if listed)

☐ Full title, including the subtitle

☐ Name and location of the publisher

☐ Copyright date

☐ Page numbers for passages that you quote, summarize, or paraphrase

For each article you consult, record the following:

☐ Author

☐ Editor (if listed)

☐ Translator (if listed)

☐ Full title, including the subtitle

☐ Name of the periodical

☐ Volume number

☐ Issue number

☐ Issue date

☐ Page numbers for passages that you quote, summarize, or paraphrase

For each computer-based source you consult (CD-ROMs and Internet documents), record the following:

☐ Author

☐ Editor (if listed)

☐ Translator (if listed)

☐ Full title of the page or article, including the subtitle

☐ Name of the organization that posted the site or published the CD-ROM

☐ Dates when the page or other document was published and revised

☐ Date when you accessed the source

☐ URL for Web pages (the uniform resource locator, or Web site address, which often starts with http://)

☐ Version number (for CD-ROMs)

☐ Volume, issue number, and date for online journals

Note: Computer-based sources may not list all the above information. For Web pages, at a minimum, record the date you accessed the source and the URL.

For each interview you conduct, record the following:

☐ Name of the person you interviewed

☐ Professional title of the person you interviewed

☐ Contact information for the person you interviewed—mailing address, phone number, e-mail address

☐ Date of the interview

Enroll your instructor in your education

Thinkstock/Getty

FACED WITH AN instructor you don't like, you have two basic choices. One is to label the instructor a "dud" and let it go at that. When you make this choice, you get to endure class and complain to other students. This choice puts you at the mercy of circumstance. It gives your instructor sole responsibility for the quality of your education and the value of your tuition payments.

There is another option. Don't give away your power. Instead, take responsibility for your education.

Show interest in class. Students give teachers moment-by-moment feedback in class. That feedback comes through posture, eye contact, responses to questions, and participation in class discussions. If you find a class boring, recreate the instructor through a massive display of interest. Ask lots of questions. Sit up straight, make eye contact, and take detailed notes. Your enthusiasm might enliven your instructor. If not, you are still creating a more enjoyable class for yourself.

Release judgments. Maybe your instructor reminds you of someone you don't like—your annoying Aunt Edna, a rude store clerk, or the fifth-grade teacher who kept you after school. Your attitudes are in your own head and beyond the instructor's control. Likewise, an instructor's beliefs about politics or religion are not related to teaching ability. Being aware of such things can help you let go of negative judgments.

Get to know the instructor. Meet with your instructor during office hours. Teachers who seem boring in class can be fascinating in person.

Students who do well in higher education often get to know at least one instructor outside of class. In some cases, these instructors become mentors and informal advisors.

Open up to diversity. Sometimes students can create their instructors by letting go of pictures about different races and ethnic groups. According to one picture, a Hispanic person cannot teach English literature. According to other pictures, a white teacher cannot have anything valid to say about African music, a teacher in a wheelchair cannot command the attention of a hundred people in a lecture hall, and a male instructor cannot speak credibly about feminism. All of those pictures can clash with reality. Releasing them can open up new opportunities for understanding and appreciation.

Separate liking from learning. You don't have to like an instructor to learn from one. See if you can focus on the instructor's content instead of form. *Form* is the way something is organized or presented. If you are irritated at the sound of an instructor's voice, you're focusing on form. When you put aside your concern about her voice and turn your attention to the points she's making, you're focusing on *content*.

Seek alternatives. You might feel more comfortable with another teacher's style or method of organizing course materials. Consider changing teachers, asking another teacher for help outside class, or attending an additional section taught by a different instructor. You can also learn from other students, courses, tutors, study groups, books, and DVDs. Be a master student, even when you have teachers you don't like. Your education is your own creation.

Avoid excuses. Instructors know every excuse. Most teachers can see a snow job coming before the first flake hits the ground. Accept responsibility for your own mistakes, and avoid thinking that you can fool the teacher.

Submit professional work. Prepare papers and projects as if you were submitting them to an employer. Imagine that your work will determine whether you get a promotion and pay raise. Instructors often grade hundreds of papers during a term. Your neat, orderly, well-organized paper can stand out and lift a teacher's spirits. ✳

 Discover more ways to create positive relationships with instructors online.

When a speaker talks *fast*

Take more time to prepare for class. Familiarity with a subject increases your ability to pick up on key points. If an instructor lectures quickly or is difficult to understand, conduct a thorough preview of the material to be covered.

Be willing to make choices. When an instructor talks fast, focus your attention on key points. Instead of trying to write everything down, choose what you think is important. Occasionally, you will make a wrong choice and neglect an important point. Worse things could happen. Stay with the lecture, write down keywords, and revise your notes immediately after class.

Exchange photocopies of notes with classmates. Your fellow students might write down something you missed. At the same time, your notes might help them. Exchanging photocopies can fill in the gaps.

Leave large empty spaces in your notes. Leave plenty of room for filling in information you missed. Use a symbol that signals you've missed something, so you can remember to come back to it.

See the instructor after class. Take your class notes with you, and show the instructor what you missed.

Use an audio recorder. Recording a lecture gives you a chance to hear it again whenever you choose. Some audio recording software allows you to vary the speed of the recording. With this feature, you can perform magic and actually slow down the instructor's speech.

Before class, take notes on your reading assignment. You can take detailed notes on the text before class. Leave plenty of blank space. Take these notes with you to class, and simply add your lecture notes to them.

Go to the lecture again. Many classes are taught in multiple sections. That gives you the chance to hear a lecture at least twice—once in your regular class and again in another section of the class.

Learn shorthand. Some note-taking systems, known as shorthand, are specifically designed for getting ideas down fast. Books and courses are available to help you learn these systems. You can also devise your own shorthand method by inventing one- or two-letter symbols for common words and phrases.

Ask questions—even if you're totally lost. Many instructors allow a question session. This is the time to ask about the points you missed.

At times you might feel so lost that you can't even formulate a question. That's OK. One option is to report this fact to the instructor. He can often guide you to a clear question. Another option is to ask a related question. Doing so might lead you to the question you really wanted to ask.

Ask the instructor to slow down. This solution is the most obvious. If asking the instructor to slow down doesn't work, ask her to repeat what you missed. ✳

Meeting with your instructor

Meeting with an instructor outside class can save hours of study time and help your grade. To get the most from these meetings, consider doing the following:

- Schedule a meeting time during the instructor's office hours.

- If you need to cancel or reschedule, let your instructor know well in advance.

- Ask about ways to prepare for upcoming exams.

- If the course is in a subject area that interests you, ask about the possibilities of declaring a major in that area and the possible careers that are associated with that major.

- Avoid questions that might offend your instructor—for example, "I missed class on Monday. Did we do anything important?"

- When the meeting is over, thank your instructor for making time for you.

Discovery/Intention Statement

Reflect on notes from school and work

Choose a set of notes that you've taken in class recently. Next to it, place notes that you took during a meeting at work.

Now compare the two sets of notes. Look past their content and consider their format. What visual differences do you see between the notes from work and the notes from class?

I discovered that . . .

_____

_____

_____

_____

Also think about the *process* of taking notes in these two settings. Did you find it easier or more difficult to take notes at work than in class?

I discovered that . . .

_____

_____

_____

_____

_____

_____

After comparing these two sets of notes, reflect on what you can do differently in the future to take more effective notes at work.

I intend to . . .

_____

_____

_____

_____

_____

_____

_____

23 critical thinking exercise
Television note taking

You can use evening news broadcasts to practice listening for keywords, writing quickly, focusing your attention, and reviewing. The more you practice, the better you become.

The next time you watch the news, use pen and paper to jot down keywords and information. During the commercials, review and revise your notes. At the end of the broadcast, spend five minutes reviewing all of your notes. Create a mind map of a few news stories, then sum up the news of the day for a friend.

This exercise will help you develop an ear for keywords. Since you can't ask questions or request that the speaker slow down, you train yourself to stay totally in the moment.

If you get behind, relax, leave a space, and return your attention to the broadcast.

Don't be discouraged if you miss a lot the first time around. Do this exercise several times, and observe how your mind works.

If you find it too difficult to take notes during a fast-paced television news show, check your local broadcast schedule for a news documentary. Documentaries are often slower paced. Another option is to record a program and then take notes. You can stop the recording at any point to review your notes. You can also ask a classmate to do the same exercise, and then compare notes the next day.

I Create It All

This article describes a powerful tool for times of trouble. In a crisis, "I create it all" can lead the way to solutions. "I create it all" means treating experiences, events, and circumstances in your life *as if* you created them.

"I create it all" is one of the most unusual and bizarre suggestions in this book. It certainly is not a belief. Use it when it works. Don't when it doesn't.

Keeping that in mind, consider how powerful this Power Process can be. It is really about the difference between two distinct positions in life: being a victim or being responsible.

A victim of circumstances is controlled by outside forces. We've all felt like victims at one time or another. Sometimes we felt helpless.

In contrast, we can take responsibility. Responsibility is "response-ability"—the ability to choose a *response* to any event. You can choose your *response* to any event, even when the event itself is beyond your control.

Many students approach grades from the position of being victims. When the student who sees the world this way gets an F, she reacts something like this:

"Another F! That teacher couldn't teach her way out of a wet paper bag. She can't teach English for anything. And that textbook—what a bore!"

The problem with this viewpoint is that in looking for excuses, the student is robbing herself of the power to get any grade other than an F. She's giving all of her power to a bad teacher and a boring textbook.

There is another way; it is called *taking responsibility*. You can recognize that you choose your grades by choosing your actions. Then you are the source, rather than the result, of the grades you get. The student who got an F could react like this:

"Another F! Oh, shoot! Well, hmmm. . . . What did I do to create it?"

Now, that's power. By asking, "How did I contribute to this outcome?" you are no longer the victim. This student might continue by saying, "Well, let's see. I didn't review my notes after class. That might have done it." Or "I went out with my friends the night before the test. Well, that probably helped me fulfill some of the requirements for getting an F."

The point is this: When the F is the result of your friends, the book, or the teacher, you probably can't do anything about it. However, if you *chose* the F, you can choose a different grade next time. You are in charge.

Learn more about using this Power Process online.

Goodshoot/RF/Jupiter Images

Career Application

Hanae Niigata is a part-time receptionist at a large cardiovascular clinic. Her responsibilities include handling incoming calls, scheduling patient visits, maintaining medical records, and completing other tasks assigned by her office manager.

sozaijiten/Datacraft/Getty

Hanae's career focus is health care. She has worked as a home health aide and is currently enrolled in school. Her goal is to complete an Associate in Science degree in nursing and work as a registered nurse.

Hanae has a reputation as a hard worker. Even in a noisy environment with frequent interruptions, she completes tasks that require attention to detail and sustained concentration. She catches errors on medical records that her coworkers tend to miss. In addition, Hanae is often the first person in the office to whom people turn when they have a problem to solve. Even in the most difficult circumstances, she can generate a list of options—including solutions that occur to no one else.

Today, the office manager asked Hanae to attend a two-hour course on a new telephone system soon to be installed in her office. She was told to take good notes so she could teach the other five receptionists. Hanae was shocked that the old system was being replaced. In her opinion, it was user-friendly.

As the training session began, Hanae diligently attempted to write down almost everything the instructor said. While doing so, she repeatedly found herself distracted by the thought that her manager was replacing a perfectly good phone system with some "sure-to-be-a-nightmare, high-tech garbage."

After completing the course, Hanae sat down with her manager to fill him in on the new system. As she thumbed through her notes, she realized they didn't make much sense to her, even though she had just finished writing them. She couldn't recall much of the course from memory either, leaving her with little information to share with her manager.

Reflecting on this scenario

List two or three suggestions for Hanae that could make her note taking more effective. Be specific.

_____

_____

_____

_____

_____

_____

_____

_____

_____

_____

Quiz

Name _____   Date ____/____/____

1. What are the three major steps of effective note taking as explained in this chapter? Summarize each step in one sentence.

2. According to the text, neat handwriting and a knowledge of outlining are the only requirements for taking effective notes. True or false? Explain your answer.

3. What are some advantages of sitting in the front and center of the classroom?

4. Instructors sometimes give clues that the material they are presenting is important. List three of these clues.

5. Postponing debate while taking notes means that you have to agree with everything that the instructor says. True or false? Explain your answer.

6. Graphic signals include which of the following?
   (a) Brackets and parentheses
   (b) Stars and arrows
   (c) Underlining and connecting lines
   (d) Equal signs, greater-than signs, and less-than signs
   (e) All of the above

7. Describe the two main types of keywords. Then write down at least five keywords from this chapter.

8. Describe a way to apply the Power Process: "Be Here Now" to the job of taking notes in class.

9. Describe three strategies for reviewing notes.

10. Briefly define the word *responsibility* as it is used in the Power Process: "I Create It All."

Focus on Transferable Skills

The Discovery Wheel in Chapter 1 includes a section labeled "Notes." Take a few minutes right now to go beyond your initial responses to that exercise. Take a snapshot of your skills as they exist today, after reading and doing this chapter. Then choose a new skill to develop—one that you can use in school and at work.

You might want to prepare for this exercise by reviewing the articles "Jumpstart Your Education with Transferable Skills" on page 58 and "101 Transferable Skills" on page 60.

OBSERVING

If my attention wanders while taking notes, I refocus by . . .

When I strongly disagree with the opinion of a speaker or author, I respond by . . .

RECORDING

The formats I usually use to take notes are . . .

A note-taking format that I'd like to experiment with is . . .

REVIEWING

If asked to rate the overall quality of the notes that I've taken in the last week, I would say that . . .

In general, I find my notes to be most useful when they . . .

NEXT ACTION

The biggest change I'd like to make in the way I take notes is . . .

To make this change, I intend to . . .

Master Student PROFILE

Faye Wattleton
. . . is willing to participate

© Maiman Rick/CORBIS SYGMA

I don't ever recall not wanting to be a nurse, or not saying I wanted to be a nurse. This was, in part, certainly my mother's influence. She wanted me to be a missionary nurse. It wasn't sufficient just to be a nurse, I had to commit to a religious cause as well. Missionary nurses work in church hospitals, in Africa and all over the world. I suspect this was suggested to me before I even understood the power of suggestion, and I always grew up saying I was going to be a nurse. I earned two degrees in nursing, but never practiced as a nurse. In the broadest sense of the word, you can say I have nursed all the time, but not in the technical sense. After undergraduate school, I taught nursing for two years. Then I went to graduate school at Columbia University and earned my master's degree. Following that I moved to Dayton, Ohio, to work in a public health department. There, I was asked to join the board of the local Planned Parenthood. Two years later, I became executive director of the local chapter. Then, seven years later, I became the national president of the organization.

I'm sure the suggestion to become a nurse was colored by the limitation on women's options in those years. Women were nurses, social workers, or teachers. I don't ever remember being explicitly told, "Oh, you can't be that because you're a girl." It just was. . . . It was never conveyed to me there were any limitations on what I could do and what my work could be, although I'm sure the idea that I be a nurse, as opposed to a doctor or something else, was due to the limitations on the role of women at that time.

Even though we lived in a working class community, there wasn't as much integration, so blacks of all economic levels lived in the black community. My father was a laborer, and my mother was a seamstress, but I went to nursing school with our doctor's son. The doctor's family lived a few blocks from us. This was before the Civil Rights movement, and before blacks moved into white or integrated neighborhoods. That experience also played a very important role in my sense of who I am ethnically, as well as what the possibilities were for me. We lived next door to professionals, as well as the housepainter who had the most beautiful house on the block because he painted and decorated it beautifully.

I try to find the best people I can in various specialties so I can learn from them. I want people who are better than me in their specialties, maybe not better than me in running the whole shebang, but better than me in the communications field or legal field. Stitching everything together to make it work as a [piece of] machinery is, for me, the challenge and the excitement.

I try very hard to listen. If there is conflict, I want to hear what the other side says. . . . As long as I feel there is mutual respect, it does not hurt me to listen to someone with whom I am really in conflict, to hear what they are saying even if I disagree. If it's a conflict I really want to resolve, I try to find ways we can come to mutual points of agreement. One thing I always believe is if you talk long enough you can almost always reach a resolution. Just the process of talking has a de-fanging influence. I have great faith in human beings finding ways to relate if they have enough contact with each other.

Lucinda Watson, *How They Achieved: Stories of Personal Achievement and Business Success.* Copyright © 2001, pp. 208–212, John Wiley & Sons. Reprinted with permission.

(1943–)
President of the Planned Parenthood Federation of America from 1978 until 1992. She is currently the founder and president of the Center for the Advancement of Women.

Learn more about Faye Wattleton and other master students at the Master Student Hall of Fame.

7 Tests

Master Student Map

as you read, ask yourself

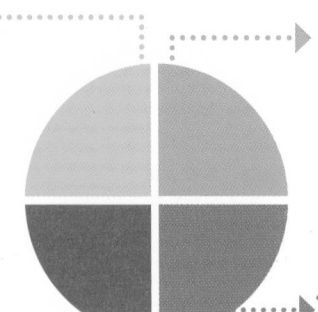

what if . . .

I could let go of stress over tests—or anything else?

why this chapter matters . . .

Adopting a few simple techniques can change your experience of tests—and make a difference in how you manage stress of any type.

how

you can use this chapter . . .

- Predict test questions and use your study time more effectively.
- Harness the power of cooperative learning by studying with other people.
- Learn to look on an F as *feedback* rather than *failure*.
- Create value from performance reviews at work.

what is included . . .

MASTER EMPLOYEE in *action*

When I first became a manager, I dreaded conducting the annual performance reviews for my group. I expected my employees—many of whom had been with the company far longer than I had—to resent me evaluating their performances. But for the most part, I was happily surprised. Most people genuinely wanted ideas about how they could improve their performance. After all, if we can't accept constructive criticism, none of us would be able to hold onto our jobs for long.

—JEFF ROGERS, RESEARCH MANAGER

Photo courtesy of Jeff Rogers

Disarm tests

ON THE SURFACE, tests don't look dangerous. Maybe that's why we sometimes treat them as if they were land mines. Suppose a stranger walked up to you on the street and asked, "Does a finite abelian P-group have a basis?" Would you break out in a cold sweat? Would your muscles tense up? Would your breathing become shallow?

Probably not. Even if you had never heard of a finite abelian P-group, you probably would remain coolly detached. However, if you find the same question on a test and you have never heard of a finite abelian P-group, your hands might get clammy.

Grades (A to F) are what we use to give power to tests. However, there are lots of misconceptions about what grades are. Grades are not a measure of intelligence or creativity. They are not an indication of our ability to contribute to society. Grades are simply a measure of how well we do on tests.

Some people think that a test score measures what a student has accomplished in a course. This idea is false. A test score is a measure of what a student scored on a test. If you are anxious about a test and blank out, the grade cannot measure what you've learned. The reverse is also true: If you are good at taking tests and you are a lucky guesser, the score won't be an accurate reflection of what you know.

Grades are not a measure of self-worth. Yet we tend to give test scores the power to determine how we feel about ourselves. Common thoughts include "If I fail a test, I am a failure" or "If I do badly on a test, I am a bad person." The truth is that if you do badly on a test, you are a person who did badly on a test. That's all.

Carrying around misconceptions about tests and grades can put undue pressure on your performance. It's like balancing on a railroad track. Many people can walk along the rail and stay balanced for long periods. Yet the task seems entirely different if the rail is placed between two buildings, 52 stories up.

It is easier to do well on exams if you don't put too much pressure on yourself. Don't give the test some magical power over your own worth as a human being. Academic tests are not a matter of life and death. Scoring low on important tests—standardized tests, medical school exams, bar exams, CPA exams—usually means only a delay.

Whether the chance of doing poorly is real or exaggerated, worrying about it can become paralyzing. The way to deal with tests is to keep them in perspective. Keep the railroad track on the ground. ✳

Discovery/Intention Statement

Transform your experience of tests

Mentally re-create a time when you had difficulty taking a test. Do anything that helps you re-experience this event. Briefly describe that experience in the following space. You could draw a picture of yourself in this situation, list some of the questions you had difficulty answering, or explain how you felt after finding out your score on the test.

I discovered that I . . .

_____

_____

_____

Now wipe your mental slate clean, and declare your intention to replace it with a new scenario. Describe how you want your experience of test taking to change. For example, you might write: "I intend to walk into every test I take feeling well rested and thoroughly prepared."

I intend to . . .

_____

_____

_____

Preview this chapter, looking for at least five strategies that can help you accomplish your goal. List those strategies in the following space, and note the page numbers where you can find out more about them.

Strategy	Page number

7

TESTS

What to do *before* the test

Do daily reviews. Daily reviews include short preclass and postclass reviews of lecture notes. You should also conduct brief daily reviews with textbooks: Before reading a new assignment, scan your notes and the sections you underlined or highlighted in the previous assignment. In addition, use the time you spend waiting for the bus or doing the laundry to conduct short reviews.

Concentrate daily reviews on two kinds of material. One is material you have just learned, either in class or in your reading. The other is material that involves simple memorization—equations, formulas, dates, and definitions.

Begin to review on the first day of class. Most instructors outline the whole course at that time. You can even start reviewing within seconds after learning. During a lull in class, go over the notes you just took. Immediately after class, review your notes again.

Do weekly reviews. Review each subject at least once a week, allowing about one hour per subject. Include reviews of assigned reading and lecture notes. Look over any mind map summaries or flash cards you have created. You should also practice working on sample problems.

Do major reviews. Major reviews are usually most helpful when conducted the week before finals or other critical exams. They help you integrate concepts and deepen your understanding of material presented throughout the term. These are longer review periods than a daily or weekly review—two to five hours at a stretch, with sufficient breaks. Remember that the effectiveness of your review begins to drop after an hour or so unless you give yourself a short rest.

After a certain point, short breaks every hour might not be enough to refresh you. That's when it's time to quit. Learn your limits by being conscious of the quality of your concentration.

During long sessions, study the most difficult subjects when you are the most alert: at the beginning of the session.

Schedule reviews. Schedule specific times in your calendar for reviews. Start reviewing key topics at least five days before you'll be tested on them. This allows plenty of time to find the answers to questions and close any gaps in your understanding.

© Gaetano Images Inc./Alamy

Create study checklists. You can use study checklists the way a pilot uses a preflight checklist. Pilots go through a standard routine before they take off. They physically mark off each item: test flaps, check magnetos, check fuel tanks, adjust instruments, check rudder. A written list helps them to be sure they don't miss anything. Once they are in the air, it's too late. Taking an exam is like flying a plane. Once the test begins, it's too late to memorize that one equation you forgot to include in your review.

Make a checklist for each subject. List reading assignments by chapters or page numbers. List dates of lecture notes. Write down various types of problems you will need to solve. Write down other skills to master. Include major ideas, definitions, theories, formulas, and equations. For math and science tests, choose some problems and do them over again as a way to review for the test.

Remember that a study checklist is not a review sheet; it is a to-do list. Checklists contain the briefest possible description of each item to study.

Instead of a checklist, you may want to use a test prep plan. This written plan goes beyond a study checklist to include the following:

- The date and time of each test, along with the name of the course and instructor.

- The type of items—such as essay or multiple choice—that are likely to appear on each test.

- Specific dates and times that you intend to study for each test (which you then enter on your calendar).

- Specific strategies that you intend to use while studying for each test.

Create mind map summary sheets. There are several ways to make a mind map as you study for tests. Start by creating a map totally from memory. You might be surprised by how much you already know. After you have gone as far as you can using recall alone, go over your notes and text, and fill in the rest of the map. Another option is to go through your notes and write down keywords as you pick them out. Then, without looking at your notes, create a mind map of everything you can recall about each keyword. Finally, go back to your notes and fill in material you left out.

Create flash cards. Flash cards can be used to make portable test questions. On one side of some 3×5 cards, write questions. On the other side, write the answers. It's that simple. Always carry a pack of flash cards with you, and review them whenever you have a minute to spare. Use flash cards for formulas, definitions, theories, keywords from your notes, axioms, dates, foreign language phrases, hypotheses, and sample problems. Create flash cards regularly as the term progresses. Buy an inexpensive card file to keep your flash cards arranged by subject.

Monitor your reviews. Each day that you prepare for a test, assess what you have learned and what you still want to learn. See how many items you've covered from your study checklist. Look at the tables of contents in your textbooks, and write an X next to the sections that you've summarized. This helps you gauge the thoroughness of your reviews and alerts you to areas that still need attention.

Take a practice test. Write up your own questions to make a practice test. Take this practice test several times before the actual exam. You might type this "test" so that it looks like the real thing. If possible, take your practice test in the same room where you will take the actual test.

In addition, meet with your instructor to go over your practice test. Ask whether your questions focus on appropriate topics and represent the kind of items you can expect to see. The instructor might decline to give you any of this information. More often, though, instructors will answer some or all of your questions about an upcoming test.

Get copies of old exams. Copies of previous exams for the class might be available from the instructor, the instructor's department, the library, or the counseling office. Old tests can help you plan a review strategy. One caution: If you rely on old tests exclusively, you might gloss over material the instructor has added since the last test. Also, check your school's policy about making past tests available to students. Some schools might not allow it. ✳

 See examples of mind map summary sheets and other review tools online.

How to cram . . . even though you shouldn't

Know the limitations of cramming, and be aware of its costs. Cramming won't work if you've neglected all of the reading assignments, or if you've skipped most of the lectures and daydreamed through the rest. The more courses you have to cram for, the less effective cramming will be. Also, cramming is not the same as learning: You won't remember what you cram.

If you *are* going to cram, however, then avoid telling yourself that you *should* have studied earlier, you *should* have read the assignments, or you *should* have been more conscientious. All those shoulds get you nowhere. Instead, write an Intention Statement about how you will change your study habits. Give yourself permission to be the fallible human being you are. Then make the best of the situation.

Make choices Pick out a *few* of the most important elements of the course and learn them backward, forward, and upside down. For example, devote most of your attention to the topic sentences, tables, and charts in a long reading assignment.

Make a plan After you've chosen what elements you want to study, determine how much time to spend on each one.

Recite and recite again The key to cramming is repetition. Go over your material again and again.

Ways to predict test questions

PREDICTING TEST QUESTIONS can do more than get you a better grade. It can also keep you focused on the purpose of a course and help you design your learning strategies. Making predictions can be fun, too—especially when they turn out to be accurate.

Ask about the nature of the test. Eliminate as much guesswork as possible. Ask your instructor to describe upcoming tests. Do this early in the term so you can be alert for possible test questions throughout the course. Some questions to ask are:

- What course material will the test cover—readings, lectures, lab sessions, or a combination?
- Will the test be cumulative, or will it cover just the most recent material you've studied?
- Will the test focus on facts and details or major themes and relationships?
- Will the test call on you to solve problems or apply concepts?
- Will you have choices about which questions to answer?
- What types of questions will be on the test—true/false, multiple choice, short answer, essay?

Note: In order to study appropriately for essay tests, find out how much detail the instructor wants in your answers. Ask how much time you'll be allowed for the test and about the length of essay answers (number of pages, blue books, or word limit). Having that information before you begin studying can help you gauge your depth for learning the material.

Put yourself in your instructor's shoes. If you were teaching the course, what kinds of questions would you put on an exam? Make up practice test questions and answer them. You can also brainstorm test questions with other students—this is a great activity for study groups.

Look for possible test questions in your notes and readings. Label a separate section in your notebook "Test questions." Add several questions to this section after every lecture and assignment. You can also create your own code or graphic signal—such as a *T!* in a circle—to flag possible test questions in your notes. Use the same symbol to flag review questions and problems in your textbooks that could appear on a test.

See the boxed feature "Words to Watch for in Essay Questions" on page 197. Use it as a guide to turn the keywords in your notes into test questions.

Look for clues to possible questions during class. During lectures, you can predict test questions by observing what an instructor says and how he says it. Instructors often give clues. They might repeat important points several times, write them on the board, or return to them in later classes.

Gestures can indicate critical points. For example, your instructor might pause, look at notes, or read passages word for word.

Notice whether your teacher has any strong points of view on certain issues. Questions on those issues are likely to appear on a test. Also pay attention to questions the instructor poses to students, and note questions that other students ask.

When material from reading assignments is covered extensively in class, it is likely to be on a test. For science courses and other courses involving problem solving, work on sample problems using different variables.

Save all quizzes, papers, lab sheets, and graded materials of any kind. Quiz questions have a way of reappearing, in slightly altered form, on final exams. If copies of previous exams and other graded materials are available, use them to predict test questions.

Apply your predictions. To get the most value from your predictions, use them to guide your review sessions.

Remember the obvious. Be on the lookout for these words: *This material will be on the test.* ✳

Cooperative learning: Working in teams

Yuri Arcurs/Shutterstock

STUDY GROUPS CAN lift your mood on days when you just don't feel like working. If you skip a solo study session, no one else will know. If you declare your intention to study with others who are depending on you, your intention gains strength.

Study groups are especially important if going to school has thrown you into a new culture. Joining a study group with people you already know can help ease the transition. To multiply the benefits of working with study groups, seek out people of other backgrounds, cultures, races, and ethnic groups. You can get a whole new perspective on the world, along with some valuable new friends. You can also experience what it's like to be part of a diverse team, which is an important asset in today's job market.

Form a study group

Choose a focus for your group. Many students assume that the purpose of a study group is to help its members prepare for a test. That's one valid purpose—but there are others. Through his research on cooperative learning, psychologist Joe Cuseo has identified several kinds of study groups.[1] For instance, members of *test review* groups compare answers and help one another discover sources of errors. *Note-taking* groups focus on comparing and editing notes, often meeting directly after the day's class. Members of *research* groups meet to help one another find, evaluate, and take notes on background materials for papers and presentations. *Reading* groups can be useful for courses in which test questions are based largely on textbooks. Meet with classmates to compare the passages you underlined or highlighted and the notes you made in the margins of your books.

Look for dedicated students. Find people you are comfortable with and who share your academic goals. Look for students who pay attention, participate in class, and actively take notes. Invite them to join your group.

Of course, you can recruit members in other ways. One way is to make an announcement during class. Another option is to post signs asking interested students to contact you. You can also pass around a sign-up sheet before class. These methods can reach many people, but they do take more time to achieve results. In addition, you have less control over who applies to join the group.

Limit groups to four people. Research on cooperative learning indicates that four people is an ideal group size.[2] Larger ones can be unwieldy.

Studying with friends is fine, but if your common interests are pizza and jokes, you might find it hard to focus.

In addition, remember that you'll gain the most benefit from study groups if you continue to take personal responsibility for your learning. Study group members can give you feedback, ask questions, and offer support. However, they cannot read, write papers, or take tests for you.

Hold a planning session. Ask two or three people to get together for a snack and talk about the group. You may define its goals, set up meeting times and locations, and clarify other logistics. You don't have to make an immediate commitment.

As you brainstorm about places to meet, aim for a quiet meeting room with plenty of space to spread out materials.

Do a trial run. Test the group first by planning a one-time session. If that session works, plan another. After a few successful sessions, you can schedule regular meetings.

Conduct your group

Ask your instructor for guidelines on study group activity. Many instructors welcome and encourage study groups. However, they have different ideas about what kinds of collaboration are acceptable. Some activities—such as sharing test items or writing papers from a shared outline—are considered cheating and can have serious consequences. Let your instructor know that you're forming a group, and ask for clear guidelines.

Set an agenda for each meeting. At the beginning of each meeting, reach an agreement on what you intend to do. Set a time limit for each agenda item, and determine a quitting time. End each meeting with assignments for all members to complete before the next meeting.

Assign roles. To make the most of your time, ask one member to lead each group meeting. The leader's role is to keep the discussion focused on the agenda and ask for contributions from all members. Assign another person to act as recorder. This person will take notes on the meeting, recording possible test questions, answers, and main points from group discussions. Rotate both of these roles so that every group member takes a turn.

Cycle through learning styles. As you assign roles, think about the learning styles present in your group. Some people excel at raising questions and creating lots of ideas. Others prefer to gather information and think critically. Some like to answer questions and make decisions, while others excel at taking action. Each of these distinct modes of learning are explained in "Learning Styles: Discovering How You Learn" on page 32. To create an effective group, match people with their preferred activities. You should also change roles within the group periodically. This gives group members a chance to explore new learning styles.

Teach each other. Teaching is a great way to learn something. Turn the material you're studying into a list of topics and assign a specific topic to each person, who will then teach it to the group. When you're done presenting your topic, ask for questions or comments. Prompt each other to explain ideas more clearly, find gaps in understanding, consider other points of view, and apply concepts to settings outside the classroom.

Test one another. During your meeting, take a practice test created from questions contributed by group members. When you're finished, compare answers. You can also turn testing into a game by pretending you're on a television game show. Use sample test questions to quiz one another.

Compare notes. Make sure that all the group's members heard the same thing in class and that you all recorded the important information. Ask others to help explain material in your notes that is confusing to you.

Create wall-size mind maps or concept maps to summarize a textbook or series of lectures. Work on large sheets of butcher paper, or tape together pieces of construction paper. When creating a mind map, assign one branch to each member of the study group. Use a different colored pen or marker for each branch of the mind map. (For more information on concept maps and mind maps, see Chapter 6: "Notes.")

Monitor effectiveness. On your meeting agenda, include an occasional discussion about your group's effectiveness. Are you meeting consistently? Is the group helping members succeed in class?

Use this time to address any issues that are affecting the group as a whole. If certain members are routinely unprepared for study sessions, brainstorm ways to get them involved. If one person tends to dominate meetings, reel her in by reminding her that everyone's voice needs to be heard.

To resolve conflict among group members, keep the conversation constructive. Focus on solutions. Move from vague complaints ("You're never prepared") to specific requests ("Will you commit to bringing 10 sample test questions next time?"). Asking a "problem" member to lead the next meeting might make an immediate difference. ✳

journal entry 17

Intention Statement

Start a study group

In the following space, outline a plan to form a study group. Explain the steps you will take to get the group organized and set a first meeting date. Also describe the reward you anticipate for acting on this intention.

I intend to . . .

_____

_____

_____

_____

_____

_____

_____

© image100/Corbis

What to do during the test

PREPARE YOURSELF FOR the test by arriving early. Being early often leaves time to do a relaxation exercise. While you're waiting for the test to begin and talking with classmates, avoid asking the question, "How much did you study for the test?" This question might fuel anxious thoughts that you didn't study enough.

As you begin

Ask the teacher or test administrator if you can use scratch paper during the test. (If you use a separate sheet of paper without permission, you might appear to be cheating.) If you *do* get permission, use this paper to jot down memory aids, formulas, equations, definitions, facts, or other material you know you'll need and might forget. An alternative is to make quick notes in the margins of the test sheet.

Pay attention to verbal directions given as a test is distributed. Then scan the whole test immediately. Evaluate the importance of each section. Notice how many points each part of the test is worth; then estimate how much time you'll need for each section, using its point value as your guide. For example, don't budget 20 percent of your time for a section that is worth only 10 percent of the points.

Read the directions slowly. Then reread them. It can be agonizing to discover that you lost points on a test merely because you failed to follow the directions. When the directions are confusing, ask to have them clarified.

Now you are ready to begin the test. If necessary, allow yourself a minute or two of "panic" time. Notice any tension you feel, and apply one of the techniques explained in the article "Let Go of Test Anxiety" later in this chapter.

Answer the easiest, shortest questions first. This gives you the experience of success. It also stimulates associations and prepares you for more difficult questions. Pace yourself, and watch the time. If you can't think of an answer, move on. Follow your time plan.

Multiple-choice questions

- *Answer each question in your head first.* Do this step before you look at the possible answers. If you come up with an answer that you're confident is right, look for that answer in the list of choices.

- *Read all possible answers before selecting one.* Sometimes two answers will be similar and only one will be correct.

- *Test each possible answer.* Remember that multiple-choice questions consist of two parts: the stem (an incomplete statement or question at the beginning) and a list of possible answers. Each answer, when combined with the stem, makes a complete statement or question-and-answer pair that is either true or false. When you combine the stem with each possible answer, you are turning each multiple-choice question into a small series of true/false questions. Choose the answer that makes a true statement.

- *Eliminate incorrect answers.* Cross off the answers that are clearly not correct. The answer you cannot eliminate is probably the best choice.

True/false questions

- *Read the entire question.* Separate the statement into its grammatical parts—individual clauses and phrases—and then test each part. If any part is false, the entire statement is false.

- *Look for qualifiers.* Qualifiers include words such as *all, most, sometimes,* or *rarely.* Absolute qualifiers such as *always* or *never* generally indicate a false statement.

- *Find the devil in the details.* Double-check each number, fact, and date in a true/false statement. Look for numbers that have been transposed or facts that have been slightly altered. These are signals of a false statement.

- *Watch for negatives.* Look for words such as *not* and *cannot.* Read the sentence without these words and see if you come up with a true or false statement. Then reinsert the negative words and see if the statement makes more sense. Watch especially for sentences with two negative words. As in math operations, two negatives cancel each other out: *We cannot say that Chekhov never succeeded at short story writing* means the same as *Chekhov succeeded at short story writing.*

Computer-graded tests

- Make sure that the answer you mark corresponds to the question you are answering.

- Check the test booklet against the answer sheet whenever you switch sections and whenever you come to the top of a column.

- Watch for stray marks on the answer sheet; they can look like answers.

- If you change an answer, be sure to erase the wrong answer thoroughly, removing all pencil marks completely.

Open-book tests

- Carefully organize your notes, readings, and any other materials you plan to consult when writing answers.

- Write down any formulas you will need on a separate sheet of paper.

- Bookmark the table of contents and index in each of your textbooks. Place sticky notes and stick-on tabs or paper clips on other important pages of books (pages with tables, for instance).

- Create an informal table of contents or index for the notes you took in class.

- Predict which material will be covered on the test, and highlight relevant sections in your readings and notes.

Short-answer/fill-in-the-blank tests

- Concentrate on keywords and facts. Be brief.

- Remember that overlearning material can really pay off. When you know a subject backward and forward, you can answer this type of question almost as fast as you can write.

Matching tests

- Begin by reading through each column, starting with the one with fewer items. Check the number of items in each column to see if they're equal. If they're not, look for an item in one column that you can match with two or more items in the other column.

- Look for any items with similar wording, and make special note of the differences between these items.

- Match words that are similar grammatically. For example, match verbs with verbs and nouns with nouns.

- When matching individual words with phrases, first read a phrase. Then look for the word that logically completes the phrase.

- Cross out items in each column when you are through with them.

What to do when you get stuck on a test question

- **Read it again.** Eliminate the simplest sources of confusion, such as misreading the question.

- **Skip the question for now.** This advice is simple—and it works. Let your subconscious mind work on the answer while you respond to other questions.

- **Look for answers in other test questions.** A term, name, date, or other fact that escapes you might appear in another question on the test itself.

- **Treat intuitions with care.** In quick-answer questions (multiple choice, true/false), go with your first instinct as to which answer is correct. If you think your first answer is wrong because you misread the question, do change your answer.

- **Rewrite the question.** See if you can put a confusing question into your own words. Doing so might release the answer.

- **Free-write.** On scratch paper or in the margins of your test booklet, record any response to the test question that pops into your head. Instead of just sitting there, stumped, you're doing something—a fact that can reduce anxiety. Writing might also trigger a mental association that answers the question.

- **Write a close answer.** Answer the question as best as you can, even if you don't think your answer is fully correct. This technique might help you get partial credit for short-answer questions, essay questions, and problems on math or science tests.

Essay questions

Managing your time is crucial in answering essay questions. Note how many questions you have to answer, and monitor your progress during the test period. Writing shorter answers and completing all of the questions on an essay test will probably yield a better score than leaving some questions blank.

Find out what an essay question is asking—precisely. If a question asks you to *compare* the ideas of Sigmund Freud and Karl Marx, no matter how eloquently you *explain* them, you are on a one-way trip to No Credit City.

Before you write, make a quick outline. An outline can help speed up the writing of your detailed answer. You're then less likely to leave out important facts. Even if you don't have time to finish your answer, your outline could win you some points. To use test time efficiently, keep your outline brief. Focus on keywords to use in your answer.

Introduce your answer by getting to the point. General statements such as "There are many interesting facets to this difficult question" can cause acute irritation to teachers grading dozens of tests.

One way to get to the point is to begin your answer with part of the question. Suppose the question is, "Discuss how increasing the city police budget might or might not contribute to a decrease in street crime." Your first sentence might be this: "An increase in police expenditures will not have a significant effect on street crime for the following reasons." Your position is clear. You are on your way to an answer.

Next, expand your answer with supporting ideas and facts. Start out with the most solid points. Be brief and avoid filler sentences.

Write legibly. Grading essay questions is in large part a subjective process. Sloppy, difficult-to-read handwriting might actually lower your grade.

Write on one side of the paper only. If you write on both sides of the paper, writing may show through and obscure the words on the other side. If necessary, use the blank side to add points you missed. Leave a generous left-hand margin and plenty of space between your answers, in case you want to add points that you missed later on.

Finally, if you have time, review your answers for grammar and spelling errors, clarity, and legibility. ✳

Words to watch for in essay questions

The following words are commonly found in essay test questions. They give you precise directions about what to include in your answer. Get to know these words well. When you see them on a test, underline them. Also look for them in your notes. Locating such keywords can help you predict test questions.

Analyze. Break into separate parts and discuss, examine, or interpret each part. Then give your opinion.

Compare. Examine two or more items. Identify similarities and differences.

Contrast. Show differences. Set in opposition.

Criticize. Make judgments. Evaluate comparative worth. Criticism often involves analysis.

Define. Explain the exact meaning—usually, a meaning specific to the course or subject. Definitions are usually short.

Describe. Give a detailed account. Make a picture with words. List characteristics, qualities, and parts.

Discuss. Consider and debate or argue the pros and cons of an issue. Write about any conflict. Compare and contrast.

Explain. Make an idea clear. Show logically how a concept is developed. Give the reasons for an event.

Prove. Support with facts (especially facts presented in class or in the text).

Relate. Show the connections between ideas or events. Provide a larger context for seeing the big picture.

State. Explain precisely.

Summarize. Give a brief, condensed account. Include conclusions. Avoid unnecessary details.

Trace. Show the order of events or the progress of a subject or event.

Notice how these words differ. For example, *compare* asks you to do something different than *contrast*. Likewise, *criticize* and *explain* call for different responses. If any of these terms are still unclear to you, look them up in an unabridged dictionary.

The test isn't over until . . .

MANY STUDENTS BELIEVE that a test is over as soon as they turn it in. Consider another point of view: You're not done with a test until you know the answer to any question that you missed—and why you missed it.

This point of view offers major benefits. Tests in many courses are cumulative. In other words, the content included on the first test is assumed to be working knowledge for future tests. When you understand the reason for lost points you learn something—and you greatly increase your odds of achieving better scores later in the course.

To get the most value from any test, take control of what you do at two critical points: immediately following the test and when the test is returned to you.

Immediately following the test. After finishing a test, your first thought might be to nap, snack, or celebrate with friends. Restrain those impulses for a short while so that you can reflect on the test. The time you invest now carries the potential to raise your grades in the future.

To begin with, sit down in a quiet place. Take a few minutes to write some Discovery Statements related to your experience. Describe how you felt about taking the test, how effective your review strategies were, and whether you accurately predicted the questions that appeared.

Follow up with an Intention Statement or two. State what you will do differently to prepare for the next test.

When the test is returned. First, make sure that the point totals add up correctly, and double-check for any other errors in grading. Even the best teachers make an occasional mistake.

Next, ask these questions:

- On what material did the teacher base test questions—readings, lectures, discussions, or other class activities?

- What types of questions appeared in the test— objective (such as matching items, true/false questions, or multiple choice), short answer, or essay?

- What types of questions did you miss?

- What can you learn from the instructor's comments that will help you prepare for the next test?

- How will you prepare differently for your next test?

Also see if you can correct any answers that lost points. Consult the following chart for help. ✳

Source of test error	Possible solutions
Study errors—studying material that was not included on the test, or spending too little time on material that *did* appear on the test	• Ask your teacher about specific topics that will be included on a test. • Practice predicting test questions. • Form a study group with class members to create mock tests.
Careless errors, such as skipping or misreading directions	• Read directions more carefully—especially when tests are divided into several sections. • Set aside time during the next test to proofread your answers.
Concept errors—mistakes made when you do not understand the underlying principles needed to answer a question or solve a problem	• Look for patterns in the questions you missed. • Make sure that you complete all assigned readings, attend all lectures, and show up for laboratory sessions. • Ask your teacher for help with specific questions.
Application errors—mistakes made when you understand underlying principles but fail to apply them correctly	• Rewrite your answers correctly. • Spend more time solving sample problems. • Predict application questions that will appear in future tests, and practice answering them.
Test mechanics errors—missing more questions in certain parts of the test than others, changing correct answers to incorrect ones at the last minute, leaving items blank, miscopying answers from scratch paper to the answer sheet	• Set time limits for taking each section of a test. • Proofread your test answers carefully. • Look for patterns in the kind of answers you change at the last minute. • Change answers only if you can state a clear and compelling reason to do so.

Let go of test anxiety

If you freeze during tests and flub questions when you know the answers, you might be dealing with test anxiety.

© Masterfile Royalty Free

A LITTLE TENSION before a test is fine. That tingly, butterflies-in-the-stomach feeling you get from extra adrenaline can sharpen your awareness and keep you alert. You can enjoy the benefits of a little tension while you stay confident and relaxed.

Sometimes, however, tension is persistent and extreme. If it interferes with your daily life and consistently prevents you from doing your best in school, you might be suffering from test anxiety.

Symptoms of anxiety include the following:[3]

- Inability to concentrate
- Insomnia
- Sweating
- Shortness of breath
- Fatigue
- Irritability
- Stomachache
- Diarrhea
- Headache

Anxiety has mental, physical, and emotional elements. The mental element includes your thoughts, including predictions of failure. The physical component includes physical sensations such as shallow breathing and muscle tension. The emotional element occurs when thoughts and physical sensations combine. The following techniques can help you deal with these elements of stress in *any* situation, from test anxiety to stage fright.

Dealing with thoughts

Yell "Stop!" When you notice that your mind is consumed with worries and fears—that your thoughts are spinning out of control—mentally yell "Stop!" If you're in a situation that allows it, yell it out loud. This

action can allow you to redirect your thoughts. Once you've broken the cycle of worry or panic, you can use any of the following techniques.

Dispute your thoughts. Certain thoughts tend to increase test anxiety. They often boil down to this statement: *Getting a low grade on a test is a disaster.* Do the math, however: A four-year degree often involves taking about 32 courses (eight courses per year over four years for a full-time student). This means that your final grade on any one course amounts to about only 3 percent of your total grade point average.

Also consider that your final grade in any one course is usually based on more than one test. This means that

F is for feedback, not failure

When some students get an F on an assignment, they interpret that letter as a message: "You are a failure." That interpretation is not accurate. Getting an F means only that you failed a test—not that you failed your life.

From now on, imagine that the letter F when used as a grade represents another word: *feedback.* An F is an indication that you didn't understand the material well enough. It's a message to do something differently before the next test or assignment.

If you interpret F as *failure,* you don't get to change anything. But if you interpret F as *feedback,* you can change your thinking and behavior in ways that promote your success.

a single test score is not going to make or break your college career.

This argument is not meant to convince you to stop preparing for tests. It *is* an argument to keep each test in perspective—and to dispute thoughts that only serve to create anxiety.

Praise yourself. Talk to yourself in a positive way. Many of us take the first opportunity to belittle ourselves: "Way to go, dummy! You don't even know the answer to the first question on the test." We wouldn't dream of treating a friend this way, yet we do it to ourselves. An alternative is to give yourself some encouragement. Treat yourself as if you were your own best friend. Consider telling yourself, "I am prepared. I can do a great job on this test."

Consider the worst. Rather than trying to put a stop to your worrying, consider the very worst thing that could happen. Take your fear to the limit of absurdity.

Imagine the catastrophic problems that might occur if you were to fail the test. You might say to yourself, "Well, if I fail this test, I might fail the course, lose my financial aid, and get kicked out of school. Then I won't be able to get a job, so the bank will repossess my car, and I'll start drinking." Keep going until you see the absurdity of your predictions. After you stop chuckling, you can backtrack to discover a reasonable level of concern. Your worry about failing the entire course if you fail the test might be justified. At that point, ask yourself, "Can I live with that?" Unless you are taking a test in parachute packing and the final question involves jumping out of a plane, the answer will almost always be yes. (If the answer is no, use another anxiety-relieving technique. In fact, use several other techniques.)

Dealing with physical sensations

Breathe. You can calm physical sensations within your body by focusing your attention on your breathing. Concentrate on the air going in and out of your lungs. Experience it as it passes through your nose and mouth. Do this exercise for two to five minutes. If you notice that you are taking short, shallow breaths, begin to take longer and deeper breaths. Imagine your lungs to be a pair of bagpipes. Expand your chest to bring in as much air as possible. Then listen to the plaintive chords as you slowly release the air.

Describe sensations. In your mind, describe your anxiety to yourself in detail; don't resist it. Think about all the ways in which your anxiety manifests itself. When you completely experience a physical sensation, it will often disappear. People suffering from chronic pain have also used this technique successfully.[4]

Scan your body. Simple awareness is an effective response to unpleasant physical sensations. Discover this for yourself by bringing awareness to each area of your body.

To begin, sit comfortably and close your eyes. Focus your attention on the muscles in your feet, and notice if they are relaxed. Tell the muscles in your feet that they can relax.

Move up to your ankles, and repeat the procedure. Next, go to your calves and thighs and buttocks, telling each group of muscles to relax.

Do the same for your lower back, diaphragm, chest, upper arms, lower arms, fingers, upper back, shoulders, neck, jaw, face, and scalp.

Use guided imagery. Relax completely, and take a quick fantasy trip. Close your eyes, free your body of tension, and imagine yourself in a beautiful, peaceful, natural setting. Create as much of the scene as you can. Be specific. Use all of your senses.

For example, you might imagine yourself at a beach. Hear the surf rolling in and the seagulls calling to each other. Feel the sun on your face and the hot sand between your toes. Smell the sea breeze. Taste the salty mist from the surf. Notice the ships on the horizon and the rolling sand dunes. Use all of your senses to create a vivid imaginary trip.

Find a place that works for you, and practice getting there. When you become proficient, you can return to it quickly for trips that might last only a few seconds.

With practice, you can use this technique even while you are taking a test.

Exercise aerobically. Performing aerobic exercise is one technique that won't work in the classroom or while you're taking a test. Yet it is an excellent way to reduce body tension. Exercise regularly during the days you review for a test. See what effect it has on your ability to focus and relax during the test.

Do some kind of exercise that will get your heart beating at twice your normal rate and keep it beating at that rate for 15 or 20 minutes. Aerobic exercise includes rapid walking, jogging, swimming, bicycling, playing basketball, and anything else that elevates your heart rate and keeps it elevated.

Find alternatives to chemicals. When faced with stress, some people turn to relief in the form of a pill, a drink, or a drug in some other form. Chemicals such as caffeine and alcohol *can* change the way you feel. They also come with costs that go beyond money. For example, drinking alcohol can relax you *and* interfere with your attention and memory. Caffeine or energy drinks might make you feel more confident in the short term. Watch what happens, though, when you start to come down from a caffeine-induced high. You might feel even more irritable than you did *before* drinking that double espresso.

All moral lectures aside, chemicals that you take without a prescription are ineffective ways to manage anxiety. Use other techniques instead.

Dealing with emotions

Accept emotions—whatever they are. Consider our typical response to problems. If a car has a flat tire, that's a problem. The solution is to repair or replace the tire. If a bathroom faucet drips, that's a problem. The solution is to repair or replace part of the faucet.

This problem–solution approach often works well when applied to events outside us. It does not work so well, however, when applied to events *inside* us. When we define anger, sadness, fear, or any emotion as a problem, we tend to search for a solution. However, emotions respond differently than flat tires and drippy faucets.

Typical attempts to "solve" unpleasant emotions include eating, drinking, watching TV, or surfing the Internet. These are actually attempts to resist the emotions and try to make them go away. For a short time, this strategy might work. Over the long term, however, our efforts to repair or replace emotions often have the opposite effect: The emotions persist or even get stronger. Our solutions actually become part of the problem.

An alternative to problem solving is *acceptance*. We can stop seeing emotions as problems. This attitude frees us from having to search for solutions (which often fail anyway).

Acceptance means just letting our emotions be. It means releasing any resistance to emotions. This approach is a wise one, since what we *resist* usually *persists*. Our emotions are just bundles of thoughts and physical sensations. Even the most unpleasant ones fade sooner or later.

The next time you are feeling anxious before a test, simply let that feeling arise and then pass away.

Practice detachment. To *detach* means to step back from something and see it as separate from ourselves. When we detach from an emotion, we no longer identify with it. We no longer say, "*I* am afraid" or "*I* am sad." We say something like "There's fear again" or "I feel sadness right now." Using language such as this offers us a way to step back from our internal experiences and keep them in perspective.

Before a test, you might find it especially useful to detach from your thoughts. Borrow some ideas from Acceptance and Commitment Therapy (ACT), which is used by a growing number of therapists.[5] Take an anxiety-producing thought—such as *I always screw up on tests*—and do any of the following:

- Repeat the thought over and over again out loud until it becomes just a meaningless series of sounds.

- Repeat the thought while using the voice of a cartoon character such as Mickey Mouse or Homer Simpson.

- Rephrase the thought so that you can sing it to the tune of a nursery rhyme or the song "Happy Birthday."

- Preface the thought with "I'm having the thought that . . ." (For example, *I'm having the thought that I always screw up on tests.*)

- Talk back to your mind by saying, "That's an interesting thought, mind; thanks a lot for sharing." Or simply say, "Thanks, mind."

Make contact with the present moment. If you feel anxious, see if you can focus your attention on a specific sight, sound, or other sensation that's happening in the present moment. Examine the details of a painting. Study the branches on a tree. Observe the face of your watch right down to the tiny scratches in the glass. During an exam, take a few seconds to listen to the sounds of squeaking chairs, the scratching of pencils, the muted coughs. Touch the surface of your desk and notice the texture. Focus all of your attention on one point—anything other than the flow of thoughts through your head. Focusing in this manner is one way to use the Power Process: "Be Here Now."

Get help. If you use any of the previous techniques for a couple of weeks and they fail to work, then turn to other people. Sometimes help with a specific situation—such as a lack of money—can relieve a source of stress that affects your test performance. Turn to the appropriate campus resource, such as the financial aid office.

If you become withdrawn, have thoughts about death or suicide, feel depressed for more than a few days, or have prolonged feelings of hopelessness, then see your doctor or a counselor at your student health center. No matter what the source of anxiety, help is always available. ✳

24 critical thinking exercise
20 things I like to do

One way to relieve tension is to mentally yell "Stop!" and substitute a pleasant daydream for the stressful thoughts and emotions you are experiencing.

To create a supply of pleasant images to recall during times of stress, conduct an 8-minute brainstorm about things you like to do. Your goal is to generate at least 20 ideas. Time yourself, and write as fast as you can in the following space.

When you have completed your list, study it. Pick out two activities that seem especially pleasant, and elaborate on them by creating a mind map. Write down all of the memories you have about that activity.

You can use these images to calm yourself in stressful situations.

Have some FUN!

Contrary to popular belief, finals week does not have to be a drag.

In fact, if you have used the techniques in this chapter, exam week can be fun. You will have done most of your studying long before finals arrive.

When you are well prepared for tests, you can even use fun as a technique to enhance your performance.

The day before a final, go for a run or play a game of basketball. Take in a movie or a concert. A relaxed brain is a more effective brain. If you have studied for a test, your mind will continue to prepare itself even while you're at the movies.

Get plenty of rest, too. There's no need to cram until 3 a.m. when you have reviewed material throughout the term.

On the first day of finals, you can wake up refreshed, have a good breakfast, and walk into the exam room with a smile on your face. You can also leave with a smile on your face, knowing that you are going to have a fun week. It's your reward for studying regularly throughout the term.

journal entry 18

Discovery/Intention Statement

Notice your excuses and let them go

Do a timed, four-minute brainstorm of all the reasons, rationalizations, justifications, and excuses you have used to avoid studying. Be creative. List your thoughts in the following space and continue them on a separate sheet if needed:

_____

_____

_____

_____

_____

_____

_____

_____

Now write a Discovery Statement about the list you just created.

I discovered that I . . .

_____

_____

_____

_____

Next, review your list, pick the excuse that you use the most, and circle it. In the following space, write an Intention Statement about what you will do to begin eliminating your favorite excuse. Make this Intention Statement one that you can keep, with a timeline and a reward.

I intend to . . .

_____

_____

_____

journal entry 19

Discovery Statement

Explore your feelings about tests

Complete the following sentences.

As exam time gets closer, one thing I notice that I do is . . .

_____

_____

When it comes to taking tests, I have trouble . . .

_____

_____

The night before a test, I usually feel . . .

_____

_____

The morning of a test, I usually feel . . .

_____

_____

During a test, I usually feel . . .

_____

_____

After a test, I usually feel . . .

_____

_____

When I learn a test score, I usually feel . . .

_____

_____

(www) An online version of this exercise is available.

Getting ready for math tests

MANY STUDENTS WHO could succeed in math shy away from the subject. Some had negative experiences in past courses. Others believe that math is only for gifted students.

At some level, however, math is open to all students. There's more to this subject than memorizing formulas and manipulating numbers. Imagination, creativity, and problem-solving skills are important, too.

Consider a three-part program for math success. Begin with strategies for overcoming math anxiety. Next, boost your study skills. Finally, let your knowledge shine during tests.

Overcome math anxiety

Many schools offer courses in overcoming math anxiety. Ask your advisor about resources on your campus. You can also experiment with the following suggestions.

Connect math to life. Think of the benefits of mastering math courses. You'll have more options for choosing a major and a career. Math skills can also put you at ease in everyday situations—for example, calculating the tip for a waiter, balancing your checkbook, or working with a spreadsheet on a computer. If you follow baseball statistics, cook, do construction work, or snap pictures with a camera, you'll use math. In addition, speaking the language of math can help you feel at home in a world driven by technology.

Pause occasionally to get an overview of the branch of math that you're studying. What's it all about? What basic problems is it designed to solve? How do people apply this knowledge in daily life? For example, many architects, engineers, and space scientists use calculus daily.

Take a first step. Math is cumulative. Concepts build upon each other in a certain order. If you struggled with algebra, you may have trouble with trigonometry or calculus.

To ensure that you have an adequate base of knowledge, tell the truth about your current level of knowledge and skill. Before you register for a math course, locate assigned texts for the prerequisite courses. If the material in those books seems new or difficult for you, see the instructor. Ask for suggestions on ways to prepare for the course.

Remember that it's OK to continue your study of math from your current level of ability, whatever that level might be.

Notice your pictures about math. Sometimes what keeps people from succeeding at math is their mental picture of mathematicians. They see a man dressed in a baggy plaid shirt and brown wingtip shoes. He's got a calculator on his belt and six pencils jammed in his shirt pocket.

These pictures are far from realistic. Succeeding in math won't turn you into a nerd. Actually, you'll be able to enjoy school more, and your friends will still like you.

Mental pictures about math can be funny, but they can have serious effects. If math is seen as a field for white males, then women and people of color are likely to get excluded. Promoting math success for all students helps to overcome racism and sexism.

Change your conversation about math. When students fear math, they often say negative things to themselves about their abilities in this subject. Many times this self-talk includes statements such as *I'll never be fast enough at solving math problems* or *I'm good with words, so I can't be good with numbers.*

Get such statements out in the open, and apply some emergency critical thinking. You'll find two self-defeating assumptions lurking there: *Everybody else is better at math and science than I am* and *Since I don't understand a math concept right now, I'll never understand it.* Both of these statements are illogical.

Replace negative beliefs with logical, realistic statements that affirm your ability to succeed in math: *Any confusion I feel now can be resolved. I learn math without comparing myself to others.* And *I ask whatever questions are needed to aid my understanding.*

TESTS

7

Choose your response to stress. Math anxiety is seldom just "in your head." It can also register as sweaty palms, shallow breathing, tightness in the chest, or a mild headache. Instead of trying to ignore these sensations, just notice them without judgment. Over time, simple awareness decreases their power.

In addition, use stress management techniques. "Let Go of Test Anxiety" on page 199 offers a bundle of them.

No matter what you do, remember to breathe. You can relax in any moment just by making your breath slower and deeper. Practice doing this while you study math. It will come in handy at test time.

Boost study skills for math

Choose teachers with care. Whenever possible, find a math teacher whose approach to math matches your learning style. Talk with several teachers until you find one you enjoy.

Another option is to ask around. Maybe your academic advisor can recommend math teachers. You can also ask classmates to name their favorite math teachers—and to explain the reasons for their choices.

In some cases, only one teacher will be offering the math course you need. The suggestions that follow can be used to learn from a teacher regardless of her teaching style.

Take math courses back to back. Approach math in the same way that you learn a foreign language. If you take a year off in between Spanish I and Spanish II, you won't gain much fluency. To master a language, you take courses back to back. It works the same way with math, which is a language in itself.

Form a study group. During the first week of each math course, organize a study group. Ask each member to bring five problems to group meetings, along with solutions. You should also exchange contact information so that you can stay in touch via e-mail, phone, and text messaging.

Avoid short courses. Courses that you take during summer school or another shortened term are condensed. You might find yourself doing far more reading and homework each week than you do in longer courses. If you enjoy math, the extra intensity can provide a stimulus to learn. However, if math is not your favorite subject, give yourself extra time. Enroll in courses spread out over more calendar days.

Participate in class. Success in math depends on your active involvement. Attend class regularly. Complete homework assignments *when they're due*— not just before the test. If you're confused, get help right away from an instructor, tutor, or study group. Instructors' office hours, free on-campus tutoring, and classmates are just a few of the resources available to you. In addition, support your class participation with time for homework. Make daily contact with math.

Prepare for several types of tests. Math tests often involve lists of problems to solve. Ask your instructor about what types of tests to expect. Then prepare for the tests using strategies from this chapter.

Ask questions fearlessly. It's a cliché, but it's true: In math, there are no dumb questions. Ask whatever questions will aid your understanding. Keep a running list of them, and bring the list to class.

Make your text your top priority. Math courses are often text driven. Class activities closely follow the book. This fact underscores the importance of completing your reading assignments. Master one

Succeeding in science courses

Many of the strategies that help you prepare for math tests can also help you succeed in science courses. For example, forming small study groups can be a fun way to learn these subjects. Following are some additional ideas.

Relate science to your career interests and daily life People in many professions—from dentists to gardeners—rely on science to do their job. Even if you don't choose a science-driven career, you will live in a world that's driven by technology. Understanding how scientists observe, collect data, and arrive at conclusions can help you feel more at home in this world.

Prepare for variety Remember that the word *science* refers to a vast range of subjects—astronomy, biology, chemistry, physics, physiology, geology, ecology, geography, and more. Most of these subjects include math as one of their tools. Beyond that, however, are many differences.

You can take advantage of this variety. Choose science courses that match your personal interests and comfort level for technical subjects.

Prepare for lab sessions Laboratory work is crucial to many science classes. To get the most out of these sessions, be prepared. Complete required reading before you enter the lab. Be sure you also gather the materials you'll need ahead of time.

 Find more strategies for succeeding in science online.

1: Prepare

- Read each problem two or three times, slowly and out loud whenever possible.
- Consider creating a chart with three columns labeled *What I already know*, *What I want to find out*, and *What connects the two.* The third column is the place to record a formula that can help you solve the problem.
- Determine which arithmetic operations (addition, subtraction, multiplication, division) or formulas you will use to solve the problem.
- See if you can estimate the answer before you compute it.

2: Compute

- Reduce the number of unknowns as much as you can. Consider creating a separate equation to solve each unknown.
- When solving equations, carry out the algebra as far as you can before plugging in the actual numbers.
- Cancel and combine. For example, if the same term appears in both dividend and divisor, they will cancel each other out.
- Remember that it's OK to make several attempts at solving the problem before you find an answer.

3: Check

- Plug your answer back into the original equation or problem and see if it works out correctly.
- Ask yourself if your answer seems likely when compared with your estimate. For example, if you're asked to apply a discount to an item, that item should cost less in your solution.
- Perform opposite operations. If a problem involves multiplication, check your work by division; add, then subtract; factor, then multiply; find the square root, then the square; differentiate, then integrate.
- Keep units of measurement clear. Say that you're calculating the velocity of an object. If you're measuring distance in meters and time in seconds, the final velocity should be in meters per second.

concept before going on to the next, and stay current with your reading. Be willing to read slowly and reread sections as needed.

Read actively. To get the most out of your math texts, read with paper and pencil in hand. Work out examples. Copy diagrams, formulas, and equations. Use chapter summaries and introductory outlines to organize your learning.

From time to time, stop, close your book, and mentally reconstruct the steps in solving a problem. Before you memorize a formula, understand the basic concepts behind it.

Practice solving problems. To get ready for math tests, work *lots* of problems. Find out if practice problems or previous tests are on file in the library, in the math department, or with your math teacher.

Isolate the types of problems that you find the most difficult. Practice them more often. Be sure to get help with these kinds of problems *before* exhaustion or frustration sets in.

To prepare for tests, practice working problems fast. Time yourself. This activity is a great one for math study groups.

Approach problem solving with a three-step process, as shown in the chart on this page. During each step, apply an appropriate strategy.

Use tests to show what you know

Practice test taking. Part of preparing for any math test is rehearsal. Instead of passively reading through your text or scanning class notes, do a practice test:

- Print out a set of practice problems, and set a timer for the same length of time as your testing period.
- Whenever possible, work practice problems in the same room where you will take the actual test.
- Use only the kinds of supporting materials—such as scratch paper or lists of formulas—that will be allowed during the test.
- As you work problems, use deep breathing or another technique to enter a more relaxed state.

Ask appropriate questions. During the test, if you don't understand a test item, ask for clarification. The worst that can happen is that an instructor or proctor will politely decline to answer your question.

Write legibly. Put yourself in the instructor's place. Imagine the prospect of grading stacks of illegible answer sheets. Make your answers easy to read. If you show your work, underline key sections and circle your answer.

Do your best. There are no secrets involved in getting ready for math tests. Master some stress management techniques, do your homework, get answers to your questions, and work sample problems. If you've done those things, you're ready for the test and deserve to do well. If you haven't done all those things, just do the best you can.

Remember that your personal best can vary from test to test, and even from day to day. Even if you don't answer all test questions correctly, you can demonstrate what you *do* know right now.

During the test, notice when solutions come easily. Savor the times when you feel relaxed and confident. If you ever feel math anxiety in the future, these are the times to remember.[6] ✳

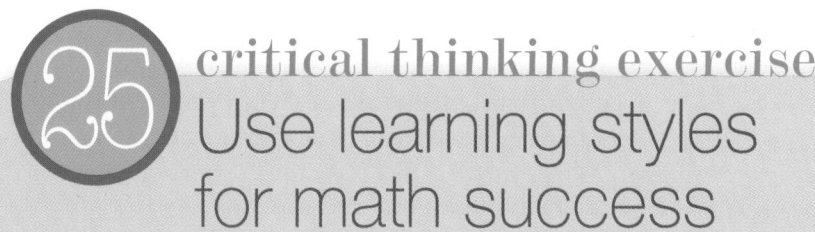

25 critical thinking exercise
Use learning styles for math success

Review the articles about learning styles in Chapter 1: "First Steps." Look for strategies that could promote your success in math. Modify any of the suggested strategies so that they work for you.

See if you can invent techniques that work especially well for math courses. If you're a visual learner, for example, you might color code your notes by writing key terms

and formulas in red ink. If you like to learn by speaking and listening, then consider reading key passages in your textbooks out loud. Alternatively, if you're a kinesthetic learner, use "manipulatives"—such as magnetic boards with letters and numbers—when you study math.

Whatever you choose, commit to using at least one new strategy. In the following space, describe what you will do.

© Lawrence Manning/Corbis

Make performance reviews work for you

PERFORMANCE REVIEWS usually take place in a meeting with your direct supervisor at work. These meetings follow various formats, and many organizations have their own systems for rating performance. Yet the basic idea in any case is for you to walk away with answers to three questions: *What am I doing well? What could I do better?* and *How can I develop the skills to do better?* When handled with skill, performance reviews are tools for taking charge of your career.

Set goals early. Your organization may schedule performance reviews only once or twice per year. However, effective performance review is a continuous process. For optimum results, begin this process on your first day at work. When you start a new job, meet with your direct supervisor to define exactly what "effective performance" means for you.

Set work-related goals that you can achieve (see Chapter 3: "Time"). State them in specific, measurable terms, as explained later in this article. Whenever possible, include a specific date to meet each goal. Put your goals in writing and share them with your supervisor.

Prepare for the review. As the date of your performance review approaches, anticipate the kinds of questions your supervisor will ask. For example:

- What was your biggest accomplishment since your last performance review?
- In light of your stated goals, how did you feel about your performance?
- What prevented you from performing well or meeting any of your goals?
- What can you do to overcome those obstacles?
- What can coworkers and managers do to help you overcome those obstacles?

Keep the tone positive. When you meet with your supervisor, refer to your list of goals and note which ones you met. Take time to celebrate your accomplishments and set new goals.

If you missed a goal, talk about how that happened. Instead of focusing on failure or placing blame, take a problem-solving approach. If you made a mistake, talk about what you learned from the experience and what you intend to do differently in the future. Revise the goal and create a new plan for achieving it.

Effective performance reviews include time for you to *give* feedback as well as receive it. Discuss what you like about your job and what you would like to change. If meeting your goals calls for extra resources or changes in your job description, then ask for them.

Instead of complaining about working conditions, make suggestions. "My office is way too noisy for me to be productive" is a complaint. "Let's set up a quiet room in our building where people can go to do work that requires long periods of concentration" is a suggestion. Suggestions are easier to hear than complaints and naturally lend themselves to follow-up action.

Create a focused plan for personal development. Performance reviews often end with a development plan that includes specific ways to improve performance. Standard advice from many self-development "experts" is to focus this plan on identifying your greatest personal weakness and changing that right away.

Think critically about this advice for three reasons. First, tackling your biggest weakness first can feel threatening and lead to procrastination. Second, this weakness may be hard to change before your next performance review. And third, eliminating this weakness might affect your life outside work but have little or no impact on your career.

Another option is to focus your development plan on your strengths. Think about any of your recent accomplishments at work. Describe them in writing, including specific details about what you did and the results of your actions.

Next, set a goal to build on one of these accomplishments. Say that you made a suggestion to change the work flow in your department, and this change allowed your team to finish a project well before the scheduled due date. Consider setting a goal to make this a permanent change in your department's procedures. You could also set a goal to find other time-saving procedures.

Of course, you can always set a goal that targets one of your weaknesses. Just stay positive. Instead of focusing on a current behavior that you want to *stop*, for example, describe a new behavior that you want to *start*. Change "I will stop taking unclear notes at meetings" to "I will review my meeting notes to clarify the major agreements we made and next actions to take."

In any case, focus your development plan on goals that you can actually achieve in the near future, leading to clear benefits at work. Translate your goal into concrete behaviors. Ask yourself: What exactly will I *do* differently based on my goal? And how will I *monitor* this behavior?

If you did the Time Monitor/Time Plan exercise in Chapter 3: "Time," you already have some experience with monitoring your behavior. You can monitor your progress toward any goal, no matter how ambitious. To monitor listening skills, for example, you could count the number of times each day that you interrupt other people.

Remember that the point of monitoring your behavior is not to become a cold-blooded measurement machine. Rather, the idea is to make a change that really makes a difference over the long term. The behaviors that we measure are the ones most likely to change.

As you monitor your behavior, suspend all self-judgment. Just record the facts. If you deviate from your plan, just look for the next opportunity to practice your new behavior.

Act on your plan every day. For your development plan, choose a behavior that you can do every day at work. Also describe how you will record the measurements that you make while monitoring your behavior. For instance, you could tally the number of your work breaks on a 3×5 card.

Do a daily debriefing on your way home from work. This can take only a minute or two. Estimate how often you're succeeding at changing your behavior. Make any adjustments to your plan that seem necessary. Then set a clear intention about when and where you will practice a new behavior at work tomorrow. By creating a continuous cycle of planning and monitoring, you set yourself up for long-term success at work.

Based on this feedback about performance in your current job, you can define the next job you want. Every performance review can be one more step to the career of your dreams. ✳

journal entry 20

Intention Statement

Set a goal for personal development

Reflect for a few minutes on your recent performance at your current job, or your overall performance at a previous job. In a single sentence, describe one success that you experienced—any goal that you were proud to meet or any task that you did especially well:

_____

_____

_____

Now reflect on this experience by completing the following sentences:

In creating this success, the attitude or behavior that helped me most was . . .

_____

_____

To experience this kind of success on a more consistent basis, I intend to . . .

_____

_____

Celebrate mistakes

PKruger/Shutterstock

A CREATIVE ENVIRONMENT is one in which failure is not fatal. Businesses striving to be on the cutting edge of competition desperately seek innovative changes. They know that innovation requires risk taking, despite the chance of failure.

This is not idle talk. There are people who actually celebrate mistakes:[7]

- The Coca-Cola company launched a number of beverages that bombed—including Choglit, OK Soda, Surge, and New Coke. But at the company's annual meeting in 2006, chair and chief executive officer E. Neville Isdell told investors to accept failures as a way to regenerate the company.

- Scott Anthony, director of a consulting firm named Innosight, coaches companies to fumble to success by failing early and cheaply as they develop new products.

- Thomas D. Kuczmarski, a Chicago-based consultant, suggests that companies hold "failure parties" to reward mistakes that lead to better products.

This is *not* an argument in favor of making mistakes. Rather, the goal is to learn from mistakes that happen as we aim for success. In fact, there are several reasons that we can even celebrate mistakes.

Celebration allows us to notice the mistake. Covering up mistakes or blaming others for them takes a lot of energy. That energy could be channeled into correcting errors instead. Celebrating mistakes gets them out into the open.

Mistakes are valuable feedback. There's an old story about the manager of a major corporation who made a mistake that cost his company $100,000. The manager predicted that he would be fired. Instead, his boss said, "Fire you? I can't afford to do that. I just spent $100,000 training you." This story may be fictional, but it makes a point: Mistakes are part of the learning process. In fact, mistakes are often more interesting and more instructive than are successes.

Mistakes demonstrate that we're taking risks. People who play it safe make few mistakes. Making mistakes can be evidence that we're stretching to the limit of our abilities—growing, risking, and learning. Fear of making mistakes can paralyze us into inaction. Celebrating mistakes helps us move into gear and get things done.

Celebrating mistakes includes everyone. Celebrating mistakes reminds us that the exclusive club named the Perfect Performance Society has no members. All of us make mistakes. When we notice them, we can work together to find a solution. ✳

Notable failures

As you experiment with new techniques, you may try a few that fail at crucial moments—such as during a test. Just remember that many people before you have failed miserably before succeeding brilliantly. Consider a few examples:

In his first professional race, cyclist *Lance Armstrong* finished last.

The first time *Jerry Seinfeld* walked onstage at a comedy club as a professional comic, he looked out at the audience and froze.

In high school, actor and comic *Robin Williams* was voted "Least Likely to Succeed."

Walt Disney was fired by a newspaper editor because "he lacked imagination and had no good ideas."

R. H. Macy failed seven times before his store in New York City caught on.

Decca Records turned down a recording contract with *The Beatles* with an unprophetic evaluation: "We don't like their sound. Groups of guitars are on their way out."

In 1954, Jimmy Denny, manager of the Grand Ole Opry, fired *Elvis Presley* after one performance.

Babe Ruth is famous for his past home run record, but for decades he also held the record for strikeouts. *Mark McGwire* broke that record.

Adapted from "But They Did Not Give Up," www.des.emory.edu/mfp/OnFailingG.html (accessed November 11, 2009).

DETACH

This Power Process helps you release the powerful, natural student within you. It is especially useful whenever negative emotions are getting in your way.

Attachments are addictions. When we are attached to something, we think we cannot live without it, just as a drug addict feels he cannot live without drugs. We believe our well-being depends on maintaining our attachments.

We can be attached to just about anything: beliefs, emotions, people, roles, objects. The list is endless.

One person, for example, might be so attached to his car that he takes an accident as a personal attack. Pity the poor unfortunate who backs into this person's car. He might as well have backed into the owner himself.

Another person might be attached to her job. Her identity and sense of well-being depend on it. She could become deeply depressed, almost to the point of suicide, if she ever gets fired.

When we are attached and things don't go our way, we can feel angry, sad, afraid, or confused.

Suppose you are attached to getting an A on your physics test. You feel as though your success in life depends on getting that A. As the clock ticks away, you work harder on the test, getting more stuck. That voice in your head gets louder: "I must get an A. I MUST get an A. I MUST GET AN A!"

Now is a time to detach. Practice observer consciousness. See if you can just *observe* what's going on, letting go of all your judgments. When you just observe, you reach a quiet state above and beyond your usual thoughts. This is a place where you can be aware of being aware. It's a tranquil spot, apart from your emotions. From here, you can observe yourself objectively, as if you were someone else. Pay attention to your thoughts and physical sensations. If you are confused and feeling stuck, tell yourself, "Here I am, confused and stuck." If your palms are sweaty and your stomach is one big knot, admit it. Put your current circumstances into a broader perspective. View your personal issues within the larger context of your community, nation, or even planet.

Practice breathing. Calm your mind and body with relaxation techniques.

Practice detaching before the big test. The key is to let go of automatic emotional reactions when you don't get what you want.

Caution: Giving up an *attachment* to being an A student does not mean giving up *being* an A student. Giving up an attachment to a job doesn't mean giving up the job. When you detach, you get to keep your values and goals. However, you know that you will be OK even if you fail to achieve a goal. You are more than your goals. You are more than your thoughts and feelings. You are more than your current circumstances. These things come and go. Meanwhile, the part of you that can just *observe* everything that happens and learn from it is always there and always safe, no matter what happens.

Behind your attachments is a master student. Release that mastery. Detach.

 Learn more about using this Power Process online.

Career Application

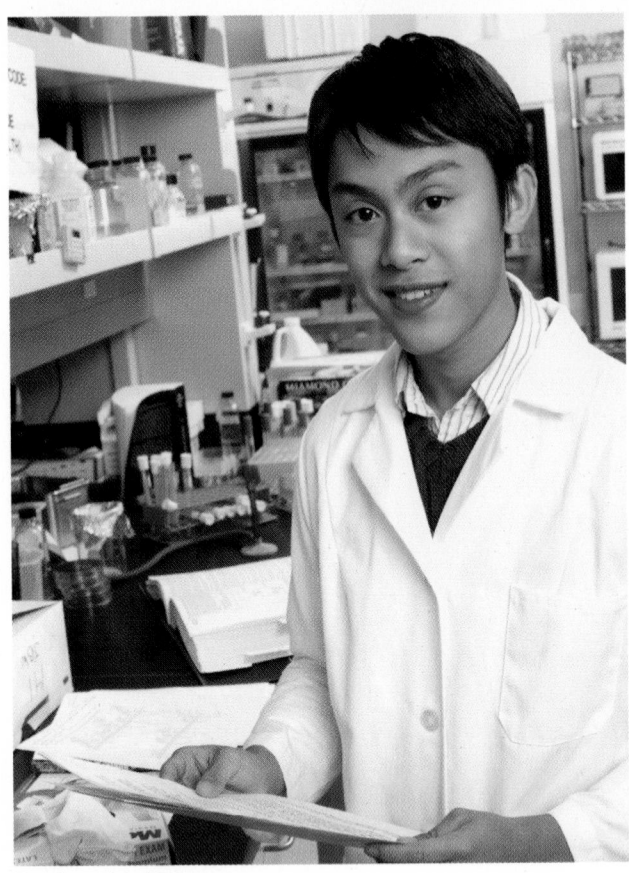

Red Chopsticks/Getty

During his senior year of high school, Chang Lee read about the favorable job market for medical assistants. He set a goal to enroll in a local community college and earn his A.A. degree in medical assisting. This was a logical choice for Chang. His mother worked as a psychiatric nurse, and he'd always been interested in health care. He figured that his degree would equip him with marketable skills and a way to contribute to society.

Chang's choice paid off. He excelled in his classes. With his career goal in mind, he often asked himself: *How could I use this information to become a better medical assistant?*

During his second year of college, Chang landed an internship with a large medical clinic near campus. The clinic offered him a job after he graduated, and he accepted.

Chang enjoyed the day-to-day tasks of medical assisting. He helped doctors run medical tests and perform physical exams. In addition, he ordered lab work and updated medical records.

After three months on the job, Chang was on a first-name basis with many of the clinic's regular patients. No matter how busy the clinic's schedule, Chang made time for people. When they finished describing their symptoms, he frequently asked, "Is there anything else that's on your mind?" Then he listened without interrupting. Chang's ability to put people at ease made him popular with patients, who often asked specifically to see him.

The only part of his job that Chang dreaded was performance reviews, which took place twice during each year of employment. Even though he was respected by coworkers, Chang felt nervous whenever the topic of evaluating work performance came up. "It just reminds me too much of final exams during school," he said. "I like my job and I try to do it well every day. Having a performance review just raises my anxiety level and doesn't really benefit me."

Reflecting on this scenario

Briefly describe three strategies from this chapter that Chang could use to change his experience of performance reviews. Be specific about how he could use each strategy.

_____

_____

_____

_____

_____

_____

_____

_____

_____

_____

_____

_____

_____

_____

_____

_____

_____

Quiz

Name _____   Date ____/____/____

1. According to the text, test scores measure your intelligence. True or false? Explain your answer.

2. When answering multiple-choice questions, it is generally effective to read all of the possible answers before answering the question in your head. True or false? Explain your answer.

3. The presence of absolute qualifiers, such as *always* or *never,* generally indicates a false statement. True or false? Explain your answer.

4. Briefly explain the difference between a daily review and a major review.

5. Define the term *study checklist,* and give three examples of what to include on such checklists.

6. Describe how using the Power Process: "Detach" differs from giving up.

7. Study groups can focus on which of the following?
   (a) Comparing and editing class notes.
   (b) Doing research to prepare for papers and presentations.
   (c) Finding and understanding key passages in assigned readings.
   (d) Creating and taking practice tests.
   (e) All of the above.

8. Give an example of "changing your conversation" about learning math.

9. Describe three techniques for dealing with the thoughts connected to test anxiety.

10. Describe three techniques for dealing with the physical sensations or emotions connected to test anxiety.

Focus on Transferable Skills

Now that you've had some concrete experience with the strategies presented in this chapter, take a minute to reflect on your responses to the "Tests" section of the Discovery Wheel in Chapter 1: "First Steps." Think about your current skills in this area and plan to expand on them.

You might want to prepare for this exercise by reviewing the articles "Jumpstart Your Education with Transferable Skills" on page 58 and "101 Transferable Skills" on page 60.

PREPARING FOR TESTS

When studying for a test, the first thing I usually do is to . . .

In addition, I . . .

TAKING TESTS

One strategy that helps me with objective tests (true/false and multiple choice) is . . .

One strategy that helps me with short-answer and essay tests is . . .

MANAGING MY RESPONSE TO TESTS AND PERFORMANCE REVIEWS

On the day of a test, my level of confidence is generally . . .

For a performance review at work, my level of confidence is generally . . .

NEXT ACTION

The skill related to tests and performance reviews that I would most like to develop is . . .

To develop this skill, the most important thing I can do next is to . . .

Master Student PROFILE

Al Gore

. . . is optimistic

© Joseph Sohm/Visions of America/Corbis

One hundred and nineteen years ago, a wealthy inventor read his own obituary, mistakenly published years before his death. Wrongly believing the inventor had just died, a newspaper printed a harsh judgment of his life's work, unfairly labeling him "The Merchant of Death" because of his invention—dynamite. Shaken by this condemnation, the inventor made a fateful choice to serve the cause of peace.

Seven years later, Alfred Nobel created this prize and the others that bear his name.

Seven years ago tomorrow, I read my own political obituary in a judgment that seemed to me harsh and mistaken—if not premature. But that unwelcome verdict also brought a precious if painful gift: an opportunity to search for fresh new ways to serve my purpose.

Unexpectedly, that quest has brought me here. Even though I fear my words cannot match this moment, I pray what I am feeling in my heart will be communicated clearly enough that those who hear me will say, "We must act." . . .

In the last few months, it has been harder and harder to misinterpret the signs that our world is spinning out of kilter. Major cities in North and South America, Asia and Australia are nearly out of water due to massive droughts and melting glaciers. Desperate farmers are losing their livelihoods. Peoples in the frozen Arctic and on low-lying Pacific islands are planning evacuations of places they have long called home. Unprecedented wildfires have forced a half million people from their homes in one country and caused a national emergency that almost brought down the government in another. Climate refugees have migrated into areas already inhabited by people with different cultures, religions, and traditions, increasing the potential for

conflict. Stronger storms in the Pacific and Atlantic have threatened whole cities. Millions have been displaced by massive flooding in South Asia, Mexico, and 18 countries in Africa. As temperature extremes have increased, tens of thousands have lost their lives. We are recklessly burning and clearing our forests and driving more and more species into extinction.

There is an African proverb that says, "If you want to go quickly, go alone. If you want to go far, go together." We need to go far, quickly. . . .

Fifteen years ago, I made that case at the "Earth Summit" in Rio de Janeiro. Ten years ago, I presented it in Kyoto. This week, I will urge the delegates in Bali to adopt a bold mandate for a treaty that establishes a universal global cap on emissions and uses the market in emissions trading to efficiently allocate resources to the most effective opportunities for speedy reductions.

This treaty should be ratified and brought into effect everywhere in the world by the beginning of 2010—two years sooner than presently contemplated. The pace of our response must be accelerated to match the accelerating pace of the crisis itself. . . .

The future is knocking at our door right now. Make no mistake, the next generation will ask us one of two questions. Either they will ask: "What were you thinking; why didn't you act?" Or they will ask instead: "How did you find the moral courage to rise and successfully resolve a crisis that so many said was impossible to solve?"

© The Nobel Foundation 2007. Reprinted with permission.

(1948–) Former vice president of the United States, Gore refocused his career on climate change, won a Nobel Peace Prize, and—in the film *An Inconvenient Truth*—invented a new type of documentary.

Learn more about Al Gore and other master students at the Master Student Hall of Fame.

8 Thinking

Master Student Map

as you read, ask yourself

what if . . .
I could solve problems more creatively and make decisions in every area of life with more confidence?

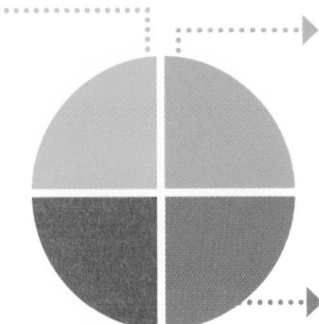

why this chapter matters . . .
The ability to think helps you succeed in school and promotes many skills that transfer to the workplace—including reading, writing, speaking, and listening.

how

you can use this chapter . . .

- Learn to create and refine ideas.
- Choose attitudes that promote your success.
- Avoid common mistakes in thinking.
- Enhance your success in problem solving.
- Put your thinking skills to practical use in making decisions.

what is included . . .

MASTER EMPLOYEE in *action*

I am lucky to work for a company that actively encourages creativity. Although we are expected to fulfill all the responsibilities of our position, there is also time set aside during which we can pursue more free-thinking activities. I stay motivated by remembering that there is an outlet for my creativity and always come back to the more mundane tasks with a renewed energy.

—KATE CHIU, ASSOCIATE DIRECTOR OF COMMUNICATIONS

Photo courtesy of Kate Chiu

Critical thinking:
A survival skill

SOCIETY DEPENDS ON persuasion. Advertisers want us to spend money on their products. Political candidates want us to "buy" their stands on the issues. Teachers want us to agree that their classes are vital to our success. Parents want us to accept their values. Authors want us to read their books. Broadcasters want us to spend our time in front of the radio or television, consuming their programs and not those of the competition. The business of persuasion has an impact on all of us.

A typical American sees thousands of television commercials each year—and TV is just one medium of communication. Add to that the writers and speakers who enter our lives through radio shows, magazines, books, billboards, brochures, Internet sites, and fund-raising appeals—all with a product, service, cause, or opinion for us to embrace.

This flood of appeals leaves us with hundreds of choices about what to buy, where to go, and who to be. It's easy to lose our heads in the crosscurrent of competing ideas—unless we develop skills in critical thinking. When we think critically, we can make choices with open eyes.

Uses of critical thinking. *Critical thinking informs reading, writing, speaking, and listening.* These elements are the basis of communication—a process that occupies most of our waking hours.

Critical thinking promotes social change. The institutions in any society—courts, governments, schools, businesses, nonprofit groups—are the products of cultural customs and trends. All social movements—from the American Revolution to the Civil Rights movement—came about through the work of engaged individuals who actively participated in their communities and questioned what was going on around them. As critical thinkers, we strive to understand and influence the institutions in our society.

Critical thinking uncovers bias and prejudice. Working through our preconceived notions is a first step toward communicating with people of other races, ethnic backgrounds, and cultures.

Critical thinking reveals long-term consequences. Crises occur when our thinking fails to keep pace with reality. An example is the world's ecological crisis, which arose when people polluted the earth, air, and water without considering the long-term consequences.

8

THINKING

Imagine how different our world would be if our leaders had thought like the first female chief of the Cherokees. Asked about the best advice her elders had given her, she replied, "Look forward. Turn what has been done into a better path. If you are a leader, think about the impact of your decision on seven generations into the future."

Critical thinking reveals nonsense. Novelist Ernest Hemingway once said that anyone who wants to be a great writer must have a built-in, shockproof "crap" detector.[1] That inelegant comment points to a basic truth: As critical thinkers, we are constantly on the lookout for thinking that's inaccurate, sloppy, or misleading.

Critical thinking is a skill that will never go out of style. At various times in human history, nonsense has been taken for the truth. For example, people have believed the following:

- Use of blood-sucking leeches is the only recommended treatment for disease.

- Illness results from an imbalance in the four vital fluids: blood, phlegm, water, and bile.

- Caucasians are inherently more intelligent than people of other races.

- Racial intermarriage will lead to genetically inferior children.

- Racial integration of the armed forces will lead to destruction of soldiers' morale.

- Women are incapable of voting intelligently.

- We will never invent anything smaller than a transistor. (That was before the computer chip.)

- Computer technology will usher in the age of the paperless office.

The critical thinkers of history arose to challenge short-sighted ideas such as those in the previous list. These courageous men and women pointed out that, metaphorically speaking, the emperor had no clothes.

Even in mathematics and the hard sciences, the greatest advances take place when people reexamine age-old beliefs. Scientists continually uncover things that contradict everyday certainties. For example, physics presents us with a world where solid objects are made of atoms spinning around in empty space, where matter and energy are two forms of the same substance. At a moment's notice, the world can deviate from the "laws of nature." That is because those "laws" exist in our heads, not in the world.

Critical thinking is a path to freedom from half-truths and deception. You have the right to question everything that you see, hear, and read. Acquiring this ability is a major goal of a liberal education.

Critical thinking as thorough thinking. For some people, the term *critical thinking* has negative connotations. If you prefer, use *thorough thinking* instead. Both terms point to the same activities: sorting out conflicting claims, weighing the evidence, letting go of personal biases, and arriving at reasonable conclusions. These activities add up to an ongoing conversation—a constant process, not a final product.

We live in a culture that values quick answers and certainty. These concepts are often at odds with effective thinking. Thorough thinking is the ability to examine and reexamine ideas that might seem obvious. This kind of thinking takes time and the willingness to say three subversive words: *I don't know.*

Thorough thinking is also the willingness to change our opinions as we continue to examine a problem. This calls for courage and detachment. Just ask anyone who has given up a cherished point of view in light of new evidence.

Thorough thinking is the basis for much of what you do in school—reading, writing, speaking, listening, note taking, test taking, problem solving, and other forms of decision making. Skilled students have strategies for accomplishing all of these tasks. They distinguish between opinion and fact. They ask probing questions and make detailed observations. They uncover assumptions and define their terms. They make assertions carefully, basing them on sound logic and solid evidence. Almost everything that we call *knowledge* is a result of these activities. This means that critical thinking and learning are intimately linked.

One kind of thorough thinking—planning—has the power to lift the quality of our lives almost immediately. When you plan, you are the equal of the greatest sculptor, painter, or playwright. More than creating a work of art, you are designing your life. *From Master Student to Master Employee* invites you to participate in this form of thinking by choosing your major, planning your career, and setting long-term goals.

It's been said that human beings are rational creatures. Yet no one is born a thorough thinker. Critical thinking is a learned skill. Use the suggestions in this chapter to claim the thinking powers that are your birthright. The critical thinker is one aspect of the master student who lives inside you. ✳

Becoming a critical thinker

Critical thinking is a path to intellectual adventure. Although there are dozens of possible approaches, the process boils down to asking and answering questions.

© Steve Cole/Getty

ACCORDING TO "Learning Styles: Discovering How You Learn" (p. 32) there are four modes of learning based on four questions: *Why? What? How?* and *What if?* These questions are also powerful guides to critical thinking. Following are a variety of tools for answering those questions. For more handy implements, see *Becoming a Critical Thinker* by Vincent Ryan Ruggiero.

1 Why am I considering this issue? Critical thinking and personal passion go together. Begin critical thinking with a question that matters to you. Seek a rationale for your learning. Understand why it is important for you to think about a specific topic. You might want to arrive at a new conclusion, make a prediction, or solve a problem. By finding a personal connection with an issue, your interest in acquiring and retaining new information increases.

2 What are various points of view on this issue? Imagine Karl Marx, Cesar Chavez, and Warren Buffett assembled in one room to choose the most desirable economic system. Picture Mahatma Gandhi, Nelson Mandela, and General George Patton lecturing at a United Nations conference on conflict resolution. Visualize Al Gore, Bill Gates, and Ban Ki-moon in a discussion about distributing the world's resources equitably. When seeking out alternative points of view, let such scenarios unfold in your mind.

Dozens of viewpoints exist on every important issue—reducing crime, ending world hunger, preventing war, educating our children, and countless other concerns. In fact, few problems have any single, permanent solution. Each generation produces its own answers to critical questions, based on current conditions. Our search for answers is a conversation that spans centuries. On each question, many voices are waiting to be heard.

You can take advantage of this diversity by seeking out alternative views with an open mind. When talking to another person, be willing to walk away with a new point of view—even if it's the one you brought to the table, but now supported with new evidence.

Examining different points of view is an exercise in analysis, which you can do with the suggestions that follow.

Define terms. Imagine a situation in which two people are arguing about whether an employer should limit health care benefits to members of a family. To one person, the word *family* means a mother, father, and children; to the other person, the word *family* applies to any individuals who live together in a long-term, supportive relationship. Chances are, the debate will go nowhere until these two people realize that they're defining the same word in different ways.

Conflicts of opinion can often be resolved—or at least clarified—when we define our key terms up front. This is especially true with abstract, emotion-laden terms such as *freedom, peace, progress,* or *justice.* Blood has been shed over the meaning of those words. Define them with care.

Look for assertions. Speakers and writers present their key terms in a larger context called an *assertion.* An assertion is a complete sentence that directly answers a key question. For example, consider this sentence from the article "The Master Student" in Chapter 1: "Mastery means attaining a level of skill that goes beyond technique." This sentence is an assertion that answers an important question: How do we recognize mastery?

Look for at least three viewpoints. When asking questions, let go of the temptation to settle for just a single answer. Once you have come up with an answer, say to yourself, "Yes, that is one answer. Now what's another?" Using this approach can sustain honest inquiry, fuel creativity, and lead to conceptual breakthroughs. Be prepared: The world is complicated, and critical thinking is a complex business. Some of your answers might contradict others. Resist the temptation to have all of your ideas fit together in a neat, orderly bundle.

Practice tolerance. One path to critical thinking is tolerance for a wide range of opinions. Taking a position on important issues is natural. When we stop having an opinion on things, we've probably stopped breathing.

Problems occur when we become so attached to our current viewpoints that we refuse to consider alternatives. Many ideas that are widely accepted in Western cultures—for example, civil liberties for people of color and the rights of women to vote—once were considered dangerous. Viewpoints that seem outlandish today might become widely accepted a century, a decade, or even a year from now. Remembering this idea can help us practice tolerance for differing beliefs and, in doing so, make room for new ideas that might alter our lives.

3 How well is each point of view supported? Uncritical thinkers shield themselves from new information and ideas. As an alternative, you can follow the example of scientists, who constantly search for evidence that contradicts their theories. The following suggestions can help you do so.

Look for logic and evidence. The aim of using logic is to make statements that are clear, consistent, and coherent. As you examine a speaker's or writer's assertions, you might find errors in logic—assertions that contradict each other or assumptions that are unfounded.

Also assess the evidence used to support points of view. Evidence comes in several forms, including facts, expert testimony, and examples. To think critically about evidence, ask questions such as the following:

- Are all or most of the relevant facts presented?
- Are the facts consistent with one another?
- Are facts presented accurately—or in a misleading way?
- Are enough examples included to make a solid case for the viewpoint?
- Do the examples truly support the viewpoint?

- Are the examples typical? That is, could the author or speaker support the assertion with other examples that are similar?
- Is the expert credible—in other words, is the expert truly knowledgeable about the topic?

Consider the source. Carefully consider that article on the problems of manufacturing cars powered by natural gas. It might have been written by an executive from an oil company. Check out the expert who disputes the connection between smoking and lung cancer. That "expert" might be the president of a tobacco company.

This is not to say that we should dismiss the ideas of people who have a vested interest in a topic or keep them from stating their opinions. Rather, we should take their self-interest into account as we consider their ideas.

Understand before criticizing. Polished debaters are good at summing up their opponents' viewpoints—in fact, they are often better than the people who support those viewpoints themselves. Likewise, critical thinkers take the time to understand a statement of opinion before agreeing or disagreeing with it.

Effective understanding calls for listening without judgment. Enter another person's world by expressing her viewpoint in your own words. If you're conversing with that person, keep revising your summary until she agrees that you've stated her position accurately. If you're reading an article, write a short summary of it. Then scan the article again, checking to see if your synopsis is on target.

Watch for hot spots. Many people have mental "hot spots"—topics that provoke strong opinions and feelings. Examples are abortion, homosexuality, gun control, and the death penalty.

To become more skilled at examining various points of view, notice your own particular hot spots. Make a clear intention to accept your feelings about these topics and to continue using critical thinking techniques in relation to them.

One way to cool down our hot spots is to remember that we can change—or even give up—our current opinions without giving up ourselves. That's a key message behind the Power Processes: "Ideas Are Tools" and "Detach." These articles remind us that human beings are much more than the sum of their current opinions.

Be willing to be uncertain. Some of the most profound thinkers have practiced the art of thinking by using a magic sentence: "I'm not sure yet."

Those are words that many people do not like to hear. Our society rewards quick answers and quotable sound bites. We're under considerable pressure to utter the truth in 10 seconds or less.

In such a society, it is courageous and unusual to take the time to pause, to look, to examine, to be thoughtful, to consider many points of view—and to be unsure. A society that adopts half-truths in a blind rush for certainty is likely to falter. A willingness to embrace uncertainty can move us forward.

4 What if I could combine various points of view or create a new one? The search for truth is like painting a barn door by tossing an open can of paint at it. Few people who throw paint at the door miss it entirely. Yet no one can cover the whole door in a single toss.

People who express a viewpoint are seeking the truth. No reasonable person claims to understand the whole truth about anything. Instead, each viewpoint can be seen as one approach among many possible alternatives. If you don't think that any one opinion is complete, combine different perspectives on the issue. Experiment with the following strategies.

Create a critical thinking "spreadsheet." When you consult authorities with different stands on an issue, you might feel confused about how to sort, evaluate, and combine their points of view. To overcome confusion, create a critical thinking "spreadsheet." List the authorities (and yourself) across the top of a page and key questions down the left side. Then indicate each authority's answer to each question, along with your own answers.

For example, the following spreadsheet clarifies different points of view on the issue of whether to outlaw boxing.

You could state your own viewpoint by combining your answers to the questions in the previous spreadsheet: "I favor legalized boxing. Although boxing poses dangers, so do other sports. And like other sports, the risk of injury can be reduced when boxers get proper training."

Write about it. Thoughts can move at blinding speed. Writing slows down that process. Gaps in logic that slip by us in thought or speech are often exposed when we commit the same ideas to paper. Writing down our thoughts allows us to compare, contrast, and combine points of view more clearly—and therefore to think more thoroughly.

Accept your changing perspectives. Researcher William Perry found that students in higher education move through stages of intellectual development.[2] In earlier stages, students tend to think there is only one correct viewpoint on each issue, and they look to their instructors to reveal that truth. Later, students acknowledge a variety of opinions on issues and construct their own viewpoints.

Monitor changes in your thinking processes as you combine viewpoints. Distinguish between opinions that you accept from authorities and opinions that are based on your own use of logic and your search for evidence. Also look for opinions that result from objective procedures (such as using the *Why? What? How?* and *What if?* questions in this article) and personal sources (using intuition or "gut feelings").

Remember that the process of becoming a critical thinker will take you through a variety of stages. Give yourself time, and celebrate your growing mastery. ✳

Find more strategies for becoming a critical thinker online.

Excerpts from Becoming a Critical Thinker, Fifth Edition by Vincent Ryan Ruggiero, © 2006, pp. 76–77.

	Medical doctor	Former boxer	Sports journalist	Me
Is boxing a sport?	No	Yes	Yes	Yes
Is boxing dangerous?	Yes	Yes	Yes	Yes
Is boxing more dangerous than other sports?	Yes	No	Yes	No
Can the risk of injury be overcome by proper training?	No	No	No	Yes

Source: Vincent Ryan Ruggiero, *Becoming a Critical Thinker,* Sixth Edition. Copyright © 2009 by Cengage Learning. Reprinted with permission.

THINKING

8

Attitudes, affirmations, and visualizations

> **I'M A GREAT STUDENT!**

"I HAVE A BAD ATTITUDE." Some of us say this as if we were talking about having the flu. An attitude is certainly as strong as the flu, but it isn't something we have to succumb to or accept.

Attitudes are powerful. They mold behavior. If your attitude is that you're not interesting at a party, then your behavior will probably match your attitude. If your attitude is that you are fun at a party, then your behavior is more likely to be playful.

> **I AM AWESOME**

Visible measures of success—such as top grades and résumés filled with accomplishments—start with invisible assets called attitudes. Some attitudes will help you benefit from all the money and time you invest in higher education. Other attitudes will render your investment worthless.

You can change your attitudes through regular practice with affirmations and visualizations.

Affirm it. An affirmation is a statement describing what you want. The most effective affirmations are personal, positive, and written in the present tense.

To use affirmations, first determine what you want; then describe yourself as if you already have it. To get what you want from your education, you could write, "I, Malika Jones, am a master student. I take full responsibility for my education. I learn with joy, and I use my experiences in each course to create the life that I want."

If you decide that you want a wonderful job, you might write, "I, Peter Webster, have a wonderful job. I respect and love my colleagues, and they feel the same way about me. I look forward to going to work each day."

Effective affirmations include detail. Use brand names, people's names, and your own name. Involve all of your senses—sight, sound, smell, taste, and touch. Take a positive approach. Instead of saying, "I am not fat," say, "I am slender."

Once you have written an affirmation, repeat it. Practice saying it out loud several times a day. Do this at a regular time, such as just before you go to sleep or just after you wake up. Sit in a chair in a relaxed position. Take a few deep and relaxing breaths, and then repeat your affirmation with emotion. It's also effective to look in a mirror while saying the affirmation. Keep looking and repeating until you are saying your affirmation with conviction.

Attitude replacements

You can use affirmations to replace a negative attitude with a positive one. There are no limitations, other than your imagination and your willingness to practice. Here are some sample affirmations. Modify them to suit your individual hopes and dreams, and then practice them.

I, _____, have abundant energy and vitality throughout the day.

I, _____, exercise regularly.

I, _____, work effectively with many different kinds of people.

I, _____, eat wisely.

I, _____, plan my days and use time wisely.

I, _____, have a powerful memory.

I, _____, take tests calmly and confidently.

I, _____, fall asleep quickly and sleep soundly.

I, _____, have relationships that are mutually satisfying.

I, _____, contribute to other people through my job.

I, _____, know ways to play and have fun.

I, _____, focus my attention easily.

I, _____, like myself.

I, _____, have an income that far exceeds my expenses.

I, _____, live my life in positive ways for the highest good of all people.

Visualize it. You can improve your golf swing, tennis serve, or batting average while lying in bed. You can become a better driver, speaker, or cook while sitting silently in a chair. While you're in line at the grocery store, you can improve your ability to type or to take tests. This is all possible through visualization—the technique of seeing yourself being successful.

I am a Loving Parent!

Here's one way to begin. Choose what you want to improve. Then describe in writing what it would look like, sound like, and feel like to have that improvement in your life. If you are learning to play the piano, write down briefly what you would see, hear, and feel if you were playing skillfully. If you want to improve your relationships with your children, write down what you would see, hear, and feel if you were communicating with them successfully.

Practice at least once a day. Once you have a sketch of what it would be like to be successful, practice it in your imagination. Whenever you shoot the basketball, it swishes through the net. Every time you invite someone out on a date, the person says yes. Each test the teacher hands back to you is graded an A. Practice at least once a day. Then wait for the results to unfold in your life.

You can also use visualizations to replay errors. When you make a mistake, replay it in your imagination. After a bad golf shot, stop and imagine yourself making that same shot again, this time successfully. If you just had a discussion with your roommate that turned into a fight, replay it successfully.

Visualizations and affirmations can restructure your attitudes and behaviors. Be clear about what you want—and then practice it. ✳

Attitudes of a critical thinker

The American Philosophical Association invited a panel of 46 scholars from the United States and Canada to come up with answers to the following two questions: "What is college-level critical thinking?" and "What leads us to conclude that a person is an effective critical thinker?"[3] After two years of work, this panel concluded that critical thinkers share the attitudes summarized in the following chart.

Attitude	Sample statement
Truth seeking	"Let's follow this idea and see where it leads, even if we feel uncomfortable with what we find out."
Open minded	"I have a point of view on this subject, and I'm anxious to hear yours as well."
Analytical	"Taking a stand on the issue commits me to take some new action."
Systematic	"The speaker made several interesting points, and I'd like to hear some more evidence to support each one."
Self-confident	"After reading the book for the first time, I was confused. I'll be able to understand it after studying the book some more."
Inquisitive	"When I first saw that painting, I wanted to know what was going on in the artist's life when she painted it."
Mature	"I'll wait until I gather some more facts before reaching a conclusion on this issue."

critical thinking exercise
26 Reprogram your attitude

Affirmations and visualizations can be used to successfully reprogram your attitudes and behaviors. Use this exercise to change your approach to any situation in your life.

Step 1
Pick something in your life that you would like to change. It can be related to anything—relationships, work, money, or personal skills. In the following space, write a brief description of what you choose to change.

Step 2
Add more details about the change you described in Step 1. Write down how you would like the change to come about. Be outlandish. Imagine that you are about to ask your fairy godmother for a wish that you know she will grant. Be detailed in your description of your wish.

Step 3
Here comes the fairy godmother. Use affirmations and visualizations to start yourself on the path to creating exactly what you wrote about in Step 2. In the following space, write at least two affirmations that describe your dream wish. Also, briefly outline a visualization that you can use to picture your wish. Be specific, detailed, and positive.

Step 4
Put your new attitudes to work. Set up a schedule to practice them. Let the first time you practice be right now. Then set up at least five other times and places where you intend to practice your affirmations and visualizations.

I intend to relax and practice my affirmations and visualizations for at least 5 minutes on the following dates and at the time(s) and location(s) given.

	Date	Time	Location
1.			
2.			
3.			
4.			
5.			

 Complete this exercise online.

www.cengage.com/success/MSME3e

Ways to create ideas

CREATIVE THINKING can give you an edge in the job market. In the face of global competition, employers are looking for people who can create new products, develop new services, and think in fresh ways about what customers and clients want.

Anyone can think creatively. Use the following techniques to generate ideas about anything—whether you're studying math problems, remodeling a house, or writing a best seller.

Conduct a brainstorm

Brainstorming is a technique for creating plans, finding solutions, and discovering new ideas. When you are stuck on a problem, brainstorming can break the logjam. For example, if you run out of money two days before payday every week, you can brainstorm ways to make your money last longer. You can brainstorm ways to pay for your education. You can brainstorm ways to find a job.

The overall purpose of brainstorming is to generate as many solutions as possible. Sometimes the craziest, most outlandish ideas, while unworkable in themselves, can lead to new ways to solve problems. Use the following steps to try out the brainstorming process:

- *Focus on a single problem or issue.* State your focus as a question. Open-ended questions that start with the words *what, how, who, where,* and *when* often make effective focusing questions.

- *Relax.* Creativity is enhanced by a state of relaxed alertness. If you are tense or anxious, use relaxation techniques such as those described in "Let Go of Test Anxiety" in Chapter 7: "Tests."

- *Set a quota or goal for the number of solutions you want to generate.* Goals give your subconscious mind something to aim for.

(woman) Floresco Productions/OJO Images/Getty, (words) Shutterstock

- *Set a time limit.* Use a clock to time your brainstorming session to the minute. Digital sports watches with built-in stopwatches work well. Experiment with various lengths of time. Both short and long brainstorms can be powerful.

- *Allow all answers.* Brainstorming is based on attitudes of permissiveness and patience. Accept every idea. If it pops into your head, put it down on paper. Quantity, not quality, is the goal. Avoid making judgments and evaluations during the brainstorming session. If you get stuck, think of an outlandish idea, and write it down. One crazy idea can unleash a flood of other, more workable solutions.

- *Brainstorm with others.* Group brainstorming is a powerful technique. Group brainstorms take on lives of their own. Assign one member of the group to write down solutions. Feed off the ideas of others, and remember to avoid evaluating or judging anyone's ideas during the brainstorm.

Focus and let go

Focusing and letting go are alternating parts of the same process. Intense focus taps the resources of your conscious mind. Letting go gives your subconscious mind time to work. When you focus for intense periods and then let go for a while, the conscious and subconscious parts of your brain work in harmony.

Focusing attention means being in the here and now. To focus your attention on a project, notice when you pay attention and when your mind starts to wander. Be sure to involve all of your senses. For example, if you are having difficulty writing a paper at a computer, practice focusing by listening to the sounds as you type. Notice the feel of the keys as you strike them. When you know the sights, sounds, and sensations you associate with being truly in focus, you'll be able to repeat the experience and return to your paper more easily.

Be willing to recognize conflict, tension, and discomfort in yourself. Notice them and fully accept them rather than fight against them. Look for the specific thoughts and body sensations that make up the discomfort. Allow them to come fully into your awareness, and then let them pass.

You might not be focused all of the time. Periods of inspiration might last only seconds. Be gentle with yourself when you notice that your concentration has lapsed. In fact, that might be a time to let go. *Letting go* means not forcing yourself to be creative. Practice focusing for short periods at first, and then give yourself a break. Take a nap when you are tired. Thomas Edison took frequent naps. Then the light bulb clicked on.

Cultivate creative serendipity

The word *serendipity* was coined by the English author Horace Walpole from the title of an ancient Persian fairy tale, "The Three Princes of Serendip." The princes had a knack for making lucky discoveries. Serendipity is that knack, and it involves more than luck. It is the ability to see something valuable that you weren't looking for.

History is full of people who make serendipitous discoveries. Country doctor Edward Jenner noticed "by accident" that milkmaids seldom got smallpox. As a result, he discovered that mild cases of cowpox immunized them. Penicillin was also discovered "by accident." Scottish scientist Alexander Fleming was growing bacteria in a laboratory petri dish. A spore of *Penicillium notatum*, a kind of mold, blew in the window and landed in the dish, killing the bacteria. Fleming isolated the active ingredient. A few years later,

during World War II, penicillin saved thousands of lives. Had Fleming not been alert to the possibility, the discovery might never have been made.

You can train yourself in the art of serendipity. Keep your eyes open. You might find a solution to an accounting problem in a Saturday morning cartoon. You might discover a topic for your term paper at the corner convenience store. Multiply your contacts with the world. Resolve to meet new people. Join a study or discussion group. Read. Go to plays, concerts, art shows, lectures, and movies. Watch television programs you normally wouldn't watch.

Also expect discoveries. One secret for success is being prepared to recognize "luck" when you see it.

Keep idea files

We all have ideas. People who treat their ideas with care are often labeled "creative." They recognize ideas, record them, *and* follow up on them.

Safeguard your ideas when they occur to you, even if you're pressed for time. One method is to write them down on 3×5 cards. Jotting down four or five words is often enough to capture the essence of an idea. If you carry 3×5 cards in a pocket or purse, you can record ideas while standing in line or sitting in a waiting room.

You can also use digital tools to capture ideas. Google Notebook, Zoho Notebook, and similar applications allow you to "clip" images and text from various Web pages, categorize all this content, and add your own notes. Personal information managers such as Evernote and Yojimbo serve a similar purpose. Some of them allow you to add "offline" content, such as digital photos of business cards and receipts. You can search through all this content by using tags and keywords.

No matter what method you use, collect powerful quotations, random insights, notes on your reading, and useful ideas that you encounter in class. Collect jokes, too.

27 critical thinking exercise
Fix-the-world brainstorm

This exercise works well with four to six people. Pick a major world problem such as hunger, nuclear proliferation, poverty, terrorism, overpopulation, or pollution. Then conduct a 10-minute brainstorm about the steps an individual could take to contribute to solving the problem.

Use the brainstorming techniques explained earlier in this chapter. Remember not to evaluate or judge the solutions

during the process. The purpose of a brainstorm is to generate a flow of ideas and record them all.

After the brainstorming session, discuss the process and the solutions that it generated. Did you feel any energy from the group? Was a long list of ideas generated? Are several of them worth pursuing?

Keep a journal. It doesn't have to be exclusively about your own thoughts and feelings. You can record observations about the world around you, conversations with friends, important or offbeat ideas—anything.

To fuel your creativity, read voraciously, including newspapers and magazines. Keep a clip file of interesting articles. Explore beyond mainstream journalism. There are hundreds of low-circulation specialty magazines and online news journals that cover almost any subject you can imagine.

Review your files regularly. Some amusing thought that came to you in November might be the perfect solution to a problem in March.

Collect and play with data

Look from all sides at the data you collect. Switch your attention from one aspect to another. Examine each fact, and avoid getting stuck on one particular part of a problem. Turn a problem upside down by picking a solution first and then working backward. Ask other people to look at the data. Solicit opinions.

Living with the problem invites a solution. Write down data, possible solutions, or a formulation of the problem on 3×5 cards and carry them with you. Look at them before you go to bed at night. Review them when you are waiting for the bus. Make them part of your life, and think about them frequently.

Look for the obvious solutions or the obvious "truths" about the problem—then toss them out. Ask yourself, "Well, I know X is true, but if X were *not* true, what would happen?" Or ask the reverse: "If that *were* true, what would follow next?"

Put unrelated facts next to each other and invent a relationship between them, even if it seems absurd at first. In *The Act of Creation,* novelist Arthur Koestler says that finding a context in which to combine opposites is the essence of creativity.[4]

Make imaginary pictures with the data. Condense it. Categorize it. Put it in chronological order. Put it

in alphabetical order. Put it in random order. Order it from most to least complex. Reverse all of those orders. Look for opposites.

It has been said that there are no new ideas—only new ways to combine old ideas. Creativity is the ability to discover those new combinations.

Create while you sleep

A part of our mind works as we sleep. You've experienced this fact directly if you've ever fallen asleep with a problem on your mind and awakened the next morning with a solution. For some of us, the solution appears in a dream or just before we fall asleep or wake up.

You can experiment with this process. Ask yourself a question as you fall asleep. Keep pencil and paper or a recorder near your bed. The moment you wake up, begin writing or speaking, and see if an answer to your question emerges.

Refine ideas and follow through

Many of us ignore the part of the creative process that involves refining ideas and following through. How many great moneymaking schemes have we had that we never pursued? How many good ideas have we had for short stories that we never wrote? How many times have we said to ourselves, "You know, what they ought to do is attach two handles to one of those things, paint it orange, and sell it to police departments. They'd make a fortune." The thing is, we never realize that we are "they."

One powerful tool you can use to follow through is the Discovery and Intention Journal Entry system. First write down your idea in a Discovery Statement, and then write what you intend to do about it in an Intention Statement. Genius resides in the follow through—the application of perspiration to inspiration. ✳

Discovering assumptions

ASSUMPTIONS CAN EVEN BE embedded in physical spaces. For example, go into any large lecture hall and take a look around. You'll probably see row after row of seats that face a lectern or platform in front of the room. This layout is based on some assumptions, such as:

Learning takes place in large groups.

Learning happens when one person does most of the talking and everyone else listens.

People learn best when they are sitting down.

Learning takes place in a quiet, private space rather than a busy, public space such as a workplace.

Spotting assumptions can be tricky. They are usually unstated and offered without evidence. In addition, we can hold many assumptions at the same time.

Assumptions might even contradict each other, resulting in muddled thinking and confused behavior. This makes uncovering assumptions a feat worthy of the greatest detective.

Assumptions can undermine us

Letting assumptions remain in our subconscious can erect barriers to our success. Take the person who says, "I don't worry about saving money for the future. I think life is meant to be enjoyed today—not later." This statement rests on at least two assumptions: *saving money is not enjoyable* and *we can enjoy ourselves only when we're spending money.*

It would be no surprise to find out that this person runs out of money near the end of each month and depends on cash advances from high-interest credit cards. He is shielding himself from some ideas that could actually help to erase his debt: Saving money can be a source of satisfaction, and many enjoyable activities cost nothing.

The stakes in uncovering assumptions are high. Prejudice thrives on the beliefs that certain people are inferior or dangerous due to their skin color, ethnic background, or sexual orientation. Those beliefs have led to flawed assumptions such as *mixing the blood of the races will lead to genetically inferior offspring* and *opening the armed forces to gay and lesbian people will destroy morale.*

Our thinking and behavior are guided by assumptions. These are often invisible, powerful, and unconscious. People can remain unaware of their most basic and far-reaching assumptions—the very ideas that shape their lives.

When we remain ignorant of our assumptions, we also make it easier for people with hidden agendas to do our thinking for us. Demagogues and unethical advertisers know that unchallenged assumptions are potent tools for influencing our attitudes and behavior.

Assumptions can create conflict

Heated conflict and hard feelings often result when people argue on the level of opinions—forgetting that the real conflict lies at the level of their assumptions.

An example is the question about whether the government should fund public works programs that create jobs during a recession. People who advocate such programs might assume that creating such jobs is an appropriate task for the federal government. In contrast, people who argue against such programs might assume that the government has no business interfering with the free workings of the economy. There's little hope of resolving this conflict of opinion unless we deal with something more basic: our assumptions about the proper role of government.

Look for assumptions

In summary, you can follow a three-step method for testing the validity of any viewpoint:

1. Look for the assumptions—the assertions implied by that viewpoint.

2. Write down these assumptions.

3. See if you can find exceptions to any of the assumptions.

This technique helps detect many errors in logic. Use these three steps to liberate yourself from half-truths, think more powerfully, and create new possibilities for your life. ✳

Ways to fool yourself: Common mistakes in logic

Rich Reed/National Geographic/Getty

EFFECTIVE REASONING IS NOT JUST an idle pastime for unemployed philosophers. When you think logically, you take your reading, writing, speaking, and listening skills to a higher level.

Over the last 2,500 years, specialists have listed some classic land mines in the field of logic—common mistakes in thinking that are called *fallacies*. The following examples will help you in understanding fallacies.

Jumping to conclusions. Jumping to conclusions is the only exercise that some lazy thinkers get. This fallacy involves drawing conclusions without sufficient evidence. Take the bank officer who hears that a student failed to pay back an education loan. After that, the officer turns down all loan applications from students. This person has formed a rigid opinion on the basis of hearsay. Jumping to conclusions—also called *hasty generalization*—is at work here.

Following are more examples of this fallacy:

- *When I went to Mexico for spring break, I felt sick the whole time. Mexican food makes people sick.*

- *Google's mission is to "organize the world's information." Their employees must be on a real power trip.*

- *During a recession, more people go to the movies. People just want to sit in the dark and forget about their money problems.*

Each item in this list includes two statements, and the second statement does not necessarily follow from the first. More evidence is needed to make any possible connection.

Attacking the person. People who indulge in personal attacks are attempting an intellectual sleight of hand to divert our attention away from the truly relevant issues. The mistake of attacking the person is common at election time. An example is the candidate who claims that her opponent has failed to attend church regularly during the campaign.

Appealing to authority. A professional athlete endorses a brand of breakfast cereal. A famous musician features a soft drink company's product in a music video. The promotional brochure for an advertising agency lists all of the large companies that have used its services.

In each case, the people involved are trying to win your confidence—and your dollars—by citing authorities. The underlying assumption is usually this: *Famous people and organizations use our product. Therefore, you should use it, too.* Or: *You should accept this idea merely because someone who's well known says it's true.*

Appealing to authority is usually a substitute for producing real evidence. It invites sloppy thinking. When our only evidence for a viewpoint is an appeal to authority, it's time to think more thoroughly.

Pointing to a false cause. The fact that one event follows another does not necessarily mean that the two events have a cause-and-effect relationship. All we can accurately say is that the events might be correlated. For example, as children's vocabularies improve, they tend to get more cavities. This does not mean that cavities are the result of an improved vocabulary. Instead, the increase in cavities is due to other factors, such as physical maturation and changes in diet or personal care.

Thinking in all-or-nothing terms. Consider these statements: *Doctors are greedy. . . . You can't trust politicians. . . . Students these days are in school just to get high-paying jobs; they lack ideals. . . . Homeless people* *don't want to work.* These opinions imply the word *all.* They gloss over individual differences, claiming that all members of a group are exactly alike. They also ignore key facts—for instance, that some doctors volunteer their time at free medical clinics and that many homeless people are children who are too young to work. All-or-nothing thinking is one of the most common errors in logic.

Basing arguments on emotion. The politician who ends every campaign speech with flag waving and slides of his mother eating apple pie is staking his future on appeals to emotion. So is the candidate who paints a grim scenario of the disaster and ruination that will transpire unless she is elected. Get past the fluff and histrionics to see if you can uncover any worthwhile ideas.

Creating a straw man. The name of this fallacy comes from the scarecrows traditionally placed in gardens to ward off birds. A scarecrow works because it looks like a man. Likewise, a person can attack ideas that sound *like* his opponent's ideas but are actually absurd. For example, some legislators attacked the Equal Rights Amendment by describing it as a measure to abolish separate bathrooms for men and women. In fact, supporters of this amendment proposed no such thing.

Begging the question. Speakers and writers beg the question when their colorful language glosses over an idea that is unclear or unproven. Consider this statement: *Support the American tradition of individual liberty and oppose mandatory seat belt laws!* Anyone who makes such a statement "begs" (fails to answer) a key question: Are laws that require drivers to use seat belts actually a violation of individual liberty?

Creating a red herring. When hunters want to throw a dog off a trail, they can drag a smoked red herring (or some other food with a strong odor) over the ground in the opposite direction. This distracts the dog, who is fooled into following a false trail. Likewise, people can send our thinking on false trails by raising irrelevant issues. Case in point: Some people who opposed a presidential campaign by U.S. Senator Barack Obama emphasized his middle name: Hussein. This was an irrelevant attempt to link the senator to Saddam Hussein, the dictator and former ruler of Iraq.

Appealing to tradition. Arguments based on an appeal to tradition take a classic form: *Our current beliefs and behaviors have a long history; therefore, they are correct.* This argument has been used to justify the divine right of kings, feudalism, witch burnings, slavery, child labor, and a host of other traditions that are now rejected in most parts of the world. Appeals to tradition ignore the fact that unsound ideas can survive for centuries before human beings realize that they are being fooled.

Sliding a slippery slope. The fallacy of sliding a slippery slope implies that if one undesired event occurs, then other, far more serious events will follow: *If we restrict our right to own guns, then all of our rights will soon be taken away. . . . If people keep downloading music for free, pretty soon they'll demand to get everything online for free. . . . I notice that more independent bookstores are closing; it's just a matter of time before people stop reading.* When people slide a slippery slope, they assume that different types of events have a single cause. They also assume that a particular cause will operate indefinitely. In reality, the world is far more complex. Grand predictions about the future often turn out to be wrong. ✳

 Practice hunting for fallacies online.

(28) critical thinking exercise
Explore emotional reactions

Each of us has certain "hot spots"—issues that trigger strong emotional reactions. These topics may include abortion, gay and lesbian rights, capital punishment, and funding for welfare programs. There are many other examples, varying from person to person.

Examine your own hot spots on a separate sheet of paper by writing a word or short phrase summarizing each issue about which you feel very strongly. Then describe what you typically say or do when each issue comes up in conversation.

After you have completed your list, think about what you can do to become a more effective thinker when you encounter one of these issues. For example, you could breathe deeply and count to five before you offer your own point of view. Or you might preface your opinion by saying, "There are many valid points of view on this issue. Here's the way I see it, and I'm open to your ideas."

Think critically about information on the Internet

SOURCES OF INFORMATION on the Internet range from the reputable (such as the Library of Congress) to the flamboyant (such as the *National Enquirer*). This fact underscores the need for thinking critically about everything you see online. Taking a few simple precautions when you surf the Net can keep you from crashing onto the rocky shore of misinformation.

Look for overall quality. Examine the features of the Web site in general. Notice the effectiveness of the text and visuals as a whole. Also note how well the site is organized and whether you can navigate the site's features with ease.

Look for the date that crucial information was posted, and determine how often the site is updated. Check individual pages for revision dates and notice how recent they are. If you're looking for facts, then avoid undated sources of information.

Next, take a more detailed look at the site's content. Examine several of the site's pages, and look for consistency of facts, quality of information, and competency with grammar and spelling. See whether links within the site are easy to navigate.

In addition, evaluate the site's links to related Web pages. Look for links to pages of reputable organizations. Click on a few of those links. If they lead you to dead ends, it might indicate that the site you're evaluating is not updated often—a clue that it's not a reliable source for current information.

Look at the source. Think about the credibility of the person or organization that posts the Web site. Look for a list of author credentials and publications. Go to **Amazon.com** and the Library of Congress (**catalog.loc.gov**) to see if the author has published other works.

Notice if the site shows any evidence of bias or special interest. Perhaps the site's sponsoring organization wants you to buy a service, a product, or a point of view. This fact might suggest that the information on the site is not objective, and therefore is questionable.

The domain in the uniform resource locator (URL) for a Web site can give you clues about sources of information and possible bias. For example, distinguish among information from a for-profit commercial enterprise (URL ending in .com); a nonprofit organization (.org); a government agency (.gov); and a school, college, or university (.edu).

Note: Wikis (peer-edited sites) such as Wikipedia do not employ editors to screen out errors or scrutinize questionable material before publication. Do not use these sites when researching a paper or presentation.

Also, be cautious about citing blogs. Blog authors might not review their posts for accuracy or base articles on careful research.

Look for documentation. When you encounter an assertion on a Web page or some other Internet resource, note the types and quality of the evidence offered. Look for credible examples, quotations from authorities in the field, documented statistics, or summaries of scientific studies. ✳

29 critical thinking exercise
Evaluate search sites

Access several popular search sites on the Web, such as:

Alta Vista	**www.altavista.com**
Ask.com	**www.ask.com**
Bing	**www.bing.com**
Dogpile	**www.dogpile.com**
Excite	**www.excite.com**
Google	**www.google.com**
HotBot	**www.hotbot.com**
Yahoo!	**www.yahoo.com**

Find more options by entering the keywords *search engines* into any of the sites mentioned in the list.

Next, choose a specific topic that you'd like to research—preferably one related to a paper or other assignment that you will complete this term. Identify keywords for this topic and enter them in several search sites. (Open up a different window or tab in your browser for each site.) Be sure to use the same keywords each time that you search.

Finally, evaluate the search sites by comparing the results that you get. Based on this evaluation, keep a list of your favorite search sites.

Overcome stereotypes with critical thinking

CONSIDER ASSERTIONS SUCH AS THESE:
"College students like to drink heavily," and "Americans who criticize the president are unpatriotic."

These assertions are examples of stereotyping—generalizing about a group of people based on the behavior of isolated group members. When we stereotype, we gloss over individual differences and assume that every member of a group is the same. Generalizations that divide the people of the world into "us" versus "them" are often based on prejudice. You can take several steps to free yourself from such stereotypes.

Look for errors in thinking. Some of the most common errors in thinking are the following:

- *Selective perception.* Stereotypes can literally change the way we see the world. If we assume that homeless people are lazy, for instance, we tend to notice only the examples that support our opinion. Stories about homeless people who are too young or too ill to work will probably escape our attention.

- *Self-fulfilling prophecy.* When we interact with people based on stereotypes, we set them up in ways that confirm our thinking. For example, when people of color were denied access to higher education based on stereotypes about their intelligence, they were deprived of opportunities to demonstrate their intellectual gifts.

Create categories in a more flexible way. Stereotyping has been described as a case of "hardening of the categories." Avoid this problem by making your categories broader. Instead of seeing people based on their skin color, you could look at them on the basis of their heredity. (People of all races share most of the same genes.) Or you could make your categories narrower. Instead of talking about "religious extremists," look for subgroups among the people who adopt a certain religion. Distinguish between groups that advocate violence and those that shun it.

Test your generalizations about people through action. You can test your generalizations by actually meeting people of other cultures. It's easy to believe almost anything about certain groups of people as long as we never deal directly with individuals. Inaccurate pictures tend to die when people from different cultures study together, work together, and live together.

Be willing to see your own stereotypes. The Power Process: "Notice Your Pictures and Let Them Go" can help you see your own stereotypes. One belief about yourself that you can shed is *I have no pictures about people from other cultures.* Even people with the best of intentions can harbor subtle biases. Admitting this possibility allows you to look inward even more deeply for stereotypes. Every time we notice an inaccurate picture buried in our mind and let it go, we take a personal step toward embracing diversity. ✳

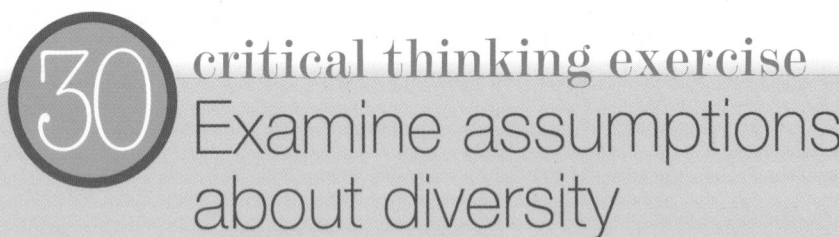

30 critical thinking exercise
Examine assumptions about diversity

On a separate sheet of paper, write down the first words that come to mind when you hear the terms in the following list. Do this now.

Musician

Homeless people

Football players

Computer programmers

Disabled person

Retired person

Adult learner

Next, exchange your responses to this exercise with a friend. Did you discover stereotypes or other examples of bias? What counts as evidence of this bias? Summarize your answers on a separate sheet of paper.

Gaining skill at *decision making*

WE MAKE DECISIONS ALL THE TIME, whether we realize it or not. Even avoiding decisions is a form of decision making. The student who puts off studying for a test until the last minute might really be saying, "I've decided this course is not important" or "I've decided not to give this course much time." In order to better understand the decision-making process, decide right now to experiment with the following suggestions.

Recognize decisions. Decisions are more than wishes or desires. There's a world of difference between "I wish I could be a better student" and "I will take more powerful notes, read with greater retention, and review my class notes daily." Decisions are specific and lead to focused action. When we decide, we narrow down. We give up actions that are inconsistent with our decision. Deciding to eat fruit for dessert instead of ice cream rules out the next trip to the ice cream store.

Establish priorities. Some decisions are trivial. No matter what the outcome, your life is not affected much. Other decisions can shape your circumstances for years. Devote more time and energy to the decisions with big outcomes.

Base your decisions on a life plan. The benefit of having long-term goals for our lives is that they provide a basis for many of our daily decisions. Being certain about what we want to accomplish this year and this month makes today's choices clearer.

Balance learning styles in decision making. To make decisions more effectively, use all four modes of learning explained in Chapter 1: "First Steps." The key is to balance reflection with action, and balance thinking with experience. First, take the time to think creatively and generate many options. Then think critically about the possible consequences of each option before choosing one. Remember, however, that thinking is no substitute for experience. Act on your chosen option, and notice what happens. If you're not getting the results that you want, then quickly return to creative thinking to invent new options.

Choose an overall strategy. Every time you make a decision, you choose a strategy, even when you're not aware of it. Effective decision makers can articulate and choose from among several strategies. For example:

- *Find all of the available options, and choose one deliberately.* Save this strategy for times when you have a relatively small number of options, each of which leads to noticeably different results.

- *Find all of the available options, and choose one randomly.* This strategy can be risky. Save it for times when your options are basically similar and fairness is the main issue.

- *Limit the options, and then choose.* This strategy works best when the number of options is overwhelming. For example, when deciding which search engine to use on the World Wide Web, visit many sites and then narrow the list down to two or three that you choose.

Use time as an ally. Sometimes we face dilemmas—situations in which any course of action leads to undesirable consequences. In such cases, consider putting a decision on hold. Wait it out. Do nothing until the circumstances change, making one alternative clearly preferable to another.

Use intuition. Some decisions seem to make themselves. A solution pops into our mind, and we gain newfound clarity. Using intuition is not the same as forgetting about the decision or refusing to make it. Intuitive decisions usually arrive after we've gathered the relevant facts and faced a problem for some time.

Evaluate your decision. Hindsight is a source of insight. After you act on a decision, observe the consequences over time. Reflect on how well your decision worked and what you might have done differently.

Think *choices*. This final suggestion involves some creative thinking. Consider that the word *decide* derives from the same roots as *suicide* and *homicide*. In the spirit of those words, a decision forever "kills" all other options. That's kind of heavy. Instead, use the word *choice,* and see if it frees up your thinking. When you *choose,* you express a preference for one option over others. However, those options remain live possibilities for the future. Choose for today, knowing that as you gain more wisdom and experience, you can choose again. ✳

8

THINKING

Four ways to solve problems

THINK OF PROBLEM SOLVING as a process with four Ps: Define the *problem*, generate *possibilities*, create a *plan*, and *perform* your plan.

1 **Define the problem.** To define a problem effectively, understand what a problem is—a mismatch between what you want and what you have. Problem solving is all about reducing the gap between these two factors.

Start with what you have. Tell the truth about what's present in your life right now, without shame or blame. For example: "I often get sleepy while reading my physics assignments, and after closing the book I cannot remember what I just read."

Next, describe in detail what you want. Go for specifics: "I want to remain alert as I read about physics. I also want to accurately summarize each chapter I read."

Remember that when we define a problem in limiting ways, our solutions merely generate new problems. As Albert Einstein said, "The world we have made is a result of the level of thinking we have done thus far. We cannot solve problems at the same level at which we created them."[5]

This idea has many applications for success in school. An example is the student who struggles with note taking. The problem, she thinks, is that her notes are too sketchy. The logical solution, she decides, is to take more notes, and her new goal is to write down almost everything her instructors say. However, no matter how fast and furiously she writes, she cannot capture all of the instructors' comments.

Consider what happens when this student defines the problem in a new way. After more thought, she decides that her dilemma is not the *quantity* of her notes but their *quality*. She adopts a new format for taking notes, dividing her notepaper into two columns. In the right-hand column, she writes down only the main points of each lecture. In the left-hand column, she notes two or three supporting details for each point.

Over time, this student makes the joyous discovery that there are usually just three or four core ideas to remember from each lecture. She originally thought the solution was to take more notes. What really worked was taking notes in a new way.

2 **Generate possibilities.** Now put on your creative thinking hat. Open up. Brainstorm as many possible solutions to the problem as you can. At this stage, quantity counts. As you generate possibilities, gather relevant facts. For example, when you're faced with a dilemma about what courses to take next term, get information on class times, locations, and instructors. If you haven't decided which summer job offer to accept, gather information on each job's salary, benefits, and working conditions.

3 **Create a plan.** After rereading your problem definition and list of possible solutions, choose the solution that seems most workable. Think about specific actions that will reduce the gap between what you have and what you want. Visualize the steps you will take to make this solution a reality, and arrange them in chronological order. To make your plan even more powerful, put it in writing.

4 **Perform your plan.** This step gets you off your chair and out into the world. Now you actually *do* what you have planned. Ultimately, your skill in solving problems lies in how well you perform your plan. Through the quality of your actions, you become the architect of your own success.

Note that the four Ps of this problem-solving process closely parallel the four key questions listed in the article "Becoming a Critical Thinker."

Define the **problem**	**What** is the problem?
Generate **possibilities**	**What if** there are several possible solutions?
Create a **plan**	**How** would this possible solution work?
Perform your plan	**Why** is one solution more workable than another?

When facing problems, experiment with these four Ps, and remember that the order of steps is not absolute. Also remember that any solution has the potential to create new problems. If that happens, cycle through the four Ps of problem solving again. ✳

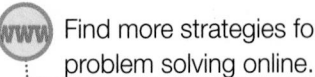 Find more strategies for problem solving online.

Define your values, align your actions

Values are the things in life that you want for their own sake. They influence and guide your choices, including your moment-by-moment decisions about what to do and what to buy. You can tell a lot about your values by looking at the ways you spend time and money.

VALUES DIFFER FROM GOALS. A goal is an outcome that you can achieve. For example, you can set a goal to lose 10 pounds, replace your car, or get a new job. Once you've achieved a goal, you can cross it off your list and replace it with a new goal.

Values, on the other hand, are constant. Instead of describing *what* we want to do or have, they describe *how* we achieve our goals. We can achieve our goals in ways that exploit other people, or we can achieve them in ways that create loving relationships. *Loving* is one example of a value. Like other values, it is never fully achieved or crossed off a list.

Some people are guided by values that they automatically adopt from others or by values that remain largely unconscious. Other people focus on short-term gain and forget about how their behavior violates their values over the long term. (This is a perspective that helped to create the recent economic recession.) When people forget or ignore their values, they miss the opportunity to live a life that's truly of their own choosing.

From Master Student to Master Employee is based on a particular set of values:

- Focused attention
- Self-responsibility
- Integrity
- Risk taking
- Contributing

You'll find these values and related ones directly stated in the Power Processes throughout the text. For instance:

"Discover What You Want" is about the importance of living a purpose-based life.

"Ideas Are Tools" points to the benefits of being willing to experiment with new ideas.

"Risk Being a Fool" is about courage—the willingness to take risks for the sake of learning something new.

"Be Here Now" expresses the value of focused attention.

"Love Your Problems (and Experience Your Barriers)" is about seeing difficulties as opportunities to develop new skills.

"Notice Your Pictures and Let Them Go" is about adopting an attitude of open-mindedness.

"I Create It All" is about taking responsibility for our beliefs and behaviors.

"Detach" reminds us that our core identity and value as a person does not depend on our possessions, our circumstances, or even our accomplishments.

"Find a Bigger Problem" is about living in ways that contribute to the happiness of others.

"Employ Your Word" expresses the value of making and keeping agreements.

"Choose Your Conversations (and Your Community)" reminds us of the power of language, and that we can reshape our lives by taking charge of our thoughts.

"Surrender" points to the value of human community and the power of asking for help.

"Be It" is specifically about the power of attitudes—the idea that change proceeds from the inside out as we learn to see ourselves in new ways.

In addition, most of the skills you read about in these pages have their source in values. The Time Monitor/Time Plan process, for example, calls for focused attention. Even the simple act of sharing your notes with a student who missed a class is an example of contributing.

Values are abstract. They do not refer to things that we can directly see, hear, or touch. To define your values, translate them into goals and visible actions that you can put on your daily to-do list.

Say that one of your values is to be healthy. To define that value, you could set a goal to exercise daily. Then you could plan to walk for 45 minutes this afternoon.

THINKING

8

One set of values

Think of values as your ultimate commitments. One way to start defining your values is to brainstorm endings for this sentence: *I am committed to being . . .*

Following is a sample list of values. Don't read it with the idea that it is the "right" set of values for you. Instead, use this list as a point of departure in creating your own list.

Value: Be accountable   This means being:

- Honest
- Reliable
- Trustworthy
- Ethical
- Dependable
- Responsible
- Able to make and keep agreements

Value: Be loving   This means being:

- Affectionate
- Devoted
- Accepting
- Considerate
- Respectful
- Inclusive
- Ethical
- Dedicated
- Equitable
- Gentle
- Forgiving
- Friendly
- Fair

Value: Be promotive   This means being:

- Nurturing
- Contributing
- Frugal
- Helpful
- Encouraging
- Reasonable
- Judicious
- Cooperative
- Appreciative

Value: Be candid   This means being:

- Honest
- Genuine
- Frank
- Spontaneous
- Free of deceit
- Able to avoid false modesty without arrogance
- Self-disclosing
- Open about strengths and weaknesses
- Authentic
- Self-expressed
- Outspoken
- Sincere

Value: Be detached   This means being:

- Impartial
- Experimental
- Open-minded
- Adaptable
- Trusting
- Joyful
- Unbiased
- Satisfied
- Patient
- Without distress
- Tolerant
- Willing to surrender

Value: Be aware of the possible   This means being:

- Creative
- Resourceful
- Foresighted
- Visionary
- Audacious
- Imaginative
- Inventive
- Holistic
- Inquisitive
- Adventurous

One wonderful aspect of defining your values is that you can start living them today. There is nothing you have to gain or buy *before* you can start being loving or honest. It might take you weeks, months, or years to achieve just one of your goals. However, you can start acting in ways that are loving and honest right now.

Defining your values and aligning your actions has a lot to do with leading a life of fulfillment and happiness. Many people define happiness as a feeling of pleasure. The problem with that definition is that we don't always control the things that happen to us or the way we feel.

In contrast, we *can* usually control our behavior. If we define happiness as taking action in the service of our values, then we can lead a worthwhile life even when circumstances and emotions are difficult.

Defining your values is also a way to create a legacy that will outlast your life. When someone dies, what we reflect on is not what they earned or what they owned. We think about what they stood for and how they showed up for life. We recall their kindness, their wisdom, their commitments, and their contributions. In other words, we focus on their values.

Gaining a liberal education is all about choosing values and then setting goals that bring those values out into the world. As you begin to define your values, consider the people who have gone before you. In creeds, scriptures, philosophies, myths, and sacred stories, the human race has left a vast and varied record of values. Be willing to look everywhere, including sources that are close to home. Another way to define your values is to describe the qualities of people you admire.

In any case, start defining your values and aligning your actions today. ✳

Making ethical decisions

EVERY DAY THAT YOU attend classes or go to work, you make choices that either reinforce or violate your core values. Your employers, coworkers, and instructors want to know that they can trust you in making these choices. Earn their trust by thinking through some potential issues now.

Making ethical choices at work

Some workplace behaviors are widely acknowledged to be unethical. Examples are submitting false expense reports, operating machinery while intoxicated, stealing from a cash drawer, diverting corporate funds for personal uses, or using work time to download explicit sexual images from the Internet.

You might find it easier to stop unethical behavior in its early stages—before it becomes habitual or widespread. According to *Setting the Standard*, published by the Office of Ethics and Business Conduct at Lockheed Martin Corporation, people might be walking on thin ethical ice when they make the following statements to justify an action:

- "It doesn't matter how the job gets done as long as it gets done."
- "Everyone does it."
- "Shred that document."
- "We can hide it."
- "No one will get hurt."
- "This will destroy the competition."
- "We didn't have this conversation."[6]

Making ethical decisions at school

Students in higher education face many situations that call for ethical decision making. While living away from home for the first time, some students choose to have casual sex, use illegal drugs, or drink alcohol before they reach the legal drinking age.

To get practice in ethical decision making, think through an issue that directly affects your grades and prospects for graduation: cheating.

Cheating on tests can be a tempting strategy. It offers the chance to get a good grade without having to study. Instead of studying, we could spend more time watching TV, partying, sleeping, or doing anything that seems like more fun. Another benefit is that we could avoid the risk of doing poorly on a test, which could happen even if we *do* study.

Cheating carries costs. Here are some intentions, actions, and consequences to consider.

We risk failing the course or getting expelled from school. The consequences for cheating are serious. Cheating can result in failing the assignment, failing the entire course, getting suspended, or getting expelled from college entirely. Documentation of cheating may also prevent you from being accepted to other colleges.

We learn less. While we might think that some courses offer little or no value, we can create value from any course. If we look deeply enough, we can discover some idea or acquire some skill to prepare us for future courses or a career after graduation.

We lose time and money. Getting an education costs a lot of money. It also calls for years of sustained effort. Cheating sabotages our purchase. We pay full tuition and invest our energy without getting full value for it.

Fear of getting caught promotes stress. When we're fully aware of our emotions about cheating, we might discover intense stress. Even if we're not fully aware of our emotions, we're likely to feel some level of discomfort about getting caught.

Violating our values promotes stress. Even if we don't get caught cheating, we can feel stress about violating our own ethical standards. Stress can compromise our physical health and overall quality of life.

Cheating on tests can make it easier to violate our integrity again. Human beings become comfortable with behaviors that they repeat. Cheating is no exception. Think about the first time you drove a car. You might have felt excited—even a little frightened. Now driving is probably second nature, and you don't give it much thought. Repeated experience with driving creates familiarity, which lessens the intense feelings you had during your first time at the wheel.

We can experience the same process with almost any behavior. Cheating once will make it easier to cheat again. Furthermore, if we become comfortable with compromising our integrity in one area of life, we might find it easier to compromise in other areas.

Cheating lowers our self-concept. Whether or not we are fully aware of it, cheating sends us the message that we are not smart enough or responsible enough to make it on our own. We deny ourselves the celebration and satisfaction of authentic success.

An alternative to cheating is to become a master student. Ways to do this are described on every page of this book.

Create an ethics checklist

You don't have to be a philosopher in order to make sound ethical decisions at work and school. Start with the working definition of ethics as using moral standards to guide your behavior. Next, turn your own moral standards into a checklist of pointed questions. Then use your checklist to make choices in daily life.

Although there is no formula for making ethical decisions, you can gain clarity with questions that can be answered either yes or no. Following is a sample checklist:

Is this action legal? [ ]Yes [ ]No

Is this action consistent with my organization's mission, goals, and policies? [ ]Yes [ ]No

Is this action consistent with my personal values? [ ]Yes [ ]No

If I continue to make choices such as this, will I be happy with the kind of person I become? [ ]Yes [ ]No

Will this action stand the test of time? Will I be able to defend this action tomorrow, next month, and next year? [ ]Yes [ ]No

In taking this action, am I setting an example that I wish others to follow? [ ]Yes [ ]No

Am I willing to make this decision public—to share it wholeheartedly with my boss, my family, and my friends? Would I feel confident if an article about my decision was published in tomorrow's newspaper? [ ]Yes [ ]No

Has everyone who will be affected by this decision had the chance to voice his or her concerns? [ ]Yes [ ]No

Avoiding plagiarism

Using another person's words, images, or other original creations without giving proper credit is called *plagiarism*. Plagiarism amounts to taking someone else's work and presenting it as your own. This is the equivalent of cheating on a test. Consequences of plagiarism can range from a failing grade to expulsion from school.

The basic guideline for preventing plagiarism is to cite a source for each phrase, sequence of ideas, or visual image created by another person. While ideas cannot be copyrighted, the way that any idea is *expressed* can be. The goal is to clearly distinguish your own work from the expressions of others.

Identify direct quotes If you're taking notes and use a direct quote from another writer or speaker, then put that person's words in quotation marks. Do the same when copying sentences or paragraphs from a Web page and pasting them directly into your notes.

Paraphrase carefully Instead of using a direct quote, you might choose to paraphrase or summarize an

author's words. Paraphrasing means restating the original passage in your own words, usually making it shorter and simpler. Remember that copying a passage and then just rearranging or deleting a few words creates a serious risk of plagiarism. Cite a source for paraphrases and summaries, just as you do for direct quotes.

Note details about each of your sources Include the author, title, publisher, publication date, and page number (for printed materials). Ask your instructor for what details to record about online sources. Also ask about how to cite your sources—as endnotes or footnotes—and get examples of the format to use.

Submit only your own work Turning in materials that have been written or revised by someone else puts your education at risk.

 Find more ways to prevent plagiarism online.

THINKING

8

Find a Bigger Problem

It is impossible to live a life that's free of problems. Besides, problems serve a purpose. They provide opportunities to participate in life. Problems stimulate us and pull us forward.

When problems are seen from this perspective, our goal becomes not to eliminate them, but to find problems that are worthy of us. Worthy problems are those that draw on our talents, move us toward our purpose, and increase our skills. Solving these problems offers the greatest benefits for others and ourselves. Viewed in this way, bigger problems give more meaning to our lives.

Problems expand to fill whatever space is available. Suppose that your only problem for today is to write a follow-up letter to a job interview. You could spend the entire day thinking about what you're going to say, writing the letter, finding a stamp, going to the post office—and then thinking about all of the things you forgot to say.

Now suppose that you get a phone call with an urgent message: A close friend has been admitted to the hospital and wants you to come right away. It's amazing how quickly and easily that letter can get finished when there's a bigger problem on your plate. True, the smaller problems still need to be solved. The goal is simply to solve them in less time and with less energy.

Bigger problems are easy to find—world hunger, child abuse, environmental pollution, terrorism, human rights violations, drug abuse, street crime, energy shortages, poverty, and wars. These problems await your attention and involvement.

Tackling a bigger problem does not have to be depressing. In fact, it can be energizing—a reason for getting up in the morning. A huge project can channel your passion and purpose.

When we take on a bigger problem, we play full out. We do justice to our potentials. We then love what we do and do what we love. We're awake, alert, and engaged. Playing full out means living our lives as if our lives depended on it.

Perhaps a little voice in your mind is saying, "That's crazy. I can't do anything about global problems." In the spirit of critical thinking, put that idea to the test. Get involved in solving a bigger problem. Then notice how you can, indeed, make a difference. And just as important, notice how your other problems dwindle—or even vanish.

 Learn more about finding bigger problems online.

Career Application

Maria Sanchez graduated with an associate's degree in legal assistance and has been working for two years as a paralegal at a large law firm.

Maria's work is supervised by an attorney who is ultimately responsible for the documents she produces. As a paralegal, she cannot set legal fees, give legal advice, or present cases in court. Except for these restrictions, however, she does many of the same things that lawyers do. Maria's current job centers on legal research—identifying laws, judicial decisions, legal articles, and other materials that are relevant to her assigned cases.

Maria is one of three paralegals who work with her supervising attorney. Recently she applied for a new paralegal job that opened up in the firm. In addition to legal research, this job involves drafting legal arguments and motions to be filed in court. Getting this job would mean a promotion and a raise for Maria.

Maria has formally applied for the job and expressed strong interest in it. She believes that her chances are excellent. One of the paralegals she works with is not interested in the job, and she knows that the other one plans to announce next month that she's quitting the firm to attend law school.

One day, Maria finds the first draft of an e-mail that her supervisor has printed out and accidentally placed in a stack of legal documents for Maria to file. The e-mail is a note of congratulations that offers the new paralegal job to the person who plans to quit.

© Andresr/Shutterstock

Reflecting on this scenario

Does Maria face an ethical dilemma in this situation? Explain your answer.

_____

_____

_____

_____

_____

Review the guidelines for decision making given in this chapter—particularly the suggestions for ethical decision making. Choose one and explain how Maria could apply it.

_____

_____

_____

_____

_____

_____

_____

_____

_____

_____

_____

Quiz

Name _____   Date ____/____/____

1. List the four questions from this chapter that can guide you to becoming a critical thinker.

2. Briefly describe one strategy for answering each question you just listed.

3. Define the word *plagiarism* and explain one method for preventing it.

4. The goal of the Power Process in this chapter is to help you eliminate problems. True or false? Explain your answer.

5. Briefly describe three strategies for creative thinking.

6. Explain the difference between values and goals.

7. List two types of logical fallacies, and give an example of each type.

8. List an assumption behind the following statement: "Why save money? I want to enjoy life today."

9. Name a logical fallacy involved in this statement: "Everyone who's ever visited this school agrees that it's the best in the state."

10. According to the text, the words *choose* and *decide* have the same meaning. True or false? Explain your answer.

Focus on Transferable Skills

Now that you've experimented with some new strategies for thinking, take a few minutes to revisit your responses to the "Thinking" section of the Discovery Wheel in Chapter 1: "First Steps." Also reflect on ways to extend your thinking skills.

You might want to prepare for this exercise by reviewing the articles "Jumpstart Your Education with Transferable Skills" on page 58 and "101 Transferable Skills" on page 60.

CREATIVE AND CRITICAL THINKING

When I'm asked to come up with a topic for a paper or speech, the first thing I do is . . .

When choosing how to vote in an election, the first thing I take into account about a candidate is . . .

PROBLEM SOLVING AND DECISION MAKING

When faced with a major decision, such as choosing a career or declaring my major, my first step is usually to . . .

One of the biggest problems I face right now is . . .

To come up with a solution for this problem, I will . . .

NEXT ACTION

The most important thing I could do to become a more skilled thinker is . . .

To develop this skill, I intend to . . .

Master Student PROFILE

Irshad Manji
. . . is courageous

© Colin McPherson/CORBIS

It's to be expected that an author with a book on the verge of publication will lose her cool over a last-minute detail or two. Some might get nervous that their facts won't hold up and run a paranoid, final check. Others might worry about what to wear to their book party. When Irshad Manji's book was about to hit the stands, her concern was a bit different. She feared for her life.

Certain her incendiary book *The Trouble with Islam* would set off outrage in the Muslim community, she called the police, told them she was working on a book that was highly critical of Islam, and asked if they could advise her on safety precautions.

They came to visit her Toronto apartment building several times and suggested she install a state-of-the-art security system, bulletproof windows, and hire a counterterrorism expert to act as her personal bodyguard.

In her short, plucky book she comes down hard on modern-day Islam, charging that the religion's mainstream has come to be synonymous with literalism. Since the 13th century, she said, the faith hasn't encouraged—or tolerated—independent thinking (or as it's known in the faith, *ijtihad*).

The book, which is written like a letter, is both thoughtful and confrontational. In person, Ms. Manji embodied the same conflicting spirit. She was affable and wore a broad smile. Her upbeat, nervous energy rose to the task of filling in every potentially awkward pause. (One of her favorite factoids: "Prophet Mohammed was quite a feminist.")

Her journey scrutinizing Islam started when she was an 8-year-old and taking weekly religious classes at a *madrasa* (religious school) in suburban Vancouver. Her anti-Semitic teacher Mr. Khaki never took her questions seriously; he merely told her to accept everything because it was in the Koran. She wanted to know why she had

to study it in Arabic, which she didn't understand, and was told the answers were "in the Koran."

Her questioning ended up getting her kicked out of school at 14, and she embarked on a 20-year-long private study of the religion. While she finds the treatment poured on women and foreigners in Islamic nations indefensible, she said that she continues to be a believer because the religion provides her with her values. "And I'm so glad I did because it was then I came to realize that there was this really progressive side of my religion and it was this tradition of critical thinking called *ijtihad*. This is what allows me to stay within the faith."

She calls herself a "Muslim refusenik" because she remains committed to the religion and yet she doesn't accept what's expected of Muslim women. As terrorist acts and suicide bombings refuse to subside, she said it's high time for serious reform within the Islamic faith.

She said many young Muslim supporters are still afraid to come out about their support of her. "Even before 9/11 it was the young Muslims who were emerging out of these audiences and gathering at the side of the stage. They'd walk over and say, 'Irshad, we need voices such as yours to help us open up this religion of ours because if it doesn't open up, we're leaving the mosques.'"

She wants Muslims to start thinking critically about their religion and to start asking more questions. "Most Muslims have never been introduced to the possibility, let alone the virtue, of asking questions about our holy book," she said. "We have never been taught the virtue of interpreting the Koran in different ways."

Lauren Mechling, "The Trouble with Writing About Islam," as appeared in *New York Sun*, November 26, 2004. Copyright © 2004. Reprinted with permission of the author.

**(1969–)
Controversial journalist, broadcaster, and author of *The Trouble with Islam*, who uses her "Muslim voice of reform, to concerned citizens worldwide" in an effort to explore faith and community, and the diversity of ideas.**

Learn more about Irshad Manji and other master students at the Master Student Hall of Fame.

Master Student Map

as you read, ask yourself

what if . . .

I could consistently create the kind of relationships that I've always wanted?

why this chapter matters . . .

Your communication abilities are as important to your success as your technical skills.

what is included . . .

how you can use this chapter . . .

- Listen, speak, and write more effectively.
- Create more satisfying relationships.
- Prevent and resolve conflict with other people.
- Use your capacity to make and keep agreements as a tool for creating your future.

MASTER EMPLOYEE in *action*

Every day there are challenges in communication between doctors and nurses, nurses and nurses, and nurses and nurses' aides. The tiniest miscommunication can lead to absolute catastrophe. During college, good communication was pushed as an essential skill to have in the workplace. Without these skills taught to me at college, I would be unable to perform effective care of my clients, and would therefore be an ineffective nurse.

—BONNIE PLAYER, NURSE

Photo courtesy of Bonnie Player

Communicating in a diverse world

ACCORDING TO THE National Association of Colleges and Employers, what interviewers look for most of all in job applicants is skill in communicating—the ability to write and speak clearly and persuasively. Coincidentally, this is also the skill that they find most consistently missing in new graduates.[1]

Communication can be defined as the process of creating shared meaning. When two people agree about the meaning of an event, they stand on common ground. They've communicated.

However, communication is a constant challenge. When people speak or listen, they don't exchange meaning. They exchange only symbols—words, images, gestures—which are open to interpretation. This means that communication is always flawed to some extent. We can never be sure that the message we send is the message that others receive.

Also remember that people differ in more ways than we can measure. The people sitting next to you in class or at work may come from many cultures. Each of them has a unique bundle of life experiences. Each of them creates meaning in a unique way. Adapting to diversity is a challenge that's always present in communication.

In the workplace, you will face diversity. Your coworkers might span three, four, or even five generations. Their race, ethnic group, religion, sexual orientation, and level of physical ability might differ greatly from yours. According to the U.S. Census Bureau, members of minority groups are the fastest growing part of the labor force.[2]

In addition, you will join an international workplace. American companies in the twenty-first century will buy from the world and sell to the world. You might work on project teams with people located in another city, state, or country.

Misunderstandings between people of different cultures can add noise to their interactions. In communication theory, the term *noise* refers to any factor that distorts meaning. Noise can be external (a lawn mower outside a classroom) or internal (fear, anger, false assumptions, or lack of information).

Communication ultimately works best when each of us has plenty of time to receive what others send *and* the opportunity to send a complete message when it's our turn. This is more challenging than it sounds. When emotions run high, people can totally forget when it's their job to receive and when it's their turn to send. Everyone talks and nobody listens.

However, with practice we can overcome many of the difficulties inherent in human communication. That's what this chapter is about. As you enhance your skills at listening, speaking, and writing, you can enter a diverse world with confidence. ✳

journal entry 22

Discovery/Intention Statement

Commit to create value from this chapter

Think of a time when you experienced an emotionally charged conflict with another person. Were you able to resolve this dispute effectively? If so, list the strategies you used in the following space.

I discovered that I . . .

_____

_____

_____

_____

Now scan this chapter for ideas that can help you get your feelings and ideas across more skillfully in similar situations. List at least four ideas here, along with the page numbers where you can read more about them.

Strategy   **Page number**

_____

_____

_____

_____

Describe an upcoming situation in which you intend to apply these techniques. If possible, choose a situation that will occur within the next week.

I intend to . . .

_____

_____

_____

_____

Choosing to listen

Observe a person in a conversation who is not talking. Is he listening? Maybe. Maybe not. Is he focusing on the speaker? Preparing his response? Daydreaming?

EFFECTIVE LISTENING IS NOT EASY. It calls for concentration and energy. But it's worth the trouble. People love a good listener. The best salespeople, managers, coworkers, teachers, parents, and friends are the best listeners.

Through skilled listening, you can gain insight into other people and yourself. You can also translate your listening skills into more powerful notes, more productive study groups, and better relationships with instructors and coworkers.

One powerful technique for listening is to separate the roles of sending and receiving. Communication channels get blocked when we try to send and receive messages at the same time. Instead, be aware of when you are the receiver and when you are the sender. If you are receiving (listening), just receive. Avoid switching into the sending (speaking) mode. When someone else talks, just listen.

You can also benefit from a clear intention. *Choose to listen well.* Once you've made this choice, you can discover more ways to become effective at listening.

Notice that the following techniques start with nonverbal listening. Next come suggestions for verbal responses that can help you fully receive a speaker's message.

Nonverbal listening

Be quiet. Silence is more than staying quiet while someone is speaking. Allowing several seconds to pass before you begin to talk gives the speaker time to catch her breath and gather her thoughts. She might want to continue. Someone who talks nonstop might fear she will lose the floor if she pauses.

If the message being sent is complete, this short break gives you time to form your response and helps you avoid the biggest barrier to listening—listening with your answer running. If you make up a response before the person is finished, you might miss the end of the message, which is often the main point.

In some circumstances, pausing for several seconds might be inappropriate. Ignore this suggestion

Ariel Skelley/Blend Images/Getty

completely when someone asks in a panic where to find the nearest phone to call the fire department.

Maintain eye contact. Look at the other person while he speaks. Maintaining eye contact demonstrates your attentiveness and helps keep your mind from wandering. Your eyes also let you observe the speaker's body language and behavior. If you avoid eye contact, you can fail to see *and* fail to listen.

This idea is not an absolute. Maintaining eye contact is valued more in some cultures than others. Also, some people learn primarily by hearing; they can listen more effectively by turning off the visual input once in a while.

Display openness. You can display openness through your facial expression and body position. Uncross your arms and legs. Sit up straight. Face the other person, and remove any physical barriers between you, such as a pile of books.

Send acknowledgments. Let the speaker know periodically that you are still there. Words and nonverbal gestures of acknowledgment convey to the speaker that you are interested and that you are receiving his message. These words and gestures include "Umhum," "OK," "Yes," and head nods.

These acknowledgments do not imply your agreement. When people tell you what they don't like about you, your head nod doesn't mean that you agree. It just indicates that you are listening.

Release distractions. Even when your intention is to listen, you might find your mind wandering. Thoughts about what *you* want to say or something you want to do later might claim your attention. There's a simple solution: Notice your wandering mind without judgment. Then bring your attention back to the act of listening.

Another option is to ask for a quick break so that you can make a written note about what's on your mind. Tell the speaker that you're writing so that you can clear your mind and return to full listening.

Comstock/Getty

Suspend judgments. Listening and agreeing are two different activities. As listeners, our goal is to fully receive another person's message. This does not mean that we're obligated to agree with the message. Once you're confident that you accurately understand a speaker's point of view, you are free to agree or disagree with it. The key to effective listening is understanding *before* evaluating.

Verbal listening

Choose when to speak. When we listen to another person, we often interrupt with our own stories, opinions, suggestions, and comments. Consider the following dialogue:

"Oh, I'm so excited! I just found out that I've been nominated to be in *Who's Who in American Musicians.*"

"Yeah, that's neat. My Uncle Elmer got into *Who's Who in American Veterinarians.* He sure has an interesting job. One time I went along when he was treating a cow, and you'll never believe what happened next. . . ."

To avoid this kind of one-sided conversation, delay your verbal responses. This does not mean that you remain totally silent while listening. It means that you wait for an *appropriate* moment to respond.

Watch your nonverbal responses, too. A look of "Good grief!" from you can deter the other person from finishing his message.

Feed back meaning. Sometimes you can help a speaker clarify her message by paraphrasing it. This does not mean parroting what she says. Instead, briefly summarize. Psychotherapist Carl Rogers referred to this technique as *reflection.*[3]

Feed back what you see as the essence of the person's message: "Let me see if I understood what you said. . . ." or "What I'm hearing you say is. . . ." Often, the other person will say, "No, that's not what I meant. What I said was. . . ."

There will be no doubt when you get it right. The sender will say, "Yeah, that's it," and either continue with another message or stop sending when he knows you understand.

When you feed back meaning, be concise. This is not a time to stop the other person by talking on and on about what you think you heard.

Notice verbal and nonverbal messages. You might point out that the speaker's body language seems to convey the exact opposite of what her words do. For example: "I noticed you said you are excited, but you look bored."

Keep in mind that the same nonverbal behavior can have various meanings across cultures. Someone who looks bored might simply be listening in a different way.

Hear complaints as requests and intentions. An effective way to listen to complaints is to look for the request hidden in them. "This class is a waste of my time" can be heard as "Please tell me what I'll gain if I participate actively in class." "The instructor talks too fast" can translate to "What strategies can I use to take notes when the instructor covers material rapidly?"

We can even transform complaints into intentions. Take this complaint: "The parking lot by the dorms is so dark at night that I'm afraid to go to my car." This complaint can lead to a plan for having a light installed in the parking lot.

Viewing complaints as requests gives us more choices. We can decide whether to grant the request or help the person translate his own complaint into an action plan. This is an alternative to responding with defensiveness ("What does he know anyway?"), resignation ("It's always been this way and always will be"), or indifference ("It's not my job").

Allow emotion. In the presence of full listening, some people will share things that they feel deeply about. They might shed a few tears, cry, shake, or sob. If you feel uncomfortable when this happens, see if you can accept the discomfort for a little while longer. Emotional release can bring relief and trigger unexpected insights.

Ask for more. Full listening with unconditional acceptance is a rare gift. Many people have never experienced it. They are used to being greeted with resistance, so they habitually stop short of saying what they truly think and feel. Help them shed this habit by routinely asking, "Is there anything more you want to say about that?" This question sends the speaker a message that you truly value what she has to say.

Be careful with questions and advice. Questions are directive. They can take conversations in a new direction, which may not be where the speaker wants to go. Ask questions only to clarify the speaker's message. Later, when it's your turn to speak, you can introduce any topic that you want.

Also be cautious about giving advice. Unsolicited advice can be taken as condescending or even insulting. Skilled listeners recognize that people are different, and they do not assume that they know what's best for someone else.

Take care of yourself. People seek good listeners, but there are times when you don't want to listen. You might be distracted with your own concerns.

Be honest. Don't pretend to listen. You can say, "What you're telling me is important, but I'm pressed for time right now. Can we set aside another time to talk about this?" It's OK not to listen.

Stay open to the adventure of listening. Receiving what another person has to say is an act of courage. Listening fully—truly opening yourself to the way another person sees the world—means taking risks. Your opinions may be challenged. You may be less certain or less comfortable than you were before.

Along with the risks come rewards. Listening in an unguarded way can take your relationships to a new depth and level of honesty. This kind of listening can open up new possibilities for thinking, feeling, and behaving. In addition, when you practice full listening, other people are more likely to receive when it's your turn to send. ✳

 Find more strategies for full listening online.

Choosing to speak

You have been talking with people for most of your life, and you usually manage to get your messages across. There are times, though, when you don't. Often, these times are emotionally charged.

WE ALL HAVE THIS PROBLEM. Sometimes we feel wonderful or rotten or sad or scared, and we want to express it. Emotions, though, can get in the way of the message. Although you can send almost any message through tears, laughter, fist pounding, or hugging, sometimes words are better. Begin with a sincere intention to reach common ground with your listener. Then experiment with the suggestions that follow.

Replace "you" messages with "I" messages. It can be difficult to disagree with someone without his becoming angry or your becoming upset. When conflict occurs, we often make statements about the other person, or "you" messages:

"You are rude."

"You make me mad."

"You must be crazy."

"You don't love me anymore."

This kind of communication results in defensiveness. The responses might be similar to these:

"I am not rude."

"I don't care."

"No, *you* are crazy."

"No, *you* don't love *me!*"

"You" messages are hard to listen to. They label, judge, blame, and assume things that might or might not be true. They demand rebuttal. Even praise can sometimes be an ineffective "you" message. "You" messages don't work.

Psychologist Thomas Gordon suggests that when communication is emotionally charged, you should consider limiting your statements to descriptions about yourself.[4] Replace "you" messages with "I" messages:

"You are rude" might become "I feel upset."

"You make me mad" could be "I feel angry."

"You must be crazy" can be "I don't understand."

"You don't love me anymore" could become "I'm afraid we're drifting apart."

Suppose a friend asks you to pick her up at the airport. You drive 20 miles and wait for the plane. No friend. You decide your friend missed her plane, so you wait three hours for the next flight. No friend. Perplexed and worried, you drive home. The next day, you see your friend downtown.

"What happened?" you ask.

"Oh, I caught an earlier flight."

"You are a rude person," you reply.

Look for and talk about the facts—the observable behavior. Everyone will agree that your friend asked you to pick her up, that she did take an earlier flight, and that you did not receive a call from her. But the idea that she is rude is not a fact, it's a judgment.

She might go on to say, "I called your home, and no one answered. My mom had a stroke and was rushed to Valley View. I caught the earliest flight I could get." Your judgment no longer fits.

When you saw your friend, you might have said, "I waited and waited at the airport. I was worried about you. I didn't get a call. I feel angry and hurt. I don't want to waste my time. Next time, you can call me when your flight arrives, and I'll be happy to pick you up."

"I" messages don't judge, blame, criticize, or insult. They don't invite the other person to counterattack with more of the same. "I" messages are also more accurate. They report our own thoughts and feelings.

At first, "I" messages might feel uncomfortable or seem forced. That's OK. You can use the five ways to say "I" explained on page 250 to help you develop this skill.

Remember that questions are not always questions. You've heard these "questions" before. A parent asks, "Don't you want to look nice?" Translation: "I wish you'd cut your hair, lose the blue jeans, and put on a tie." Or how about this question from a spouse: "Honey, wouldn't you love to go to an exciting hockey game tonight?" Translation: "I've already bought tickets."

We use questions that aren't questions to sneak our opinions and requests into conversations. "Doesn't it upset you?" means "It upsets me," and "Shouldn't we hang the picture over here?" means "I want to hang the picture over here."

Communication improves when we say, "I'm upset" and "Let's hang the picture over here."

Choose your nonverbal messages. How you say something can be more important than what you say. Your tone of voice and gestures add up to a silent message that you send. This message can support, modify, or contradict your words. Your posture, the way you dress, how often you shower, and even the poster hanging on your wall can negate your words before you say them.

Most nonverbal behavior is unconscious. We can learn to be aware of it and choose our nonverbal messages. We can get clear about what we want to say and commit to sending that message. Then our inflections, gestures, and words work together.

Speak candidly. When we brood on negative thoughts and refuse to speak them out loud, we lose perspective. Likewise, when we keep joys to ourselves, we diminish our satisfaction. A solution is to share regularly what we think and feel.

Sometimes candid speaking can save a life. For example, if you think a friend is addicted to drugs, you can tell her so in a supportive, nonjudgmental way.

Imagine a community in which people freely and lovingly speak their minds—without fear or defensiveness. That can be your community.

Remember two key points. First, there is a big difference between speaking candidly about your problems and griping about them. Gripers usually don't seek solutions. They just want everyone to know how unhappy they are. Instead, talk about problems as a way to start searching for solutions.

Second, avoid bragging. We are usually turned off when someone makes constant references to his status, money, and success. There is a difference between sharing excitement and being obnoxious.

Notice barriers to sending messages. Sometimes fear stops us from sending messages. We are afraid of other people's reactions, sometimes justifiably.

Assumptions can also be used as excuses for not sending messages. "He already knows this," we tell ourselves. Or, "He'll never do anything about it, even if I tell him."

However, we can be truthful and still be insensitive to the impact that our messages have on others. Tact is a virtue; letting fear prevent communication is not.

If you have fear or some other concern about sending a message, be aware of it. Also realize that you can communicate even with your concerns. Make them part of your message: "I am going to tell you how I feel, and I'm afraid that you will think it's stupid."

Five ways to say "I"

An "I" message can include any or all of the following five elements. Be careful when including the last two elements, though, because they can contain hidden judgments or threats.

Observations. Describe the facts—the indisputable, observable realities. Talk about what you, or anyone else, can see, hear, smell, taste, or touch. Avoid judgments, interpretations, or opinions. Instead of saying, "You're a slob," say, "Last night's lasagna pan was still on the stove this morning."

Feelings. Describe your own feelings. It is easier to listen to "I feel frustrated" than to "You never help me." Stating how you feel about another's actions can be valuable feedback for that person.

Wants. You are far more likely to get what you want if you say what you want. If someone doesn't know what you want, she doesn't have a chance to help you get it.

Ask clearly. Instead of saying, "Do the dishes when it's your turn, or else!" say, "I want to divide the housework fairly." Also avoid demanding or using the word *need* when you make your request. Most people like to feel helpful, not obligated.

Thoughts. Communicate your thoughts, and use caution. Beginning your statement with the word *I* doesn't automatically make it an "I" message. "I think you are a slob" is a "you" judgment in disguise. Instead, say, "I'd have more time to study if I didn't have to clean up so often."

Intentions. The last part of an "I" message is a statement about what you intend to do. Have a plan that doesn't depend on the other person. For example, instead of saying "From now on we're going to split the dishwashing evenly," you could say, "I intend to do my share of the housework and leave the rest."

Discovery/Intention Statement

Re-create a relationship

Think about one of your relationships for a few minutes. It can involve a parent, sibling, spouse, child, friend, hairdresser, a coworker, or anyone else. In the following space, write down some things that are not working in the relationship. What bugs you? What do you find irritating or unsatisfying?

I discovered that . . .

_____

_____

_____

_____

_____

_____

_____

_____

_____

_____

_____

Now think for a moment about what you want from this relationship. More attention? Less nagging? Better cooperation? More openness, trust, financial security, or freedom? Choose a suggestion from this chapter, and describe how you could use it to make the relationship work.

I intend to . . .

_____

_____

_____

_____

_____

_____

_____

_____

_____

_____

_____

Overcoming such barriers could be a matter of educational survival. Sometimes a short talk with an advisor, a teacher, a friend, or a family member can solve a problem that otherwise could jeopardize your education.

Speak up! Look for opportunities to practice speaking strategies. Join class discussions. Start conversations about topics that excite you. Ask for information and clarification. Ask for feedback on your skills.

Also speak up when you want support. Consider creating a team of people who help one another succeed. Such a team can develop naturally from a study group that works well. Ask members if they would be willing to accept and receive support in achieving a wide range of academic and personal goals. Meet regularly to do goal-setting exercises from this book and brainstorm success strategies.

After you have a clear statement of your goals and a plan for achieving them, let family members and friends know. When appropriate, let them know how they can help. You may be surprised at how often people respond to a genuine request for support. ✳

 Find more strategies for speaking your mind.

9

COMMUNICATING

Thriving with diversity

Communicating with people of other cultures is a learned skill. Once you are willing to embrace diversity and talk openly about it, you can make creative use of the following suggestions and invent more of your own.

(woman with glass) © Sven Hagolani/zefa/Corbis, (woman in hijab) Peter Dazeley/Photographer's Choice/Getty

PEOPLE FROM DIFFERENT CULTURES read differently, write differently, think differently, eat differently, and learn differently than you. If you know this from the beginning, you can be more effective with your classmates, coworkers, and neighbors.

One key to understanding styles is to look for several possible interpretations of any behavior. For example:

Learn about other cultures.

- Consider the hand signal that signifies *OK* to many Americans—thumb and index finger forming a circle. In France, that signal denotes the number zero. In Japan, it is a symbol for money. And in Brazil, it is considered an obscene gesture.

- When Americans see a speaker who puts her hands in her pockets, they seldom attribute any meaning to this behavior. But in many countries—such as Germany, Indonesia, and Austria—this gesture is considered rude.

- During a conversation, you might prefer having a little distance between yourself and another person. But in Iran, people may often get so close to you that you can feel their breath.[5]

These examples could be extended to cover many areas—posture, eye contact, physical contact, facial expressions, and more. The various ways of interpreting these behaviors are neither right nor wrong. They simply represent differing styles in making meaning out of what we see.

You might find yourself fascinated by the interpretations of a particular culture. Consider learning as much about that culture as possible. Immerse yourself in it. Read novels, see plays, go to concerts, listen to music, look at art, take courses, and learn the language.

Look for differences between individualist and collectivist cultures. Individualist cultures flourish in the United States, Canada, and Western Europe. If your family has deep roots in one of these areas, you were probably raised to value personal fulfillment and personal success. You received recognition or rewards when you stood out from your peers by earning the highest grades in your class, scoring the most points during a basketball season, or demonstrating another form of individual achievement.

In contrast, collectivist cultures value cooperation over competition. Group progress is more important than individual success. Credit for an achievement is widely shared. If you were raised in such a culture, you probably place a high value on your family and were taught to respect your elders. Collectivist cultures dominate Asia, Africa, and Latin America.

In short, individualist cultures often emphasize "I." Collectivist cultures tend to emphasize "we." Forgetting about the differences between them can strain a friendship or wreck an international business deal.

If you were raised in an individualist culture, following are a few things to keep in mind when communicating with someone from a collectivist culture:

- *Remember that someone from a collectivist culture may place a high value on "saving face."* This idea involves more than simply avoiding embarrassment. This person may *not* want to be singled out from other members of a group, even for a positive achievement. If you have a direct request for this person or want to share something that could be taken as a personal criticism, save it for a private conversation.

- *Respect titles and last names.* Although Americans often like to use first names immediately after meeting someone, in some cultures this practice is acceptable only among family members. Especially in work settings, use last names and job titles during your first meetings. Allow time for informal relationships to develop.

- *Put messages in context.* For members of collectivist cultures, words convey only part of an intended message. Notice gestures and other nonverbal communication as well.

If you were raised in a collectivist culture, you can creatively "reverse" the items in this list. Keep in mind that direct questions from an American student or coworker are meant not to offend but only to clarify an idea. Don't be surprised if you are called by a nickname, if no one asks about your family, or if you are rewarded for a personal achievement. In social situations, remember that indirect cues might not get another person's attention. Practice asking clearly and directly for what you want.

Look for common ground. Students in higher education often find that they worry about many of the same things—including tuition bills, the quality of dormitory food, and the shortage of on-campus parking spaces. More important, our fundamental goals as human beings, such as health, physical safety, and economic security—cross culture lines.

The key is to honor the differences among people while remembering what we have in common. Diversity is not just about our differences—it's also about our similarities. On a biological level, less than 1 percent of the human genome accounts for visible characteristics such as skin color. In terms of our genetic blueprint, we are more than 99 percent the same.[6]

Look for individuals, not group representatives. Sometimes the way we speak glosses over differences among individuals and reinforces stereotypes. For example, a student who is worried about her grade in math may express concern over "all those Asian students who are skewing the class curve." Or a white music major may assume that her black classmate knows a lot about jazz or hip-hop music. We can avoid such errors by seeing people as individuals, not spokespersons for an entire group.

Be willing to accept feedback. Members of another culture might let you know that some of your words or actions had a meaning other than what you intended. A comment that seems harmless to you may be offensive to them, and they may tell you directly about it.

Avoid responding to such feedback with comments such as "Don't get me wrong," "You're taking this way too seriously," or "You're too sensitive." Instead, listen without resistance. Open yourself to what others have to say. Remember to distinguish between the *intention* of your behavior and its actual *impact* on other people. Then take the feedback you receive, and ask yourself how you can use it to communicate more effectively in the future.

You can also interpret such feedback positively as a sign that others believe you can change and that they see the possibility of a better relationship with you.

If you are new at responding to diversity, expect to make some mistakes along the way. However, as long as you approach people in a spirit of tolerance, your words and actions can always be changed.

Speak up against discrimination. You might find yourself in the presence of someone who tells a racist joke, makes a homophobic comment, or utters an ethnic slur. When this happens, you have a right to state what you observe, share what you think, and communicate how you feel. Depending on the circumstance, you might say:

- "That's a stereotype, and we don't have to fall for it."

- "Other people are going to take offense at that. Let's tell jokes that don't put people down."

- "I realize that you don't mean to offend anybody, but I feel hurt and angry by what you just said."

Also keep in mind that someone from a specific ethnic or cultural background can also be the source of negative comments about that culture. Be mindful of discriminatory comments from any source.

Speak up for change. Throughout recent history, social change has been fueled by students. When it comes to ending discrimination based on race, ethnicity, gender, or sexual orientation, you are in an environment where you can make a difference. Run for student government. Write for school publications. Speak at rallies. Express your viewpoint. This is training for citizenship in a multicultural world. ✳

Developing emotional intelligence

EMOTIONAL INTELLIGENCE MEANS recognizing feelings and responding to them in skillful ways. Daniel Goleman, author of *Emotional Intelligence: Why It Can Matter More Than IQ*, concludes that "IQ washes out when it comes to predicting who, among a talented pool of candidates *within* an intellectually demanding profession will become the strongest leader." At that point, emotional intelligence starts to become more important.[7]

If you're emotionally intelligent, you're probably described as someone with good "people skills." That's shorthand for being aware of your feelings, acting in thoughtful ways, showing concern for others, resolving conflict, and making responsible decisions. You can deepen these skills with the following strategies.

Recognize three elements of emotion

Even the strongest emotion consists of just three elements: physical sensations, thoughts, and action. Usually they happen so fast that you can barely distinguish them. Imagine that you suddenly perceive a threat—such as a supervisor who's screaming at you. Immediately your heart starts beating double time and your stomach muscles clench (physical sensations). Then thoughts race through your head: *This is a disaster. She hates me. And everyone's watching.* Finally, you take action, which could mean staring at her, yelling back, or running away.

Becoming aware of these elements is a first step toward emotional intelligence. This allows you to slow down, fully experience the sensations and thoughts, and then take your time to choose a more constructive action.

Name your emotions

Naming your emotions is a First Step to going beyond the "fight or flight" reaction to any emotion. Naming gives you power. The second that you attach a word to an emotion, you start to gain perspective. People with emotional intelligence have a rich vocabulary to describe a wide range of emotions. For example, do an Internet search with the keywords *feeling list*. Read through the lists you find for examples of ways that you can name your feelings in the future.

Accept your emotions

Another step toward emotional intelligence is accepting your emotions—*all* of them. This can be challenging if you've been taught that some emotions are "good" while others are "bad." Experiment with another viewpoint:

Emotions are complicated. They have many causes that are beyond your control, including what *other* people do. Because you do not choose your emotional reactions from moment to moment, you cannot be held morally responsible for them. However, you can be held responsible for what you *do* in response to any emotion.

Express your emotions

One possible response to any emotion is expressing it. The key is to speak without blaming others for the way you feel. The basic tool for doing so is using "I" messages, as described on page 250.

Respond rather than react

The heart of emotional intelligence is moving from mindless reactions to mindful actions. See if you can introduce an intentional gap between sensations and thoughts on the one hand and your next action on the other hand. To do this more often:

- *Run a "mood meter."* Check in with your moods several times each day. On a 3×5 card, note the time of day and your emotional state at that point. Rate your mood on a scale of 1 (relaxed and positive) to 10 (very angry, sad, or afraid).

- *Write Discovery Statements.* In your journal, write about situations in daily life that trigger strong emotions. Describe these events, and your usual responses to them, in detail.

- *Write Intention Statements.* After seeing patterns in your emotions, you can consciously choose to behave in new ways. Instead of yelling back at the angry supervisor, for example, make it your intention to simply remain silent and breathe deeply until he finishes. Then say, "I'll wait to respond until we've both had a chance to cool down."

Make decisions with emotional intelligence

Emotional intelligence can help you make decisions. When considering a possible choice, ask yourself, "How am I likely to feel if I do this?" You can use "gut feelings" to tell when an action might violate your values or hurt someone.

Think of emotions as energy. Anger, sadness, and fear send currents of sensation through your whole body. Ask yourself how you can channel that energy into constructive action. ✳

 Learn more ways to develop emotional intelligence.

Managing conflict

Conflict management is one of the most practical skills you'll ever learn. Here are strategies that can help. To bring these strategies to life, think of ways to use them in managing a conflict that you face right now.

© Masterfile Royalty Free

Back up to common ground. Conflict heightens the differences between people. When this happens, it's easy to forget how much we still agree with each other.

As a first step in managing conflict, back up to common ground. List all of the points on which you are *not* in conflict: "I know that we disagree about how much to spend on a new car, but we do agree that the old one needs to be replaced." Often, such comments put the problem in perspective and pave the way for a solution.

State the problem. Using "I" messages, as explained earlier in this chapter, state the problem. Tell people what you observe, feel, think, want, and intend to do. Allow the other people in a particular conflict to do the same.

Each person might have a different perception of the problem. That's fine. Let the conflict come into clear focus. It's hard to fix something unless people agree on what's broken.

Remember that the way you state the problem largely determines the solution. Defining the problem in a new way can open up a world of possibilities. For example, "I need a new roommate" is a problem statement that dictates one solution. "We could use some agreements about who cleans the apartment" opens up more options, such as resolving a conflict about who will wash the dishes tonight.

State all points of view. If you want to defuse tension or defensiveness, set aside your opinions for a moment. Take the time to understand the other points of view. Sum up those viewpoints in words that the other parties can accept. When people feel that they've been heard, they're often more willing to listen.

Ask for complete communication. In times of conflict, we often say one thing and mean another. So before responding to what the other person says, use active listening. Check to see if you have correctly received that person's message by saying, "What I'm hearing you say is. . . . Did I get it correctly?"

Focus on solutions. After stating the problem, dream up as many solutions as you can. Be outrageous. Don't hold back. Quantity—not quality—is the key. If you get stuck, restate the problem and continue brainstorming.

Next, evaluate the solutions you brainstormed. Discard the unacceptable ones. Talk about which solutions will work and how difficult they will be to implement. You might hit upon a totally new solution.

Choose one solution that is most acceptable to everyone involved, and implement it. Agree on who is going to do what by when. Then keep your agreements.

Finally, evaluate the effectiveness of your solution. If it works, pat yourselves on the back. If not, make changes or implement a new solution.

Focus on the future. Instead of rehashing the past, talk about new possibilities. Think about what you can do to prevent problems in the future. State how you intend to change, and ask others for their contributions to the solution.

Commit to the relationship. The thorniest conflicts usually arise between people who genuinely care for each other. Begin by affirming your commitment to the other person: "I care about you, and I want this relationship to last. So I'm willing to do whatever it takes to resolve this problem." Also ask the other person for a similar commitment.

Allow strong feelings. Permitting conflict can also mean permitting emotion. Being upset is all right. Feeling angry is often appropriate. Crying is OK. Allowing other people to see the strength of our feelings can help resolve the conflict. This suggestion can be especially useful during times when differences are so extreme that reaching common ground seems possible.

Expressing the full range of your feelings can transform the conflict. Often what's on the far side of anger is love. When we express and release resentment, we might discover genuine compassion in its place.

Notice your need to be "right." Some people approach conflict as a situation where only one person wins. That person has the "right" point of view. Everyone else loses.

When this happens, step back. See if you can approach the situation in a neutral way. Define the conflict as a problem to be solved, not as a contest to be won. Explore the possibility that you might be mistaken. There might be more than one acceptable solution. The other person might simply have a different learning style than yours. Let go of being "right," and aim for being effective instead.

Sometimes this means apologizing. Conflict sometimes arises from our own errors. Others might move quickly to end the conflict when we acknowledge this fact and ask for forgiveness.

© Masterfile Royalty Free

Slow down the communication. In times of great conflict, people often talk all at once. Words fly like speeding bullets, and no one listens. Chances for resolving the conflict take a nosedive.

When everyone is talking at once, choose either to listen or to talk—not both at the same time. Just send your message. Or just receive the other person's message. Usually, this technique slows down the pace and allows everyone to become more levelheaded.

To slow down the communication even more, take a break. Depending on the level of conflict, this might mean anything from a few minutes to a few days.

A related suggestion is to do something nonthreatening together. Share an activity with the others involved that's not a source of conflict.

Communicate in writing. What can be difficult to say to another person face to face might be effectively communicated in writing. When people in conflict write letters or e-mails to each other, they automatically apply many of the suggestions in this article. Writing is a way to slow down the communication and ensure that only one person at a time is sending a message.

There is a drawback to this tactic, though: It's possible for people to misunderstand what you say in a letter or e-mail. To avoid further problems, make clear

③① critical thinking exercise
Write an "I" message

First, pick something about school that irritates you. Then pretend that you are talking to a person who is associated with this irritation. In the following space, write down what you would say to this person as a "you" message.

Now write the same complaint as an "I" message. Include at least the first three elements suggested in "Five Ways to Say 'I'" on page 250.

COMMUNICATING

9

what you are *not* saying: "I am saying that I want to be alone for a few days. I am *not* saying that I want you to stay away forever." Saying what you are *not* saying is often useful in face-to-face communication as well.

Before you send your letter or e-mail, put yourself in the shoes of the person who will receive it. Imagine how your comments could be misinterpreted. Then rewrite your note, correcting any wording that might be open to misinterpretation.

There's another way to get the problem off your chest, especially when strong, negative feelings are involved: Write the nastiest, meanest e-mail response you can imagine, leaving off the address of the recipient so you don't accidentally send it. Let all of your frustration, anger, and venom flow onto the page. Be as mean and blaming as possible. When you have cooled off, see if there is anything else you want to add.

Then destroy the letter or delete the e-mail. Your writing has served its purpose. Chances are that you've calmed down and are ready to engage in skillful conflict management.

Get an objective viewpoint. With the agreement of everyone involved, set up a video camera and record a conversation about the conflict. In the midst of a raging argument, when emotions run high, it's almost impossible to see ourselves objectively. Let the camera be your unbiased observer.

Another way to get an objective viewpoint is to use a mediator, an objective, unbiased third party. Even an untrained mediator, as long as it's someone who is not a party to the conflict—can do much to decrease tension. Mediators can help everyone get their point of view across. The mediator's role is not to give advice but to keep the discussion on track and moving toward a solution.

Allow for cultural differences. People respond to conflict in different ways, depending on their cultural background. Some stand close, speak loudly, and make direct eye contact. Other people avert their eyes, mute their voices, and increase physical distance.

When it seems to you that other people are sidestepping or escalating a conflict, consider whether your reaction is based on cultural bias.

Agree to disagree. Sometimes we say all we have to say on an issue. We do all of the problem solving we can do. We get all points of view across. Nonetheless, the conflict still remains, staring us right in the face.

What's left is to recognize that honest disagreement is a fact of life. We can peacefully coexist with other people—and respect them—even though we don't agree on fundamental issues. Conflict can be accepted even when it is not resolved.

See the conflict within you. Sometimes the turmoil we see in the outside world has its source in our own inner world. A cofounder of Alcoholics Anonymous put it this way: "It is a spiritual axiom that every time we are disturbed, no matter what the cause, there is something awry with us."[8]

When we're angry or upset, we can take a minute to look inside. Perhaps we are ready to take offense— waiting to pounce on something the other person said. Perhaps, without realizing it, we did something to create the conflict. Or maybe the other person is simply saying what we don't want to admit is true.

When these things happen, we can shine a light on our own thinking. A simple spot-check might help the conflict disappear right before our eyes. ✳

 Discover more ways to manage conflicts online.

Big Cheese Photo LLC/Alamy

Join a diverse workplace

THE ECONOMIES OF THE WORLD are gradually becoming one. Some time during the first third of this century, goods and services from China, India, and Japan could represent one-half of the world's gross domestic product.[9] Twenty percent of jobs in the United States are currently linked to international trade, and this percentage is expected to increase.[10]

As American companies look for ways to gain overseas market share, they will look for people who enter this global environment with ease. Diversity in the workplace will be seen as good for people and good for business. People of all races and cultures can use several strategies to reach common ground at work.

Expect differences

To begin, remember an obvious fact: People differ. Obvious as it is, this fact is easy to forget. Most of us unconsciously judge others by a single set of standards—our own. That can lead to communication breakdown. Consider some examples:

- A man in Costa Rica works for a multinational company. He turns down a promotion that would take his family to California. This choice mystifies the company's executives. Yet the man has grandparents who are in ill health, and leaving them behind would be taboo in his country.

- A Native American woman avoids eye contact with her superiors. Her coworkers see her as aloof. However, she comes from a culture where people seldom make eye contact with their superiors.

- A woman from Ohio travels to Mexico City on business. She shows up promptly for a 9 a.m. meeting and finds that it starts 30 minutes late and goes an hour beyond its scheduled ending time. She's entered a culture with a flexible sense of time.

- An American executive schedules a meeting over dinner with people from his company's office in Italy. As soon as the group orders food, the executive launches into a discussion of his agenda items. He

notices that his coworkers from Italy seem unusually silent, and he wonders if they feel offended. He forgets that they come from a culture where people ease into business discussions slowly—only after building a relationship through "small talk."

To prevent misunderstandings, remember that culture touches every aspect of human behavior, ranging from the ways people greet one another to the ways they resolve conflict. Differences in culture could affect any encounter you have with another person. Expecting differences up front helps you keep an open mind.

Mind the details

Pay attention to details that people from any culture will use to form first impressions of you. Lydia Ramsey, author of *Manners That Sell: Adding the Polish That Builds Profits*, suggests the following practices. You might find them especially useful if you travel overseas for your job:

- *Shake hands appropriately.* Although the handshake is a near-universal form of greeting, people do it differently across the world. You might have been coached to take a firm grip, make eye contact, pump twice, and then let go. In other countries, however, people might prefer a lighter grip or longer contact. When traveling to the Middle East, you might even be greeted with a kiss or hug. Observe closely to discover the norm.

- *When in doubt, dress up.* Americans are relatively informal about workplace fashion. In many cultures, there are no "casual days." Formal business wear is expected every day. Dress up unless it's clearly OK to do otherwise.

- *Treat business cards carefully.* In many cultures, the way that you exchange cards conveys your respect for others. When someone gives you a card, take a second to look at it. Then offer your thanks and place the card in a folder or briefcase with other work-

9

COMMUNICATING

related documents. Don't stash it quickly in a pocket or purse.

- *Respect titles and names.* Although Americans like to do business on a first-name basis, this is acceptable in some cultures only among family members. Avoid misunderstandings by using last names and job titles when you greet people in work settings.[11]

Use language with care

Even people who speak the same language sometimes use simple words that can be confused with each other. For instance, giving someone a "mickey" can mean pulling a practical joke or slipping a drug into someone's drink. We can find it tough to communicate simple observations, let alone abstract concepts.

You can help by communicating simply and directly. When meeting with people who speak English as a Second Language, think twice before using figures of speech or slang expressions. Stick to standard English and enunciate clearly.

Also remember that nonverbal language differs across cultures. For example, people from India may shake their head from side to side to indicate agreement, not disagreement.

Put messages in context

When speaking to people of another culture, you might find that words carry only part of an intended message. In many countries, strong networks of shared assumptions form a context for communication.

As an example, people from some Asian and Arabic countries might not include every detail of an agreement in a written contract. These people often place a high value on keeping verbal promises. Spelling out all the details in writing might be considered an insult. Knowing such facts can help you prevent and resolve conflicts in the workplace.

32 critical thinking exercise
Enter the global economy

In his classic book *The World Is Flat: A Brief History of the Twenty-First Century,* Thomas Friedman describes a new world economy driven by two major forces—globalization and technology.[12] He argues that the world economy is becoming "flat" in the sense of offering a more level playing field. The Internet and workflow software allow people across the world to collaborate on team projects. Digital technology also allows American employers to outsource jobs by hiring people in other countries to fill them.

Take a few minutes to think about how you can succeed in this new world. One option is to develop your communication skills. For example, you might choose to learn a second language that could help you travel overseas on business. You could learn to communicate across cultures by joining a project team that involves a diverse group of people. Or you could plan to take courses in sales or public speaking. Having these skills could make it more difficult for an employer to ship your job overseas to someone sitting behind a computer.

In the following space, brainstorm what *you* could do to prosper in a "flat" global economy. Fill the following space and continue on additional paper as needed.

Now, review the list you just created and choose the idea that interests you most—one that has the potential to make a real difference in your long-term career plan. In the following space, write a goal based on this idea and list three action steps you can take to meet this goal.

Test for understanding

To promote cross-cultural understanding, look for signs that your message got through clearly. Ask questions without talking down to your audience: *Am I making myself clear? Is there anything that doesn't make sense?* Watch for nonverbal cues of understanding, such as a nod or smile.

Learn about another culture

You can also promote cross-cultural understanding through the path of knowledge. Consider learning everything you can about another culture. Read about that culture and take related classes. Cultivate friends from that culture and take part in their community events. Get a feel for the customs, music, and art that members of the group share. If appropriate, travel abroad to learn more. Also ask about foreign language training; it might be offered by your company.

Follow up with action at work. Join project teams with diverse members. Experiencing diversity firsthand can be a positive experience when you're working with others to meet a common goal.

Expand networks

People with narrow circles of relationships can be at a disadvantage when trying to change jobs or enter a new field. For maximum flexibility in your career path, stay connected to people of your own culture—*and* cultivate contacts with people of other cultures.

Counter bias and discrimination

In the United States, laws dating back to the Equal Pay Act of 1963 and Title VII of the Civil Rights Act of 1964 ban discrimination in nearly all aspects of the work world, from hiring and firing to transfers and promotions. Congress set up the Equal Employment Opportunity Commission (EEOC) to enforce these laws. You can get more information from the EEOC Web site at **www.eeoc.gov**.

If you think that you've been the subject of discrimination, take time to examine the facts. Before filing a lawsuit, exhaust other options. Start by bringing the problem to your supervisor, your company's equal employment officer, or someone from the EEOC.

Stereotypes based on race, ethnicity, gender, and disability are likely to fade as the workplace becomes more diverse. As they do, disprove stereotypes through your behavior. Set high standards for yourself and meet them. Seek out key projects that make you visible in the organization, and then perform effectively. These are useful success strategies for anyone in the workplace.

Also keep records of your performance. Log your achievements. Ask for copies of your performance evaluations and make sure they're accurate. Having a stack of favorable evaluations can help you make your case when bringing a complaint or resolving conflict.

Be willing to bridge gaps

Simply being *willing* to bridge culture gaps can be just as crucial as knowing about another group's customs or learning their language. People from other cultures might sense your attitude and be willing to reach out to you.

Begin by displaying some key attributes of a critical thinker. Be open-minded and willing to suspend judgment. Notice when you make assumptions based on another person's accent, race, religion, or gender. Become willing to discover your own biases, listen fully to people with other points of view, enter new cultural territory, and even feel uncomfortable at times.

It's worth it. Bridging to people of other cultures means that you gain new chances to learn, make contacts, increase your career options, and expand your friendships. The ability to work with people of many cultures is a marketable skill—and a way to enlarge your world. ✱

COMMUNICATING

9

33 critical thinking exercise
V.I.P.s (very important persons)

Step 1. Under the column below titled "Name," write the names of at least seven people who have positively influenced your life. They might be relatives, friends, teachers, or perhaps persons you have never met. (Complete each step before moving on.)

Step 2. In the next column, rate your gratitude for this person's influence (from 1 to 5, with 1 being a little grateful and 5 being extremely grateful.

Step 3. In the third column, rate how fully you have communicated your appreciation to this person (again, 1 to 5, with 1 being not communicated and 5 being fully communicated).

Step 4. In the final column, put a U to indicate the persons with whom you have unfinished business (such as an important communication that you have not yet sent).

Name	Grateful (1–5)	Communicate Appreciation (1–5)	U

Step 5. Now select two persons with a U beside their name, and write each of them a letter or e-mail. Express the love, tenderness, and joy you feel toward them. Tell them exactly how they have helped change your life and how glad you are that they did.

Step 6. You also have an impact on others. Write in the following space the names of people whose lives you have influenced. Consider sharing with these people why you enjoy being a part of their lives.

Create high-performing teams

WORKING IN TEAMS helps you to develop several transferable skills. One is sociability—taking an interest in people, valuing what they think, and understanding how they feel. Another is understanding social systems in organizations and operating effectively in them. Teamwork also gives you a chance to practice all the communication skills explored in this chapter.

In the workplace, teams abound. To research their book *When Teams Work Best,* Frank LaFasto and Carl Larson studied 600 teams. These ranged from the Mount Everest climbing team to the teams that produced the Boeing 747 airplane—the world's largest aircraft and a product of 75,000 blueprints.[13]

Know the pitfalls

Research indicates many potential problems with teams, including[14]

- Dependence on a dominant leader.
- "Group think" that excludes new ideas.
- Fear of taking risks.
- "Social loafing"—the tendency of people to take less action when working as part of a group than when working alone.
- Taking on too many goals.
- Adopting ideas that most group members disagree with because members choose not to share their true thoughts and feelings.

Apply the cycle of learning to teams

One way to prevent such problems is to select team members based on the cycle of learning as described in Chapter 1: "First Steps." Psychologist David Kolb proposed that people learn from experience through four kinds of activity that occur in a repeating cycle. Teams learn in the same way. To create a successful team, choose members who will:

- Get fully involved with the team and commit to its purpose (concrete experience).
- Talk about the team's experiences and stay open to new ideas (reflective observation).
- Think critically about which agreements and actions will achieve the team's purpose (abstract conceptualization).
- Make decisions and take action (active experimentation).

Not everyone will have all these skills, so invite members with a variety of learning styles. Look beyond your circle of friends and people who tend to think and act alike. Your team is more likely to succeed with a variety of people who can choose tasks based on their strengths and preferences.

Moving through the cycle of learning is easier when the team is an optimal size. Think carefully about how many people to include. There is no magic number that will guarantee a successful team. Keep it small enough to manage and large enough to achieve the team's goals.

Your team members might say that they are too busy to bother with the full cycle of learning. As an alternative, simply ask them to reflect on their prior experience. During your first meeting, set aside time to talk about everyone's prior experience with teams. Share your best and worst experiences. Based on that discussion, create your own list of what makes for a successful team. Then make some basic agreements about ways to prevent the problems you've experienced with teams in the past.

Even out the work load

One potential trap for teams is that one person ends up doing most of the work. This person might feel resentful and complain.

If you find yourself in this situation, transform your complaint into a request. Instead of scolding team members for being lazy, request help. Ask team members to take over tasks that you've been doing. Delegate specific jobs.

Share roles

Teams often begin by choosing a leader with a vision, charisma, and expertise. As your team matures, however, consider letting other members take turns in a leadership role. This is one way to encourage a diversity of viewpoints and help people expand their learning styles.

Apply the Power Processes

People talk a lot about *empowering* teams. One answer is to take your cue from the word *empowered* and see if you can apply the Power Processes in this book to team work. Following are examples to get you started.

Discover what you want. When forming a team, look for a fit between individual goals and the team's mission. Team members might want formal recognition for taking part in the project and meeting its objectives. People naturally ask, "What's in this for me?" Provide answers to that question. Emphasize the chance to develop marketable skills by joining the team.

Equally important is ensuring that the organization knows what it wants from the team. To promote effective results, define your team's purpose, its expected results, and how it will be held accountable.

Also ask for enough support—in terms of time, money, and other resources—to produce what the team wants. To get down to specifics, ask four questions based on the Master Student Map that begins each chapter of this book:

- *Why* is this project being done?

- *What* would a successful outcome for this project look like?

- *How* are we going to create a bridge from our current reality to that successful outcome?

- *What if* we truly made this outcome a high priority? What is the very next action that each of us would take to make it happen?

Ideas are tools. Teams tend to fizzle when they create new ideas that meet with immediate skepticism or outright rejection. After proposing changes to a company's existing policies and procedures, team members might face resistance: "This suggestion will never work." "That's just not the way we do things around here." "We can't break with tradition." These responses are examples of groupthink, which happens when a team automatically rules out new options simply because they're . . . well, *new*.

(people) Photodisc, (lightbulb) Comstock Klips

Managers can prevent this outcome by asking pointed questions before a team convenes its first meeting: Are we truly interested in change? Are we willing to act on what the team recommends? Or are we just looking for a team to reinforce our current practices?

People who want a team to succeed will treat its ideas as tools. Instead of automatically looking for what's wrong with a proposal, look for potential applications. Even a proposal that seems outlandish at first might become workable with a few modifications.

In an empowered team, all ideas are welcome, problems are freely admitted, and any item is open for discussion. During meetings, allow members to fully express any idea before thinking critically about it. Speak openly about personal conflicts and resolve them quickly.

Be here now. Concentration and focused attention are attributes of effective students—and effective teams. When a team tries to tackle too many problems or achieve too many goals, it gets distracted. Members can forget the team's purpose and lose their enthusiasm for the project. You can help restore focus by asking: "What is the single most important goal that our team can meet?" and "What is the single most important thing we can do *now* to meet that goal?"

Another source of team distraction is a member who doesn't perform—someone who comes to meetings unprepared, consistently fails to complete individual assignments, or attacks new ideas. Effective teams have a leader who focuses the group on its agenda and tactfully asks nonperforming members to change their behavior.

Notice your pictures. During much of the previous century, many large businesses and nonprofit organizations were organized as hierarchies with multiple layers—executives, middle-level managers, supervisors, and employees. People who worked for such a company had jobs with clearly defined and limited responsibilities. Collaborations among employees in different departments were rare.

Teams present a different picture of how to operate a workplace, and old pictures die hard. Companies may give lip service to the idea of teams and yet fall back into traditional practices. Managers might set up teams but offer little training to help people function in this new working environment.

You can prepare for this situation now. While you are in school, seize opportunities to work collaboratively. Form study groups. Enroll in classes that include group projects. Show up for your next job with teamwork skills. At the same time, remember that some of your coworkers may not share your assumptions about the value of teams. By demonstrating your abilities, you help them to form new pictures. ✳

Three paths to clear writing

Writing skills are essential to your success in school and in the workplace. Papers, presentations, online courses, reports, e-mails, and social networking call for your ability to communicate ideas with force and clarity.

Digital Vision/Getty

THIS CHAPTER OUTLINES a three-phase process for writing anything: First, get ready to write. Second, write a first draft. Finally, revise your draft.

PHASE 1: Get ready to write

Schedule and list writing tasks

To overcome procrastination, divide a big writing project—such as a 20-page paper—into smaller steps. Then set a due date for each step and add those dates to your calendar. Build in a little time to spare.

Say that the paper is due to your instructor on December 1, and you have about three months to finish it. Plan to complete your phase 1 activities by October 1. Then set a due date of November 1 for your first draft and November 25 for your final draft. That leaves you with five extra days to catch up before the final paper is due.

Choose a topic and working title

Using your instructor's guidelines, write down a list of topics that interest you. Write as many of these ideas as you can think of in two minutes. Then choose one topic. If you can't decide, use scissors to cut your list into single items, put them in a box, and pull one out. To avoid getting stuck on this step, set a precise timeline: "I will choose a topic by 4 p.m. on Wednesday."

The most common pitfall is selecting a topic that's too broad. "Success" is probably not a useful topic for a paper. Instead, consider "The Meaning of Success." Your topic statement can function as a working title.

Write a thesis statement

Clarify what you want to say by summarizing it in one concise sentence. This sentence, called a *thesis statement,* refines your working title. It also helps in making a preliminary outline.

You might write a thesis statement such as, "The meaning of success lies in setting and achieving goals." A thesis statement that's clear and to the point can make your paper easier to write. You can always rewrite your thesis statement as you learn more about your topic.

A thesis statement is not the same as a topic. Like newspaper headlines, a thesis statement makes a point or describes an action. It is expressed in a complete sentence, including a verb. "Diversity" is a topic. "Cultural diversity is valuable" is a thesis statement.

Consider your purpose

Effective writing flows from a purpose. Discuss the purpose of your assignment with your instructor. Also think about how you'd like your reader or listener to respond after considering your ideas. Do you want your audience to think differently, to feel differently, or to take a certain action?

To clarify your purpose, state it in one sentence. For instance, "The purpose of this paper is to define the term *success* in such a clear and convincing way that I win a scholarship from the publisher of this textbook."

Do initial research

At this stage, the aim of your research is not to uncover specific facts about your topic. That comes later. First, you want to gain an overview of the subject. Say, for example, that you want to persuade the reader to vote for a certain candidate. Begin by learning enough about this person to summarize his background and state his stands on key issues.

Outline

An outline keeps you from wandering off the topic. Start by gathering a stack of 3×5 cards. Using the information gathered from your initial research, brainstorm ideas you want to include in your paper. Write one phrase or sentence per card.

Next, experiment with the cards. Group them into separate stacks, with each stack representing one major category of ideas that relate to your topic. After that, arrange the stacks in order. Finally, arrange the cards within each stack in a logical order. Rearrange them until you discover an organization that you like. If you write on a computer, find out whether your word-processing software has an outlining feature that allows you to list and sort ideas in a similar way.

Do in-depth research

For suggestions on research techniques, see "Taking Notes While Reading" on page 178 and "Gaining Information Literacy" on page 152.

PHASE 2: Write a first draft

To create a first draft, gather your notes and arrange them to follow your outline. Then expand your notes into paragraphs that flow in a logical order. Focus on one point per paragraph.

Remember that the first draft can be rough. Worry about quality later, when you revise. Your goal at this point is simply to create a complete draft. Just get it done.

Some people find that it works well to forget the word *writing* when assembling a draft. Instead, they free associate, cluster, meditate, daydream, doodle, draw

diagrams, or talk into a voice recorder and transcribe the recording. These are all ways to get ideas out of your head and capture them on the paper or computer.

Also forget about inspiration. Simply schedule a block of time to write your first draft. The very act of writing can breed inspiration.

PHASE 3: Revise your draft

Schedule time for rewrites before you begin, and schedule at least one day between revisions so that you can let the material sit. On Tuesday night, you might think your writing sings the song of beautiful language. On Wednesday, you will see that those same words, such as the phrase "sings the song of beautiful language," belong in the trash.

Plan to revise a paper two or three times. Let the last revised draft sit for at least three or four days, and then look at it one more time. Keep in mind the saying, "Write in haste; revise at leisure." When you edit and revise, slow down and take a microscope to your work. Allow plenty of time for this phase.

An effective way to revise your paper is to read it out loud. The eyes tend to fill in the blanks in our own writing. The combination of voice and ears forces us to pay attention to the details.

Another technique is to have a friend look over your paper. Although this is never a substitute for your own review, a friend can often see mistakes you miss.

Remember, when other people criticize or review your work, they're not attacking you. They're just commenting on your paper. With a little practice, you can actually learn to welcome feedback.

Reading aloud and having a friend comment on your paper are techniques that can help you in each step of revising: cut, paste, fix, prepare, and proof.

Cut

Look for excess baggage. Avoid at all costs and at all times the really, really terrible mistake of using way too many unnecessary words, a mistake that some student writers often make when

> ☐ Avoid ~~at all costs and at all times the really, really terrible mistake of~~ using ~~way too many~~ unnecessary words, ~~a mistake that some student writers often make when they sit down to write papers for the various courses in which they participate at the fine institutions of higher learning which they are fortunate to attend.~~

they sit down to write papers for the various courses in which they participate at the fine institutions of higher learning that they are fortunate enough to attend. (Example: The previous sentence could be edited to "Avoid unnecessary words.")

Paste

In deleting both larger and smaller passages in your first draft, you've probably removed some of the original transitions and connecting ideas. The next task is to rearrange what's left of your paper or speech so that it flows logically. Look for consistency within paragraphs and for transitions from paragraph to paragraph. Rearrange paragraphs as needed.

Fix

Now it's time to look at individual words and phrases. Define any terms that the reader might not know, putting them in plain English whenever you can.

In general, rely on nouns and verbs. Using too many adjectives and adverbs weakens your message and adds unnecessary bulk to your writing.

You can add force to your writing by using the active voice rather than the passive voice. For example, change "A project was initiated" to "The team began a project."

Specifics add power to your writing. Consider this sentence: "The speaker made effective use of the medium, asking that we change our belief systems." See if you can add specifics: "The reformed criminal stared straight into the television camera and shouted: *Take a good look at what you're doing! Will it get you what you really want?*"

Prepare

In a sense, any paper is a sales effort. If you hand in a paper that is wearing wrinkled jeans, its hair tangled and unwashed and its shoes untied, your instructor is less likely to buy. To avoid this situation, format your paper following accepted standards for margin widths, citations, title pages, and other details.

Proof

Read your revised document from start to finish to get a big picture view. Make sure that it aligns with your thesis statement and achieves your purpose. Then read the whole thing again to correct any spelling and grammar mistakes.

When you're done, take a minute to savor the result. You've just witnessed a miracle—your mind attaining clarity and contributing new ideas to the world. That's the *aha!* moment in writing. ✳

 Find more paths to effective writing online.

Writing for the workplace

The skills that you develop in writing for teachers will also help you write clearly for coworkers. Remember, however, that readers at work are often pressed for time. Do them a courtesy with the following strategies.

Get to the point, pronto! Don't worry about warming up to your point with an introduction. Put your main idea in the first paragraph—if possible, the first sentence. If your document will go over two pages, then add a summary at the top. Keep this to one paragraph and place the key "take away" idea there.

Answer key questions. Put yourself in your reader's place. She may be reading your document after a long day of meetings and still have 50 items on her to-do list. When she sees your report, she's likely to ask: What's the problem you're addressing? What's your solution? And why should I care? Organize your document so that it directly answers such questions.

Make it clear how you want readers to respond. You might want them to schedule a meeting, approve your budget, give a green light to your project plan, or give you a raise. Whatever your purpose, make a polite and clear request.

Let the text breathe. Allow white space between paragraphs. For long documents, include each of your main points in a large, newspaper-style headline. For ideas that come in a series, use numbered or bulleted lists.

Write e-mail that gets results. Send e-mail messages only to the people who need them, and only when necessary. Also write an informative subject line: Rather than offering a generic description of your message, include a complete sentence with the main point. Above all, think short. Keep your subject line short, your paragraphs short, and your message as a whole short.

© Masterfile Royalty Free

Mastering public speaking

Some people tune out during a presentation. Just think of all the times you have listened to instructors, lecturers, and politicians. Remember all the wonderful daydreams you had during their speeches.

YOUR AUDIENCES ARE LIKE YOU. The way you plan and present your speech can determine the number of audience members who will stay with you until the end.

Polishing your speaking and presentation skills can also help you think on your feet and communicate clearly. You can use these skills in any course and in any career you choose.

Analyze your audience

Developing a speech is similar to writing a paper. Begin by writing out your topic, purpose, and thesis statement as described in "Three Paths to Clear Writing" on page 264. Then carefully analyze your audience by using the strategies in the chart below.

Remember that audiences generally have one question in mind: *So what?* Relate your presentation to something that they want. Think of your main topic or point. Then see if you can complete this sentence: *I'm telling you this because . . . .*

If your topic is new to listeners . . .	• Explain why your topic matters to them. • Relate the topic to something that listeners already know and care about. • Define any terms that listeners might not know.
If listeners already know about your topic . . .	• Acknowledge this fact at the beginning of your speech. • Find a narrow aspect of the topic that may be new to listeners. • Offer a new perspective on the topic, or connect it to an unfamiliar topic.
If listeners disagree with your thesis . . .	• Tactfully admit your differences of opinion. • Reinforce points on which you and your audience agree. • Build credibility by explaining your qualifications to speak on your topic. • Quote expert figures that agree with your thesis—people whom your audience is likely to admire. • Explain that their current viewpoint has costs for them, and that a slight adjustment in their thinking will bring significant benefits.
If listeners may be uninterested in your topic . . .	• Explain how listening to your speech can help them gain something that matters deeply to them. • Explain ways to apply your ideas in daily life.

Consider the length of your presentation. Plan on delivering about a hundred words per minute. This is only a general guideline, however, so time yourself as you practice your presentation. Aim for a lean presentation—enough words to make your point but not so many as to make your audience restless. Leave your listeners wanting more.

Write an introduction. Rambling speeches with no clear point or organization put audiences to sleep. Solve this problem with your introduction. The following introduction, for example, reveals the thesis and exactly what's coming. It reveals that the speech will have three distinct parts, each in logical order:

Dog fighting is a cruel sport. I intend to describe exactly what happens to the animals, tell you who is doing this, and show you how you can stop this inhumane practice.

9

COMMUNICATING

Whenever possible, talk about things that hold your interest. Include your personal experiences and start with a bang. Consider this introduction to a speech on the subject of world hunger:

I'm honored to be here with you today. I intend to talk about malnutrition and starvation. First, I want to outline the extent of these problems, then I will discuss some basic assumptions concerning world hunger, and finally I will propose some solutions.

You can almost hear the snores from the audience. Following is a rewrite:

More people have died from hunger in the past five years than have been killed in all of the wars, revolutions, and murders in the past 150 years. Yet there is enough food to go around. I'm honored to be here with you today to discuss solutions to this problem.

Some members of an audience will begin to drift during any speech, but most people pay attention for at least the first few seconds. Highlight your main points in the beginning sentences of your speech.

Create the main body. The main body makes up 70 to 90 percent of most speeches. In the main body, you develop your ideas in much the same way that you develop a written paper.

Transitions are especially important. Give your audience a signal when you change points. Do this by using meaningful pauses and transitional phrases: "On the other hand . . ." or "The second reason is. . . ."

In long speeches, recap from time to time. Also preview what's to come. Hold your audience's attention by using facts, descriptions, expert opinions, and statistics.

Create the conclusion. You started with a bang. Now finish with drama. The first and last parts of a speech are the most important. Make it clear to your audience when you've reached the end. Summarize your points and draw your conclusion.

Avoid endings such as "This is the end of my speech." A simple standby is "So in conclusion, I want to reiterate three points: First, . . ."

When you are finished, stop talking.

Create speaking notes. Some professional speakers recommend writing out your speech in full, and then putting keywords or main points on a few 3×5 cards. Number the cards so that if you drop them, you can quickly put them in order again. As you finish the information on each card, move it to the back of the pile. Write information clearly and in letters large enough to be seen from a distance.

Some speakers prefer to use standard outlined notes. Another option is mind mapping. Even an hour-long speech can be mapped on one sheet of paper. You can also use memory techniques from Chapter 4: "Memory" to remember the outline of your speech.

Create supporting visuals. Presentations often include visuals such as overhead transparencies, flip charts, or slides created with presentation software. These visuals can reinforce your main points and help your audience understand how your presentation is

Making the grade in group presentations

When preparing group presentations, you can use three strategies for making a memorable impression.

Get organized. As soon as you get the assignment, select a group leader and exchange contact information. Schedule specific times and places for planning, researching, writing, and practicing your presentation.

At your first meeting, write a to-do list that includes all of the tasks involved in completing the assignment. Then ask the leader to distribute tasks fairly, paying attention to the strengths of individuals in your group. For example, some people excel at brainstorming, while others prefer researching.

One powerful way to get started is to define clearly the topic and thesis, or main point, of your presentation. Support your thesis by looking for the most powerful facts, quotations, and anecdotes you can find.

As you get organized, remember how your presentation will be evaluated. If the instructor doesn't give grading criteria, create your own.

Get coordinated. Coordinate your presentation so that you have transitions between individual speakers. Practice making those transitions smooth.

Also practice using visuals such as flip charts, posters, video, or slides. To give visuals their full impact, make them appropriate for the room where you will present. Make sure that the text is large enough to be seen from the back of the room. For bigger rooms, consider using presentation software.

Get cooperation. Presentations that get top scores take teamwork and planning—not egos. Communicate with group members in an open and sensitive way. Contribute your ideas, and be responsive to the viewpoints of other members. When you cooperate, your group is on the way to an effective presentation.

organized. Remember that effective visuals *complement* rather than *replace* your speaking:

- Use fewer visuals rather than more. Save them for illustrations, photos, charts, and concepts that are hard to express in words. For a 15-minute presentation, a total of 5 to 10 slides is enough.
- Limit the amount of text on each visual to keywords.
- Use a consistent set of plain fonts that are large enough for all audience members to see.
- Stick with a simple, coherent color scheme.

Reduce fear of public speaking. For starters, research your topic thoroughly. Knowing your topic inside and out can create a baseline of confidence. To make a strong start, memorize the first four sentences that you plan to deliver, and practice them many times.

Also accept your physical sensations. Maybe you've got stage fright: dry mouth, a pounding heart, sweaty hands, muscle jitters, shortness of breath, and a shaky voice. If you feel these sensations, simply notice them and keep speaking. Tell yourself: *Yes, my hands are clammy. Yes, my stomach is upset. Also, my face feels numb. And I am going to continue this presentation.*

Instead of thinking about yourself during your presentation, just focus on your message. Forget about giving a "speech." Just give people valuable ideas and information.

Practice your presentation. The key to successful public speaking is practice. Do this in a loud voice. Your voice sounds different when you talk loudly, and this fact can be unnerving. Get used to it early on.

Whenever possible, practice in the room in which you will deliver your speech. Hear what your voice sounds like over a sound system. Also make sure that the materials you will need for your speech, including any audio-visual equipment, will be available when you want them.

Many schools have video recording equipment available for student use. Use it while you practice. Then view the finished recording to evaluate your presentation.

Listen to yourself for repeated words and phrases. Examples include *you know, kind of,* and *really,* plus any little *uh's, umm's,* and *ah's.* To get rid of them, remind yourself that you don't use those words anymore.

As you practice, avoid speaking as if you were reading a script. Deliver your ideas in a natural way.

Practice your presentation until you can deliver it in your sleep. Then run through it a few more times.

Deliver your presentation. Dress for the occasion. The clothing you choose to wear on the day of your speech delivers a message that's as loud as your words. Consider how your audience will be dressed, and then choose a wardrobe based on the impression you want to make.

When it's your turn to speak, get the audience's attention. Then, when all eyes are on you, begin.

When you speak, talk loudly enough to be heard. Avoid leaning over your notes or the podium.

Also maintain eye contact. When you look at people, they become less frightening. In addition, it is easier for the audience to listen to someone when that person is looking at them. Find a few friendly faces around the room, and imagine that you are talking to each of these people individually.

During your presentation, notice your nonverbal communication. Be aware of what your body is telling your audience. Contrived or staged gestures will look dishonest. Be natural. If you don't know what to do with your hands, notice that. Then don't do anything with them.

In addition, notice the time. You can increase the impact of your words by keeping track of the time during your speech. It's better to end early than to run late.

Feel free to pause when appropriate. Beginners sometimes feel that they have to fill every moment with the sound of their voice. Release that expectation. Give your listeners a chance to make notes and absorb what you say.

Above all, have fun. If you lighten up and enjoy your presentation, so will your listeners.

Reflect on your presentation. After your presentation, review your performance. Did you finish on time? Did you cover all of the points you intended to cover? Was the audience attentive? Did you handle any nervousness effectively?

Welcome evaluations from others. Most of us find it difficult to hear criticism about our speaking. Be aware of resisting such criticism, and then let go of your resistance. Learning from feedback puts you on the fast track to better speaking skills. ✳

Safe social networking

Stay in charge of your safety, reputation, and integrity any time you use Facebook, Myspace, Twitter, or a similar service.

Post only what you want made public and permanent. The Internet as a whole is a public medium. This is true of its online communities as well. Post only the kind of information about yourself that you *want* to be made public.

Friends, relatives, university administrators, potential employers, and police officers might be able to access your online profile. Don't post anything that could embarrass you later. Act today to protect the person that you want to be four or five years from now.

Remember that there is no delete key for the Internet. Web sites such as the Internet Archive and its "Wayback Machine" almost guarantee that anything you post online will stay online for a long time. Anyone with Internet access can take your words and images and post them on a Web site or distribute them via e-mail to damage your reputation. In the virtual world, you never know who's following you.

To avoid unwanted encounters with members of online communities, avoid posting the following:

- Your home address
- Your school address
- Your home phone number
- Your birth date
- Your screen name for instant messaging
- Your class schedule
- Your financial information, such as bank account numbers, credit card numbers, your social security number, or information about an eBay or PayPal account
- The state where you were born—a detail that can be used to find your social security number
- Information about places that you regularly go at certain times of the day
- Details about a planned trip ("Going on vacation this weekend—looking forward to being away from home")
- Information about trips you are planning to take
- Provocative pictures or messages with sexual innuendos

Also consider limiting the details of your work history on sites such as LinkedIn. Committed hackers might use such information to guess one of your passwords or even fill out a loan application. Include just enough history to interest a potential employer in contacting you directly.

Use similar caution and common sense when joining groups. Signing up for a group with a name like *Binge Drinking Forever* can have consequences for years to come.

Use privacy features. Several social networking sites allow you to create both private and public profiles. Look for links titled "Frequently Asked Questions," "Security Features," "Account Settings," or "Privacy Settings." Using such features may allow you to control comments or other messages from strangers. For further protection, review and update your list of contacts on a regular basis.

Be cautious about meeting community members in person. People can give misleading or false information about themselves online. If you do opt for a face-to-face meeting, choose a public place, and bring along a friend you trust.

Report malicious content. If you find online content that you consider offensive or dangerous, report it to site administrators. In many online communities, you can do this anonymously.

You can help to prevent online forms of intolerance, prejudice, and discrimination. Set a positive counterexample by posting messages that demonstrate acceptance of diversity.

Remember "netiquette." To promote a cordial online community:

- Respect others' time by limiting the length of your messages.
- Proofread your messages for spelling and grammar— just as you would a printed message.
- Avoid typing passages in ALL UPPERCASE LETTERS—the online equivalent of shouting.
- Avoid attachments that take a long time to download, tying up your recipient's computer.

The cornerstone of netiquette is to remember that anyone sitting at a computer is a human being. Whenever you're sending a message online, ask yourself: "Would I say that to this person's face?" ✳

 Learn more about smart social networking online.

Employ Your Word

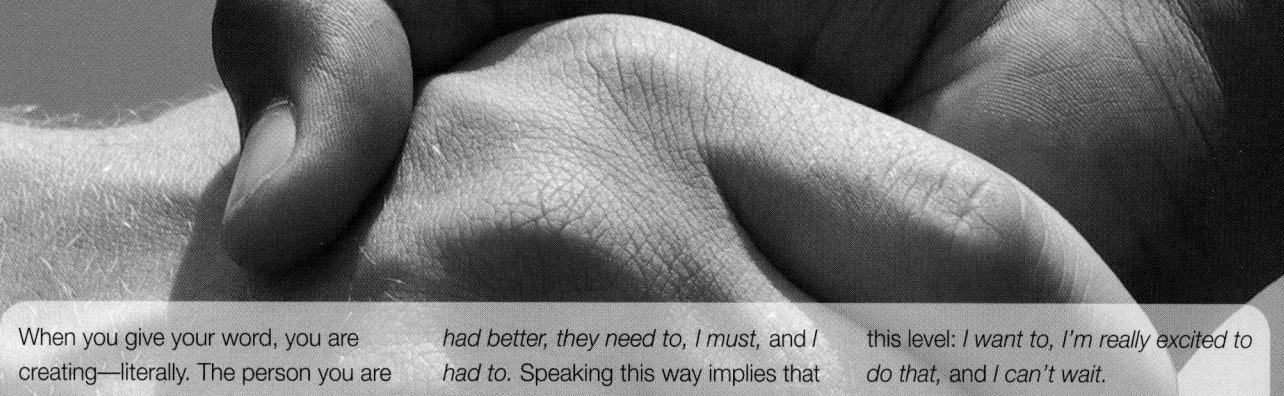

When you give your word, you are creating—literally. The person you are is, for the most part, a result of the agreements you make. Others know who you are by your words and your commitments. Therefore, you can learn who you are by observing which commitments you choose to keep and which ones you choose to avoid.

Relationships are built on agreements. When we break a promise to be faithful to a spouse, to help a friend move to a new apartment, or to pay a bill on time, relationships are strained.

The words we use to make agreements can be placed onto several different levels. We can think of each level as one rung on a ladder—the ladder of powerful speaking. As we move up the ladder, our speaking becomes more effective.

The lowest rung on the ladder is *obligation*. Words used at this level include *I should, he ought to, someone had better, they need to, I must,* and *I had to.* Speaking this way implies that something other than ourselves is in control of our lives. When we live at the level of obligation, we speak as if we are victims.

The next rung up is *possibility*. At this level, we examine new options. We play with new ideas, possible solutions, and alternative courses of action. As we do, we learn that we can make choices that dramatically affect the quality of our lives. We are not the victims of circumstance. Phrases that signal this level include *I might, I could, I'll consider, I hope to,* and *maybe.*

From possibility, we can move up to *preference*. Here we begin the process of choice. The words *I prefer* signal that we're moving toward one set of possibilities over another, perhaps setting the stage for eventual action.

Above preference is a rung called *passion*. Again, certain words signal this level: *I want to, I'm really excited to do that,* and *I can't wait.*

Action is preceded by the next rung—*planning.* When people use phrases such as *I intend to, my goal is to, I plan to,* and *I'll try like mad to,* they're at the level of planning. The Intention Statements you write in this book are examples of planning.

The highest rung on the ladder is *promising.* This is where the power of your word really comes into play. At this level, it's common to use phrases such as these: *I will, I promise to, I am committed,* and *you can count on it.* Promising is where we bridge from possibility and planning to action. Promising brings with it all of the rewards of employing your word.

Find more ways online to employ your word.

 Find more ways online to employ your words.

Career Application

After Mark Hyland earned his associate degree in dental hygiene, he applied to work with his family's dentist. He got the job the day after he graduated.

Mark welcomed the chance to apply the skills he'd gained in school. He examined patients' teeth and gums. He removed stains and plaque. Mark asked if he could expand his job duties to include taking and developing dental X-rays. The dentist who hired him agreed.

Everyone in the dental office admitted that Mark's technical skills were superb. His communication skills were another matter. Several long-term patients complained that Mark's manner was condescending—even harsh at times.

One day, the dentist who hired Mark overheard him talking to a patient.

"You can't expect to have white teeth if you drink coffee," Mark told the patient.

The patient tried to make light of the situation. "Oh well," she said, "we all have our vices, and. . . ."

"Yeah, but it's your teeth we're talking about here," Mark said, interrupting her. "Tea is just as bad, and hot chocolate is even worse. On top of that, you've got a lot of plaque on your upper teeth. Do you *ever* floss?"

The dentist winced. He feared he was about to lose a valued patient. On the other hand, he'd known Mark for years and counted his parents as friends. He wanted to meet with Mark and give him feedback about his "chair-side manner." Yet the dentist knew that this conversation would be awkward for both of them. He found this meeting an easy thing to put off.

Reflecting on this scenario

Review the suggestions given in this chapter for creating "I" messages. Then write an "I" message that the dentist could use to express his concerns with Mark.

_____

_____

_____

_____

_____

_____

_____

_____

_____

List another suggestion for sending or receiving messages that the dentist could use.

_____

_____

_____

_____

_____

_____

_____

_____

Sanna Lindberg/PhotoAlto Agency RF Collections/Getty

Quiz

Name _____   Date ____/____/____

1. According to the text, human communication is always flawed to some extent. True or false? Explain your answer.

2. Potential problems with asking questions and giving advice include:
   (a) Questions can be directive and control the conversation.
   (b) Advice can be heard as condescending.
   (c) Advice can be heard as insulting.
   (d) All of the above.

3. This chapter suggests techniques for nonverbal listening and verbal listening. Briefly explain the difference between these two approaches and give one example of each approach.

4. Reword the following complaint as a request: "You always interrupt when I talk!"

5. List the five parts of an "I" message (the five ways to say "I").

6. You can listen skillfully to a speaker even when you disagree with that person's viewpoint. True or false? Explain your answer.

7. Which of the following is an effective thesis statement? Explain your answer.
   (a) Two types of thinking.
   (b) Critical thinking and creative thinking go hand in hand.
   (c) The relationship between critical thinking and creative thinking.

8. Effective conflict resolution takes place only when people are face-to-face and not communicating through writing. True or false? Explain your answer.

9. Describe at least three techniques for preparing and delivering a speech.

10. Write one example of a statement on the lowest rung of the ladder of powerful speaking and one example of a statement on the highest rung.

Focus on Transferable Skills

By now you've had a chance to read this chapter and apply some of the suggestions it includes. Take a few minutes to revisit your responses to the "Communicating" section of the Discovery Wheel exercise in Chapter 1: First Steps." Also declare your intention to expand your communication skills.

You might want to prepare for this exercise by reviewing the articles "Jumpstart Your Education with Transferable Skills" on page 58 and "101 Transferable Skills" on page 60.

LISTENING, SPEAKING, AND WRITING

The technique that has made the biggest difference in my skill at listening is . . .

When I hear an accomplished public speaker, the skill that I notice first and most admire is . . .

When given a writing assignment, my first response is usually to . . .

OTHER COMMUNICATION SKILLS

When I've been effective at managing conflict, I've remembered to . . .

When I'm in a social setting with people from other cultures, I usually feel . . .

NEXT ACTION

I'll know that I've reached a new level of mastery with communication skills when I can . . .

To reach that level of mastery, the most important thing I promise to do is . . .

Master Student PROFILE

Cesar Chavez

. . . was caring

© Bettmann/CORBIS

**(1927–1993)
Leader of the
United Farm
Workers (UFW)
who organized
strikes, boycotts,
and fasts to improve
conditions for
migrant workers.**

A few men and women have engraved their names in the annals of change through nonviolence, but none have experienced the grinding childhood poverty that Chavez did after the Depression-struck family farm on the Gila River was foreclosed in 1937. Chavez was 10. His parents and the five children took to the picking fields as migrant workers.

Chavez's faith sustained him, but it is likely that it was both knowing and witnessing poverty and the sheer drudgery and helplessness of the migrant life that drove him.

He never lost the outreach that he had learned from his mother, who, despite the family's poverty, told her children to invite any hungry people in the area home to share what rice, beans, and tortillas the family had.

He left school to work. He attended 65 elementary schools but never graduated from high school . . . .

It was in the fields, in the 1950s, that Chavez met his wife, Helen. The couple and their eight children gave much to "La Huelga," the strike call that became the UFW trademark, from their eventual permanent home near Bakersfield. Chavez did not own the home . . . but paid rent out of his $900 a month as a union official.

Yet, in the fields in the 1930s, something happened that changed Chavez's life. He was 12 when a Congress of Industrial Organizations union began organizing dried-fruit industry workers, including his father and uncle. The young boy learned about strikes, pickets, and organizing.

For two years during World War II, Chavez served in the U.S. Navy; then it was back to the fields and organizing. There were other movements gaining strength in the United States during those years, including community organizing.

From 1952 to 1962, Chavez was active outside the fields, in voter registration drives and in challenging police and immigration abuse of Mexicans and Mexican-Americans.

At first, in the 1960s, only one movement had a noticeable symbol: the peace movement. By the time the decade ended, the United Farm Workers, originally established as the National Farm Workers Association, gave history a second flag: the black Aztec eagle on the red background.

In eight years, a migrant worker son of migrants helped change a nation's perception through nonviolent resistance. It took courage, imagination, and the ability to withstand physical and other abuse.

The facts are well-known now. During the 1968 grape boycott, farmers and growers fought him, but Chavez stood firm. Shoppers hesitated, then pushed their carts past grape counters without buying. The growers were forced to negotiate.

The UFW as a Mexican-American civil rights movement in time might outweigh the achievements of the UFW as a labor movement, for Chavez also represented something equally powerful to urban Mexican-Americans and immigrants—a nonviolent leader who had achieved great change from the most humble beginnings.

Word of Chavez's death spread to the union halls decorated with the Virgin of Guadalupe and UFW flag, to the fields, to the small towns and larger cities. And stories about the short, compact man with the ready smile, the iron determination, the genuine humility and the deep faith were being told amid the tears.

Reprinted by permission of the National Catholic Reporter, 115 E Armour Blvd, Kansas City, MO 64111 www.ncronline.org and Arthur Jones.

Learn more about Cesar Chavez and other master students at the Master Student Hall of Fame.

10 Money

Master Student Map

as you read, ask yourself

what if . . .

I could adopt habits that would free me from money worries for the rest of my life?

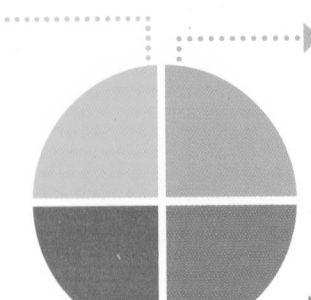

why this chapter matters . . .

Money no longer has to be a barrier to getting what you want from school—and from your life.

what is included . . .

how you can use this chapter . . .

- Discover the details about how money flows in and out of your life.
- Experiment with ways to increase your income and decrease expenses.
- Gain strategies for saving money and reducing debt.
- Find ways to pay for your education.

MASTER EMPLOYEE in *action*

The budgeting work that I do in the office has made me a better money manager in my own life. It has taught me that money is just a way to ascribe value, and not a value in and of itself. I've been better able to evaluate the things I care about and the things I can do without.

—BILL WHITE, CONSTRUCTION MANAGER

Photo courtesy of Bill White

Three paths to financial freedom

"I CAN'T AFFORD IT" is a common reason that students give for dropping out of school. Actually, "I don't know how to pay for it" or "I don't think it's worth it" are probably more accurate.

Money produces more unnecessary conflict and worry than almost anything else. It doesn't really seem to matter how much money a person has. Money worries can upset people even if they're millionaires.[1]

Most money problems result from spending more than is available. It's that simple, even though we often do everything we can to make the problem much more complicated.

The solution also is simple: *Don't spend more than you have.* If you are spending more than you have, then increase your income, decrease your spending, or do both. This idea has never won a Nobel Prize in Economics, but you won't go broke applying it.

Money management may be based on a simple idea, but there is a big incentive for us to make it seem more complicated than it really is. If we don't understand money, then we don't have to be responsible for it. After all, if you don't know how to change a flat tire, then you don't have to be the one responsible for fixing it. It works the same way with money. But many students enter higher education because they want to fix or enhance their finances. After graduating, they want to get a better job. Over the long term, they want a career path with more options, more income, and more satisfaction.

If that's what you want, then this chapter is for you. It's full of ways to make your money life work, starting with the next exercise and continuing for the rest of your life.

The strategies you're about to learn are not complicated. In fact, they're not even new. The strategies are all based on the cycle of discovery, intention, and action that you've already practiced with the Journal Entries in this book. With these strategies and the abilities to add and subtract, you have everything you need to manage your money.

There are three main steps in money management:

- First, tell the truth about how much money you have and how much you spend (discovery).

- Second, commit to spend less than you have (intention).

- Finally, apply the suggestions for earning more money, spending less money, or both (action).

If you do these three things consistently, you can eventually say goodbye to most money worries. You'll discover something that even millionaires can forget—ways to control money instead of letting money control you.

 Find more perspectives on the nature of financial freedom online.

journal entry 24

Discovery/Intention Statement

Commit to a new experience of money

Reflect on your overall experience of money. List any statements you've made about your money during the last month—anything from "I never have enough" to "I have some extra money to invest, and I'm wondering where to put it." Write your statements here.

When speaking about my money life, I discovered that I . . .

_____

_____

_____

_____

_____

Now scan this chapter with an eye for strategies that could help you increase your income, decrease your expenses, or both. List three money strategies that you'd like to use right away.

I intend to . . .

_____

_____

_____

_____

_____

10

MONEY

Many of us find it easy to lose track of money. It likes to escape when no one is looking. Unfortunately, usually no one *is* looking. That's why the simple act of monitoring your expenses is so useful. You'll discover exactly how much money flows out of your life—and where it all goes. With that awareness, you can start making informed choices about what to spend next week, next month, and next year.

Your goal with this exercise is to record all the money you spend over the course of one week. That sounds like a big task, but it's simpler than you might think. In addition, monitoring expenses is a transferable skill that will help you file tax returns, fill out expense forms at work, and handle many other financial tasks. Use the following steps to begin.

1. Make a copy of the Money Monitor form on the following page

Use this form whenever you want to monitor your weekly spending.

2. Choose a way to record your expenses

Use any method that works for you. Be sure to keep it simple.

One option is to carry 3x5 cards in your pocket, purse, backpack, or briefcase. Every time you buy something or pay a bill, make a note on a card. List the date and describe what you bought or paid for. Consider using a separate card for each expense. This makes it easier to sort your cards into the categories listed on the Money Monitor form.

Another option is to save all your receipts and file them. Although this method does not require you to carry any 3x5 cards, it does require that you keep a record of every payment. Every time you buy something, ask for a receipt. Then stick it in your wallet, purse, or pocket. When you get home, file the receipts in a folder labeled with the current week (for example, *01/03/12 to 01/09/12*). If you do not get a receipt or record of payment, then whip out a 3x5 card and create one of your own. Stick the card in the folder.

A third option is to use a computer. Perhaps you have a checking account that offers online services. If so, take advantage of the records that the bank is already keeping for you. Every time you write a check or use a debit card, the transaction will show up online. Use a computer to log in to your account and view these transactions each week. Or, use software such as Quicken to record expenses and sort them into categories.

Experiment with these options and settle into one that feels most comfortable to you. You can also create a method of your own. *Anything will work, as long as you get an exact and accurate record of your expenses.*

3. Fill out your Money Monitor

Pull out a blank Money Monitor. Next to *Period*, write in the dates for the week that you're monitoring (for example, *1/10/12 to 1/16/12*). Then fill out the rest of this form using your expense records for that week.

The left column of the Money Monitor includes categories of expenses. Write your total for each category in the right column. For example, if you spent $30 at the grocery store during the week, write that amount in the column next to *Groceries*.

Use your receipts and other records to split expenses when necessary. Suppose that you used your credit card to buy a sweater, pay for a restaurant meal, and buy a tank of gas for your car. Write the amount you paid for the sweater next to *Clothes*. Write the total you spent at the restaurant next to *Eating Out*. Finally, write the total for your gas stop next to *Gas*.

Perhaps you have expenses that do not fit into any of the categories listed in the Money Monitor. No problem. Use the blank columns to create additional categories of your own. Use *Miscellaneous* for expenses that don't seem to fit in any other category.

Finally, add up all your expenses and list that amount under *Total Expenses* at the bottom of the form. Behold—this is what you spent during one week of your life. This exercise should be completed after monitoring a week of spending using Critical Thinking Exercise 34: The Money Monitor.

 Do this exercise online and find printable copies of the Money Monitor.

10

MONEY

Money Monitor
Period:_____ Notes:

Books and Supplies	
Car Maintenance	
Car Payment	
Clothes	
Eating Out	
Entertainment	
Gas	
Groceries	
Insurance	
Laundry	
Phone	
Rent/Mortgage Payment	
Tuition and Fees	
Utilities	
Total Expenses	

This exercise should be completed after monitoring a week of spending using Critical Thinking Exercise 34: The Money Monitor. The purpose of this exercise is to make specific and immediate changes in what you spend.

Many people look at the Money Plan and call it a budget. The mere mention of that word can make students cringe. To them, budgeting is associated with scarcity, drudgery, and guilt. A budget conjures up images of a penny-pinching Ebenezer Scrooge shaking a bony, wrinkled finger at them and screaming, "You spent too much, you loser!"

That's not the idea behind this exercise. No one is pointing a finger at you. As with the First Step and Discovery Wheel exercises in Chapter 1: "First Steps," there's no shame and no blame. Instead, this exercise is an opportunity for you to set and achieve goals related to spending money. That's where the magic happens.

To begin, make a copy of the blank Money Plan on the next page. Next to *Period*, fill in the dates for the upcoming week.

You'll notice that the categories listed in the Money Plan are exactly the same as those listed on the Money Monitor. If you created additional categories for the Money Monitor, then add those same categories to the Money Plan.

Review the Money Monitor that you filled out for the previous week. Based on that information, set specific dollar goals for your spending during the upcoming week. Say that you spent $30 eating out last week, and for the next week you'd like to decrease that amount. Write $20 (or whatever amount you want to spend) in the column next to *Eating Out*.

Perhaps your expenses for next week will fall into different categories than the categories you filled out for last week's Money Monitor. That's fine. Just set goals in any category you choose.

Also remember that you don't have to set goals for every category. Even if you reduce your spending in just one category next week, you'll notice the difference at the end of the month.

After you've filled out your first Money Monitor and Money Plan, take a moment to congratulate yourself. No matter how the numbers add up, you are starting to take conscious control of your money. Keep doing these exercises and you will be on a lifelong path to financial freedom.

Also consider the following ways to expand the power of the Money Monitor and Money Plan.

Compare your Money Monitor and Money Plan

Take your Money Monitor for any week and compare it to your Money Plan for the same week. Determine whether you actually met the goals that you set for that week's spending. If you spent more than you planned, then see "Spend Less Money" on page 284 for suggestions.

Monitor and plan over a longer period

Many bills, such as rent and utilities, fall on a monthly cycle. Consider monitoring and planning your expenses for an entire month at a time. You might get more meaningful results.

Add notes

The Money Monitor and Money Plan forms include blank space for making notes. Use this space to record other useful ideas and information. For example, write Discovery and Intention Statements related to money.

You can also list your sources of income and the amount that you received from each source during the period at the top of the form. This allows you to compare your total expenses for that period with your total income. You'll soon discover whether you're spending less than you earn. If you want to increase your income, then see "Make More Money" on page 282.

 Do this exercise online and find printable copies of the Money Monitor.

Money Plan

Period: _____

Notes:

Expense	Amount
Books and Supplies	
Car Maintenance	
Car Payment	
Clothes	
Eating Out	
Entertainment	
Gas	
Groceries	
Insurance	
Laundry	
Phone	
Rent/Mortgage Payment	
Tuition and Fees	
Utilities	
Total Expenses	

10

MONEY

Make more money

FOR MANY PEOPLE, finding a way to increase income is the most appealing way to fix a money problem. This approach is reasonable, but it has a potential problem: When their income increases, many people continue to spend more than they make. This means that money problems persist, even at higher incomes. To avoid this problem, manage your expenses no matter how much money you make.

If you do succeed at controlling your expenses over the long term, then increasing your income is definitely a way to build wealth. Among the ways to make more money are to focus on your education, consider financial aid, work while you're in school, and do your best at every job.

Focus on your education. Your most important assets are not your bank accounts, your car, or your house—they are your skills. That's why your education is so important. Right now, you're developing knowledge, experience, and abilities that you can use to create income for the rest of your life.

Once you graduate and land a job in your chosen field, continue your education. Look for ways to gain additional skills or certifications that lead to higher earnings and more fulfilling work assignments.

Consider financial aid. Student grants and loans can play a major role in your college success by freeing you up from having to work full-time or even part-time. Many students erroneously assume they don't qualify for educational grants or low-interest student loans.

Remember, though, that loans can burden students with payments after they complete their degrees. This is true even for student loans at reduced interest rates. Consider loans with caution.

Work while you're in school. If you work while you're in school, you earn more than money. You gain experience, establish references, interact with a variety of people, and make contact with people who might hire you in the future. Regular income in any amount can also make a difference in your monthly cash flow.

Many students work full-time or part-time jobs. Work and school don't have to conflict, especially if you plan carefully (see Chapter 3: "Time") and ask for your employer's support.

On most campuses, the financial aid office employs a person who helps students find work while they're in

RAYES/Getty

school. See that person. In addition, check into career planning services at your school for information on internships or other work options. Using these resources can greatly multiply your job options.

Many jobs are never advertised. In fact, a key source of information about new jobs is people—friends, relatives, coworkers, and fellow students—rather than classified advertising. Tell all of them that you're looking for a job.

In addition, make a list of several places where you would like to work. Then go to each place on your list and contact the Human Resources department about job openings. They might say that they don't have a job available. No problem. Ask to be considered for future job openings. Then check back periodically.

See if you can find a job related to your chosen career. Even an entry-level job in your field can provide valuable experience. Once you've been in such a job for a while, explore the possibilities for getting a promotion or a higher-paying job with another employer.

Some part-time jobs are just made for students. Serving or delivering food may not be glamorous, but the tips can make a real difference in your monthly income. Other jobs, such as working the reference desk at the campus library or monitoring the front desk in

MONEY

10

a dorm, can offer quiet times that are ideal for doing some extra studying.

Another option is to start your own business. Consider a service you could offer—anything from lawn mowing to computer consulting. Students can boost their income in many other ways, such as running errands, giving guitar lessons, walking pets, or house sitting. Charge reasonable rates, provide impeccable service, and ask your clients for referrals.

Self-employment during higher education can blossom into amazing careers. For example, David Filo and Jerry Yang started making lists of their favorite Web sites while they were graduate students. They went on to create Yahoo!, which became the world's most popular search engine.[2]

Do your best at every job. Once you get a job, make it your intention to excel as an employee. A positive work experience can pay off for years by leading to other jobs, recommendations, and contacts.

No matter what job you have, be as productive as possible. Look for ways to boost sales, increase quality, or accomplish tasks in less time. Every day, ask yourself how you can create value for your employer by solving a problem, reducing costs, improving service, or attracting new clients or customers.

To maximize your earning power, keep honing your job-hunting and career-planning skills. You can find a wealth of ideas on these topics in Chapter 12: "Working."

Finally, keep things in perspective. If your job is lucrative and rewarding, great. If not, remember that almost any job can support you in becoming a master student and reaching your educational goals. ✳

 Discover more ways to increase your income.

36 critical thinking exercise
Show me the money

See if you can use *From Master Student to Master Employee* to create a financial gain that is many times more than the cost of the book. Scan the entire text, and look for suggestions that could help you save money or increase income in significant ways; for example:

- Use suggestions for career planning and job hunting in Chapter 12: "Working" to find your next job more quickly—and start earning money sooner.

- Negotiate a higher salary for your next job using strategies from the article "Use Interviews to Hire Yourself an Employer" on page 330.

- Use suggestions for goal setting from Chapter 3: "Time" to acquire a skill that will make it easier for you to get a higher-paying job.

In the following space, write your ideas for creating more money from your experience of this book. Use additional paper as needed.

Spend less money

Stockbyte/Getty

Look to small-ticket items. Reducing or eliminating the money you spend on low-cost purchases can make the difference between saving money or going into debt. For example, $3 spent at the coffee shop every day adds up to $1,095 over a year. That kind of spending can give anyone the jitters.

Ask for student discounts. Movie theaters, restaurants, bars, shopping centers, and other businesses sometimes discount prices for students. Also go to your bank, and ask whether you can open a student checking and savings account with online banking. The fees and minimum required amounts could be lower. Go online to check your balances weekly so that you avoid overdraft fees.

Do comparison shopping. Prices vary dramatically. Shop around, wait for off-season sales, and use coupons. Check out secondhand stores, thrift stores, and garage sales. Before plunking down the full retail price for a new item, consider whether you could buy it used. You can find "preowned" clothes, CDs, furniture, sports equipment, audio equipment, and computer hardware in retail stores and on the Internet.

Be aware of quality. The cheapest product is not always the least expensive over the long run. Sometimes, a slightly more expensive item is the best buy because it will last longer. However, there is no correlation between the value of something and the amount of money spent to advertise it. Carefully inspect things you are considering to buy, and see if they are well made.

Save money on food. This single suggestion could significantly lower your expenses. Instead of hitting a restaurant or bar, head to the grocery store. Fresh fruits, fresh vegetables, and whole grains are better for you than processed food. They also cost less. In addition, clip food coupons. Sign up for shopper's discount cards.

Cooking for yourself doesn't need to take much time if you do a little menu planning. Create a list of your five favorite home-cooked meals. Learn how to prepare them. Then make sure to always keep ingredients for these meals on hand. To reduce grocery bills, buy these ingredients in bulk.

If you live in a dorm, review the different meal plans you can buy. Some schools offer meal plans for students who live off campus. These plans might be cheaper than eating in restaurants while you're on campus.

Lower your phone bills. If you use a cell phone, pull out a copy of your latest bill. Review how many minutes you used last month. Perhaps you could get by

CONTROLLING YOUR EXPENSES is something you can do right away, and it's usually easier than increasing your income. Use ideas from the following list, and invent more of your own.

Look to big-ticket items. When you look for places to cut expenses, start with the items that cost the most. Choices about where to live, for example, can save you thousands of dollars. Sometimes a place a little farther from campus, or a smaller house or apartment, will be much less expensive. You can also keep your housing costs down by finding a roommate. Offer to do repairs or maintenance in exchange for reduced rent. Pay your rent on time, and treat property with respect.

Another high-ticket item is a car. Take the cost of buying or leasing and then add expenses for parking, insurance, repairs, gas, maintenance, and tires. You might find that it makes more sense to walk, bike, ride a campus shuttle, and call for an occasional taxi ride. Another option is carpooling. Find friends with a car to ride along with and chip in for gas. Also see if you can get student rates on public transportation.

Focus on a few major areas where you can reduce spending while continuing to pay your fixed monthly bills, such as rent and tuition.

10

MONEY

with a less expensive phone, fewer minutes, fewer text messages, and a cheaper plan. Do an Internet search on *cell phone plan comparison,* and see if you could save money by switching providers.

There are more options. Consider a family calling plan, which might cost less than a separate plan for each person. In addition, consider whether you need a home phone (a land line) *and* a cell phone. Dropping the home phone could save you money right away.

Go "green." To conserve energy and save money on utility bills, turn out the lights when you leave a room. Keep windows and doors closed in winter. In summer, keep windows open early in the day to invite lots of cool air into your living space. Then close up the apartment or house to keep it cool during the hotter hours of the day. Leave air-conditioning set at 72°F or above. In cool weather, dress warmly and keep the house at 68°F or less. In hot weather, take shorter, cooler showers.

Unplug any electric appliances that are not in use. Appliances like microwaves, audio systems, and cell phone chargers use energy when plugged in even when they're not in use. Also, plug computer equipment into power strips that you can turn off while you sleep.

Explore budget plans for monthly payments that fluctuate, such as those for heating your home. These plans average your yearly expenses so you pay the same amount each month.

Pay cash. To avoid interest charges, deal in cash or debit card rather than credit. If you don't have the money, don't buy. Buying on credit makes it more difficult to monitor spending. You can easily bust next month's money plan with this month's credit card purchases.

Postpone purchases. If you plan to buy something, leave your checkbook or credit card at home when you first go shopping. Look at all the possibilities. Then go home and make your decision when you don't feel pressured. Look up reviews online to determine whether this is the right choice. When you are ready to buy, wait a few days, even if the salesperson pressures you. What

seems like a necessity today may not even cross your mind the day after tomorrow.

Notice what you spend on "fun." Blowing your money on fun is fun. It is also a fast way to blow your savings. When you spend money on entertainment, ask yourself what the benefits will be and whether you could get the same benefits for less money. You can read magazines for free at the library, for example. Most libraries also loan CDs and DVDs for free.

Use the envelope system. After reviewing your income and expenses, for example, put a certain amount of cash each week in an envelope labeled *Entertainment/ Eating Out.* When the envelope is empty, stop spending money on these items for the rest of the week. If you use online banking, see if you can create separate accounts for various spending categories. Then deposit a fixed amount of money into each of those accounts. This is an electronic version of the envelope system.

Don't compete with big spenders. When you watch other people spend their money, remember that you don't know the whole story. Some students have parents with deep pockets. Others head to Mexico every year for spring break but finance the trips with high-interest credit cards. If you find yourself feeling pressured to spend money so that you can keep up with other people, stop to think about how much it will cost over the long run. Maybe it's time to shop around for some new friends.

Spend less, and feel the power. Cutting your spending might be challenging at first. Give it time. Spending less is not about sacrificing pleasure. It's about something that money can't buy—the satisfaction of choosing exactly where your money goes and building a secure financial future. Every dollar that you save on a frivolous expense is a dollar you can invest in something that truly matters to you. ✳

 Discover more cost-cutting strategies online.

10

MONEY

Discovery/Intention Statement

Reflect on monitoring and planning

Take a few minutes to think about your experience with the Money Monitor and Money Plan exercises included earlier in this chapter. Reflect on what you've learned and your next step in creating a new relationship with money.

After monitoring my expenses, I was surprised to discover that . . .

_____

_____

_____

_____

_____

_____

When it comes to money, I am skilled at . . .

_____

_____

_____

_____

_____

_____

_____

When it comes to money, I am *not* so skilled at . . .

_____

_____

_____

_____

_____

I could increase my income by . . .

_____

_____

_____

_____

_____

_____

I could spend less money on . . .

_____

_____

_____

_____

_____

_____

After thinking about the most powerful step I can take right now to improve my finances, I intend to . . .

_____

_____

_____

_____

_____

_____

_____

10

MONEY

Take charge of your credit

A GOOD CREDIT RATING will serve you for a lifetime. With this asset, you'll be able to borrow money any time you need it. A poor credit rating, however, can keep you from getting a car or a house in the future. You might also have to pay higher insurance rates, and you could even be turned down for a job.

To take charge of your credit, borrow money only when truly necessary. If you do borrow, make all of your required payments on time. This is especially important for managing credit cards and student loans.

Use credit cards with caution. Credit cards do offer potential benefits. Having one means that you don't have to carry around a checkbook or large amounts of cash, and they're pretty handy in emergencies. Getting a card is one way to establish a credit record. Some cards offer rewards, such as frequent flier miles and car rental discounts.

Used unwisely, however, credit cards can create a debt that takes decades to repay. This debt can seriously delay other goals—paying off student loans, financing a new car, buying a home, or saving for retirement.

The Credit Card Accountability, Responsibility, and Disclosure (CARD) Act of 2009 placed limits on hidden fees and rate hikes charged by credit card companies. It also requires a co-signer on credit card applications for people under age 21, unless they prove that they have a job and can make monthly payments. Ask someone at your school's financial aid office for more information.

Also use the following strategies to take control of your credit cards. Write these ideas on a 3×5 card, and don't leave home without it.

Pay off the balance each month. An unpaid credit card balance is a sure sign that you are spending more money than you have. To avoid this outcome, keep track of how much you spend with credit cards each month. Pay off the card balance each month, on time, and avoid finance or late charges.

If you do accumulate a large credit card balance, go to your bank and ask about ways to get a loan with a lower interest rate. Use this loan to pay off your credit cards. Then promise yourself never to accumulate credit card debt again.

Scrutinize credit card offers. Beware of cards offering low interest rates. These rates are often only temporary. After a few months, they could double or

© Michele Constantini, PhotoAlto/Getty

even triple. Also look for annual fees, late fees, and other charges buried in the fine print.

Be especially wary of credit card offers made to students. Remember that the companies who willingly dispense cards on campus are not there to offer an educational service. They are in business to make money by charging you interest.

Avoid cash advances. Due to their high interest rates and fees, credit cards are not a great source of spare cash. Even when you get cash advances on these cards from an ATM, it's still borrowed money. As an alternative, get a debit card tied to a checking account, and use that card when you need cash on the go.

Check statements against your records. File your credit card receipts each month. When you get the bill for each card, check it against your receipts for accuracy. Mistakes in billing are rare, but they can happen. In addition, checking your statement reveals the interest rate and fees that are being applied to your account.

Use just one credit card. To simplify your financial life and take charge of your credit, consider using only one card. Choose a card with no annual fee and the lowest interest rate. Don't be swayed by offers of free T-shirts or coffee mugs. Consider the bottom line, and be selective.

Get a copy of your credit report. A credit report is a record of your payment history and other credit-related items. You are entitled to get a free copy each year. Go to your bank and ask someone there how to do this. You can also request a copy of your credit report online at **www.annualcreditreport.com**. This site was created by three nationwide consumer credit-reporting companies—Equifax, Experian, and TransUnion. Check your report carefully for errors or accounts that you did not open. Do this now, before you're in financial trouble.

Protect your credit score. Whenever you apply for a loan, the first thing a lender will do is check your credit score. The higher your score, the more money you can borrow at lower interest rates. To protect your credit score, pay all your bills on time, hold on to credit cards that you've had for a while, and avoid applying for new credit cards. Pay off your credit card balance every month. Pay your bills on time. Never charge more than your limit.

Manage student loans. A college degree is one of the best investments you can make. However, you don't have to go broke to get that education. You can make that investment with the lowest debt possible.

Choose schools with costs in mind. If you decide to transfer to another school, you can save thousands of dollars the moment you sign your application for admission. In addition to choosing schools on the basis of reputation, consider how much they cost and the financial aid packages that they offer.

Avoid debt when possible. The surest way to manage debt is to avoid it altogether. If you do take out loans, borrow only the amount that you cannot get from other sources—scholarships, grants, employment, gifts from relatives, and personal savings.

In addition, set a target date for graduation and stick to it. The fewer years you go to school, the lower your debt.

Shop carefully for loans. Go to the financial aid office and ask if you can get a Stafford loan. These are fixed-rate, low-interest loans from the federal government. If you qualify for a subsidized Stafford loan, the government pays the interest due while you're in school. Unsubsidized Stafford loans do not offer this benefit, but they are still one of the cheapest student loans you can get. Remember that *anyone* can apply for a Stafford loan. Take full advantage of this program before you look into other loans. For more information on the loans that are available to you, visit **www.studentaid.ed.gov**.

If your parents are helping to pay for your education, they can apply for a PLUS loan. There is no income limit, and parents can borrow up to the total cost of their children's education. With these loans, your parents—not you—are the borrowers. A new option allows borrowers to defer repayment until after you

If you're in trouble . . .

Financial problems are common. Solve them in ways that protect you for the future.

Get specific data. Complete the Money Monitor exercise included earlier in this chapter.

Be honest with creditors. Determine the amount that you are sure you can repay each month, and ask the creditor if that would work for your case.

Go for credit counseling. Most cities have agencies with professional advisors who can help straighten out your financial problems.

Change your spending patterns. If you have a history of overspending (or underearning), change *is* possible. This chapter is full of suggestions.

graduate. PLUS loans cost more than Stafford loans but are still usually less expensive than private loans. If at all possible, avoid private loans.

Some lenders will forgive all or part of a student loan if you agree to take a certain job for a few years—for example, teaching in a public school in a low-income neighborhood or working as a nurse in a rural community. This arrangement is called an *income-based repayment plan*. Talk to someone in the financial aid office to see if there is such a program that applies to you.

If you take out student loans, find out exactly when the first payment is due on each of them. Don't assume that you can wait to start repayment until you find a job. Any bill payments that you miss will hammer your credit score.

You should also ask your financial aid office about whether you can consolidate your loans. This means that you lump them all together and owe just one payment every month. Loan consolidation makes it easier to stay on top of your payments and protect your credit score. ✳

 Find more strategies online for credit mastery.

You can pay for school

MILLIONS OF DOLLARS are waiting for people who take part in higher education. However, the funds flow only to students who know how to find them.

There are many ways to pay for school. The kind of help you get depends on your financial need. In general, financial need equals the cost of your schooling minus what you can reasonably be expected to pay.

Financial aid includes money you don't pay back (grants and scholarships), money you do pay back (loans), and work-study programs. Most students who get financial aid receive a package that includes several examples of each type.

To find out more, visit your school's financial aid office on a regular basis. Also go online. Start with Student Aid on the Web at **www.studentaid.ed.gov**.

Once you've lined up financial aid, keep it flowing. Find out the requirements for renewing loans, grants, and scholarships. Remember that many financial aid packages depend on your making "satisfactory academic progress." Also, programs change constantly. Money may be limited, and application deadlines are critical.

Scholarships, grants, and loans backed by the federal government are key sources of money for students. (For more information on loans, refer back to the article "Take Charge of Your Credit" earlier in this chapter.) State governments often provide grants and scholarships as well. So do credit unions, service organizations such as Kiwanis International, and local chambers of commerce. Sometimes relatives will provide financial help.

Determine how much money you need to complete your education and where you will get it. Having a plan for paying for your entire education makes it easier to finish your degree. ✳

 Discover more ways online to pay for school.

Education is worth it

Education is one of the few things you can buy that will last a lifetime. It can't rust, corrode, break down, or wear out. It can't be stolen, burned, repossessed, or destroyed. Once you have a degree, no one can take it away. That makes your education a safer investment than real estate, gold, oil, diamonds, or stocks.

Think about all the services and resources that your tuition money buys: academic advising to help you choose classes and select a major; access to the student health center and counseling services; career planning and job placement offices that you can visit even after you graduate; athletic, arts, and entertainment events at a central location; and a student center where you can meet people and socialize.

If you live on campus, you also get a place to stay with meals provided, all for less than the cost of an average hotel room. And by the way, don't forget that you get to attend classes. Consider how much nonstudents would have to pay for such an array of services. You can see that higher education is a bargain.

The benefits go even further. A 2007 study released by the College Board reports that higher levels of education are associated with:

- Higher incomes for both men and women in all racial and ethnic groups.
- Higher levels of volunteer work and voting.
- Higher tax revenues for governments, which fund libraries, schools, parks, and other public goods.
- Lower levels of unemployment and dependence on social services, as well as lower smoking rates.[3]

In short, education is a good deal for you and for society. It's worth investing in it periodically to update your skills, reach your goals, and get more of what you want in life.

10

MONEY

Using technology to manage money

IF YOU OWN A COMPUTER, you can use it in a variety of ways to make peace with money. Consider the following options

Sign up for direct deposit

Your employer might offer to deposit paychecks directly to a bank or credit union account. This saves you time—no waiting for checks to arrive, no waiting in line to make deposits in person, and no waiting for checks to clear.

Bank online

Many banks, credit unions, and brokerage firms now offer online services. These services typically allow you to view account activity, access account statements, transfer funds, and pay bills. You may have the choice of paying bills manually or setting up automatic payments. With either method, be sure to schedule payments at least five days before each bill's due date.

Use personal finance software

Products such as Quicken and Microsoft Money allow you to:

- Keep detailed records of activity related to your bank accounts, credit cards, mortgage, and investments.
- Reconcile your records with bank and credit card statements.
- Move money between accounts.
- Sort your income and expenses into categories.
- Organize records needed to prepare tax returns.
- Print reports and graphs that show your income and expenses.
- Compare your actual expenses to budgeted amounts.
- Receive notices of low balances and potential overdraft fees.

- Plan for major purchases and long-term financial goals, such as retirement.
- Create reminders for when bills are due.
- Print checks.

If you bank online, you can download account transactions directly from your bank's Web site to your personal finance software. This reduces the time needed to enter data.

Avoid scams

Con artists have been around ever since money was invented. Today, they're active online, looking for high-tech ways to peddle their schemes. Don't fall for them.

One scheme is called *phishing*. It works like this: You receive an e-mail that looks as if it came from a bank or credit card company. The e-mail asks you to supply your account number and password by clicking on a link.

If you get such a message, trash it. No reputable person or business would send such an e-mail.

Prevent identity theft

Identity theft takes place when someone steals personal information—such as your social security number, PIN numbers, credit card numbers, or passport data—to gain access to your money. Take the following steps to prevent this form of stealing:

- Keep your social security number private.
- For online money transactions, use Web sites with an address (URL) that begins with https:// rather than http://. The extra *s* stands for "secure," meaning that any data you send will be encrypted and nearly impossible to steal.
- Check the lower right-hand corner of your Web browser for an icon that looks like a closed lock. This also indicates a secure site.
- Don't manage your money on public computers. Other users could see your information displayed on the screen and watch the keyboard as you type in passwords.
- Don't let your Web browser store passwords and other login information for sites that you use to manage money. People who know how to access this information could hack into your accounts.
- Shred any financial documents you print out or receive in the mail before throwing them away.

If any of your confidential information is stolen, file a police report right away. Also contact your bank and credit card companies. Afterward, keep checking your bank statements and credit card bills to make sure that problem has stopped. For more help, go online to the Federal Trade Commission's identity theft site at **www.ftc.gov/bcp/edu/microsites/idtheft**.

In addition, use a strong password whenever you pay bills or buy something online. Strong passwords will look like a string of random characters to anyone but you. To create a strong password, make it at least eight characters long, and include a combination of letters, numbers, and symbols. Choose characters from across the entire keyboard rather than characters that are located close together.

Also consider using a *pass phrase*—several words with a space between each word. Choose a phrase that's easy for you to remember but difficult for anyone else to guess. ✳

critical thinking exercise
37 Education by the hour

Determine exactly what it costs you to go to school. Fill in the following blanks using totals for a semester, quarter, or whatever term system your school uses.

Note: Include only the costs that relate directly to going to school. For example, under *Transportation*, list only the amount that you pay for gas to drive back and forth to school—not the total amount you spend on gas for a semester.

Tuition	$_____
Books	$_____
Fees	$_____
Transportation	$_____
Clothing	$_____
Food	$_____
Housing	$_____
Entertainment	$_____
Other expenses (such as insurance, medical costs, and child care)	$_____
Subtotal	$_____
Salary you could earn per term if you weren't in school	$_____
Total (A)	$_____

Now figure out how many classes you attend in one term. This is the number of your scheduled class periods per week multiplied by the number of weeks in your school term. Put that figure below:

Total (B) _____

Divide the **Total (B)** into the **Total (A)**, and put that amount here:

$_____

This is what it costs you to go to one class one time.

On a separate sheet of paper, describe your responses to discovering this figure. Also list anything you will do differently as a result of knowing the cost of your education.

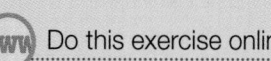 Do this exercise online.

Practicing money skills at work

THE EXPERTISE YOU DEVELOP NOW IN MONITORING MONEY, increasing income, and decreasing expenses can help you succeed professionally. Look for ways to practice these skills on the job. The following examples can stimulate your thinking.

Develop financial literacy now

Your next job may require you to prepare budgets, keep money records, make financial forecasts, and adjust income and expenses in order to meet an organization's financial goals. The ability to handle such tasks successfully is called *workplace financial literacy*.

Organizations from the smallest nonprofits to the largest multinational corporations all need to raise money, develop products and services, attract customers and clients, hire people, pay salaries and benefits, set financial goals, create budgets, and manage expenses. Knowing something about these processes can help you connect to future employers and get promoted to higher-paying jobs. Even if your career plan is to become a self-employed artist, learn about ways to fund your chosen lifestyle and make it economically viable.

Think about the ways you'll be handling money in your chosen career. If you plan to become an architect, for example, then you'll need to estimate costs for a building project, request bids from contractors, and evaluate those bids. Find out more by interviewing people who work in your field. Ask them how they handle money on the job.

After listing the financial skills that you need, consider which courses you'll take to develop them. You might benefit from classes in business management or accounting.

Another option is to learn about writing business plans. These documents follow a standard format that includes a description of the proposed business along with goals for marketing, finance, and management. If you can make sense of a business plan, then you've gained a high degree of financial literacy. In addition, you might get ideas for starting your own business some day. For more information, go online to the U.S. Small Business Administration at **www.sba.gov**. This Web site includes tutorials and links to examples of real business plans.

Get continuing financial education at work

Stress related to personal finances can have a negative impact on an employee's productivity. Recognizing this, many companies offer free workshops on financial topics. These include classes on retirement planning, insurance planning, investing, college funding, and estate planning.

Keep records of financial success

Throughout your career, keep track of the positive outcomes you produce at work, including financial successes. Summarize these results in a sentence or two and add them to your résumé as well.

You can take this technique to a deeper level with a journal. Whenever you deliver a project on time and on budget, write Discovery Statements about how you created that result. Follow up with Intention Statements about ways to be even more effective on your next project.

Learn spreadsheet software

With spreadsheet programs such as Microsoft's Excel, you can enter data into charts with rows and columns and then apply various formulas. This makes it possible to create budgets, income reports, expense records, and investment projections. Master this software now and you'll have a marketable skill to add to your résumé.

Consider income and expenses related to your career choices

Your career plan can include estimates of how much money you'll earn in various jobs in your field. In addition, think about the possible expenses involved in your career choice. If you're planning a career that requires graduate school, for example, then consider how you will pay for that education.

Perhaps advancement in your career calls for additional certifications or course work. Examples are continuing education credits for teachers and board certifications for nurses and physicians. Start thinking now about how you'll meet such requirements.

An equally important consideration is your choice about where to live after graduating from school. Given the high cost of living in certain cities, this choice can have a big impact on your personal finances.

Some career choices call for living in a major metropolitan area with high housing and transportation costs. If this is true for you, then set salary goals that will help you cover such costs, with money to spare. ✳

10

MONEY

Choose Your Conversations (and Your Community)

Conversations can exist in many forms. One form involves people talking out loud to each other. At other times, when the conversation takes place inside our own heads, we call it *thinking*. We are even having a conversation when we read a magazine or book, watch a television show or movie, or write a letter or report. This observation has three implications that wind their way through every aspect of our lives.

One implication is that conversations exercise incredible power over what we think, feel, and do. They shape our attitudes, our decisions, our opinions, our emotions, and our actions. If you want clues as to what a person will be like tomorrow, listen to what she's talking about today.

Second, given that conversations are so powerful, it's amazing that few people act on this fact. Most of us swim in a constant sea of conversations, almost none of which we carefully and thoughtfully choose.

The real power of this process lies in a third discovery: We can choose our conversations. Certain conversations create real value for us. They give us fuel for reaching our goals. Other conversations distract us from what we want. They might even create lasting unhappiness and frustration.

Suppose that you meet with an instructor to ask about some guidelines for writing a term paper. She launches into a tirade about your writing skills and lack of preparation for higher education. This presents you with several options. One possibility is to talk about what a jerk the instructor is and give up on the idea of learning to write well. Another option is to refocus the conversation on what you can do to improve your writing skills, such as working with a writing tutor or taking a basic composition class. These two sets of conversations will have vastly different consequences for your success in school.

Another important fact about your conversations is that they are dramatically influenced by the people you associate with. If you want to change your attitudes about almost anything—prejudice, politics, religion, humor—choose your conversations by choosing your community. Spend time with people who speak about and live consistently with the attitudes you value. Use conversations to change habits and create new options in your life.

When we choose our conversations, we discover a tool of unsurpassed power. This tool has the capacity to remake our thoughts—and thus our lives. It's as simple as choosing the next article you read or the next topic you discuss with a friend.

Begin applying this Power Process today. Start choosing your conversations, and watch what happens.

 Learn more about choosing your conversations.

Career Application

Gordon McGinnis, assistant dean and director of student activities at Mountain State University, had vehemently banned credit card solicitations during his five-year tenure. Over the years, a number of credit card companies and banks had approached him, offering deals to market their cards on campus that would generate good income for the university.

Yet Gordon had heard stories from his colleagues at other colleges of students cutting back on classes or dropping out to earn money to pay off debt. He also knew bad credit histories often hurt students when seeking their first jobs. Many of them had both student loan and credit card debt.

Gordon had tried to convince the business school to offer basic courses on this topic for students who weren't business majors. So far, he'd had no luck.

Despite his successes in keeping the credit card hawkers at bay, Gordon faced a new challenge when he got a call from Elsie Lombardi, the university's treasurer and vice president for finance.

"I just got an offer I don't think we can refuse," Elsie began. "The credit card division at Highland Bank Corporation wants us to enter into an exclusive credit card marketing program with them. They'll pay us $5 million over the next seven years to allow them to be the only bank card issuer allowed to market on campus."

"While we could really use the money, I'm afraid I'll have to say no," replied Gordon, "I'm philosophically opposed to marketing credit cards on campus."

"I didn't know you were a philosopher," said Elsie. "Listen, this is a service that students want in a world where, like it or not, plastic is important. Having a credit card helps students establish a credit history. Besides, most students handle cards as responsibly as adults."

Gordon paused. "Those are good points, Elsie. And if there's one thing that we can agree on, it's that our student organizations could always use a financial boost. Tell you what: I'd like to sleep on this before making a decision. Would you give me 24 hours to sleep on this? I'll get back to you tomorrow."[4]

Photodisc/Getty

Reflecting on this scenario

Identify at least one transferable skill that Gordon demonstrates.

_____

_____

_____

_____

_____

One option for Gordon is to create a financial literacy program for students at his school. List three major skills that you'd like to see students gain from such a program.

_____

_____

_____

_____

_____

_____

Quiz

Name _____   Date ____/____/____

1. According to the text, skills at managing money are hard to learn and require advanced mathematics. True or **false**? Explain your answer.

2. List three ways to decrease your expenses while you are in school.

3. Briefly explain three techniques for monitoring your expenses.

4. Which of the following is *not* a recommended strategy for using credit cards?
   (a) Scrutinize credit card offers.
   (b) Avoid cash advances.
   (c) Check statements against your records.
   (d) Use three to five credit cards.

5. List the three main steps suggested in this chapter for managing your money.

6. Give examples of *conversation* as defined in the Power Process for this chapter.

7. Define *identity theft* and explain at least one way to prevent it.

8. Define the term *income-based repayment plan.*

9. List some possible consequences of having a poor credit rating.

10. Explain the difference between PLUS loans and Stafford loans.

Focus on Transferable Skills

Now that you've reflected on the ideas in this chapter and experimented with some new strategies, go beyond your responses to the "Money" section of the Discovery Wheel exercise in Chapter 1: "First Steps." Also think about a skill you could develop in the near future to free yourself from money worries.

You might want to prepare for this exercise by reviewing the articles "Jumpstart Your Education with Transferable Skills" on page 58 and "101 Transferable Skills" on page 60.

MANAGING INCOME AND EXPENSES

Right now my main sources of income are . . .

My three biggest expenses each month are . . .

One monthly expense that I could reduce right away is . . .

To begin to reduce this expense immediately, I could . . .

PAYING FOR SCHOOL

I plan to graduate by (month and year) . . .

I plan to pay for my education next year by . . .

TAKING THE NEXT ACTION

I'll know that I've reached a new level of mastery with money when I can . . .

To reach that level of mastery, the most important thing I can do next is to . . .

Master Student PROFILE

Kat James

. . . is self-aware

Kat James had never gone to college, so she felt very lucky that the long boom years carried her up into the ranks of successful professionals. She worked for a public relations agency in London. The hours were long and demanding, and she'd often wonder, "What am I after? What do I want?" Her rote answer: someday, one of her clients would offer her a big salary and a Vice Presidency. She wanted to move up—or assumed she did. Didn't everyone? . . .

A year and a half ago, at a time when many people in high-tech felt lucky to have any job at all, Kat was offered a job running the P.R. department at one of the hottest telecoms in the UK. To convince her, they offered to *double* her salary. Double it!

At first she said yes, instinctively.

But the offer to double her salary had an unintended effect. It made it crystal clear that if she were to take this job, she would be doing it for the money. Not because it would be fun and interesting. For the money, plain and simple.

Over the next three weeks, she stalled. She told the telecom she was reconsidering.

She thought, *if I accept this, where will it end?*

This was not what she wanted the rest of her life.

. . . She had one thought. She barely let herself consider it. Ever since she was six years old, Kat had said that if money were no object, and if status didn't matter, and if there were nothing in the way . . . she would be a landscape gardener.

Why not go do the thing she'd always wanted to do?

. . . A few days later, she went to a music festival, and between bands she had a Tarot card reading performed, somewhat as a joke. Kat didn't believe in that stuff. Up turned goddess cards and earth cards. The Tarot reader looked at these cards and pronounced, "You would be really good at tending people's gardens."

Wow! Was it that obvious, that a complete stranger could see this in her?

The next day, she recounted the amazing coincidence to a neighbor.

"Are you thinking about doing it?" the neighbor asked.

"I'm thinking," Kat said.

The neighbor said she had just thrown into the trash a catalog for courses at Brighton City College. "I'll go get it," she offered. Kat took the catalog into her house. The college offered an extensive horticulture program that awarded two-year vocational certification. The first class began the next week, and the enrollment session for the class *was that very afternoon.*

Guided by another in the string of coincidences, Kat went down to enroll immediately. She felt light and happy and excited about what she was doing.

Classes were from nine a.m. to five p.m., three days a week. A third of each day was spent in the classroom, two thirds outdoors. She loved it.

. . . Does she ever regret not taking that doubled salary?

She said many people in her shoes would have taken the double salary in order to save up for the leap into garden design, believing that money is the path to freedom. She didn't, and she's found that true freedom comes from the confidence she can live within her means, whatever those means may be.

Profiled in *What Should I Do with My Life?*—a book by Po Bronson about people who transformed their lives by asking that question.

Learn more about Kat James and other master students at the Master Student Hall of Fame.

11 Health

Master Student Map

as you read, ask yourself

what if . . .

I could meet the demands of daily life with energy and optimism to spare?

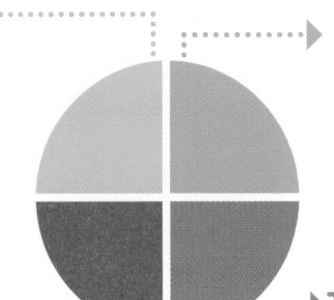

why this chapter matters . . .

Succeeding in higher education and the workplace calls for a baseline of physical and emotional well-being.

what is included . . .

- Wake up to health   299
- Choose your fuel   300
- Choose to exercise   302
- Choose mental health   303
- Living in balance   305
- Choose to stay safe   306
- Choose sexual health: Prevent infection   307
- From dependence to recovery   311
- Power Process: Surrender   313
- Master Student Profile: Randy Pausch   317

how you can use this chapter . . .

- Expand your physical and mental energy.
- Adopt habits that reduce your risk of disease.
- Make decisions about alcohol and other drugs that align with your values.

MASTER EMPLOYEE in *action*

In college I always enjoyed running. It helped me stay healthy and clear my head. It is even more important to me now since it helps me deal with the pressures of my job while also countering the fact that the majority of my time at work is spent sitting at a desk.

—JANE CASSON, COPYWRITER

Photo courtesy of Jane Casson

Wake up to health

SOME PEOPLE SEE HEALTH as just a matter of common sense. These people might see little value in reading a health chapter. No one needs to tell them that alcohol abuse, cigarette smoking, unprotected sex, lack of exercise, and lack of sleep can sap them of their energy. They already know that.

Yet *knowing* and *doing* are two different things. Health information does not always translate into healthy behaviors. Mastery means closing the gap between information and action.

We expect to experience health challenges as we age. Even youth, however, is no guarantee of good health. Over the last three decades, obesity among young adults has tripled. In addition, 29 percent of young men smoke. Furthermore, 70 percent of deaths among adults age 18 to 29 result from unintentional injuries, accidents, homicide, and suicide.[1]

Your success in school is directly tied to your health. Lack of sleep and lack of exercise have been associated with lower grade point averages among undergraduate students. So have alcohol use, tobacco use, gambling, and chronic health conditions.[2]

Taking charge of your health can boost your career. When asked what qualities they value in employees, employers often mention alertness, enthusiasm, optimism, and energy. These are words that describe a high level of health. Demonstrating these qualities might help you get hired and promoted.

Healthy people meet the demands of daily life with energy to spare. Illness or stress might slow them down for a while, but then they bounce back. They know how to relax, create loving relationships, find satisfaction in their work, and discover meaning in life. Health in this larger sense includes all dimensions of life—body, mind, and spirit.

Taking charge of your health might seem like a big project. Yet changing even a few behaviors can make a difference. One study found that people lengthened their lives an average of 14 years by adopting just four habits: staying tobacco-free, eating more fruits and vegetables, exercising regularly, and drinking alcohol in moderation if at all.[3]

You can become aware of current habits (discovery), choose new habits that align with your values (intention), and practice them every day.

Health is a choice you make in every moment, with each action that you take. Wake up to this possibility by experimenting with the suggestions in this chapter. ✳

journal entry 26

Discovery Statement

Choose a new level of health

Summarize your top three health concerns in the following space.

I discovered that . . .

Now scan the articles in this chapter. In the following space, list some suggestions that could help you respond positively to your health concerns:

I discovered that . . .

Finally, based on your quick review of this chapter, list three suggestions that you will explore in more detail:

I intend to . . .

Choose your fuel

WHAT YOU EAT CAN HAVE IMMEDIATE and long-term effects on your performance as a student. That giant jelly donut can make you drowsy within minutes. A steady diet of them can affect the amount of energy you have available to meet and juggle the demands of classes, family members, jobs, extracurricular activities, and other commitments.

Food is your primary fuel for body and mind. Even though you've been eating all your life, entering higher education is bound to change the way that you fuel yourself. Fast foods can be tempting when you're pressed for time, even though a steady diet of them can expand your waistline and drain your budget. It's easy to feel out of control in this area of your life.

There have been hundreds of books written about nutrition. Some say don't drink milk. Others say buy a cow. Although the debate seems confusing, take comfort. There is actually wide agreement about how to fuel yourself for health.

Build your pyramid

Today, federal nutrition guidelines are summarized visually as a *food pyramid*. The idea is to eat more of the foods shown in the bigger sections of the pyramid and less of those in the smaller sections. To see an example and build your personal food pyramid, go online to **www.mypyramid.gov**.

The various food pyramids agree on several core guidelines:[4]

- Emphasize fruits, vegetables, whole grains, and fat-free or low-fat milk and milk products.
- Include lean meats, poultry, fish, beans, eggs, and nuts.
- Choose foods that are low in saturated fats, trans fats, cholesterol, salt (sodium), and added sugars.

Keep it simple

Michael Pollan, a writer for the *New York Times Magazine,* spent several years sorting out the scientific literature on nutrition.[5] He boiled the key guidelines down to seven words in three sentences:

- *Eat food.* In other words, choose whole, fresh foods over processed products with a lot of artificial ingredients.
- *Not too much.* If you want to manage your weight, then control how much you eat. Notice portion sizes. Pass on snacks, seconds, and desserts—or indulge just occasionally.

© Iconotec/ Wonderfile

- *Mostly plants.* Fruits, vegetables, and grains are loaded with chemicals that help to prevent disease. Plant-based foods, on the whole, are also lower in calories than foods from animals (meat and dairy products).

If you're concerned about getting enough protein, remember that you can get plenty of it from low-fat dairy products, occasional lean meats, and soy foods.

You can still enjoy fats and sweets. Just do them in moderation.

Also, your body is mostly water, so drink plenty of it.

Pass up diets

If you want to lose weight, then avoid people who offer a quick fix. Even if that "Lose 20 pounds in 20 days!" diet works at first, you're likely to gain the weight back. In addition, diets are often complicated and hard to maintain.

For most of us, the path to weight loss is simple, though not always easy: Eat better food, eat less food, and exercise regularly. To find safe weight-loss and nutrition programs, visit your doctor or campus health service. Look for a program that provides peer support.

How you eat can matter as much as *what* you eat. If you want to eat less, then eat slowly. Savor each bite. Stop when you're satisfied instead of when you feel full. Use meal times as a chance to relax, reduce stress, and connect with people.

Cook at home

To save money and promote health, prepare meals at home. Center them on whole grains, fruits, and vegetables.

You can eat healthfully even when you're pressed for time. Cut up a bunch of vegetables, stir-fry them with lean meat or tofu, and season them just the way you like. Or, load those vegetables into a tortilla, add a little cheese, heat it all up, and enjoy. For variation, throw the

11

HEALTH

same ingredients on flat bread and heat it in the oven for a few minutes—you've made a delicious, homemade pizza.

For another set of easy and nutritious meals, combine low-fat pasta with pestos or spaghetti sauces. Also remember that low-fat smoothies and cereals with skim milk are satisfying snacks that you can eat with few worries.

Watch portion sizes—especially when eating out

Restaurant portions—especially at fast-food places—have swelled in recent decades. Since McDonald's opened, the calories in a serving of its French fries have tripled. A quarter pounder with cheese, large fries, and large soda may weigh in at over 1,300 calories, which is all that most of us need for an entire day.[6]

If you want to lose weight, start by eating smaller portions and eliminating second servings. Even using smaller plates, bowls, and utensils may help.

When you eat out, reduce portions. Remember that splitting a meal with someone reduces both cost and calories.

Prevent and treat eating disorders

Eating disorders affect many students. These disorders involve serious disturbances in eating behavior. Examples are overeating or extreme reduction of food intake, as well as irrational concern about body shape or weight. Women are much more likely to develop these disorders than are men, though cases are on the rise among males.

Bulimia involves cycles of excessive eating and forced purges. A person with this disorder might gorge on a pizza, doughnuts, and ice cream and then force herself to vomit. Or she might compensate for overeating with excessive use of laxatives, enemas, or diuretics.

Anorexia nervosa is a potentially fatal illness marked by self-starvation. People with anorexia may practice extended fasting or eat only one kind of food for weeks at a time.

These disorders are not due to a failure of willpower. They are real illnesses in which harmful patterns of eating take on a life of their own.

Eating disorders can lead to many complications, including life-threatening heart conditions and kidney failure. Many people with eating disorders also struggle with depression, substance abuse, and anxiety. They need immediate treatment to stabilize their health. This is usually followed by continuing medical care, counseling, and medication to promote a full recovery.

If you're worried you might have an eating disorder, visit a doctor, campus health service, or local public health clinic. If you see signs of an eating disorder in someone else, express your concern with "I" messages, as explained in Chapter 9: "Communicating."

For more information, contact the National Eating Disorders Association at 1-800-931-2237 or online at **www.nationaleatingdisorders.org**. ✳

 Discover more strategies online for fueling your body.

Maybe it's the company you keep

Peer pressure is real. Researchers Nicholas A. Christakis and James H. Fowler discovered that health-related behaviors can "pass" from person to person. This conclusion is based on data from the Framingham Heart Study, an investigation that began in 1948 and still continues, with thousands of participants.

Christakis and Fowler found that conditions such as obesity and unhappiness spread across networks of friends. So do healthy habits such as exercising and quitting smoking.[7] In short, healthy people who keep in close, regular contact with healthy peers tend to thrive as they age. This is a positive form of contagion.

The take-away message from this research is clear: To protect your health, associate with healthy people. If you want to exercise regularly, for example, then join a gym or start a walking group. If you want to change the way you eat, then socialize with people who enjoy nutritious meals. Making health a social affair can add a fun factor and raise your level of commitment.

© Brand X (X Collection)/Wonderfile

Choose to exercise

OUR BODIES WERE MADE TO MOVE. The world ran on muscle power back in the days when we had to hunt down a woolly mammoth every few weeks and drag it back to the cave. Now we can grab a burger at a drive-up window. Today exercising calls for special planning.

It's worth it. Exercise promotes weight control and reduces the symptoms of depression. It also helps to prevent heart attack, diabetes, and several forms of cancer.[8]

An added benefit is that exercise refreshes your body and your mind. If you're stuck on a math problem or blocked on writing a paper, take an exercise break. You'll come back with a fresh perspective.

If you get moving, you'll start to create lean muscles, a strong heart, and an alert brain. You don't have to train for the Boston Marathon, however. And if the word *exercise* turns you off, think *physical activity* instead. An hour of daily activity is ideal, but do whatever you can. Some activity is better than none. Following are some things you can do.

Stay active throughout the day. Whenever possible, walk. Walk between classes or while taking a study break. Instead of meeting a friend for a restaurant meal or movie, go for a walk. If you commute, then park a little farther from campus and cover the extra blocks on foot.

Also take the stairs instead of riding elevators, especially if you're going up just one or two flights. For an extra workout, climb two stairs at a time. Stair climbing is a highly aerobic form of exercise.

Keep some one- to five-pound weights by your desk. Instead of reaching for another cup of coffee or a sugary snack, restore alertness with a quick set of repetitions.

Use your campus environment. Look for exercise facilities on campus. Search for classes in aerobics, swimming, volleyball, basketball, golf, tennis, and other sports. Intramural sports are another option. School can be a great place to get in shape.

Do what you enjoy. Stay active over the long term with aerobic activities that you enjoy. You might enjoy martial arts, kickboxing, yoga, ballroom dance classes, stage combat classes, or mountain climbing. Check your school catalog for such courses.

Vary your routine. Find several activities that you enjoy, and rotate them throughout the year. Your main form of activity during winter might be ballroom dancing, riding an exercise bike, or skiing. In summer, you could switch to outdoor sports. Whenever possible, choose weight-bearing activities such as walking, running, or stair climbing.

Get active early. Work out first thing in the morning. Then it's done for the day. Make it part of your daily routine, just like brushing your teeth.

Look for gradual results. If your goal is to lose weight, be patient. Since 1 pound equals 3,500 calories, you might feel tempted to reduce weight loss to a simple formula: *Let's see . . . if I burn away just 100 calories each day through exercise, I should lose 1 pound every 35 days.*

Actually, the relationship between exercise and weight loss is complex. Many factors—including individual differences in metabolism and the type of exercise you do—affect the amount of weight you lose.[9]

When you step on the bathroom scale, look for small changes over time rather than sudden, dramatic losses. Gradual weight loss is more healthy, anyway—and easier to sustain over the long term.

Before beginning any vigorous exercise program, consult a healthcare professional. This is critical if you are overweight, over age 60, in poor condition, or a heavy smoker, or if you have a chronic health condition. ✳

 Discover more ways online to follow through on your exercise goals.

Choose mental health

THE NUMBER OF students in higher education who have mental health problems is steadily increasing.[10] According to the American College Health Association, 31 percent of college students report that they have felt so depressed that it was difficult to function. Almost half of the students say that they've felt overwhelming anxiety, and 60 percent report that they've felt very lonely.[11]

Managing your mental health depends on many factors: your skill at managing stress, your ability to build loving relationships, your capacity to meet the demands of school and work, and your beliefs about your ability to succeed. People with mental illness have thoughts, emotions, or behaviors that consistently interfere with these areas of life.

You can take simple and immediate steps to prevent mental health problems or cope with them if they do occur. To begin, take care of your body. Your thoughts and emotions can get scrambled if you go too long feeling hungry or tired. Follow the suggestions in this chapter for eating, exercise, and sleep. You can also experiment with the following ideas.

Solve problems. Although you can't "fix" a bad feeling in the same way that you can fix a machine, you can choose to change a situation associated with that feeling. You might be able to identify a problem associated with that feeling. You might be able to identify a problem that is causing you stress or emotional pain.

Describe the problem in detail. Then brainstorm solutions, and choose one to implement. Reducing your course load, cutting back on hours at work, getting more financial aid, delegating a task, or taking some other concrete action might solve the problem and help you feel better over the long run.

Share what you're thinking and feeling. There are times when negative thoughts and emotions persist even after you take appropriate action. Tell a family member or friend about them. The simple act of describing a problem can sometimes reveal a solution or give you a fresh perspective.

Don't believe everything you think. According to Albert Ellis and other cognitive psychologists, stress results not from events in our lives but from the way we *think* about those events.[12] If we believe that people should always behave in exactly the way we expect

ZenShui/Alix Minde/Getty

them to, then we set ourselves up for misery. The same happens if we believe that events should always turn out exactly as we want.

A more sane option is to dispute such irrational beliefs and replace them with more rational ones: *I can control my own behavior but not the behavior of others.* And: *Some events are beyond my control.* Changing our beliefs can reduce our stress significantly.

Another way to deal with stressful thoughts is to release them altogether. Meditation is a way to do this. While meditating, you simply notice your thoughts as they arise and pass. Instead of reacting to them, you observe them. Eventually, your stream of thinking slows down. You might enter a state of deep relaxation that also yields life-changing insights.

Allow yourself to feel bad. This suggestion is not a joke or a piece of "reverse psychology." The point is simply that mental health is possible only if you allow yourself to feel the full range of your emotions— pleasant as well as unpleasant.

Sometimes bad is an appropriate way to feel. When you leave a place you love, sadness is natural. When you lose a friend or lover, misery might be in order. When someone treats you badly, it is probably appropriate to feel angry. When a loved one dies, it is necessary to grieve. There is nothing wrong with such emotional pain. It is natural, it is temporary, and it doesn't have to be fixed.

If depression, sadness, or anger persist and interfere with your ability to carry out the tasks of daily life, then get help. Otherwise, allow yourself to experience unpleasant emotions. They can be appropriate and necessary for personal growth.

Believe it or not, you can actually play with this suggestion (assuming that your mental health is basically strong and stable). Suppose that you wake up one day and feel absolutely useless, ugly, and unlovable. Look in the mirror and tell yourself over and over again how useless, ugly, and unlovable you are. It might be hard to berate yourself for very long and keep a straight face.

If you are determined to feel sorry for yourself, then go all the way. Increase your misery by studying a few extra hours. You'll get some extra studying done, and you also might start feeling like a good student. You could even start feeling pleased with yourself. Notice what happens to your misery.

Stay active. Another strategy for coping with unpleasant feelings is to do something—*anything*—that's constructive. For example, mop the kitchen floor. Clean out your dresser drawers. Iron your shirts. This sounds silly, but it often works.

The basic principle is that you can separate emotions from actions. It is appropriate to feel miserable when you do. It's normal to cry and express your feelings. It is also possible to go to class, study, work, eat, and feel miserable at the same time. Unless you have a diagnosable problem such as anxiety or depression, you can continue your normal activities until the misery passes.

Japanese psychiatrist Morita Masatake, a contemporary of Sigmund Freud, based his whole approach to treatment on this insight: We can face our emotional pain directly and still take constructive action. One of Masatake's favorite suggestions for people who felt depressed was that they tend a garden.[13]

Prevent suicide. Suicide is the second leading cause of death on college campuses.[14] Most often, suicide can be prevented. If you think that someone you know is considering suicide, do whatever it takes to ensure the person's safety.

If you ever begin to think about committing suicide, then seek out someone you trust. Tell this person how you feel. If necessary, make an appointment to see a counselor, and ask someone to accompany you. When you're at risk, you deserve the same compassion that you'd willingly extend to another person.

Find out more on this topic from the American Foundation for Suicide Prevention at 1-800-273-8255 or **www.afsp.org**.

Find resources on or off campus. Student health centers are not just for treating colds, allergies, and flu symptoms. Counselors can help students deal with their adjustment to campus, changes in mood, academic problems, and drug abuse and dependence. Students with anxiety disorders, clinical depression, bipolar disorder, and other diagnoses might get referred to a psychiatrist or psychologist who works off campus. The referral process can take time, so seek help right away.

Your tuition helps to pay for mental health services. It's smart to use them now.

You can find resources to promote mental health even if your campus doesn't offer counseling services. First, find a personal physician—one person who can coordinate all of your health care. A personal physician can refer you to a mental health professional if it seems appropriate.

Also remember a basic guideline about *when* to seek help: whenever problems with your thoughts, moods, or behaviors consistently interfere with your ability to sleep, eat, go to class, work, or create positive relationships.

These suggestions can also work after you graduate. Promoting mental health is a skill to use for the rest of your life. ✳

 Find more pathways to robust mental health online.

Choose to rest

A lack of rest can decrease your immunity to illness and impair your performance in school. You still might be tempted to cut back drastically on your sleep once in a while for an all-night study session. Instead, read Chapter 3: "Time" for some time management ideas. Depriving yourself of sleep is a choice you can avoid.

If you have trouble falling asleep, experiment with the following suggestions:

- Exercise daily, taking care to finish several hours before you want to go to sleep.
- Avoid naps during the daytime.
- Monitor your caffeine intake, especially in the afternoon and evening.
- Avoid using alcohol to induce sleepiness.
- Develop a sleep ritual—a regular sequence of calming activities that end your day.
- Keep your sleeping room cool.
- Keep a regular schedule for going to sleep and waking up.
- Sleep in the same place each night.
- Practice relaxation techniques while lying in bed, such as counting your breaths and releasing thoughts as they arise.
- If you lie in bed awake for more than 30 minutes, get up and read until you're tired.
- See a doctor if sleeplessness persists.

Living in balance

STUDENTS EXPERIENCE EXTRAORDINARY demands on their time, especially when juggling classes and studying with time spent on family, friends, and work. Following are some ideas to use when 24 hours a day and 168 hours a week just don't seem like enough.

Monitor and plan

If you have not done Critical Thinking Exercise 14: "The Time Monitor/Time Plan Process" on page 88, then turn back to it now. Yes, this exercise takes a little time. However, the payoff comes in creating a more sane schedule. Monitoring will let you know which activities consume the most time, and which produce the least value. You can use that information to plan more effectively. After all, a big part of planning is choosing what *not* to do.

In his book *Full-Catastrophe Living: Using the Wisdom of Your Body and Mind to Face Stress, Pain, and Illness*, Job Kabat-Zinn recalls a stress-reduction program he conducted for judges. One judge in particular complained about his overwhelming case load. After monitoring his time, this judge discovered that he spent two to three hours each day reading newspapers and watching the news on TV. He chose to reduce his news gathering activities to one hour per day, freeing up nearly two hours for other activities. That's the power of monitoring and planning.[15]

Harness the power of one

Students in higher education sometimes struggle with "option overload": There are so many courses that would be fun to take, as well as so many events on campus and so many extracurricular activities to consider.

Whenever possible, look for areas where you can reduce the available options to one. For example, register for *one* course with a heavy reading or writing load next term. Declare *one* major. Choose *one* extracurricular activity.

You don't need a long list of activities on your résumé to impress a future employer. Instead, focus on developing excellence in a few special interests.

Lower your standards in some areas

Perhaps you don't have a spotless house and the laundry is piled a little higher than usual. Big deal. You are in school, investing time and money in your skills, your career, and the future prosperity of your family. Given the power of those goals, it makes sense to cut back on time for some household chores. See if you can delegate

(students working together) Supernova/Getty, (woman with football) Dave & Les Jacobs/Getty

them to other people in your household or do them less often.

Say no with grace

An inability to say no can spring from the assumption that you'll lose friends if you say no to a time-demanding request. Consider this: If you cannot say no, then you are not in charge of your time. You've given that right to someone else. The people who really care about you will understand when you decline a request because you are busy educating yourself.

You might find it easier to say no when you don't have to grasp for words. Craft your refusals in advance. For example: "Thanks for inviting me to the party, but I have a huge test tomorrow and want to study."

Guard your fun time

One thing that you can say "yes" to is regular doses of fun. Set aside a "date night" with your spouse, a play day with your children, or an occasional day off with no commitments.

You might find it useful to actually block out time in your calendar for activities that recharge and relax you. If you monitor your time, you'll discover ways to set aside those times while still meeting your work, school, and family commitments.

Let go of perfection

Instead of trying to find the perfect balance between all the areas of your life, just experiment with simple changes in behavior like those just listed. Notice which ones actually lower your stress level, even in small ways. Subtle changes over time can add up to a life that feels a lot more in balance. ✳

Choose to stay safe

© George Shelley/Masterfile

WHILE ON CAMPUS, you might feel insulated from the outside world and believe that you have special protection. Yet there are people who know how to take advantage of this belief. Some criminals target students who are alone. Others monitor dorm activity. They know that rooms are often unlocked and filled with computers and other valuables.

Take general precautions

Three simple actions can significantly increase your personal safety.

One is to always lock doors when you're away from home. If you live in a dorm, follow the policies for keeping the front doors secure. Don't let an unauthorized person walk in behind you. If you commute to school or have a car on campus, keep your car doors locked.

The second action is to avoid walking alone, especially at night. Many schools offer shuttle buses to central campus locations. Use them. As a backup, carry enough spare cash for a taxi ride.

Third, plan for emergencies. Look for emergency phones along the campus routes that you normally walk. If you have a cell phone, you can always call 9-1-1 for help.

Prevent sexual assault

Both women and men can take the following steps to prevent rape and other forms of sexual assault:

- Get together with a group of people for a tour of the campus. Make a special note of danger spots, such as unlighted paths and unguarded buildings. Keep in mind, however, that rape can also occur during daylight and in well-lit places.

- Ask if your school has escort services for people taking evening classes. These might include personal escorts, car escorts, or both. If you do take an evening class, ask if there are security officers on duty before and after the class.

- Take a course or seminar on self-defense and rape prevention. To find these courses, check with your student counseling service or local library.

If you are raped, get medical care right away. Go to the nearest rape crisis center, hospital, student health service, or police station. Also arrange for follow-up counseling.

It's your decision whether to report the crime. Filing a report does not mean that you have to press charges. However, if you do choose to press charges later, having a report on file can help your case.

Date rape—the act of forcing sex on a date—is a common form of rape among college students. Date rape is still rape. It is a crime.

Drugs such as Rohypnol (flunitrazepam) and GHB (gamma-hydroxybutyrate) have been used in date rape crimes. These drugs, which can be secretly slipped into a drink, reduce resistance to sexual advances and produce an effect similar to amnesia. People who take these drugs might not remember the circumstances that led to their being raped. To protect yourself, don't leave your drinks unattended, and don't let someone else get drinks for you.

Take further steps to protect yourself from sexual assault. Decide what kind of sexual relationships you want. Then set firm limits, and communicate them clearly and assertively. Make sure that your nonverbal messages match your verbal messages. If someone refuses to respect your limits, then stay away from that person.

Prevent accidents

Accidents due to unsafe conditions and behaviors can lead to disability and even death. Following are ways you can greatly reduce the odds of accidents:

- Don't drive after drinking alcohol or using psychoactive drugs.

- Drive with the realization that other drivers may be preoccupied, intoxicated, or careless.

- Put poisons out of reach of children, and label poisons clearly. Also, remember that poisoning takes a larger toll on people age 15 to 45 than on children.

- Keep stairs, halls, doorways, and other pathways clear of shoes, toys, newspapers, and other clutter.

- Keep a fire extinguisher handy.

- Install smoke detectors where you live and work. Most run on batteries that need occasional replacement. Follow the manufacturer's guidelines. ✳

Choose sexual health: Prevent infection

PEOPLE WITH A sexually transmitted infection (STI) might feel no symptoms for years and not even discover that they are infected. Know how to protect yourself.

STIs can result from vaginal sex, oral sex, anal sex, or any other way that people contact semen, vaginal secretions, and blood. Without treatment, some of these infections can lead to blindness, infertility, cancer, heart disease, or even death.[16]

There are at least 25 kinds of STIs. Common examples are chlamydia, gonorrhea, and syphilis. Sexual contact can also spread the human papillomavirus (HPV, the most common cause of cervical cancer) and the human immunodeficiency virus (HIV, the virus that causes AIDS).

Most STIs can be cured if treated early. (Herpes and AIDS are important exceptions.) Prevention is a better course of action. Some guidelines for prevention follow.

Abstain from sex. Abstain from sex, or have sex exclusively with one person who is free of infection and has no other sex partners. These are the only ways to be absolutely safe from STIs.

Talk to your partner. Before you have sex with someone, talk about the risk of STIs. If you are infected, tell your partner.

Use condoms. Male condoms are thin membranes stretched over the penis prior to intercourse. Condoms prevent semen from entering the vagina. For the most protection, use latex condoms—not ones made of lambskin or polyurethane. Use a condom every time you have sex, and for any type of sex.

Condoms are not guaranteed to work all of the time. They can break, leak, or slip off. In addition, condoms cannot protect you from STIs that are spread by contact with herpes sores or warts.

Talk to your doctor before using condoms, lubricants, spermicides, and other products that contain nonoxynol-9. This chemical can irritate a woman's vagina and cervix and actually increase the risk of STIs.

Stay sober. People are more likely to have unsafe sex when drunk or high.

Do not share needles. Sharing needles or other paraphernalia with other drug users can spread STIs.

Take action soon after you have sex. Urinate soon after you have sex. Wash your genitals with soap and water.

Get vaccinated. Vaccines are available to prevent hepatitis B and HPV infection. See your doctor.

Get screened for STIs. The only way to find out whether you're infected with an STI is to be tested by a healthcare professional. If you have sex with more than one person, get screened for STIs at least once each year. Do this even if you have no symptoms. Remember that many schools offer free STI screening.

The more people you have sex with, the greater your risk of STIs. You are at risk even if you have sex only once with one person who is infected.

The U.S. Centers for Disease Control and Prevention recommends chlamydia screening for all sexually active women under age 26. Women age 25 and older should be screened if they have a new sex partner or multiple sex partners.[17]

Recognize the symptoms of STIs. Symptoms can include swollen glands with fever and aching; itching around the vagina; vaginal discharge; pain during sex or when urinating; sore throat following oral sex; anal pain after anal sex; sores, blisters, scabs, or warts on the genitals, anus, tongue, or throat; rashes on the palms of your hands or soles of your feet; dark urine; loose and light-colored stools; and unexplained fatigue, weight loss, and night sweats.

Get treated right away. If you think you have an STI, go to your doctor, campus health service, or local public health clinic. Early treatment might prevent serious health problems. To avoid infecting other people, abstain from sex until you are treated and cured.

Prevent pregnancy

You and your partner can avoid unwanted pregnancy. There are many options for doing so, and choosing among them can be a challenge. Think about whether you want to have children someday, the number of sexual partners you have, your comfort with using a birth control method, possible side effects, and your overall health.

Abstinence is always an option. This means choosing *not* to have sex—vaginal, oral, or anal. When practiced without exception, this is the *only* sure way to prevent pregnancy and STIs.

You might feel pressured to reject abstinence as an option. However, many people exist happily without having sex for a certain period of time. For some, the choice is permanent.

If you are sexually active, then make conscious choices about birth control. There are many methods to consider. They vary greatly in cost, convenience, and effectiveness.

Some birth control methods require practice and special techniques. For example, male condoms have an inside and outside surface. They also work best when there's a little space left at the tip for fluid.

Also keep in mind that the effectiveness rate for any method of birth control can only be estimated. Estimates depend on many factors—for example, the health of the people using them, their number of sex partners, and how often they have sex.

Be sure you know how to use your chosen method of birth control. A doctor might assume that you already have this knowledge. If you don't, then ask questions freely.

Even birth control methods that are usually effective can fail when used incorrectly. To prevent pregnancy, make sure you understand your chosen method. Then use it *every* time you have sex.

Get the latest information about birth control from your doctor or campus health service. You can also go online to **www.womenshealth.gov/faq/birth-control-methods.cfm**. ✳

 Learn more about choosing sexual health.

Observe thyself

You are an expert on your body. You are more likely to notice changes before anyone else does. Pay attention to these changes. They are often your first clues about the need for medical treatment or intervention.

Watch for the following signs:

- Weight loss of more than 10 pounds in 10 weeks with no apparent cause
- A sore, scab, or ulcer that does not heal in three weeks
- A skin blemish or mole that bleeds; itches; or changes size, shape, or color
- Persistent or severe headaches
- Sudden vomiting that is not preceded by nausea
- Fainting spells
- Double vision
- Difficulty swallowing
- Persistent hoarseness or a nagging cough
- Blood that is coughed up or vomited

- Shortness of breath for no apparent reason
- Persistent indigestion or abdominal pain
- A big change in normal bowel habits, such as alternating diarrhea and constipation
- Black and tarry bowel movements
- Rectal bleeding
- Pink, red, or unusually cloudy urine
- Discomfort or difficulty when urinating or during sexual intercourse
- Lumps or thickening in a breast
- Vaginal bleeding between menstrual periods or after menopause

If you are experiencing any of these symptoms, get help. Even if you don't think the situation is serious, consult a medical professional about it. Without timely and proper treatment, a minor illness or injury can lead to serious problems. Begin with your doctor or school health service.

People who have problems with drugs and alcohol can hide this fact from themselves and from others. It can also be hard for a friend or family member to admit that a loved one has a problem.

The purpose of this exercise is to give you an objective way to look at your relationship with drugs or alcohol. There are signals that indicate when drug or alcohol use has become abusive or even addictive. This exercise can also help you determine if a friend might be addicted.

Answer the following questions quickly and honestly with yes, no, or n/a (not applicable). If you are concerned about someone else, rephrase each question using that person's name.

_____ Are you uncomfortable discussing drug abuse or addiction?

_____ Are you worried about your own drug or alcohol use?

_____ Are any of your friends worried about your drug or alcohol use?

_____ Have you ever hidden from a friend, spouse, employer, or coworker the fact that you were drinking? (Pretended you were sober? Covered up alcohol breath?)

_____ Do you sometimes use alcohol or drugs to escape lows rather than to produce highs?

_____ Have you ever gotten angry when confronted about your use?

_____ Do you brag about how much you consume? ("I drank her under the table.")

_____ Do you think about or do drugs when you are alone?

_____ Do you store up alcohol, drugs, cigarettes, or caffeine (in coffee or soft drinks) to be sure you won't run out?

_____ Does having a party almost always include alcohol or drugs?

_____ Do you try to control your drinking so that it won't be a problem? ("I drink only on weekends now." "I never drink before 5 p.m." "I drink only beer.")

_____ Do you often explain to other people why you are drinking? ("It's my birthday." "It's my friend's birthday." "It's Veterans Day." "It sure is a hot day.")

_____ Have you changed friends to accommodate your drinking or drug use? ("She's OK, but she isn't excited about getting high.")

_____ Has your behavior changed in the last several months? (Grades slipping? Lack of interest in a hobby? Change of values or moral standards?)

_____ Do you drink or use drugs to relieve tension? ("What a day! I need a drink.")

_____ Do you have medical problems (stomach trouble, malnutrition, liver problems, anemia) that could be related to drinking or drugs?

_____ Have you ever decided to quit drugs or alcohol and then changed your mind?

_____ Have you had any fights, accidents, or similar incidents related to drinking or drugs in the last year?

_____ Has your drinking or drug use ever caused a problem at home?

_____ Do you envy people who go overboard with alcohol or drugs?

_____ Have you ever told yourself you can quit at any time?

_____ Have you ever been in trouble with the police after or while you were drinking?

_____ Have you ever missed school or work because you had a hangover?

_____ Have you ever had a blackout (a period you can't remember) during or after drinking?

_____ Do you wish that people would mind their own business when it comes to your use of alcohol or drugs?

_____ Is the cost of alcohol or other drugs taxing your budget or resulting in financial stress?

_____ Do you need increasing amounts of a drug to produce the desired effect?

_____ When you stop taking a drug, do you experience withdrawal?

_____ Do you spend a great deal of time obtaining and using alcohol or other drugs?

_____ Have you used alcohol or another drug when it was physically dangerous to do so (such as when driving a car or working with machines)?

_____ Have you been arrested or had other legal problems resulting from the use of a substance?

Now count the number of questions you answered yes. If you answered yes more than once, then talk with a professional. This does not necessarily mean that you are addicted. It does point out that alcohol or other drugs could be adversely affecting your life. Talk to someone with training in recovery from chemical dependency. Do not rely on the opinion of anyone who lacks such training.

If you filled out this questionnaire about another person and you answered yes two or more times, then your friend might need help. You probably can't provide that help alone. Seek out a counselor or a support group such as Al-Anon. Call the local Alcoholics Anonymous chapter to find out about an Al-Anon meeting near you.

Setting limits on screen time

When left unchecked, addiction to the internet and other online outlets can have an adverse effect on your work. Access to online communication offers easy ways to procrastinate. We call it "surfing," "texting," "IMing"—and sometimes "researching" or "working." Author Edward Hallowell coined a word to describe these activities when done compulsively—*screensucking*.[18]

Digital devices create value. With a computer you can stream music, watch videos, listen to podcasts, scan newspapers, read books, check e-mail, and send instant messages. With a cell phone you can be available to key people when it counts. Any of these activities can become compulsive distractions.

Discover how much time you spend online.
To get an accurate picture of your involvement in social networking and other online activity, use the Time Monitor/Time Plan exercise included in Chapter 3: "Time." Then make conscious choices about how much time you want to spend online and on the phone. Don't let social networking distract you from meeting personal and academic goals. People who update their MySpace or Facebook page every hour may be sending an unintended message—that they have no life offline.

Go offline to send the message that other people matter. It's hard to pay attention to the person who is right in front of you when you're hammering out text messages or updating your Twitter stream. You can also tell when someone else is doing these things and only half-listening to you.

An alternative is to close up your devices and "be here now." You can do this with any activity. When you're eating, stop answering the phone. Notice how the food tastes. When you're with a friend, close up your laptop. Hear every word he says. Instead of using a computer or cell phone for a conversation about the past or present, rediscover where life actually takes place—in the present moment, and often face-to-face.

Developing interpersonal intelligence requires being with people and away from a computer or cell phone. People who break up with a partner through text messaging are not developing that intelligence. True friends know when to go offline and head across campus to resolve a conflict, and when to go home for a crucial conversation with a family member. When it counts, your presence is your greatest present.

From dependence to recovery

© Geoff Manasse/Photodisc/Getty

THE TECHNICAL TERM FOR DRUG ADDICTION is *drug dependence.* This disease is defined by the following:

- *Loss of control*—continued substance use or activity in spite of adverse consequences.
- *Pattern of relapse*—vowing to quit or limit the activity or substance use and continually failing to do so.
- *Tolerance*—the need to take increasing amounts of a substance to produce the desired effect.
- *Withdrawal*—signs and symptoms of physical and mental discomfort or illness when the substance is taken away.[19]

This list can help you determine if dependence is a barrier for you right now. The previous items can apply to anything from cocaine use to internet addiction.

If you have a problem with dependence in any form, consider the following suggestions.

Use responsibly. Show people that you can have a good time without alcohol or other drugs. If you do choose to drink, then consume alcohol with food. Pace yourself. Take time between drinks.

Avoid promotions that encourage excess drinking. "Ladies Drink Free" nights are especially dangerous. Women are affected more quickly by alcohol, making them targets for rape. Also stay out of games that encourage people to guzzle. In addition, avoid people who make fun of you for choosing not to drink.

Pay attention. Whenever you use alcohol or another drug, do so with awareness. Then pay attention to the consequences. Act with deliberate intention based on what you've learned rather than out of habit or under pressure from others.

Look at the costs. There is always a tradeoff to dependence. Drinking six beers might result in a temporary high, and you will probably remember that feeling. You might feel terrible the morning after consuming six beers, but some people find it easier to forget *that* feeling.

Before going out to a restaurant or bar, set a limit for the number of drinks you will consume. If you consistently break this promise to yourself and experience negative consequences afterward, then you have a problem.

Admit the problem. People with active dependencies are a varied group—rich and poor, young and old, successful and unsuccessful. Often these people do have one thing in common: They are masters of denial. They deny that they are unhappy. They deny that they have hurt anyone. They are convinced that they can quit any time they want. They sometimes become so skilled at hiding the problem from themselves that they die.

Take responsibility for recovery. Nobody plans to become an addict, just like nobody plans to get pneumonia. If you have pneumonia, you seek treatment and recover without guilt or shame. Approach drug dependence in the same way. You can take responsibility for your recovery without self-blame.

Get help. People cannot treat dependence on their own. Behaviors tied to dependence are often symptoms of an illness that needs treatment.

11

HEALTH

Two broad options exist for getting help. One is the growing self-help movement. The other is formal treatment. People recovering from dependence often combine the two.

Many self-help groups are modeled after Alcoholics Anonymous (AA). AA is made up of recovering alcoholics and addicts. These people understand the problems of abuse firsthand, and they follow a systematic, 12-step approach to living without it. AA is one of the oldest and most successful self-help programs in the world. Chapters of AA welcome people from all walks of life, and you don't have to be an alcoholic to attend most meetings. Programs based on AA principles exist for many other forms of dependence as well.

Some people feel uncomfortable with the AA approach. Other resources exist for them, including private therapy and group therapy. You should also investigate organizations such as Women for Sobriety, the Secular Organizations for Sobriety, and Rational Recovery. Use whatever works for you.

Treatment programs are available in almost every community. They might be residential (you live there for weeks or months at a time) or outpatient (you visit several hours a day). Find out where these treatment centers are located by calling a doctor, a mental health professional, or a local hospital. If you don't have insurance, it is usually possible to arrange some other payment program. Cost is no reason to avoid treatment.

Get help for a friend or family member. You might know someone whose behavior meets the criteria for dependence. If so, you have every right to express your concern to that person. Wait until the person is clearheaded. Then mention specific incidents. For example: "Last night you drank five beers when we were at my apartment, and then you wanted to drive home. When I offered to call a cab for you instead, you refused." Be prepared to offer a source of help, such as the phone number of a local treatment center. ✳

 Learn more online about recovery from dependence.

Succeed in quitting smoking

There is no magic formula for becoming tobacco-free. However, you can take steps to succeed sooner rather than later. The American Cancer Society suggests the following.[20]

Make a firm choice to quit. All plans for quitting depend on this step. If you're not ready to quit yet, then admit it. Take another look at how smoking affects your health, finances, and relationships.

Set a date. Choose a "quit day" within the next month. That's close enough for a sense of urgency—and time to prepare. Pick a day that's close enough to give you a sense of urgency, but far enough out to give you time to prepare. Let friends and family members know about the big day.

Get personal support. Involve other people. Sign up for a quit smoking class. Attend Nicotine Anonymous or a similar group.

Consider medication. Medication can double your chances of quitting successfully.[21] Options include bupropion hydrochloride (Zyban) and varenicline (Chantix), as well as the nicotine patch, gum, nasal spray, inhaler, and lozenge.

Prepare the environment. Right before your quit day, get rid of all cigarettes and ashtrays at home and at work. Stock up on oral substitutes such as sugarless gum, candy, and low-fat snacks.

Deal with cravings for cigarettes. Distract yourself with exercise or another physical activity. Breathe deeply. Tell yourself that you can wait just a little while longer until the craving passes. Even the strongest urges to smoke will pass. Avoid alcohol use, which can increase cravings.

Learn from relapses. If you break down and light up a cigarette, don't judge yourself. Quitting often requires several attempts. Think back over your past plans for quitting and how to improve on them. Every relapse contains a lesson about how to succeed next time.

Surrender

Life can be magnificent and satisfying. It can also be devastating.

Sometimes there is too much pain or confusion. Problems can be too big and too numerous. Life can bring us to our knees in a pitiful, helpless, and hopeless state. A broken relationship with a loved one, a sudden diagnosis of cancer, total frustration with a child's behavior problem, or even the prospect of several long years of school are situations that can leave us feeling overwhelmed—powerless.

In these troubling situations, the first thing we can do is to admit that we don't have the resources to handle the problem. No matter how hard we try and no matter what skills we bring to bear, some problems remain out of our control. When this is the case, we can tell the truth: "It's too big and too mean. I can't handle it."

Desperately struggling to control a problem can easily result in the problem controlling us. Surrender is letting go of being the master in order to avoid becoming the slave.

Many traditions make note of this idea. Western religions speak of surrendering to God. Hindus say surrender to the Self. Members of Alcoholics Anonymous talk about turning their lives over to a Higher Power. Agnostics might suggest surrendering to the ultimate source of power. Others might speak of following their intuition, their inner guide, or their conscience.

In any case, surrender means being receptive to help. Once we admit that we're at the end of our rope, we open ourselves up to receiving help. We learn that we don't have to go it alone. We find out that other people have

faced similar problems and survived. We give up our old habits of thinking and behaving as if we have to be in control of everything. We stop acting as general manager of the universe. We surrender. And that creates a space for something new in our lives.

Surrendering is not "giving up." It is not a suggestion to quit and do nothing about your problems. Giving up is fatalistic and accomplishes nothing. You have many skills and resources. Use them. You can apply all of your energy to handling a situation and still surrender at the same time. Surrender includes doing whatever you can in a positive, trusting spirit. So let go and recognize when the true source of control lies beyond you.

Learn more about the power of this Power Process online.

Yasuhide Fumoto/Getty

Career Application

For weeks David had been bothered by aching muscles, loss of appetite, restless sleep, and fatigue. Eventually he became so short-tempered and irritable that his wife insisted he get a checkup.

Sitting in the doctor's office, David barely noticed when Theresa took the seat beside him. They had been good friends when she was an assistant in the front office at the factory where he worked. He hadn't seen her since she left three years ago to take a different job. Her gentle poke in the ribs brought him around. Within minutes they were talking freely.

"You got out just in time," he told her. "Since the reorganization at the plant, nobody feels safe. There were a lot of layoffs. And they still expect the same production rates, even though two guys are now usually doing the work of three. We're so backed up that I'm working 12-hour shifts six days a week. Guys are calling in sick just to get a break."

"Well, I really miss you guys," she said. "In my new job in customer service, a computer routes calls to me automatically, and they never stop. I even have to schedule my bathroom breaks. All I hear the whole day are complaints from unhappy customers. I try to be helpful and sympathetic, but I can't promise anything until I get my boss's approval. Most of the time I'm caught between what the customer wants and company policy. And the other reps are so uptight and tense they don't even talk to one another. We all go to our own little cubicles and stay there until quitting time. No wonder I'm in here with migraine headaches and high blood pressure."

Image Source/Getty

David and Theresa are using a powerful strategy to reduce stress and promote health—talking about how they feel with a person they trust. Describe three other strategies that might be useful to them:

_____

_____

_____

_____

_____

_____

_____

_____

_____

_____

_____

_____

_____

_____

_____

_____

_____

_____

_____

_____

_____

_____

_____

_____

_____

Quiz

Name _____ Date _____/_____/_____

1. According to the text, taking charge of your health can promote your success in school but has little effect on your career. True or false? Explain your answer.

2. Key signs of dependence include
   (a) Loss of control
   (b) A pattern of relapse
   (c) Tolerance
   (d) Withdrawal
   (e) All of the above

3. How is the Power Process: "Surrender" different from giving up?

4. A person with a sexually transmitted infection might have no symptoms for months—or sometimes years. True or false? Explain your answer.

5. Define *date rape,* and describe two ways to protect yourself against it.

6. Explain the meaning of "don't believe everything you think" as a strategy for promoting mental health.

7. Explain some potential problems with dieting and suggest a better option for weight control.

8. Name at least three methods for preventing sexually transmitted infection.

9. Explain a possible connection between lowering your standards and achieving more balance in your life.

10. The only option for long-term recovery from dependence is treatment based on the steps of Alcoholics Anonymous. True or false? Explain your answer.

Focus on Transferable Skills

Now that you've reflected on the ideas in this chapter and experimented with some new strategies, revisit your responses to the "Health" section of the Discovery Wheel exercise on page 27. Think about the most powerful action you could take to master a new skill in this area of your life.

DISCOVERY

To monitor my current level of health, I look for specific changes in . . .

After reading and doing this chapter, my top three health concerns are . . .

INTENTION

My top three intentions for responding to these concerns are . . .

NEXT ACTION

The most important health-related habit that I can change right now is . . .

My plan for changing this habit is . . .

Master Student PROFILE

Randy Pausch
. . . was energetic

© ABCNews.com

It's a thrill to fulfill your own childhood dreams, but as you get older, you may find that enabling the dreams of others is even more fun.

When I was teaching at the University of Virginia in 1993, a twenty-two-year-old artist-turned-computer-graphics-wiz named Tommy Burnett wanted a job on my research team. After we talked about his life and goals, he suddenly said, "Oh, and I have always had this childhood dream."

Anyone who uses "childhood" and "dream" in the same sentence usually gets my attention.

"And what is your dream, Tommy?" I asked.

"I want to work on the next *Star Wars* film," he said.

Remember, this was in 1993. The last *Star Wars* movie had been made in 1983, and there were no concrete plans to make any more. I explained this. "That's a tough dream to have because it'll be hard to see it through," I told him. "Word is that they're finished making *Star Wars* films."

"No," he said, "they're going to make more, and when they do, I'm going to work on them. That's my plan."

Tommy was six years old when the first *Star Wars* film came out in 1977. "Other kids wanted to be Han Solo," he told me. "Not me. I wanted to be the guy who made the special effects—the space ships, the planets, the robots."

He told me that, as a boy, he read the most technical *Star Wars* articles he could find. He had all the books that explained how the models were built, and how the special effects were achieved. . . . I figured Tommy's big dream would never happen, but it might serve him well somehow. I could use a dreamer like that. I knew from my NFL desires that even if he didn't achieve his, they could serve him well, so I asked him to join our research team. . . .

When I moved to Carnegie Mellon, every member of my team from the University of Virginia came with me—everyone except Tommy. He couldn't make the move. Why? Because he had been hired by producer/director George Lucas' company, Industrial Light & Magic. And it's worth noting that they didn't hire him for his dream; they hired him for his skills. In his time with our research group, he had become an outstanding programmer in the Python language, which as luck would have it, was the language of choice in their shop. Luck is indeed where preparation meets opportunity.

It's not hard to guess where this story is going. Three new *Star Wars* films would be made—in 1999, 2002, and 2005—and Tommy ended up working on all of them.

On *Star Wars Episode II: Attack of the Clones*, Tommy was a lead technical director. There was an incredible fifteen-minute battle scene on a rocky red planet, pitting clones against droids, and Tommy was the guy who planned it all out. He and his team used photos of the Utah desert to create a virtual landscape for the battle. Talk about cool jobs. Tommy had one that let him spend each day on another planet.

From the book *The Last Lecture* by Randy Pausch with Jeffrey Zaslow, pp. 117–119. Copyright (c) 2008 Randy Pausch. Reprinted by permission of Hyperion. All rights reserved.

(1960–2008) Carnegie Mellon University professor who once dreamed of playing professional football. Shortly after being diagnosed with pancreatic cancer, he gave a "last lecture"—a reflection on his personal and professional journey—that became a hit on YouTube (this lecture was later adapted into a book of the same title). He devoted the remaining nine months of his life to creating a legacy.

Learn more about Randy Pausch and other master students at the Master Student Hall of Fame.

12 Working

Master Student Map

as you read, ask yourself

what if . . .

I could find work that expresses my core values and connects with my passions?

why this chapter matters . . .

You can gain strategies to succeed as a job hunter and employee.

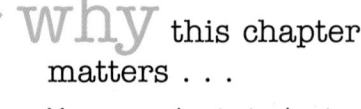

what is included . . .

how you can use this chapter . . .

- Learn effective strategies for job hunting.
- Create résumés that lead to job interviews.
- Go into job interviews fully prepared.
- Build satisfying relationships with coworkers.

MASTER EMPLOYEE in *action*

> I have read through literally thousands of résumés. The résumés that shine are those that are submitted by applicants who are aware of their strengths and weaknesses, and are able to highlight the former while being honest about the latter.
>
> **—KEN NGO, HUMAN RESOURCES**

Photo courtesy of Ken Ngo

The master employee

THE TITLE OF this book—*From Master Student to Master Employee*—implies that these two types of mastery have something in common. There's some pretty hard-nosed evidence for this idea. One piece of evidence is the fact that higher levels of education are correlated with higher levels of income.[1] Another is that mastery in school and in work seems to rest on a common set of transferable skills.

Consider the Secretary's Commission on Achieving Necessary Skills (SCANS) issued by the U.S. Department of Labor.[2] According to this document, one crucial skill for the workplace is a personal quality called *responsibility*. This skill is demonstrated by any employee who:

- "Exerts a high level of effort and perseverance toward goal attainment.
- "Works hard to become excellent at doing tasks by setting high standards, paying attention to details, working well, and displaying a high level of concentration even when assigned an unpleasant task.
- "Displays high standards of attendance, punctuality, enthusiasm, vitality, and optimism in approaching and completing tasks."

A better definition of mastery would be hard to find. If you've ever exerted a high level of effort to complete an assignment, paid attention to the details of a lecture, or displayed a high level of concentration while reading a tough textbook, then you've already demonstrated mastery.

When you graduate from school, you don't leave your capacity for mastery locked inside a classroom. Excellence in one setting paves the way for excellence in other settings.

For example, a student who knows how to show up for class on time is ready to show up for work on time. The student who knows how to focus attention during a lecture is ready to focus attention during a training session at work. And a student who's worked cooperatively in a study group brings a lot of skills to the table when joining a workplace team.

A master employee embraces change, takes risks, and looks for chances to lead others while contributing to the quality of their lives. A master employee completes tasks efficiently, communicates openly and respectfully, and commits to lifelong learning. You can learn to do all

this, and more. *Master student* and *master employee* are names for qualities that already exist in you, waiting to be expressed as you embrace new ideas and experiment with new behaviors.

You are about to make another transition—not just to another chapter of this book, but to the next chapter of your life. Each article in this chapter is about creating the work you love through the skills you've gained in this course. Use the following pages to choose your next steps. ✳

journal entry 27

Discovery/Intention Statement

Reflect on your experience of working

Reflect on all the jobs you've held in your life. What aspect of working would you most like to change? Answers might include job hunting with less frustration, resolving conflicts with coworkers, building a better relationship with your boss, or coping with office politics. Describe the change that would make the biggest positive difference in your job satisfaction over the long run.

I discovered that I . . .

_____

_____

_____

_____

_____

Now preview this chapter for ideas that could help you make the positive change you just described. List three to five suggestions in the following space, along with the page numbers where you intend to read more about them.

Strategy	Page number
_____	_____
_____	_____
_____	_____
_____	_____

WORKING

12

(man) Photodisc,
(group) Corbis

Use power tools for finding work

ONE OF THE MOST USEFUL JOB SKILLS you can ever develop is the art of *finding* a job. The more you develop this skill, the less you need to fear getting fired, laid off, or stuck in a job that no longer interests you. Remember that all of the following tools are at your disposal.

Tool #1: Think like an employer

Imagine yourself working as the hiring manager for a small business or head of human resources for a larger company. Your organization has a job opening, and your job is to fill it as soon as possible. You have the following options:

1. Hiring someone you know—a current or former employee or intern—with appropriate qualifications.

2. Hiring someone who is *recommended* by a current or former employee or intern.

3. Asking other members of your professional network to recommend a person for the job.

4. Hiring someone else who has already contacted you and demonstrated that he or she has the appropriate qualifications.

5. Contracting with an employment agency to screen potential applicants.

6. Running blind "help-wanted" ads and preparing for the dreaded onslaught of résumés.

If you're like most people in charge of hiring new employees, you'll choose from options 1 to 4 whenever possible, and in roughly that order. This makes logical

sense: You'd prefer to hire someone you know well, or have met. This is probably safer than risking your luck on a total stranger.

Now consider the traditional approach to *finding* a job, which usually relies on tasks that follow in a different order:

1. Responding blindly to help-wanted ads with a résumé and cover letter.

2. Contacting employment agencies.

3. Making direct contact with people who have the power to hire you, even when their organization does not have an advertised job opening.

4. Asking people in your professional network if they know of job openings that match your qualifications.

5. Asking people who work in your chosen field to recommend you for job openings.

6. Asking a current or former employer about job openings and opportunities to get promoted.

Carefully compare these two numbered lists. The traditional job-hunting method proceeds in *exactly the opposite direction* that employers use. Employers prefer to hire someone that they know, but many job seekers rely on help-wanted ads to connect with potential employers that they've never met. It's no wonder that people find the process of hiring and getting hired to be so frustrating.

To prevent this disconnection, think like an employer. Get to know people. Use your professional contacts to find out about job openings *before* they are advertised. (Most never are.) Do research to discover organizations that interest you. Find out who does the hiring at those organizations, and make direct contact with those people right away. Instead of sending out a stack of résumés to people you don't know and hoping for the best, build a professional network. For specific strategies, see "Tell Everyone You Know: The Art of Networking" on page 323.

Note: This is not to say that help-wanted ads and employment agencies are a waste of time. They might work. The suggestion here is simply not to rely on them exclusively. To succeed at job hunting, you should be flexible and use a variety of methods.

WORKING

12

Tool #2: Offer a limited amount of work for free

If you really want to get a potential employer's attention, then offer to work for free. This is not a joke. When done with care, working for free offers a low-risk way for you and an employer to get to know each other. If it works out, you could get hired full-time and start earning a salary. If it doesn't work out, the employer loses nothing. You get to walk away from the company on friendly terms and learn something from the experience as well.

There are four caveats to this suggestion. First, be sure to do your homework. Go online to find companies and entrepreneurs that really interest you. Supplement this with library research. Also ask people you know for suggestions.

Second, make sure that you have something to offer these companies and individuals. Find out what kinds of products and services they want to develop. Then look for a match between their wants and your skills.

Third, set a limit on the amount of time that you're willing to work for free. Put this limit in writing and ask the potential employer to agree to it. You might send an e-mail that goes something like this: "I have some specific ideas for the home page of your company's Web site that could increase the number of customer responses and raise its ranking on Google and other search engines. Over the next two weeks I will develop some prototypes for a new home page. If you like my ideas, then I'd like to meet with you about getting hired on a contract or full-time basis to implement them."

Finally, develop another source of income to pay the bills. Work part-time at another job. Another option is to find a full-time job with a flexible schedule that allows you to "moonlight" for potential employers. Doing this might mean reducing your expenses and learning to live on a bare-bones budget for a short time. See Chapter 10: "Money" for suggestions.

Tool #3: Use the Internet to power your job search

Millions of people go online to inventory their job skills, take career assessments, research potential employers, find job openings, post résumés, and submit applications. These activities offer many benefits. They also have limitations. For example, the haphazard organization of the Internet makes it hard for potential employers to find your résumé online. In addition, many job openings are not listed on the Internet (or anywhere else for that matter).

This is not meant to disparage the Internet as a tool for job hunters. To get better results, supplement the Internet with face-to-face contact. Get out and talk to people in your career field, including those who can hire you someday. View the Internet as just one source of information and contacts.

Tool #4: When job offers are scarce, stay flexible

Some people are lucky enough to graduate from higher education with a job offer or two in hand. However, many new graduates plan to spend their first weeks after the commencement party in an all-out job hunt.

If you're in this situation, you won't be alone. And if you've done career planning as suggested in Chapter 2: "Careers," you'll have a head start on finding work.

Stay in contact with classmates who are job hunting or those who have just found jobs. These people, especially those with similar career interests, can be excellent sources of referrals.

Perhaps you'll find out about an entry-level job that's related to your chosen career—but not quite the job you envisioned. Consider the possible benefits of taking it. This choice might pay off if you're weeks or months into your job search. Perhaps the position offers a chance to "step up" to a position that's more in tune with your career plan.

Tool #5: Make job hunting a full-time job

Successful job hunters know how to tap the "hidden job market"—the vast majority of openings that are never advertised. This means working as hard at your job hunt as you would at a full-time job. Plan to use many of the suggestions in this article and spend 40 hours per week on your job search.

Tool #6: Cope with emotional ups and downs

Job hunting and rejection go hand-in-hand. If you've been turned down for several job offers but are still getting interviews, then your job hunting methods are basically working well. Remember that you can perform well in an interview and still get turned down for a job, especially when there are several equally qualified applicants.

Coping with rejections can pose many challenges. Your self-confidence can crack when people don't return your calls, or when job applications disappear into the void with no response.

Whatever your feelings, take a First Step about them. There's power in telling the truth to yourself and to a good listener. You can go into more depth by writing Discovery Statements about your changing moods.

Follow up with Intention Statements about the next strategies that you will use for your job search. One cornerstone of mental health is that you can *do* something constructive even when you *feel* sad or mad. Moving into action can change your mood and bring you closer to the job you've been waiting for. ✳

Rehearse your job search

Imagine that you've completed your education as of today. Your next task is to find a job in a field of interest to you. The following questions will help you rehearse this job hunt.

If you are unsure of an answer, write down your best guess. Write your answers in the space following each question.

1. What kind of job will you apply for? If you choose self-employment, what product or service will you offer?

2. Where will you go to find a job? Will you approach an existing company or choose self-employment? If you opt for self-employment, how will you find potential customers or clients?

3. What kind of training, education, and experience is required for the kind of work that you want?

4. Next, visualize your job interview. Who will interview you? What questions will this person ask? What questions will you ask the interviewer?

5. Will this job be your "dream job"? If not, how long will it take you to find that ideal job?

Finally, review what you've just written. Does any of it suggest changes to make in your current course work or major? If so, describe the specific changes you intend to make.

WORKING

12

Tell everyone you know: The art of networking

NETWORKING MEANS STAYING in touch with people to share career-planning ideas and track job openings. It's possible that more jobs are filled through networking than through any other method.

Start by listing contacts

A *contact* is anyone who can help you implement your career plan. Contacts can include classmates, roommates, teachers, friends, relatives, and *their* friends. You can also add to the list former employers current employers, and people who met you for information interviews.

Start your contact list now. List each person's name, phone number, and e-mail address on a separate 3×5 card or Rolodex card. Another option is to keep your list on a computer, using word processing, database, or contact management software.

Whenever you speak to someone on your contact list, make brief notes about what you discussed. You should also jot down any further actions you'll take to follow up on your discussion.

Craft your "elevator speech"

Develop a short statement of your career plan that you can easily share with people. Make it short enough to deliver in 30 seconds or less. This is what you will say if someone asks "What do you do?" while you're riding an elevator or waiting in line to grab a cup of coffee.

An effective elevator speech has three main parts. First, state your name. (So far, so good.) Second, say what you do in an intriguing way, focusing on the main benefit that you create. Third, explain in a more straightforward way how you create that benefit.

For example: "I am Tanisha Jones. My job is to help people think *inside* the box. My company helps people and businesses find off-site storage space."

Write out your speech. Revise and rehearse it until it sounds natural.

By the way, avoid "I am a government fund-raiser." That's already been taken by an IRS agent.

Meet contacts in person

Any gathering of people—from a family gathering to a chance conversation at the bus stop—can become a place and time to network. Of course, formal gatherings such as an alumni event at your school are great places to network.

(hand) Photodisc

Consider joining a professional association related to your career plan. These exist for just about every profession, from the American Dental Association to the Association for Women in Communication. These groups are tailor-made for networking. Many associations have student chapters, and perhaps one already meets on your campus.

When you talk to people, avoid asking for a job outright. Instead, say something like, "I'm in the job market right now" or, "If you hear about anyone who's hiring, would you please keep me in mind?"

Have some business cards printed with your name and contact information. This makes it easy for people to follow up with you when they *do* hear of something.

Another way to connect people is through the Internet. LinkedIn is designed for professional networking, and Facebook and Twitter are being used for the same purpose. Search for blogs related to your career and notice who comments on articles. You might be able to find contact information for these people through a search engine such as pipl (**pipl.com**), PeekYou (**www.peekyou.com**), or wink (**wink.com**).

Remember that networking is a two-way street. See if you can share information that will help people meet *their* career goals. Ask them what kind of work they'd like to be doing one year, five years, and even ten years from today. Then listen fully to what they say. When you allow people to talk about the kinds of jobs that excite them, you help them create a compelling and detailed vision for the future. This is a form of contribution. Furthermore, when you can put people in touch with someone *you* know, you add even more value to the relationship. ✳

Write a résumé that gets noticed

A RÉSUMÉ IS A PIECE OF PERSUASIVE WRITING, not a laundry list of previous jobs or a dry recitation of facts. This document has one purpose: to get you to the next step in the hiring process, usually an interview.

When writing a résumé, consider your audience. Picture a person who has a hundred résumés to plow through, and almost no time for it. She may spend only 20 seconds scanning each résumé before making a decision about who to call for interviews. Your goal is to get past this first cut. Neatness, organization, and correct grammar and punctuation are essential. Meet these goals, and then make an even stronger impression with the following strategies.

There is no formula for a great résumé. Employers have many different preferences for what they want to see. Just remember that an effective résumé does two things. First, it states how you can benefit a potential employer. Second, it offers evidence that you can deliver those benefits. Make sure that every word in your résumé serves those goals.

The following suggestions will guide you through a common résumé format. Plan to keep revising your résumé and see which version generates the most interviews.

Let people know how to contact you

Start your résumé with contact information. This includes your name, mailing address, e-mail address, and phone number. If you have a Web site, add that as well.

State your objective

Many résumés follow the contact information with an *objective*. This is a description of the job that you want. Keep this to one sentence, and tailor it to the specific position for which you're applying.

Craft your objective to get attention. Ask yourself: *From an employer's perspective, what kind of person would make an ideal candidate for this job?* Then write your objective to directly answer this question with two or three specific qualities that you can demonstrate.

Focus the objective on what you can do for the employer. Here is the first place to state the benefits you can deliver. Avoid self-centered phrases like "a job in the software industry where I can develop my sales skills." Instead, state your objective as "a sales position for a software company that wants to continually generate new customers and exceed its revenue goals."

Highlight your experience and education

Follow your objective with the body of your résumé. Common headings are *experience* and *education*.

Write your "experience" section carefully. Here is where you give a few relevant details about your past jobs, listed in order. This is the heart of a *chronological* résumé.

Employers pay special attention to this section. They read it with several questions in mind: How long did you stay at each job? Were your jobs related? Did you develop new skills and gain new responsibilities over time? What kind of contribution can you make to our company?

List details that answer these questions. Include your past job titles, names of your employers, and job duties. Whenever possible, use phrases that start with an active verb when describing your duties: "*supervised* three people," "*generated* leads for sales calls," "*wrote* speeches and *edited* annual reports," "*designed* a process that reduced production expenses by 20 percent."

Active verbs refer directly to your skills. Make them relevant to the job you're seeking, and tie them to specific accomplishments whenever possible. Be prepared to discuss these accomplishments during a job interview.

Note: An alternative to the chronological format is the *functional* résumé. It highlights the functions, or skills, that you developed and used rather than the jobs you held. This format might be useful for people with limited experience or gaps in their work history.

End your résumé by listing any degree(s) that you attained beyond high school. Mention your academic major here, along with any minors you may have. If you achieved any honors or gained other recognition while you were in school, include that as well.

WORKING

12

Cut the fluff

Leave out information that could possibly eliminate you from the hiring process and send your résumé hurtling into the circular file. Some items to consider for deletion include:

- Boilerplate language—stock wording or vague phrases such as "proven success in a high-stress environment," "highly motivated self-starter," or "a demonstrated capacity for strategic thinking."
- The date you're available to start a new job.
- Salary information, including what you've earned in the past and want to earn now.
- Details about jobs you held over 10 years ago.
- Reasons for leaving previous jobs.

Note that employers cannot legally discriminate against job applicants based on personal information such as age, national origin, race, religion, disability, and pregnancy status. Including this kind of information on your résumé might even hurt your job prospects. To learn more about types of job discrimination, access the U.S. Equal Employment Opportunity Commission (EEOC) at **www.eeoc.gov**. This Web site also explains how to file a charge of discrimination.

Get feedback

Ask friends and family members if your résumé is persuasive and easy to understand. You should also get feedback from someone at your school's career-planning center. Revise your résumé based on their comments. Then revise some more. Create sparkling prose that will intrigue a potential employer enough to call you for an interview.

Get noticed in the digital world

While you're preparing a résumé, take a break to type your name into an Internet search engine such as Google and see what results you get. These search results make up your larger résumé in the digital world.

Begin by keeping your career plan in mind when you use sites such as Facebook, MySpace, and Twitter. Future employers will check these sites to learn about you, so remember this when you post content. Add updates about your academic achievements, extracurricular activities, and internships.

In addition, create a personal Web site with samples of your work and information about your career goals. Consider adding a blog and writing a post every two weeks or so. Search for blogs by people with similar interests and add constructive comments to their posts.

Combine your résumé with other strategies

If you just send out résumés and neglect to make personal contacts, you will be disappointed with the results. Instead, research companies and do informational interviews. Contact potential employers directly—even if they don't have a job opening at the moment. Find people who have the power to hire you. Then use every job contact you have to introduce yourself to those people and schedule an interview. To get the most from your résumé, use it to support a variety of job-hunting strategies. ✳

 Get more tips for résumé writing.

Keys to scannable résumés

Write your résumé so that it's easy to skim. Make key facts leap off the page. Use short paragraphs and short sentences. Use bulleted lists for key points.

Also avoid filling the page with ink. Instead, leave some blank space between the major sections of your résumé.

Many companies use software to scan résumés and search for keywords. Including appropriate keywords on your résumé can help it stand out from others. Review job postings to find common terms used in your career and include these words on your résumé.

Print your scannable résumé on one side of an 8½" × 11" sheet of plain white paper with an easy-to-read font and layout. If your résumé is more than one page in length, be sure your name and contact information appear on both sheets of paper. Avoid using italics, boldface, or underlining and other special text formatting.

Do not staple or fold your résumé. Instead, deliver it by hand or send it in an oversized envelope.

If you plan to submit your résumé via e-mail or post it online, then save a plain text version of it (.txt). Review this file for any formatting errors and correct them.

12

Sample résumés

Susan Chang
susangeorgia276@aol.com
2500 North Highland Avenue, Atlanta, GA 30306
770-899-8707

Objective: A position as a personal banker that blends customer service, product development, and programs to increase customer loyalty.

Work Experience: **LAND Enterprises, Inc., Atlanta, GA**
Administrative Assistant: January 2008–present
- Support national sales manager and three district managers in creating monthly reports for nationwide sales staff.
- Create, prepare, and maintain Excel spreadsheets with weekly sales data.
- Manage calendars of events for 20 sales representatives in Lotus Notes database.

Peachtree Bank, Macon, GA
Teller: May 2002–December 2007
- Received deposits, processed withdrawals, and accepted loan payments.
- Communicated with customers and provided account balance and savings and loan information.
- Trained new employees in customer service.

Education: **Macon State Community College, Macon, GA**
AA—Communications and Information Technology, May 2007
Overall GPA—3.0

Volunteer: **Macon Chamber of Commerce**
Events Coordinator 2000–2006
- Managed Chamber of Commerce budget for social events.
- Raised money from local businesses to support 70 events over 7 years.
- Exceeded fund-raising goals for 3 consecutive years.

Computer Skills: Microsoft Word, Microsoft Excel, Microsoft Access, Lotus Notes, PowerPoint.

Lamont Jackson
2250 First Avenue, #3 • New York, NY 10029 • (212) 222-5555
Lamont_Jackson44@hotmail.com

OBJECTIVE
Work as a public relations associate for a firm developing new media for social marketing.

EDUCATION
Rutgers University, New Brunswick, NJ
BA in English, minor in Business Communication; May 2010
Major GPA — 3.2; Minor GPA — 3.3

EXPERIENCE
The Medium, Rutgers University, New Brunswick, NJ
Contributing Writer, August 2008 to May 2010
- Wrote and edited feature articles about campus programs to promote diversity and cultural competence.
- Wrote weekly feature about developments in social networking.

Shandwick Public Relations, New York, NY
Intern, Summer 2008
- Coordinated biweekly mass mailings of press releases to medical community.
- Conducted health surveys focusing on nutrition habits of senior citizens in the tri-state area; organized data from 1,000 respondents.
- Answered telephone inquiries from Shandwick clients.

ACTIVITIES
- Intramural Soccer Team, Spring 2009
- Habitat for Humanity, *Treasurer*, Fall 2008–Spring 2009
- Rutgers University Orientation Leader, Summer 2008

TECHNICAL SKILLS
- Working knowledge of PC and Macintosh platforms and Microsoft Office software.
- Expertise in using third-party software for Twitter, Facebook, MySpace, and other social networking Web sites.
- Fluency in Spanish—oral and written competency.

HONORS
Rutgers University Dean's List, Fall 2007, Spring 2010

Sell your résumé with an effective cover letter

AN EFFECTIVE COVER LETTER can leave a prospective employer waiting with bated breath to read your résumé. An ineffective letter, however, can propel your résumé to a stack of papers to be read "later." In some cases, a well-written letter alone can land you an interview.

Many cover letters are little more than a list of stock phrases. In essence, they say: "I want that job you listed. Here's my résumé. Read it, dude."

You can avoid this trap. Present your cover letter as a response to a specific job opening—not just a form letter. Also write with a tone that's professional *and* conversational. Avoid jargon such as "attached please find my résumé for your perusal," or "I am writing in regard to the aforementioned position." Sound like a human being instead.

Remember the primary question in an employer's mind: What do you have to offer us? Using a three-part structure can help you answer this question.

1. Gain attention

In your first sentence, address the person who can hire you and grab that person's attention. Make a statement that appeals directly to her self-interest. Write something that moves a potential employer to say, "We can't afford to pass this person up. Call him right away to set up an appointment."

To come up with ideas for your opening, complete the following sentence: "The main benefit that I can bring to your organization are. . . ." Another option: "My work experience ties directly to several points mentioned in your job description. First, ..."

Perhaps someone the employer knows told you about this job opening. Mention this person in your opening paragraph, especially if she has a positive reputation in the organization.

2. Build interest

Add a fact or two to back up your opening sentence. If you're applying for a specific job opening, state this. If you're not, then offer an idea that will intrigue the employer enough to respond anyway. Another option is to give a summary of your key qualifications for a specific job. Briefly refer to your experience and highlight a few key achievements.

3. Take care of business

Refer the reader to your résumé. Mention that you'll call at a specific point to follow up. Then make good on your promise.

Use these additional suggestions for making your cover letter a "must read":

- Address your letter to a specific individual. Make sure to use the correct title and mailing address. Mistakes in such details could detract from your credibility.

- Use a simple typeface that is easy to read.

- Tailor each letter you write to the specific company and position you are applying for.

- Be honest. During an interview, an employer may choose to ask you questions about information you present in your résumé or cover letter. Be prepared to expand upon and support your statements. The ability to do this enhances your reputation as an ethical employee.

- Thank your reader for her time and consideration.

- Check for typographical, grammatical, and word usage errors. Do not rely on your computer to spell check.

- Ask someone to read your letter before you send it out. An extra pair of eyes may help you uncover errors.

- Use high-quality paper stock for your hard-copy letters.

- When sending cover letters via e-mail, use a meaningful subject header and a professional tone. Do not use emoticons like :-). Be sure to include your phone number in case the contact prefers to follow up with you via phone.

- When faxing a cover letter and résumé, indicate the total number of pages in the transmission.

Like your résumé, your cover letters may never hit paper. Chances are that they will be processed digitally. With this fact in mind, write cover letters that include no special formatting—boldface, italics, special fonts, and so on. Save a plain text (.txt) version of each cover letter. (Plain text files are most easily read across computer systems.) Inspect it to ensure that there are no stray characters or formatting errors. ✱

WORKING

12

Sample cover letters

Example 1

My recent experience qualifies me as a candidate for editorial assistant at *Seventeen* magazine. I held three positions at my college's alumni magazine: features editor, campus correspondent, and copy editor. In my senior year, I initiated a new section in our magazine, *Style File*, featuring local clothing and accessories stores. A similar section presenting fashion from different cities across the nation would be an intriguing addition to your magazine. More details about my experience are in my résumé.

I will call you in a few days to see if we can schedule a time to talk in person. At that time I can share with you my writing portfolio. Thank you.

Example 2

The position of program coordinator at the UC International House interests me because I have skills that are well suited for working with people from many countries. I am fluent in Spanish, French, and English. As explained in the attached résumé, I've taken specific courses to support those skills. In addition, my experience as a vendor in an Argentina zoo and my current job as unit manager at the UN Communications Center are two examples of the diverse background I would bring to this position.

As directed in the job announcement, I am requesting an appointment for an interview on March 28, between 2 p.m. and 6 p.m., at a time convenient for you. Please contact me if another time is more appropriate. Thank you for your time and consideration.

Example 3

Your Chief Financial Officer, Elena Perez, told me recently that you were looking for an MIS director. Because of my background, she encouraged me to contact you directly. I am impressed with the growth of your company during the last two years. With that kind of expansion, I can understand your need to create a separate MIS department.

My current position for Murphy and Sons, LLP, has given me a skill set that I can transfer directly to your company. Please see my résumé for more details.

I welcome the opportunity to meet with you to talk about the next step in applying for this position. Thank you for your time and consideration.

Use interviews to hire yourself an employer

JOB INTERVIEWS CAN BE EXHILARATING. They offer a way to meet new people. They give you a chance to present your skills. They can expand your network of contacts. And they can lead directly to a job that you love.

If you've written a career plan and prepared a résumé, you've already done much of the preparation for a successful interview. You probably have specific ideas about *what* job skills you want to use and *where* you want to use them. By the time you get to a job interview, you'll be able to see if the job is something that you really want. An interview is a chance for you to assess a potential job and work environment. By interviewing, you're "hiring" yourself an employer.

Prepare for common questions

Job interviewers ask many questions. Most of them boil down to a few major concerns:

- Would we be comfortable working with you?
- How did you find out about us?
- How can you help us?
- Will you learn to do this job quickly?
- What makes you different from other applicants?

Before your interview, rehearse some answers to questions such as these. Answer each question directly. Know the main points you want to make, and be brief.

To make the most favorable impression on an interviewer, avoid canned answers. These are easy to detect. Remember that genuine enthusiasm for a job counts as much as carefully composed answers. Before convincing an employer that you want a job and can do the job, convince yourself. When you're authentic, it will show.

If you get turned down for the job after your interview, write a Discovery Statement that describes your feelings about this event. You can also describe what you learned from the experience. Follow up with an Intention Statement that describes how you can interview more effectively next time. Every interview is a source of feedback about what works—and what doesn't work—when meeting with employers.

© Thinkstock/Alamy

Start on a positive note

Many interviewers make their decision about an applicant early on. These decisions can come within the first five minutes of the interview.

With this in mind, start on a strong note. Do everything you can to create a positive impression early in the interview. Even if you're nervous, you can be outgoing and attentive. Explain how your research led you to the company. Focus on how you can contribute to the employer. Talk about skills or experiences that make you stand out from the crowd of other applicants.

Once you hit a positive note, do everything possible to stay there. When speaking about other people, for example, be courteous. If you find it hard to say something positive about a previous coworker or supervisor, shift the focus back to the interviewer's questions.

Manage nonverbal language

One way to create a favorable first impression is through the way you look. Be well groomed. Wear clothing that's appropriate for the work environment.

Also give a firm handshake and make eye contact (without looking like a zombie). Sit in a way that says you're at ease with people and have a high energy level. During the interview, seize opportunities to smile or even tell an amusing story, as long as it's relevant and positive.

Find common ground

As the interview gets rolling, search for common ground. Finding out that you share an interest in jazz guitar with an interviewer can make the conversation sail—and put you closer to a job offer.

Be here now

You can demonstrate interest through focused attention. Listen carefully to everything interviewers say. Few of them will mind if you take notes. This might even impress them.

Offer your skills as solutions

As the interviewer speaks, listen for challenges that the company faces. Then paint yourself as someone who can help meet those challenges. Explain how you've solved similar problems in the past—and what you can do for the employer right now. To support your claims, mention a detail or two about your accomplishments and refer the interviewer to your résumé for more.

If you really want to get an interviewer's attention, then adopt the mindset of someone who *already works for the company* and has a solution to offer. For example: "I've already found a way to double the traffic to this company's Web site. The first step we could take is to. . . ."

When appropriate, take the initiative

The interviewer might be uncomfortable with her role. Few people have training in this skill. Interviewers may dominate the conversation, interrupt you, or forget what they want to ask.

When things like this happen, take the initiative. Ask for time to get your questions answered. Sum up your qualifications, and ask for a detailed job description.

Ask open-ended questions and listen

Come with your own list of questions for the interviewer. Skilled interviewers will leave time for these. Some questions you can consider asking are:

- If I take this job, what kind of training will it include?
- Does this job offer opportunities for advancement?
- Who would be my supervisor, and to whom does that person report?
- Who would be my direct coworkers, and can you tell me a little about them?
- Can I have a short tour of the area where I'd be working?
- What would be the best way for me to follow up on this interview?

After you ask a question, give the interviewer plenty of time to talk. Listen at least 50 percent of the time.

If the interview has gone well, consider asking one more question: "Do you have any concerns about hiring me?" Some variations of this question are "What

 Go online to discover more job-hunting strategies.

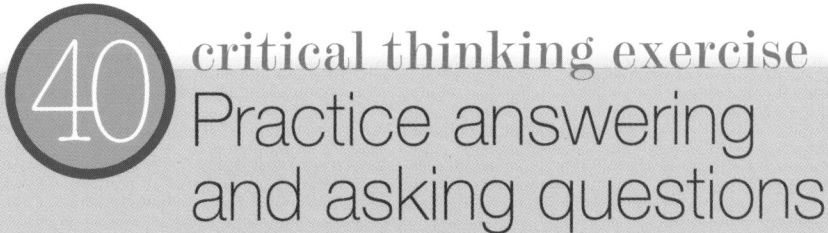

critical thinking exercise
40 Practice answering and asking questions

Before your next job interview, set up situations where you can practice answering common interview questions. Enroll a friend to play the part of an interviewer and ask you the following:

Tell me about yourself.

What are your most important strengths?

What are your most important areas for improvement?

Why do you want this job?

Why should I hire you?

Why did you leave your previous job?

What do you see yourself doing five years from now?

What was a key problem you faced on your last job, and how did you solve it?

How well do you get along with people?

You can prepare your answers to these questions by focusing on keywords from the four learning style questions explained in Chapter 1: "First Steps." In other words, your job during an interview is to explain *Why* you are an ideal candidate for the job, *What* skills and experience you bring to the company, *How* well you will get along with other employees, and *What* specific benefits an employer can expect to gain *if* she hires you.

During your practice interview, keep your speaking brief and to the point. See if you can respond to each question in two minutes or less.

Be alert to any inconsistencies in your answers. For example, if you say that you're a "team player" but prefer to work independently, be prepared to explain. When you're done, ask your friend for feedback about your answers.

happens next?" and "Based on our conversation today, would you be willing to offer me this job?"

Some interviewers might see these questions as too bold. Others might see them as a sign of initiative and give you an honest answer. The benefit is that you get a chance to address their concerns immediately. The very fact that you asked such a question could distinguish you from other applicants.

Give yourself a raise before you start work

Effective salary discussion can make a huge difference to your financial well-being. Consider the long-term impact of making just an extra $1,000 per year. Over the next decade, that's an extra $10,000 dollars in pretax income, even if you get no other raises.

It's possible to discuss salary too early in the interview process. Let the interviewer bring up this topic. In many cases, an ideal time to talk about salary is when the interviewer is ready to offer you a job. This often takes place during a second or even third interview. At this point the employer might be willing to part with some more money.

Many interviewers use a standard negotiating strategy: They come to the interview with a salary range in mind. Then they offer a starting salary at the lower end of that range.

This strategy holds an important message for you: Salaries are sometimes flexible. You do not have to accept the first salary offer.

When you finally get down to money, be prepared. Begin by knowing the income that you want. First, figure out how much money you need to maintain your desired standard of living. Then add some margin for comfort. If you're working a job that's comparable to the one you're applying for, consider adding 10 percent to your current salary. As you do this, take into account the value of any benefits the employer provides. Also consider stating a desired salary range at first rather than a fixed figure.

Find out the salary range for the job you want. This information might be available online. Start with America's Career InfoNet at **www.careerinfonet.org** and click on Occupation Information. You can also go to your favorite Internet search engine and key in the term *salary ranges*.

Other sources of salary information are friends who work in your field and notes from your informational interviews. Another option is the obvious one—directly asking interviewers what salary range they have in mind.

Once you know that range, aim higher rather than lower. Name a figure toward the upper end and see how the interviewer responds. Starting high gives you some room to negotiate. See if you can get a raise now rather than later.

Salary negotiation gives you an opening to ask about benefits. Depending on the company and the job involved, these might include vacation time, health insurance, life insurance, disability plans, use of a company car, reimbursement for travel expenses, retirement plans, and tuition reimbursement.

Use each *no* to come closer to *yes*

Almost everyone who's ever applied for a job knows the lines: "We have no job openings right now." "We'll keep your résumé on file." "There were many qualified applicants for this position." "Even though you did not get the job, thanks for applying." "Best of luck to you as you pursue other career opportunities."

Each of those statements is a different way of saying no. And they can hurt.

However, *no* does not have to be the final word. Focus on the future. If you're turned down for one job, consider ways to turn that *no* into a *yes* next time. Could you present yourself differently during the interview? Could you do more thorough research? Can you fine-tune your career goals? You might even ask the interviewer for suggestions. Also ask for referrals to other companies that might be hiring.

Think about what a job rejection really means. It's not an eternal judgment of your character. It only reflects what happened between you and one potential employer, often over just a few hours or even a few minutes. It means no for right now, for this job, for today—not for every job, forever.

Eventually, an employer or client will hire you. It's just a matter of time before the inevitable *yes*. When you're turned down for a job, that is just one more *no* that's out of the way. ✳

WORKING

Finding work in a tough job market

"Wow, this is a tough market—there just aren't any jobs out there." That statement sounds reasonable, especially during a recession. There's just one problem: It's not true.

WHILE EMPLOYMENT RATES RISE AND FALL, certain facts about the workforce remain constant: People retire, shift to part-time work, quit working to raise a family, or die. Other people get promoted to new jobs, which leaves their old jobs vacant. In addition, new businesses are starting up and hiring. The fact is, there are *always* jobs out there.

To cope with a tough economy, begin with the idea that you are in charge. Be willing to work hard at your job search and give it plenty of time. Then experiment with the following strategies.

Create a personal safety net

Review the suggestions in Chapter 10: "Money" for earning more money, spending less money, and saving any money that's left over. If you set aside enough to live on for several months after losing a job, then you can approach tough times with peace of mind. Even if you do not succeed at saving money, you will gain skills at living more simply.

Focus on creating value

When you're job hunting, the first thing that probably comes to your mind is *I need work*. See if you can shift your conversation to *I create value*. This means taking an inventory of your technical and transferable skills and finding out which jobs allow you to use those skills. (See Chapter 2: "Careers.") Document how you used those skills in the past to solve problems, reduce costs, develop new products or services, or create value in other ways for employers. Armed with this self-knowledge, you can approach your job search with more confidence.

Clarify what you want

Imagine that someone approaches you at a networking event and says, "I need a job—do you know of any?" Later, someone else walks up to you and says, "I am a journalist with 10 years of experience as a business reporter. I'm starting a new career as a freelance writer and I'd like to meet editors of Web sites and community newspapers with a business focus. Could you please let me know if you hear of any?" Chances are that you'll find the second person easier to answer than the first one.

To get the job that you want, know exactly what you want. Be able to explain the work that you're looking for in precise terms. The more details that you provide, the easier you make it for other people to assist you.

Take charge of your personal presence

No matter how you feel about your job search, you can add a personal touch. Express appreciation to everyone who mentions a job opening. Write thank-you notes to job interviewers.

In addition, take the time to define the skills that you are passionate about using. Faced with a choice between a job candidate who has the necessary skills and one who has the skills *plus* enthusiasm, an employer is more likely to choose the latter.

Use a new approach

When people say "There are no jobs," maybe what they really mean is, "My current job hunting method is not working." There's a world of difference between those statements. The first one kills options. The second one *creates* options. If your current job-hunting method is not working, then you can always use another method.

During your job search, take an hour each week to reflect on your current strategies. If you're relying on classified ads to find job openings, for example, then do more networking next week. If you've been posting your résumé online and waiting for responses, then consider making more phone calls.

Even in the best job market, there will be competition for jobs. Use tough times to experiment with new strategies and get more skilled at job hunting. One key to staying positive during tough times is always to have another option at hand. ✳

Succeeding as a new employee

YOUR FIRST YEAR at a new job represents a distinct stage in your life, especially if it's your first job after getting a degree. You're no longer a student. Nor are you a seasoned professional in your new position. You've left one world behind and your new world is still an unknown.

The way that you manage this year might affect your entire career. Coworkers' early impressions of you can create lasting attitudes. These attitudes influence your chances for advancement, leading to long-term effects on your job satisfaction and income. Make the most of this key transition period with the following strategies.

Prepare for culture clash

If you're a new graduate and just beginning your career, prepare for a radical change. After mastering the culture of higher education, you are in a game with entirely new rules. Here are a few examples:

- You might be used to structured courses with lots of direction from teachers but find yourself in an unstructured workplace with little direction from your supervisor.

- You might be used to a flexible schedule but find yourself saddled with a tight "eight to five" schedule.

- You might thrive on mastering ideas and facts but find yourself forced to master office politics.

- You might be used to focusing on your individual development but now find yourself focusing on team results.

- You might be used to moving in groups of people who know about your academic accomplishments but now find yourself among strangers.

One powerful way to prepare for this clash of cultures is to simply know that it's coming. In addition, review the Introduction to this book for suggestions about mastering the transition to higher education. The strategies presented there—such as admitting your feelings, giving yourself time, and taking constructive action—can help you as you make *any* transition, including the transition to a new job.

Focus on attitudes first

As a new employee, your first concern might be succeeding at job *tasks*. The top questions on your mind might be: "Am I really prepared to *do* this job?" and "Can I actually complete the projects that my boss gives me?"

Meanwhile, your boss's top concern might be *attitudes*. She's probably asking herself: "Is this new person open to coaching?" and "Will he fit in with our team?" If your boss could talk candidly about her desires for "new hires," she might say: "Send me someone with a positive attitude, a work ethic, and plenty of energy. We'll teach him everything else he needs to know."

Remember that your boss scoped out your qualifications *before* you got hired. Because she hired you, she's probably confident that you can handle job tasks now or learn to do them within a reasonable period. To really shine as a new employee, remember the "soft" skills—those that relate to personality and people.

People in 12 Step programs such as Alcoholics Anonymous talk about the usefulness of HOW attitudes—Honesty, Openness, and Willingness. This is also a useful acronym for succeeding as a new employee. Here are some attitudes it points to:

- Being honest when you don't understand directions and being willing to ask questions.

- Being open to feedback about your performance and being willing to change your behavior on the basis of the feedback.

- Being willing to complete the mundane tasks that are part of almost every job and understanding what it means to "pay your dues."

Another thing to keep in mind: Technical skills help people get hired. However, the lack of transferable skills—such as listening well, speaking clearly, and thinking thoroughly—can get them fired.

Decode the culture

Every organization, large or small, develops its own culture. One way to succeed in the workplace is to "decode" corporate cultures—the basic assumptions and shared values that shape human behavior in the workplace every day.

You can use this knowledge to prevent misunderstanding, resolve conflict, and forge lasting relationships.

Start by observing. Being culturally savvy starts with discovering "the way we do things around here"—the beliefs and behaviors that are widely shared by your coworkers. In terms of the cycle of learning explained in Chapter 1: "First Steps," this means that your efforts to decode corporate culture begin with the stage of reflective observation.

In other words, keep your eyes open. See what actions are rewarded and which are punished. Observe what people do and say to gain credibility in your organization.

WORKING

12

You may disagree with what you see and find yourself making negative judgments about your coworkers. Start by noticing those judgments and letting them go. You cannot fully observe behaviors and judge them at the same time. Play the role of a social scientist and collect facts impartially.

Create theories about unwritten rules. Next, create theories about how people succeed in your organization. In terms of the learning cycle, this is the stage of abstract conceptualization. In particular, notice the unwritten "rules" that govern your workplace. Your coworkers may behave on the basis of beliefs such as:

- Never make the boss look bad.
- Some commitments are not meant to be kept.
- If you want to get promoted, then be visible.
- Everyone is expected to work some overtime.
- Before you try to change the rules around here, prove that you know what you're doing.
- Before we assign you to a big project, build a solid track record of small successes.

Once you understand the norms and standards of your company, you can consciously choose to accept them. You can also choose to challenge them by actively

Surviving your first day

You've landed a new job. Congratulations! Now prepare to walk into the office and make a place for yourself.

Well-meaning people may advise you to "just be yourself" when you show up for your first day of work. Following are a few more specifics.

Dress the part Many students cultivate an eclectic wardrobe that won't pass the test for a new job. Even employers with "casual days" prefer to meet new employees in standard business attire. Think back to what people in the office were wearing when you showed up for your job interview. To make a positive impression, put special effort into looking your best on your first day.

Arrive early Don't underestimate the power of this simple suggestion. Arriving late for your first day of work sends mixed messages. To you, it may be a simple mistake. Your supervisor might interpret it as being careless or having an "attitude." Remove all possibility of misunderstanding by showing up with at least 15 minutes to spare.

Notice your "nonverbals" Remember to shake hands firmly and say hello in a friendly voice. Make eye contact and smile. Also check out your other nonverbal messages. In meetings, for example, check to see if your posture says, *I'm here now and paying attention to what you say.*

Remember names Occasionally, we find ourselves in situations where we're introduced to many people at the same time: "Let's take a tour so you can meet all 32 people in this department."

When meeting a group of people, concentrate on remembering just two or three names. Free yourself from feeling obligated to remember everyone. Few of the people in mass introductions expect you to remember their names.

Another way to avoid memory overload is to limit yourself to learning just first names. Last names can come later.

In some cases, you might be able to get photos of the people you meet on your first day at work. For example, a small business where you apply for a job might have a brochure with employee pictures.

Ask for individual or group photos and write in the names if they're not included. You can use these photos as "flash cards" as you drill yourself on names.

Take notes During your first day you'll cover lots of details. First, there's the obvious stuff—where to sit, where to park, where to eat, where to make photocopies, where to take breaks, where to go to the bathroom. Then there's the higher level stuff, such as phone numbers, user IDs, and passwords for Internet access.

Be prepared with paper and pen to write this stuff down. Besides aiding your memory, taking notes gives you something to do with your hands if you feel nervous.

Pack a briefcase Companies just love to push paper at new employees—brochures, forms, maps, manuals, and more. When you receive this stuff, look at it for a few seconds. This communicates in a small and significant way that you pay attention to details. Then place the papers in a professional-looking folder or briefcase.

Go easy on yourself Notice whether there's a self-critical voice in your head that's saying something like: "You're not fooling anyone—you really have no idea what you're doing here." No one else hears that voice, just like no one expects you to perform to perfection on your first day. If you hear a self-critical voice, just notice it and let it go.

Do not say these words: "Wow, that's not how we did things at my last job" This invites an inevitable response: "Well, then why did you leave that job?" Expect procedures to differ from job to job, and look for chances to suggest improvements in the future.

experimenting with new behaviors and immersing yourself in new experiences. In any case, changing any organization begins with a First Step—telling the truth about how it works right now.

Cope with office politics. The unspoken rules for getting recognized and rewarded are usually what people mean when they talk about *office politics*. One way to deal with office politics is to pretend they don't exist. The downfall of this strategy is that politics are a fact of life.

Another option is to be politically savvy *and* still hold fast to your values. You can move through the echelons of power and meet ethical career goals at the same time. Here are some specific strategies:

- *Grow "industry-smart."* Read trade journals and newsletters related to your field. Keep up with current developments. Speak the language shared by the decision makers in your organization.

- *Promote your boss.* During your first year with an organization, the single most important person in your work life could be your boss. This is the person who most closely monitors your performance. This is also the person who can become your biggest advocate. Find out what this person needs and wants. Learn about her goals and then assist her to meet them.

- *Get close to the power centers.* People who advance to top positions are often those who know the language of sales, marketing, accounting, and information technology. These departments are power centers. They directly affect the bottom line. You can enhance your company's profitability no matter what position you hold. Look for ways to save money and time. Suggest workable ways to streamline procedures or reduce costs. Focus on solutions to problems, no matter how small, and you'll play the ultimate political game—making a contribution.

- *Be visible.* To gain credibility in your organization, get involved in a high-profile project that you believe in. Then perform well. Go beyond the minimum standards. Meet the project goals—and deliver even more. ✳

journal entry 28

Discovery/Intention Statement

Create a new perspective on your work

You can use this journal entry any time that you feel unhappy at work. Complete the following sentences, using additional paper as needed. To spark your creative thinking, see "Loving Your Next Job" on page 342.

I discovered that:

If I could change one thing about this job, I would . . .

_____

_____

_____

Something I *do* like about this job is . . .

_____

_____

_____

The transferable skills I am learning on this job include . . .

_____

_____

_____

The technical skills that I am learning on this job include . . .

_____

_____

_____

Some aspects of this job that I do not control include . . .

_____

_____

_____

Some aspects of this job that I *do* control include . . .

_____

_____

_____

I intend to make this job more satisfying by . . .

_____

_____

_____

Learning on the job

BESIDES A PAYCHECK, the workplace offers constant opportunities for learning. Employers value the person who is a "quick study"—someone who can get up to speed at a new job in minimum time. In addition, some of the information you acquired in school might become quickly outdated. Learning how to learn—a key transferable skill—is a necessity if you want to survive in the job market and advance in your career.

Let go of old ideas about learning. Educational literature is full of distinctions such as "theory versus application" and "beginner versus advanced." These distinctions are useful. But if you want to learn on the job, you can often benefit by letting them go. In workplace-based learning, for example:

- There is no "finish" line such as a graduation ceremony. Rather, you learn continuously, taking periodic progress checks to assess your current skills.
- Outside of formal training programs, there are no course divisions. A new job might call on you to integrate knowledge of several subjects at once.
- There is no syllabus for learning a subject with assignments carefully laid out in a planned sequence. You might learn concepts in an "illogical" order as dictated by the day-to-day demands of a job.

If all this sounds like a prescription for chaos, consider that it reflects the ways you've always learned outside the classroom. Teaching yourself anything from a new golf swing to a new song on the guitar has a lot in common with the way you teach yourself on the job.

Seize informal opportunities to learn. At work, your learning may take place in unplanned, informal ways. Look for opportunities to do the following:

- Do self-directed reading on topics related to new job tasks.
- Observe people who demonstrate a skill that you would like to develop.
- Ask questions on the spot.
- Attend trade shows for new products or services offered by your company's competitors.
- Join professional organizations in your field that offer workshops and seminars.

image100/Alamy

- Make yourself into the company expert on a new product or procedure by digging into brochures, Web sites, professional journals, technical manuals, and other sources of information that your coworkers may have overlooked.

Create a development plan. Some organizations require their employees to create a professional development plan. If your employer does not require such a plan, create one anyway. You can do this by answering several "W questions":

- *What* skill or specialized base of knowledge is most essential for you to acquire now in order to do your job more effectively?
- *Who* has acquired this knowledge or demonstrated this skill and would be willing to share their expertise? Perhaps one of these people would be willing to mentor you.
- If learning your desired knowledge or skill requires experiences outside your work environment, *where* will you go to pursue those experiences? Answers might include a night class at a local business school or a company-sponsored training session.
- *When* would you like to demonstrate mastery of your new knowledge or skill? Give yourself a due date for meeting each professional development goal.

In addition, ask *how* you will know that you've mastered the new knowledge or skill. List specifically what you will say or do differently as a result of your development.

As you answer these questions, keep focused. If you try to develop too many skills at once, you might end with few gains over the long run. Consider setting and achieving one major development goal each year.

Act on your plan every day. Remember that the word *learning* is often defined as an enduring change in behavior. Focus on a new work-related behavior— such as creating a to-do list or overcoming procrastination—that will make a significant, positive, and immediate difference in your performance. Then do it. Every day, implement one new behavior or practice one new habit. In the workplace, learning means doing. ✳

Working with a mentor

ONE STRATEGY FOR planning your career and succeeding in the workplace is to find a mentor—a partner in your professional and personal development. Many people will be flattered to take on such a role in your life.

Start with a development plan

Before you ask someone to mentor you, reflect on your goals for this relationship. Begin with *what* you want to gain rather than *who* to ask for mentoring. List the specific skills that you want to develop with a mentor's involvement. Over time you might work with several mentors, each with different expertise, to develop a variety of skills.

For maximum clarity, put your development plan in writing. Consider using the Discovery and Intention Journal Entry System. Write Discovery Statements to list your current skills, recent examples of how you've used them, and insights from your mentor.

Whenever possible, create a way to measure your progress. For example, you could note the number of times you practice a new habit. Or you could summarize ratings from your performance reviews at work. Include these measurements in your Discovery Statements and share them with your mentor.

Follow up with Intention Statements that describe exactly what new behaviors you want to implement, along with ongoing updates to your development plan.

In your Intention Statements, include a timeline. Use your goal-setting skills to set due dates for acquiring new skills or producing new outcomes in your life. Also state when you want to begin and end the mentoring sessions. Keep in mind that many mentoring relationships are short-term, taking place over weeks or months rather than years.

Approach potential mentors

Identify several people who have demonstrated competence in the skills you want to gain, along with the energy and desire to take on a mentee—that is, you. If you can find someone at work who has a positive reputation and influence in your organization, that's an added plus.

Next, contact each person on your list and mention that you're seeking a mentor. Summarize your development plan and timetable. Also suggest ways that you can create value for a mentor, such as helping that person complete a project or achieve one of *his* development goals. The more you give to the mentor relationship, the more you'll get out of it.

If a potential mentor is too busy to work with you right now, ask if she can refer you to someone else. After meeting with several people, choose one person to work with.

Accept your mentor's feedback

Remember that a mentor is not a boss, parent, or taskmaster. Instead, you're looking for coaching. A coach helps you clarify your goals and then offers nonjudgmental observations of your behavior along with suggestions for improvement. However, the responsibility for your day-to-day performance and long-term development lies with you.

Schedule regular meetings with your mentor

During these meetings, put all your listening skills to work. Resist the temptation to debate, argue, or justify your behavior. Simply receive what your mentor has to say. Ask questions to clarify anything you don't understand.

Remember that when you asked for mentoring, you signed on for objective feedback and suggestions—including ideas you may have resisted in the past. A commitment to change implies the willingness to think, speak, and act in new ways. Stay open to suggestions.

Beyond listening, move into action. When your mentor offers an insight, look for an immediate way to apply it. Experiment with a new behavior every day.

Seek closure—and continue

When you've come to the end of a mentoring relationship, offer your thanks and celebrate your accomplishments. Solidify your learning by listing the top five insights or skills you gained.

In addition, choose your next step. List upcoming opportunities to practice your newly acquired skills. Also consider the benefits of working with a mentor again in the future. This is a development tool that you can use for the rest of your life. ✳

Adapting to styles in the workplace

AS THE WORKPLACE becomes more diverse and technology creates a global marketplace, you'll meet people who differ from you in profound ways. Your coworkers will behave in ways that express a variety of preferences for perceiving information, processing ideas, and acting on what they learn.

For example, consider the person who talks continually on the phone about a project. This person prefers to learn by listening, talking, and forging key relationships.

Then there's the supervisor who wants to see detailed project plans and budgets submitted in writing, well before a project swings into high gear. This person excels at abstract conceptualization.

At some point you'll probably work with a team member who always takes the initiative, manages the discussion, and delegates the work. This person prefers to lead by active experimentation.

The more you can adapt to differences in style, the more likely you are to enjoy your job, forge positive work relationships, and meet your career goals.

Look for specific clues to another person's style

You can learn a lot about other people's styles of learning simply by observing them during the work day. Consider the following:

Approaches to a task that requires learning

Some people process new information and ideas by sitting quietly and reading or writing. When learning to use a piece of equipment, such as a new computer, they'll read the instruction manual first. Others will skip the manual, unpack all the boxes, and start setting up equipment. Others might ask a more experienced colleague to guide them in person, step by step.

Word choice

Some people like to process information visually. You might hear them say, "I'll look into that" or "Give me the big picture first." Others like to solve problems verbally: "Let's talk through this problem" or "I hear you!" In contrast, some people focus on body sensations ("This product feels great") or actions ("Let's run with this idea and see what happens.").

Body language

Notice how often coworkers or classmates make eye contact with you and how close they sit or stand next to you. Observe their gestures, as well as the volume and tone of their voices.

Content preferences

Notice what subjects coworkers or classmates openly discuss and which topics they avoid. Some people talk freely about their feelings, their families, and even their personal finances. Others choose to remain silent on such topics and stick to work-related matters.

Process preferences

Look for patterns in the way that your coworkers and classmates meet goals. When attending meetings, for example, some of them might stick closely to the agenda and keep an eye on the clock. Other people might prefer to "go with the flow," even if it means working an extra hour or scrapping the agenda.

Resolve conflict with respect for styles

When people's styles clash in work settings, you have several options. One is to throw up your hands and resign yourself to "personality conflicts." Another option is to recognize differences, accept them, and discover new ways to meet common goals:

Introduce a conversation about learning styles

Attend a workshop on learning styles. Then bring such training directly to your classroom or office.

Let people take on tasks that fit their learning styles

People gravitate toward the kinds of tasks they've succeeded at in the past. Ask people for their preferences and see if you can accommodate them.

Remember that learning styles are stable *and* dynamic. People can also broaden their styles by tackling new tasks to reinforce different modes of learning.

Resolve conflict within yourself

You might have mental pictures that characterize workplaces as places where people are all "supposed" to have the same style. Notice if you have those pictures and gently let them go.

If you *expect* to find differences in styles, you can more easily respect those differences. ✳

WORKING

12

Dealing with sexism and sexual harassment

Sexism and sexual harassment are real. Incidents that are illegal or violate organizational policies occur throughout the year at schools and in workplaces.

UNTIL THE EARLY NINETEENTH CENTURY, women in the United States were banned from attending colleges and universities. Today women make up the majority of first-year students in higher education, yet they still encounter bias based on gender. Although men also can be subjects of sexism and sexual harassment, women are more likely to experience this form of discrimination.

Bias based on gender can take many forms. For example, instructors might gloss over the contributions of women. Students in philosophy class might never hear of a woman named Hypatia, an ancient Greek philosopher and mathematician. Those majoring in computer science might never learn about Rear Admiral Grace Murray Hopper, who pioneered the development of a computer language named COBOL. And your art history textbook might not mention the Mexican painter Frida Kahlo or the American painter Georgia O'Keeffe. A supervisor might assign a leadership role to a male employee despite his inexperience compared with a female coworker.

Even the most well-intentioned people might behave in ways that hurt or discount women. Sexism is a factor in these situations:

- Instructors use only masculine pronouns—*he, his,* and *him*—to refer to both men and women.
- Career counselors hint that careers in mathematics and science are not appropriate for women.
- Students pay more attention to feedback from a male teacher than from a female teacher.
- Clients assume that a male employee is in a superior position compared to a female coworker.
- Women are not called on in class, their comments are ignored, or they are overly praised for answering the simplest questions.
- People assume that middle-aged women who return to school have too many family commitments to study adequately or do well in their classes.

Many kinds of behavior—both verbal and physical—can be categorized as sexual harassment. This kind of discrimination involves unwelcome sexual conduct.

Eric Audras/Getty

Examples of such conduct in a school or workplace setting include the following:

- Sexual advances
- Any other unwanted touch
- Displaying or distributing sexually explicit materials
- Sexual gestures or jokes
- Pressure for sexual favors
- Spreading rumors about someone's sexual activity or rating someone's sexual performance

Suppose that a supervisor demands sexual favors as a condition for getting a promotion. This is an example of *quid pro quo harassment*. The term also applies when students believe that an educational decision depends on submitting to unwelcome sexual conduct. *Hostile environment harassment* takes place when such incidents are severe, persistent, or pervasive.

The feminist movement has raised awareness about both forms of harassment. We can now respond to such incidents in the places we live, work, and go to school. Specific strategies follow.

Point out sexist language and behavior. When you see examples of sexism, point them out. Your message can be more effective if you use "I" messages instead of personal attacks, as explained in Chapter 9: "Communicating."

Indicate the specific statements and behaviors that you consider sexist. To help others understand sexism, you might rephrase a sexist comment so that it targets another group, such as Jews or African Americans. People sometimes spot anti-Semitism or racism more readily than sexism.

Keep in mind that men can also be subjected to sexism, ranging from antagonistic humor to exclusion from jobs that have traditionally been done by women.

Observe your own language and behavior. Looking for sexist behavior in others is a good first step in dealing with it. Detecting it in yourself can be just as powerful. Write a Discovery Statement about specific comments that could be interpreted as sexist. Then notice if you say any of these things. Also ask people you know to point out occasions when you use similar statements. Follow up with an Intention Statement that describes how you plan to change your speaking or behavior.

You can also write Discovery Statements about the current level of intimacy (physical and verbal) in any of your relationships at home, work, or school. Be sure that any increase in the level of intimacy is mutually agreed upon.

Encourage support for women. Through networks, women can work to overcome the effects of sexism. Strategies include study groups for women, women's job networks, and professional organizations, such as the Association for Women in Communications. Other examples are counseling services and health centers for women, family planning agencies, and rape prevention centers.

If your school or workplace does not have the women's networks you want, you can help form them. Help set up a conference on women's issues. Create a discussion or reading group for the women in your class, office, department, residence hall, union, or neighborhood.

Take action. If you are sexually harassed, take action. Title IX of the Education Amendments of 1972 prohibits sexual harassment and other forms of sex discrimination. The law also requires schools to have grievance procedures in place for dealing with such discrimination. If you believe that you've been sexually harassed, report the incident to a school official. This person can be a teacher, administrator, or campus security officer. Check to see if your school has someone specially designated to handle your complaint, such as an affirmative action officer or Title IX coordinator. If the harassment occurs at work, report the incident to someone in your human resources department.

You can also file a complaint with the Office for Civil Rights (OCR), a federal agency that makes sure schools and workplaces comply with Title IX. In your complaint, include your name, address, and daytime phone number, along with the date of the incident and a description of it. Do this within 180 days of the incident. You can contact the OCR at 1-800-421-3481, or go online to **wdcrobcolp01.ed.gov/CFAPPS/OCR/contactus.cfm**.

Your community might offer more resources to protect against sexual discrimination. Examples are public interest law firms, legal aid societies, and unions that employ lawyers to represent students and individuals. ✴

Strategies for nonsexist communication

When speaking and writing, use language that includes both women and men. Following are some ways you can do this without twisting yourself into verbal knots.

1. Use gender-neutral terms Instead of *policeman* or *chairman,* for example, use *police officer* or *chairperson.* In many cases, there's no need to identify the gender or marital status of a person. This fact allows us to dispose of expressions such as *female driver, male nurse,* and *lady doctor.*

2. Use examples that include both men and women Effective writing and speaking thrives on examples and illustrations. As you search for details to support your main points, include the stories and accomplishments of women as well as men.

3. Alternate pronoun gender In an attempt to be gender fair, some people make a point of mentioning both sexes whenever they refer to gender. Another method is to alternate male and female pronouns throughout a text or speech—the strategy used in this book.

4. Switch to plural With this approach, a sentence such as *The writer has many tools at her disposal* becomes *Writers have many tools at their disposal.*

5. Avoid words that imply sexist stereotypes Included here are terms such as *tomboy, sissy, office boy, advertising man, man-eater, mama's boy, old lady,* and *powder puff.*

WORKING

12

FROM MASTER STUDENT TO MASTER EMPLOYEE 341

Loving your next job

JOB DISAPPOINTMENT has countless symptoms, including statements such as "My boss is a jerk," "I'm so bored," and "This is too hard." Faced with such sentiments, there's a tempting short-term solution: "I quit." Sometimes that is a reasonable option. In many cases of job dissatisfaction, however, there are solutions that do less damage to your immediate income and your long-term job prospects.

Manage your expectations

Instead of changing jobs, consider changing the way you think. If you were planning to run the company within six months after joining it, then perhaps your expectations were unrealistic.

Managing your expectations is especially useful if you've just graduated from school and find yourself working in an entry-level position in your field. Students who are used to stimulating class discussions and teachers with a passion for their subject might be shocked by the realities of the workplace: people who hide behind a cubicle and avoid human contact, managers with technical skills but no people skills, and coworkers who get promoted on the basis of political favors rather than demonstrated skills.

If you're unhappy at work, then review the Power Process: "Notice Your Pictures and Let Them Go" on page 159. Ask which of your work-related pictures might be related to the reasons you are upset. Perhaps you're operating on the basis of unrealistic "shoulds" such as:

- My first job after graduating *should* draw on all the skills I developed in school.
- Everyone I meet on a job *should* be interesting, competent, and kind.
- Every task that I perform at work *should* be enjoyable.
- My work environment *should* be problem-free.

See if you can replace the *should* in such statements with *can* or *could*. For example: "Even though I'm not using all my skills, I *can* use this job to learn about corporate culture and coping with office politics." Or, "I *could* use this job to develop at least one skill that I can transfer to my next job."

Practice problem solving

Sometimes you can benefit by adjusting more than your attitude. Apply your transferable skills at problem solving. Write Discovery Statements about the following:

- How you felt when you started the job.
- When you started feeling unhappy with the job.
- Any specific events that triggered your dissatisfaction.

This writing can help you pinpoint the sources of job dissatisfaction. Possibilities include conflict with coworkers, a mismatch between your skills and the job requirements, or a mismatch between your personal values and the values promoted in the workplace.

No matter what the problem, you can brainstorm solutions. Ask friends and family members for help. If you're bored with work, for example, then propose a project that will create value for your boss and offer to lead it. If your supervisor seems unhappy with your performance, ask for coaching to do better.

Reread this book for possible solutions. If you feel stressed, review the stress-management techniques in Chapter 7: "Tests" and Chapter 11: "Health." Choose at least one technique to use on a daily basis. When you're in conflict with a coworker, apply strategies for resolving conflict presented in Chapter 9: "Communicating." If you want more challenging assignments, then ask for them.

Moving into action to solve the problem leads to a key discovery: You—not your boss or coworkers—are in charge of the quality of your life.

Focus on process

Practice shifting your focus from the content of your job to the process you use—from *what* you do to *how* you do it. Even if a task seems boring or beneath you, see if you can do it impeccably and with total attention. As you do, project a professional image in everything from the way you dress to the way you speak. One strategy for handling a dead-end job is to do it so well that you get noticed and promoted to a new job. ✱

12

Leadership in a diverse world

THE U.S. CENSUS BUREAU PREDICTS that the groups once classified as minorities—Hispanics, African Americans, East Asians, and South Asians—will become the majority by the year 2042. By the year 2023, the majority of Americans under age 18 will belong to one of these groups.[3] Translation: Your next boss or coworker could be a person whose life experiences and views of the world differ radically from yours.

We live in a world where Barack Obama, a man with ancestors from Kenya and Kansas, became president of the United States; where Bobby Jindal, the son of immigrants from India, became governor of Louisiana; and where Oprah Winfrey, an African American woman, can propel a book to the top of the best seller list simply by recommending it on her television show. These people set examples of diversity in leadership that many others will follow. Prepare to apply your own leadership skills in a multicultural world.

No one is born knowing how to lead. We acquire the skills over time. To become a more effective leader, understand the many ways you can influence others. The following strategies can help you have a positive impact on your relationships with your friends, family members, and coworkers.

Own your leadership. Let go of the reluctance that many of us feel toward assuming leadership. It's impossible to escape leadership. Every time you speak, you lead others in some small or large way. Every time you take action, you lead others through your example. Every time you ask someone to do something, you are in essence leading that person. Leadership becomes more effective when it is consciously applied.

Be willing to be uncomfortable. Leadership is a courageous act. Leaders often are not appreciated or even liked. They can feel isolated—cut off from their colleagues. This isolation can sometimes lead to self-doubt and even fear. Before you take on a leadership role, be aware that you might experience such feelings. Also remember that none of them needs to stop you from leading.

Allow huge mistakes. The more important and influential you are, the more likely it is that your mistakes will have huge consequences. The chief financial officer for a large company can make a mistake that costs thousands or even millions of dollars. A physician's error could cost a life. At the same time, these people are in a position to make huge changes for the better—to save thousands of dollars or lives through their power, skill, and influence.

People in leadership positions can become paralyzed and ineffective if they fear making a mistake. It's necessary for them to act even when information is incomplete or when they know a catastrophic mistake is a possible outcome.

Take on big projects. Leaders make promises. Furthermore, effective leaders make big promises. These words—*I will do it* and *You can count on me*—distinguish a leader.

Look around your world to see what needs to be done, then take it on. Consider taking on the biggest project you can think of—ending world hunger, eliminating nuclear weapons, wiping out poverty, or promoting universal literacy. Think about how you'd spend your life if you knew that you could make a difference regarding these overwhelming problems. Then take the actions you considered. See what a difference they can make for you and for others. Campuses offer continual opportunities to gain leadership skills. Volunteer for clubs, organizations, and student government. Look for opportunities to tutor, or to become a peer advisor or mentor.

Tackle projects that stretch you to your limits—projects that are worthy of your time and talents.

Provide feedback. An effective leader is a mirror to others. Share what you see. Talk with others about what they are doing effectively—and what they are doing ineffectively.

Keep in mind that people might not enjoy your feedback. Some would probably rather not hear it at all. Two things can help. One is to let people know up front that if they sign on to work with you, they can expect feedback. Also give your feedback with skill. Use "I" messages as explained in Chapter 9: "Communicating." Back up any criticisms with specific observations and facts. When people complete a task with exceptional skill, point that out, too.

Paint a vision. Help others see the big picture—the ultimate purpose of a project. Speak a lot about the end result and the potential value of what you're doing.

There's a biblical saying: "Without vision, the people perish." Long-term goals usually involve many intermediate steps. Unless we're reminded of the purpose for those day-to-day actions, our work can feel like a grind. Leadership is the art of helping others lift their eyes to the horizon—keeping them in touch with the ultimate value and purpose of a project.

WORKING

12

Model your values. "Be the change you want to see" is a useful motto for leaders. Perhaps you want to see integrity, focused attention, and productivity in the people around you. Begin by modeling these qualities yourself. It's easy to excite others about a goal when you are enthusiastic about it yourself. Having fun while being productive is contagious. If you bring these qualities to a project, others might follow suit.

Make requests—lots of them. An effective leader is a request machine. Making requests—both large and small—is an act of respect. When we ask a lot from others, we demonstrate our respect for them and our confidence in their abilities.

At first, some people might get angry when we make requests of them. Over time, however, many will see that requests are compliments and opportunities to expand their skills. Ask a lot from others, and they might appreciate you because of it.

Follow up. What we don't inspect, people don't respect. When other people agree to do a job for you, follow up to see how it is going. You can do so in a way that communicates your respect and interest—not your fear that the project might flounder. When you display a genuine interest in other people and their work, they are more likely to view you as a partner in achieving a shared goal.

Focus on problems, not people. Sometimes projects do not go as planned. Big mistakes occur. If this happens, focus on the project and the mistakes—not the personal faults of your colleagues. People do not make mistakes on purpose. If they did, we would call them "on-purposes," not mistakes. Most people will join you in solving a problem if your focus is on the problem, not on what they did wrong.

Acknowledge others. Express genuine appreciation for the energy and creativity that others have put into their work. Take the time to be interested in what others have done and to care about the results they have accomplished. Thank and acknowledge them with your eyes, your words, and the tone of your voice.

Share credit. As a leader, constantly give away the praise and acknowledgment that you receive. When you're congratulated for your performance, pass the praise on to others. Share the credit with the group. Doing so is essential if you want to continue to count on the support of others in the future.

Delegate. Ask a coworker or classmate to take on a job that you'd like to see done. Ask the same of your family or friends. Delegate tasks to the mayor of your town, the governor of your state, and the leaders of your country.

Take on projects that are important to you. Then find people who can lead the effort. You can do this even when you have no formal role as a leader.

We often see delegation as a tool that's available only to those above us in the chain of command. Actually, delegating up or across an organization can be just as effective. Consider delegating a project to your boss. That is, ask him to take on a job that you'd like to see accomplished. It might be a job that you cannot do, given your position in the company.

Balance styles. Think for a moment about your own learning style. To lead effectively, assess your strengths and look for people who can complement them. If you excel at gathering information and setting goals, for example, then recruit people who like to make decisions and take action. You can also enlist people who think creatively and generate different points of view.

Look for different styles in the people who work with you. Remember that learning results from a balance between reflection, action, abstract thinking, and concrete experience. (For more information, see "Learning Styles: Discovering How You Learn" on page 32.) The people you lead will combine these characteristics in infinite variety. Welcome that variety, and accommodate it.

You can defuse and prevent many conflicts simply by acknowledging differences in style. Doing so opens up more options than blaming the differences on "politics" or "personality problems."

Listen. As a leader, be aware of what other people are thinking, feeling, and wanting. Listen fully to their concerns and joys. Before you criticize their views or make personal judgments, take the time to understand what's going on inside them. This is not merely a personal favor to the people you work with. The more you know about your coworkers or classmates, the more effectively you can lead them.

Practice. Leadership is an acquired skill. No one is born knowing how to make requests, give feedback, create budgets, do long-range planning, or delegate tasks. We learn these things over time, with practice, by seeing what works and what doesn't.

As a process of constant learning, leadership calls for all of the skills of master students. Look for areas in which you can make a difference, and experiment with these strategies. Right now there's something worth doing that calls for your leadership. Take action, and others will join you. ✳

 Gain more perspectives on leadership.

41 Discovery Wheel— coming full circle

This book doesn't work. It is worthless. Only you can work. Only you can make a difference and use this book to become more effective as a student.

The purpose of this book is to give you the opportunity to change your behavior. The fact that something seems like a good idea doesn't necessarily mean that you will put it into practice. This exercise gives you a chance to see what behaviors you have changed on your journey toward becoming a master student.

Answer each question quickly and honestly. Record your results on the following Discovery Wheel. Then compare your new wheel with the one you completed in Chapter 1: "First Steps."

The scores on this Discovery Wheel indicate your current strengths and weaknesses on your path toward mastery. As you complete this self-evaluation, keep in mind that your *scores might be lower here than on your earlier Discovery Wheel.* That's OK. Lower scores might result from increased self-awareness and honesty, as well as other valuable assets.

Note: The online version of this exercise does not include number ratings, so the results will be formatted differently than described here. If you did your previous Discovery Wheel online, do it online again. This will help you compare your two sets of responses more accurately.

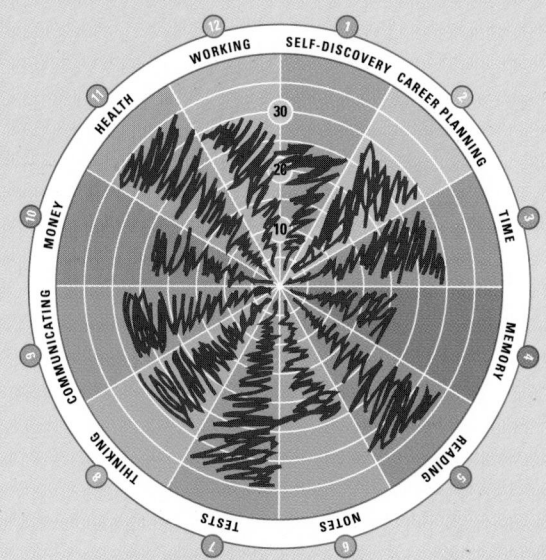

5 points: This statement is always or almost always true of me.

4 points: This statement is often true of me.

3 points: This statement is true of me about half the time.

2 points: This statement is seldom true of me.

1 point: This statement is never or almost never true of me.

 Complete this exercise online.

1. _____ I enjoy learning.

2. _____ I understand and apply the concept of multiple intelligences.

3. _____ I connect my courses to my purpose for being in school.

4. _____ I make a habit of assessing my personal strengths and areas for improvement.

5. _____ I am satisfied with how I am progressing toward achieving my goals.

6. _____ I use my knowledge of learning styles to support my success in school.

7. _____ I am willing to consider any idea that can help me succeed in school—even if I initially disagree with that idea.

8. _____ I regularly remind myself of the benefits I intend to get from my education.

_____ **Total score (1) Self-discovery**

1. _____ I relate school to what I plan to do for the rest of my life.

2. _____ I plan my career with a detailed knowledge of my skills.

3. _____ I relate my career plan to my interests, attitudes, and core values.

WORKING

12

4. _____ I can effectively use a variety of resources to research possible careers.

5. _____ I use the career planning services offered by my school.

6. _____ I am planning a career that contributes something worthwhile to the world.

7. _____ I have a written career plan and I update it regularly.

8. _____ I use internships, extracurricular activities, information interviews, and on-the-job experiences to test and refine my career plan.

_____ **Total score (2) Career Planning**

1. _____ I set long-term goals and periodically review them.

2. _____ I set short-term goals to support my long-term goals.

3. _____ I write a plan for each day and each week.

4. _____ I assign priorities to what I choose to do each day.

5. _____ I plan review time so I don't have to cram before tests.

6. _____ I plan regular recreation time.

7. _____ I adjust my study time to meet the demands of individual courses.

8. _____ I have adequate time each day to accomplish what I plan.

_____ **Total score (3) Time**

1. _____ I am confident of my ability to remember.

2. _____ I can remember people's names.

3. _____ At the end of a lecture, I can summarize what was presented.

4. _____ I apply techniques that enhance my memory skills.

5. _____ I can recall information when I'm under pressure.

6. _____ I remember important information clearly and easily.

7. _____ I can jog my memory when I have difficulty recalling.

8. _____ I can relate new information to what I've already learned.

_____ **Total score (4) Memory**

1. _____ I preview and review reading assignments.

2. _____ When reading, I ask myself questions about the material.

3. _____ I underline or highlight important passages when reading.

4. _____ When I read textbooks, I am alert and awake.

5. _____ I relate what I read to my life.

6. _____ I select a reading strategy to fit the type of material I'm reading.

7. _____ I take effective notes when I read.

8. _____ When I don't understand what I'm reading, I note my questions and find answers.

_____ **Total score (5) Reading**

1. _____ When I am in class, I focus my attention.

2. _____ I take notes in class.

3. _____ I am aware of various methods for taking notes and choose those that work best for me.

4. _____ I distinguish important material and note key phrases in a lecture.

5. _____ I copy down material that the instructor writes outs and displays to the class.

6. _____ I can put important concepts into my own words.

7. _____ My notes are valuable for review.

8. _____ I review class notes within 24 hours.

_____ **Total score (6) Notes**

1. _____ I use techniques to manage stress related to exams.

2. _____ I manage my time during exams and am able to complete them.

3. _____ I am able to predict test questions.

4. _____ I adapt my test-taking strategy to the kind of test I'm taking.

5. _____ I understand what essay questions ask and can answer them completely and accurately.

6. _____ I start reviewing for tests at the beginning of the term.

7. _____ I continue reviewing for tests throughout the term.

12

8. _____ My sense of personal worth is independent of my test scores.

> _____ **Total score (7) Tests**

1. _____ I have flashes of insight and think of solutions to problems at unusual times.

2. _____ I use brainstorming to generate solutions to a variety of problems.

3. _____ When I get stuck on a creative project, I use specific methods to get unstuck.

4. _____ I see problems and tough choices as opportunities for learning and personal growth.

5. _____ I am willing to consider different points of view and alternative solutions.

6. _____ I can detect common errors in logic.

7. _____ I construct viewpoints by drawing on information and ideas from many sources.

8. _____ As I share my viewpoints with others, I am open to their feedback.

> _____ **Total score (8) Thinking**

1. _____ I am candid with others about who I am, what I feel, and what I want.

2. _____ Other people tell me that I am a good listener.

3. _____ I can communicate my upset and anger without blaming others.

4. _____ I can make friends and create valuable relationships in a new setting.

5. _____ I am open to being with people I don't especially like in order to learn from them.

6. _____ I can effectively plan and research a large writing assignment.

7. _____ I create first drafts without criticizing my writing, then edit later for clarity, accuracy, and coherence.

8. _____ I know ways to prepare and deliver effective speeches.

> _____ **Total score (9) Communicating**

1. _____ I am in control of my personal finances.

2. _____ I can access a variety of resources to finance my education.

3. _____ I am confident that I will have enough money to complete my education.

4. _____ I take on debts carefully and repay them on time.

5. _____ I have long-range financial goals and a plan to meet them.

6. _____ I make regular deposits to a savings account.

7. _____ I pay off the balance on credit card accounts each month.

8. _____ I can have fun without spending money.

> _____ **Total score (10) Money**

1. _____ I have enough energy to study and work—and still enjoy other areas of my life.

2. _____ If the situation calls for it, I have enough reserve energy to put in a long day.

3. _____ The way I eat supports my long-term health.

4. _____ The way I eat is independent of my feelings of self-worth.

5. _____ I exercise regularly to maintain a healthy weight.

6. _____ My emotional health supports my ability to learn.

7. _____ I notice changes in my physical condition and respond effectively.

8. _____ I am in control of any alcohol or other drugs I put into my body.

> _____ **Total score (11) Health**

1. _____ In work settings, I look for models of success and cultivate mentors.

2. _____ My work creates value for my employer.

3. _____ I see working as a way to pursue my interests, expand my skills, and develop mastery.

4. _____ I support other people in their career planning and job hunting—and am willing to accept their support.

5. _____ I can function effectively in corporate cultures and cope positively with office politics.

6. _____ I am skilled at discovering job openings and moving through the hiring process.

7. _____ I regularly update and take action on my career plan.

8. _____ I see learning as a lifelong process that includes experiences inside and outside the classroom.

_____ **Total score (12) Working**

Filling In Your Discovery Wheel

Using the total score from each category, shade in each section of the Discovery Wheel. Use different colors, if you want. For example, you could use green to denote areas you want to work on. When you have finished, complete Journal Entry 29, which follows this exercise.

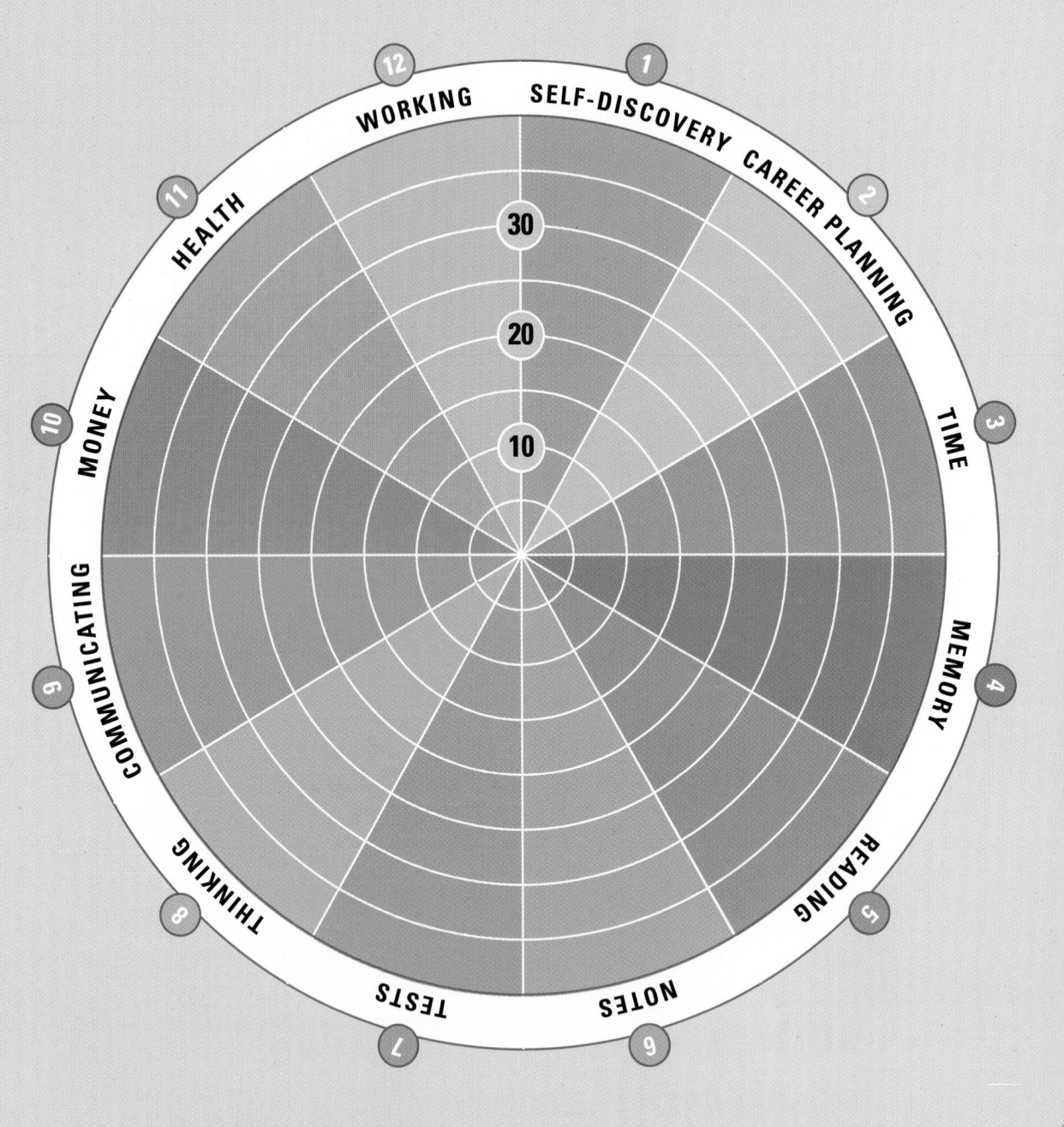

www.cengage.com/success/MSME3e

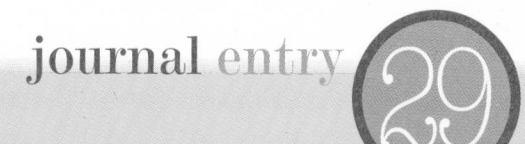

Discovery/Intention Statement

Revisiting your Discovery Wheels

The purpose of this Journal Entry is to (1) review both of the Discovery Wheels you completed in this book, (2) summarize your insights from doing them, and (3) declare how you will use these insights to promote your continued success in school.

   Again, a lower score on the second Discovery Wheel does not necessarily indicate decreased personal effectiveness. Instead, the lower score could result from increased honesty and greater self-awareness.

   Enter your Discovery Wheel scores from both chapters in the space below.

	Chapter 1	Chapter 12
Self-discovery	_____	_____
Career planning	_____	_____
Time	_____	_____
Memory	_____	_____
Reading	_____	_____
Notes	_____	_____
Tests	_____	_____
Thinking	_____	_____
Communicating	_____	_____
Money	_____	_____
Health	_____	_____
Working	_____	_____

   Comparing the Discovery Wheel in this chapter with the Discovery Wheel in Chapter 1, I discovered that I . . .

_____

_____

_____

_____

_____

_____

_____

_____

_____

_____

_____

_____

_____

_____

_____

_____

_____

_____

_____

_____

_____

_____

   In the next 6 months, I intend to review the following articles from this book for additional suggestions I could use:

_____

_____

_____

_____

_____

_____

_____

_____

_____

_____

_____

_____

_____

_____

_____

_____

WORKING

12

Keep your career plan alive

NEW JOBS AND CAREER PATHWAYS are constantly being added to the workplace. To thrive in this world of constant change, create a career plan that includes lifelong learning and skill updating. Then put your plan into action.

Creating a plan and keeping it alive acknowledges a key fact: *You* are in charge of your career. No other person or organization can take on this task. Effective career planners routinely watch for new work opportunities, take responsibility for their long-term financial security, plan for job transitions, and expect to change careers. You can now benefit by ultimately thinking of yourself as self-employed—even when you work for someone else.

Keep thinking about what you want in all areas of your life, including your career. Then use a variety of techniques to transform your written plan into real change.

(images) Photodisc

Display your goals

Without reminders, even skilled planners can forget their goals. One solution is to post written goals in prominent locations—the bathroom, bedroom, hall mirror, or office door. You can also write goals on 3×5 cards and tape them to walls or store them next to your bed. Review the cards every morning and night.

You can make goals even more visible. Create an elaborate poster or collage that displays your life purpose. Use frames, color, graphics, and other visual devices to rivet your attention on your goals.

Add to your plan

Goals might pop into your mind at the oddest moments—while you're waiting in line, riding the bus, or stuck in rush-hour traffic. With a little preparation, you can capture those fleeting goals. Carry around a few 3×5 cards and a pen in your pocket or purse. You can also pack a small voice recorder with you. That way you can speak your goals and preserve them for the ages.

Schedule time for career planning

Schedule regular times for career planning. This is an important appointment with yourself. Treat it as seriously as an appointment with your doctor.

Remember that planning does not have to take a lot of time. You can do the following in just one hour or less:

- Review and revise your career plan.
- Update your résumé.
- Visit the career center at your school.
- Do an informational interview with someone working in a job related to your major.
- Brainstorm a list of places where you'd like to do an internship.
- Rehearse your answers to common questions asked during job interviews.
- Call or e-mail one of your contacts.

To get more benefit from planning and create the most options for your future, see career planning as a constant activity. This is not something to put off until your last year of school. Begin now.

Advertise your career plan

When it comes to achieving your goals, everyone you know is a potential ally. Take a tip from Madison Avenue and advertise. Tell friends and family members about what you plan to be, do, or have. Make your career plan public.

Enlist support

People might criticize your goals: "You want to promote world peace *and* become a millionaire? That's crazy." Remember that there are ways to deal with resistance.

One is to ask directly for support from friends and contacts. Explain how much your goal means to you and what you'll do to achieve it. Mention that you're willing to revise your goal as circumstances change. Also *keep* talking about your vision. Goals that sound outlandish at first can become easier to accept over time.

Get coaching

You can hire a personal life coach to assist with goal setting and achievement. The principle is the same as hiring a personal trainer to set and meet fitness goals. A life coach engages you in a conversation about goals for all areas of your life—work, family, finances, education, spirituality, and more. To find such a person, key the words *life coach* into your favorite search site on the Web. National organizations for life coaches have their own sites, which can link you with resources in your own area.

Teach career planning

There's a saying: We teach what we most want to learn. You can turn this idea into an incentive for creating your future. Explain the process of career planning to friends and family. Volunteer to lead an informal seminar or workshop on this topic. If you have children, help them to set and meet goals.

Enjoy the rewards

Break large, long-term career goals into small tasks that you can finish in one hour or less. Savor the feeling that comes with crossing off items on a to-do list. Experience accomplishment often.

At least once each year, list the career goals that you achieved and celebrate. Do the same with goals in all areas of your life. Let the thrill of meeting one goal lead you to setting more. ✳

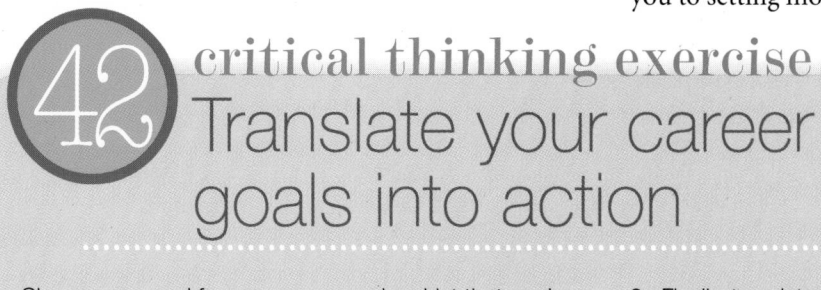

42 critical thinking exercise
Translate your career goals into action

1. Choose one goal from your career plan. List that goal here:

_____

_____

_____

_____

2. Next, list some follow-up actions. Ask yourself: "What will it really take for me to meet this goal?" List at least five ideas below:

_____

_____

_____

_____

_____

_____

_____

_____

_____

_____

3. Finally, translate any action you just listed into immediate steps—the kind of items that you would include on a daily to-do list or planning calendar. Think of tasks that you could complete in less than one hour, or start within the next 24 hours.

_____

_____

_____

_____

_____

_____

_____

_____

_____

_____

_____

You can apply this three-step technique to any goal for your career or the rest of your life. The point is to move from ideas into action.

12

43 critical thinking exercise
Create your next semester or term

This exercise offers a chance to celebrate your successes during the past term and to think in specific ways about what you want to create next term.

Part 1: Update your First Step

Looking back on this past semester or term, you might be surprised at how quickly it went by. You might also be surprised at how much you learned, both inside and outside the classroom.

In the following space, list three things that you did well during the current term. Perhaps you took the initiative to meet a new person or created an effective way to take notes in class. Write down any success that you find personally significant, no matter how small it might seem to others. Use additional paper as needed.

1. _____

2. _____

3. _____

Now take a moment to write about three things that did not go as well as you wanted during the past term. Give yourself permission to explore whatever comes to mind—anything from a simple embarrassment to a major mistake. If you missed a class because you set your alarm for 7 p.m. instead of 7 a.m., you can write about that. If you failed a test, you might describe that experience as well.

As you practice truth telling, remember to keep it light. It's fine to acknowledge breakdowns and to laugh at yourself as you do.

1. _____

2. _____

3. _____

Part 2: Determine what you want next

You've come a long way since first setting foot on campus. Now consider where you want to go next term. Brainstorm some intentions in several areas of your life. Then channel them into some new behaviors.

Do this activity by building on the writing you did in Part 1 of this exercise. Reflect on ways to maintain or expand on the successes you listed. You should also consider ways to change or prevent some of the experiences you didn't like.

Determine what you want from academics. For instance, you could set a goal to raise your grade point average to a specific number, or to declare your major by a certain date. Complete the following sentence.

In my academic life, I want to . . .

_____

_____

Now consider your social life. Perhaps you want to resolve a conflict with an instructor or roommate. You might also want to deepen a connection with someone you already know and make this person a friend for life. Put such goals in writing by completing the following sentence.

In my social life, I want to . . .

_____

_____

Finally, brainstorm a list of specific actions you can take to meet the goals you just described. Write these actions in the following space. Reflect on which ones might work best for you and record them in your calendar or to-do list. For more suggestions on goal setting, see Chapter 3: "Time."

_____

_____

_____

journal entry 30

Discovery/Intention Statement

You've done a lot of writing during this course. To retain your key insights from this experience, review your responses to the Critical Thinking Exercises and Journal Entries in this book.

On a separate sheet of paper, summarize your key discoveries. List any intentions that call for further action. Write any new Discovery Statements or Intention Statements that seem appropriate.

WORKING

12

Be It

Use this Power Process to enhance all of the techniques in this book.

Consider that most of our choices in life fall into three categories. We can choose to do the following:

- Increase our material wealth (what we have).
- Improve our skills (what we do).
- Develop our "being" (who we are).

Many people devote their entire lives to the first two categories. They act as if they are "human havings" instead of human beings. For them, quality of life hinges on what they have. They devote most of their waking hours to getting more—more clothes, more cars, more relationships, more degrees, more trophies. "Human havings" define themselves by looking at the circumstances in their lives—what they have.

Some people escape this materialist trap by adding another dimension to their identities. In addition to living

as "human havings," they also live as "human doings." They thrive on working hard and doing everything well. They define themselves by how efficiently they do their jobs, how effectively they raise their children, and how actively they participate in clubs and organizations. Their thoughts are constantly about methods, techniques, and skills.

In addition to focusing on what we have and what we do, we can also focus on our being. That last word describes how we *see* ourselves. All of the techniques in this book can be worthless if you operate with the idea that you see yourself as an ineffective student. You might do almost everything this book suggests and still never achieve the success in school that you desire.

Instead, picture yourself as a master student right now. Through higher education, you are simply gaining

knowledge and skills that reflect and reinforce this view of yourself. Change the way you see yourself. Then watch your actions and results shift as if by magic.

Remember that "Be It" is not positive thinking or mental cheerleading. This Power Process works well when you take a First Step—when you tell the truth about your current abilities. The very act of accepting who you are and what you can do right now unleashes a powerful force for personal change.

If you can first visualize where you want to be, if you can go there in your imagination, if you can *be* it today, then you set yourself up to succeed.

If you want it, be it.

 Learn more about this Power Process online.

Career Application

Duane Bigeagle earned his B.A. in Elementary Education and found a job teaching kindergarten in an urban public school.

To his surprise, the hardest thing about the job was not interacting with students—whom he enjoyed greatly—but interacting with his coworkers. Though Duane had heard of office politics, he did not expect them to be so strong in an educational setting.

Duane's greatest concern was a colleague named Reneé, a teacher with 25 years of experience. During weekly staff meetings, the school's principal asked teachers to share any problems they were experiencing with students and collectively brainstorm solutions. Reneé smiled a lot, offered suggestions, and freely offered praise for anyone who was willing to share a problem. During informal conversations with Duane before or after school, however, Reneé complained bitterly about other teachers on staff—including those whom she'd just praised during staff meetings.

Being new to the school and a first-year teacher, Duane decided that he wanted to avoid making enemies. His goal in relating to staff members was simply to learn everything he could from them. With that goal in mind, Duane adopted the habits of carefully observing the classroom strategies used by other teachers and listening without judgment to any coaching they offered him.

Reneé talked with Duane every day and, after gossiping about other teachers, freely offered her advice for managing his classroom. By the end of the school year, Duane had enough of this. He worried that Reneé was taking on the role of a self-appointed mentor to him, and he disagreed with many of her ideas about teaching. He also worried that other teachers would perceive him and Reneé as a "team" and that her reputation for backstabbing would reflect negatively on him as well.

Reflecting on this scenario

Describe a transferable skill that Duane demonstrates.

_____

_____

_____

_____

_____

_____

_____

_____

_____

_____

List two or three suggestions for Duane that could help him cope with office politics and solve his problem with Reneé.

_____

_____

_____

_____

_____

_____

_____

_____

_____

_____

© Ed Kashi/CORBIS

Quiz

Name _____   Date ____/____/____

1. According to the article "Use Power Tools for Finding Work," the way that people traditionally *hunt* for jobs closely matches the way that employers like to *hire* people. True or false? Explain your answer.

2. List the three parts of an "elevator speech" and give an example of such a speech.

3. Explain the importance of getting noticed in the digital world and give an example for doing this.

4. According to the text, it is possible to escape leadership. True or false? Explain your answer.

5. Summarize a three-part structure for writing effective cover letters.

6. List three strategies for keeping your career plan alive.

7. List three examples of information to *omit* from your résumé.

8. Explain the suggestion to "give yourself a raise before you start work."

9. Using the Power Process: "Be It" eliminates the need to take a First Step. True or false? Explain your answer.

10. If your scores are lower on the Discovery Wheel the second time you complete it, that means your study skills have not improved. True or false? Explain your answer.

Focus on Transferable Skills

Jerry Seinfeld told one aspiring comedian that "the way to be a better comic was to create better jokes and the way to create better jokes was to write every day."[4] Seinfeld also revealed his own system for creating a writing habit: He bought a big wall calendar that displayed the whole year on one page. On each day that he wrote jokes, Seinfeld marked a big red "X" on the appropriate day on the wall calendar. He knew that he'd established a new habit when he looked at the calendar and saw an unbroken chain of "X's."

So much of success boils down to changing habits. Take a snapshot of your habits as they exist today, after reading and doing this book. Then take the next step toward mastery by committing to change a specific habit in the near future.

DISCOVERY

During this course, it has been my intention to change the following habits . . .

I would describe my skill at changing those habits as . . .

INTENTION

Three habits that I am committed to changing in the future are . . .

NEXT ACTION

Of the three habits listed above, the one I would like to focus on next is . . .

To experience success at making this habit change, I will . . .

Master Student PROFILE

Ruth Handler

. . . was creative

© Bettmann/Corbis

When Ruth Handler first proposed the idea of a grown-up doll to the toy designers at Mattel—the company she and her husband ran—the designers thought she was crazy. Little girls want to pretend to be mommies, she was told.

No, said Handler. Little girls want to pretend to be bigger girls. And she knew this because she spent a lot of time observing one little girl in particular—her daughter, Barbara, nicknamed "Barbie."

All her life, Ruth has considered the word "no" just another challenge.

When Ruth graduated from East Denver High School and announced her intention to attend college, her family didn't give her a lot of encouragement. Marrying her high-school sweetheart—a broke-but-talented artist named Elliot Handler—was more traditional than going to college. But she ended up at the University of Denver. And she married Elliot anyway. When she took two semesters of business education at the University of California at Los Angeles, she was the only married woman in her class. And she became the first woman to complete the program.

Ruth fell in love with Southern California and was hired as a stenographer at Paramount Studios in Hollywood. The year was 1937. Ruth worked at Paramount until 1941, when she became pregnant with Barbara, and stayed home until after the birth of her son, Ken, in 1944. Staying home made Ruth restless; she wanted to help [her husband] Elliot run his giftware and costume jewelry business. "You make something; I'll sell it," she told him.

In 1944, while the United States was embroiled in World War II, Elliot designed a new style of picture frame made out of the then-revolutionary new plastics. His partner,

Harold "Matt" Matson, built samples and Ruth took the frames to a chain of photography studios and got a large order. The three celebrated, calling their new business "Mattel" after MATT and ELliot.

Soon after, plastic was needed for the war effort and became unavailable for civilian use. Fortunately, Elliot came up with the idea of making frames out of scrap wood. Ruth took the samples back to the photography studio and got an even bigger order. Mattel could continue operating. The leftover wood from the picture frames led to a thriving business making doll house furniture.

Worldwide, Mattel sold millions of Ruth Handler's Barbie dolls, boosting the company's sales to $18 million. Within ten years, customers had bought $500 million worth of Barbie products.

Over the years, Ruth moved up from cofounder of the company to executive vice president to president to cochairman of the board of directors. These titles were practically unheard of for women in the 1960s.

Handler remembers one episode that occurred despite her executive status. A brokerage house was holding a meeting with the investment community at a private club, and Handler was to be the keynote speaker. When she arrived at the club, the program planners ushered her into the club through the alley and kitchen. Later, she discovered that she was sneaked into the building because the club didn't allow women.

From Ethlie Ann Vare and Greg Placek, *Women Inventors and Their Discoveries*. Copyright © 1993. Reprinted by permission of The Oliver Press.

(1916–2002) Co-founder of Mattel who invented the Barbie doll in 1959. After being diagnosed with breast cancer and undergoing a mastectomy, she designed a prosthetic breast that was later patented as Nearly Me.

Learn more about Ruth Handler and other master students at the Master Student Hall of Fame.

Endnotes

Introduction

1. John Henry Newman, *Newman Reader*, "Discourse 5. Knowledge Its Own End," http://www.newmanreader.org/works/idea/discourse5.html (accessed October 25, 2009).
2. Fordcarz.com, "Quotations from Henry Ford," http://www.fordcarz.com/henry_ford_quotes.htm (accessed October 25, 2009).
3. U.S. Department of Labor, Bureau of Labor Statistics, "Education Pays . . . ," March 6, 2009, http://www.bls.gov/emp/emptab7.htm (accessed October 25, 2009).
4. William James, *Talks to Teachers on Psychology; And to Students on Some of Life's Ideals* (Project Gutenberg e-book), http://www.gutenberg.org/files/16287/16287-h/16287-h.htm (accessed October 30, 2009).
5. Robert Mager, *Preparing Instructional Objectives* (Belmont, CA: Fearon, 1975).
6. Ezra Pound, *The ABC of Reading* (New York: New Directions, 1934).
7. Robert Hutchins, "The Tradition of the West," in *The Great Conversation: The Substance of a Liberal Education, Vol. 1, The Great Books of the Western World* (Chicago: Encyclopaedia Britannica, 1952).
8. Randy Moore, "The Importance of Admissions Scores and Attendance to First-Year Performance," *Journal of the First-Year Experience & Students in Transition*, 2006, Vol. 18, No. 1 (2006): pp. 105–125.
9. Albert Bandura, *Social Foundations of Thought and Action* (Englewood Cliffs, NJ: Prentice-Hall, 1986).
10. Deborah Davis, *The Adult Learner's Companion* (Boston: Houghton Mifflin, 2007).
11. Abraham Maslow, *The Further Reaches of Human Nature* (New York: Viking, 1971).
12. Excerpts from *Creating Your Future*. Copyright © 1998 by David B. Ellis. Adapted by permission of Houghton Mifflin Company. All rights reserved.

Chapter 1

1. David A. Kolb, *Experiential Learning: Experience as the Source of Learning and Development* (Englewood Cliffs, NJ: Prentice-Hall, 1984).
2. Douglas A. Bernstein, Louis A. Penner, Alison Clarke-Stewart, and Edward J. Roy, *Psychology* (Boston: Houghton Mifflin, 2006), pp. 368–369.
3. Howard Gardner, *Frames of Mind: The Theory of Multiple Intelligences* (New York: Basic Books, 1993).
4. Neil Fleming, "VARK: A Guide to Learning Styles," 2009, http://www.vark-learn.com (accessed October 26, 2009).
5. Mihaly Csikszentmihalyi, *Flow: The Psychology of Optimal Experience* (New York: Harper, 1991), pp. 31–32.
6. Carl Rogers, *Freedom to Learn* (Columbus, OH: Merrill, 1969).
7. Richard Malott, "Self Management Checklist," Counselling Services, University of Victoria, 2008, http://www.coun.uvic.ca/learning/motivation/self-management.html (accessed October 26, 2009).
8. B. F. Skinner, *Science and Human Behavior* (Boston: Free Press, 1965).

Chapter 2

1. Adapted from Dave Ellis, Stan Lankowitz, Ed Stupka, and Doug Toft, *Career Planning*, Third Edition. Copyright © 2003 by Houghton Mifflin Company. Reprinted by permission.
2. Ibid.
3. Ibid.
4. Ibid.
5. Ibid.
6. Ibid.
7. Ibid.
8. Ibid.
9. National Center on Education and the Economy, *Tough Choices or Tough Times: The Report of the New Commission on the Skills of the American Workforce* (San Francisco: Jossey-Bass, 2007).
10. Frank Levy and Richard J. Murnane, *The New Division of Labor: How Computers Are Creating the Next Job Market* (Princeton, NJ: Princeton University Press, 2004), pp. 47–48.
11. Adapted from Dave Ellis, Stan Lankowitz, Ed Stupka, and Doug Toft, *Career Planning*, Third Edition. Copyright © 2003 by Houghton Mifflin Company. Reprinted by permission.
12. Ibid.
13. Joe Cuseo, "Academic-Support Strategies for Promoting Student Retention and Achievement During the First Year of College," University of Ulster, *Student Transition and Retention*, http://www.ulster.ac.uk/star/resources/acdemic_support_strat_first_years.pdf (accessed October 26, 2009).
14. National Committee for Latin and Greek, March 5, 2006, http://www.promotelatin.org/Default.htm#famous (accessed October 29, 2009).
15. U.S. Department of Labor, Bureau of Labor Statistics, *Occupational Outlook Handbook 2008-09 Edition*, "Computer Programmers," http://www.bls.gov/oco/ocos110.htm (accessed October 26, 2009).

Chapter 3

1. Alan Lakein, *How to Get Control of Your Time and Your Life* (New York: New American Library, 1973; reissue 1996).
2. Linda Sapadin, with Jack Maguire, *It's About Time! The Six Styles of Procrastination and How to Overcome Them* (New York: Penguin, 1997).
3. Stephen R. Covey, *The Seven Habits of Highly Effective People: Restoring the Character Ethic* (New York: Simon & Schuster, 1990).

Chapter 4

1. Donald Hebb, quoted in D. J. Siegel, "Memory: An Overview," *Journal of the American Academy of Child and Adolescent Psychiatry*, Vol. 40, No. 9 (2001): pp. 997–1011.
2. Donald Hebb, *Essay on Mind* (Hillsdale, NJ: Erlbaum, 1980).
3. Daniel L. Schacter, *The Seven Sins of Memory: How the Mind Forgets and Remembers* (Boston: Houghton Mifflin, 2001), p. 14.
4. From *Information Anxiety* by Richard Saul Wurman. Copyright © 1989 by Richard Saul Wurman. Used by permission of Doubleday, a division of Bantam Doubleday Dell Publishing Group, Inc.
5. D. J. Siegel, "Memory: An Overview," *Journal of the American Academy of Child and Adolescent Psychiatry*, Vol. 40, No. 9 (2001): pp. 997–1011.
6. Schacter, *The Seven Sins of Memory*, p. 14.
7. Alzheimer's Association, "Brain Health," 2009, http://www.alz .org/brainhealth/overview.asp (accessed February 19, 2009).

Chapter 5

1. Adapted from *Master Student Guide to Academic Success* (Boston: Houghton Mifflin, 2005), p. 115.
2. Ibid.

Chapter 6

1. Walter Pauk and Ross J. Q. Owens, *How to Study in College*, Eighth Edition (Boston: Houghton Mifflin, 2005).
2. Tony Buzan, *Use Both Sides of Your Brain*, Third Edition (New York: Dutton, 1991).
3. Gabrielle Rico, *Writing the Natural Way* (Los Angeles: J. P. Tarcher, 2000).
4. Joseph Novak and D. Bob Gowin, *Learning How to Learn* (New York: Cambridge University Press, 1984).

Chapter 7

1. Joe Cuseo, "Academic-Support Strategies for Promoting Student Retention and Achievement during the First Year of College," University of Ulster Office of Student Transition and Retention, www.ulster.ac.uk/star/data/cuseoretention.htm (accessed September 4, 2003).
2. Ibid.
3. MayoClinic.com, "Generalized Anxiety Disorder," www.mayoclinic.com/health/generalized-anxiety-disorder/ DS00502/DSECTION=symptoms, June 23, 2009 (accessed November 13, 2009).
4. Jon Kabat-Zin, *Full Catastrophe Living: How to Cope with Stress, Pain and Illness Using Mindfulness Meditation* (London: Piatkus Books, 2001).
5. Steven C. Hayes, *Get Out of Your Mind and Into Your Life: The New Acceptance and Commitment Therapy* (Oakland, CA: New Harbinger, 2004).
6. This article incorporates detailed suggestions from reviewer Frank Baker.
7. Jena McGregor, William C. Symonds, Dean Foust, Diane Brady, and Moira Herbst, "How Failure Breeds Success," *Business Week*, July 10, 2006, www.businessweek.com/magazine/ content/06_28/b3992001.htm (accessed November 11, 2009).

Chapter 8

1. Quoted in Theodore A. Rees Cheney, *Getting the Words Right: How to Rewrite, Edit and Revise*, reprint (Cincinnati, OH: Writer's Digest Books, 1990).
2. William G. Perry, Jr., *Forms of Intellectual and Ethical Development in the College Years: A Scheme* (New York: Holt, Rinehart, and Winston, 1970).
3. Peter A. Facione, *Critical Thinking: A Statement of Expert Consensus for Purposes of Educational Assessment and Instruction* (Millbrae, CA: California Academic Press, 1990).
4. Arthur Koestler, *The Act of Creation* (New York: Dell, 1964).
5. Quoted in Alice Calaprice, ed., *The Expanded Quotable Einstein* (Princeton, NJ: Princeton University Press, 2000).
6. *Setting the Standard*, Office of Ethics and Business Conduct, Lockheed Martin Corporation, 2003, actrav.itcilo.org/ actrav-english/telearn/global/ilo/code/lockheed.htm (accessed November 13, 2009).

Chapter 9

1. "How You Fit Into the Tight Job Market," National Association of Colleges and Employers, 2009, http://www.jobweb.org/ studentarticles.aspx?id=2121 (accessed November 27, 2009).
2. "Working in the 21st Century," U.S. Bureau of Labor Statistics, http://www.bls.gov/opub/working/page4a.htm (accessed November 27, 2009).
3. Carl Rogers, *On Becoming a Person* (Boston: Houghton Mifflin, 1961).
4. Thomas Gordon, *Parent Effectiveness Training: The Tested New Way to Raise Responsible Children* (New York: New American Library, 1975).
5. Vincent A. Miller, *Guidebook for International Trainers in Business and Industry* (New York: Van Nostrand Reinhold, 1979), pp. 46–51.
6. Maia Szalavitz, "Race and the Genome," Howard University Human Genome Center, March 2, 2001, www.genomecenter .howard.edu/article.htm (accessed March 27, 2009).
7. Daniel Goleman, *Emotional Intelligence: Why It Can Matter More Than IQ* (New York: Bantam, 1995), pp. xiv–xv.
8. *Twelve Steps and Twelve Traditions* (New York: Alcoholics Anonymous World Services, 1981), p. 90.
9. W. T. Wilson, *The Dawn of the India Century: Why India Is Poised to Challenge China and the United States for Global Economic Hegemony in the 21st Century* (Chicago: Keystone India, 2005).
10. "Exports from Manufacturing Establishments: 2001," Table 2, U.S. Census Bureau, July 2004, http://www.census.gov/mcd/ exports/ar01.pdf (accessed November 18, 2009).
11. Lydia Ramsey, "Minding Your Global Manners," 2008, http://www.mannersthatsell.com/articles/globalmanners.html (accessed November 27, 2009).
12. Thomas Friedman, *The World Is Flat: A Brief History of the Twenty-First Century* (New York: Farrar, Straus, and Giroux, 2005).
13. Frank LaFasto, "The Zen of Brilliant Teams," Center for Association Leadership, July 2002, www.asaecenter.org/ PublicationsResources/articledetail.cfm?ItemNumber=13295 (accessed March 17, 2009).

14. Anna B. Adams, D. Christopher Kayes, and David A. Kolb, "Experiential Learning in Teams," *Experience-Based Learning Systems*, 2004, http://www.learningfromexperience.com/images/uploads/experiential-learning-in-teams.pdf (accessed March 18, 2009).

Chapter 10

1. Jonathan Chevreaux, "Even Young Millionaires on Skates Need to Worry about Financial Planning, *National Post*, June 26, 2009, http://network.nationalpost.com/np/blogs/wealthyboomer/archive/2009/06/26/even-young-millionaires-on-skate-need-to-worry-about-financial-planning.aspx (accessed November 27, 2009).

2. Saul Hansell, "Yahoo Feels Breath on Neck; These Days, No. 1 Portal Seems to Be a Step Behind," *New York Times*, October 11, 2006.

3. Sandy Baum and Jennifer Ma, "Education Pays 2007: The Benefits of Higher Education for Individuals and Society," *College Board*, 2007, http://www.collegeboard.com/prod_downloads/about/news_info/cbsenior/yr2007/ed-pays-2007.pdf (accessed November 19, 2009).

4. Adapted from O. C. Ferrell, John Fraedrich, and Linda Ferrell, *Business Ethics: Ethical Decision Making and Cases* (Boston: Houghton Mifflin, 2005), pp. 161–163. Used by permission.

Chapter 11

1. Centers for Disease Control and Prevention, "Health Habits of Adults Aged 18–29 Highlighted in Report on Nation's Health," February 18, 2009, www.cdc.gov/media/pressrel/2009/r090218.htm (accessed April 10, 2009).

2. University of Minnesota, "Health and Academic Performance: Minnesota Undergraduate Students," 2007, www.bhs.umn.edu/reports/HealthAcademicPerformanceReport_2007.pdf, (accessed April 10, 2009).

3. Kay-Tee Khaw, Nicholas Wareham, Sheila Bingham, Ailsa Welch, Robert Luben, and Nicholas Day, "Combined Impact of Health Behaviours and Mortality in Men and Women: The EPIC-Norfolk Prospective Population Study," *PLoS Medicine*, Vol. 5, No. 1 (2008), www.plosmedicine.org/article/info:doi/10.1371/journal.pmed.0050012 (accessed April 10, 2009).

4. U.S. Department of Agriculture, "MyPyramid.gov," 2009, mypyramid.gov/guidelines/index.html (accessed April 10, 2009).

5. Michael Pollan, "Unhappy Meals," *New York Times*, January 28, 2007, www.nytimes.com/2007/01/28/magazine/28nutritionism.t.html (accessed April 10, 2009).

6. Harvard Medical School, "Portion Distortion," *HEALTHbeat*, January 3, 2007, http://www.health.harvard.edu/healthbeat/HEALTHbeat_010307.htm (accessed November 27, 2009).

7. Nicholas A. Christakis and James H. Fowler, *Connected: The Surprising Power of Our Social Networks and How They Shape Our Lives* (Boston: Little, Brown & Company, 2009).

8. Harvard Medical School, *HEALTHbeat: 20 No-Sweat Ways to Get More Exercise* (Boston: Harvard Health Publications, October 14, 2008).

9. Jane Brody, "Exercise = Weight Loss, Except When It Doesn't," *New York Times*, September 12, 2006, www.nytimes.com/2006/09/12/health/nutrition/12brody.html (accessed April 9, 2009).

10. Mary Duenwald, "The Dorms May Be Great, but How's the Counseling?" *New York Times*, October 26, 2004, www.nytimes.com/2004/10/26/health/psychology/26cons.html?_r=1 (accessed April 9, 2009).

11. American College Health Association, *American College Health Association–National College Health Assessment II: Reference Group, Executive Summary Fall 2008*, 2009, www.acha-ncha.org/docs/ACHA NCHA_Reference_Group_ExecutiveSummary_Fall2008.pdf (accessed April 9, 2009).

12. Albert Ellis, *Overcoming Destructive Beliefs, Feelings, and Behaviors: New Directions for Rational Emotive Behavior Therapy* (Amherst, NY: Prometheus, 2001).

13. Morita Masatake's ideas are discussed in David Reynolds, *A Handbook for Constructive Living* (New York: Morrow, 1995), p. 98.

14. M. Schaffer, E. L. Jeglic, and B. Stanley, "The Relationship between Suicidal Behavior, Ideation, and Binge Drinking among College Students," *Archives of Suicide Research*, Vol. 12, No. 2 (2008): pp. 124–132.

15. Job Kabat-Zinn, *Full-Catastrophe Living: Using the Wisdom of Your Body and Mind to Face Stress, Pain, and Illness* (New York: Bantam Doubleday Dell, 1990), p. 359.

16. Centers for Disease Control and Prevention, "Trends in Reportable Sexually Transmitted Diseases in the United States, 2007," 2009, www.cdc.gov/nchhstp/newsroom/docs/STDTrendsFactSheet.pdf (accessed April 9, 2009).

17. Centers for Disease Control and Prevention, "CDC Fact Sheet: Most Widely Reported, Curable STDs Remain Significant Health Threat," 2009, www.cdc.gov/nchhstp/newsroom/docs/STDFastFacts-3.27.09-508%20Compliant.pdf (accessed April 9, 2009).

18. Edward Hallowell, *Crazy Busy: Overstretched, Overbooked, and About to Snap!* (New York: Ballantine, 2006), pp. 71–85.

19. American Psychological Association, *Diagnostic and Statistical Manual of Psychoactive Substance Abuse Disorders* (Washington, DC: American Psychological Association, 1994).

20. American Cancer Society, "Guide to Quitting Smoking," 2008, www.cancer.org/docroot/PED/content/PED_10_13X_Guide_for_Quitting_Smoking.asp (accessed April 10, 2009).

21. American Cancer Society, "Double Your Chances of Quitting Smoking," 2008, www.cancer.org/docroot/PED/content/PED_10_3x_Double_Your_Chances.asp (accessed April 10, 2009).

Chapter 12

1. U.S. Department of Labor, Bureau of Labor Statistics, "Education Pays . . . ," March 6, 2009, http://www.bls.gov/emp/emptab7.htm (accessed October 25, 2009).

2. U.S. Department of Labor, "Secretary's Commission on Achieving Necessary Skills (SCANS)," March 9, 2006, http://wdr.doleta.gov/SCANS/ (accessed November 27, 2009).

3. U.S. Census Bureau, "An Older and More Diverse Nation by Midcentury," August 14, 2008, www.census.gov/Press-Release/www/releases/archives/population/012496.html (accessed March 27, 2009).

4. Brad Isaac, "Jerry Seinfeld's Productivity Secret," *Lifehacker*, July 24, 2007, http://lifehacker.com/software/motivation/jerry-seinfelds-productivity-secret-281626.php (accessed April 15, 2009).

Additional Reading

Adler, Mortimer, and Charles Van Doren. *How to Read a Book*. New York: Touchstone, 1972.

Allen, David. *Getting Things Done: The Art of Stress-Free Productivity*. New York: Penguin, 2001.

Bolles, Richard N. *What Color Is Your Parachute? A Practical Manual for Job-Hunters and Career-Changers*. Berkeley, CA: Ten Speed, updated annually.

Bronson, Po. *What Should I Do with My Life? The True Story of People Who Answered the Ultimate Question*. New York: Random House, 2003.

Buzan, Tony, and Barry Buzan. *The Mind Map Book*. London: BBC Active, 2006.

Chaffee, John. *Thinking Critically*. Florence, KY: Cengage Learning, 2009.

Coplin, Bill. *10 Things Employers Want You to Learn in College: The Know-How You Need to Succeed*. Berkeley, CA: Ten Speed, 2004.

Covey, Stephen R. *First Things First*. New York: Simon & Schuster, 1994.

Cushman, Kathleen. *First in the Family: Advice About College From First-Generation Students*. Providence, RI: Next Generation Press, 2006.

Davis, Deborah. *The Adult Learner's Companion*. Florence, KY: Cengage Learning, 2007.

Dominguez, Joe, and Vicki Robin. *Your Money or Your Life: Transforming Your Relationship with Money and Achieving Financial Independence*. New York: Viking Penguin, 1992.

Dreikurs, Rudolf, with Vicki Soltz. *Children: The Challenge*. New York: Plume, 1991.

Elgin, Duane. *The Living Universe: Where Are We? Who Are We? Where Are We Going?* San Francisco, CA: Berrett-Koehler, 2009.

Elgin, Duane. *Voluntary Simplicity: Toward a Way of Life That Is Outwardly Simple, Inwardly Rich*. New York: William Morrow, 1998.

Ellis, Dave. *Becoming a Master Student*. Florence, KY: Cengage Learning, 2011.

Ellis, Dave. *Falling Awake: Creating the Life of Your Dreams*. Rapid City, SD: Breakthrough Enterprises, 2000.

Ellis, Dave, Stan Lankowitz, Ed Stupka, and Doug Toft. *Career Planning*. Boston: Houghton Mifflin, 2003.

Facione, Peter. *Critical Thinking: What It Is and Why It Counts*. Millbrae, CA: California Academic Press, 2010.

Ferrell, O. C., John Fraedrich, and Linda Ferrell. *Business Ethics: Ethical Decision Making and Cases*. Florence, KY: Cengage Learning, 2011.

Friedman, Thomas. *The World Is Flat: A Brief History of the Twenty-First Century*. New York: Farrar, Straus, and Giroux, 2005.

Gawain, Shakti. *Creative Visualization: Using the Power of Your Imagination to Create What You Want in Your Life*. New York: New World Library, 2002.

Golas, Thaddeus. *The Lazy Man's Guide to Enlightenment*. Layton, UT: Gibbs Smith, 1997.

Greene, Susan D., and Melanie C. L. Martel. *The Ultimate Job Hunter's Guidebook*. Florence, KY: Cengage Learning, 2008.

Grinder, Richard, and John Bandler. *Frogs Into Princes: Neuro Linguistic Programming*. Boulder, CO: Real People Press, 1979.

Hales, Diana. *An Invitation to Health*. Florence, KY: Cengage Learning, 2010.

Higbee, Kenneth L. *Your Memory: How It Works and How to Improve It*. New York: Marlowe & Company, 2001.

Keyes, Ken. *Handbook to Higher Consciousness*. Berkeley, CA: Living Love Center, 1975.

Kolb, David A. *Experiential Learning: Experience as the Source of Learning and Development*. Englewood Cliffs, NJ: Prentice Hall, 1984.

Levy, Frank, and Richard J. Murnane. *The New Division of Labor: How Computers Are Creating the Next Job Market*. Princeton, NJ: Princeton University Press, 2004.

Light, Richard J. *Making the Most of College: Students Speak Their Minds*. Cambridge, MA: Harvard University Press, 2001.

Nolting, Paul D. *Math Study Skills Workbook*. Florence, KY: Cengage Learning, 2008.

Orman, Suze. *2009 Action Plan: Keeping Your Money Safe & Sound*. New York: Spiegel & Grau, 2009.

Pauk, Walter, and Ross J. Q. Owens. *How to Study in College*. Florence, KY: Cengage Learning, 2011.

Peddy, Shirley, Ph.D. *The Art of Mentoring: Lead, Follow and Get Out of the Way*. Houston, TX: Bullion Books, 2001.

Pirsig, Robert. *Zen and the Art of Motorcycle Maintenance*. New York: Perennial Classics, 2000.

Raimes, Anne, and Maria Jerskey. *Universal Keys for Writers*. Florence, KY: Cengage Learning, 2008.

Robbins, John. *Diet for a New America: How Your Food Choices Affect Your Health, Happiness and the Future of Life on Earth*. New York: H. J. Kramer, 1998.

Ruggiero, Vincent Ryan. *Becoming a Critical Thinker*. Florence, KY: Cengage Learning, 2009.

Schacter, Daniel L. *Searching for Memory: The Brain, the Mind, and the Past*. New York: HarperCollins, 1997.

Schlosser, Eric. *Fast Food Nation*. Boston: Houghton Mifflin, 2001.

Strunk, William, Jr., and E. B. White. *The Elements of Style*. Harlow, Essex, UK: Pearson Education, 1999.

Toft, Doug, ed. *Master Student Guide to Academic Success*. Florence, KY: Cengage Learning, 2005.

Ueland, Brenda. *If You Want to Write: A Book About Art, Independence and Spirit*. St. Paul, MN: Graywolf, 1987.

Watkins, Ryan, and Michael Corry. *E-learning Companion: A Student's Guide to Online Success*. Florence, KY: Cengage Learning, 2011.

Welch, David. *Decisions, Decisions: The Art of Effective Decision Making*. Amherst, NY: Prometheus, 2002.

Wurman, Richard Saul. *Information Anxiety 2*. Indianapolis: QUE, 2001.

Gordon, Thomas, 249
Gore, Al, 215
Government, as resource, 17
Gowin, D. Bob, 177
Grades, 189, 199
Grants, 289
Graphic organizers, 123–124. *See also* Charts
Griping, vs. candor, 250
Group presentations, 268
Groups. *See* Study group

Habits
   changing, 46–47
   in reading, 147
Handler, Ruth, 357
Handshake, 258
Handwriting, 176
Harassment, sexual, 340–341
Hardware, for online learning, 148–149
Headings, in outlines, 173
Health
   addiction questionnaire and, 309–310
   alcohol and, 311
   balanced lifestyle and, 305
   behaviors in, 299
   of brain, 128
   drugs and, 311–312
   eating disorders and, 301
   emotional pain and, 313, 314
   exercise and, 302
   foods for, 300–301
   of master students, 42
   mental health and, 303–304
   resources for, 304
   rest and, 304
   safety and, 306
   self-observation and, 308
   sexual, 307
   skills for, 61
   smoking and, 312
   stress and, 303, 305
   suicide prevention and, 304
   transferable skills on, 316
Heart, brain health and, 128
Heiferman, Scott, 137
Hemingway, Ernest, 218
Hepatitis B, 307
Hierarchy of needs (Maslow), 20
Higher education
   employer support for, 20
   language of, 14
   succeeding in, 19–20
   transition to, 13–16
   value of, 11–12
High-performing teams, 262–263
HOMES mnemonic device, 129
Hopper, Grace Murray, 340
Hostile environment harassment, 340
Hotlines, 17
Hot spots, critical thinking and, 220
HOW attitudes (Honesty, Openness, and Willingness), 334
How To Get Control of Your Time and Your Life (Lakein), 97
Human papillomavirus (HPV), 307
Hunger to learn, of master students, 43
Hutchins, Robert, 12

"I"
   five ways to say, 250
   in individualist cultures, 252
   messages, 249, 255, 341
I Create It All (PowerProcess), 183
Idea of a University, The (Newman), 1
Ideas
   creating, 225–227
   files of, 226
   as tools, 49, 263
Ideas Are Tools (Power Process), 49
Identity theft, preventing, 290–291
Illness. *See* Health
Images, manufacturing by brain, 159
Income
   career choice-related, 292
   increasing, 282–283
Income-based repayment plan, 288
Inconvenient Truth, An (documentary film), 215
Independence, 13
Independent study programs, academic major and, 79
Index cards, for notes, 170, 175
Individualist cultures, collectivist cultures and, 252–253
Individuals, communicating with, 253
Inference, in reading, 146
Information
   about academic major, 78
   quality of Internet information, 231
   about salaries, 332
Information Anxiety (Wurman), 122
Information interview, 67, 75
Information literacy, 152–154
Inquisitiveness, of master students, 42
Inquisitive thinkers, 223
Instructors
   attending to, 167
   discussing reading assignment with, 145, 149
   enrolling in education process, 180
   judgments about lecture styles, 168
   meeting with, 16, 181
Intelligence
   emotional, 254
   interpersonal, 310
   multiple, 37, 38
   types of, 37
Intentions. *See also* Discovery and Intention Journal Entry System; Discovery/Intention Statement
   communicating, 250
Intention Statement, 254. *See also* Discovery/Intention Statement
   after job interview, 330
Interests, discovering, 11
Internal dialogue, during class, 167–168
Internet. *See also* Online learning; Web sites
   addiction to, 310
   for career information, 64
   critical thinking about information on, 231

evaluating search sites, 232
   job search on, 321
   networking via, 323
   research on, 152–154
   social networking and, 270
Internships, 76
Interpersonal intelligence, 37, 38, 310
Interviewing skills, 58
Interviews
   information, 75
   for jobs, 330–332
Intrapersonal intelligence, 37, 38
Introduction, to speech, 267
Intuition, in decision making, 233
Intuitiveness, of master students, 43
IPMAT mnemonic device, 129

Jacobs, Bert and John, 163
James, Kat, 297
James, William, 6
Jenner, Edward, 226
Job(s). *See also* Employment
   creation of new, 350
   finding in tough job market, 333
   learning on, 337
   naming of, 66
   part-time, 282–283
   reading related to, 160
   résumé for, 324–325
   sources of, 69
Job discrimination, 325
Job hunting, 320
   as full-time job, 321
   résumé as strategy, 325
   skills for, 282, 283
Job interview, 330–332
   answering and asking questions in, 331
   salary discussion in, 332
Job market, entering, 75
Job placement offices, 17
Job satisfaction, 342
Job search
   in Internet, 321
   networking in, 323
   rehearsing, 322
Job titles, 56, 65
Journal entry system, 7–8. *See also* Discovery/Intention Statement
Judgments, about instructors, 180
Jumping to conclusions fallacy, 229
"Just do it" method, 147

Kabat-Zinn, Job, *Full-Catastrophe Living:…*, 305
Keirsey Temperament Sorter, 74
Keywords
   as cues to recitation, 174
   in mind maps, 172
   in online searches, 152, 153
Kinesthetic learning, 39, 40
Knowledge workers, 152
Koestler, Arthur, *Act of Creation, The,* 227
Kolb, David, 32
Kuczmarski, Thomas D., mistakes celebrated by, 210

Lab work, in science, 205
LaFasto, Frank, *When Teams Work Best,* 262

Lakein, Alan, *How to Get Control of Your Time and Your Life,* 97
Language. *See also* Communication
   careful use of, 259
   of higher education, 14
   nonverbal, in job interview, 330
   sexist, 340–341
Larson, Carl, *When Teams Work Best,* 262
Leadership
   developing, 16
   diversity and, 343–344
Learners
   adult, 19–20
   self-regulated, 16
Learning. *See also* Reading
   active, 123
   about careers, 64
   cooperative, 193–194
   distributing, 126
   on job, 337
   memory and, 121
   natural learners and, 2–3
   online, 148–151
   opinion of instructors and, 180
   service-learning, 77
   VAK system for, 39–40
   VARK system for, 40
Learning cycle, teams and, 262
Learning modes, 33, 35–36
Learning style(s)
   for career exploration, 36
   in decision making, 233
   discovering how you learn, 32–34
   for math success, 207
   as transferable skill, 52
   using profile for success, 35–38
Learning Style Inventory (LSI), 34
Lectures
   clues to test questions in, 192
   instructor speed during, 181
   judgments about styles of, 168
   main concept of, 172
   recording, 171, 181
Legal aid services, 17
Leisure, guarding, 305
Length of speech, 267
Leonardo da Vinci, 41
Letters
   for conflict management, 256–257
   cover letter for résumé, 328, 329
Letting go, 225–226
Levy, Frank, 73
Liberal arts, mastering, 11
Libraries, resources and, 17, 152–153
Library of Congress online catalog, 231
Life coach, 351
Life plan, for decision making, 233
Lifestyle
   balanced, 305
   ideal, 66
LinkedIn, 323
Links
   in concept maps, 177
   in mind maps, 172
   to work world, 6
Listening
   choosing to, 246–248
   in ESL studies, 155

by leaders, 344
verbal, 247–248
Listening skills, 58
Lists
in reading, 146
in writing, 264
Literacy
financial, 292
information, 152–154
Literature, familiarity with, 11–12
Loans, 289
Location, naming of, 66
Loci system, for remembering, 130
Logic
common mistakes in, 229–230
in critical thinking, 220
Long-term goals, 95, 96
academic major and, 78
Long-term memory, 120
Long-term planner, 110–112
Love Your Problems (And
Experience Your Barriers)
(Power Process), 133

Macy, R. H., failure by, 210
Major subject
choosing, 78–79, 80
critical thinking about, 79, 80
Make a Trial Choice of Major
(exercise), 80
Malott, Richard, 46
Manji, Irshad, 243
*Manners That Sell: Adding the Polish
that Builds Profits* (Ramsey),
258–259
Maps. *See also* specific types
to summarize, 194
Marking up
of ebooks, 150
of text, 143
Masatake, Morita, 304
Maslow, Abraham, 20
Master employee, 1, 319
Master monthly calendar (exercise),
108–109
Master Student, 1, 42–43
Anderson, Richard, 117
Chavez, Cesar, 275
Csikszentmihalyi, Mihaly, 41
Gore, Al, 215
Handler, Ruth, 357
Heiferman, Scott, 137
Jacobs, Bert and John, 163
James, Kat, 297
Manji, Irshad, 243
to Master Employee, 2–3, 33
Pausch, Randy, 317
Price, Lisa, 85
profiles of, 48
Wattleton, Faye, 187
Yang, Jerry, 53
Master Student Map, 24, 54, 86,
118, 138, 164, 188, 216, 244,
263, 276
Mastery, 319
Matching tests, 196
Math
boosting skills for, 205
overcoming anxiety over,
204–205
tests in, 204–207
Mathematical/logical intelligence,
37, 38

Mattel toys, Handler, Ruth, and, 357
Mature thinkers, 223
Meaning
feeding back, 247
as memory techniques, 122
Meditation, 303
Meetings
with instructors, 181
with mentors, 338
note taking during, 176
Memory
attitudes and, 126, 127
context-dependent, 127
critical thinking about, 128
Ebbinghaus forgetting curve
and, 175
as jungle, 120–121
learning and, 121
long-term, 120
for names, 131, 136
as process, 119
setting trap for, 126
short-term, 119, 120
skills for, 60
storage in, 119
styles of, 127
testing of, 175
transferable skills for, 136
Memory techniques, 122–127
acronyms as, 129
acrostics as, 129
active learning as, 123
associations as, 122–123, 131
brain used in, 125–126
distribute learning and, 126
drawing as, 123
elaboration and, 126
emotions and, 125
graphic organizers and, 123–125
intention to remember as,
126–127, 131
loci system as, 130
meaning as, 122
mnemonic devices as, 129–130,
131
overlearning as, 125–126
peg system as, 130
photos for remembering, 131
pictures and, 123–125
recall as, 120, 127
recite and repeat as, 124–125,
131
relaxation as, 123
rhymes and songs as, 112, 129
selectivity as, 122
visualization as, 120–121, 131
write it down as, 125
Mental health, 228, 303–304
Mentors, 338
Messages
barriers to, 250
context of, 253, 259
sending, 245
verbal and nonverbal, 246–248
"you" and "I," 249
Meta-search engines, 153
Mid-term goals, 95, 96
Mind maps, 107, 172
for career plans, 71
summaries from, 175, 191
Minorities
in labor force, 245
as majority, 343

Minor subject, 79
Mistakes
allowing in leadership, 343
celebrating, 210
in logic, 229–230
Misunderstanding, in
communication, 245
Mnemonic devices, 129–130, 131.
See also Memory techniques
Modeling, as motivation, 45
Modes of learning, 33, 35–36
Money. *See also* Finances
controlling expenses and,
284–285
increasing income and, 282–283
as personal safety net, 333
plan for, 280
practicing skills at work, 292
Money management
technology for, 290–291
transferable skills on, 296
Money Monitor, 278, 279, 280, 281
Money Plan, 280
Money problems, 277
Money skills, 61
Monthly calendar, 108–109
Mood meter, 254
"Moonlighting," 321
Mosques, 17
Motivation, 44–45
Move from problems to solutions
(exercise), 132
Multiple-choice tests, 195
Multiple intelligences, 37, 38
Murnane, Richard J., 73
Muscle Reading, 139, 140, 144
for ebooks, 150
Musical/rhythmic intelligence,
37, 38
Myers-Briggs Type Indicator, 74
MySpace, 325

Names
culture and, 253, 259
remembering, 131, 136
Naturalist intelligence, 37, 38
Natural learners, 2–3
Navigation tools, for ebooks, 150
Needs hierarchy, of Maslow, 20
Negotiating skills, 58
Netiquette, 270
Networking, 323
Neural traces, 120
*New Division of Labor, The: How
Computers Are Creating the
Next Job Market* (Levy and
Murnane), 73
Newman, John Henry, 1
Newspapers, 17
Ngo, Ken, 318
Noise
avoiding, 102
in communication, 245
Nonsense, critical thinking and, 218
Nonsexist communication, 341
Nonverbal communication, in
speeches, 269
Nonverbal language, in job
interviews, 330
Nonverbal listening, 246–247
Nonverbal messages, 259
in speaking, 250
Norms, of workplace, 335–336

Note cards
for data, 227
for ideas, 226
Notes. *See also* Note cards
abbreviations in, 170
blank spaces in, 170
on "cheat sheet," 175
color in, 170
comparing in study groups, 194
editing, 174
graphic signals in, 170
on income and expenses, 280
index cards for, 170, 175
instructor lecture clues and, 168
labeling, numbering, and dating,
170
mind maps for, 172
from missed classes, 167
one side of paper for, 170
paraphrasing in, 178
plagiarism and, 178–179
possible test questions in, 192
research, 178–179
review of, 166–167, 174–175,
176, 178
for speech, 268
speed of instructor lecturing
and, 181
three-ring binders for, 170
Note taking. *See also* Note-taking
techniques
Cornell method of, 171–172, 173
critical thinking about, 182
for ebooks, 150
Intention Statement and, 167
observe, record, and review at
work, 176
outlining in, 173
in paragraph format, 170
PowerPoint and, 170
preclass review before, 166–167
process of, 165, 166–168, 174–175
during reading, 178–179
recording during, 171
setting stage for, 166–167
summary in, 171
for television programs, 182
transferable skills on, 186
in workplace, 184, 335
Note-taking groups, 193
Note-taking skills, 60
Note-taking techniques. *See also*
Note-taking
combining formats as, 173
copying material from board
and PowerPoint as, 170
keywords and, 169
mind maps and, 172
separating thoughts as, 170
visuals and, 169
writing notes in paragraphs, 169
Notice Your Pictures and Let Them
Go (Power Process), 159
Novak, Joseph, 177
Nutrition, 300

Oats, Kristen, 24
Objectives, of résumé, 324
Objective viewpoint, in conflict
management, 257
Observations
communicating, 250
in note-taking process, 176

Occupational Information Network, 69

Occupational Outlook Handbook, 66

OCEAN mnemonic device, 129

Office for Civil Rights (OCR), 341

Office politics, 336

Olivo, Raul, 118

O*NET OnLine system, 57

Online banking, 290

Online learning, 148–151
  applications for creating and editing documents, 151
  backing up files, 149
  building into courses, 151
  connecting with other students in, 150
  ebook reading and, 150
  organization of, 149
  research skills for, 152–154
  timely completion of assignments, 149

On-the-job learning, 337

Open-book tests, 196

Open minded thinkers, 223

Openness, in listening, 246

Optimism, of master students, 43

Organization
  of master students, 42
  as memory technique, 122

Organizational culture, 334–336

Outlining
  in note taking, 173
  before reading an assignment, 141
  for writing, 265

Out-of-class time management, 15, 16

Overdoers, procrastination by, 99

Overlearning, as memory technique, 125–126

Pain, emotional, 313

Paradox, master student acceptance of, 43

Paraphrasing, 178, 238

Part-time jobs, 282–283, 321

Pass phrase, for bill payment and online purchases, 291

Password, for bill payment and online purchases, 291

Pasting, in written paper, 266

Pauk, Walter, 171

Pausch, Randy, 317

PBwiki, 151

Peer pressure, eating habits and, 301

Peg system, for remembering, 130

Penicillin, discovery of, 226

People skills, 58

Perceiving, 32–33

Perfectionists, procrastination by, 99

Performance, of transferable skills, 59

Performance reviews, 208–209, 212

Peripatetic students, 12

Personal finance software, 290

Personal information managers, 226

Personal meetings, in social networking, 270

Persuasion, importance of, 217

Phishing, 290

Phone. *See* Telephone

Photos, for memory, 131

Physical activity, 128, 302

Pictures, as memory technique, 123–125

Pie charts, for career plans, 71

Plagiarism, avoiding, 178–179, 238

Planning
  career, 350
  long-term planner for, 110–112
  for money, 280
  in problem solving, 234
  skills for, 58
  in teams, 193
  time management and, 107
  as transferable skill, 116

Player, Bonnie, 244

Plurals, for nonsexist communication, 341

PLUS loans, 288

Point of view
  in critical thinking, 220, 221
  testing validity of, 228

Point to false cause fallacy, 229

Pollan, Michael, 300

Positive attitude, 42

Pound, Ezra, 11

Power Process
  Be Here Now, 113, 167
  Be It, 353
  Choose Your Conversations (and Your Community), 293
  detaching from attachments, 211
  Discover What You Want, 23
  Employ Your Word, 271
  Find a Bigger Problem, 239
  guide to, 22
  I Create It All, 183
  Ideas Are Tools, 49
  Love Your Problems (And Experience Your Barriers), 133
  Notice Your Pictures and Let Them Go, 159
  Risk Being a Fool, 81
  Surrender, 313
  in teams, 262–263

Practice test, 191

Practicing
  of leadership skills, 344
  of new behaviors, 47

Practicum, 76

Pregnancy, preventing unwanted, 307–308

Prejudice
  critical thinking and, 217
  online, 270

Preparation
  note-taking process flow and, 166–167
  for studying, 102
  for writing, 264–265
  of written paper, 266

Presentation
  group, 268
  practicing speeches, 269

Presley, Elvis, failure by, 210

Pressure, as motivation, 45

Prevention, of accidents, 306

Previewing, before reading an assignment, 141, 144

Price, Lisa, 85

Primary sources, 153

Printing, from ebooks, 150

Prioritizing
  of career plans, 71
  rating tasks and, 97–98
  for study time, 103

Privacy, in social networking, 270

Problem solving. *See also* Critical thinking
  critical thinking about, 132
  job satisfaction and, 342
  for math tests, 206
  mental health and, 303
  procedures for, 234
  transferable skills on, 242

Process, job satisfaction through, 342

Processing, 32–33

Procrastination, 44
  overcoming, 45–47
  7-day antiprocrastination plan, 105
  skills for overcoming, 116
  stopping, 99

Professional associations, 323

Professional development plan, at work, 337, 338

Professionalism, in papers, 180

Progress, at work, 338

Promises, to finish tasks, 105

Pronoun gender, 341

Proofing, of written paper, 266

Publications, for career information, 64

Public speaking
  mastering, 267–269
  reducing fear of, 269

Purpose, of writing, 264

Questioning
  in information literacy, 152
  modes of learning and, 33
  and note taking, 181
  before reading an assignment, 141, 144
  for transferable skills, 59

Questions. *See also* Test(s)
  getting stuck on tests, 196
  in job interviews, 330, 331
  listening and, 248
  predicting for tests, 192
  that are not questions, 250

Quid pro quo harassment, 340

Racism, 341

Ramsey, Lydia, *Manners That Sell: Adding the Polish that Builds Profits,* 258–259

Rape, 306

Rational Recovery, 312

Reading. *See also* Learning
  active, 139
  activities after, 144
  activities during, 142–143
  activities prior to, 141
  answering questions during, 143, 144
  with children nearby, 156–157
  context clues in, 146
  difficulties with, 145
  of ebooks, 150
  eye movements in, 147
  job-related, 160
  "just do it" method of, 147

marking up text during, 142, 143
  for math tests, 206
  Muscle Reading, 139, 140, 144
  note taking during, 178–179
  out loud, 142, 145
  reciting and, 144
  re-reading, 145
  reviewing in, 144, 145
  skimming in, 147
  speed of, 147
  strategies for, 145
  transferable skills on, 162
  underlining during, 142, 143
  visualization during, 142
  vocabulary building for, 146

Reading aloud, of written paper, 265

Reading groups, 193

Reading skills, 60

Recall, memory and, 120, 127

Receiving, in communication, 245

Reciting
  in cramming for tests, 191
  as memory technique, 124–125, 131
  from notes, 174
  as reading technique, 144

Recording, in note-taking process, 176

Records, financial, 292

Recovery, from addiction, 311

Red herring fallacy, 230

Reflecting
  on online source materials, 154
  on presentations, 269

Reflection technique, in communication, 247

Reflective observation, 32, 35

Regressions, in eye movements, 147

Rehearse your job search (exercise), 322

Relationships
  giving one's word and, 271
  re-creating, 251

Relax (exercise), 147

Relaxation
  critical thinking and, 147
  as memory technique, 123

Remembering your car key—or anything else (exercise), 128

Repeating, as memory technique, 125, 131

Repetition
  in cramming, 191
  as memory technique, 125

Research
  note taking for, 178–179
  recording source information for, 179
  for writing, 265

Research groups, 193

Research paper, skills needed for, 58

Research skills, 58
  online, 152–154

Resources, 17. *See also* Source(s)
  for ESL students, 155
  in higher education, 14
  in libraries, 152–153

Respect, communicating, 15

Responsibility
  of master students, 42
  taking, 183
  as workplace quality, 319

Rest, health and, 304